INSIDERS' GUIDE® SERIES

D0596579

INSIDERS' GUIDE® TO
THE TWIN CITIES

SIXTH EDITION

TODD R. BERGER

INSIDERS' GUIDE®

GUILFORD, CONNECTICUT
AN IMPRINT OF THE GLOBE PEQUOT PRESS

The prices and rates in this guidebook were confirmed at press time. We recommend, however, that you call establishments before traveling to obtain current information.

INSIDERS' GUIDE®

Text design by Nancy Freeborn
Maps by XNR Productions, Inc. © Morris Book Publishing, LLC

ISSN 1525-7460
ISBN 978-0-7627-4788-7

Printed in the United States of America
10 9 8 7 6 5 4 3 2 1

CONTENTS

CONTENTS

Directory of Maps

Twin Cities and Metro Area

Downtown St. Paul

St. Paul Skyway

Legend:
- Skyway
- Tunnel

N

Scale: 0, 0.1, 0.2 km | 0, 0.1, 0.2 mi.

Highways: 52, 5, 3, 94, 35E, 52, 12

Streets and labels:
12TH ST., 11TH ST., 10TH ST., 9TH ST., 8TH ST., 7TH ST., 6TH ST., 5TH ST., 4TH ST.

BROADWAY ST., WALL ST., WACOUTA ST., SIBLEY ST., JACKSON ST., ROBERT ST., MINNESOTA ST., CEDAR ST., WABASHA ST., ST. PETER ST., EXCHANGE ST., KELLOGG BLVD., 7TH PL.

Landmarks:
Mears Park, Mears Park Plaza, First Trust Center, KTCA, Galtier Plaza, Warren Burger Federal Courts Building, Kellogg Square, Metro Square, Helmar Building, Firstar Center, First National, Town Square, U.S. Bank Center, Wells Fargo Place, Macy's, Hamm Building, Victory Ramp, Lowry Square, City Hall, Crowne Plaza Northstar Hotel, Saint Paul Hotel, Science Museum of Minnesota, Xcel Energy Center

Mississippi River

Downtown Minneapolis

Minneapolis Skyway

N
0   0.1   0.2 km
0   0.1   0.2 mi.

Skyway

HOW TO USE THIS BOOK

For the most part, those who live in the Twin Cities don't consider themselves Twin Cities residents—in the Metro you're either from Minneapolis or St. Paul. While both cities have much in common, differences in architecture, city layout, history, and industry set St. Paul and Minneapolis apart. Each could fill a separate guidebook by itself.

The *Insiders' Guide to the Twin Cities* is organized so that information can be accessed as quickly as possible. In addition to the comprehensive table of contents and index, each separate chapter includes multiple subheadings. Chapters are divided by city where appropriate for easier navigation through the Cities and suburbs. Other chapters are organized alphabetically by subject or chronologically by event. You'll also find interesting tips scattered throughout the text, flagged with the **i** symbol. Look for the close-up features for an in-depth look at what makes the Cities special.

The book is structured with the reader in mind: It is written from the point of view of someone moving to or visiting the Twin Cities for the first time, or someone visiting a given establishment for the first time. Accurate, useful information was the standard, and although perfection is never attainable, excellence is. You can feel confident that this book will steer you in the right direction 99 percent of the time as you use it to make choices based on your own preferences. Negative comments are few; if a certain restaurant, attraction, store, park, or hotel would rate negative words, it is not listed here. Why recommend rudeness, poor service, lousy food, boring inventory, bad atmosphere, or uninteresting "attractions"? That said, there are numerous worthy establishments in the Cities that do not appear in these pages because of time constraints and space constraints or because they are yet to be visited by the author. Although we encourage you to use this guidebook and are confident that you will find it useful in choosing places to your liking, we also encourage you to stop by that intriguing Ethiopian restaurant, visit that interesting shop selling bobblehead dolls or what have you, or buy a house in a neighborhood that "feels right," whether or not it is included in this book. This book is a diving board to get you into the pool; once there, you can swim wherever you like.

AREA OVERVIEW

Legend has it that the many lakes that cover the face of Minnesota are actually the filled-in footprints of Paul Bunyan and his mighty blue ox, Babe, created as they stomped around the countryside when Paul was just a boy. If this is true, then he must have been doing jumping jacks in the Twin Cities: St. Paul and Minneapolis alone have 22 lakes within their borders, with many more just outside their borders. Just about everywhere you go, you're bound to drive by, cross over, or end up at one of the Metro's lakes, not to mention the mighty Mississippi.

Even with all their historic buildings, bridges, and more recent whimsical experiments in architecture, the most remarkable physical feature about the Twin Cities has always been their natural beauty. Where else can you find wildlife preservations, rich fossil beds, and fishing lakes, all within a short walk from either downtown?

This, of course, was not always so. Minneapolis was partially built on the lumber industry, and thousands and thousands of old-growth trees were leveled and shipped out of state, almost completely destroying the Big Woods, a maple, oak, and basswood forest that once covered most of southern Minnesota. The Mississippi River valley Native American populations were decimated along with the forests that had been their home for thousands of years, and many of their spiritual centers, including the ill-fated Spirit Island that once rose out of the Mississippi River below St. Anthony Falls, were either gutted or dynamited in the name of progress.

With the founding of the two cities in the mid-1800s, however, a new level of civility and sophistication came to the residents. Multiple parks boards were established to protect wildlife areas, and even more groomed areas were set aside for outdoor activities. Today Twin Citians have the luxury of being able to walk past wetlands full of migratory waterfowl and turtles on their way to downtown Minneapolis, or through thickly forested areas housing species of rare native animals and birds just minutes from downtown St. Paul. Kids who grow up in the Twin Cities get to share in pleasures usually reserved for children who grow up in the country, whether it be fishing in one of the many regularly stocked urban lakes, berry picking, or just enjoying being surrounded by trees, songbirds, and wildflowers in parks practically in their own backyards.

THE PERSONALITY OF THE CITIES

Minnesota has long suffered a reputation of being an American Siberia peopled with blond-haired, blue-eyed Scandinavian types. And while it's true that some parts of the state do have six-month cold seasons, often complete with snow for the entire six months, the Twin Cities have been particularly blessed with relatively mild temperatures, partly due to our proximity to the swift-moving Mississippi River. Summers can top the scale at 100 degrees occasionally, and, conversely, winters can drop well below zero. A good rule of thumb is to just be prepared for it to get cold in the winter and warm in the summer, and dress accordingly.

While most residents of the Twin Cities will go on and on about how much we love the changing of the seasons, to the point of ridiculing visitors who complain about "a little snow," fact is, as soon as any of us have enough money to take a vacation somewhere warm during the winter, we're gone. Our snowbird migrations—RV-driving senior citizens who winter in the South and summer in Minnesota—are legendary. A brief jaunt to a tropical clime in the dead of winter is not an act of infidelity on any level—rather, we just want to protect the treasured memories we have of glorious trees covered with palm-sized green or flame-colored leaves, of hordes of Canada geese sunning themselves along the shores of the Mississippi, or of the way the brilliant white riverboats look heading down the St. Croix River in the middle of summer, mirror-reflected in the clear, tannin-tinted waters.

As soon as the weather is nice, however, anyone who can go outside, is outside. City parks get used here in the Twin Cities, from huge group picnics to locally organized volleyball and baseball games. Many neighborhood parks have a splash pool for kids, and at any given time during the summer, families can be seen splashing around in the ridiculously shallow waters. At night the streets of downtown Minneapolis and St. Paul are full of people either out for a late-night walk in the balmy evening air or heading out on foot for a night on the town.

HOLLYWOOD AND THE TWIN CITIES

Minnesota has long been a favorite filming spot for moviemakers, especially those who need to shoot in snowy, cold areas with lots of open spaces. The Twin Cities are a logical spot to find actors and actresses to fill these scenes, as both Minneapolis and St. Paul have more than enough talent trained on the many professional and amateur theater stages in the area. Some of the films that have been shot in the Twin Cities metro area include *Airport, Beautiful Girls, Drop Dead Fred, Equinox, Fargo, Feeling Minnesota, Foolin' Around, Grumpy Old Men, Grumpier Old Men, Jingle All the Way, Mall Rats, The Mighty Ducks (I, II, and III), The Personals, A Prairie Home Companion, A Simple Plan, Twenty Bucks,* and *Untamed Heart.* Brothers Joel and Ethan Coen, film directors and producers of such films as *Raising Arizona, Blood Simple, Fargo, O Brother Where Art Thou,* and *No Country for Old Men,* are from here, as is *Twin Peaks* producer Mark Frost and director of *The Sting,* George Roy Hill.

Television and big-picture actors and actresses who hail from the Twin Cities include Eddie Albert (*Roman Holiday, Green Acres*), Loni Anderson (*WKRP in Cincinnati*), Richard Dean Anderson (*General Hospital, MacGyver, Stargate SG–1*), James Arness (*Gunsmoke*), Julia Duffy (*Newhart, Designing Women*), Mike Farrell (*M*A*S*H, Providence*), Terry Gilliam (*Monty Python*), Peter Graves (*Mission: Impossible*), Tippi Hedren (*The Birds*), Josh Hartnett (*Pearl Harbor*), Charlie Korsmo (*Hook, Dick Tracy*), Dorothy Lyman (*All My Children, Mama's Family*), Kelly Lynch (*Drugstore Cowboy*), Mike Nelson (*Mystery Science Theater*), Kevin Sorbo (*Hercules, Andromeda*), Lea Thompson (*Back to the Future I, II, III; Howard the Duck, Caroline in the City*), Robert Vaughn (*The Man from U.N.C.L.E.*), and Vince Vaughn (*Into the Wild, The Break-Up*).

LITERATURE AND MUSIC

There's nothing like a long, Minnesota winter to make you want to curl up with a good book—or sit down and write one. Some literary luminaries from the Twin Cities area have included *Prairie Home Companion*'s Garrison Keillor, Sinclair Lewis, F. Scott Fitzgerald, Meridel Le Sueur, Harvey Mackay, Robert Bly, Tim O'Brien, Gordon Parks, cartoonist Charles Schultz, and journalist Eric Severeid. Folksinger Bob Dylan; blues legends Koerner, Ray, and Glover; former Replacements' lead singer Paul Westerberg; Soul Asylum singer Dave Pirner; and Prince also made Minneapolis or St. Paul their home at one time or another.

GEOLOGY

The state of Minnesota is known throughout the world for its once-productive iron mines as well as its quarries of beautiful St. Peter

3

Twin Cities Timeline

1680: Father Louis Hennepin, after being held captive in a village of the Mille Lacs Dakotas, is the first European to see the Falls of St. Anthony.

1819: The United States establishes Fort St. Anthony (renamed Fort Snelling in 1825) to protect the confluence of the Minnesota and Mississippi Rivers.

1837: Governor Henry Dodge of Wisconsin signs a treaty at Fort Snelling with the Ojibwes, who agree to cede all their pinelands on the St. Croix River and its tributaries. A treaty is also signed at Washington, D.C., with representatives of the Dakotas for their lands east of the Mississippi. These treaties lead the way for extensive white settlements within the area of what would become Minnesota.

1838: Franklin Steele establishes a claim at the Falls of St. Anthony in what is today Minneapolis; Pierre "Pig's Eye" Parrant builds a shanty and settles on the present site of the city of St. Paul, then called Pig's Eye.

1841: The Chapel of St. Paul is built and consecrated, giving the name to the future capital of the state.

1848: On August 26, after the admission of Wisconsin to the Union, the Stillwater Convention adopts measures calling for a separate territory to be named Minnesota. On October 30, Henry Hastings Sibley is elected the delegate to Congress for the Minnesota Territory.

1855: On January 23 the first bridge to span the main channel of the Mississippi River anywhere along its length is opened between Minneapolis and St. Anthony.

1858: Minnesota becomes the 32nd state on May 11. At the time of its entry, Minnesota is the third-largest state in land area—only Texas and California are larger.

1861: On April 14 Governor Alexander Ramsey offers President Abraham Lincoln 1,000 men for the Civil War effort, making Minnesota the first state to offer troops to the Union. The first Minnesota regiment leaves Fort Snelling on June 22.

1862: The first railroad in Minnesota is opened between Minneapolis and St. Paul.

1881: Technological advances in flour milling made during the 1870s help turn Minneapolis into the flour milling capital of the world.

1883: The Northern Pacific Railroad completes its transcontinental route from Minnesota to the Pacific.

1884: The first iron ore is shipped from Minnesota, a product of the Soudan Mine on the Vermillion Range. Six years later iron is discovered on the Mesabi Range and shipped from there beginning in 1892.

1894: The town of Hinckley, Minnesota, about 80 miles north of St. Paul, and six neighboring communities are destroyed by an apocalyptic forest fire. More than 600 people lose their lives.

1914: Minneapolis becomes home to the Ninth District Federal Reserve Bank, one of 12 Federal Reserve Banks founded after Congress passed and President Woodrow Wilson signed the 1913 Federal Reserve Act.

1927: Charles Lindbergh, originally from Little Falls, Minnesota, becomes the first person to fly nonstop across the Atlantic Ocean alone.

1930: Minnesotan Frank B. Kellogg, serving as U.S. secretary of state, is awarded the Nobel Peace Prize for his work on the Kellogg-Briand Peace Pact, signed in Paris in 1928.

1944: The Democratic and Farmer-Labor Parties merge to form the Minnesota Democratic-Farmer-Labor Party (DFL).

1947: Engineering Research Associates, Inc., designs the ATLAS—the beginning of Minnesota's computer industry.

1947: The NBA's Minneapolis Lakers, originally part of the National Basketball League, begin play. The Lakers, led by big man George Mikan, win several league championships in Minneapolis before moving to lake-less Los Angeles in 1960.

1948: The value of manufactured products exceeds cash farm receipts in the state for the first time.

1958: Prince Rogers Nelson, better known as the often purple and always funky musician Prince, is born in Minneapolis.

1965: Hubert H. Humphrey becomes the first Minnesotan to win election to national executive office when he is sworn in as vice president on January 20.

1968: Minnesota politicians play a central role in the 1968 presidential campaign, as both Vice President Humphrey and U.S. Senator Eugene McCarthy of Minnesota seek the Democratic nomination. Humphrey wins the nomination, but Richard Nixon wins the general election.

1969: Warren Burger of St. Paul becomes chief justice of the United States Supreme Court.

1970: Minnesotan Harry Blackmun is named to the United States Supreme Court.

1977: Walter Mondale becomes the second Minnesotan to win election to national executive office when he is sworn in as vice president on January 20.

1977: Rosalie Wahl becomes the first woman to serve on the state supreme court.

1987: The Minnesota Twins win the World Series.

1990: The Minnesota Supreme Court becomes the first state supreme court in the nation to have a majority of women seated as justices, following the appointment of Appeals Court Judge Sandra Gardebring.

1991: Casino gambling becomes legal in and around Minnesota's Indian reservations.

1991: The Minnesota Twins win their second world championship in five years.

1992: The Mall of America, the nation's largest shopping and entertainment complex, opens in Bloomington.

1993: Minnesota loses professional hockey when the Minnesota North Stars move to Dallas.

1993: Sharon Sayles Belton is elected mayor of Minneapolis, the first African-American woman to preside over a major American city.

CONTINUED

1999: On January 3 Reform Party candidate Jesse Ventura, whose only previous political experience was as the mayor of the Minneapolis suburb of Brooklyn Park, is sworn in as Minnesota's governor.

1999: On March 10, the *St. Paul Pioneer Press* breaks the story of widespread academic misconduct involving players, coaches, and support staff of the University of Minnesota basketball team, including hundreds of term papers written for players by an academic tutor. After a nine-month investigation, the university fires men's basketball coach Clem Haskins. The NCAA later forces the university to forfeit all of its postseason games played between 1993 and 1998, including all of the games leading up to their 1997 trip to the Final Four, and to surrender 90 percent of the school's earnings from those postseason appearances. George Dohrmann, the *Pioneer Press* reporter who broke the original story, won the 1999 Pulitzer Prize for Beat Reporting.

2000: NHL hockey returns to Minnesota on September 29 when the Minnesota Wild play their first game before a sold-out crowd at the brand-new Xcel Energy Center in downtown St. Paul.

2002: On October 25, 11 days before the election, U.S. Senator Paul Wellstone of Minnesota, his wife, daughter, three campaign workers, and two pilots die in a plane crash in northern Minnesota.

2004: The Twin Cities' first light-rail line, which runs between downtown Minneapolis and the Mall of America, opens on June 26.

2007: The bridge carrying Interstate 35W over the Mississippi River in downtown Minneapolis collapses during the evening rush hour on August 1, dumping some 100 cars and trucks into the river. Thirteen people are killed.

sandstone and marble deposits. Of more scientific interest, some of the oldest exposed rock known in the world can be found in the Minnesota River valley, the Morton gneiss, which was formed approximately 3,600 million years ago. The Morton gneiss and "younger" (1,700- to 1,800-million-year-old) quarries of Minnesota granite and basalt have been prized as building materials throughout the world for years, as have St. Peter sandstone, marble, and fossil-rich kaolinite clay.

Millions of years ago the area now known as Minnesota lay submerged beneath shallow continental seas. During the Ordovician period (505 to 438 million years ago), Minnesota was located 10 to 40 degrees south of the equator, making the area about as tropical as Hawaii is today. The waters were rich with primitive animal life, much of which can be seen today as layers in the fossil record at paleontology digs throughout the state. Large amounts of corals, trilobites, snails, mussel and clam shells, and the ancestors of modern-day octopi and squid have been unearthed at sites such as Harriet Island/Lilydale Park and Shadow Falls in St. Paul and near Cannon Falls in Goodhue County.

Most of Minnesota is part of the Canadian Shield—a core of Precambrian rocks that contains the record of the history of the North American continent from about 3,600 million to 600 million years ago. Much of this ancient shield had been protected by the covering of the Ordovician seas, and later by layers of sediment and earth, but was again exposed by the eroding progress of glaciers over a mile thick that last covered the area more than 12,000 years ago—the same glaciers that eventually carved out the 15,000-plus lakes and rivers that pockmark the face of the state today.

THE ORIGINAL SETTLERS

Before European settlement, Dakota (Sioux) and Ojibwe (Chippewa) tribes populated the Twin Cities area, and before that, an amalgam of people known as the Woodland Indians (or Hopewell Indians), who left behind thousands of burial mounds throughout the Midwest, six of which can still be seen at Mounds Park in St. Paul. The Mississippian cultures of the Dakotas and Ojibwes replaced these American Indians circa A.D. 800 to 1000.

While the Ojibwes' origins were to the east and north, the Dakotas were western Plains Indians who at the time of European exploration occupied the Twin Cities area, western and southern Minnesota, and much of present-day North and South Dakota. The French referred to the Dakotas as Sioux, a meaningless abridgement of the Ojibwe term *Nadouissouix,* which meant "little viper" or "lesser enemy." The derogatory name stuck for centuries until recently, when the tribe began referring to itself by its original name. Both the Dakotas and Ojibwes were hunting societies, and their hunting techniques evolved by incorporating European tools, wares, and implements such as guns, hatchets, blankets, knives, and kettles. On a cultural level, the European introduction of glass beads and colored cloth and yarn to the Native peoples resulted in a revolution in American Indian artwork, producing the spectacular woven blankets and intricate beadwork that we associate with American Indian craftwork today.

The Twin Cities are home to the largest urban population of American Indians in the United States and are the birthplace of the American Indian Movement (AIM). AIM produces locally and nationally distributed literature that addresses Indian concerns on everything from legal issues to finding hospitals that practice Native American medicine.

St. Paul

Home to thousands of American Indians for centuries, the earliest known name for St. Paul is that given by the Indians: *Im-in-i-ja ska,* which translated into English means "White Rock," taken from the high limestone bluffs in the area. Fort Snelling (originally named Fort St. Anthony), the first European settlement in the area, was completed in 1825, and soon after, seeking the nearby protection of the fort, the community of St. Peter's (today known as Mendota) was established.

Soon the more privileged military officers and the residents of St. Peter's became disturbed at the lifestyle of the residents of the squatter camp, most of whom were refugees from the ill-fated Selkirk Colony in Manitoba. They were especially disturbed about the activities of a notorious and highly popular retired fur trapper whose talents had been turned to moonshining, Pierre "Pig's Eye" Parrant. The whiskey trade quickly infuriated the straitlaced Major Lawrence Taliaferro, Fort Snelling's Indian agent, who issued a proclamation banishing the squatters from lands controlled by the fort. This forced them to move down the river to the northeast, just outside the fort's jurisdiction.

This site, then known as Fountain Cave, was located near what is now the southern part of St. Paul. A small monument today marks a spot on the riverbank near where the small group settled. Soon after they set up their new squatter camp, Major Taliaferro decided they were not quite far enough out of his sight and extended the jurisdiction of the fort to include the Fountain Cave site, sending his soldiers to burn the Fountain Cave encampment. The settlers were again forced to move farther down the river, this time settling on the north bank in what is now part of downtown St. Paul.

Institutions such as government and the Roman Catholic Church have been central to St. Paul's history since its earliest days. Since the beginnings of Minnesota Territory in 1849, St. Paul has served as the capital. At about

Twin Cities Vital Statistics

Founded:
Minneapolis: 1856;
St. Paul: 1819

Incorporated: Minneapolis: 1867; St. Paul: 1854

Size: Minneapolis: 54.9 square miles; St. Paul: 52.8 square miles

Elevation: 824 feet above sea level

Population:
Minneapolis: 382,618;
St. Paul: 287,151

Mayor:
Minneapolis: R. T. Rybak;
St. Paul: Chris Coleman

Governor: Tim Pawlenty

Airport: Minneapolis–St. Paul International Airport

Average temperatures:
July: 72 degrees F
January: 12 degrees F

Average yearly precipitation: 26.5 inches

Colleges and universities:
Minneapolis: Augsburg College, Capella University, Dunwoody College of Technology, Minneapolis College of Art and Design, Minneapolis Community and Technical College, Northwestern Health Science University, the University of Minnesota–Twin Cities
St. Paul: Bethel College and Seminary, the College of St. Catherine, Concordia University–St. Paul, Hamline University, Luther Seminary, Macalester College, McNally Smith College of Music, Metropolitan State University, William Mitchell College of Law, Northwestern College, St. Paul College, University of Minnesota–Twin Cities, University of St. Thomas

Daily newspapers: *StarTribune, St. Paul Pioneer Press*

Radio stations: 48

Television stations: 9

Driving laws: Driver's license at age 16; maximum speed limit on interstate freeways varies from 55 mph to 70 mph; seat belts mandatory for driver and all passengers; child seats mandatory for children under age five or under 45 pounds; helmets mandatory for motorcycle riders.

the same time, it also became a Catholic diocese established by Father Lucian Galtier, who had come to save the souls in the crassly named settlement of "Pig's Eye."

Industry and technology were paramount in the historical development of St. Paul. Minnesota Mining and Manufacturing Company (3M) is one of the Cities' most important companies. 3M's history began in 1902 in Two Harbors, a small town north of Duluth, as a manufacturer of sandpaper. The company relocated to St. Paul in 1909, where sandpaper is one of the most important 3M products today. 3M has always placed a premium on producing and developing diverse and innovative products, such as Scotch brand tape and Post-it Notes. As time has passed 3M has grown into an international corporation but remains essentially a St. Paul company, even after relocating its headquarters to the adjoining suburb of Maplewood.

Minneapolis

The emergence of the other Twin City, Minneapolis, was far less colorful. In 1680 Father Louis Hennepin happened upon St. Anthony Falls, and 140 years later soldiers from nearby Fort Snelling constructed a sawmill and flour mill at the falls. Fort Snelling retained control of the current site of downtown Minneapolis until 1852, but the across-the-river town of St. Anthony was founded in 1849 as a milling and lumbering center. Minneapolis and St. Anthony were linked by a bridge in 1855, the first suspension bridge to span the Mississippi; today, downtown Minneapolis' Hennepin Avenue Bridge sits on the site of the 1855 span. The town of Minneapolis formed in 1856 on the opposite bank of the Mississippi from St. Anthony. Minneapolis's name was formed from a derivative of *minnehaha*, which means "waterfall" in the Dakota language, and *polis*, the Greek suffix for "city." Literally speaking, Minneapolis means "city of waters." The city of Minneapolis was incorporated in 1867, and in 1872 Minneapolis and St. Anthony were united to form one city.

Minneapolis was founded to mill Minnesota grain with the tremendous power-generating capabilities of St. Anthony Falls, and by the late 19th century, Minneapolis became nationally known as the Mill City. To businessmen in the area, the falls represented an unbridled source of energy for milling the vast Midwestern wheat crops, which rapidly expanded as Minnesota and the upper Midwest were settled. The milling industry became increasingly decentralized as the largest and most successful Twin Cities milling companies gradually diversified into related industries.

> **i** The Wabasha Street Caves used to be a St. Paul gangster hideout. Now they're a popular place to hold weddings and other events.

THE CITIES TOGETHER

Since the beginning of the 20th century, the Twin Cities economy has become increasingly diverse, depending less on a single industry—such as lumber, milling, or mining—and expanding into the technological, medical, retail, and agricultural fields.

Some companies' roots reach back to industry and manufacturing that began in the late 19th and early 20th centuries, as is the case with the 3M Corporation, while others quickly became important businesses because of technological innovation. Medtronic founder Earl Bakken began his company in a northeast Minneapolis garage in 1949, and it was the first of many medical supply companies that have made their home in the Twin Cities.

The Twin Cities is also home to one of the nation's largest retailers, the Target Corporation. For most of its long history in the Twin Cities, Target was known as the Dayton Corporation, and later the Dayton Hudson Corporation. George Dayton opened the first Dayton's department store in downtown Minneapolis in 1902, and in 1962 the Dayton Corporation opened the first Target store in nearby Roseville. Dayton Hudson officially changed its name to the Target Corporation in 2000.

Recent immigration is transforming the composition of the Twin Cities, much as it did in the late 19th and early 20th centuries. These new immigrant populations include Vietnamese, Laotians, Khmers (Cambodia), Hmong (Laos), East Africans, Russians, Bosnians, and many other nationalities. With the exception of the Russians and Bosnians, Europeans are a relatively small component of the new immigration. The Twin Cities, centered in St. Paul, have the largest Hmong population in the nation. The Hmong and other Southeast Asians have started more than 400 area businesses and have transformed St. Paul's

Frogtown and Midway neighborhoods.

The new wave of immigration is just one parallel linking the Twin Cities past and present. Both Minneapolis and St. Paul are reviving important elements of their past on the Mississippi riverfront. Since the late 1980s Minneapolis has focused on regaining its greatest historical assets—the Mississippi River and the Mill District. Down the river in St. Paul, the renovated Harriet Island Regional Park celebrates its city's rich history.

THE SEVEN-COUNTY METRO AREA

Anoka County

Anoka County's history starts as far back as 1849, when the Minnesota territorial legislature organized the counties of Washington, Ramsey, and Benton. What is now Anoka County was originally parts of both Ramsey and Benton Counties, with the Rum River dividing the two. As more settlers came into the area, the plot of land bordering the Rum River's shores was given the name Anoka. The name originated from a Dakota word meaning "on both sides."

Anoka County was formed from Ramsey County on May 23, 1857. The original eight townships included Anoka, Watertown (Ramsey), Round Lake (Andover), Bethel, Columbus, St. Francis, Oak Grove, and Centerville. The original boundaries of Anoka County were the same as today except for a small portion of the southeastern tip of the county along the Mississippi River. This strip was a tiny county created from Ramsey County, possibly by a surveying miscalculation, the same day Anoka County was created. This tiny county was given the name of Manomin and occupied only about one-third of a congressional township; it functioned as an organized county until abolished and attached to Anoka County by constitutional amendment on November 2, 1869. As an organized township of Anoka County, Manomin kept this name until it was changed to Fridley in 1879.

Anoka County has grown from a largely rural area in 1857 to the present-day urban center. It is one of the largest and fastest-growing counties in the state. Anoka County, with its county seat in the city of Anoka, encompasses a 424-square-mile area, has a population of approximately 327,000, and is the fourth-largest county in Minnesota. Anoka County is also the third most densely populated county in the state, following Ramsey and Hennepin Counties, and includes the cities of Andover, Anoka, Bethel, Blaine, Burns, Centerville, Circle Pines, Columbia Heights, Columbus, Coon Rapids, East Bethel, Fridley, Ham Lake, Hilltop, Lexington, Lino Lakes, Linwood, Oak Grove, Ramsey, St. Francis, and Spring Lake Park within its borders.

Carver County

With the signing of the Treaty of Traverse de Sioux in 1851, the formerly Dakota lands that soon became Carver County were opened for settlement by white pioneers. The county was named in honor of the 16th-century English explorer of the Upper Midwest, Jonathan Carver. The original county seat was in San Francisco Township, but in 1856 voters moved it to Chaska, where it remains today.

Many of Carver County's initial settlers were from the East Coast, but by the 1860s new settlers in the county were often immigrants from Germany or Sweden. The Germans founded towns like Hamburg, New Germany, and Cologne, while the Swedes settled in East Union and Watertown.

Farming was the chief occupation of Carver County for 100 years. While many residents grew crops, others were dairy farmers, and creameries were so numerous that the county started calling itself the "Golden Buckle of the Dairy Belt." Oak Grove Dairy in Norwood–Young America and Bongards Creameries are still important forces in the dairy industry.

Carver County was home to the farmer Wendelin Grimm, a German immigrant who settled in Chanhassen in the 1850s. Grimm

Calling in the Metro Area

The Twin Cities metropolitan area has four area codes (612, 651, 763, and 952), but callers do not have to dial "1" before calling phone numbers in the other area codes. You can dial the seven-digit phone number for calls within your area code or the ten-digit number (area code plus phone number) for calls to areas outside your area code within the Metro. Your call will still go through if you dial "1" first, but you will be charged for a long-distance call.

created his own strain of hardy alfalfa, named Grimm alfalfa, which was at the time considered to be the most winter-hardy strain available. Grimm alfalfa was used throughout North America between 1910 and 1940. Grimm died in 1890, never knowing the impact his alfalfa strain had on American agriculture.

Today Carver County has a population of approximately 88,000 people, divided among the cities of Carver, Chanhassen, Chaska, Cologne, Hamburg, Mayer, New Germany, Norwood, Norwood–Young America, Victoria, Waconia, and Watertown.

Dakota County

Located minutes south of the Twin Cities, Dakota County offers the amenities of the metropolitan area with the charm and serenity of a small town. Approximately 388,000 people live within the county's limits, making it the third most populous county in the state of Minnesota. Yet one-half of its land remains undeveloped or rural.

The quality of life in Dakota County is high due to its excellent schools, its proximity to renowned health care facilities, and pleasant neighborhoods. Parks, fishing lakes, trail systems, and recreation areas are in abundance, as well as the spacious grounds of the Min-

nesota Zoo, the second-largest zoo in the country. Businesses with roots and holdings in Dakota County include Northwest Airlines, West Publishing, ConAgra, Hudson Manufacturing, Alexis Baily, Vineyard, Mead Paper, and Gumby Fancy, providing long-term employment for residents of the area.

Dakota County cities include Apple Valley, Burnsville, Eagan, Farmington, Hastings, Inver Grove Heights, Lakeville, Lilydale, Mendota, Mendota Heights, Miesville, New Trier, Randolph, Rosemount, South St. Paul, Sunfish Lake, and West St. Paul.

Hennepin County

Hennepin County, incorporated in 1852, forms part of one of the nation's major metropolitan areas, with Minneapolis as its largest city and county seat. The county has a broad-based economy with strong trade, service, and manufacturing sectors, and many major corporations are headquartered in the county. The employment base is diverse, and employment remains relatively stable. The county's unemployment rate has consistently remained below the state and national averages.

More than 1,122,000 people live in the 557 square miles that make up Hennepin County, with the greatest percentage living in Minneapolis and the rest distributed among the cities of Bloomington, Brooklyn Center, Brooklyn Park, Champlin, Chanhassen, Corcoran, Crystal, Dayton, Deephaven, Eden Prairie, Edina, Excelsior, Golden Valley, Greenfield, Hamel, Hanover, Hopkins, Howard Lake, Independence, Long Lake, Loretto, Maple Grove, Maple Plain, Medicine Lake, Medina, Minnetonka, Minnetonka Beach, Minnetonka Mills, Minnetrista, Mound, Navarre, New Hope, Orono, Osseo, Plymouth, Richfield, Robbinsdale, Rockford, Rogers, Saint Anthony, Saint Bonifacius, Saint Louis Park, Spring Park, Tonka Bay, Wayzata, Woodland, and Young America.

The largest employers with holdings in Hennepin County include the state government, the University of Minnesota, General Mills, Cargill, Target Corporation, and the U.S. Postal Service.

Ramsey County

Ramsey County, established in 1849, is home to Minnesota's state capital, the city of St. Paul. More than 493,000 people live in the 156 square miles that make up the county, which includes the cities of Arden Hills, Blaine, Falcon Heights, Gem Lake, Lauderdale, Little Canada, Maplewood, Mounds View, New Brighton, North Oaks, North St. Paul, Roseville, St. Anthony, St. Paul, Shoreview, Spring Lake Park, Vadnais Heights, and White Bear Lake.

Ramsey County is the site of many popular attractions, both man-made and natural, including Como Park Zoo and Conservatory, Indian Mounds Park, Harriet Island and Lilydale Parks, and the Alexander Ramsey House. St. Paul's suburbs are built around lakes and parks for summer and winter recreation alike.

Scott County

Scott County, established in 1853 and named after War of 1812 and Mexican-American War General Winfield Scott, is an area of 357 square miles located in the southwest corner of the Twin Cities metro area. The Minnesota River forms the northern border of the county, while the broad river valley cuts though glacial sediment into some of the oldest exposed rock beds in the state. The savanna that makes up most of Scott County once bordered the Big Woods, a hardwood forest that covered a majority of the state before it was logged in the mid-19th century.

Shakopee, the county seat, began in 1851 as a trading post near the Dakota village of Chief Shakopee (or Shakpay). Town sites were established along transportation routes provided by the Minnesota River and the numerous oxcart trails that crisscrossed the region. Years later the railroad was the choice of transport in Minnesota, and still later, highways developed along the oxcart trails and between communities.

Today urban sprawl and suburbanization are threatening this primarily rural county.

Industry has taken hold, and transportation issues play a primary role in development decisions, just as they did in the past.

The county currently has a population of approximately 124,000. Located within the county lines are the cities of Elko, Jordan, New Prague, Prior Lake, and Savage.

Washington County

Washington County is located on the eastern edge of the Metro. Incorporated in 1849, its 392 square miles now house more than 225,000 people divided among the cities of Afton, Bayport, Birchwood, Cottage Grove, Dellwood, Forest Lake, Hastings, Hugo, Lake Elmo, Lake St. Croix Beach, Lakeland, Lakeland Shores, Landfall, Marine on St. Croix, Newport, Oak Park Heights, Oakdale, Pine Springs, St. Mary's Point, St. Paul Park, Scandia, Stillwater, Willernie, and Woodbury. The county seat is located in Stillwater, along the St. Croix River. Originally full of lumber towns, with an economy fueled by the lumber industry and made possible by the St. Croix River, industry in Washington County has grown to include major employers such as Anderson Windows, State Farm Insurance, 3M, and the Minnesota Correctional Facilities in Bayport and Oak Park Heights.

In 1849 the Minnesota territorial legislature met in Stillwater (at 102 South Main Street) and created nine counties in the new Minnesota Territory, including Washington County. Other historic places in the county include Gammelgården, Scandia, the site of the first Swedish settlement in Minnesota, and Cottage Grove, the birthplace of commercial agriculture in Minnesota.

Washington County has more than its share of beautiful natural areas. Located within county lines are Afton State Park, Lake Elmo Park Reserve, St. Croix Bluffs Regional Park, and Square Lake Park, as well as dozens of smaller protected wilderness areas. The county is bordered by the Lower St. Croix National Scenic Riverway.

GETTING HERE, GETTING AROUND

Transportation has long played a crucial role in shaping the Twin Cities. In the beginning the Mississippi, Minnesota, and St. Croix Rivers all made the lumber industry possible in Minnesota, turning communities like Stillwater, St. Anthony, and Minneapolis into important centers of commerce and trade. The rivers were also important in transporting iron, granite, sandstone, and marble from Minnesota to the rest of the world, and for bringing military supplies and luxury items from the rest of the world to Minnesota. Trains later replaced boats as the preferred means of transporting raw materials, and commuter trains became Twin Cities residents' favorite means of personal transportation. The Great Northern Depot in St. Paul, built in 1914, connected passengers to nearby resort destinations like Minnehaha Park and White Bear Lake as well as to the East and West Coasts.

Electric streetcars made their debut in the Twin Cities in 1889, and by the 1920s Minneapolis and St. Paul were home to one of the largest streetcar systems in the world. More than 1,000 cars on 500 miles of track took commuters to work and back home again each day, and the system was so extensive that it was possible to take a streetcar from downtown Minneapolis all the way to Stillwater or Excelsior. Unfortunately the streetcar system was abandoned in the 1950s. In 1954 street buses replaced the electric streetcars, and the electric tracks that crisscrossed the metro area were paved over to facilitate automobile use. The Twin Cities have recently begun to restore streetcar service in the modern-day guise of light-rail trains; Minneapolis launched a light-rail line from downtown Minneapolis to the airport and on to the Mall of America in 2004, and Metro Transit is now in the planning stages of a light-rail line between downtown Minneapolis and downtown St. Paul along University Avenue.

Today, in addition to light rail, the Twin Cities are home to one large international airport and six smaller ones and a bus line that runs 24 hours a day in the busy downtown areas. Even if you're new to the area, fleets of friendly, reliable taxicabs and helpful bus drivers and information operators will make sure you get to your destination safely.

AIR TRAVEL

Minneapolis–St. Paul International Airport
Charles A. Lindbergh Terminal
4300 Glumack Drive, St. Paul
(612) 726-5555

Hubert H. Humphrey Terminal
7150 Humphrey Drive, Minneapolis
(612) 726-5800
www.mspairport.com
Minneapolis–St. Paul International Airport (MSP) is a sprawling complex of two terminals serving 21 passenger airlines, 17 cargo airlines, and 36 million people annually. The airport is located between Minneapolis and St. Paul on the southern side of the Metro, with relatively quick access to both downtowns and the rest of the Twin Cities region. MSP is a hub for Northwest Airlines (the company is based in Eagan, a St. Paul suburb) and, with a steady stream of takeoffs and landings, ranks as the eighth-busiest airport in the nation.

Getting to the Airport

MSP encompasses two terminals—the Lindbergh Terminal and the Humphrey Terminal. The Lindbergh Terminal is accessible from Minnesota Highway 5 via the Lindbergh Terminal exit. The Humphrey Terminal is accessible from Interstate 494 via the 34th Avenue South exit. You can also reach the Lindbergh Terminal by city bus, and both terminals by light rail (visit www.metrotransit.org for schedules and routes). Most commercial passenger airlines fly into Lindbergh, while Humphrey is the landing site for many charter airlines. Check your ticket carefully to determine your terminal before driving to the airport or instructing someone where to pick you up, although if you end up at the wrong terminal, you can hop on the light rail—free of charge between terminals—to quickly get back on track.

Design

If you haven't been through MSP for a few years, you probably won't recognize either of the terminals today. MSP and the six reliever airports operated by the Metropolitan Airports Commission (MAC) are wrapping up a $3.1 billion reconstruction project known as MSP 2010, and things have come a long way since work began in 1996.

Despite the changes, it is not difficult to find your way around either the Lindbergh or Humphrey Terminal. The top level of the Lindbergh Terminal is for ticketing and departures. You can be dropped off at this level via the elevated roadway just outside the doors. The gate concourses at Lindbergh are lettered sequentially, A through G. Generally, if your concourse letter is A through E, you will veer right after passing through the security checkpoints in between the check-in counters; if your concourse letter is F or G, you will veer left. You can easily find your gate by observing the concourse number and gate (for example, E8 would be Gate 8 on Concourse E). The lower the number of the gate, the shorter your walk down the concourse. Note that Concourses A and B, designated for smaller commuter airlines, are at the end of Concourse C.

People-mover walkways carry passengers down Concourses C and G, the two longest at MSP, and across the Skyway Connector

between Concourses C and G. An aboveground shuttle tram also carries passengers the length of Concourse C, with several stops along the way, and an underground Hub Tram runs from Level T, two floors below the ticketing and departures concourse, to escalators leading to the Skyway Connector. This tram also carries passengers to the outer Blue and Red parking ramps and to the Transit Center, where you will find the rental car counters, city bus stop, and the light-rail station.

At Lindbergh the baggage claim area is one floor below the ticketing and departures concourse. Electronic displays on this level indicate which of the 14 baggage carousels will deliver the luggage from your flight.

The much-smaller Humphrey Terminal will not make your feet as sore. Ticketing and departure counters, as well as the baggage claim area, are all located on the first floor of the terminal. The gates are one floor up and accessible via a short escalator ride. Taxis and shuttles to rental car agencies can be found on the commercial roadway on the first level of the parking ramp.

Airlines

As noted, MSP is a hub for Northwest Airlines, and the carrier controls more than 60 percent of the local market. But Northwest has had recent troubles, including filing for Chapter 11 bankruptcy protection in September 2005. The airline emerged from bankruptcy in May 2007 with a leaner, lower-paid workforce; fewer flights and fuller airplanes; and somewhat higher ticket fares, on average. Then again, MSP's renewed status as a Northwest hub means that Twin Citians and visitors continue to enjoy a large selection of nonstop flights to and from destinations worldwide. If you are flexible about your departure time, plan far enough in advance, and look for sale fares online, you'll be less likely to experience sticker shock flying in or out of MSP.

Given the dominance of Northwest in Minneapolis–St. Paul, it is worth checking the airline's Web site (www.nwa.com) for cyberdeals if you are planning a trip to or from the Twin Cities. The airline offers specials, released every Wednesday, and if the special happens to be to or from your city, you can get a steep discount on your seat. On the Web site you can sign up for e-mail notices of these special offers.

Of course, Northwest isn't the only game in town. With the exception of Southwest Airlines, all major American carriers serve MSP, as do three international airlines and five charter airlines. When looking for a flight, be certain to check the Web site of Sun Country Airlines (www.suncountry.com), which also has a hub in the Twin Cities and often has discount fares on direct flights, although on a limited flight schedule. Often, charter flights can also mean a deal on your airline seat, although in Minneapolis–St. Paul most charter flights are from the Cities to warm-weather destinations, particularly in winter.

Domestic Airlines

AirTran Airways, (800) 247-8726; www.airtran.com

American Airlines, (800) 433-7300; www.aa.com

Comair Airlines (operated by Delta), (800) 354-9822; www.comair.com

Continental Airlines, (800) 525-0280; www.continental.com

Delta Airlines, (800) 221-1212; www.delta.com

Frontier Airlines, (800) 432-1359; www.frontierairlines.com

Mesaba Airlines (Northwest Airlink), (800) 225-2525; www.mesaba.com

Midwest Airlines, (800) 452-2022; www.midwestairlines.com

Northwest Airlines, (800) 225-2525; www.nwa.com

SkyWest Airlines, (800) 221-1212 or (435) 624-3400; www.skywest.com

Sun Country Airlines, (800) 359-6786; www.suncountry.com

United Airlines, (800) 241-6522; www.ual.com

US Airways, (800) 428-4322; www.usairways.com

International Airlines

Air Canada, (888) 247-2262; www.aircanada.com

Icelandair, (800) 223-5500; www.icelandair.com

KLM Royal Dutch Airlines, (800) 374-7747; www.klm.com

Charter Airlines

Champion Air, (800) 922-2606; www.championair.com

Miami Air International, (305) 876-3600; www.miamiair.com

Omni Air International, (877) 718-8901; www.omniairintl.com

Ryan International, (888) 443-7926; www.flyryan.com

Xtra Airways, (800) 258-8800; www.xtraairways.com

Ground Transportation

You can get to or from the airport via a variety of means. For the Lindbergh Terminal: For car rentals, city buses, hotel shuttles, or light rail, take the Hub Tram on Level T to the Transit Center.

Once at the Transit Center, follow the signs on Level T to the escalators to reach the taxi station. Also follow the signs for car rental agencies, although the signage can be a little confusing; check around for a sign with your rental agency on it before getting on an escalator or walking out a door. At the Humphrey Terminal, you can find the rental car counters in the Ground Transport Center on the bottom floor of the parking ramp directly across from the terminal building. Car rental agencies that have rental locations at the airport (at both terminals) are **National Car Rental** (800-227-7368; www.nationalcar.com); **Budget Car & Truck Rental** (800-527-0700; www.budget.com); **Avis Rent A Car** (800-831-2847; www.avis.com); **Alamo** (800-327-9633; www .alamo.com); **Dollar Rent A Car** (800-800-4000; www.dollar.com); **Enterprise Rent-A-Car** (800-325-8007; www .enterprise.com); and **Hertz** (800-654-3131; www.hertz.com). Car rental agencies with off-airport locations are **Payless** (www.paylesscarrental.com; 800-729-5377) and **Thrifty** (www .thrifty.com; 800-367-2277. At the Lindbergh Terminal's Transit Center, you can catch a shuttle bus designated for your agency. At the Humphrey Terminal, you must arrange pickup by using the call boards in the baggage claim area to contact your agency for pickup.

You can catch taxis at the Lindbergh Terminal in the Transit Center, one level up from the Tram Level. At the Humphrey Terminal, taxis queue up at the Ground Transport Center on the bottom floor of the parking ramp directly across from the terminal building. Let the attendant know if you have special needs, such as a cab that takes credit cards. For a list of taxi companies and their contact information, see the Taxis section later in this chapter.

City buses and the light-rail transit (LRT) are far and away the cheapest ways to get to and from the airport. If you're traveling light and in no big hurry, you can catch a city bus at the Transit Center (Humphrey Terminal passengers arriving by bus or riding a bus to their Twin Cities destination must take the LRT between terminals, which is free between the airport stops). As a faster option, if your destination or starting point happens to be along

its path, the LRT stops at the Lindbergh Terminal's Transit Center and the Humphrey Terminal's Ground Transport Center on its way to and from the Mall of America and downtown Minneapolis. Contact **Metro Transit** at (612) 373-3333 or visit www.metrotransit.org for route and schedule information for buses or light rail. For more information on both, see the Public Transportation section later in this chapter.

Parking

The Lindbergh Terminal offers short-term, long-term, and valet parking in the four ramps surrounded by the terminal concourses. Follow the signs as you enter the terminal area. Short-term parking is designed for stays of less than two hours; long-term parking is designed for stays longer than two hours. Receive $2 off short- or long-term parking with epark, a self-pay system used by inserting your credit card into a machine when you enter and exit. You can access the terminal from any of the ramps via enclosed skyways, the Hub Tram (accessible from the Transit Center), or Level T.

The Humphrey Terminal offers short- and long-term parking in the ramp across the street from the terminal. Travelers can get to the terminal by walking across the street or using the enclosed skyway on the second level.

For off-airport parking, the following lots offer shuttle transportation to and from MSP every 5 to 10 minutes, 24 hours a day:

EZ Air Park (651-777-7275; www.ezairpark.com); at 2804 Lexington Avenue, Eagan

Park 'N Fly (952-854-0606; www.pnf.com); 3700 American Boulevard East, Bloomington

Park 'N Go (952-854-3386; www.parkngo.net); 7901 International Drive, Bloomington

Team Parking, (651-690-1265); 1400 Davern Street and Shepard Road, St. Paul

For parking availability and information, call the MSP Parking Information Line at (877) 359-7275 or visit www.mspairport.com/msp/parking/realtime.aspx.

Amenities

With the last big series of expansions made to MSP in the 1990s, the Lindbergh Terminal's waiting area went from being a midsize airport to a mall of shops and restaurant courts. The centerpiece of the terminal's lobby is Northstar Crossing, a collection of more than 100 retail shops and restaurants. The area features Minnesota-themed shops and nationally known retailers, including the first airport-based Lands' End. Throughout the terminal can be found McDonald's, Burger King, Cinnabon, Pizza Hut, Ben & Jerry's, Stage Deli, the first airport D.Q. Grill and Chill, and more. For libations (Lindbergh Terminal only) there are several City Martinis, a PS Air Pub, and the MSP Brewhouse. The Humphrey Terminal offers more limited services, with Lord Fletcher's restaurant, Dunn Bros. Coffee and Cafe, plus two shops selling magazines, newspapers, snacks, and gifts.

For passengers with disabilities, all airlines operating out of MSP provide wheelchairs for the flight. For carts, wheelchairs, or medical transportation, airline passengers should contact their travel agent, ticketing agents, flight attendants, or gate agents. **Travelers Assistance** (TA) can also help with wheelchair requests. TA volunteers may be reached by calling (612) 726-5500. Wheelchairs are also available for checkout at the information booth on Level T and at security checkpoints.

If you lose something at either of the terminals, call **Airport Lost and Found** at (612) 726-5141. The Lost and Found Office is located in the Lindbergh Terminal on the Mezzanine Level, one floor above the ticketing area.

TRAIN TRAVEL

Amtrak
Twin Cities Passenger Station
730 Transfer Road, St. Paul
(651) 644-1127 or (800) 872-7245
www.amtrak.com
The Twin Cities share a train station in the industrial Midway District of St. Paul. To get to the station, take the Cretin Avenue/Vandalia Street exit from Interstate 94 and turn north at the stoplights. Turn east (right) at University Avenue, and then turn north (left) at the next stoplight (Cleveland/Transfer Road). The station is about a block up on the right. You can also get to the station from downtown Minneapolis or St. Paul on Metro Transit bus route 16 along University Avenue. The station and ticket counter are open 6:00 a.m. to 12:30 p.m. daily.

A single passenger train, the Empire Builder between Chicago and Seattle, stops at the station twice a day (once in each direction). If you're headed for points far afield, you can make connections in Chicago or Seattle to stations throughout the country.

Within Minnesota, the Empire Builder stops at Winona, Red Wing, St. Cloud, Staples, Detroit Lakes, and Fargo-Moorhead. While the train can be a fine option for travel to and from Red Wing and Winona, it's less convenient for the stations north of the Cities, where you arrive or depart in the middle of the night, regardless of whether you are on the east- or westbound train. See the Amtrak Web site for detailed schedules and routes.

BUS TRAVEL

Greyhound Lines
166 West University Avenue, St. Paul
(651) 222-0507

950 Hawthorne Avenue, Minneapolis
(612) 371-3325
www.greyhound.com
Greyhound is a Minnesota company, founded in Hibbing on northern Minnesota's Iron Range in 1914. St. Paul and Minneapolis each have a Greyhound station. St. Paul's station is just west of the State Capitol building on University Avenue and is open 6:45 a.m. to 7:30 p.m. daily. The downtown Minneapolis station is next to the Hawthorne Transportation Center, a few blocks west of Target Center (First Avenue becomes Hawthorne Avenue as it heads west), and is open 6:00 a.m. to midnight daily. Greyhound also picks up and drops off (but doesn't sell tickets) at the

Amtrak Station, 730 Transfer Road, St. Paul (651-644-0616); at the Student Center at the University of Minnesota–St. Paul Campus, 2017 Buford Avenue, St. Paul (612-625-9794); and at several locations in the Twin Cities suburbs.

Jefferson Lines serves both Greyhound terminals, the St. Paul Amtrak Station, the Lindbergh Terminal at Minneapolis–St. Paul International Airport, the University of Minnesota, Burnsville, and Anoka. Call (888) 864-2832 or visit www.jeffersonlines.com for more information.

CAR TRAVEL

Highways

Minneapolis–St. Paul has well-thought-out arterial and surrounding highways. However, politics and not-so-well-thought-out plans limit the number of lanes on many area highways, causing traffic jams and bottlenecks with predictable frequency. If you are driving to your destination in the Twin Cities, be aware that some major highways become parking lots during the morning and evening rush hours.

On August 1, 2007, the Mississippi River bridge carrying Interstate 35W collapsed, killing 13 people. The horrific disaster stunned the nation, but it also posed a major transportation conundrum as the bridge was the busiest in Minnesota, carrying some 140,000 cars and trucks daily to and from downtown Minneapolis. A replacement bridge is under construction and is expected to be completed in late 2008. If you need to get to downtown Minneapolis from the northern Metro, follow Minnesota Highway 36/I-35W to Minnesota Highway 280 in Roseville, exit on Highway 280 going south, join I-94 going west at the terminus of Highway 280, and follow I-94 into downtown Minneapolis. Reverse the route to commute back to the northern suburbs. I-35W north of the Mississippi remains open as far as University Avenue and is open once again at 3rd Street south of the river. Contact the Minnesota Department of Transportation at (800) 657-3774 or www.dot.state.mn.us for

the latest information.

The Twin Cities are ringed by the Interstate 494/Interstate 694 loop. I-494 starts at the interchange with I-94 in the eastern suburb of Woodbury; arcs south around South St. Paul; heads due west through Eagan, Bloomington, and Eden Prairie; and then swings north through the western suburbs to reunite with I-94 in the suburb of Maple Grove northwest of Minneapolis. I-694 also starts at the intersection with I-94 in Woodbury but heads north through Oakdale, swings west to the intersection with Interstate 35E in Little Canada, and then meanders roughly northwest through the suburbs of New Brighton, Fridley, Brooklyn Center, Brooklyn Park, and Maple Grove, where it meets I-94 again.

The ragged rectangle made by the I-494/I-694 loop is sliced by two branches of I-35 heading north–south through the Metro. I-35 splits into I-35W and I-35E in the southern suburb of Burnsville. I-35W heads due north through the western part of the Metro (note the ongoing construction around the intersection with Minnesota Highway 62 makes the commute on I-35W south of downtown Minneapolis ponderous). Eventually, you'll reach downtown as far as Third Street. Due to the 2007 bridge collapse, I-35W is closed between Third Street and University Avenue, after which the artery wiggles northeast of downtown through the northern suburbs to merge with I-35E in Columbus Township and becomes I-35 again. I-35E heads northeast from Burnsville into downtown St. Paul and then shoots north to briefly merge with I-694 before stretching north again for its eventual reunion with I-35W.

I-94 and I-394 split the I-494/I-694 rectangle east–west. I-94 rolls into the eastern Metro from Wisconsin, passing through downtown St. Paul and downtown Minneapolis before abruptly swinging north, where it merges for a few miles with I-694 in Brooklyn Center before going it alone again in its long march westward. Interstate 394 runs from the western suburbs to downtown Minneapolis. The newest of the Twin Cities freeways, I-394 includes separate carpool lanes (open during times of heavy congestion), as well as Minnesota's only pay-per-use highway. Solo drivers in a hurry can use the carpool lanes as long as they have a MnPASS account and a transponder, which can be electronically read by highway sensors, and you'll then be automatically charged a toll that varies based on traffic levels and on where you enter or exit the highway. (For more information about MnPASS, contact the Minnesota Department of Transportation MnPASS Service Center at 866-394-4334 or www.mnpass.net.) Whether you choose to use the MnPASS, are driving with more than one person, or are willing to drive on the free noncarpool, non-MnPASS lanes, I-394 will take you from the western Metro right into the heart of downtown Minneapolis's Warehouse District and back again.

Several other federal and state highways crosshatch the I-494/I-694 loop. U.S. Highway 169 arrives in the Metro from southwestern Minnesota in the suburb of Eden Prairie, on the southwestern edge of the Cities, and then shoots due north through the western suburbs, crossing I-694 in Maple Grove just east of the intersection of I-694 and I-494. US 169 and the roughly parallel Minnesota Highway 100 are the principal north–south routes in the western suburbs.

Minnesota Highway 62 is the major east–west route through the southern Metro north of I-494. MN 62, referred to locally as the Crosstown, runs from its intersection with US 169 in Minnetonka in the southwestern Metro to its intersection with Minnesota Highway 55, just north of the Minneapolis–St. Paul International Airport. The Crosstown looks convenient on a map, but the highway briefly merges with I-35W in Richfield, and the resulting bottleneck is considered one of the worst in the nation. Current construction along I-35W, which will one day separate the two highways and relieve the bottleneck, is slowing things down even more.

Other useful highways in the south-central Metro include Minnesota Highway 77, which runs from the southern suburb of Apple Val-

ley to its intersection with the Crosstown in the Lake Nokomis area of south Minneapolis. This highway passes, among other things, the Minnesota Zoo, the Mall of America, and MSP airport. MN 55 stretches all the way from the town of Hastings, 20 miles southeast of St. Paul, to downtown Minneapolis, passing over the Minnesota River via the 4,119-foot concrete-arch Fort Snelling–Mendota Bridge and skirting Fort Snelling State Park, MSP airport, and Minnehaha Park before gliding through the commercial districts of south Minneapolis. Known as Hiawatha Avenue along its path inside Minneapolis, this road is the route of the Hiawatha light-rail transit (LRT) leg from downtown Minneapolis to the airport. There are stoplights along parts of this route, but it can be a quick alternative to get downtown from the southeastern Metro.

The principal highways in the eastern Metro include Minnesota Highway 110, which starts at its intersection with I-494 just west of the intersection with U.S. Highway 52, then takes a short tour of the St. Paul suburbs of Inver Grove Heights, Sunfish Lake, West St. Paul, and Mendota Heights before intersecting with MN 55 just before the Fort Snelling–Mendota Bridge over the Minnesota River.

US 52 is perhaps more useful, arriving from southern Minnesota and intersecting I-494 in the southern St. Paul suburb of Inver Grove Heights. From there the highway conveniently heads through the suburbs of South St. Paul and West St. Paul right to downtown St. Paul, passing St. Paul Downtown Holman Field airport and crossing the Mississippi River in the process. The route into the city along US 52, particularly at night, provides some of the most spectacular views of the St. Paul skyline.

U.S. Highways 10 and 61 unite in Hastings and follow the Mississippi River to I-94 just

i   Twin Citians are notorious for the speeds at which they enter city highways. They definitely try to merge onto the freeway already traveling at freeway speed—and they expect that you will accelerate rapidly, too.

Interstate 94 winds its way through downtown St. Paul and on to Minneapolis. TODD R. BERGER

east of downtown St. Paul, passing through the suburbs of Cottage Grove, St. Paul Park, and Newport in the process. From there, US 61 veers north at Arcade Street, following city streets until hitting the suburb of Maplewood and then spiking north through the suburbs of Mahtomedi, Gem Lake, White Bear Lake, and Hugo before ending just north of Forest Lake about 25 miles north of downtown St. Paul. US 61 roughly parallels I-35E in the northern suburbs, and the interstate is almost always a better choice except during heavy rush-hour traffic.

US 10 takes the easy route after intersecting I-94 by merging with the interstate in the westbound direction, then turning north and merging with I-35E for a few miles, and then merging with I-694 and heading northwest to the northern suburb of Arden Hills. From there US 10 briefly follows its own route northwest, then merges with I-35W in Mounds View for a few miles, finally going it alone through the suburbs of Blaine, Coon Rapids, Anoka, Ramsey, and Elk River before skipping out of the Metro.

Minnesota Highway 36 is another useful eastern highway, running from its intersection with I-35W in the northern suburb of Roseville through Little Canada, Maplewood, North St. Paul, and Oakdale all the way to Stillwater on the St. Croix River. MN 36 is the quickest outlet to the St. Croix Valley and a convenient artery leading to many shopping areas in the first-tier northern suburbs.

Minnesota Highway 280 provides an appreciated shortcut for motorists on I-94 on the western edges of St. Paul intent on reaching the northern suburbs and for commuters trying to reach downtown Minneapolis from the north. The highway runs from its intersection with I-94 just east of the Minneapolis city boundary due north through Lauderdale to intersect I-35W in Roseville after just a few miles. The highway provides access not only to the retail outlets of Roseville but also to the University of Minnesota–St. Paul Campus and

Luther Seminary. MN 280 is the principal detour to get around the fallen bridge on I-35W, so be prepared for very heavy traffic and some closed cross-street access points along MN 280 while the I-35W bridge is being rebuilt.

Twin Cities Streets

Minneapolis and St. Paul are two distinctly governed municipalities, separated along much of one boundary by the Mississippi River. For this reason, Minneapolis and St. Paul share a few important streets, which include University and Como Avenues. However, several streets change their names when crossing the county line. Most notably, Larpenteur Avenue in St. Paul becomes East Hennepin Avenue in Minneapolis, and Marshall Avenue in St. Paul turns into Lake Street after crossing the Mississippi into Minneapolis. More confusingly, both cities have streets that share names but are not connected to their counterparts across the river, including Minnehaha and Grand Avenues. These things happen when urban centers develop next to one another. Try to keep this in mind when navigating Twin Cities streets.

St. Paul Streets

It felt like all of St. Paul was mad at then-Minnesota governor Jesse Ventura after he complained to David Letterman on national television that the downtown streets seemed to have been designed by drunken Irishmen. But people have been complaining about St. Paul's street plan for ages, and anyone thinking Governor Ventura was in the habit of softening the blows should remember that the man was a pro wrestler.

The street plan really isn't that confounding, but it does get a little tricky where main thoroughfare Kellogg Boulevard takes a southeasterly bend to run along the Mississippi River. Kellogg connects the action at the southeastern end of the city (Xcel Energy Center, the Science Museum of Minnesota) with the artsy Lowertown district. The main streets unfolding away from the river, or northwest of Kellogg, are numbered beginning with 4th and

i Parking ramp availability signs are conveniently located on downtown St. Paul streets. The signs post the number of available parking spots and are helpful in guiding drivers to lots with spaces open.

reach 11th just before I-94 and I-35E rein in downtown St. Paul. These numbered streets are labeled "west" and "east" depending on which side of Wabasha Street they are. Wabasha is a main northwest–southeast thoroughfare, and it, along with Robert and Smith Streets, crosses the Mississippi River to what's called St. Paul's West Side (it's actually on the city's south side), which is the premier Twin Cities Latino neighborhood. Seventh Street (again, labeled east or west in relation to Wabasha) is the main northeast–southwest route. It and all the other major arteries named here are prone to congestion during rush hour or major Xcel Energy Center events, though St. Paul generally has less traffic than Minneapolis.

Another of St. Paul's main streets, Snelling Avenue (Minnesota Highway 51), starts on far western Seventh Street, northeast of MSP airport. It then runs north past the St. Paul neighborhood of Highland Park and through the university-riddled west side of the city, where it intersects major avenues such as Randolph, Grand, Summit, and University, as well as I-94, before continuing past the Minnesota State Fairgrounds into St. Paul's northern suburbs. Snelling is often busy, as is cross street University Avenue, which starts near the Minnesota State Capitol just north of downtown St. Paul, then parallels I-94 west on into Minneapolis.

East–west-running Grand and Summit Avenues are good to know, too. They begin on a bluff on the northwest side of downtown, just 1 block from one another—Summit is the world's longest stretch of intact original Victorian housing, and Grand is St. Paul's main shopping and dining street.

Minneapolis Streets

Four key pieces of advice for drivers new to downtown Minneapolis. One: Get your numbered avenues and streets straight. Two: The myriad one-way streets generally alternate. Three: Keep your eyes peeled for the light rail on Fifth Street. Four: Never drive on Nicollet Mall, the city's pedestrian-friendly shopping artery.

We'll start with the numbers thing. The streets run northwest–southeast, beginning with First Street along the Mississippi River. They're named north or south depending on which side of the main thoroughfare Hennepin Avenue (aka Theater Row) they lie. Avenues, such as Hennepin, run northeast–southwest, and they have names more often than numbers. Downtown Minneapolis is bound by I-94, which runs east–west below Minneapolis before angling north–south along the city's west edge. Both Hennepin and Third Avenues have bridges across the Mississippi into St. Anthony and the hip Northeast neighborhood, with lots of locally owned shops, restaurants, and bars. The beautiful Stone Arch Bridge, like Nicollet Mall, is for people and bikes only. All of downtown is congested during rush hours and when events are happening at the Metrodome (on the southeast side of downtown) or Target Center (on the northwest).

Things get easier both northeast and southwest of the city when the grid straightens out. At that point streets run plain-old north–south, and the avenues go, for the most part, east–west. Take Hennepin southwest out of downtown, for example, and you're headed to Loring Park, the Walker Art Center, and, once the street curves south, the Uptown shopping and dining district. Lake Street and Hennepin Avenue are at the heart of Uptown—follow Lake Street west a few blocks and you're at Lake Calhoun (one of this area's many lakes). Follow Lake Street east and you'll cross major north–south-running Lyndale Avenue, I-35W, Chicago Avenue, and Hiawatha Avenue (home to the

LRT line) before eventually crossing the Mississippi into St. Paul.

SNOW EMERGENCY INFORMATION

Although the words "snow emergency" may sound ominous to the uninitiated, such events are declared so that the city of Minneapolis or St. Paul can get people to park their cars in the proper places to allow plows through. Declaration of an "emergency" does not (necessarily) mean that you will need to stock up on batteries or canned chipped beef. Both Minneapolis and St. Paul have extensive (and different) snow emergency ordinances. In some situations, not complying with snow removal rules will result in the towing of your vehicle, a hefty fine, or both, so beware. Snow emergencies are announced through the local media. You can also check to see if restrictions are in effect in Minneapolis by calling (612) 348-SNOW or visiting www.ci.minneapolis.mn.us/snow/parking-info. For St. Paul call (651) 266-PLOW, or check the Web at www.stpaul.gov/depts/publicworks/snowplow. It is your responsibility to know if a snow emergency has been declared; pleading ignorance will not get you out of paying a fine or towing fees. The following is a list of guidelines and helpful hints for snow emergencies.

Minneapolis

Minneapolis does not set a minimum amount of snowfall to declare a snow emergency other than to describe it as "significant." Once a snow emergency is declared before 6:00 p.m., the entire city enters a three-day cycle that dictates where you can park your car. On the first day of a snow emergency, from 9:00 p.m. to 8:00 a.m., the city allows no parking on either side of Snow Emergency Routes, which are marked with red signs along the side of the street or blue street-name signs (non–snow emergency routes have green or brown street-name

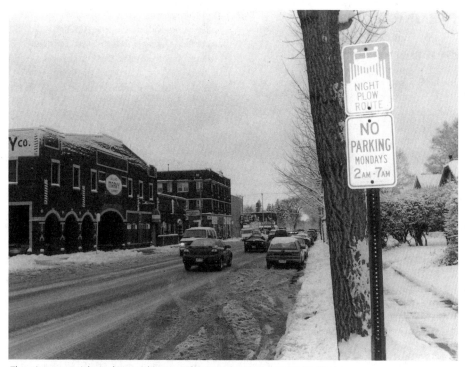

There is no overnight parking on this street during snow emergencies in St. Paul. TODD R. BERGER

signs). You can park on either side of any non–snow emergency route and on parkways. On the second day of the snow emergency, from 8:00 a.m. to 8:00 p.m., there is no parking on either side of parkways or on the even-numbered side of non–snow emergency routes; however, you can now park on plowed Snow Emergency Routes. From 8:00 p.m. to 8:00 a.m. on the second night of the snow emergency, you cannot park on the odd-numbered side of non–snow emergency routes. On the third day of the snow emergency, the parking ban continues on the odd-numbered side of non–snow emergency routes until the street is plowed to the curb.

Minneapolis offers free or reduced-fee parking on the first night of a snow emergency at five parking ramps near downtown and around the University of Minnesota. Call the Minneapolis snow emergency line or check out the Web site for more information.

St. Paul

St. Paul declares snow emergencies after 3 or more inches of snow accumulate at once, or accumulate over days. St. Paul divides its streets into "night plow" and "day plow" routes. The night plow routes are plowed between 9:00 p.m. and 6:00 a.m. on the night the snow emergency is declared. These routes are marked with Night Plow Route signs. All downtown streets are plowed the first night. Note that some north–south residential streets have signs reading NIGHT PLOW ROUTE THIS SIDE OF STREET. You can park on the nonsigned sides of these streets during the first night of a snow emergency. The snow is removed on day plow routes from 8:00 a.m. to 5:00 p.m. These routes, which are not marked with signs, include east–west residential streets and north–south residential streets without Night Plow Route signs.

PARKING

The rates at downtown Minneapolis and St. Paul parking ramps and lots range widely based on location, time of day, the owner of the facility, and whether a sporting event or other major happening is occurring in the area. Generally you can expect to pay $4 to $7 minimum for the first hour at downtown lots in either city, but there's usually a maximum amount you'll pay—likely somewhere between $8 and $20. To get the best price, look for surface lots near event sites or ramps/lots on the fringes of either city's downtown. For many ramps in downtown Minneapolis, parking charges can be avoided by patronizing stores and restaurants that participate in the "Do the Town" parking program, where a $20 purchase after 4:00 p.m. and all day on weekends will get you a parking validation.

Both cities have many parking meters. Rates and enforcement times vary, so check the signs carefully and carry plenty of quarters. It's illegal to replug in both cities.

Keep in mind when parking in either downtown that you do not necessarily have to park right next to your destination when the winter winds blow and the temperatures plummet. In both downtown Minneapolis and downtown St. Paul, many buildings and parking ramps are connected through the Cities' respective skyway systems.

The skyway systems provide an added bonus in the summer, too—walking over the main pedestrian thoroughfares means you don't have to stop for traffic lights or crosswalks, or watch out for puddles or rogue automobiles.

Park-and-Ride Lots

Thousands of free parking spaces are available for city bus and LRT passengers at more than 100 Park-and-Ride lots throughout the Twin Cities metro area. For locations, call Metro Transit at (612) 373-3333, or visit their Web site at www.metrotransit.org/service Info/parkRide.

i Numerous Twin Cities events offer park-and-ride opportunities. For example, the Minnesota State Fair has park-and-ride lots at the University of Minnesota, Har Mar Mall (in Roseville), and at other locations. Park and ride is an excellent way to avoid traffic and the hassle of commuting to popular Twin Cities events.

PUBLIC TRANSPORTATION
City Buses

Metro Transit
(612) 373-3333
www.metrotransit.org

Metro Transit, the principal transportation provider in the Minneapolis and St. Paul area, is one of the country's largest transit systems. Each weekday, customers board Metro Transit buses and LRT trains an average of 240,000 times. Buses run between the Cities and the suburbs every day and evening—some downtown Minneapolis lines even run 24 hours a day. The system is made up of 118 routes served by a fleet of 821 buses, and Metro Transit has its own police department.

Adult rates for Metro Transit buses are $1.50 during non–rush-hour times and $2.00 for rush-hour times for local bus routes and $2.00 outside rush hour and $2.75 during rush hour for express routes. Rush hour is defined as 6:00 to 9:00 a.m. and 3:00 to 6:30 p.m., Monday through Friday (except holidays). Seniors over 65 and youths under 12 can ride at reduced fares during non–rush-hour times. Persons with disabilities can ride for 50 cents anytime.

Metro Transit buses are reliable and travel widely dispersed routes within the cities of Minneapolis and St. Paul, and it is very possible to live in either St. Paul or Minneapolis and not own a car. Service to the outer suburbs is less frequent, with only a few lines running out of town each day—usually one an hour at most. Downtown Minneapolis, downtown St. Paul, Uptown Minneapolis, the

Chicago Lake Transit Center, the Columbia Heights Transit Center, the Rosedale Transit Center, the Southdale Transit Center, and the Mall of America are Metro Transit's eight main hubs, where most routes converge and transfers are easy to make. A quick phone call to Metro Transit will put you in touch with an operator who will plan your trip or mail you all the schedules you need to get around the area. Transit System maps are also available from Metro Transit.

On Metro Transit's Web site, you can determine routes, view route maps, print schedules, and plan itineraries by entering origination and destination addresses, landmarks, or nearest street intersections.

Light-Rail

Metro Transit
(612) 373-3333
www.metrotransit.org
The Twin Cities first light-rail line, the Hiawatha LRT, opened in 2004. The line stretches 12 miles from downtown Minneapolis, past the Metrodome and near the University of Minnesota West Bank Campus, and then follows Hiawatha Avenue through south Minneapolis past Lake Street, tunnels under Minnehaha Park, resurfaces to pause at the Veterans' Administration Medical Center, and then moves on to Fort Snelling State Park. The line dives underground again via tunnels to the Lindbergh Terminal and emerges to stop at the Humphrey Terminal at MSP airport, then travels to the Mall of America in Bloomington.

The line features 17 stations, all individually designed to fit in with the surrounding neighborhoods. Train fares are $2.00 during

Light-rail transit, known as the LRT, in downtown Minneapolis. GREATER MINNEAPOLIS CONVENTION & VISITORS ASSOCIATION

rush hours and $1.50 at other times—the same fares as local bus service. Rail riders must pay this fare before boarding trains and show proof of payment to transit police officers when asked. Ticket vending machines are available on rail platforms.

The Hiawatha LRT line was a source of great public debate for many years in the Twin Cities and in Minnesota state government—not surprising given the project's $715 million price tag. However, not long after the first south Minneapolis residents rode to the Mall of America, the first conventioneers boarded a train at the airport that dropped them off near their downtown Minneapolis hotels, and the first Metro commuters took advantage of the several park-and-ride lots for quick trips to their downtown jobs, the arguments were over. During the first 15 months of service, customers took 8.5 million rides—67 percent higher than projections, and Metro Transit is now planning future expansions of LRT lines.

> **i** Some of the buses in downtown Minneapolis run 24 hours a day year-round. Within the "Downtown Zones" of Minneapolis and St. Paul, bus fares are 50 cents. Simply tell the driver you will be riding only in the Downtown Zone to get the reduced fare. Call Metro Transit at (612) 373-3333 for specific bus schedules and route information.

Suburban Bus Systems

Several suburban areas have smaller bus systems serving outlying communities, with connections to the larger Metro Transit system in the Twin Cities. For more information on bus service in specific areas, contact the following organizations.

Northwestern suburbs

Maple Grove Transit
(763) 494-6005
www.ci.maple-grove.mn.us

Northstar Commuter Coach
(888) 528-8880
www.commutercoach.org
Northstar Commuter Coach connects the communities of Elk River and Coon Rapids with downtown Minneapolis.

Plymouth Metrolink
(763) 509-5535
www2.ci.plymouth.mn.us

Southern suburbs

Minnesota Valley Transit Authority
(952) 882-7500
www.mvta.com
The Minnesota Valley Transit Authority serves five southern suburbs just south of the Minnesota River: Apple Valley, Burnsville, Eagan, Rosemount, and Savage.

Southwestern suburbs

SouthWest Metro Transit
(952) 949-2287
www.swtransit.org
SouthWest Metro Transit serves the communities of Eden Prairie, Chanhassen, and Chaska.

i Are you concerned about road conditions? Check out the Minnesota Department of Transportation Web site (www.dot.state.mn.us) or call (651) 296-3000 or (800) 657-3774.

Taxis

While taxicabs are a common sight in both downtown Minneapolis and St. Paul, flagging one down on the street is nearly impossible. Your best bet is to call a cab company and have it send a ride over to you.

The one exception to this rule is at the airport. Parked cabs waiting for fares line up at the taxi station at Lindbergh Terminal and at the curb in front of Humphrey Terminal.

The following taxi companies provide service in both the Twin Cities. Consult the Minneapolis or St. Paul Yellow Pages for further options, but understand that most companies don't have cabs in both cities.

Green & White/Suburban Taxi
Minneapolis Service: (612) 522-2222
St. Paul Service: (651) 222-2222

Yellow Checker Taxi
Minneapolis Service: (763) 586-9999
St. Paul Service: (651) 777-1111

HISTORY

The Twin Cities were built on their abundant natural resources and fecund lands. Milling, mining, and lumbering were the cornerstones of the early Twin Cities economy. The number of farmers, millers, and lumberjacks may have dramatically decreased, but it is the basis of the area's early history. And at least indirectly, it continues to affect the personal and economic livelihood of Twin Citians.

THE ORIGINS OF THE TWIN CITIES

The history of the Twin Cities begins with two cities, Minneapolis and St. Paul, each with distinct yet similar developments. Minneapolis is nicknamed the "City of Lakes" and the "Mill City." In stark contrast, St. Paul is the "Saintly City" and the "Capital City." But there are more similarities than differences between the cities. One commonality is the first inhabitants of the area: American Indians.

Human habitation of the Twin Cities area dates back at least 11,500 years to the Paleo-Indians, who hunted big game such as woolly mammoths, then abundant in Minnesota. Archeologists and historians actually know more about the Woodland Indians because of the rich fossil record they left behind. Woodland Indian burial mounds were scattered throughout Minnesota when the state was settled. Indian Mounds Park, overlooking downtown St. Paul, has some of the area's finest examples of Hopewell and Dakota Indian mounds. The Mississippian cultures of the Dakotas and Ojibwes replaced these early peoples. Archeologists posit that this occurred between A.D. 800 and 1000. The mounds and their human remains, tools, and other artifacts are protected as the historical record of the first Twin Citians.

In the past, the Ojibwes, or Ojibwas, were often referred to as the Chippewas and had origins in the area near Sault Ste. Marie, Michigan. The skilled hunters' territories expanded to include parts of the northern metropolitan Twin Cities. While the Ojibwes' origins were to the east and north, the Dakotas were western Plains Indians, who at the time of European exploration occupied the Twin Cities, western and southern Minnesota, and much of present-day North Dakota and South Dakota. The French referred to the Dakotas as Sioux, a meaningless abridgement of the Ojibwe term *Nadouissouix*. The word translates as "little viper" or "lesser enemy." The derogatory name stuck for centuries, until recently when the tribe was called the more respectful name Dakota. Both the Dakotas and Ojibwes were hunting societies, and they evolved tremendously by incorporating European tools, wares, and implements such as guns, hatchets, blankets, knives, and kettles. The contact and cultural exchange transformed the local American Indians and the Europeans. The Europeans rapidly pushed the less densely populated American Indians from their lands through treaties and warfare. Frequently internecine warfare occurred between the Dakotas, usually supported and supplied by the British, and the Ojibwes, supported by the French. However, the French voyageurs were the first Europeans to leave a mark on the area, even if they did not establish a permanent settlement.

The names of French explorers and traders are found on the streets, avenues, counties, and institutions in the Twin Cities. Father Louis Hennepin, a Belgian, explored French territories that included the area that became the Twin Cities in 1680 and three years later wrote the then-best-selling book

Description of Louisiana, in which he exaggerated the splendor of the area's natural wonders. During his visit he named the Falls of St. Anthony after his patron saint. The town of St. Anthony, today a Minneapolis neighborhood, is located across the Mississippi River from the later birthplace of Minneapolis. In 1872 St. Anthony and Minneapolis merged. Hennepin's name is commemorated in Minneapolis's most famous thoroughfare, Hennepin Avenue, and the county of the same name. Fur trapping remained important in the area for well over a century, but a permanent settlement in the area did not occur until the United States won independence from England.

Fort Snelling was the first site permanently settled in Minnesota. The federal government established the fort to protect the then-northwestern edge of the United States. Lt. Col. Henry Leavenworth came to the present site of Fort Snelling in 1819, at the confluence of the Mississippi and Minnesota Rivers. Today the fort adjoins Minneapolis–St. Paul International Airport. Leavenworth didn't care for Minnesota winters, however, and he was reassigned to Florida in 1820. Command of the distant outpost went to Col. Josiah Snelling, and Snelling oversaw the construction of what was first known as Fort St. Anthony. The fort was completed in 1825 and was renamed in honor of its commander that same year. The fort sits on a cliff overlooking the rivers and remains one of the Twin Cities' grandest overlooks. When Fort Snelling was constructed, civilians began squatting in the area to serve the needs of soldiers and take advantage of the protection of the U.S. military.

The birth of St. Paul was a colorful page of Twin Cities history. Pierre "Pig's Eye" Parrant, a 60-year-old former voyageur, was the liquor bootlegger for the soldiers and citizens in and around Fort Snelling. Parrant's nickname was the result of his disfigured and blind eye; "Pig's Eye" was the original name given to St. Paul. Not surprisingly, the porcine name for the city did not last. In 1840 a young Catholic priest, Lucian Galtier, arrived in Pig's Eye, where he christened the Chapel of St.

Paul. Afterward the city was generally referred to as St. Paul's Landing. Following the arrival of the post office in 1846, the city's name was shortened to St. Paul.

Just up the Mississippi, the emergence of the other twin city, Minneapolis, was less colorful. The town of St. Anthony was founded in 1849 as a milling and lumbering center; settlers also inhabited the area that now comprises downtown Minneapolis in the 1840s, just across the Mississippi River from St. Anthony. The village of Minneapolis was not officially founded until 1856, four years after Congress rescinded 26,000 acres from Fort Snelling's control. This allowed squatters such as Col. John H. Stevens to claim and develop the land that would become downtown Minneapolis.

Minneapolis's name has interesting origins. It is an amalgam of words from two languages, the Dakota word *minne,* meaning "waters," and *polis,* the Greek word for "city." Minneapolis was founded on the west bank of the Mississippi River and St. Anthony on the east bank. In the 21st century it is difficult to believe that St. Anthony's importance early in its history eclipsed Minneapolis's, which had a relatively late start and was not chartered as a city until 1867. But as time marched on, Minneapolis's growth significantly outpaced St. Anthony's. In 1855 a suspension bridge was constructed to link the two communities. It was the first permanent bridge across the Mississippi River, and it created extensive commercial and civic ties between the rapidly expanding urban centers. The two cities merged in 1872, which established a much larger Minneapolis. The Twin Cities' growth had a significant impact on Minnesota, which became a territory in 1849 and the 32nd state in 1858.

THE MILL CITY

In the late 19th and early 20th centuries, Minneapolis became nationally prominent as the "Mill City." The emergence of milling came as the lumbering industry began to decline because of competition from the west. The ascendancy of milling created numerous allied industries and was important to the development of the diverse Minneapolis economy in the 20th century.

Milling began in Minneapolis and St. Anthony because of the proximity to St. Anthony Falls. Since the 19th century, industry and government programs have tamed much of the turbulence of the falls. To businessmen in the area, the falls represented a source of energy for milling the vast wheat crops in the area, which rapidly expanded as Minnesota and the upper Midwest were settled. As time progressed, each succeeding generation of mills became larger. This led to further consolidation, and industry leaders, internationally recognizable even today, emerged to dominate Minneapolis's market.

Innovations were instrumental in the development and dominance of General Mills. The corporation emerged gradually after a succession of mergers in Minneapolis's milling industry. Washburn-Crosby and Company is the major original component of General Mills. The star of the company skyrocketed following an important innovation, "new process flour," which originated in Paris but was brought to Washburn-Crosby and Company in 1871, where millers improved upon the method. The revolutionary new process flour involved milling spring wheat into white flour. No longer was winter wheat preferred. Quickly many Minneapolis mills acquired the revolutionary technology for producing new process flour. Many competitors acquired the information by dubious means. Washburn-Crosby and Company found tremendous success again in 1880, when they won the gold medal at the Millers' Exhibition in Cincinnati; thereafter the company marketed the Gold Medal brand of flour. The new technology catapulted Washburn-Crosby and Company and other Minneapolis mills to prominence as the nation's leading milling companies. By 1890 Minneapolis was the largest wheat market in the nation.

Minneapolis spawned many of the world's largest and most important mills, and they

i Before becoming Minnesota Territory in 1849, the future state of Minnesota was part of Illinois, Indiana, Michigan, Missouri, Wisconsin, and Iowa Territories at some time during its history.

have had a profound impact on the Cities' development. Pillsbury is another Minnesota-based company, and it began milling on the Mississippi in Minneapolis. The world's largest agribusiness company—Cargill—also has origins in Minneapolis; today, Cargill is headquartered in Minnetonka, a Minneapolis suburb. Milling's influence still deeply pervades Minneapolis culture. The city's minor-league baseball team between 1884 and 1960 was named the Millers. Moreover, the call letters of one of Minneapolis's radio and television stations is WCCO. The station takes its name from Washburn-Crosby and Company, an early owner of the station.

THE CAPITAL CITY

The institution of government has been central to St. Paul's history. Since the beginnings of the Minnesota Territory in 1849, St. Paul has served as the capital city, although it almost lost the capital to St. Peter in 1857. Joe Rolette, a territorial councilman, pocketed a bill passed by both houses of the legislature calling for relocating the territorial capital to St. Peter (south of the Twin Cities on the Minnesota River). Rolette hid with the bill for a week, but a copy of the bill was passed on to the governor, who signed it. Fortunately for St. Paul, the territorial governor was not reappointed. Later a federal district judge ruled that Minnesota Territory could not name another capital site. The capital remained in St. Paul.

The Roman Catholic Church is another important institution in the city's history. Catholicism has always found more adherents in St. Paul than in Minneapolis. The city includes large populations of Irish and German Catholics, and a small but significant number of Italian immigrants, while Minneapolis's immigration in the 19th century was dominated by Scandinavian and German Lutherans. Catholicism's influence began with the arrival of Father Lucian Galtier, who came to save the souls in "Pig's Eye." St. Paul was established as a diocese by 1850, and in 1888 it was expanded to become the archdiocese of St. Paul. Today known as the archdiocese of St. Paul and Minneapolis, it remains head-quartered in St. Paul. The spectacular Cathedral of St. Paul, which held its first mass in 1915, is one of the city's most prominent landmarks.

Industry and technology were paramount in the historical development of St. Paul. Minnesota Mining and Manufacturing Company (3M) is one of the Cities' most important companies. 3M's history began in Two Harbors, a small town northeast of Duluth, in 1902 as a manufacturer of sandpaper. The company relocated to St. Paul in 1909. Over time 3M has grown into an international corporation and remains essentially a St. Paul company, even after relocating its headquarters to the adjoining suburb of Maplewood.

EUROPEANS SETTLE THE TWIN CITIES

Minnesota immigration in the 19th and early 20th centuries for the most part mirrored patterns throughout the United States. However, there were exceptions specific to the state of Minnesota and the Twin Cities. The national perception of Minnesota is of a state dominated by Scandinavians. This generalization is fairly accurate, if slightly exaggerated. German heritage is the most common ethnic background, followed closely by Norwegian, Swedish, and Irish ancestry.

Germans came to the state in greatest numbers from 1875 to 1900. Germans' contributions have been significant, especially in communities like New Ulm. In the south and west metropolitan area, there are numerous communities with German names and origins, such as New Germany, Hamburg, and Heidelberg.

Minnesota's second most-numerous group of immigrants were Norwegians, whose legacy is felt to this day. From 1875 until 1910 Norwegian immigrants came to Minnesota in the greatest numbers. O. E. Rolvaag was among this immigrant group. He wrote *Giants in the Earth* (1927), a classic novel about Norwegian immigrant farmers. His son, Karl Rolvaag, served as governor of Minnesota.

The Swedish are the third-largest ancestral group in Minnesota. The Swedes followed similar immigration patterns as the Norwegians, and the two quickly became largely indistinguishable to outsiders. The legacy of Scandinavians is manifest in the cities they founded and settled, for example, Scandia and Lindstrom. Moreover, public facilities bear the name of important past citizens of Scandinavian heritage. Olson Memorial Highway is named after governor Floyd B. Olson, who died suddenly in 1936 while running for the U.S. Senate.

Scandinavians dominated Minnesota politics during much of the state's history. Since Knute Nelson was elected governor in 1893, there have been 25 additional heads of state, and of this number only 6 were not of Scandinavian heritage. Even today Scandinavian heritage is an asset for Minnesota politicians. Congressman Martin Olav Sabo of Minneapolis makes his ancestry apparent by emphasizing his Scandinavian middle name.

The Irish are also an essential component of Minnesota's ethnic heritage. The Irish were influential in the development of St. Paul, especially in the formation of the Catholic Church under the leadership of Archbishop John Ireland. Heavy Irish immigration began in the 1860s and ended about 1890. The ethnic group quickly integrated into the community and ascended to government positions.

Additional immigrant groups came to Minnesota and the Twin Cities. From 1820 to 1890 small groups of Swiss, Belgians, and Dutch settled in the area. Later, echoing national trends, southern, central, and eastern Europeans came to the Twin Cities. Compared with ℹ️ Several excellent Minnesota history books are available. The most recent, concise survey is *A Popular History of Minnesota* by Norman K. Risjord, available from the Minnesota Historical Society Press.

many other areas of the nation, they were smaller in number. However, they were a significant immigrant group from 1890 until 1920. Primarily Russians and various groups from the Austro-Hungarian Empire were included in this wave of immigrants. Unlike many other areas of the country, Italians and Greeks were a relatively insignificant immigrant group during this time in Minnesota. Since the 1960s Twin Cities immigrants are predominately non-European. Today, the Twin Cities has the largest population of Somali and Hmong peoples in the United States.

THE DIVERSE TWIN CITIES' 20TH-CENTURY ECONOMY

In the 20th century the Twin Cities diversified and developed an economy consistently among the strongest in the United States.

The milling industry became increasingly decentralized, as the largest and most successful Twin Cities milling companies gradually diversified into related industries. The decline of Minneapolis milling occurred fairly rapidly, and in the 1920s flour production was halved from the production levels of the glory years before and immediately after the turn of the 20th century. Today Minneapolis is once again the largest producer of flour in the United States but holds considerably less domination over the industry, where it accounts for only 10 percent of the national total.

Washburn-Crosby and Company changed its name to General Mills in 1928. The corporation had developed Wheaties breakfast cereal in 1924 and Betty Crocker, a globally recognized cake mix, in 1921. The name change represented the growing national focus of the company. General Mills moved into other food-related businesses, including numerous breakfast foods, dough mixes, and frozen foods.

Pillsbury followed a similar path, diversifying its food lines and businesses throughout the 20th century. The home of the Pillsbury Doughboy moved into prepared doughs as well as frozen and canned foods. The company entered the restaurant business in 1967, acquiring Burger King, and later became involved in additional restaurant ventures. Pillsbury was acquired by London-based Grand Metropolitan PLC (later known as Diageo PLC) in 1989 and became a subsidiary of General Mills in 2001.

As the traditional industries of the Twin Cities diversified, new high-tech businesses asserted themselves as an important component of the local economy. Some companies' roots reach back to industry and manufacturing that began in the late 19th and early 20th centuries, as is the case with the 3M Corporation, while others quickly became important businesses in the area because of technological innovation.

One such Twin Cities company is Medtronic Inc. Earl Bakken, a University of Minnesota graduate student, began his company in a northeast Minneapolis garage in 1949. Medtronic's first big success came with the development of an implantable pacemaker in 1960. Medtronic diversified into numerous medical technology fields and today is an internationally recognized corporation.

Honeywell is another important Twin Cities high-technology company. The origins of Honeywell date from a failed spring-powered thermostat company developed by A. M. Butz in 1885. Over time the fledgling company honed its technological devices. After success with its thermostat line, the company moved into heating, air-conditioning, and varied technological devices for industry and Cold War defense programs. Honeywell's military products became an important component of the company's revenues. As the Cold War came to an end, however, Honeywell ran into economic hard times.

Close-up

Larry Millett, Author

"I always tell people the most interesting place in the world is the place where you grew up," says Larry Millett, author of the award-winning books *Lost Twin Cities* and *Twin Cities Then and Now*, as well as several Sherlock Holmes mysteries that take place in Minnesota. "I've been a fan of local history for a long time because I find it intriguing. I grew up in the Cities and went to school in downtown Minneapolis and saw first-hand the demolition of the Gateway District. My father's family goes way back in Minneapolis—my grandfather owned a bar on Washington Avenue, and his wife was the granddaughter of one of the early founders of the city. So I have deep roots in this area."

Millett, who worked as a reporter and editor at the *St. Paul Pioneer Press* for more than 30 years, has taken his love for architecture and history to write some of the most amazing and heartbreaking literary tours of the Twin Cities. Using photos kept on record at the Minnesota History Center for more than 150 years, Millett's books show in great detail how much the cities have both changed and stayed the same over the past century. *Lost Twin Cities* is composed completely of photographs and the histories of the many architectural wonders that were destroyed over the years—including the beautiful Gateway Park, which became a hangout for homeless people during the Depression—while *Twin Cities Then and Now* provides side-by-side pictures of Twin Cities neighborhoods and business districts at various points in time.

"The cities are not hugely distinctive from each other architecturally, I think," says Millett about the Twin Cities today. "What happened historically is that there was a different set of architects for St. Paul and Minneapolis, so there were initial differences from the individual hands involved. But what's hap-

The Twin Cities are also home to one of the nation's largest retailers, the Target Corporation. For most of its long history in the Twin Cities, Target was known as the Dayton Company, and later the Dayton Hudson Corporation. The Dayton Company opened for business in downtown Minneapolis in 1902. The company started its most nationally recognized retail store, Target, in suburban Roseville, in 1962. Dayton Hudson officially changed its name to the Target Corporation in 2000.

As the 20th century came to a close, the Twin Cities saw significant corporate reorganization. Larger domestic and multinational corporations acquired several local firms. Several Twin Cities economists questioned the vitality of the area's economy, while many others felt the event was simply emblematic of global restructuring of the economy.

THE TWIN CITIES ENTER THE NEW MILLENNIUM

The Twin Cities underwent a substantial transformation during the late 1990s. The economy is still a topic of conversation because of acquisitions and mergers of several blue chip Twin Cities firms.

Corporations outside the Twin Cities acquired several area firms. In 1998, Norwest, a bank headquartered in the Twin Cities, was pened in St. Paul since is that it's probably got a better stock of historic buildings than Minneapolis, while Minneapolis probably has a better stock of newer buildings. St. Paul has been more fortunate in preserving its historic housing stock than Minneapolis, and there are reasons for that that have more to do with relative lack of development and change than any great historic sentiment, I think. Minneapolis, since the turn of the century, has been a more dynamic city, and the more dynamic a city is, the more quickly its architecture tends to change."

Millett's favorite buildings today? "I love St. Paul's city hall," he says. "I think it's one of our country's great art deco buildings, as is the county courthouse. The public library in St. Paul, and the Hill Reference Library, which is next door and is part of the same building but a different institution. Of course Landmark Center, the State Capitol, St. Paul Cathedral, the basics. In Minneapolis, I'm very fond of the IDS building, I think that's a nationally and internationally significant skyscraper, and the Norwest Tower (renamed the Wells Fargo Center) is very nice for its kind, too.

"It's amazing as a researcher to find out how many places aren't documented," finishes Millett. "There are places in both cities where basically there's no clue to how it looked 100 years ago because there are no pictures in the public collection. That's especially true of some of the residential neighborhoods. The downtowns of both cities are well documented, but once you get out to the residential districts, the documentation is much spottier. It all depends on how good a job the city's photographer did at the time. The Minnesota Historical Society has more than 190,000 images on their Web site (www.mnhs.org), so you can cruise through all those on their Web site now. It's really phenomenal what they have, all the images of the Twin Cities in particular."

purchased by Wells Fargo of San Francisco. Honeywell merged with New Jersey–based Allied-Signal in 1999 and then was bought by General Electric in 2001. Minneapolis-based ReliaStar, a financial products firm, was purchased by ING Group of the Netherlands in 2000.

Reflecting the strength of the local economy, there was a sharp increase in immigration over the past decade. The most recent Twin Cities immigrants are largely from Asia, Africa, and areas of the world that before the late 1970s were absent from area demographics. The dynamic new immigrant population has significantly contributed to the complex of Twin Cities ethnicity. The new immigrant populations are largely émigrés who came to the United States to escape political tumult, repression, and warfare. The first group to arrive were displaced Vietnamese, who were followed by numerous other Southeast Asian groups, which included Laotians, Khmers (Cambodia), and the Hmong (Laos). With the exception of Bosnians and Russians, Europeans are a relatively small component.

The Hmong are a significant immigrant group in the Twin Cities. Since the late 1970s they have come from Laos, or relocated to the area from other American cities, to take advantage of the area's low unemployment and booming economy. Today there are more than 200,000 Hmong living in the United

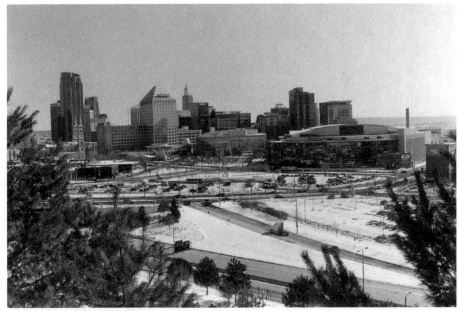

Rapid growth and new construction, particularly around the Xcel Energy Center, have fueled new businesses in downtown St. Paul. TODD R. BERGER

States. The Twin Cities, in particular St. Paul, have the largest Hmong population in the nation. The Hmong and other Southeast Asians have started more than 400 area businesses and have transformed St. Paul's Frogtown and Midway neighborhoods.

A more recent trend has seen East Africans settling in the Twin Cities. The first significant wave of African immigrants came from Ethiopia and Eritrea in the late 1980s and early 1990s. Today, Ethiopian and Eritrean restaurant businesses are scattered throughout the Twin Cities, and many of the former immigrants now hold government positions.

An estimated 40,000 Somalis currently live in the United States, and approximately 20,000 reside in Minnesota. However, members of the Somali community feel the government numbers are low and believe there may be as many as 90,000 in Minnesota. The Somalis' presence is felt in the many small businesses owned and operated by the community.

The new wave of immigration is just one parallel linking the Twin Cities' past and present. Both Minneapolis and St. Paul are reviving important elements of their past on the Mississippi riverfront.

Since the late 1980s, Minneapolis has focused on regaining its greatest historical assets—the Mississippi River and the Mill District. It began with the restoration of the James J. Hill Stone Arch Bridge—one of Minneapolis's most scenic vistas—and the Minneapolis riverfront is now home to the Mill City Museum, founded in 2003, and the new Guthrie Theater, opened in 2006. In addition, the Minneapolis Park and Recreation Board completed Mill Ruins Park in 2001.

Downriver in St. Paul the renovated Harriet Island Regional Park celebrates its city's rich history. During late summer 2000 more than 50,000 citizens attended the reopening of the park. The park represents the Cities' commitment to the riverfront.

ARCHITECTURE

The Twin Cities are composed of two cities with distinctly different histories and perspectives on architecture. Both cities draw architectural inspiration from different sources, and it is reflected in their respective architecture.

St. Paul has always looked to the East, and in particular Boston, as a source for civic inspiration. The design of the city reflects this perspective and was in large part developed by transplanted old-stock New Englanders. The streets, like Boston's, were platted much narrower than in Minneapolis. St. Paul views itself as a city of tradition and as the "Capital City." With a few exceptions, most notably Wells Fargo Place, St. Paul's architecture has concerned itself with human-scale structures of elegance.

St. Paul's rival across the river has taken a considerably different approach to architecture. Minneapolis has always embraced progress and modernity. This distinction between the cities has only been exacerbated as Minneapolis architecture has increasingly grown vertically. But Minneapolis is also home to some smaller modernist architectural masterpieces, including the Frederick R. Weisman Art Museum and the new Guthrie Theater.

FUNCTION FIRST: THE BIRTH OF THE TWIN CITIES

Early Twin Cities architecture reflected national trends. When America was settled, functionality was of primary importance. Homes and civic structures were erected with safety and survival as main concerns. European settlers wanted protection from American Indians and from the severe Minnesota winters. Most early structures in the Twin Cities were log cabins, sod houses, and simple wooden structures.

Fort Snelling was the first permanent white settlement in the Twin Cities. Completed in 1825, it protected the northwestern-most edge of the United States. Thereafter, small wooden buildings were constructed in the two fledgling cities. Father Lucian Galtier dedicated a small log chapel in honor of St. Paul in November of 1841. Down the Mississippi almost a decade later, John Stevens created the first humble structure in the area that would soon be named Minneapolis. The little white house was soon surrounded by many similar structures.

Minneapolis and St. Paul rapidly developed into nationally prominent cities. During this epoch, buildings were constructed as quickly as possible to meet the needs of the expanding cities. As the cities developed, municipal institutions became necessary. Public buildings were the first opulent pieces of architecture in both cities, and they were public declarations of the importance of the Cities.

THE EMERGENCE OF THE TWIN CITIES

The Minneapolis City Hall (1906) represented the Cities' emergence as a nationally prominent municipality. In 1856 Minneapolis's population was 4,607, but by 1895 it had swelled to 192,823 and the city was the 18th largest in the nation.

St. Paul created structures to celebrate the Cities' ascendancy at the turn of the 20th century. The most significant architectural work was the Minnesota State Capitol, completed in 1904. Cass Gilbert designed the neoclassical structure. It is one of several outstanding pieces of government architecture in St. Paul.

Government and institutional structures marked St. Paul's entrance into the modern age. In contrast, Minneapolis was poised to begin its ascent skyward, which began with the Foshay Tower.

The Foshay Tower was the first skyscraper constructed in the Twin Cities. When it was completed in 1929, it was considered one of the greatest feats of modern architecture. The 32-story obelisk was the tallest building in the Twin Cities for more than 40 years. During the late 19th and early 20th centuries, both cities expanded upward with large concrete and metal structures, but none were as grand in scale as the Foshay.

In 1973 the IDS Center exceeded the Foshay by 25 stories, and the IDS was briefly lonesome atop the skyline. In the 1980s and 1990s new skyscrapers constructed of glass, concrete, and steel began to dominate downtown. The architecture is an eclectic modern mix of styles ranging from the interesting art deco–influenced Wells Fargo Center to less distinctive massive glass structures like the Piper Jaffray Tower.

St. Paul also expanded upward in the late 20th century, but skyscrapers are not as prominent. The sixth-tallest building in Minneapolis, the U.S. Bank Plaza (formerly known as the Pillsbury Center), is taller than any building in St. Paul. The best architecture in downtown St. Paul is the city's government buildings. The St. Paul City Hall is a stunning structure, particularly its lobby, a fine example of art deco/moderne design. The Cathedral of Saint Paul is another architectural masterpiece; the baroque interior of the building suggests Europe rather than Minnesota. St. Paul architecture is not as vertical as Minneapolis; however, the Minnesota State Capitol and the Cathedral of Saint Paul make up for it in sheer size.

INTO THE 21ST CENTURY

As the Twin Cities enter the 21st century, both cities have recommitted themselves to their historic riverfronts. Architecture and landscape design in the last decade have emphasized the Mississippi River.

In St. Paul the new Science Museum of Minnesota opened on the bluff above the river. The state-of-the-art museum makes fine use of its location with several scenic overviews of the river. In addition, the city reopened one of its most scenic parks, Harriet Island, across the river from downtown. Landscape architecture restored the park's links to the river through such features as the large concrete steps leading down to the river. Plans to redevelop the beautiful riverfront property to make better use of the river are in various stages of implementation. There is also a plan for residential development in the historic Irvine Park neighborhood on the Mississippi.

Minneapolis has shown a commitment to redeveloping the Mississippi riverfront with projects of its own. The first major project was the James J. Hill Stone Arch Bridge, which was renovated in 1994 by the Minnesota Department of Transportation. Then in 2003 the city opened the ambitious Mill City Museum (see the close-up later in this chapter for further details). The Minneapolis firm of Meyer, Scherer, and Rockcastle Ltd. created the design for the museum. In 2006 the new Guthrie Theater opened, and its remarkable "endless bridge" has quickly catapulted the theater to the level of architectural masterpiece.

TWIN CITIES ARCHITECTURE IN DETAIL

The Downtown Minneapolis Skyline

Campbell Mithun Tower
222 South Ninth Street, Minneapolis
(612) 342-2222
www.campbellmithuntower.com
Immense glass skyscrapers have transformed the look of downtown Minneapolis. Looking down Ninth Street, the chasm between the past and present is highly visible. On the corner of Marquette Avenue and Ninth is the 32-story Foshay Tower. Continuing down Ninth

Street to Third Avenue South is the Campbell Mithun Tower. By no means is it one of the most well-known pieces of architecture in Minneapolis, yet the structure easily eclipses the once-giant Foshay Tower in sheer size. Rising 42 stories, the Campbell Mithun Tower is the fifth-tallest building in the city. Constructed in 1985, it was an early addition to the skyward growth of downtown.

Dain Rauscher Plaza
60 South Sixth Street, Minneapolis

Dain Rauscher Plaza is one of the many large glass skyscrapers erected in downtown Minneapolis in the '90s. Like all of the recent additions to the Minneapolis skyline, it has a system of skyways, which connect it to the second and fourth levels of the Wells Fargo Center. At 539 feet and 40 stories, Dain Rauscher is the seventh-tallest building in Minneapolis.

The Foshay Tower
821 Marquette Avenue South, Minneapolis
(612) 359-3030

It is difficult to imagine that this obelisk once stood as the tallest skyscraper west of Chicago. The 448-foot building dominated the Minneapolis skyline and was the tallest building in the Twin Cities until the completion of the 792-foot IDS Center in 1973. Today the Foshay Tower is surrounded by modern glass-and-steel giants, which dwarf what is now the sixteenth-tallest building in the city.

The Foshay Tower draws its name from the financier behind its construction, Wilbur H. Foshay. Foshay, a utilities magnate, became wealthy enough during the boom of the Roaring Twenties to construct a building modeled on the Washington Monument. The 32-story obelisk was topped with 10-foot-high letters that spelled out Foshay. The Foshay's dedication in 1929 was one of the most lavish in the city's history. The festivities included fireworks and a 75-piece brass band conducted by John Philip Sousa, which included his composition "Foshay Tower–Washington Memorial March."

Unfortunately for Foshay, the good times were not to last. Shortly after the dedication the stock market crashed. Foshay's finances were decimated; in addition, he was convicted of fraud and sentenced to 15 years at Fort Leavenworth. President Franklin Delano Roosevelt pardoned Foshay after he had served three years.

Today the Foshay is one of the Twin Cities' memorable sights, with its lights illuminating the Minneapolis sky. And it does this despite its relatively diminutive stature alongside the many larger skyscrapers built in the wake of the '80s and '90s. The open-air observatory, the only outdoor observation deck in Minneapolis, offers a spectacular panoramic view of Minneapolis. The Foshay is presently undergoing renovations to become a 229-room hotel, slated to open in 2008. The new hotel, when completed, will still allow access to the observation deck.

Hennepin County Government Center
300 South Sixth Street, Minneapolis
(612) 348-3000

The twin-tower exterior of the Hennepin County Government Center is unassuming enough. However, the 24-story atrium provides a truly spectacular view, which grows as you ascend the 403-foot building. There is another interesting feature to the building—Sixth Street passes directly under the structure.

The building was completed in 1977, and it serves Hennepin County (Minneapolis and suburbs) well. In addition to the wonderful atrium, the building includes an immense water fountain.

IDS Center
80 South Eighth Street, Minneapolis
(612) 376-8000
www.ids-center.com

The IDS Center supplanted the Foshay Tower as the tallest building in the Twin Cities when it opened in 1973—a position it has not relinquished. The IDS Center is arguably the most well-known building in the Twin Cities and is recognized as the centerpiece of the Minneapolis skyline. Seen from downtown Minneapolis and even the suburbs, the IDS Center looms large.

The IDS Center distinguishes itself in several other ways. The 57-story, 792-foot structure has more than 42,000 panes of glass as well as a 105-foot waterfall, which was added during the 1998 renovation. Designed by world-renowned architects Philip Johnson and John Burgee, the skyscraper has frequently attracted national attention.

The grandeur of the Crystal Court was featured in the Mary Tyler Moore Show and two motion pictures. The Crystal Court is still one of the most beautiful shopping areas in the Twin Cities, and the IDS Center remains the centerpiece of the Minneapolis skyline.

225 South Sixth
225 South Sixth Street, Minneapolis
(612) 672-3011
www.225southsixth.com

225 South Sixth is recognizable throughout Minneapolis by the crown that sits atop the large glass skyscraper. The 776-foot building is the second tallest in Minneapolis. It was completed in 1992 as First Bank Place. The nationally respected firm of Pei, Cobb, Freed and Partners designed the 56-story building, which, despite its size and unusual architecture, receives far less attention than the Wells Fargo Center and the IDS Center.

US Bank Plaza
200 South Sixth Street, Minneapolis

Minneapolis was known throughout the nation as the Mill City during the 19th and early 20th centuries. As time has passed, the importance of milling has been de-emphasized, and the "City of Lakes" nickname has moved to the forefront. However, milling and its many allied services and industries remain a vital part of the area's dynamic economy.

The US Bank Plaza, which has two towers, was originally built as the Pillsbury headquarters. Pillsbury Center was completed in 1981. In 2001, Pillsbury was acquired by General Mills, which relocated the company to its suburban Golden Valley campus. US Bank took up the empty space in Pillsbury Center, and soon thereafter the building was renamed to reflect this change. US Bank Plaza is in the heart of downtown Minneapolis, where the 40-story and 22-story towers overlook the city with their immense neighbors. The beautiful atrium distinguishes it from other structures, with its eight stories of enclosed open space.

Wells Fargo Center
90 South Seventh Street, Minneapolis
(612) 344-1200
www.wellsfargocenter.com

The Wells Fargo Center sits at the heart of downtown and is perhaps Minneapolis's most recognizable building, with its golden-hued glow and art deco look. The third-tallest building in the Twin Cities, the Wells Fargo Center, is 57 stories high, the same number of stories as the neighboring IDS Center, although it is 18 feet shorter. The building was completed in 1988 as the Norwest Center. The name changed when the Norwest and Wells Fargo banks merged in 1998.

The Wells Fargo Center was constructed in the ashes of tragedy. A Thanksgiving 1982 fire destroyed the Northwestern National Bank Building. The structure itself was not as important a piece of architecture to the community as the 157-foot "weatherball," which sat atop the building and changed color to reflect the weather forecast. Norwest set out to construct a replacement for their destroyed headquarters.

The Wells Fargo Center was completed in 1989. The Cesar Pelli–designed building features a 100-foot-high domed ceiling rotunda as well as a gorgeous lobby that hearkens back to the 1920s. The golden color of the building is created by the Kasota Limestone used in its façade.

Minneapolis Architectural Landmarks

American Swedish Institute
2600 Park Avenue, Minneapolis
(612) 871-4907
www.americanswedishinst.org

A hundred years ago, Minneapolis's wealthy resided on Park Avenue beside the American Swedish Institute. The affluent relocated many years ago and left behind the elegant American Swedish Institute.

Completed in 1908, the palatial 33-room mansion was once a single-family residence. The châteauesque mansion was constructed for Swan and Christina Turnblad and their daughter, Lillian. The Turnblad family amassed their fortune through the *Svenska Amerikanska Posten,* a Swedish-language newspaper with a circulation of 40,000 at its zenith. In 1929, the Turnblads donated the mansion to the American Institute for Swedish Arts, Literature, and Science, which later changed its name to the American Swedish Institute. The rooms inside the mansion display interesting architectural details. For example, there is a rococo revival salon, a two-story fireplace in the Grand Hall made of carved mahogany, and 11 Swedish *kakelugnar* (porcelain stoves) in various rooms. The institute is the oldest museum of Swedish-American history and culture in the United States. The American Swedish Institute shines on as one of the best reminders of the Park Avenue's architectural history.

Butler Square
Sixth Street and First Avenue, Minneapolis
(612) 339-4343

Butler Square is perhaps the finest example of a renovated warehouse in Minneapolis. The building, formerly known as Butler Brothers Warehouse, is situated on the southwestern edge of the historic Warehouse District. The Warehouse District is filled with classic buildings that once housed Minneapolis's bustling industrial and shipping sector.

The Warehouse District, like much of the city, was neglected in the era following World War II as people flocked to the suburbs. Many businesses closed or left the warehouses for the suburbs, and much of the district sat dormant, which was a fate much better than the neighboring Gateway District of downtown, which was largely torn down. The Warehouse

District was spared the wrecking ball because the area was too far from downtown and was not considered financially lucrative. In the 1970s, urban revitalization gradually began in the Warehouse District, and Butler Square was the first converted for modern use. Today the once-moribund section of Minneapolis is filled with converted warehouses that serve as office space, restaurants, bars, art galleries, and retail shops.

Butler Square's architecture is based on its past strengths combined with a superb renovation in 1973. The exterior is dark brick, and it distinguishes itself with a Moorish-style turret atop the building. The interior is where the building sets itself apart. The renovation maximized the building's open space. The original wood beams were cleaned and left exposed, and windows were installed to gaze out at the atrium. There are two large atriums from floor to ceiling, and sculptures such as George Segal's *Acrobats* accent the interior's striking beauty. After the success of Butler Square, many other renovations followed in the Warehouse District, but none have matched its architectural grandeur.

Hennepin Center for the Arts
528 Hennepin Avenue, Minneapolis
(612) 332-4478
www.mnshubert.org

An example of 19th-century Richardsonian romanesque architecture, the Hennepin Center for the Arts was completed in 1889 as a Masonic Temple. Like its neighbor the Lumber Exchange, it is an excellent example of the architecture that coexisted with the Hennepin Avenue Theater District until the mid-1940s. Thereafter it was neglected and the architecture modified. The onion dome on the top corner facing Fifth Street and Hennepin Avenue was lopped off. However, after years of neglect, parts of downtown were reborn. Today the Hennepin Center for the Arts thrives as a performance arts building. In 2007 the building became part of the Minnesota Shubert Performing Arts and Education Center, a three-building complex that is home to several ballet and modern dance companies, as well as the Minneapolis home of the St. Paul Chamber Orchestra.

Lumber Exchange Building
425 Hennepin Avenue, Minneapolis
(612) 334-3011

In the late 19th century, downtown Minneapolis was lined with large stone structures like the Lumber Exchange Building. Completed in 1890, the 11-story building was one of Minneapolis's first "skyscrapers." Today downtown is dominated by immense glass, steel, and concrete buildings occupied by large corporations. The Lumber Exchange retains the character of the city when it first rose to prominence, and it exudes the ambience that once pervaded the city.

Minneapolis City Hall
350 South Fifth Street, Minneapolis
(612) 673-3000

The Minneapolis City Hall was an extraordinarily expensive and time-consuming project that marked the city's arrival on the national scene. Constructed between 1888 and 1906, the city hall came at great financial costs but symbolically represented much more for the fledgling city. The city hall covers an entire city block and is distinguished by its 341-foot-high clock tower, which rings daily throughout downtown.

Minneapolis Post Office
100 South First Street, Minneapolis
(612) 321-5957

The Minneapolis Post Office is a colossal 2-block art moderne structure located in the heart of the birthplace of the city. The building was completed in 1933, and the architecture reflects its Works Progress Administration (WPA) origins.

The site of the post office was once the home of Col. John H. Stevens's white frame house, the first structure in Minneapolis. This important piece of architecture was relocated to Minnehaha Park in south Minneapolis, where it can be visited today.

The post office is an excellent example of the fine government structures built by the WPA. The interior is particularly stunning. The lobby includes plenty of fine stone, brass, and glass, which is immaculately maintained. The exterior is more subdued and is constructed of stone with large metal grilles over the two entrances. The post office exudes the confidence that was necessary during the darkest days of the Great Depression.

Shubert Theater
Fifth Street and Hennepin Avenue, Minneapolis
www.mnshubert.org

The 1910 Shubert Theater is one of the Twin Cities' most contentious pieces of architecture. The grand old theater sat vacant for years on the corner of Seventh Street and First Avenue, where it was once a part of Minneapolis's extensive Hennepin Avenue and Seventh Street theater district. But much had changed since the Shubert's construction, and the Shubert had fallen from glory.

Local leaders and business interests called for the theater's demolition, especially in light of its location on the lucrative, vacant, and, until recently, undeveloped Block E. The theater stood in the way of development on the highly sought piece of property. A plan made for the theater's destruction was met by resistance from local arts organizations. Fortunately, the theater was spared; in 1999, it was moved 2 blocks away and placed beside the Hennepin Center for the Arts. The Shubert weighs an astounding 5,816,000 pounds or 2,908 tons, and its move set a world record for the largest structure relocated.

In 2007 the building became part of the Minnesota Shubert Performing Arts and Education Center, a three-building complex that is home to several ballet and modern dance companies, as well as the Minneapolis home of the St. Paul Chamber Orchestra.

Both downtown Minneapolis and St. Paul have skyway systems between buildings, allowing people to get around most of the downtowns without ever setting foot outside. GREATER MINNEAPOLIS CONVENTION & VISITORS ASSOCIATION

University of Minnesota—Twin Cities: Minneapolis Campus

Civil and Mineral Engineering Building
500 Pillsbury Drive SE, Minneapolis
(612) 625-5522

Civil Engineering stands in stark contrast to the variations of classic architecture that dominate the campus. More than 95 percent of the building was constructed underground, and it extends 110 feet below the surface. Civil Engineering was planned during the OPEC oil embargo of 1974, when the building was simultaneously an architectural curiosity and a source for research into more efficient energy and land use. The Minnesota Legislature allocated funds for numerous experimental features in the structure, which was completed in 1983. Both active and passive solar heating are included for research purposes.

Frederick R. Weisman Art Museum
333 East River Road, Minneapolis
(612) 625-9494
www.weisman.umn.edu

The Frederick R. Weisman Art Museum is one of the Twin Cities' most distinctive pieces of architecture. Opinions on the museum vary widely. Detractors have called the structure an ugly, discombobulated homage to the tin man in *The Wizard of Oz,* while enthusiasts glow incessantly about Frank Gehry's internationally acclaimed style. However, one fact is for certain: Gehry created a museum that is not, in the words of a former University of Minnesota president, Nils Hasselmo, "another brick lump."

Art critics from as far away as New York have lauded the Weisman. The museum features brushed stainless steel arranged in bold, undulating angles. Gehry links the

Close-up

Mill City Museum

Minneapolis is most commonly known to visitors as the City of Lakes. But the city's first nickname, the "Mill City," was the nickname that elevated the city to national prominence. In recent years, the Minneapolis riverfront has undergone a renaissance as, piece by piece, elements of Minneapolis's past have been revived. The Mill City Museum, which opened in 2003, reclaimed the once-buried and nearly forgotten history of the city and restored it to the prominent position it deserves as the birthplace of a world-class city.

The Mill City Museum is located in the heart of Minneapolis's historic milling district. Shortly after the town of Minneapolis was founded in 1856, small mills congregated on both the east bank (until 1872, St. Anthony) and the west bank of the Mississippi River near St. Anthony Falls. At this, the only waterfall on the Mississippi, the river provided an exceptional source of power for milling the increasingly limitless wheat of the upper Midwest, and the number and size of the mills swelled. By 1890 Minneapolis had established itself as the nation's largest wheat market, and Washburn-Crosby and Company (the antecedent of General Mills) was among the Cities' leaders in the industry with its nationally recognized trademark, Gold Medal Flour.

To serve these needs, the company constructed the Washburn A Mill. Like its predecessor, the A Mill was plagued by fire, but none as deadly as the May 2, 1878, explosion, which killed 18. The mill was rebuilt and remained in operation until 1965; for many years thereafter, the A Mill was left dormant, during which time the structure was seriously damaged. Parts of the old mill were destroyed and enormous gaping holes were left, exposing the structure to Minneapolis's harsh weather. In 1991 another fire nearly destroyed the vacant building. This

museum to the more architecturally conservative buildings with terra-cotta bricks on the south and east sides. The interior of the museum includes extensive use of natural lighting sources, whether it is the skylights or large windows tastefully framing the view of downtown Minneapolis. The Weisman houses five galleries. Gehry designed an expansion of the museum (including a new gallery wing and a café), which was begun in 2007 and is scheduled to be completed in 2009.

The Weisman Art Museum has housed the University of Minnesota's art collection since 1934, although the current building opened in 1993. The museum emphasizes art of the recent vintage, just as the building is

among the Twin Cities' most ambitious pieces of modern architecture. The Weisman is definitely worth a visit both for its fine galleries as well as its astounding architecture. The Weisman is on the campus' East Bank where Washington Avenue crosses over East River Parkway. Admission is free, although the parking garage will set you back a few bucks.

McNamara Alumni Center
200 Oak Street SE, Minneapolis
(612) 624-7570
www.alumicenter.umn.edu
The McNamara Alumni Center, completed in 2000, is the most recent addition to the Minneapolis campus of the University of

was the challenge for the Minneapolis architectural firm of Meyer, Scherer & Rockcastle Ltd., which designed the Mill City Museum to incorporate the ruins of the Washburn A Mill.

The Mill City Museum design retained many elements of the old mill: milling machinery, flour bins, rail corridor, engine house, and wheat house. While much of the mill has been restored, in some cases the architect has exploited scenic views created by fire damage, including a breathtaking view of St. Anthony Falls.

Architect Tom Meyer adapted this unique structure for the numerous attractions at the Mill City Museum. The museum emphasizes hands-on experiences, like those offered by the Minnesota Historical Society, and includes a waterpower laboratory and a test kitchen. The eight-story "Flour Tower" ride features regional history. Another attraction is the open-air courtyard within the walls of the mill ruins.

The museum features several historical exhibits beyond milling, examining the influence of waterpower both in milling and in allied industries on the Mississippi River. The museum demonstrates the role of milling in the development of Minneapolis's dynamic economy and its impact on immigration patterns, railroad development, and agriculture.

The structure includes a bookstore, classrooms, and a restaurant. The mill also incorporates lofts on the top five floors, with spectacular views of downtown Minneapolis and St. Anthony Falls.

The Mill City Museum is located on the Minneapolis riverfront at 704 South Second Street near the intersection with Portland Avenue. For more information, you can contact the museum at (612) 341-7555 or visit the museum on the Web at www.millcitymuseum.org.

Minnesota. The structure is an apt bridge between the alumni and present students and contains something for the admirers of both the school's august history and daring architecture.

Until the 1980s the McNamara Alumni Center was the site of Memorial Stadium. The stadium served as the home for the Minnesota Golden Gophers football team. Today the restored Memorial Stadium arch serves as the entrance to the Curtis L. and Arleen M. Carlson Heritage Gallery, where the University of Minnesota's alumni and faculty are honored with artifacts, images, and stories.

The McNamara is a domed 90-foot geode on the eastern edge of the campus 1 block south of the intersection of Oak Street SE and University Avenue SE. The McNamara Alumni Center is a $45 million monument to the school's alumni.

Northrop Memorial Auditorium
84 Church Street SE, Minneapolis
(651) 624-2345
www1.umn.edu/umato/
Northrop Memorial Auditorium stands out elegantly on the north end of the Northrop Mall, a long grassy area at the heart of the Minneapolis campus. The mall is lined with stunning architecture, and it was the dream of architect Cass Gilbert that the mall would stretch to the banks of the Mississippi River.

Unfortunately his dreams were thwarted when the Coffman Memorial Union was completed at the base of the Mall in 1940. Since then the union has stared across the mall at the Northrop Memorial Auditorium, and Gilbert's plan has not been revived.

The neoclassical building is among the most beautiful and storied on campus. The large brick structure features a 10-column facade and was named after University of Minnesota president Cyrus Northrop (1884–1911). Completed in 1929, Northrop Memorial Auditorium serves as an auditorium and concert hall. And with more than 4,800 seats, the auditorium is one of the area's most beautiful venues. Today the auditorium hosts dance and jazz performances, as well as other special events.

Walter Library
Pleasant Avenue SE, Minneapolis
(612) 626-2227
www.lib.umn.edu

Walter Library, which underwent a $63.4 million renovation between 1999 and 2002, is a building important in the history of the campus and the Twin Cities. Constructed in 1924, it was the third principal library. The recent renovation included restoring the staircase, lobby, and reading rooms to their original glory, and creating spaces for the Digital Technology Center, the Science and Engineering Library, the Learning Resources Center, and the Minnesota Supercomputing Institute. The structure is built in the Roman Renaissance style, the dominant style of the campus's architectural epicenter, Northrop Mall. It has the most decorative façade on the mall, making use of red brick and limestone trim.

St. Paul's Architectural Treasures

Bandana Square
1021 East Bandana Boulevard, St. Paul
(651) 642-1509

During the past century the site of present-day Bandana Square has served several roles. The structure was constructed to serve as a train repair shop. As the railroad industry declined, the repair shop closed. After sitting vacant the huge building was renovated in the 1980s and reopened as a shopping mall. Unfortunately, the beautiful shopping center did not fare well. A few businesses have remained, but offices are the most common tenants at Bandana Square. Bandana Square hosts a link to its past—the Twin Cities Model Railroad Club—where fans of architecture can revisit the old train garage in miniature surrounded by façades of the historic Twin Cities.

Fort Snelling
Minnesota Highways 5 and 55, St. Paul
(651) 725-2413
www.mnhs.org/fortsnelling

Completed in 1825, Fort Snelling was the first permanent white settlement in what would become Minnesota and was once the farthest west military post in the United States. The restored fort features examples of 19th-century architecture that emphasize practical, defense-oriented designs over opulence. On the site are a hospital, forge, and a garrison for defending the confluence of the Mississippi and the Minnesota Rivers. Minnesota, like much of the Midwest, has a relatively brief history, and at Fort Snelling visitors can examine a restored version of the architecture of the first Minnesotans of European heritage.

Governor's Residence
1006 Summit Avenue, St. Paul
(651) 297-8177

The location of the governor's residence is ideal. Summit Avenue is the historical home of St. Paul's old wealth. The beautiful wide parkway is lined with trees and elegant Victorian homes and was the childhood home of F. Scott Fitzgerald and railroad baron James J. Hill.

The governor's residence is a fairly recent tradition in Minnesota. Since the 1960s Minnesota's governor has called 1006 Summit Avenue home. Before that date governors lived in their own homes and rented facilities for political events. William Channing Whitney, a prominent Twin Cities architect, designed the governor's residence in the English Tudor revival style. The interior has been renovated several times. Tours are available occasionally and by appointment.

James J. Hill House
240 Summit Avenue, St. Paul
(651) 296-6126

The James J. Hill House was once one of the largest mansions in the Midwest, appropriately built for one of St. Paul's wealthiest and most powerful men. In the age of barons of industry, Hill was one of the area's most prominent citizens. Mansions like Hill's helped create the reputation Summit Avenue retains even today—as the street where St. Paul's old money resides.

James J. Hill ironically arrived via riverboat at age 17 from Ontario, Canada, in 1838. Hill was to play a central role in the development of another conveyance, the railroad, in the rapidly developing United States. Hill built a railroad empire, the Great Northern Railroad, from his adopted home of St. Paul.

Perhaps the most impressive aspect of the Hill House is its sheer size. The beautiful home was constructed with red sandstone and has many examples of skilled craftsmanship. The carved woodwork and stained glass are of the finest quality. There are 32 rooms, 13 bathrooms, and 22 fireplaces, which were a necessity for Minnesota's harsh winters when the house was constructed in 1891. Boasting 36,000 square feet of living space, it was a fitting residence for one of Minnesota's, and the nation's, greatest railroad tycoons.

Landmark Center
75 West Fifth Street, St. Paul
(651) 292-3228

Landmark Center is one of many architectural gems in downtown St. Paul's cultural quarter, which includes the Ordway Music Theatre, the Children's Museum, and the Science Museum. Landmark Center was erected in 1906 as the Federal Courthouse, where St. Paul's famous gangsters were once prosecuted. Today Landmark Center serves as the gallery for the Minnesota Museum of American Art, but the architecture continues to convey the structure's history. The building's tower overlooks Rice Park, which is surrounded by several of St. Paul's most attractive pieces of architecture.

Marjorie McNeely Conservatory at Como Park
Estabrook Drive and Aida Place, St. Paul
(651) 632-5111

The Marjorie McNeely Conservatory at Como Park is the architectural centerpiece of this lovely St. Paul public park. The park was designed by one of St. Paul's most important landscape architects, Horace W. S. Cleveland, and a German immigrant, Frederick Nussbaumer. Later Nussbaumer drew up the plans for the conservatory, which was inspired by London's Crystal Palace in Hyde Park.

The conservatory features a palm dome in the center of this glass structure, and the building is split into several wings displaying seasonally blooming flora. The conservatory is expertly integrated into the landscape of the rolling hills, ravine, and gardens that surround the structure. In 1993 a major face-lift restored the conservatory to a splendor far eclipsing its original beauty in 1915. The combination of architecture and flowers make the conservatory a treat for Twin Citians throughout the year.

Minnesota State Capitol
75 Constitution Avenue, St. Paul
(651) 297-3521

The Minnesota State Capitol is one of the area's architectural landmarks for several reasons. The 223-foot unsupported marble dome is the largest in the world. The architectural splendor also includes statues, columns, arches, and murals.

Cass Gilbert won a capitol design competition in 1898. Gilbert designed several Twin Cities buildings and the plan for the University of Minnesota's Northrop Mall (which was significantly modified) before moving on to national prominence with designs such as the Woolworth Building in New York City. The capitol was completed in 1904, and the cost

Minnesota State Capitol. SAINT PAUL RCVA

of the new structure was the subject of great controversy. The third state capitol, most Minnesotans would agree today, was worth the hefty price tag.

St. Paul City Hall
and Ramsey County Courthouse
15 West Kellogg Boulevard, St. Paul
(651) 266-8023

St. Paul City Hall and the Ramsey County Courthouse is an exemplary combination of neoclassical and art deco. The building's facade is an example of neoclassical style, while the art deco interior is where the building shines. It shares with New York's Rockefeller Center the then-modern art deco style that is paired with unmatched attention to materials and detail.

Constructed during the middle of the Great Depression, St. Paul City Hall overflows with the finest craftsmanship. When the nation's economy hit rock bottom, many of the nation's most talented artists and artisans were unemployed. Not only did the cost of labor plummet but so did the price paid for materials. The results are breathtaking, particularly in the lobby, which glitters with black marble walls and features a 36-foot-high rotating statue named Visions of Peace. The original 1931 structure was renovated in 1993, restoring its luster.

St. Paul Public Library
80 West Fourth Street, St. Paul
(651) 227-9531

Twin Cities libraries are often distinguished by fine architecture. The St. Paul Public Library is an exceptional example, especially the James J. Hill Reference Library Reading Room. The reading room is an exemplar of Beaux-Arts classicism, and the two-story reading room is surrounded by the book stacks and Ionic columns, with abundant finely crafted woodwork and granite floors. Large comfy tables and chairs entice visitors to enjoy the resources available or quietly absorb the architecture. Recently renovated, the library is one of downtown St. Paul's many beautiful public buildings.

Union Depot
214 East Fourth Street, St. Paul

The Union Depot was constructed between 1917 and 1923. At the time the railroad was a prominent means of transportation, and a serpentine labyrinth of tracks circled the depot. Since then the importance of the railroad has dwindled, but the depot remains—although it serves a different purpose. Today the Union Depot is an awe-inspiring architectural work that takes advantage of a high ceiling, balconies, and plenty of stone. Restaurants occupy the immense lobby where passengers once arrived and departed, and visitors may dine in one of St. Paul's most historic and architecturally attractive settings.

Wells Fargo Place
30 East Seventh Street, St. Paul
(651) 229-2800

Completed in 1987, Wells Fargo Place (formerly known as the Minnesota World Trade Center) sits high atop the St. Paul skyline. It is the tallest building in St. Paul, and at 37 stories high, the building would fit in the much loftier Minneapolis skyline. The architectural design of the building is similar to many of the colossal Minneapolis structures. The exterior has plenty of dark glass, which reflects light on sunny summer days. Even in St. Paul, a city where tradition has always been emphasized, the thoroughly modern Wells Fargo Place dominates the skyline.

HOUSES OF WORSHIP

Minneapolis

The Basilica of Saint Mary
88 North 17th Street, Minneapolis
(612) 333-1381
www.mary.org

The Basilica of Saint Mary celebrated its first Mass on May 31, 1914, as a then-unique Catholic place for worship. It was the first basilica in America, an institution created to serve the needs of Minneapolis. While St. Paul held the first mass in its own breathtakingly beautiful cathedral in 1915, the other Twin City was allowed by the Vatican to construct the basilica. As with the Cathedral of Saint Paul, Emmanuel L. Masqueray (1861–1917) was the architect for the Basilica of Saint Mary.

Masqueray unveiled his design in 1906. The colossal basilica features a 200-foot dome and an impressive nave. At the time of its construction, the 140-foot by 82-foot nave was considered the widest in the world. The stained-glass windows, designed by Thomas Gaytee, are another extraordinary feature of the basilica.

The life of the namesake of the basilica, Mary, mother of Jesus, is artfully displayed on the stained-glass windows. The rose windows on both sides of the sanctuary portray the Immaculate Conception and the Crowning of Mary Queen of Heaven. Archangels in the windows of the entrance guard everyone who enters the basilica. Sculptures play a significant role in the architecture of the basilica and its grounds. The 12 apostles are depicted in the sanctuary, and there are half-scale replicas of the sculptures at Saint John Lateran in Rome. These are just a few of the sculptures, which include one of Father Louis Hennepin, who brought Catholicism to the area. His sculpture looks out on the street that today bears his name (Hennepin Avenue).

Located on the edge of downtown Minneapolis at the intersection of Hennepin Avenue and North 17th Street, the building sits across the street from Loring Park and is within walking distance of the internationally acclaimed Walker Art Center and the other two beautiful churches lining Hennepin Avenue (Hennepin Avenue United Methodist and Cathedral Church of St. Mark). All of these churches are examples of excellent Beaux-Arts architecture, but the Basilica of Saint Mary is certainly the largest in scale.

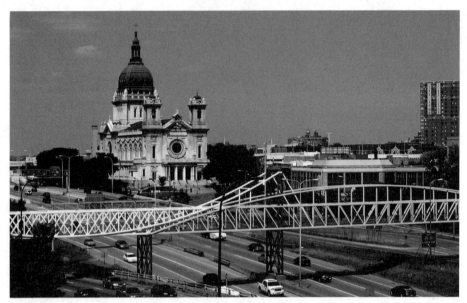

Minneapolis's Basilica of St. Mary. TODD R. AND BONNIE S. BERGER

Cathedral Church of St. Mark
519 Oak Grove Street, Minneapolis
(612) 870-7800
www.ourcathedral.org

The Cathedral Church of St. Mark was designed by one of the Twin Cities' most renowned architectural firms in the early 20th century, Brown and Hewitt. Between 1904 and 1930 the firm created several outstanding pieces of architecture, including this church, completed in 1910. Edwin H. Hewitt was the primary designer of most of the firm's work, which was heavily influenced by the eclectic Beaux-Arts style. Emphasizing revivalism in architectural designs, Beaux-Arts works are symmetrical and balanced. The style was a popular foil for modernism.

As a member of the church, Hewitt set out to create a design appropriate to his faith. Denominationally, the church is Episcopalian; the design reflects this heritage. English Gothic revival dominates the church's architectural style. The tower is inspired by the example found at Magdalen College at Oxford, albeit significantly scaled down.

Adding to the church's splendor is its location on the southern edge of Loring Park, which is one of Minneapolis's most beautiful parks. You can find the Cathedral Church of St. Mark at the intersection of Oak Grove Street and West 15th Street.

Christ Church Lutheran
3244 34th Avenue South, Minneapolis
(612) 721-6611
www.christchurchluth.org

Built in a humble working-class neighborhood in south Minneapolis, Christ Church Lutheran is the last design of Eliel Saarinen. The world-famous Finnish architect created a design for the state of Minnesota, where Scandinavian Lutherans abound.

Saarinen's great architectural pieces began with the railway station in Helsinki (1905–14). He went on to design a series of central European railway stations. Later, Saarinen immigrated to the United States, where his work culminated with the Cranbrook School (circa 1925). He was selected for the Christ Church Lutheran's design, which

St. Paul's tallest building, Wells Fargo Place (formerly the Minnesota World Trade Center), towers over the Capital City. TODD R. BERGER became his last architectural triumph, completed in 1949.

Saarinen's forté was creating excellent institutional architecture, but the church's coffers did not overflow with money for a distinctive design. Hence, Saarinen created a work of great beauty out of a relatively limited budget. The church is small and intimate, and the exterior design is composed of minimalistic blocks. As parishioners or visitors approach the church, they walk under a large stone canopy. Inside the building are two wings, with a sanctuary on one end, and a fellowship hall, offices, and classrooms on the other. The interior is finely detailed and makes abundant use of yellow brick and complementary shaded wood. The exterior of the sanctuary has four sculptures representing faith, love, church, and hope. Saarinen died in 1950, the year after Christ Church Lutheran was completed. The architect's legacy continues with one of the Twin Cities' most attractive small churches.

Christ Church Lutheran is on 34th Avenue South 2 blocks south of East Lake Street and five blocks east of Minnehaha Avenue.

Hennepin Avenue United Methodist Church
511 Groveland Avenue, Minneapolis
(612) 871-5303
www.haumc.org

The Hennepin Avenue United Methodist Church is yet another impressive piece of architecture near Hennepin Avenue. Like the Cathedral Church of St. Mark, it was designed by Hewitt and Brown and is again an example of English Gothic revival work. The octagonal base of the steeple and tall, slender spire set the church apart and position it among the Twin Cities' most spectacular architectural churches.

The church is on Groveland Avenue 1 block east of Hennepin Avenue and 1 block south of Loring Park.

Our Lady of Lourdes Church
One Lourdes Place, Minneapolis
(612) 379-2259
www.ourladyoflourdes.com

Not only is Our Lady of Lourdes the oldest standing church in Minneapolis, but it also has a simultaneously tumultuous and intriguing history. During each successive turn in the history of the church, at least minimal architectural alterations were made. Surprisingly, despite the cobbled nature of the church's construction, it is an awe-inspiring work and a landmark in historic St. Anthony.

The church dates from 1857, when the First Universalist Society completed the original structure. The front nave was built from native limestone. The original Greek temple–style church was significantly smaller than it is today. In 1877 the church was purchased by a group of Catholic French Canadian settlers in the area and rechristened Our Lady of Lourdes. The Canadians added the mansard roof, which remains on the eastern side of the church. In toto the structure was transformed into the French provincial style, which was one of the seven styles of church architecture then constructed in Quebec. Shortly thereafter, the church added a bell tower, sacristy, and a vestibule. Stained-glass windows were installed from the 1890s through the 1910s. However, the church was increasingly neglected over time.

In 1968 church leaders decided to demolish the church, but the Minneapolis city council intervened and the church was spared. Since then the church has undergone several renovations to restore it to its previous glory. In 1991 carillon bells were mounted in the church tower. Today their sonorous chiming can be heard throughout historic St. Anthony.

Our Lady of Lourdes can be found at the intersection of Hennepin Avenue East and Lourdes Place, in the St. Anthony neighborhood across the Hennepin Avenue Bridge from downtown Minneapolis.

St. Paul

Assumption Church
51 West Seventh Street, St. Paul
(651) 224-7536
The Assumption Church was constructed between 1869 and 1874. Located in an area of downtown St. Paul where architectural change has occurred at a rapid pace, the church remains a distinct and important piece of architecture.

As St. Paul developed, religious communities constructed churches to fulfill their spiritual needs. The ethnic heritage and denomination of the church often profoundly influenced the architecture of individual structures. This was certainly the case with the Assumption Church, which was formed to meet the needs of German Catholics. The Ludwigskirche in Munich, Germany, heavily influenced the German Romanesque revival design of the church. For materials, the church makes use of Minnesota limestone. The twin towers are the most distinguishable features of the church. They rise 210 feet and are a perennial landmark in the ephemeral architecture of downtown St. Paul.

Assumption Church is located at the intersection of West Seventh Street and St. Peter Street, 2 blocks northeast of the Xcel Energy Center.

Cathedral of Saint Paul
239 Selby Avenue, St. Paul
(651) 228-1766
www.cathedralsaintpaul.org
The Cathedral of Saint Paul is one of the Twin Cities' most recognizable landmarks. The sheer size of the structure is daunting, and it stands like a sentinel atop Cathedral Hill, where it overlooks downtown St. Paul, directly across the interstate from the Minnesota State Capitol.

The grand scale of the Cathedral of Saint Paul reflects its source of inspiration. The cathedral, which was designed by Emmanuel L. Masqueray, was modeled after Saint Peter's

Cathedral in Rome. Also instrumental in the erection of the cathedral was Archbishop John Ireland, who envisioned and raised the money for the cathedral as a tribute to the faith of the archdiocese. The cathedral held its first mass in 1915, although the building wasn't completed and dedicated until 1958.

The features of the cathedral are breathtaking. The interior is baroque in design, makes use of Minnesota granite and travertine, and is decorated with stained glass and paintings, including several beautiful frescoes. The dome extends 175 feet above the cathedral and can be seen from great distances. Guided tours are held Monday, Wednesday, and Friday (except holidays) at 1:00 p.m., when visitors may enjoy the Cathedral of Saint Paul's astounding beauty.

Mount Zion Temple
1300 Summit Avenue, St. Paul
(651) 698-3881
www.mzion.org
Founded in 1856 as the Mount Zion Hebrew Congregation, Mount Zion Temple was the first Jewish house of worship in the Twin Cities. The present building, the fourth to house the congregation, is located on elegant Summit Avenue. Eric Mendelsohn, an internationally renowned Bauhaus architect, designed the stylish, modern building, which was dedicated in 1954.

St. Clement's Episcopal Church
901 Portland Avenue, St. Paul
(651) 228-1164
www.stclements-stp.org
Many are surprised to hear that this attractive and quaint church was designed by Cass Gilbert, who later served as architect for the colossal Minnesota State Capitol. The structure makes fine use of material but on a much smaller scale. Intimacy is stressed. The church is constructed of slate, stone, and wood; conveys a sense of solace; and is scaled to parishioner's size. St. Clement's Episcopal Church was completed in 1894.

West

Colonial Church of Edina
6200 Colonial Way, Edina
(952) 925-2711
www.colonialchurch.org
The Colonial Church of Edina is a curiosity that stands in stark contrast to the first-tier suburban architecture in the neighborhoods just north of Minnesota Highway 62. The church was modeled on a New England colonial village. Architect Richard Hammel visited a church in Barnstable, Massachusetts, that was built by the Pilgrims in the 17th century. The Edina design, in keeping with the source architecture, is simple and subdued. The church makes use of gray with white trim and features a bell tower at the center. The colonial village design includes space for a sanctuary, lounges, and additional rooms for church activities.

East

Church of St. Michael
611 South Third Street, Stillwater
(651) 439-4400
www.stillwatercatholics.org
Catholic missionaries arrived in Stillwater in 1849, and the first Church of St. Michael was built in 1853. In 1873 the construction of the present Church of St. Michael began, and the building was completed in 1875. The yellow Kasota-stone church with its 190-foot spire sits atop a hill overlooking the city of Stillwater and the St. Croix River Valley. Over the years St. Michael's has been renovated several times to maintain its striking beauty. In a city filled with architectural treasures, the Church of St. Michael stands out as one of Stillwater's prettiest structures.

TWIN CITIES BRIDGES

With the Mississippi River winding through Minneapolis and St. Paul, the Twin Cities are blessed with many bridges. However, the most famous bridge in the Twin Cities, the Interstate 35W bridge over the Mississippi in downtown Minneapolis, no longer stands. The bridge collapsed on August 1, 2007, killing 13 people and injuring dozens. One hundred cars fell into the Mississippi during the catastrophe. Construction began on a replacement bridge just months after the collapse.

Hennepin Avenue Suspension Bridge
Main Street SE and Hennepin Avenue, Minneapolis
The original Hennepin Avenue Bridge was completed in 1855; it was the first permanent span across the Mississippi River and was necessary for the creation of the city of Minneapolis in 1872. The villages of St. Anthony (east bank) and Minneapolis (west bank) could not have merged into one city without the bridge.

The current bridge is the fourth structure on the site. It is a larger, architecturally scaled-down version of the Disneyesque first two bridges that stood here between 1855 and 1891. On the current bridge, completed in 1990, two minimally ornamented, relatively short towers sit on either side of the Mississippi, anchoring the lopping cables that support the elegant bridge. The span provides a panoramic view of downtown Minneapolis.

High Bridge
Smith Avenue, St. Paul
The High Bridge is a landmark that provides one of the best views of downtown St. Paul. The original High Bridge opened in 1889 to link St. Paul's West Seventh Street and the upper West Side. The span of the bridge was an astounding 2,770 feet, and it was constructed with more than one million pieces of iron. It was no small accomplishment for its era; however, the bridge deteriorated over the course of almost a century, and it was razed in 1985.

St. Paul completed construction of the current replica High Bridge in 1987. Once again, the 160-foot-high bridge had a steep 4 percent grade. In addition, the bridge consisted of 11 spans, the longest stretching 520 feet.

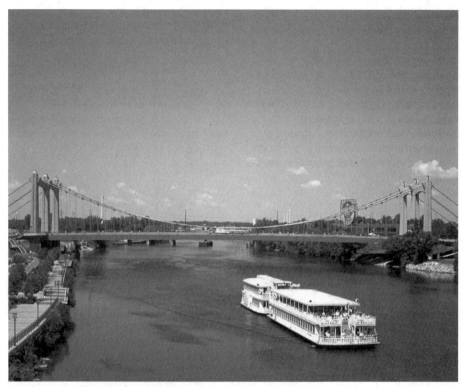

The Hennepin Avenue Suspension Bridge stands on the spot of the first bridge across the Mississippi River.
GREATER MINNEAPOLIS CONVENTION & VISITORS ASSOCIATION

Mendota Bridge
Minnesota Highway 55, Mendota

The spectacular 4,119-foot Mendota Bridge carries Minnesota Highway 55 over the Minnesota River and Fort Snelling State Park to link southeast Minneapolis with the southern suburbs of St. Paul. When the original bridge was completed in 1926, it was the longest concrete arch bridge in the world, and it remains one of the longest bridges of any kind in the United States—only New York City's Verrazano-Narrows Bridge, San Francisco's Golden Gate Bridge, and several highway trestle bridges in the Louisiana bayous are longer. The deck of the bridge was completely rebuilt in the early 1990s, a two-year project that closed the bridge entirely during construction. The Mendota Bridge is on the National Register of Historic Places.

Stillwater Lift Bridge
Wisconsin/Minnesota Highway 64 and Water Street, Stillwater

The Stillwater Lift Bridge is one of only two automotive lift bridges in Minnesota (the other is the Aerial Lift Bridge in Duluth), but its future is uncertain. The span linking Stillwater, Minnesota, to Houlton, Wisconsin, was constructed in 1931. It is a vertical-lift bridge, which rises to allow large vessels on the St. Croix River to pass under it. Despite the bridge's architectural significance, it has a questionable future because of the population growth in the western Wisconsin counties along the St. Croix. A 2007 Sierra Club lawsuit against the National Park Service (the current and potential future bridges span the St. Croix National Scenic Riverway) has halted planning on the replacement bridge, adding

another chapter to one of Minnesota's
longest-running environmental controversies.

Stone Arch Bridge
Main Street SE and Fifth Avenue, Minneapolis

The Stone Arch Bridge was constructed in
1883 for James J. Hill's Great Northern Railway. The bridge spanning the Mississippi took
two years to complete. In 1978 the bridge
was closed because of decreased train traffic.
The bridge remained dormant until the state

The Stone Arch Bridge is the best
place in Minneapolis to view both
Minneapolis's historic milling district
architecture and the city's skyline.

of Minnesota purchased it in 1992. The historic railroad bridge, the second oldest
surviving bridge over the Mississippi, was renovated to serve pedestrians and bicyclists;
the bridge reopened in 1994.

ACCOMMODATIONS

There are a few good rules to remember when trying to find hotel accommodations in the Twin Cities. First of all, winter rates for rooms are almost half that of spring and summer rates. Second, staying in St. Paul is cheaper than staying in Minneapolis, even though there are far fewer hotel options in St. Paul. Most hotels in the Cities have package plans that can knock up to a couple hundred dollars off the price of a room if you reserve a few months in advance and you plan to stay for two or more days. All major credit cards are accepted at the following establishments except where noted. Also, all the following hotels have both smoking and nonsmoking rooms unless otherwise noted; however, none of the bed-and-breakfasts listed here allow smoking inside the rooms. All hotels in the metro area are required to have wheelchair-accessible ramps outside and inside the hotels.

If you visit the Twin Cities during the chilly winter months, try to find a hotel connected to either the Minneapolis or the St. Paul skyway system. These wonderful second-floor walkways are climate controlled and link most of the downtown businesses, so you don't have to step outside unless you want to. You can enter the skyway system through the parking garages in both cities, and posted maps let you know where you are at every junction.

NOTE: Accommodations are listed alphabetically under the headings Minneapolis, St. Paul, Neighboring Communities, and Bed-and-Breakfasts.

PRICE CODE

The following rate information is based on the cost of a standard, double-occupancy room in springtime (May–June), which is generally considered to be the peak tourist season in the Twin Cities.

$	Less than $100
$$	$101–$150
$$$	$151–$200
$$$$	$201–$250
$$$$$	$251 and higher

MINNEAPOLIS

Best Western Normandy Inn $
405 South Eighth Street, Minneapolis
(612) 370-1400
www.bestwesternnormandy.com
Conveniently located in the heart of downtown Minneapolis, this hotel is equally close (5 blocks) to the Metrodome and the Minneapolis Convention Center, 3 blocks from the light-rail line's Government Plaza Station, and across the street from an entrance to the skyway system. The hotel offers guests a complimentary continental breakfast; has an indoor pool, a Jacuzzi, and a fitness room; and serves milk and chocolate chip cookies every night. Every room has free wireless Internet.

Chambers, The Luxury Art Hotel $$$$$
901 Hennepin Avenue, Minneapolis
(612) 767-6900
www.chambersminneapolis.com
Opened in September 2006, Chambers is the Midwestern sister of New York's Chambers Hotel. The small, 60-room hotel is filled with contemporary art from the collection of the hotel's owner, Ralph Burnet. The rooms are modernistic and hip with big windows, plasma screen TVs, glass-tiled bathrooms with rain showers, free wireless Internet access, 400-thread-count sheets, and art-bedecked walls. Chambers Kitchen offers the

creations of chef Jean-Georges Vongerichte (for more information on eating at Chambers Kitchen, see the Restaurants chapter), and the top floor hosts a glass-walled, balconied lounge. The hotel is located in the heart of the Hennepin Theater District and a short walk from Target Center, the Block E Entertainment Complex, and Nicollet Mall.

Crowne Plaza Northstar Hotel $$
618 Second Avenue South, Minneapolis
(612) 338-2288
www.msp-northstar.crowneplaza.com
This hotel offers a comfortable stay for tourists and business travelers alike, with a year-round fitness center and a 24-hour business center. Each room includes an oversize desk with an ergonomic chair, individually controlled heating and air-conditioning, and high-speed Internet access. The hotel is in the middle of downtown Minneapolis and minutes from all the entertainment venues and shopping.

Days Inn University $
2407 University Avenue SE, Minneapolis
(612) 623-3999
www.daysinn.com
This friendly six-story hotel is located on the eastern edge of the Minnepolis campus of the University of Minnesota and is within walking distance from Dinkytown and all its stores and restaurants. The hotel offers guests a complimentary continental breakfast, free lot parking, and complimentary shuttle service to sites within 2 miles of the hotel. The hotel is a convenient choice if your plans include the Minneapolis university area.

Embassy Suites $$$
425 South Seventh Street, Minneapolis
(612) 333-3111
www.embassysuites.com
This newly renovated all-suite hotel in downtown Minneapolis 2 blocks from the Metrodome features an open atrium and access to the skyway system. Suite amenities include a separate bedroom, living area, and a fully equipped kitchen; hotel facilities include a gym, an indoor swimming pool, a restaurant with room service, and complimentary cooked-to-order breakfasts.

The Grand Hotel Minneapolis $$$$$
615 Second Avenue South, Minneapolis
(612) 288-8888 or (866) THE-GRAND
www.grandhotelminneapolis.com
Originally the home of the historic Minneapolis Athletic Club, the Grand Hotel Minneapolis remodeled and reopened as a hotel in 2000. Based on the AAA rating system, the hotel is the top luxury hotel in downtown Minneapolis. Although you will pay for the experience, you will be pampered from the moment you step in the door. The 140 rooms of the hotel feature such indulgences as Egyptian cotton sheets, silk bathrobes, Aveda bath products, leather-topped desks, marble bathrooms, and Tuscan furniture. Guests also enjoy their choice of complimentary newspapers delivered to their door, complimentary shoe shines, the Martini BLU Restaurant and Night Club, the Martini BLU Sushi Bar, the Grand Finale Lounge, and a LifeSpa Aveda Concept Salon. Guests are allowed free use of the on-site 58,000-square-foot Minneapolis Lifetime Athletic Club, with an indoor lap pool, racquetball and squash courts, fitness center, boxing studio, sauna, and eucalyptus steam room. The hotel is connected to the skyway system and is within easy walking distance of the luxurious Gaviidae Common shopping center (anchored by such stores as Neiman Marcus and Saks Fifth Avenue), the Minneapolis Convention Center, Nicollet Mall, and the Hennepin Theater District.

Graves 601 Hotel $$$$
601 First Avenue, Minneapolis
(612) 677-1100 or (866) 523-1100
www.graves601hotel.com
Formerly Le Méridien, Graves 601 is across the street from the Target Center in the Block E entertainment and shopping complex and is connected to the skyway system. Since opening in 2003, this swank hotel has gotten rave reviews by local and national publications—

i Nicollet Mall is a prime location for hotels. For a cheaper rate that's still near the action and insulated from a Minnesota winter, look for a hotel that's a block or two off the mall and connected to the skyway.

and travelers. Rooms have features such as glass-etched, handcrafted headboards; back-lit photographs inspired by Twin Cities culture; huge plasma televisions; high-speed Internet access; and artistically designed bathrooms with rain shower features. In addition to an on-site health club, the hotel has a restaurant (Cosmos) and a street-level, futuristic lounge (Infinity).

Hilton Minneapolis $$$$$
1001 Marquette Avenue, Minneapolis
(612) 376-1000
www.minneapolis.hilton.com
The Hilton Minneapolis is located next door to Orchestra Hall in the center of downtown and is connected to the skyway system. The 25-story brick hotel has 821 rooms, all featuring large windows and hand-carved oak trim. The hotel has an on-site health club (including a full gym, whirlpool, sauna, and swimming pool); 73,000 square feet of meeting space including the new Symphony Ballroom; wireless Internet access; and more. There's a coffee cart in the lobby as well as an on-site restaurant and bar (Skywater).

Holiday Inn Metrodome $$
1500 Washington Avenue South, Minneapolis
(612) 333-4646 or (800) 448-DOME
www.metrodome.com
Located on the eastern edge of the downtown business district with the Minneapolis campus of the University of Minnesota on one side and the Metrodome on the other, the Holiday Inn Metrodome has one of the best hotel locations for sports fans in the Twin Cities. The 265-room hotel has an indoor pool, a whirlpool and sauna, a gym, and a restaurant (the Grill Room Restaurant and

Lobby Bar) and offers guests shuttle transportation within a 3-mile radius.

Hyatt Regency Hotel $$$
1300 Nicollet Mall, Minneapolis
(612) 370-1234
www.minneapolis.hyatt.com
This 24-story hotel is located right on the Nicollet Avenue pedestrian mall near Orchestra Hall, with direct access to the skyway system. The hotel has 533 guest rooms and suites, four restaurants, an indoor pool, a full-service athletic club, a business center, and a retail area that includes clothing stores, salons, gourmet coffee shops, and delis. The hotel features a bistro, Taxxi, and neighbors Manny's Steakhouse and the city's finest "flown-in daily" seafood restaurant, the Oceannaire Seafood Room.

Marquette Hotel $$$
710 Marquette Avenue, Minneapolis
(612) 333-4545 or (800) 328-4782
www.marquettehotel.com
Located in the heart of downtown Minneapolis, the Marquette has the distinct advantage of being part of the IDS Center complex, which is connected to the downtown skyway system. The rooms are large with great views of the downtown area from all sides. Amenities include Egyptian cotton sheets, luxury bath products, free wireless Internet access, a business center, and a 24-hour fitness center. The hotel has a restaurant, Basil's, which overlooks the Crystal Court of the IDS Center, and a bar, the MARC VII Lounge. The Marquette also operates Windows on Minnesota, a banquet and meeting space on the 50th floor of the IDS Center, which features 11-foot-high windows with spectacular views of the Metro.

Minneapolis Marriott City Center $$$$
30 South Seventh Street, Minneapolis
(612) 349-4000
www.marriott.com
Connected to the skyway system, this hotel is conveniently located just off Nicollet Mall with

its numerous shops and restaurants. The hotel also provides guests with a fitness center, a business center, the Lobby Bar, and an on-site restaurant—Northern Shores Grille, a casual dining establishment.

Nicollet Island Inn $$$$
95 Merriam Street, Minneapolis
(612) 331-1800
www.nicolletislandinn.com
The small, intimate Nicollet Island Inn sits in the middle of the Mississippi River on Nicollet Island across from downtown Minneapolis and is easily accessible from the Warehouse District via the Hennepin Avenue Bridge. The building that houses the inn was built in 1893 as the factory for the Island Door and Sash Company, a maker of window shades and blinds. Today the National Historic Building, which completed extensive renovations in 2007, includes 24 individually decorated guest rooms with fine linens, plasma screen TVs, Select Comfort Sleep Number beds, and gorgeous views of the downtown skyline and the river. The Nicollet Island Inn also has a romantic restaurant well known throughout the Cities for its wonderful brunch.

Radisson Plaza Hotel Minneapolis $$$$$
35 South Seventh Street, Minneapolis
(612) 339-4900
www.radisson.com/minneapolismn_plaza
This luxury hotel on Nicollet Mall is a short walk from the Hennepin Theater District and Target Center. The Radisson Plaza features a restaurant, a lounge, a 24-hour business center, and a health club. Through the connected skyway you can easily reach most of downtown Minneapolis's attractions and shopping areas. The comfortable rooms feature free high-speed Internet access, marble and granite bathrooms, and large desks.

i If you choose not to stay at the Nicollet Island Inn, try it out for dinner or drinks. The inn's restaurant and bar are perfect for romantic evenings on the town.

Radisson University $$$
615 Washington Avenue Southeast
Minneapolis
(612) 379-8888
www.radisson.com/minneapolismn_metro dome
The Radisson University is set on the University of Minnesota–Minneapolis campus. A short walk from U of M sporting venues and Dinkytown—the main college-kid hangout—this is a great place to catch most of the sports action in town, college or otherwise. The hotel offers amenities including an on-site Applebee's, a gift shop, a Starbucks, and a Great Clips salon. Guests receive free access to the university's Sports and Recreation Facility next to the hotel, complimentary shuttle service to any destination within 5 miles of the hotel on an appointment basis, and free high-speed wireless Internet access.

Ramada Inn $$
41 North 10th Street, Minneapolis
(612) 356-7500
www.ramada.com
This relatively inexpensive hotel is one of the few places in downtown Minneapolis that offers free parking to its guests. The hotel also offers a restaurant for breakfast only, a lounge in the evenings, a kiddie pool, an indoor pool, a whirlpool, and a fitness center. The rooms are somewhat Spartan but comfortable.

Residence Hotel Minneapolis Downtown at the Depot $$
425 South Second Street, Minneapolis
(612) 340-1300
www.marriott.com
This relatively inexpensive hotel is connected to the restored Historic Depot Complex in downtown Minneapolis near the riverfront and the new Guthrie Theater. The hotel, built in 2000 and last renovated in 2006, features an indoor water park and free deluxe continental breakfast, as well as suites with in-room kitchens, fold-away sofabeds, and

high-speed Internet access. More basic rooms are also available. All rooms are nonsmoking.

St. Paul

Best Western—Bandana Square $$
1010 Bandana Boulevard West, St. Paul
(651) 647-1637
www.bestwestern.com
Built inside the original shell of a Northern Pacific Railroad foundry repair shop, this beautiful yellow-brick hotel has 130-year-old train tracks running through its lobby. It's connected to Bandana Square, a dwindling mall that is home to a cool model train museum. Nearby are the Minnesota State Fairgrounds and Midway Stadium, a great open-air baseball field that is home to the St. Paul Saints, the Twin Cities' minor league baseball team. The hotel facilities include an indoor pool, kiddie pool, fitness room, and hot tub, and wireless high-speed Internet throughout. The centrally located hotel is about 5 miles away from downtown St. Paul and about 8 miles from downtown Minneapolis.

Best Western Kelly Inn $$
161 Street Anthony Avenue, St. Paul
(651) 227-8711
www.bestwesternstpaul.com
Two blocks from the State Capitol with a great view of the Cathedral of Saint Paul, this hotel offers guests comfortable, moderately priced rooms near downtown St. Paul. Amenities include an indoor swimming pool, hot tub, and fitness center, as well as high-speed Internet access, and a full-service bar/restaurant (Sweetwater) that delivers to your room. Parking is free.

Crowne Plaza Hotel St. Paul-Riverfront $$
11 East Kellogg Boulevard, St. Paul
(651) 292-1900 or (800) 333-3333
www.cpstpaul.com
Right across the street from the Mississippi River, the Crowne Plaza Hotel St. Paul-Riverfront (formerly the Radisson Riverfront) is in the heart of downtown St. Paul. The hotel offers a restaurant, coffee and sandwich

i Downtown St. Paul's pedestrian skyways are a nice way to walk around comfortably in wintertime. As in downtown Minneapolis, many shops and restaurants are on the skyway level or connected to the skyway.

counter, and lounge. Other hotel amenities include a heated indoor pool, a fitness center, a business center, and free wireless Internet access. The hotel was renovated in 2006.

Embassy Suites St. Paul $$
175 East 10th Street, St. Paul
(651) 224-5400
www.embassystpaul.com
The Embassy Suites St. Paul has 210 rooms, all two-room suites. Hotel amenities include a business center, a swimming pool, fitness club, whirlpool, sauna, downtown shuttle service, full-service restaurant (Woolley's), and an Irish sports bar (Cork's Pub), which features a nightly happy hour. The price of the room includes a cooked-to-order breakfast, and the tropical atrium belies the Northern Plains climate beyond the glass. The hotel is about 7 blocks from the heart of downtown.

Holiday Inn RiverCentre $$
175 West Seventh Street, St. Paul
(651) 225-1515
www.holiday-inn.com/stpaulmn
Located right across the street from the Xcel Energy Center, home of the Minnesota Wild NHL team, and the RiverCentre convention center, this hotel is within 4 blocks of the Science Museum of Minnesota, the Children's Museum, and the Ordway Center for the Performing Arts. It's also a short walk from the Minnesota State Capitol, the Minnesota History Center, and the Fitzgerald Theatre. The hotel was completely renovated in 2005. Guest amenities include an indoor pool and fitness center. It's attached to a wonderful Irish pub and restaurant called the Liffey, which provides room service. The Liffey has great food and a rooftop patio with an incredible view of downtown St. Paul.

The Holiday Inn RiverCentre across the street from the Xcel Energy Center in downtown St. Paul. HOLIDAY INN RIVERCENTRE AND ST. PAUL RCVA

Saint Paul Hotel $$$
350 Market Street, St. Paul
(651) 292-9292 or (800) 292-9292
www.stpaulhotel.com
Built in 1910 and located in the center of St. Paul on beautiful Rice Park, this premier luxury hotel is a member of the Historic Hotels of America. Fully restored to its original splendor (the most recent update was in 2005), the hotel offers guests a unique combination of turn-of-the-century charm and modern convenience. The hotel is within walking distance of St. Paul's RiverCentre, the Ordway Center for the Performing Arts, the Science Museum of Minnesota, and Xcel Energy Center, as well as the Mississippi River walk, plus more business and shops via the climate-controlled skyway. Amenities include a complimentary newspaper, a rooftop fitness center, a business center, and free high-speed Internet access. The hotel has two restaurants, the elegant St. Paul Grill and the M ST. café, as well as the Lobby Bar with libations and

lighter fare. (For more information on eating at the St. Paul Grill, see the Restaurants chapter.) Shuttle service to and from destinations such as the Mall of America and Minneapolis is available upon request.

NEIGHBORING COMMUNITIES

Afton House Inn $$–$$$
3291 St. Croix Trail South, Afton
(651) 436-8883 or (877) 436-8883
www.aftonhouseinn.com
The Afton House Inn is located about 20 miles east of downtown St. Paul in the quaint town of Afton on the St. Croix River. Built in 1867, the 25-room hotel is on the National Register of Historic Places. The nicely furnished rooms include such amenities as gas fireplaces and Jacuzzis. The hotel also operates Afton Hudson Cruise Lines, with several boats that ply the St. Croix. The hotel has three restaurants—two fine-dining rooms plus the casual Catfish Saloon and Café, which has outdoor seating.

Amerisuites $$–$$$
7800 International Drive, Bloomington
(952) 854-0700
www.amerisuites.com

This all-suite hotel is within a mile of the Mall of America and near Minneapolis–St. Paul (MSP) International Airport. The 128 rooms all have small kitchens and free high-speed Internet access. The hotel has an exercise room and indoor pool. Amerisuites operates a shuttle service to the airport and to the Mall of America. This is a good choice for travelers wishing to be near the airport or the mall.

Hampton Inn Airport/Mall of America $$
7745 Lyndale Avenue South, Richfield
(612) 861-1000
www.hamptoninnrichfield.com

This comfortable hotel with few frills is set up especially with the business traveler in mind, with desks and free wireless Internet access. Guests also receive a complimentary buffet breakfast, free parking, and in-room delivery of food from restaurants in the area. The hotel provides free shuttle transportation to the Mall of America and MSP airport, and there is an indoor swimming pool and whirlpool on the premises.

The Lowell Inn $$$
102 North Second Street, Stillwater
(651) 439-1100
www.lowellinn.com

The elegant Lowell Inn in Stillwater (20 miles east of downtown St. Paul) harbors 21 individually decorated rooms featuring period antiques. Elmore Lowell established the Sawyer House on the land where the Lowell Inn now stands in 1848, the year Stillwater was incorporated as the Minnesota Territory's first city. The colonial inn standing today dates from 1927, and the interior brings to mind the regal atmosphere of southern plantation homes. The Lowell has 23 unique guest rooms and four distinct dining rooms. Guests can also relax in front of the colonial fireplace in the Front Parlor.

When you get into the Twin Cities, pick up a copy of the free weekly newspaper, *City Pages*, for information on what's happening in the Twin Cities as well as for restaurant and event coupons.

Mystic Lake Casino Hotel $$
2400 Mystic Lake Boulevard, Prior Lake
(952) 445-9000 or (800) 262-7799
www.mysticlake.com

About 25 miles southwest of downtown Minneapolis, the 600-room Mystic Lake Casino Hotel rises next to the alcohol-free casino of the same name. The hotel features such amenities as an Olympic-size pool with waterslide, 18-hole golf course, fitness center, and the largest casino in the Upper Midwest, with some 4,000 slot machines and 100 blackjack tables. Major celebrities regularly headline at the Mystic Showroom, and guests can partake in the massive buffet, routinely honored as the best buffet in the Twin Cities. The hotel is near Canterbury Park, which features betting on live horse racing during the summer months and a card room year-round.

Radisson Hotel & Conference Center $$$
3131 Campus Drive, Plymouth
(763) 559-6600
www.radisson.com/minneapolismn_plymouth

The Radisson Plymouth in the western Metro is located near Interstate 494 and Minnesota Highway 55 in a parklike setting overlooking a 25-acre marshland preserve. All guest rooms include a minibar, two telephones, free high-speed Internet, and a lighted work desk. Hotel facilities include a full-service fitness center, an indoor pool, two restaurants, and a lounge.

Sofitel Minneapolis $$$
5601 West 78th Street, Bloomington
(952) 835-1900
www.sofitel.com

The French-style Sofitel is located at the intersection of I-494 and Minnesota Highway 100 on the Bloomington Strip. The hotel is about

10 minutes from the Mall of America and 15 minutes from MSP airport. The 282-room hotel also hosts two French restaurants—La Fougasse, in particular, is worthy of destination dining (see the Restaurants chapter for more information). Other amenities include a business center, wireless Internet access, and comfortable guest rooms. The entire hotel is nonsmoking. The hotel was completely renovated in 2006.

Water Park of America Grand Lodge $$$$
1700 East American Boulevard, Bloomington
(952) 854-8700
www.waterparkofamerica.com
Conveniently close to MSP airport and the Mall of America (the latter operates the waterpark), the Water Park of America Grand Lodge is an excellent (though pricey) choice for families whose younger members have a lot of energy. The main attraction is the water park, the largest indoor waterpark in the United States. The lodge has 403 rooms, some of which have views of the water park. Guests can enjoy such amenities as bunk beds for the kids, refrigerators and microwaves, and shuttle service to area attractions. The lodge has three restaurants (Split Rock Grille, Sleepy Eye Cafe, and Camp Many Point) and a lounge (Split Rock Bar).

BED-AND-BREAKFASTS

Covington Inn Bed and Breakfast $$$
100 Harriet Island Road B3, St. Paul
(651) 292-1411
www.covingtoninn.com
The only floating bed-and-breakfast in the Twin Cities, the Covington Inn is a renovated tugboat first launched in 1946 and now moored in the Mississippi River across from downtown St. Paul. Open year-round, the B&B has four comfortable rooms, all with fireplaces and private baths. The inn's common areas are trimmed in bronze, brass, and mahogany, and many salvaged fixtures suggest what it must have been like when the tug Covington

pushed barges up and down the river. You can sit out on the deck and watch the mighty river flow by gleaming downtown St. Paul. The Covington's Harriet Island dock is a short walk from the Wabasha Street Bridge, which spans the Mississippi and leads to the museums, theaters, restaurants, and shops downtown.

Wales House $
1115 Southeast Fifth Street, Minneapolis
(612) 331-3931
www.waleshouse.com
Since opening to the public in 1994, this 10-bedroom bed-and-breakfast has been providing the charm of a home for faculty, staff, and other visitors to the University of Minnesota for extremely reasonable rates. Hundreds of visitors from more than 68 countries have stayed in this antiques-furnished turn-of-the-20th-century home. The living rooms, which are open to guests, include a four-season porch, large front parlor, fireplace room, lounge, dining room, and kitchen. Outside, guests can use the front patio. Amenities include free continental breakfast, free wireless high-speed Internet access, a furnished guest kitchen, on-site laundry, and a cleaning service. The bed-and-breakfast is nonsmoking throughout.

William Sauntry Mansion $$$–$$$$
626 North Fourth Street, Stillwater
(651) 430-2653 or (800) 828-2653
www.sauntrymansion.com
Lumber baron William Sauntry had his 25-room Victorian mansion built in the booming sawmill town of Stillwater on the St. Croix River in 1881. Today this B&B, listed on the National Register of Historic Places, has six guest rooms, all with fireplaces, private baths, and double whirlpool tubs. The ornate house features wood floors, original chandeliers, stained-glass windows, and Victorian furnishings. The William Sauntry Mansion is close to downtown Stillwater, with its quaint antiques stores, lovely cafes, and antiquarian bookshops.

RESTAURANTS

With thousands of restaurants in the metropolitan area, the Twin Cities boast one of the most diverse and tastiest dining scenes in the country. Once considered the land of the smorgasbord or simple meat-and-potato fare, the Twin Cities today offer a vast array of culinary choices.

Traditional American and European fine-dining options are plentiful in the Twin Cities. Downtown Minneapolis, including the Warehouse District and Nicollet Mall, offers the highest concentration of fine-dining opportunities. St. Paul boasts fine restaurants in downtown and in the thriving Cathedral Hill neighborhood.

The Twin Cities restaurant scene reaches into cuisines not common in other parts of the country. Besides the more standard ethnic fare such as Chinese, Mexican, Thai, Middle Eastern, and Indian foods, the area boasts Kurdish, Cambodian, Afghani, Eastern European, and Ethiopian cuisine. Ethnic dining in the area starts on Nicollet Avenue, or Eat Street, which begins on Nicollet Mall in downtown Minneapolis and leads into south Minneapolis. St. Paul offers ethnic food throughout town, and has had many new establishments open up on University Avenue West.

Dining options continue to expand in the suburban Twin Cities, especially the St. Croix River Valley east of Minneapolis and St. Paul. There you'll find avant-garde cuisine, tropical flavors, and ethnic restaurants. In fact, there are many more Indian restaurants in the suburbs than in the Cities.

The chapter has been organized alphabetically by cuisine, followed by listings for sweets and treats and coffeehouses and teashops. In general each cuisine section is divided into regions: Minneapolis, St. Paul, and the suburbs north, south, east, and west.

Also listed for most restaurants are which meals are served, days of the week the restaurant is open, and reservation policies. If the listing does not say otherwise, you can assume that the restaurant accepts all major credit cards. These policies frequently change, so call the restaurant if you have any questions. Both St. Paul and Minneapolis ban smoking in all restaurants and bars.

PRICE CODE

The following price code is based on one adult dinner entrée, without beverage, gratuity, and tax.

$ .... under $10
$$ .... $11–$20
$$$ .... $21–$30
$$$$ .... $31and up

AFGHANI
St. Paul

Khyber Pass Café $$
1571 Grand Avenue, St. Paul
(651) 690-0505
www.khyberpasscafe.com
Khyber Pass Café has served delicious Afghani cuisine since 1985. When entering the restaurant, the diner is immediately struck by its personality, charm, and aesthetic sense. The restaurant has a comfortable, clean, and cobbled-together feel, which integrates potted plants and Afghani crafts with numerous tasteful paintings.

The menu is composed of well-executed entrees. The possibilities include chicken, lamb, beef, and vegetarian dishes. The *korma-e-murgh,* boneless chicken in curry sauce with potatoes and peas, is one savory option.

The Uptown Bar and Cafe (3018 Hennepin Avenue South; 612-823-4719) is a rock club, but it serves food too. The breakfasts are especially good and large (and served all day), and if you're a Bloody Mary fan, this is your place.

Another interesting choice is *kof a-chalau*, which is made of meatballs, onions, and spices. The restaurant is open for lunch Monday through Friday and for dinner Monday through Saturday.

South

Da Afghan Restaurant $$
929 West 80th Street, Bloomington
(952) 888-5824
www.daafghan.com

Da Afghan serves Southwest Asian and Middle Eastern specialties, including spring lamb chops, kabeli palow with chicken or lamb, mantou, and many kinds of kabob. The beautiful restaurant is decorated with Afghani artifacts and Afghani rugs on the tabletops. Beer and wine are served. Da Afghan is open for dinner Tuesday through Sunday and for lunch on Thursday and Friday (for lunch, Da Afghan offers a buffet).

AMERICAN

Minneapolis

Al's Breakfast $
413 14th Avenue SE, Minneapolis
(612) 331-9991

This tiny hole-in-the-wall near the University of Minnesota has been serving customers since the 1940s. It has been called the "narrowest restaurant in the Twin Cities," and when visiting this counter-seating-only diner, you'll quickly see why. College students and folks from the neighborhood have been known to line up around the block waiting for the place to open or to get a seat. Eggs, hash browns, and pancakes are served, as well as exotic omelets, many of which are named after Al's patrons or employees. Al's is open for breakfast and lunch (serving dishes off the breakfast menu) daily. Al's is a Twin Cities institution, and if you don't mind the wait or the grease, get your day started at Al's. Al's accepts no credit cards.

Aster Cafe $
125 Main Street SE, Minneapolis
(612) 379-3138

Located across the Mississippi River from downtown Minneapolis, this little cafe is the perfect place to stop by for lunch or to grab a cup of coffee or a beer in the evening. The menu includes premade sandwiches and homemade soups, cookies, focaccia bread pizzas, and dessert bars. The dining area inside is large and opens up into the art gallery next door, and there's also a beautiful fenced-in outside patio that's nice for summer lounging. The cafe often books acoustic music but entertainment is also provided by people wandering in to play the piano set up in the corner. The cafe keeps about a dozen board and card games on hand for patrons who want to hang out past lunch—and there's a bowl full of dog biscuits under the counter for hounds accompanying patrons. The Aster Cafe is open daily.

B.A.N.K. $$–$$$
88 South 6th Street
(The Westin Minneapolis), Minneapolis
(612) 656-3255
www.bankmpls.com

B.A.N.K., inside the new Westin Minneapolis, serves up modern American food in a gorgeous, though large, art deco seating area (the restaurant space once housed the Farmers and Mechanics Bank). Chef Todd Stein's menu is nontraditional yet familiar, including such things as wild duck, steamed mussels, steaks, and leg of lamb. The restaurant is open for not only lunch and dinner, but also breakfast, and a morning stop at B.A.N.K. is worth it. Omelettes, frittatas, lobster Benedict, and French toast are some of the items you are likely to see on the menu. Be prepared to spend a little more for breakfast than you might be used to, as most of B.A.N.K.'s breakfasts rise above $10. B.A.N.K. is open daily for all three meals

The Brothers Deli $
50 South Sixth Street (skyway level), Minneapolis
(612) 341-8007
www.thebrothersdeli.com

The Brothers Deli offers authentic New York–style deli fare in downtown Minneapolis. This small deli, located on a busy second-floor skyway route, serves mouthwatering delicacies composed of only the best breads, meats, toppings, and condiments. The deli has cold sandwiches, grilled sandwiches, all-vegetable sandwiches, kosher sandwiches, and even grilled-cheese sandwiches, all at pretty cheap prices for downtown Minneapolis. The deli also serves breakfast, including some very inexpensive scrambles. The deli is open weekdays for breakfast and lunch.

Bryant-Lake Bowl (BLB) $–$$
810 West Lake Street, Minneapolis
(612) 825-3737
www.bryantlakebowl.com

A bowling alley? Well, yes, but the Bryant-Lake Bowl in Uptown belies every stereotype of bowling alley eats, atmosphere, and culture. The inside of the restaurant is vintage 1940s, with beautiful woodwork and closely placed tables for intimate eating (with patrons at your neighboring table as well as your tablemates). Famous for its cheap-but-delicious breakfasts, including bison hash, several BLB scrambles (eggs scrambled with a choice of ingredients), and the ridiculously yummy Amy's Breakfast Burrito, the BLB serves lunch and dinner as well. Diners favor such specialties as the turkey, avocado, and bacon sandwich; grilled ahi tuna sandwich; and basmati rice and vegetables (with tofu or chicken optional). The BLB has a full bar, with many microbrews on tap. In addition to the 1950s-era bowling lanes, where you get to relearn the lost art of scoring your game by hand, the BLB is attached to a cabaret theater, where

you can also order from the full menu. (See the Arts chapter for more information on the Bryant-Lake Bowl Theater.) The Bryant-Lake Bowl is open 8:00 a.m. to 2:00 a.m daily.

Cafe Brenda $$
300 First Avenue North, Minneapolis
(612) 342–9230
www.cafebrenda.com

Cafe Brenda is a chic little bistro where the emphasis is on ingredients obtained, as often as possible, from local farmers and prepared in ways that emphasize the current season. This is not a vegetarian restaurant, just a place where vegetarians and vegans feel totally at home. Chef-owner Brenda Langton has been credited as one of the health-food movement's early pioneers, and this restaurant has been running in one form or another since 1978. In addition to the vegetarian dishes, there is plenty of healthy omnivorous fare, including free-range chicken and fresh fish. Cafe Brenda is open for lunch and dinner Monday through Friday and dinner only on Saturday. The restaurant is closed on Sunday. Reservations are accepted.

Chino Latino $$–$$$
2916 Hennepin Avenue South, Minneapolis
(612) 824-7878
www.chinolatino.com

A popular spot for the hip dinner crowd, the foods of Thailand, Mexico, Jamaica, Polynesia, and Korea are represented on Chino Latino's true melting pot of a menu. Chino Latino's menu changes daily, and the foods here run the gamut of these countries' spiciest cuisines, including five-spice duck, taco plates, and peppery steamed mussels. The restaurant also serves a variety of sakes and tequilas to accompany your meal—and just about the biggest banana split in the state to finish it off. The global menu is perfectly matched with the wild, complicated decor, with its cushioned orange-vinyl wall, a satay bar, giant round booths, semi-unisex bathrooms (shared sinks), and an open kitchen. Chino Latino is open daily for dinner.

French Meadow Bakery & Cafe $
2610 Lyndale Avenue South, Minneapolis
(612) 870-4740 or (877) NO YEAST
www.frenchmeadow.com

There's no disputing the quality of the food at this trendy eatery in the Wedge neighborhood, which sells organic sourdough breads, coffees, elaborate cakes, and several kinds of quiches. French Meadow uses no oil, no preservatives, and no yeast in producing chewy and flavorful organic loaves in flavors ranging from multigrain to hemp to rye with sunflower seeds. Step to the counter to order up a French Meadow sandwich and you can request any of those breads with a tasty topping of hummus, roasted eggplant, rosemary chicken salad, whitefish, or smoked turkey. With a comfortable country decor that includes simple tables and chairs, dried grapevines winding up the walls, and enough antiques to keep you intrigued but not overwhelmed, French Meadow is the perfect place to get a cup of coffee and a sandwich for lunch. French Meadow is open daily for breakfast, lunch, and dinner, and they have an extensive to-go menu.

Hell's Kitchen $–$$
89 South 10th Street, Minneapolis
(612) 33-4700
www.hellskitcheninc.com

This breakfast, brunch (on weekends), and lunch spot features wonderfully inventive dishes such as eggs Benedict with bison flank steak and tangerine jalapeño hollandaise sauce, wild-rice porridge, and walleye hash. Despite higher prices than most other breakfast places in the Twin Cities, Hell's Kitchen serves food that is a cut above the rest. Duluth-bound breakfasters can drop by Hell's Kitchen's second outlet (310 Lake Avenue South; 218-727-1620) in Canal Park a couple of blocks from the Duluth Lift Bridge.

Jax Café $$$–$$$$
1928 University Avenue NE, Minneapolis
(612) 789-7297
www.jaxcafe.com

Jax has been a strange combination of kitsch and elegance since it opened in 1933 (right after Prohibition ended), with a long wooden bar accented by a stained-glass window depicting the seven dwarfs, and a trout stream in back. The menu includes shrimp cocktail, crab cakes, gigantic aged steaks, lobster, lamb chops, and salmon. In spring and summer request a place on the outside patio. Jax is open daily for lunch and dinner.

Joe's Garage $$
1610 Harmon Place, Minneapolis
(612) 904-1163
www.joes-garage.com

Joe's integrates the culinary flavors of the world with traditional American fare, including several interesting takes on the burger. The menu includes the Greek lamb burger, a Mediterranean take on a traditional burger, with feta, black olive pesto, tomato, and spinach. Other offerings include the spicy Asian pork burger and the classic beef burger. Pasta and risotto are also prominently featured on the menu. Joe's is open for lunch and dinner Monday through Saturday, and for brunch and dinner Sunday.

The Malt Shop $–$$
809 West 50th Street, Minneapolis
(612) 824-1352

The Malt Shop serves gourmet burgers and sandwiches as well as shakes and malts. Besides the standard cheeseburgers and Reubens, there are items like the Malibu chicken, a sautéed chicken breast with Swiss cheese, bacon, and avocado. Most important are the malts and shakes, available in almost 40 flavors. They range from strawberry and chocolate to black cherry and cookies 'n' cream.

Market Bar-B-Que $$
1414 Nicollet Avenue, Minneapolis
(612) 872-1111

15320 Wayzata Boulevard, Wayzata
(952) 475-1770
www.marketbbq.com

Established in 1946 (although not always at this location), Market Bar-B-Que's been a Twin Cities family tradition for years. The menu includes fabulous, lean spareribs and beef tips, barbecue beef sandwiches, and an amazing "dessert trough" including key lime pie and grasshopper ice cream pie. The extensive wine list is printed on the side of giant empty wine bottles set on the tables. The decor is simple and comfortable, with large carved wooden booths and tables and black-and-white photographs of celebrities who have dined at Market, including Jay Leno and Willie Mays. Each table is equipped with a small jukebox that carries popular music selections from the '50s to the present. Both locations are open for lunch and dinner daily.

Matt's Bar $
3500 Cedar Avenue South, Minneapolis
(612) 722-7072
www.mattsbar.com
Matt's Bar is famous for one thing—the Jucy Lucy. And, yes, that is the correct spelling of the south Minneapolis super-cheeseburger. Matt's makes the best Jucy Lucy, although a couple of south Minneapolis bars disagree on where it was first created in the Twin Cities. The burger is composed of two beef patties sealed around a pool of American cheese. Jucy Lucy novices beware; the burger, when removed from the grill, is filled with steaming hot cheese. The menu also includes additional burger selections and sandwiches.

Modern Cafe $–$$
337 13th Avenue NE, Minneapolis
(612) 378-9882
The Modern is a magnet for arty students who miss their mom's home cooking but don't want to eat at an actual diner. The restaurant serves pot roast with carrots, pork sandwiches on apple bread, omelets, and giant malts and milk shakes. If you have a hankering for grilled cheese, have one here: they're made with Asiago cheese, Dijon mustard, and caramelized onions to create the yummiest variation on this old standby you'll

probably ever need (there may be better ones out there, but when they're this good, why bother?). To mix it up a bit, the cafe also makes walleye egg rolls, penne with goat cheese and crimini mushrooms, tomato risotto with capers and lemon zest, and heavenly chocolate crème brûlée. The Modern serves lunch and dinner Tuesday through Friday, and adds breakfast Saturday and Sunday. Closed Mondays.

Sapor Cafe and Bar $$
428 Washington Avenue North,
Minneapolis
(612) 375-1971
www.saporcafe.com
Diners in search of a sophisticated and difficult to classify fusion cuisine will love the Sapor Cafe. Entrees meld together high-quality, seemingly disparate ingredients to create piquant culinary delights. The menu changes seasonally and emphasizes local, organic ingredients. Dinners include a miso-baked salmon and a pork chop in jerk spices. The restaurant features a comfortable bar, which is frequented by a hip crowd. Sapor is open Monday through Friday for lunch, and Monday through Saturday for dinner. Closed Sundays.

Ted Cook's 19th Hole Bar-B-Que $–$$
2814 East 38th Street, Minneapolis
(612) 721-2023
Ted Cook's is a small takeout-only restaurant in south Minneapolis that serves some of the best barbecue in the Twin Cities. One of the restaurant's secrets is they cook their barbecue over a cherrywood fire. All aspects of the meats, sides, and desserts are carefully executed, and the end result is outstanding. The meats include pork ribs, beef ribs, and barbecue chicken and beef. The tender meat is accompanied by the rich and tasty barbecue sauce, which can be ordered mild or spicy. With each dinner, jo jo potatoes, coleslaw, and bread are served. Many of the barbecue meats are also available a la carte. Items from Mom's kitchen—greens with corn muffins, black-eyed peas, and red beans and rice—are

available as well as peach cobbler and sweet potato pie for dessert. Prices are very reasonable at Ted Cook's and even cheaper with lunch sandwich combinations. Hungry night owls are wise to show up for takeout shortly before the restaurant closes: The portions become humongous when the kitchen begins to shut down. Ted Cook's is open for lunch and dinner Tuesday through Saturday. Closed Mondays.

Vera's Cafe $
2901 Lyndale Avenue South, Minneapolis
(612) 822-3871
www.verascafe.com
Open until midnight seven nights a week, Vera's is a popular late-night dining establishment in the Lyn-Lake neighborhood, serving homemade soups, huge sandwiches, six kinds of scrambled eggs, and European coffees. During the summer months the gated patio is a beautiful place to take in lunch or to hang out after a movie. Inside, Vera's is outfitted with antique-looking tables, ice-cream-parlor chairs, and velvet and mohair couches. Vera's is open daily for breakfast, lunch, and dinner.

St. Paul

Cecil's Restaurant, Delicatessen
& Bakery $
651 South Cleveland Avenue, St. Paul
(651) 698-0334
www.cecilsdeli.com
Cecil's, established in 1949, is St. Paul's best deli. The front of the building is a huge deli with fresh meats, cheeses, breads, and baked goods; in the back is a modest restaurant. The food is as outstanding as it always has been and has not yielded to the prepared and

ℹ️ In summer, take a little time to check out Vera's Garden along the Midtown Greenway biking trail next to the cafe. Patrons of Vera's banded together to plant trimmings from their home gardens, and a spectacular array of flowers and other plants adorns the hillside.

health-food trends that now dominate the restaurant business. The menu contains almost every hot and cold sandwich imaginable. There are also several kosher selections. All of Cecil's food can be ordered for takeout. Cecil's Restaurant is open for lunch and dinner daily, and the delicatessen is also open seven days a week.

Day by Day Cafe $
477 West Seventh Street, St. Paul
(651) 227-0654
www.daybyday.com
Day by Day is a lovely spot just west of downtown St. Paul. The restaurant meanders through several rooms of multiple storefronts on busy West Seventh Street, and the plants, bookshelves, and tables at odd angles will make visitors feel right at home. Breakfast (served all day) highlights include homemade buckwheat cakes, the earth breakfast (two eggs scrambled with hash browns and onions and covered with melted cheese), and the breakfast burrito. For lunch and dinner the restaurant features a guacamole burger, triple-decker clubhouse sandwich, and stir-fried sesame chicken or tofu. Each menu has unique handmade cover art. Day by Day is open for early dinner Monday through Friday, and is open for breakfast and lunch seven days a week. On weekdays and Saturdays, the cafe opens at 6:00 a.m., making it popular with people (especially insomniacs) who work downtown.

Fabulous Fern's Bar & Grill $$
400 Selby Avenue, St. Paul
(651) 225-9414
www.fabulousferns.com
Located in St. Paul's historic Cathedral Hill neighborhood of brownstone townhomes, Fabulous Fern's is a casual spot with plenty of comfort food and an active bar. Restaurant specialties include wild rice and chicken salad with cranberry vinaigrette dressing, the Cajun meat loaf sandwich, Fern's pot roast, and pecan-crusted walleye. Popular with sports fans who flock to Fabulous Fern's to watch the

St. Paul's Forepaugh's restaurant is set in an 1870 Victorian mansion. SAINT PAUL RCVA

bar's 4 plasma TVs and 10 regular TVs, the place really gets hopping during Vikings games. Fern's is open for lunch and dinner seven days a week and serves their full menu until midnight every day.

Forepaugh's $$–$$$
276 South Exchange Street, St. Paul
(651) 224-5606
www.forepaughs.com

Set in a Victorian mansion and named for Joe Lybrandt Forepaugh, the dry-goods merchant who built the house in 1870, Forepaugh's is an elegant choice. Soft light in nine cozy dining rooms offers the warmth of a turn-of-the-20th-century parlor, lace curtains and all. Forepaugh's main courses include duck, lamb, veal, steak, and seafood. Forepaugh's offers a shuttle ride to and from the Ordway Theater in downtown St. Paul, very helpful if your evening includes a concert or show or if you

plan to attend a Wild game at the Xcel Energy Center next to the Ordway. Ask about the shuttle when you make your reservations, which are recommended. The restaurant is open for lunch weekdays, for dinner Monday through Saturday, and for brunch and dinner on Sunday.

Hickory Hut $
647 University Avenue West, St. Paul
(651) 224-9464

The Hickory Hut serves up great barbecue in a fast-food and take-out environment. The restaurant is light on fancy décor and heavy on practical tile, but people don't come here for pretty surroundings. They come for the tangy, meaty wings, barbecue beef sandwiches, and ribs. They come for the catfish, shrimp, and at least a dozen side dishes. They come for the large, inexpensive portions. And they come for the superb barbecue sauce.

Everyone has their reasons for coming to Hickory Hut, and they're all gastronomic. This is some seriously tasty food.

Mickey's Diner $
36 West Seventh Street, St. Paul
(651) 222-5633
Mickey's, on the National Register of Historic Places, serves up real ice-cream malts, eggs any way you like 'em, burgers and fries, Mulligan stew, and pancakes 24 hours a day. Set in a '30s-era dining car with a chrome and Formica interior, the diner has been family owned and operated since 1939. Almost inevitably, movies shot in Minnesota, including *Jingle All the Way, The Mighty Ducks,* and *A Prairie Home Companion,* feature downtown St. Paul's most camera-friendly diner.

Muffuletta Café $$
2260 Como Avenue, St. Paul
(651) 644-9116
www.muffuletta.com
Located in the beautiful St. Anthony Park neighborhood near the University of Minnesota's St. Paul campus, Muffuletta serves an eclectic menu in a colorful, casual-yet-classy atmosphere. The restaurant changes its menu daily, but you can expect to find such things as pork tenderloin, duck, gnocchi, and steaks, all prepared with great attention to detail and an eye toward succulence. Muffuletta also offers a prix fixe menu that changes weekly, with an appetizer, main course, and dessert for one price. Muffuletta serves beer and wine, including a fabulous wine list courtesy of the sommelier on staff. The restaurant is open for lunch and dinner Monday through Saturday and brunch only on Sunday.

Porky's $
1890 University Avenue West, St. Paul
(651) 644-1790
In the early 21st century, there are few drive-in restaurants, but Porky's, founded in 1953, bucks the trend. And the pickup window is

> **i** Forepaugh's is a delicious upscale restaurant housed in a gorgeous Victorian mansion that's said to be haunted. Ask the waitstaff for details— if you dare.

open regardless of Twin Cities weather. The restaurant is a modified drive-in where you have the option of ordering at the pickup window or at a counter inside the restaurant. Diners may enjoy their food in their car under the large awning or, when weather permits, on the half-dozen picnic tables provided by the restaurant. Porky's menu is filled with drive-in favorites such as hamburgers, cheeseburgers, fried chicken, chicken wings, pork sandwiches, catfish, shakes, fries, and much more. Porky's is open seven days a week for lunch and dinner.

St. Paul Grill $$$$
350 Market Street, St. Paul
(651) 224-7455
www.stpaulgrill.com
Located in the four-star Saint Paul Hotel, the St. Paul Grill overlooks elegant Rice Park, one of downtown St. Paul's loveliest blocks. The St. Paul Grill serves upscale food and spirits. The menu includes steaks, lobster, halibut, lamb chops, and much more. The food is first-rate, but you'll pay for your delight: Several entrees top $30 and the Surf & Turf tops an eye-popping $60. The restaurant features an excellent wine list, which, like the cuisine, has received countless local and national awards. The St. Paul Grill is also famous for its extensive list of cognacs, Armagnacs, single-malt scotches, and Irish whiskies, and the bartenders are also well known for their bloody Marys. The bar is a lovely place to stop for a drink before or after events at the nearby Ordway Center for the Performing Arts. Reservations are highly recommended. The St. Paul Grill is open for lunch and dinner Monday through Saturday, and for brunch and dinner on Sunday.

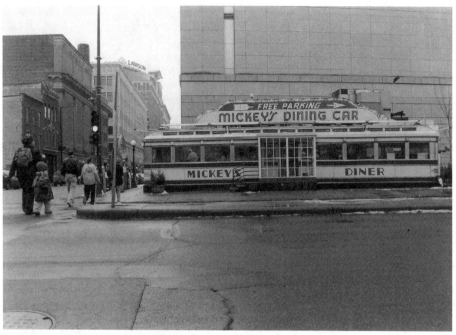

St. Paul's historic Mickey's Diner is wildly popular among the downtown lunch crowd and curious tourists.
TODD R. BERGER

Tavern on Grand $$–$$$
656 Grand Avenue, St. Paul
(651) 228-9030
www.tavernongrand.com
Tavern on Grand is a Minnesota classic, serving up plates of walleye fillets to the masses. Sure, you can also come here for sirloin, lasagna, and slow-roasted ribs, but you're unlikely to order walleye in Memphis, so get with the program and order up a plate of the exalted fish with all the trimmings. The restaurant has a north-woodsy feel like a lakefront lodge, complete with built-in fish tank, and the walleye is simply spectacular. Options abound, including a choice of a grilled or deep-fried (with "secret batter") one- or two-fillet dinner, the walleye basket, the walleye sandwich, and the Lakeshore Special, which includes a fillet and an eight-ounce steak. You can also add a flaky fillet to any meal as a side order, if spaghetti, meatballs, and walleye are your thing. The waitstaff won't bat an eye.

The Tavern on Grand is open daily for lunch and dinner.

W. A. Frost and Company $$$
374 Selby Avenue, St. Paul
(651) 224-5715
www.wafrost.com
W. A. Frost is located in the Cathedral Hill neighborhood of St. Paul in the elegant 19th-century Dacotah Building. The menu is brief but well executed and includes ahi tuna, duck, walleye, filet mignon, and more. Of particular note is the house-smoked gravlox, salmon cured in sugar, salt, and dill (the dill distinguishes gravlox from regular lox). The restaurant also serves some unusual and delightful cheeses paired with wines and sherries. Also of note is the extensive loose tea list, courtesy of St. Paul's Tea Source. If you're in the Twin Cities in summer, try to get a table on the leafy patio, which time and again is voted the best outdoor dining experi-

ence in the Twin Cities. It's refreshing and comfortable during the day, and cozy and romantic after the sun sets. W. A. Frost is open Monday through Saturday for lunch and dinner, and Sunday for brunch and dinner. Reservations are highly recommended.

East

The Bayport Cookery $$$$
328 Fifth Avenue North, Bayport
(651) 430-1066
www.bayportcookery.com
The core of the Bayport Cookery's menu, which has monthly themes and varies weekly, is avant-garde cuisine. The restaurant features several prix fixe tasting menus (varying in price based on the number of courses) that emphasize seasonal, local foods. Recent tasting menus have included beef Wellington, seared duck breast, and lemon tart brûlée. The menu is based on availability of fresh items and often changes daily due to supply. The prix fixe menu varies greatly from month to month. Reservations are required. The Bayport Cookery is open for dinner Wednesday through Sunday.

Chickadee Cottage Restaurant $–$$
9900 Valley Creek Road, Woodbury
(651) 578-8118
The Chickadee Cottage Restaurant offers an extensive menu of American and European-influenced favorites. The cottage theme pervades the restaurant, with each room having a particular cottage motif (e.g., rustic lodge or rural getaway). Chickadee's breakfast menu is enormous and includes many fresh-baked goods as well as pancakes, waffles, eggs, omelets, and much more. The lunch and dinner menus also provide plenty to choose from, including meat loaf sandwiches, scallops and shrimp, vegetable lasagna, and smoky apple pork chops. The restaurant is family friendly: Children are provided with crayons and a menu that includes pancakes or scrambled eggs for breakfast and grilled cheese or peanut butter and jelly sandwiches for dinner. Chickadee Cottage Restaurant is open Tuesday through Sunday for breakfast, lunch, and dinner.

The Lowell Inn $$–$$$
102 North Second Street, Stillwater
(651) 439-1100
www.lowellinn.com
The Lowell Inn is widely known for its Swiss cheese fondue, served in the Stillwater inn's Matterhorn Room. But at the Lowell the Swiss cheese fondue is just the starter of a four-course meal (with optional wine accompaniment) featuring beef tenderloin, duck breast, or jumbo prawns with Minnesota wild rice pilaf. Desserts include grapes Devonshire and Grand Marnier chocolate fondue for two. The whole shebang is delivered tableside for a set price. For those looking to choose individual dishes rather than a multicourse extravaganza, the Lowell's George Washington Room offers such entrees as duck breast, filet mignon, and lobster tail. (For more information on the Lowell Inn's guest rooms, see the Accommodations chapter.)

West

Park Tavern $–$$
3401 Louisiana Avenue South, St. Louis Park
(952) 929-6810
www.parktavern.net
Bar and bowling alley food is generally not highly regarded for its taste. The Park Tavern is an exception. The appetizers are tasty and edible, with or without suds for lubrication, and include nachos, quesadillas, and chicken strips. Also featured are top-notch burgers and sandwiches such as the French dip au jus and the prime melt sandwich, which features prime rib topped with sautéed onions and cheese. Salads are another option for less ravenous diners. The Park Tavern serves lunch and dinner Monday through Friday, and breakfast, lunch, and dinner on weekends.

Zaroff's Delicatessen Restaurant $–$$
11300 Wayzata Boulevard, Minnetonka
(952) 545-9090
When patrons open Zaroff's menu they first

notice the glossary of terms. Despite the restaurant's Minneapolis suburban location—Minnetonka—the menu proudly proclaims its Jewish deli roots. There are almost 20 Yiddish terms to aid patrons not yet experienced with Jewish-American culinary traditions. The extensive menu includes appetizers, numerous sandwich selections, entrees, burgers, and eggs. Just a few highlights are the hot brisket of beef, the hot pastrami sandwich, and the Hebrew national frank on a bun. Zaroff's offers a wide selection of dessert items, including chocolate cake, apple pie, and ice cream. The cakes and cheesecake are flown in from the Carnegie Deli in New York. The full-service deli also has a wine and beer list. Zaroff's is open daily for lunch and dinner.

CAJUN/SOUTHERN

Dixie's on Grand $–$$
695 Grand Avenue, St. Paul
(651) 222-7345
www.dixiesongrand.com
There are only a few Cajun and southern restaurants in the North Star State. Cajun- and Southern-cooking purists may balk at Dixie's menu since it includes such foods as calamari, Cuban black bean soup, and fusion foods like the Cajun burger. However, the menu also includes Cajun and Southern staples, such as jambalaya, blackened catfish, shrimp and crawfish étouffée, and Carolina crab cakes. The ribs are another specialty at Dixie's and are available in baby back and country-style pork ribs. Dixie's has an extensive wine list as well as a large selection of domestic and imported beers, and later in the evening, the bar can get pretty hopping (or pretty crowded and loud depending on your sensibilities). On Sunday the restaurant hosts a champagne brunch, which includes red beans and rice, corn bread, country ham, barbecue chicken, and much more. The entire menu is available for take-out. Reservations for dinner are recommended, especially on weekend evenings. Dixie's is open for lunch and dinner daily.

CAMBODIAN

Cheng Heng $
448 University Avenue West, St. Paul
(651) 222-5577
Definitely a diamond in the rough, Cheng Heng is one of the most amazing deals (and best-kept secrets) in town. Cheng Heng looks, to the casual observer, like just one more uninviting sign in a line of strip malls. But this is the only place in town where you can get a pile of beautifully steamed mussels in black bean sauce for under $10, and that's about the most expensive selection on the menu. The couple who runs the place takes hospitality to new levels, positioning fans to cool down your table when it's hot out and fussing over you as though you were their house guest and not just another restaurant customer. They offer suggestions and menus with pictures to make even the pickiest of eaters comfortable with ordering Cambodian food for the first time and are more than willing to share their cooking secrets with curious customers. This has long been a favorite place to take relatives for special occasions or wow out-of-town friends when they come to visit. Cheng Heng is open daily for breakfast, lunch, and dinner.

CARIBBEAN
Minneapolis

**Harry Singh's Original
Caribbean Restaurant** $–$$
2653 Nicollet Avenue, Minneapolis
(612) 729-6181
www.harrysinghs.com
Great prices and tasty West Indies cuisine distinguish Harry Singh's. The restaurant specializes in roti, a crepe-like Caribbean flatbread with your choice of more than a dozen curries. You can get roti with such ingredients as potatoes, chickpeas, cardamom seeds, curried beef, and jerk chicken. The servings are enormous here, often enough for two hungry diners. Harry Singh's is open for lunch and dinner Tuesday through Saturday.

St. Paul

West Indies Soul Cafe $
625 University Avenue, St. Paul
(651) 665-0115

West Indies Soul began serving the Twin Cities at annual neighborhood festivals. The savory tastes of the Caribbean created a demand for catering and later a restaurant to serve jerk chicken, curry chicken and goat, fried plantains, and roti (Caribbean breads filled with meats). Though not a fast-food restaurant, the order-in and take-out counter-style dining facilitates quick service. The restaurant serves homemade drinks of carrot punch, ginger beer, and lemonade but does not serve alcohol. West Indies Soul is open for lunch and dinner Tuesday through Saturday.

East

San Pedro Cafe $$
426 Second Street, Hudson, Wisconsin
(715) 386-4003
www.sanpedrocafe.com

The San Pedro Cafe offers Mediterranean and tropical cuisine and atmosphere in scenic Hudson, Wisconsin. The menu overflows with flavor. There are sandwiches, wraps, pastas, salads, seafood, jerk chicken, and Neapolitan pizzas. The restaurant is located in a wonderful restored building in downtown Hudson and is often packed with customers. The San Pedro Cafe is open for lunch and dinner Monday through Friday, and for all three meals on weekends.

CHINESE

Minneapolis

1st Wok $–$$
3236 West Lake Street, Minneapolis
(612) 922-8883

415 East 78th Street, Bloomington
(952) 881-2413

1st Wok features an extensive menu of Hunan- and Szechuan-style Chinese food. Fine renditions of sesame chicken, kung pao chicken, lo mein, and pepper steak are

i If you are an ethnic food novice but would like to sample the cuisine of another culture, look for ethnic restaurants with lunch buffets. The buffets provide an excellent overview of a culture's food at reasonable prices.

served, as well as numerous seafood items. The restaurant features specialties such as sesame shrimp, Double Wonder, and princess chicken and shrimp. Daily lunch specials are a steal and include an entree plus soup and fried rice. Vegetarian items include bean curd selections (kung pao bean curd and spicy bean curd Szechuan-style). 1st Wok is open daily for lunch and dinner.

Hong Kong Noodles Restaurant $–$$
901 Washington Avenue SE, Minneapolis
(612) 379-9472

Several excellent Chinese restaurants are in the vicinity of the University of Minnesota—this is arguably one of the best. The restaurant is rather small and seats no more than 50 people in an often-packed room. But it is the food that garners the restaurant accolades from its regular patrons and critics alike. With almost 300 menu items, Hong Kong Noodles offers plenty to choose from, but noodles are the restaurant's specialty. The menu is divided into extensive soup, chicken, beef, fried rice, hot pot, seafood, pork, and vegetable choices. A few standouts are the Singapore-style rice noodles, seafood lo mein, and beef brisket fun. Hong Kong Noodles is open for lunch and is open for dinner late daily, which is relatively uncommon in the Twin Cities.

Rainbow Chinese Restaurant & Bar $–$$
2739 Nicollet Avenue, Minneapolis
(612) 870-7084
www.rainbowrestaurant.com

Rainbow Chinese's menu features exciting examples of Chinese cuisine prepared with fresh ingredients. Rainbow's signature dishes include Szechuan wontons, honey walnut shrimp and Singapore chow mai fun, and fried walleye pike with black bean sauce. There are many other options, including vegetarian entrees. Alcohol is available with meals and at the lovely bar, where diners can feel free to bask in the comely decor of the restaurant, which is superbly decorated in greens and yellows. Reservations are accepted only for groups of four or more. The restaurant serves lunch and dinner daily.

Shuang Cheng Restaurant $–$$
1320 Fourth Street SE, Minneapolis
(612) 378-0208

On weekends, Shuang Cheng, which is located in Dinkytown near the U, draws huge crowds, mainly for the delicious seafood prepared with a tantalizing Chinese flair. The menu includes shrimp, crab, scallops, oysters, clams, lobster, squid, and four walleye dishes. Chicken, beef, pork, and vegetarian options are available. Daily specials are posted on a whiteboard and erased when the item sells out. Shuang Cheng is open Monday through Saturday for lunch and dinner, and Sunday for dinner only.

St. Paul

Little Szechuan $–$$
422 University Avenue West, St. Paul
(651) 222-1333
www.littleszechuan.com

The Little Szechuan restaurant on University Avenue a few blocks west of the State Capitol building got off to a rocky start just after it opened in October 2006: A kitchen fire shut the restaurant down for two months. But the restaurant bounced back and has quickly become a Twin Cities favorite. Little Szechuan has many of the "Chinese" favorites of most of us (kung pao chicken, beef strips with garlic sauce, etc.) but also has many items more common to actual restaurants in China rather than their Americanized cousins. Such succulent creations as tea-smoked duck and eel strips with spicy sauce will get your attention while dishes such as stir-fried beef entrails and tongue slices with red spicy oil will arouse your curiosity. Little Szechuan is open daily for lunch and dinner.

North

Willow Gate II $
1885 West Perimeter Drive, Roseville
(651) 628-0990

Willow Gate's menu is extensive and features several hundred Chinese and Vietnamese items. At lunch there are combination meals for under $5, which include several seafood items. The curry shrimp and chicken fried rice are two favorites. Each is accompanied by a choice of two chicken wings or cheese won-tons. Dinner offers larger combination plates as well as traditional Chinese fare, such as lo mein, egg foo young, fried rice, and seafood. Willow Gate serves beer and wine, and lunch and dinner are served daily.

West

Yangtze Chinese Restaurant $$
5625 Wayzata Boulevard, St. Louis Park
(952) 541-9469
www.yangtze.us

The Yangtze Restaurant serves Hunan, Szechuan, Cantonese, and Mandarin Chinese dishes. Specials of the house include duck, Szechuan-style leg of lamb, and tangerine beef. The extensive menu also includes everything from lobster to eggplant in a garlic sauce, moo shu pork, several version of lo mein and chow mein, two preparations including fresh Maine lobster, and much more. Yangtze Restaurant is open daily for lunch and dinner and features an excellent dim sum over the weekend lunch hours.

CUBAN

Cafe Havana $$–$$$
119 Washington Avenue North, Minneapolis
(612) 338-8484

Cafe Havana evocatively re-creates cosmopolitan Havana of the 1950s through telling details: the red carpet leading to the door, huge sprays of flowers, sumptuous velveteen chairs and curtains, the whiff of good cigars, and the black dial telephone. Fans of true Cuban food—rice and pork dishes, plantains, and creamy three-milk cakes—will love Cafe Havana, which is also home to one of the posher bar scenes in the Cities. Owners Gladys and Peter Mendoza (mother and son) say that their family recipes are faithful to the Cuban dishes they left behind in 1969. Black beans and rice, the national dish, accompany many entrees, along with fried plantains. There's no goat on the menu, but the lamb shank and the traditional *ropa vieja* (shredded beef slow-cooked in sherry tomato sauce) are satisfying and delicious. Cafe Havana is open for dinner Tuesday through Saturday. The restaurant accepts Visa and MasterCard only.

Victor's 1959 Cafe $
3756 Grand Avenue South, Minneapolis
(612) 827-8948
www.victors1959cafe.com
Serving Cuban and American breakfast and lunch cuisine, this tiny restaurant is packed with photographs and memorabilia of both Cuba and Fidel Castro. The yellow walls give a Caribbean feel to the restaurant, as does the Cuban music in the background. The menu includes eggs Havana, mango waffles, ranchero Cubano, the Bay of Pigs pork sandwich, fried yucca, both sweet plantains and fried green plantains, and Cuban coffee. The restaurant is a popular neighborhood stop, and with fewer than ten tables inside, the wait to get seated can be an hour or so. Victor's serves breakfast and lunch Tuesday through Sunday and dinner Tuesday through Saturday.

EASTERN EUROPEAN

Kramarczuk Sausage Company $
215 Hennepin Avenue East, Minneapolis
(612) 379-3018
www.kramarczuk.com
Specializing in the cuisine of Ukraine and some other countries in that neck of the steppe, the casual Kramarczuk Sausage Company serves delicious, cheap eats in their cafeteria-style restaurant across the river from downtown Minneapolis. Specialties include *varenyky* (dumplings stuffed with

meat, cheese and potato, or sauerkraut), *holubets* (cabbage rolls stuffed with rice and meat and topped with tomato sauce), *szegedin* goulash (meat, sauerkraut, and onions in a paprika sauce), and several selections of sausages. Soups include borscht and sausage vegetable, and Kramarczuk serves beer and wine. The restaurant also has an on-site deli and market. Live accordion music livens things up on Saturday night. Kramarczuk is open for breakfast and lunch Monday through Saturday, and for lunch on Sunday; the market and deli are open daily for sausages (and many other items) to take home and grill.

ETHIOPIAN
Minneapolis

Blue Nile $–$$
2027 Franklin Avenue East, Minneapolis
(612) 338-3000
Blue Nile was one of the first Ethiopian restaurants in the area. The restaurant, in Minneapolis's Seward neighborhood, is in a huge complex, including voluminous dining room, bar, and dance floor. Blue Nile's menu items include *maraka hoolaa* (lamb flavored with ginger root and other exotic spices), a shish kebab combo, and several vegetarian options, to name a few. For an overview of the culinary treats offered at the Blue Nile, try the gosa-gosa C, which is a sampler of two of the menu's vegetarian entrees and *maraka* (Ethiopian stewed meat dishes). Blue Nile is open for dinner daily.

St. Paul

Queen of Sheba Café & Restaurant $–$$
2447 West Seventh Street, St. Paul
(651) 690-0068
Queen of Sheba serves primarily Ethiopian food—stewed beef, chicken, and vegetables spiced and served with *injera* (delicious, spongy pieces of flat bread). It's a strange mixture of elegant and casual, as the restaurant is beautifully decorated with hand-embroidered tablecloths and framed

needlepoints, but all the food is prepared to be eaten with your hands alone, although if you ask, they'll gladly bring you silverware. A counter at one side of the restaurant serves Ethiopian coffee. The restaurant is open for lunch and dinner daily.

FRENCH
Minneapolis

Fugaise $$$
308 Hennepin Avenue East, Minneapolis
(612) 436-0777
www.fugaise.com

Contemporary French cuisine is the specialty at Fugaise in the St. Anthony neighborhood across the Hennepin Avenue Bridge from downtown Minneapolis. You are likely to see such main courses as *barramundi*, pork tenderloin with cherry-marcona almond bread pudding, and curried beef shortribs in what has been described by *Mpls St. Paul* magazine as some of the most creative contemporary French cuisine in town. An extensive and excellent wine list will certainly have a bottle to pair with your chosen main course, and you can also opt for a five-, seven-, or nine-course "tour of the menu." Plum tarts and dark chocolate cake with fig compote are some recent dessert highlights, and the restaurant offers many dessert wines. The restaurant is a particularly great deal for lunch, when prices for smaller entrees can be as much as a third of their nighttime cousins. Fugaise is open for lunch and dinner Monday through Friday, and for dinner only on Saturdays.

Vincent $$$
1100 Nicollet Mall, Minneapolis
(612) 630-1189
www.vincentrestaurant.com

Vincent, named for head chef and owner Vincent Francoual, is a lovely spot for casual fine dining. Beautiful oak woodwork, high ceilings, and large windows overlooking Nicollet Mall and Orchestra Hall provide the upscale atmosphere for the restaurant's French-American specialties. The menu changes every two months, but some past dishes include "porchetta" of suckling pig, rosemary-scented chevre cheese ravioli, and roasted hawaiian barracuda. Vincent is open for lunch Monday through Friday and dinner Monday through Saturday; reservations are recommended, particularly on weekends.

South

La Fougasse $$$
Sofitel Minneapolis Hotel, 5601 West 78th Street, Bloomington
(952) 835-1900
www.lafougasseminneapolis.com

This hotel restaurant serves a wide variety of elegant French dishes, including onion and caramelized fennel soup, bouillabaisse marseillaise, and a lovely collection of scrumptious desserts. The restaurant also features several Spanish dishes (including paella and empanadas) and two prix fixe tasting menus. Warm saffron, deep red, and azure blue give the restaurant a relaxing Mediterranean look. Reservations are almost always required, as the place fills up quickly with hotel guests. La Fougasse is open Monday through Saturday for lunch and dinner, and Sunday for brunch and dinner.

GERMAN
Minneapolis

Black Forest Inn $$
1 East 26th Street, Minneapolis
(612) 872-0812
www.blackforestinnmpls.com

The Black Forest Inn has been a favorite German restaurant for more than 40 years. It is located in the popular ethnic restaurant area of Eat Street (Nicollet Avenue) in south Minneapolis. The restaurant has a lovely, shaded courtyard open in the summertime. Another asset at the restaurant is the large bar stocked with imported German, Austrian, Czech, Belgian, English, Irish, and domestic beers, including several excellent pilsners and two weissbiers on tap. The hearty suds go great with the robust German food, including such specialties as wiener schnitzel (breaded veal cutlets), sauerbraten (marinated beef), *hasenpfeffer* (braised rabbit), and *kaseller rippchen* (smoked and boiled pork chop), as well as sauerkraut and spaetzle (German dumplings). Dessert is outstanding, too, especially the decadent Black Forest torte and the equally rich sacher torte. The restaurant is open for breakfast, lunch, and dinner daily.

St. Paul

Glockenspiel $–$$
605 West Seventh Street, St. Paul
(651) 292-9421
www.glockenspielrestaurant.com
When Glockenspiel opened, the Twin Cities was prepared for something special. After all, two of the restaurant's co-owners are the Wildmos, David and Mary, who own one of St. Paul's favorite restaurants, the Tavern on Grand. The location, a Czech and Slovak fraternal hall, is one of the restaurant's greatest assets. On entering the restaurant, you see a huge bar stocked with German beers. The dining area is a classy continuation of the bar and is decked out in plenty of blue against a large mural in the long, narrow, spacious dining area.

German specialties fill the large menu, including *schweinhaxe* (pork hocks), *Eisbach pfeffersteak* (a German version of sirloin steak), and *schweinrippchen* (pork spare ribs). And for those with a smaller appetite, there are *kleine speise* (lighter fare) such as bratwurst, weisswurst, *käsespätzle* (German dumplings with cheese), and *leberkäse* (German pork loaf). Stop in for the Friday Night Fish Fry, an all-you-can-eat affair available for lunch or dinner. Finally, for dessert the restaurant features tortes, cakes, and other German delights. Glockenspiel is open for lunch and dinner daily.

East

Gasthaus Bavarian Hunter $–$$
8390 Lofton Avenue North, Stillwater
(651) 439-7128
www.gasthausbavarianhunter.com
Gasthaus has specialized in the cuisine of southern Germany since 1966, and the extensive menu offers something for everyone. The restaurant has the largest variety of schnitzels (cutlets) in the Twin Cities. Also featured are sausages, sauerbraten (a tangy beef), and, for large appetites, a couple of Bavarian combination platters. Surprisingly, the meaty restaurant has two *kein fleisch* (no meat) meals—vegetable rouladen and vegetable casserole. And don't forget to wash the meal down with a German beer, especially since the restaurant does not stock domestic brews. For diners' entertainment, polka music is performed on Friday and Sunday as well as for the many German events. The Gasthaus Bavarian Hunter is open daily for lunch and dinner.

The Gasthaus packs them in for its three annual festivals: Sommerfest in June, Waldfest on Labor Day, and Oktoberfest later in September. Sommerfest and Oktoberfest feature food, German beer in traditional one-liter mugs (and in smaller sizes), and polka music under the big tent in front of the restaurant. If you plan to partake in the festivities, make sure someone in your party is the designated driver, because the beer goes down fast and the location of the rural Stillwater-area restaurant makes for an expensive taxi ride back to the Cities.

The Winzer Stube $$
516 Second Street, Hudson, Wisconsin
(715) 381-5092
www.winzerstube.net
One of the Twin Cities' best German restaurants is located in Hudson, Wisconsin, 25 miles east of downtown St. Paul. The menu features several excellent dishes. One savory item is the *roulade mit speck und gurke*. The flavorful beef rollups and smoky bacon are wrapped around a tasty pickle. Also outstanding is the *jägerschnitzel*. The fine pork cutlet is the restaurant's biggest seller and comes accompanied by spaetzle (homemade noodles) and *rotkraut* (red cabbage). The *schweinhaxe* (pork hocks) is a popular daily special that occasionally sells out during lunch. For smaller appetites there are soups and sausage platters (bratwurst, weisswurst,

bauern mettwurst, and knackwurst) on the menu. The restaurant has a children's menu (for the "little lederhosens") and outstanding dessert options such as Black Forest cake, apple strudel, and chocolate torte.

GREEK
Minneapolis

Gardens of Salonica
New Greek Cafe and Deli $–$$
19 Fifth Street NE, Minneapolis
(612) 378-0611
www.gardensofsalonica.com
Anna and Lazaros Christoforide's sunny restaurant serves fresh bread with delightful dips, like their zingy *skordalia* (potatoes, lemon juice, and garlic) and *tyro* (feta cheese blended with roasted peppers, garlic, and herbs); chicken souvlaki and lamb-and-beef gyro sandwiches; and fancier dishes like rice-stuffed squid baked in red wine sauce and the fresh artichoke-and-braised-lamb dish that's a spring special. The house specialty, popular for lunch or dessert, is *boughatsa*: phyllo pastries that come in sweet and savory varieties. Located in a turn-of-the-20th-century storefront on an obscure side street, this family-owned Greek cafe and deli draws patrons from all over the Metro. Gardens of Salonica is open for lunch and dinner Tuesday through Saturday.

It's Greek to Me $$
626 West Lake Street, Minneapolis
(612) 825-9922
This restaurant is casual and welcoming, with high pressed-tin ceilings, freshly painted wall murals, and terra-cotta–like tiled floors. It's also inexpensive, considering that a dinner-size portion of anything costs around $10 and will usually leave you enough for tomorrow's lunch. The menu offers nearly two dozen appetizers to precede classic Greek specialties such as souvlaki and spanakopita, fried smelt, octopus, chicken gyros, and flaming cheese. Every night the place bustles with couples, small families, and intimate clusters

of friends devouring spicy-hot feta cheese spread, roast leg of lamb, or vegetarian dolmades. The restaurant is open Tuesday through Sunday for lunch and dinner.

St. Paul

Acropol Inn Restaurant $
748 Grand Avenue, St. Paul
(651) 298-0151
The Acropol Inn is one of the Twin Cities' oldest Greek restaurants. The Apostolou family opened the restaurant in 1975 to serve gyros and other Greek specialties. The restaurant serves all the traditional Greek standards—moussaka (meat and eggplant), *dolmades* (grape leaves stuffed with rice and meat), and pasticcio (a Greek version of lasagna). Wash the Greek cuisine down with a cold beer or glass of wine. The Acropol Inn Restaurant is open Monday through Saturday for lunch and dinner.

Christos Greek Restaurant $$
214 East Fourth Street, St. Paul
(651) 224-6000

2632 Nicollet Avenue, Minneapolis
(612) 871-2111

15600 Highway 7, Minnetonka
(952) 912-1000
www.christos.com
Christos serves all your Greek favorites from three Twin Cities locations. The St. Paul restaurant is one of the most beautiful and historical dining spots in the area, the Union Depot Place. Christos is situated in the middle of the immense former Union Depot, atop a riser, and is surrounded by columns and plenty of big windows and marble. It's hard for a restaurant to fail with such grandeur and beauty.

All three locations feature tasty versions of Greek cuisine. The menu includes gyros, *dolmades*, spanakopita, moussaka, and many other traditional Greek dishes. The prices are reasonable, especially for lunch, when the St. Paul location serves a buffet Monday through Friday. The buffet offers a relatively inexpensive introduction for Greek food novices as well as connoisseurs. The food selections are always delicious, and the unmatched ambience is free. All three Christos restaurants are open for lunch and dinner daily.

West

Santorini $$$
9920 Wayzata Boulevard, St. Louis Park
(952) 546-6722

Greek cuisine and American specialties dominate the menu at Santorini. For lunch and dinner there are numerous choices. Sandwiches ranging from a traditional burger to the Moroccan chicken, which features a unique pepper spread, onions, and cucumbers, are served along with pastas and more elaborate entrees. Shrimp, steaks, lamb chops, and much more are available as well as Greek combination platters. Santorini is open daily for lunch and dinner.

INDIAN

Minneapolis

Passage to India $–$$
1401 West Lake Street, Minneapolis
(612) 827-7518

Minneapolis's Passage to India is a branch of the New York City restaurant of the same name, regarded as one of the best Indian restaurants in the Big Apple. And Passage to India lives up to its high expectations. The breads and tandoori choices are outstanding as are the special dinners. Each offers soup, appetizer, main course, and dessert for under $20. Passage to India is open until midnight daily—a blessing in the Twin Cities, where so few restaurants have late-night hours. The restaurant is also open for lunch daily.

North

India Palace $–$$
2570 Cleveland Avenue North, Roseville
(651) 631-1222

8362 Tamarack Village, Woodbury
(651) 731-6300
www.indiapalacemn.com

India Palace creates some of the area's best cuisine at its two locations. Featured menu items include tandoori specialties, curries, and vindaloos. Also available is the lunch buffet, where seven days a week diners may enjoy the flavors of India. In addition, the restaurant offers takeout as well as an extensive beer and wine list. Both locations are open daily for lunch and dinner.

South

Tandoor Restaurant $–$$
8062 Morgan Circle, Bloomington
(952) 885-9060
www.tandoormn.com

True to its name, the specialty of Tandoor Restaurant is the meats, seafood, and other foods cooked in the tandoor, a clay oven heated to high heat using charcoal. Favorites included tandoori chicken, tandoori naan bread, lamb rogan nosh, and chicken makhani, as well as various curry dishes. The restaurant features an all-you-can-eat lunch buffet. Tandoor Restaurant is open Monday through Saturday for lunch and dinner.

East

Taste of India $–$$
1745 Cope Avenue, Maplewood
(651) 773-5477
www.tasteofindiamn.com

This Taste of India has different ownership than the St. Louis Park location and a different menu. The restaurant features an extensive list of mainly north Indian dishes. Curries and tandoori specialties dominate the menu. The menu also has many vegetarian options. The restaurant offers a daily lunch buffet and a selection of beers, wines, and Indian drinks such as *lassi* (yogurt drink) and Indian tea. Taste of India serves lunch and dinner daily.

West

Taste of India $–$$
5617 Wayzata Boulevard, St. Louis Park
(952) 541-4865

The Taste of India in St. Louis Park, similar in spirit to the Maplewood restaurant of the same name, offers an extensive menu of excellently prepared curries and tandoori (clay-oven) specialties. The restaurant specializes in north Indian cuisine, with treats from throughout the subcontinent thrown in to enthrall the taste buds. The tandoori items are especially tasty. Indian specialty drinks (mango milk shakes, mango lassi yogurt drink, etc.) as well as wines and beers, both imported and domestic, are offered. The restaurant features a daily lunch buffet with a particularly large spread. Taste of India is open daily for lunch and dinner.

IRISH

Kieran's Irish Pub $$
330 Second Avenue South
(Towle Building), Minneapolis
(612) 339-4499
www.kierans.com
Kieran's Irish Pub is a popular place to imbibe in the gaiety of the Emerald Isle. Owner Kieran Folliard satisfies the Twin Cities' love of Irish culture by providing beer, liquor, music, and food. The menu includes such Irish classics as lamb stew and corned beef and cabbage, as well as American favorites like grilled New York strip. All menu items are influenced by Ireland; even the New York strip has an Irish flair (Irish whiskey sauce). And don't forget to order a Guinness to accompany the fare. Kieran's is especially busy during lunch and happy hour because of its location in downtown Minneapolis. The restaurant is open Monday through Saturday for lunch and dinner.

The Local $–$$
931 Nicollet Mall, Minneapolis
(612) 904-1000
www.the-local.com
The Local is another successful restaurant created by Kieran Folliard. Food is served in a lovely dining room draped with velvet curtains and a charming bar, which is amply stocked with Irish and domestic beers. The menu includes reasonably priced sandwiches and entrees. Among the sandwiches offered are

the pot roast beef, chicken breast, and an Irish specialty, corned beef (topped with Swiss cheese). For lighter appetites, diners may choose from a half-dozen salads. Entrees include salmon, sirloin steak, fish-and-chips, and lamb steak. Reservations are recommended. The Local is open Monday through Friday for lunch and dinner, and Saturday and Sunday for brunch and dinner.

ITALIAN
Minneapolis

al Vento $$$–$$$
5001 34th Avenue South, Minneapolis
(612) 724-3009
www.alventorestaurant.com
Al Vento is a trattoria serving southern Italian specialties prepared with simplicity and authenticity. This is one of the rare Italian restaurants serving dishes from the south of Italy, and the menu ingredients include plenty of tomatoes and, in many cases, the wonderful spice fennel. But this isn't a restaurant of spaghetti and meatballs (although a version with veal meatballs is often on the menu); much more experimentation is worth a try here, with some examples of recent dishes including gnocchi, bucatini, steak, pizza, and halibut. (The menu changes regularly.) Al Vento is open for lunch Monday through Friday, brunch on Sunday, and dinner Sunday through Saturday.

Broders' Cucina Italiana $
2308 West 50th Street, Minneapolis
(612) 925-3113
www.broders.com
Back in the early 1950s, Tom and Molly Broder founded this amazing neighborhood deli that served handmade pastas, imported olive oils, olives, cheese, meats, and other high-quality imported and homemade ingredients. Since then they've added spicy pizzas sold by the slice, sandwiches, take-out homemade pasta sauces, and deli treats from grilled asparagus to homemade cannolis to the menu. And they don't skimp on anything. The deli serves a full

range of desserts, including triple-chocolate cheesecake and tiramisu. The restaurant is open for lunch and dinner daily.

Broders' Pasta Bar $$
5000 Penn Avenue South, Minneapolis
(612) 925-9202
www.broders.com

Made by hand by the excellent chefs at Broders', the different styles of pasta served here are all amazingly tender and rich, complemented by sauces and toppings that range from steamed green lip mussels to broiled fish and fresh herbs. It's about as far away from ordinary spaghetti as you can get, and for a price that's more than reasonable, especially for the quality of the food Broders' serves. The one drawback is the no-reservation policy, and mere minutes after the doors open for dinner, the place is packed. But the restaurant does allow you to call an hour ahead of time to put your name on the waiting list, something you'll want to take advantage of. In summer guests can sip drinks on the modest outdoor patio while waiting for a seat, but in winter latecomers will more than likely be left out in the cold. Broders' is open for dinner daily.

Campiello $$$
1320 West Lake Street, Minneapolis
(612) 825-2222

6411 City West Parkway, Eden Prairie
(952) 941-6868
www.campiello.damico.com

Campiello is a great place to impress a date. The smart lighting makes everyone look fabulous, and the stunning presentations make everyone look like a big spender without breaking the bank. Campiello is high class without being snobby, as is the waitstaff. Bond in his tuxedo might feel a little overdressed, but everyone else, from the blue jeaned to the all in black, fits right in. On the menu the crackly thin-crusted pizzas make for stunning appetizers, the salads are solid, and the entrees (especially the pastas and the rotisserie meats) are absolutely top drawer. The Minneapolis location is open daily for din-

ner, and serves brunch as well on Sunday. The Eden Prairie location is open for lunch and dinner Monday through Friday, and dinner only on weekends.

D'Amico Cucina $$$
100 North Sixth Street, Minneapolis
(612) 338-2401
www.damico.com

The D'Amicos own restaurants throughout the Twin Cities. The D'Amico Cucina is their fine Italian dining restaurant. The restaurant offers several tasting menus paired with wines, antipasti, such delights as braised lamb ravioli and roasted lingcod, and creative, luscious desserts. The restaurant has a spectacular wine list, including many vintages found nowhere else in Minneapolis. D'Amico Cucina is open Monday through Saturday for dinner only. Reservations are highly recommended.

Davanni's Pizza & Hot Hoagies $
2500 Riverside Avenue, Minneapolis
(612) 332–5551
www.davannis.com and
20 additional Twin Cities locations

Since 1975 Davanni's has been well known for its pizzas and hot hoagies. Diners have an option of three crust types: traditional, thin, and Chicago deep dish. The deep dish is especially tasty. The thick, light crust is topped with a tangy tomato sauce, and the toppings and cheese are always fresh. Diners can also choose one of 16 hoagies, including salami, turkey, roast beef, meatball, pizza, and tuna. The calzones here are also worth a try. If you'd rather eat at home, delivery is always an option at Davanni's. The Riverside Avenue location is open daily for lunch and dinner, and stays open past midnight on the weekends.

Fat Lorenzo's $
5600 Cedar Avenue South, Minneapolis
(612) 822-2040
www.fatlorenzos.com

A southside neighborhood institution, Fat Lorenzo's tables are covered with white butcher paper for customers to doodle on with supplied crayons while they wait for their pizzas to show up. The menu features New York–style pizza and Italian specialties such as lasagna, baked rigatoni, spaghetti, and chicken cacciatore. Hot and cold hoagies (including meatball, turkey, and roast beef) round off the menu nicely. Fat Lorenzo's is open daily for lunch and dinner.

Figlio Restaurant and Bar $$
3001 Hennepin Avenue South, Minneapolis
(612) 822-1688
www.figlio.com

Located inside the Calhoun Square mall, this is where wealthy hipsters come to drink and hold power lunches. Figlio's servings are generous, and the specialty dishes are absolutely decadent. Its seafood and pasta dishes are excellent, and its desserts have won numerous awards throughout the Twin Cities. The Death by Chocolate concoction is especially wonderful: layers of soft chocolate molded around a chocolate torte filled with chocolate mousse and drenched in warm chocolate sauce. You may want to call ahead for a reservation on weekend nights or holidays—this place fills up fast. Serving a full menu until 1:00 a.m. during the week and until 2:00 a.m. on Friday and Saturday nights, Figlio is a popular stop for patrons fresh from the bars and clubs of Uptown.

Golooney's East Coast Pizza $
2329 Hennepin Avenue South, Minneapolis
(612) 377-8555

New York–style pizza shops are frequently imitated in the Twin Cities, but Golooney's East Coast Pizza is one of the best. The pizza is thick and cheesy with a fresh, piquant tomato sauce and a variety of delicious toppings. An important part of the restaurant's business is pizza by the slice, which serves the hungry, young, and hip Uptown neighborhood. For thrifty diners lunch specials are offered as well as take-out service. The menu also includes salads, sub sandwiches, and pitas. Golooney's is open daily for lunch and dinner.

Green Mill has expanded throughout the Twin Cities and to some others cities in the Midwest. The pizza parlor and brewpub serves up some of the tastiest pizza in the Metro. TODD R. BERGER

Green Mill $–$$
2626 Hennepin Avenue South, Minneapolis
(612) 374-2131 and
15 additional Twin Cities locations

Since 1976 the Green Mill has been one of the Twin Cities' favorite places for pizza. Since then the Green Mill has opened 32 franchises in four states and expanded the scope of its menu to include pasta, calzones, sandwiches, fish, fowl, and much more. The pizza remains the standout and the restaurant's best value. Green Mill offers flat, deep-dish, pescara, and numerous specialty pizzas. The Hennepin Avenue location is open daily for lunch and dinner.

Pane Vino Dolce $$–$$$
819 West 50th Street, Minneapolis
(612) 825-3201

Pane Vino Dolce offers fine Italian cuisine in a small, busy dining room. The menu includes small pizzas, risotto, ravioli, and seafood. All are prepared with fresh ingredients, and great attention is paid to presentation. Daily specials are offered. The restaurant is open daily for dinner. Pane Vino Dolce does not accept credit cards.

Pizza Lucé $–$$
119 North Fourth Street, Minneapolis
(612) 333–7359

3200 Lyndale Avenue South, Minneapolis
(612) 827–5978

2200 East Franklin Avenue, Minneapolis
(612) 332–2535

1183 Selby Avenue, St. Paul
(651) 288-0186
www.pizzaluce.com

Pizza Lucé specializes in, well, pizza, and they're pretty good at it. Including the classic taste of the Lucé, which is made of Italian sausage, onions, garlic, and extra cheese, there are many gourmet pizza choices, such as the barbecue chicken and the luau (Canadian bacon, pineapple, green onions, and mozzarella). And if the large selection of gourmet pizzas doesn't meet your needs, then build your own pizza. The menu of more than 50 fresh ingredients includes meats, seafood, vegetables, and eight cheeses. In addition to pizza, the restaurant serves hoagies, spaghetti, lasagna, mostaccioli, and several vegetarian and vegan dishes. The Lyndale location serves beer and wine; the downtown, East Franklin, and St. Paul locations have full bars. All restaurants are open daily for lunch and dinner and stay open late, making Pizza Lucé a popular post-bartime nosh spot, particularly at the downtown Minneapolis location.

Zelo $$$–$$$$
831 Nicollet Mall, Minneapolis
(612) 333-7000
www.zelomn.com

This splashy restaurant is doing everything right to please couples in search of a memorable date, combining impeccable service with an accessible menu and a nicely focused wine list. Daily fish specials are the highlight, such as flaky walleye Milanese with a golden crown of Italian bread crumbs or a lusciously rare grilled ahi tuna moistened with Chinese mustard vinaigrette and served with green wasabi mashed potatoes. Steaks, veal chops, and lemon-herb chicken round out the entrees, while commendable pizzas and pastas present more economical options. Their most popular dessert is their incredible tiramisu layered with mascarpone. Zelo is open for lunch and dinner Monday through Saturday, and dinner only on Sunday.

St. Paul

Carmelo's $$
238 South Snelling Avenue, St. Paul
(651) 699-2448

Carmelo's is a small, intimate Italian restaurant in St. Paul's Mac-Groveland neighborhood. The busy, family-run restaurant is a nice choice for a romantic evening, with a hand-picked selection of wines and beers to complement such made-from-scratch dishes as chicken carmelo, seafood canneloni, and spinach and cheese ravioli. If you can't find a parking place out front, park in the lot next to Sweeney Cleaners at the intersection of Snelling and St. Clair Avenues just south of the restaurant. Reservations are highly recommended for dinner, especially on the weekend. The restaurant is open for lunch Tuesday through Friday and dinner Monday through Saturday.

Cossetta Italian Market & Pizzeria $
211 West Seventh Street, St. Paul
(651) 222-3476

Cossetta's is one of the busiest lunch spots in St. Paul. It draws throngs of patrons because of the fine pizzas and pastas prepared for eating in or take-out. The delicious chewy thick crust of Cossetta's Chicago-style pizza is topped with a piquant marinara sauce, tasty mozzarella, and fresh ingredients. Huge pieces of pizza are ready to eat at the counter. Another counter offers lasagna, sausage and peppers, chicken marsala, sausage calabrase, chicken cacciatore, and more a la carte items. Ample seating is provided on two floors, where recordings by Italian-American singers such as Tony Bennett and Frank Sinatra are played over the sound system. A wine list is available. Michael and Irene Cossetta opened the adjoining market in 1911, where the now-sprawling market and restaurant began. Today Cossetta's does booming business for lunch and dinner daily.

Luci Ancora $$–$$$
2060 Randolph Avenue, St. Paul
(651) 698-6889
www.ristoranteluci.com

Luci Ancora has been influenced by the trend toward minimalist preparation and organic ingredients. The menu is brief, but all dishes are well executed. Each evening a four-course *prezzo fiso* (fixed price) meal is offered, which includes antipasto, soup or salad, pasta, and fish. In addition, wine and delicious desserts are offered. Call ahead for reservations. Luci Ancora is open for lunch and dinner Tuesday through Friday and for dinner only on Saturday, Sunday, and Monday.

Paisano's Pizza & Hot Hoagies $
619 Selby Avenue, St. Paul
(651) 224-3350

Paisano's deep-dish pizza is sold by the slice as well as in large, medium, and "solo" sizes. There are several specialty pizzas to choose from, and diners can also choose any of the 24 offered ingredients to build a pizza to their liking. In addition, there are eight varieties of cold and hot hoagies. For the health conscious, house, classic Caesar, and Mediterranean salads are available. Paisano's is open seven days a week for lunch and dinner.

Pazzaluna Urban Trattoria and Bar $$$
360 St. Peter Street, St. Paul
(651) 223-7000
www.pazzaluna.com

Pazzaluna serves upscale regional Italian cuisine in downtown St. Paul. Specialties of the house include risotto alla Milanese, gnocchi (the house specialty), and filleto di manzo al pepe. A full bar features many Italian wines and several varieties of grappa, as well as single-malt scotches and numerous cordials. The elegant bar has a happy hour from 4:00 to 6:00 p.m. and 9:00 to 10:00 p.m. Monday through Friday. Reservations are recommended, and valet parking is available for bar and restaurant patrons. Pazzaluna is open for dinner nightly.

Punch Neapolitan Pizza $$
704 Cleveland Avenue South, St. Paul
(651) 696-1066

210 East Hennepin Avenue, Minneapolis
(612) 623-8114

3226 West Lake Street, Minneapolis
(612) 929-0006

8353 Crystal View Road, Eden Prairie
(952) 943-9557

1313 Wayzata Boulevard, Wayzata
(952) 476-7991
www.punchpizza.com

Punch takes its plate-sized Neapolitan pizzas very seriously. Since the restaurant opened its first location, in St. Paul, in 1996, it has been a member of the Associazione Vera Pizza Napoletana, an Italian organization that regulates pizza purity. Since Punch's inception, owner John Soranno has adhered to the organization's guidelines requiring only the highest quality ingredients and methods. The result is outstanding pizza. All pizzas are thin crusted and vary only in their high-quality toppings, such as the Puttanesca, which includes

i Groups of 6 to 10 people can reserve the Chef's Table at Pazzaluna, which includes a five-course menu and an evening with the chef.

anchovies, capers, olives, onions, and oregano. With more than 20 pizzas, the choices are almost endless. Calzones and salads are other options on the menu. A wine list is also provided. Punch is open Tuesday through Saturday for dinner.

Red's Savoy Pizza $
421 East Seventh Street, St. Paul
(651) 227-1437

520 White Bear Avenue North, White Bear Lake
(651) 227-1437

1642½ Hastings Avenue, Newport
(651) 458-5212

3250 Denmark Avenue, Eagan
(651) 454-6400

14755 Victor Hugo Boulevard, Hugo
(651) 426-1355

Red's offers an excellent rendition of flat-crust pizza. The pizza has a zippy sauce and fresh cheese and ingredients. Diners may select from popular pizzas, such as pepperoni and sausage, or atypical pies, such as the tomato, bacon, and pickle. The pizzas are inexpensive, and they are available in regular or large. In addition, the restaurant serves burgers and several pastas. Another bonus at Red's is the dark and interesting ambience of the St. Paul location, which feels like a movie gangster hangout. Red's is open daily for lunch and dinner.

Ristorante Luci $$–$$$
470 Cleveland Avenue South, St. Paul
(651) 699-8258
www.ristoranteluci.com

Ristorante Luci serves spectacular classical Italian cuisine in a modestly decorated location. The restaurant is owned by the Smith family, Al and Lucille, who also own Luci Ancora, kitty-corner across Cleveland and Randolph from Ristorante Luci. Ristorante Luci specializes in pastas and seafood, which are prepared to perfection. This is one of the reasons the neighborhood restaurant is a perennial favorite. Another is the wine list and the

excellent desserts. Reservations are recommended for dinner, especially on weekends. Ristorante Luci is open for dinner Tuesday through Saturday.

South

I Nonni $$
981 Sibley Memorial Highway, Lilydale
(651) 905-1081
www.buongiornoitalia.biz

Focusing on the cuisine of central Italy, I Nonni is an elegant, romantic restaurant only minutes from downtown St. Paul via Interstate 35E South. Freshly made pastas, ingredients such as rabbit, and fresh seafood distinguish the menu, and the spectacular wine list with more than 400 options will have something for every taste and wallet size. The post-dinner menu includes 14 varieties of grappa and other wines and spirits, along with cheeses and impeccable desserts. This is a great place to take a date you wish to impress or to pamper yourself. The restaurant is connected to an Italian market and wine shop. I Nonni is open for lunch Monday through Friday, and dinner Monday through Saturday.

West

Vescio's $–$$
4001 County Road 25, St. Louis Park
(952) 920-0733

406 14th Avenue SE, Minneapolis
(612) 378-1747

Vescio's serves ravioli, rigatoni, tortellini, fettuccine, and spaghetti as well as sandwiches. The sandwiches are Italian-inspired creations that include the Big Boy Italiano (various meats and cheeses on French loaf) and the sweet fried pepper sandwich. And don't forget Vescio's pizza. The pizzas are available in small and large and include one notable specialty: Sid's Special Pizza is topped with sausage, mushrooms, pepperoni, sweet fried peppers, extra cheese, and special seasoning and is named after longtime *Minneapolis Star Tribune* sports columnist Sid Hartman, who often frequents the restaurant. Vescio's

Cucina in St. Louis Park is open daily for lunch and dinner. Vescio's Originalé in Minneapolis is open Tuesday through Sunday for lunch and dinner.

JAPANESE
Minneapolis

Fuji Ya Japanese Restaurant $$–$$$
600 West Lake Street, Minneapolis
(612) 871-4055

465 Wabasha Street, St. Paul
(651) 310-0111
www.fujiyasushi.com

Fuji Ya is located in the Lyn-Lake neighborhood of south Minneapolis. It is the fourth location in the long history of the restaurant, which first opened its doors in downtown Minneapolis in 1959. A new St. Paul location opened in 2005. Fuji Ya offers a wide array of Japanese food in all price ranges. For lunch, the restaurant's noodle soups as well as more expensive items are available, and there is also a sushi bar to satisfy lovers of the Japanese delicacy. Dinner specialties include shrimp tempura, sukiyaki, and chicken teriyaki. Fuji Ya has an extensive list of beers and wines. In Minneapolis, Fuji Ya serves dinner Tuesday through Sunday. The St. Paul location is open for lunch and dinner Monday through Friday, and dinner only on Saturday. Reservations are recommended.

Kikugawa $$–$$$
43 Main Street SE, Minneapolis
(612) 378-3006
www.kikugawa-restaurant.com

The best seats in the house are in the Kikugawa atrium, from which restaurant patrons can look out over the Mississippi and beyond to the Minneapolis skyline. Inside, the lighting is romantically dim, reflecting off the large gold-leaf fans decorating the walls. The sukiyaki (a simmered beef dish) is the best in town, and the restaurant also offers a large selection of sushi and pickled vegetable appetizers. To drink, there are Japanese beers and flavored sakes to choose from. At night (if you're lucky) drinking businessmen and big-spending hipsters take turns at the karaoke machine, belting out hits from the '60s on up. Kikugawa is open for lunch and dinner daily.

Koyi Sushi $–$$
122 North Fourth Street, Minneapolis
(612) 375-9811
www.koyisushi.com

Koyi Sushi serves fresh sushi at some of the best prices in town, with some very tasty renditions. Some of the more popular choices include the Dynamite Roll (spicy salmon and yellowtail), the Dragon Roll (cooked tuna, masago, and spicy mayo topped with unagi and avocado), and the Marilyn Monroll (grilled chicken, asparagus, and avocado). Koyi offers sushi a la carte (two pieces per serving), as well as small and large rolls. Non-sushi offerings include *kalbee* (marinated and grilled beef ribs served with Korean vegetables) and seafood tempura. The restaurant is open daily for dinner and for lunch Monday through Friday.

St. Paul

Sakura Restaurant and Sushi Bar $$–$$$
350 St. Peter Street, St. Paul
(651) 224-0185
www.sakurastpaul.com

Sakura's menu is divided into tempura, teriyaki, donburi, noodles, salads, and of course, sushi. Sushi is the most important menu item—although there are many other standouts. The sushi bar is prominently placed at the center of a large open room. With more than 30 types of the fresh sushi, connoisseurs have plenty of choices. The sushi bar offers California rolls, salmon egg, shrimp, crab, albacore tuna, scallop, sea eel, and many additional options; all are beautifully presented. The restaurant has a relaxed atmosphere and a friendly waitstaff. The excellent service resonates from owner Miyoko Omori, who frequently greets and seats customers. Reservations are recommended for dinner. Sakura is open daily for both lunch and dinner.

Tanpopo Noodle Shop $
308 Prince Street, St. Paul
(651) 209-6527
www.tanpoporestaurant.com
There are numerous Vietnamese noodle shops in the Twin Cities but few Japanese restaurants specializing in the fine delicacy. The act of making noodles is elevated to an art at Tanpopo. The menu changes seasonally, and the restaurant concentrates on a concise, inexpensive, well-executed menu for lunch and dinner composed of various *udon* (wheat flour noodles) and soba (buckwheat flour noodles) as well as teishoku (set meals). The Nabeyaki Udon is one superb selection, which includes shrimp tempura, chicken, mushrooms, vegetables, and fish cake. The noodle shop is a beautiful renovated warehouse space in St. Paul's lower arts district. Tanpopo is open for lunch Tuesday through Saturday and dinner Monday through Saturday.

KOREAN

St. Paul

Mirror of Korea $–$$
761 Snelling Avenue North, St. Paul
(651) 647-9004
Mirror of Korea's large menu belies the humbly decorated restaurant. Soups, stir-fries, and stews fill out the menu. One excellent dish is the *chop chae*, a traditional Korean dish of beef, vegetables, and rice noodles. There are also more exotic dishes, like the *yook hwae* (raw beef). The restaurant also offers Korean lunch specials. Mirror of Korea is open for lunch and dinner daily, except on Tuesday when the restaurant is closed.

Shilla Korean Restaurant $–$$
694 Snelling Avenue North, St. Paul
(651) 645-0006
Shilla Korean Restaurant is much larger than its neighbor, Mirror of Korea, just up the street, but both share many of the same menu items. The restaurant is a combination of '70s decor accented with Korean motifs and serves as the meeting place for many activities in the local Korean community. The menu is extensive. A few standout dishes are *bi bim bop* (vegetable salad with a boiled egg) and *man do* (pork and vegetable dumplings). Take out is also available. Shilla is open Tuesday through Sunday for lunch and dinner and does not accept reservations.

Sole Cafe $–$$
684 Snelling Avenue North, St. Paul
(651) 644-2068
In an area with two additional Korean restaurants within walking distance, this restaurant is certainly the most authentic and arguably the best. The Sole Cafe is a friendly mom-and-pop operation. Unlike its neighboring Korean restaurants, the menu is not extensive. It is, however, remarkably well executed. The menu includes traditional Korean favorites, such as *bulgogi* (the spicy Korean version of barbecue), *kim chi* soup, and *chop chae* (beef, vegetables, and noodles), as well as less familiar items for American diners. Soups and seafood are also prominent menu items. Sole Cafe is closed on Wednesday but open Thursday through Tuesday for lunch and dinner.

South

Hoban $
1989 Silver Bell Road, Eagan
(651) 688-3447
Hoban is a casual, small restaurant specializing in favorites such as *bi bim bop* (steamed vegetables over rice) and *kalbee* (thinly sliced marinated beef ribs that are grilled). The restaurant serves beer and wine and is open for lunch and dinner Tuesday through Sunday. The restaurant accepts Visa and MasterCard only.

KURDISH

Babani's Kurdish Restaurant $
544 St. Peter Street, St. Paul
(651) 602-9964
Babani's Kurdish is the first restaurant of its kind in the United States. The beautiful building on the outskirts of downtown St. Paul is decorated with Kurdish designs on rugs, pic-

tures, and green curtains. The restaurant provides an excellent opportunity to learn about Kurdish culture and cuisine. The servers are attentive and eager to answer questions regarding Kurdish food, which includes heavy influences of Middle Eastern, Indian, and Mediterranean cuisine. Chicken *tawa*, a sautéed chicken in lemon with vegetables over rice, is an excellent choice. The *biryani* (rice with almonds, raisins, vegetables, and spices) is also excellent and quite similar to the Indian dish of the same name. Babani's serves lunch Monday through Friday and is open for dinner seven days a week.

LATIN AMERICAN

Conga Latin Bistro $$–$$$
501 East Hennepin Avenue, Minneapolis
(612) 331-3360
The owners of Conga, the Thunstrom family, are also responsible for the perennially popular south Minneapolis Latin restaurant, El Meson. The nuevo Latino menu features a couple of paellas, the popular Spanish rice and seafood dish, as well as a wide selection of chicken, pork, beef, and seafood items. Other choices include the seafood casserole and Jamaican chicken. The beer and wine list is extensive, and there is ample opportunity for dancing. Conga is open for lunch Monday through Friday and for dinner daily.

Machu Picchu $$–$$$
2940 Lyndale Avenue South, Minneapolis
(612) 822-2125
www.machupicchurestaurante.com
Machu Picchu is a Peruvian restaurant that specializes in Latin seafood. Located in the heart of the Lyn-Lake neighborhood, an area overflowing with stores, theaters, and coffee shops, the restaurant attracts a hip crowd looking for an exotic dining experience.

Are you looking for a unique ethnic meal? Try Babani's Kurdish Restaurant in St. Paul. It is the first restaurant to serve Kurdish food in the nation.

Machu Picchu in the Lyn-Lake neighborhood of south Minneapolis. TODD R. BERGER

Machu Picchu is open for dinner Tuesday through Saturday.

MEXICAN
Minneapolis

Chiapas Restaurant $
2416 Central Avenue NE, Minneapolis
(612) 789-2971
Chiapas Restaurant serves authentic Mexican food in northeast Minneapolis. Silverio Perez, who also owns the Pancho Villa restaurant in south Minneapolis, operates this 50-seat eatery. The restaurant specialties include chile relleno, enchiladas, and fajitas. Also featured are several vegetarian items. Chiapas is open daily for late breakfast, lunch, and dinner.

Chino Latino $$$
2916 Hennepin Avenue South, Minneapolis
(612) 824-7878
www.chinolatino.com

Chino Latino is a chic hangout with a menu influenced by the food of Asia and Latin barrios. The food is often delicious and sometimes, well, interesting, such as one that caught the eyes of local animal lovers—guinea pig. Chino Latino is open for dinner (and stays open past midnight) daily.

Me Gusta Mexican Cuisine　　$–$$
1507 East Lake Street, Minneapolis
(612) 724-6007

833 South Robert Street, St. Paul
(651) 227-3533

For decades Me Gusta Mexican Cuisine has satisfied Twin Citians' needs for authentic Mexican cuisine. Today, there are numerous authentic Mexican restaurants in the area, but not that long ago Me Gusta was an oasis in a sea of bland, tasteless pseudo-Mexican eateries. Like the rest of the menu, the chips are fresh and the salsa is spicy. Then satisfy your thirst with Mexican beer, wine, or Jarritos, a sweet Mexican soda. The menu includes several burrito, fajita, and enchilada dinners and, for more adventurous diners, *nopales asados* (grilled cactus), the chile relleno, or the enchiladas en mole. Both Me Gusta locations are open daily for lunch and dinner.

Pepitos Mexi-Go Deli　　$
4820 Chicago Avenue South, Minneapolis
(612) 822-2104

4624 Nicollet Avenue South, Minneapolis
(612) 825-6311

16388 Wagner Way, Eden Prairie
(952) 934-7568
www.pepitosrestaurant.com

This small local chain of Mexican restaurants and delis carries an amazing selection of Mexican foods at reasonable prices, including vegetarian enchiladas and tacos, Azteca sandwiches served on teleta-style Mexican bread, huge nacho plates, and quesadillas made with homemade tortillas, all of which are excellent when topped with one of the six fresh-made salsas offered at the salad table. Pepitos is open daily for lunch and dinner. The Chicago Avenue location serves brunch on Sunday.

St. Paul

El Burrito Mercado–El Cafe Restaurant　　$
175 Cesar Chavez Street, St. Paul
(651) 227-2192
www.elburritomercado.com

St. Paul's District del Sol neighborhood on the city's West Side is a historically diverse area and one of the first Chicano settlements in the Twin Cities. In this enclave there is a large Mexican grocery, bakery, and the cafeteria-style restaurant, El Cafe in El Burrito Mercado. Tucked in the back of the complex, El Cafe does astounding business by serving excellent Mexican food at reasonable prices. Get in line and make a selection from the menu, which features tortas, quesadillas, tamales, tacos, and burritos. After a shorter wait than at many fast-food restaurants, take a seat and enjoy a fine Mexican meal. El Cafe also serves breakfast, and don't forget to visit the bakery and grocery.

MIDDLE EASTERN

Minneapolis

Caspian Bistro & Marketplace　　$$
2418 University Avenue SE, Minneapolis
(612) 623-1113

The Caspian Bistro specializes in kabobs, including beef, chicken, and lamb versions accompanied by basmati rice and salad. The menu also includes Middle Eastern treats such as gyros and lamb shank. Since 1986 the restaurant has served the nearby University of Minnesota with scrumptious Persian foods. The small adjoining market offers Middle Eastern delicacies and staples. The restaurant is open for lunch and dinner Tuesday through Saturday. The restaurant accepts Visa, MasterCard, and Discover.

Falafel King $
701 West Lake Street, Minneapolis
(612) 824-7887

121 South 8th Street (TCF Tower), Minneapolis
(612) 339-5560

8405 Lyndale Avenue South, Bloomington
(952) 888-3008
www.falafelking.com

The Falafel King provides Middle Eastern foods in a casual atmosphere. From the counter, diners may select from numerous appetizers, salads, sandwiches, combinations, and dinner entrees. Middle Eastern favorites such as kabobs, hummus, and falafel are served. The restaurant also serves omelets, and Greek and Middle Eastern–style breakfasts. The Falafel King is open daily and offers lunch and dinner buffets. The downtown Minneapolis location is takeout or delivery only.

Holy Land Bakery, Grocery & Deli $
2513 Central Avenue NE, Minneapolis
(612) 781-2627

Holy Land Midtown
920 East Lake Street (Global Market),
Minneapolis
(612) 870-6104
www.holylandbrand.com

Holy Land is not only one of the best specialty markets in the area, it also serves enormous portions of outstanding Middle Eastern cuisine on disposable plates. The choices include kabobs, falafel, hummus, spinach pie, *shawarma* (gyro), and much more. The menu offers large pita sandwiches and much larger dinners, which generally include a salad and rice or hummus paired with one of several meats (shawarma, kabobs, combinations, etc.) and a basket of fresh pita. Select a self-service drink, and there will be plenty of leftovers for less than $10. On request the deli offers halal meals to meet the dietary needs of Muslims. Holy Land does not serve alcohol. Both Holy Land locations are open daily for lunch and dinner.

Jerusalem's $–$$
1518 Nicollet Avenue South, Minneapolis
(612) 871-8883

Jerusalem's, a perennial Best of the Twin Cities winner among readers of *City Pages*, dishes up the flavors and ambience of the Middle East in a surprisingly intimate atmosphere. The restaurant is topped by a mosque-like onion dome, and stepping inside the otherwise unassuming building on Nicollet Avenue will transport you to another world filled with exotic spices, sights, and sounds. Jerusalem's serves a pan–Middle Eastern menu. Lovers of hummus, *kibbe* (bulgur, beef, onion, and pine nuts), and stuffed grape leaves will find plenty of satisfying choices. Desserts are simple but tasty, including baklava and krima. Do not leave the table without a demitasse of Turkish coffee; the restaurant serves a just-sweet-enough version with a floating cardamom seed that is perhaps the best this side of Ankara. If your schedule allows, come to Jerusalem's on a Friday or Saturday night, when belly dancers wiggle on stage and through the dining room, although be sure to call ahead for reservations; the small restaurant is often packed on those nights. The sword dance, in particular, is a crowd pleaser. Jerusalem's is open daily for lunch and dinner.

Trieste Cafe $
10 South Fifth Street, Minneapolis
(612) 333-4658

Trieste Cafe is an international eatery with flair. The menu includes hot hoagies, subs, gyros, hummus, falafels, spanakopita, salads, and more. The Trieste Cafe occupies a small, cramped space on the ground floor of the historic Lumber Exchange building and is open from breakfast until 6:00 p.m. on weekdays.

North

El Bustan $–$$
4757 Central Avenue NE, Columbia Heights
(763) 502-8888

This Columbia Heights restaurant features halal foods (in accordance with Islamic dietary laws), no alcohol, and hookah, a traditional water pipe. The menu is an extensive survey of Middle Eastern standards and includes delicious hummus, kabobs, and shrimp *sayyadiya*. The latter dish is a spicy combination of shrimp in tomato sauce served over a bed of rice. El Bustan is open daily and accepts Visa and MasterCard.

MOROCCAN

Barbary Fig
720 Grand Avenue, St. Paul
(651) 290-2085

Like many businesses on St. Paul's buzzing Grand Avenue, Barbary Fig operates out of an unassuming house. But chef Brahim Hadj-Moussa is doing wonderful things with the foods of north Africa in his cozy restaurant. The menu includes Morrocan-, Tunisian-, and Mediterranean-influenced specialties with savory ingredients such as figs, couscous, phyllo dough, cinnamon, pears, and apricots. Barbary Fig's *tangine* (a Moroccan stew) is a menu standout. Desserts here are also fantastic. The restaurant is open for lunch Monday and Wednesday through Saturday, and for dinner Wednesday through Monday.

NEPALI AND TIBETAN

Everest on Grand
1278 Grand Avenue, St. Paul
(651) 696-1666

Everest Cafe
920 East Lake Street (Midtown Global Market), Minneapolis
(612) 872-1203
www.hotmomo.com

Everest on Grand and its Minneapolis sister Everest Cafe serve Nepali and Tibetan dishes to tuna casserole–leaning Midwesterners. The restaurant specializes in Tibetan *momos*, tasty steamed dumplings mixed with vegetables, pork and turkey, or yak. Nepali specialties include a variety of vegetarian and meat or fish (chicken, goat, lamb, cod, or shrimp) curries and *daal-bhatt,* traditional Nepali combination meals. During the week the restaurant features a lunch buffet, allowing patrons to sample many of the kitchen's Himalayan dishes at a set price. Both locations are open daily for lunch and dinner.

PAN-ASIAN

Chambers Kitchen $$$–$$$$
901 Hennepin Avenue (Chambers Hotel), Minneapolis
(612) 767-6999
www.chambersminneapolis.com

The new Chambers Kitchen in Minneapolis's swank Chambers Hotel is an Asian-influenced restaurant in an art-filled space near the Hennepin Theater District. The menu is filled with seafood favorites such as halibut, salmon, walleye, and lobster, as well as nonseafood specialties such as grilled pork chops, rack of lamb, and beef tenderloin. But in addition to the fresh and superior-quality main ingredients, the spices and other ingredients raise Chambers Kitchen to the status of one of the top 10 restaurants in the Twin Cities. Depending on the dish, you might see wok-fried cabbage, Thai basil, tempura with jalapeños, Asian pears, sautéed shitakes, spicy plum mustard, or lemongrass. Desserts are as fabulous as you'd expect; particularly notable is the port roasted fig with cumin ice cream and sesame tuile. Chambers Kitchen is open daily for breakfast, lunch, and dinner.

20.21 $$$$
Walker Art Center
1750 Hennepin Avenue, Minneapolis
(612) 253-3410
www.wolfgangpuck.com

Founded in 2005, this Wolfgang Puck establishment serves spectacularly good Pan-Asian cuisine with a panoramic view of Loring Park, the Cathedral of St. Mary, and downtown Minneapolis from its second-floor perch in the nearly all-new Walker Art Center. (The name of the restaurant is taken from the Walker's emphasis on 20th and 21st century art.) The menu features local ingredients in season and has influences from many Asian cultures, including Chinese, Indian, Japanese, Thai, and Korean. Such dishes as miso-sake glazed black cod and grilled Mongolian lamb chops will make you feel wonderful inside, perhaps even good enough to stomach the hefty check your waitperson will bring. Desserts are also memorable here, especially when complemented with one of 20.21's many ports, single-malt scotches, cognacs, or martinis. The restaurant is open Tuesday through Saturday for lunch and dinner, and Sunday for brunch and dinner.

PUERTO RICAN

Puerta Azul $–$$
1811 Selby Avenue, St. Paul
(651) 646-7003
www.puertaazulrestaurant.com
This friendly, beautifully lit and decorated restaurant is considered by many a St. Paul treasure, serving a small but enticing menu of Puerto Rican food. Chef Sonia Gonzales Sadr grew up in Puerto Rico, and the wonderful dishes served at Puerta Azul are either from traditional recipes or her own variations. Entrees include pork kabobs or roast marinated in garlic and ginger, marinated sliced beef fried with onions, fish in Caribbean Creole sauce, mango chicken, and guava chicken. The restaurant serves beer and wine. Puerta Azul is open Monday through Friday for lunch and dinner, and Saturday for dinner only.

REGIONAL
Minneapolis
Cafe Lurcat
1624 Harmon Place, Minneapolis
(612) 486-5500
www.cafelurcat.com
Cafe Lurcat, just north of Loring Park in the building once occupied by the legendary Loring Cafe, features what the restaurant describes as regional New American cuisine. What that means in practice is fresh ingredients in dishes including such things as sea bass, pot roast, lamb shank, and oysters on the half shell. Vegetables and side dishes, including roasted cauliflower, butternut squash, and potato puree, are ordered separately. The desserts are heavenly. Cafe Lurcat is open daily for dinner.

Craftsman $$$
4300 East Lake Street, Minneapolis
(612) 722-0175
www.craftsmanrestaraunt.com
Serving what Craftsman calls "regionally inspired New American cuisine," this restaurant near the Mississippi River on East Lake Street is a great choice for a semi-casual tour of the tastiest things the Midwest has to offer. The restaurant uses organic produce, meat, and fish, the majority of which is produced locally by independent farmers. Recent notable entrees include pan-roasted rainbow trout wrapped with pancetta and served with kohlrabi puree and sautéed chard, grilled grass-fed beef steak with fries and béarnaise sauce, and potato gnocchi with green and yellow beans and crème fraiche. Craftsman also serves pizzas and burgers with Midwestern flair (one recent pizza included green bean pesto) and lovely desserts, including a crème brulee of the day. Wash it down with one of the wines on the somewhat short wine list, a beer from the much longer beer list, or a Minnesota Pickle Martini, the latter made with pickle juice, Minnesota-made vodka, olive juice, and mini-pickles.

Cue at the Guthrie $$–$$$
Guthrie Theater
806 South Second Street, Minneapolis
(612) 225-6499
www.cueatguthrie.com

Opened in the summer of 2006 in the brand-new Guthrie Theater on the Minneapolis riverfront, Cue is one of the most talked about new restaurants in the Twin Cities. Its space is wide open with huge glass windows, floor-to-ceiling photographs, and a lot of polished steel and purple pillars, as well as a kitchen cooking island that puts the chefs on stage. Cue may not be the best choice for a cozy romantic dinner, but it is an excellent choice if your evening plans include the theater. The food emphasizes local, seasonal ingredients. Some recent entrees include Wisconsin rabbit leg confit with white wine garlic sausage-flageolet bean ragoût (say that out loud real fast); Valrhona cocoa roasted rack of venison with baby broccoli, roasted red creamer potatoes, and cherry glace; and lemon-scented risotto with toasted pine nuts, golden raisins, Parmesan cream and fried parsley. And for this kind of food, the prices are not sky-high. Cue is open Tuesday through Saturday for lunch and dinner, Friday and Saturday for late night dinner (until midnight), and Sunday for brunch. Closed Monday.

Restaurant Alma $$$–$$$$
528 University Avenue SE, Minneapolis
(612) 379-4909
www.restaurantalma.com

Chef Alex Roberts, a veteran of such restaurant kitchens as New York City's Bouley and Union Square Cafe, serves up incredible New American–style dishes emphasizing seasonal, local ingredients. The menu changes often, but may feature such delights as salmon tartare, beef-ricotta ravioli, and braised lamb with spicy lamb sausage. Don't leave without having dessert; whatever you choose, you won't be disappointed. Reservations are highly recommended, especially on weekends. Restaurant Alma is open for dinner daily.

Spoonriver $$–$$$
750 South Second Street, Minneapolis
(612) 436-2236
www.spoonriver.com

The new Guthrie Theater and the Mill City Museum have unleashed a renaissance in the downtown riverfront areas of Minneapolis. Opening right across the street from the Guthrie, Spoonriver is an upscale second establishment for Minneapolis restaurateur Brenda Langton, who also owns Cafe Brenda. As at Cafe Brenda, Spoonriver features local, organic ingredients including grass-fed beef, wild mushrooms, and Lake Superior herring. (Unlike Cafe Brenda, Spoonriver serves free-range animal dishes.) The narrow restaurant with its intimate lighting and long diner counter is an interesting combination of romantic and solo-diner friendly. Open for lunch Tuesday through Friday from 11:30 a.m. to 2:00 p.m.; brunch Saturday from 8:00 a.m. (or 10:00 a.m. in winter) to 2:00 p.m. and Sunday from 10:00 a.m. to 2:00 p.m.; and dinner Tuesday through Thursday from 5:30 p.m. to 10:00 p.m., Friday and Saturday from 5:30 p.m. to 11:00 p.m., and Sunday from 5:00 p.m. to 10:00 p.m.

St. Paul

Heartland: A Comtemporary Midwestern Restaurant $$$–$$$$
1806 St. Clair Avenue, St. Paul
(651) 699-3536
www.heartlandrestaurant.com

Heartland is a special place, serving dishes with ingredients from the Midwest and south-central Canada. Whenever possible, the chefs purchase organic or naturally raised foods from small family farmers. The menu changes nightly and includes two fixed-price full meals, as well as many a la carte items. Examples of dishes the restaurant has served include a sherried-rabbit consommé with pork-rabbit meatballs and locally picked wild king bolete mushrooms; wild-leek-crusted lake cisco with cherry-tomato relish, baby Pontiac onions, and Wisconsin crayfish cream; and a Yorkshire pork chop with braised Michihili cabbage, spiced watermelon reduction, and roasted local apples. The extensive wine list allows diners to choose the perfect complement to their meal. The Arts and Crafts–style dining room and food preparation area on the dining room floor, as well as the Heartland's elegant wine bar, all add up to one of the nicest dining experiences in the Twin Cities.

SEAFOOD

Minneapolis

Cosmos $$$–$$$$
610 First Avenue North (Graves 601 Hotel), Minneapolis
(612) 312-1168
www.cosmosrestaurant.com
Cosmos can be loosely categorized as a seafood restaurant, but the modernistic restaurant with attentive service and a AAA Four Diamond rating goes well beyond such simplistic branding. The restaurant, which is in the middle of the Hennepin Theater District in the Graves 601 Hotel, features a multiple-course tasting menu, available paired with wine or alone, that changes weekly. Recent dinner entrees include wild rice crusted ahi tuna with rock shrimp, lemon sunchoke puree, and root vegetable remoulade; vanilla butter poached lobster with sweet onion risotto and red curry reduction; and a grilled Colorado lamb chop with cabbage-wrapped lamb confit, rosemary demi, and Verjus grape compote. For dessert, you're unlikely to go wrong with the heavenly chocolate fig tart. The restaurant, in a hotel, is open daily for breakfast, lunch, and dinner. Cosmos is also open on holidays with special menus. Eating at one of the earlier meals can save some money while still giving you access to Cosmos's first-class dishes.

Oceanaire Seafood Room $$$$
1300 Nicollet Mall (Hyatt Regency Hotel), Minneapolis
(612) 333-2277
www.theoceanaire.com
A sidecar, clams casino, and lobster thermi-dor are just a few factors that make up the Oceanaire's decor. The fish here is all fresh, flown in daily from both coasts, and, depending on the catch of the day, the restaurant serves meals like black bass in black butter; a zesty cioppino boasting an immense catch of mussels, clams, shrimp, and fish; yellowfin tuna with wild mushrooms and rich red-wine sauce; Chilean sea bass; and a fantastic oyster bar. The menu changes daily, according to what's available, and the fish fresh on any given day are identified at the top of the menu with a check mark. The Oceanaire is open for dinner daily.

Seafood Palace Chinese Restaurant $–$$
2523 Nicollet Avenue South, Minneapolis
(612) 874-7721
www.seafoodpalacemn.com
The Seafood Palace Chinese's menu begins with extremely reasonable lunch specials, then moves on to the dinner specialties, which include shrimp, scallops, mussels, lobster, and crab as well as traditional Chinese favorites like fried crispy duck, sweet-and-sour pork, and vegetarian dishes such as bean curd with brown sauce and mushrooms with Chinese cabbage. The restaurant is open daily for lunch and dinner.

Sea Salt Eatery $–$$
4825 Minnehaha Avenue, Minneapolis
(612) 721-8990
www.seasalteatery.com
This casual restaurant in Minnehaha Falls Park serves up cheap and tasty seafood. Specialties include several types of fish tacos, po' boys, and oysters, the latter broiled, fried, raw, or served up as part of an Oil Pan, along with shrimp and libations. You order at the counter and the food is brought to your table, either inside the small restaurant or on the patio under the shade of the park's tree canopy within earshot of Minnehaha Creek. The Sea Salt Eatery can be packed on weekend evenings; get there early, eat lunch instead of dinner, eat during the week, or bring a thick book. Open daily.

St. Paul

Mac's Fish & Chips $

1330 Larpenteur Avenue West, St. Paul
(651) 489-5299

Mac's is tiny, none too fancy, and take-out oriented, but for fish-and-chips that would make a Londoner proud, it is a must-visit restaurant in the Twin Cities. Mac's specializes in haddock fillets, and the lightly breaded, deep-fried fish pieces seem as light as clouds and taste otherworldly. You can get the best deal if you buy a basket, which includes haddock, shrimp, chicken strips, or a combination thereof, along with fries, coleslaw, bread, and a beverage. You can also buy the haddock fillets and shrimp by the piece, chicken strips in six-strip servings, half and full orders of fries, and plenty of slaw, allowing you to customize the size of your meal. Mac's harbors a few tables in its dining room, but it is best to call ahead and pick up your order, heading back to your hotel or home with a basket or two of fish-and-chips for a low-key, inexpensive, filling feast. Mac's is open daily for lunch and dinner.

SOUTHWESTERN

Minneapolis

Bar Abilene $–$$

1300 Lagoon Avenue, Minneapolis
(612) 825-2525
www.barabilene.com

The flavors of the Southwest are available in the Twin Cities at Bar Abilene. Located in the Uptown neighborhood of Minneapolis, the restaurant does brisk business and draws a hip clientele. For starters the menu features Texas tapas that include potato-pepper jack flautas, barbecue chicken quesadillas, and tortilla soup. Dinner is divided into burgers and Southwestern specialties. The restaurant features entrees such as savory jalapeño skewered shrimp, and several types of tacos, ranging from peanut-pasilla glazed chicken to crab. Bar Abilene is open daily for dinner and on Saturday and Sunday for lunch.

SPANISH

Minneapolis

Babalú

800 Washington Avenue North, Minneapolis
(612) 746-3158
www.babalu.us

Babalú's varied menu includes specialties of Spain, Cuba, and other parts of the Caribbean. This Warehouse District restaurant has a somewhat funky interior design that fits well with the Latin-Caribbean cuisine. The food here is particularly fresh and may include such dishes as tapas, Veracruz-style red snapper, and Paella Valenciana. For those looking to party beyond dinner (or without dinner), Babalú has a hopping lounge with music and dancing (including salsa and flamenco) nearly every night. Babalú is open for dinner daily.

El Meson $–$$

3450 Lyndale Avenue South, Minneapolis
(612) 822-8062
www.elmesonbistro.com

El Meson features Spanish and Caribbean cuisine in a relaxed, comfortable atmosphere. A few popular dishes include the *arroz* con *mariscos* (rice with seafood) and the paellas (a Spanish rice and seafood dish). In addition, the restaurant serves various chicken and pork dishes with savory rice and beans. For lunch the restaurant offers an ever-popular buffet of home-style Latin favorites. The restaurant has repeatedly received kudos for its delicious, nutritious cuisine. El Meson serves beer and wine. The restaurant is open Monday through Saturday for lunch and dinner, and Sunday for dinner only.

La Bodega Tapas Bar $$–$$$

3005 Lyndale Avenue South, Minneapolis
(612) 823-2661

Tapas, small servings of Spanish food, have become a trendy cuisine nationally. The Twin Cities' first tapas bar, La Bodega is a popular restaurant in the Lyn-Lake neighborhood of south Minneapolis. The tapas are small portions, and the majority of diners purchase at least two or three. Seafood is featured prominently among the tapas choices, which include fried calamari and garlic shrimp. The restaurant offers extensive wine selections to accompany the tapas as well as Spanish flamenco music and dancing on weekends. La Bodega is open daily for lunch and dinner.

SRI LANKAN

Sri Lanka Restaurant $$–$$$
3226 West Lake Street, Minneapolis
(612) 926-0110
This lovely restaurant specializes in the bounty of tastes from Sri Lanka, where fresh fruits, vegetables, meats, and spices are combined to make exciting dishes. A warning to those who are inexperienced with Sri Lankan cuisine: Spice is very important. However, the cooks will spice the dishes to meet diners' tastes. Seafood and vegetarian items are prominent on the menu. The restaurant serves a brunch on Friday, Saturday, and Sunday. The brunch is one of the best in the area and features salads, meats, vegetables, and desserts. The range of flavors and combinations of tastes are astounding. Sri Lanka Restaurant is open daily for dinner; reservations are recommended.

STEAKHOUSES
Minneapolis

Fogo de Chão $$$–$$$$
645 Hennepin Avenue (City Center), Minneapolis
(612) 338-1344
www.fogodechao.com
Fogo de Chão is part of a much welcome trend of Brazilian *churrascarias* (steakhouses) that are popping up around the country. Here, "gauchos" complete with red kerchiefs, cowboy boots, and swords (for cutting the meat) roam the dining room with multiple skewers of fire-roasted steak in several distinct cuts, as well as ribs, leg of lamb, chicken, and linguica (spicy pork sausages). Did I mention it's all-you-can-eat? The central location near Nicollet

Mall, the Hennepin Theater District, and the Target Center is about as convenient as it gets. Fogo de Chão is open Monday through Friday for lunch and dinner, and Saturday and Sunday for dinner only.

Manny's Steakhouse $$$$
1300 Nicollet Mall (Hyatt Regency Hotel), Minneapolis
(612) 339-9900
www.mannyssteakhouse.com
With the bad rap cholesterol gets these days, it's hard not to feel a little bit naughty eating here. This bustling, Manhattan-style steakhouse serves obscenely huge and gloriously tender steaks, lobster, salmon, and chops—and that's about it besides the great wine list and a couple of desserts. Be prepared to either share dinner with a companion or get a doggy bag to go, because there's almost no way for one person to eat a whole dinner entree here.

Murray's $$$–$$$$
26 South Sixth Street, Minneapolis
(612) 339-0909
www.murraysrestaurant.com
The New York strip sirloin is a tradition for Twin Cities upscale dining. Either the porterhouse or the ribeye will also make you shimmy with exultation. Other menu items are offered, but the many regulars come in droves for the steaks and the charming and elegant dining room. Reservations are a necessity. Even then, diners must compete with the regulars for a good table. Murray's serves lunch Monday through Friday and dinner every day of the week.

THAI
St. Paul

Pad Thai Grand Cafe $–$$
1659 Grand Avenue, St. Paul
(651) 690-1393
www.padthaigrand.nv.switchboard.com
The food at the Pad Thai Grand Cafe includes spring rolls with a tangy spicy fish sauce, pad

Thai, drunken noodles, and *pra ram rong song* (stir-fried meat with vegetables in a peanut sauce). The menu includes seafood and vegetarian options as well as a wine list. The service is friendly, and the chef will spice dishes according to patrons' desired heat level. Pad Thai is open Monday through Saturday for lunch and dinner and Sunday for dinner only.

Taste of Thailand $
1671 Selby Avenue, St. Paul
(651) 644-3997

1753 Old Hudson Road, St. Paul
(651) 774-6905

527 South Seventh Street, Minneapolis
(612) 333-0082

7890 University Avenue NE, Fridley
(763) 571-1188

7705 West 147th Street, Apple Valley
(952) 431-4144
www.tasteofthailandrestaurant.com
The original location of Taste of Thailand, in a residential area on Selby Avenue west of Snelling Avenue in St. Paul, won't wow you with its intimate atmosphere. But it more than makes up for lack of ambience with its extensive menu of wonderful Thai dishes. The restaurant has all the classics, including oh-so-light spring rolls, fiery *miang kham*, the house specialty *tom yum* soup, and the ever-popular pad Thai. Other notable dishes include *pad goong*, *pad med mamnang himaphane*, and *gaeng ped pla*. If it's summertime, wash it all down with a glass of Thai lemonade. All Taste of Thailand locations are open daily for lunch (there's a lunch buffet Monday through Friday) and dinner.

North

Royal Orchid $–$$
2401 Fairview Avenue, Roseville
(651) 639-9999
www.thebestthaifood.com
Royal Orchid serves delicious Thai dishes in a pleasantly purple restaurant. Instead of cooking with cliché tastes and using shortcuts, the Royal Orchid marries complex

spices, vegetables, and meats. Particularly notable are the masmon curry, pad Thai, Moslem salad, pineapple fried rice, and tri-flavored fish. Also available are many dishes with beef, chicken, pork, tofu, scallops, and shrimp, which all can be prepared with eight different sauce choices, from garlic to saffron curry, satay, and mock ginger chili with green beans. Royal Orchid accepts Visa and Master-Card only and is open for lunch and dinner Monday through Saturday.

TURKISH

Black Sea $–$$
737 Snelling Avenue North, St. Paul
(651) 917-8832
The first Turkish restaurant in Minnesota (opened in 2001) is arguably one of the best. The menu is filled with Turkish delights such as *döner* (gyros), *köfte* (meatball kabobs), shish kabobs, and several vegetarian entrees, including falafels. The seasonal cold cucumber soup and the falafel salad are also worthy of your consideration. And don't pass up the thick Turkish coffee, which is particularly tasty here. Turkish teas are also available. The restaurant does not serve alcohol. Black Sea is open for lunch and dinner Monday through Saturday.

VEGETARIAN AND VEGAN

Birchwood Cafe $
3311 East 25th Street, Minneapolis
(612) 722-4474
www.birchwoodcafe.com
Although not completely vegetarian, Birchwood often wins accolades for their largely vegetarian menu. Formerly a dairy and grocery store, Birchwood has an old-fashioned stay-a-spell sense of welcome that makes it Seward's informal community center. You can set yourself down in the 1950s-era dining room or at one of the tables on the outdoor patio in summer. Birchwood serves sandwiches on fresh country bread, rustic pizzas, daily changing entrees such as enchiladas and

curries, soups, and half a dozen salads. Known for its fresh organic ingredients and extensive vegetarian and vegan dishes, the Birchwood menu also includes nonvegetarian items. Service is semicafeteria style; you get your salads, desserts, and beverages (including wine and beer) at the counter, and hot or custom-made items are brought to your birchwood-topped table. The cafe is open for breakfast, lunch, and dinner Monday through Saturday, and for breakfast and lunch on Sunday. Birchwood accepts Visa and MasterCard only.

Ecopolitan
2409 Lyndale Avenue South, Minneapolis
(612) 874-7336
www.ecopolitan.com
Ecopolitan's menu is 100 percent organic, vegan, and raw, the only such restaurant in the Twin Cities. But it's not just the food that is good for you and the environment; Ecopolitan uses biodegradable cleaning products, generates solar/wind power on site, and used nontoxic materials to finish the restaurant and attached store. Vegans (and others) can enjoy collared greens burritos, pizzas, and several salads, among several other menu items. The restaurant and store also has an attached Oxygen Bar.

St. Martin's Table $
2001 Riverside Avenue, Minneapolis
(612) 339-3920
www.communityofstmartin.org
This small vegetarian restaurant run by the Community of St. Martin will convert even the most agnostic palates with its menu (which changes daily) of fresh-baked breads, ingenious sandwiches, savory soups, and fair-trade coffee. The restaurant uses organic produce, non–bovine growth hormone milk, and purified water in its dishes and is committed to serving simple, nutritious food that sustains our natural resources and supports growers. St. Martin's waitstaff are all volunteers, and they donate their tips to local, national, and international charities. St. Martin's Table is open for lunch only Monday through Satur-

day. The restaurant does not serve alcohol. You dine well, and all for a higher purpose.

VIETNAMESE
Minneapolis
The Lotus Restaurant $
313 Oak Street SE, Minneapolis
(612) 331-1781

113 West Grant Street, Minneapolis
(612) 870-1218

3037 Hennepin Avenue South, Minneapolis
(612) 825-2263
Each Lotus location has its own unique character. The menus include favorites such as Vietnamese beef salad, curried chicken Vietnamese-style, spring rolls, and egg rolls. Lunch specials are also offered; the mustard chicken is particularly good and includes chicken and onions in a spicy mustard sauce. The Lotus Restaurant is closed Monday but provides a casual environment for lunch and dinner the rest of the week.

Lucky Dragon Riverside Restaurant $–$$
1827 Riverside Avenue, Minneapolis
(612) 375-1690
Lucky Dragon's menu includes soups, combination meals, noodles, stir-fried entrees, and numerous Vietnamese and Chinese specialties. Vegetarian items are available, and the entire menu contains no MSG. There is a large lunch and dinner buffet Monday through Friday. The egg rolls, hot-and-spicy chicken, and beef in black bean sauce are exceptional and usually available with the buffet. Lucky Dragon is open daily for lunch and dinner.

Quang Restaurant $–$$
2719 Nicollet Avenue South, Minneapolis
(612) 870-4739
The hip Quang Restaurant serves fine renditions of Vietnamese favorites. Popular items include caramelized lemongrass chicken, grilled pork chops, and the seafood noodle soups. In addition to fine versions of egg rolls and spring rolls, the menu features such

dishes as grilled sugarcane shrimp (*banh hoi choi*). The restaurant does not serve alcohol. Quang Restaurant is closed Tuesday and open for lunch and dinner the rest of the week.

St. Paul

Saigon Restaurant & Bakery $
601 University Avenue West, St. Paul
(651) 225-8751

Saigon Restaurant is the best and most afford-able authentic Vietnamese restaurant in the Twin Cities. The specialties are *pho* and *banh mi*. Pho, the national dish of Vietnam, is a huge bowl of soup. It includes vegetables, noodles, and a choice of meats from roast pork to sev-eral delicious seafood combinations. Banh mi is a savory Vietnamese sandwich composed of pâté, cilantro, cucumber, Vietnamese mayo, and any of a number of meats combined on a fresh baguette. There is a deli counter where banh mi and baked goods are available for takeout, all at incredibly low prices. The restaurant and bakery are open Tuesday through Sunday for lunch and dinner.

Vina Highland $
756 Cleveland Avenue South, St. Paul
(651) 698-8408

Vina Vietnamese Restaurant
6401 Nicollet Avenue South, Richfield
(612) 866-5034

Vina Plus
1821 University Avenue, St. Paul
(612) 644-1384

The casual Vina serves delicious, inexpensive dishes. The menu is filled with Vietnamese favorites such as curry shrimp, egg roll salad, and hot-and-spicy chicken. The hot-and-spicy chicken is an excellent rendition of the Viet-namese favorite and is composed of chicken with onions, lemongrass, and red peppers. All items are spiced to order and contain no MSG. For lunch, Vina features more inexpen-sive combination meals, where Chinese menu items are an important part. Vina is open seven days a week for lunch and dinner. Vina accepts Visa and MasterCard.

South

Kimson Vietnamese Cuisine $
8654 Lyndale Avenue South,
Bloomington
(952) 885-0230

With more than 200 items, Kimson's menu provides plenty of pork, chicken, beef, tofu, seafood, and vegetarian selections. The restaurant offers many Vietnamese favorites, including hot-and-spicy chicken, sautéed beef over fried potatoes, curry chicken, and egg rolls. The menu includes many vegetarian dishes. There are nearly a dozen tofu entrees, which range from chow mein and sweet and sour to ginger bean curd. Kimson is open daily for lunch and dinner.

Kinhdo Restaurant $
2755 Hennepin Avenue South, Minneapolis
(612) 870-1295

2709 Winnetka Avenue North, New Hope
(763) 544-8440

Kinhdo Restaurant has two unique Twin Cities locations, but both serve excellent renditions of Vietnamese cuisine as well as a few favorite Chinese dishes. The menu features excep-tional values on Vietnamese favorites like hot-and-spicy chicken, beef and potatoes, and egg rolls with fish sauce. The menu also fea-tures such Chinese items as chow mein, egg foo young, and a great version of sweet-and-sour chicken. Both Kinhdo restaurants are open daily for lunch and dinner.

SWEETS AND TREATS

Minneapolis

Caruso's Gelato Cafe $
3001 Hennepin Avenue South
(Calhoun Square), Minneapolis
(612) 822-2629
www.carusosgelato.com

Caruso's carries more than 30 flavors of gelato, which it makes using fresh ingredients in small batches. The list of flavors is exten-sive and includes chocolate chip, balsamic fig, mango, coconut, caramel nut swirl, peanut, banana, and tiramisu, all of which can be carried out either in a waffle cone or in a cup.

Dairy Sales Room Store $
Andrew Boss Meat Science Building
University of Minnesota
1354 Eckles Avenue, St. Paul
(612) 624-7776

If your timing is right, you can find some of the best ice cream and cheeses in the Twin Cities in this little-known and rarely open outlet on the University of Minnesota's St. Paul Campus. Open only 3:00 to 5:00 p.m. Wednesdays, customers line up early to get their hands on dairy products produced by university students and researchers. Don't worry, no failed experiments make it to the sales floor, and if you're willing to make the effort to find the store, you will be treated to rich (12 percent fat!) and creamy ice cream in a variety of flavors and a range of cheeses, the weekly selection depending on what is available from the university's work and the time of year. The store may (or may not) have on hand such favorites as Gopher Gold ice cream (French vanilla and raspberry), aged cheddar, and Nuworld, a spreadable variety of blue cheese that is all white. Quantities available for sale are always limited: Arrive early for the best selection.

Sebastian Joe's $
1007 Franklin Avenue West, Minneapolis
(612) 870-0065

4321 Upton Avenue South, Minneapolis
(612) 926-7916

4301 Nicollet Avenue South, Minneapolis
(612) 824-3461

When Italian immigrant Sebastiano Pellizer arrived in the Twin Cities in the 1930s, he was almost immediately rechristened Joe by his employer, a construction-crew chief. The moniker stuck, and in 1984 when his grandchildren Mike and Todd founded this ice-cream shop, Sebastiano gave them permission to use his name. Sebastian Joe's has become nearly synonymous with handmade ice cream in the Twin Cities. The ice-cream list tops 80 flavors (15 daily) and includes both new spins and old favorites, such as basil strawberry, chocolate, fresh strawberry, vanilla made from ground vanilla beans, ginger cream, and cayenne pepper-laced Chocolate Coyote.

Wuollet Bakery $
2447 Hennepin Avenue, Minneapolis
(612) 381-9400

1080 Grand Avenue, St. Paul
(651) 292-9035
Four additional Twin Cities locations
www.wuollet.com

Wuollet is a family-run bakery, watched over by two brothers, their uncle, and a cousin. In the hands of Wuollet's cake artists, traditional white-on-white wedding cakes can ascend to seven tiers covered in white chocolate ropes, orchids, and other adornments, while soufflé cakes featuring genoise (egg-rich sponge cake) disappear under drifts of Bavarian cream. A sweets table covered in profiteroles, fancy French pastries, cheesecake, and trifle is a reception addition that uses Wuollet's skills to their tastiest advantage. The shop also sells delicious doughnuts and princess tortes layered in Bavarian cream and raspberry preserves. All six Wuollet bakeries are open Monday through Saturday.

St. Paul

Cafe Latte $
850 Grand Avenue, St. Paul
(651) 224-5687
www.cafelatte.com

Cafe Latte features cheesecakes in a myriad of flavors, including the tin roof cheesecake with layers of nuts and chocolate. Latte is also renowned for its decadent turtle cake—dark chocolate cake layers separated by and topped with buttery caramel and pecans—as well as the tart key lime pies, raspberry marzipan, and thick scones served with crème fraîche, jams, and fresh fruit. Also of particular note is the exceptionally moist tres leches cake, with three different cake layers each soaked in a different type of milk and fresh raspberries circling the cake's top. Yum. A few desserts are available as individual servings, but the restaurant primarily makes full cakes for parties and events. Cafe Latte is open daily.

Grand Ole Creamery $
750 Grand Avenue, St. Paul
(651) 293-1655
www.grandolecreamery.com
Two additional Twin Cities locations
The Grand Ole Creamery has been creating some of the most imaginative and delicious ice-cream flavors in its parlor since 1984. And the flavors, including Irish coffee eggnog and chocolate malt banana, aren't just interesting experiments in flavor, they're also very, very good. The store serves up to 32 flavors from a master list of more than 100, and customers can satisfy their chocolate, strawberry, or vanilla cravings or try the black walnut, cinnamon, or sweet cream. At the bottom of each ice-cream cone is a malted milk ball carefully placed so that the ice cream doesn't leak out onto your shirt. The store also makes thick, rich malts and shakes, banana splits, and sundaes. During the dog days of summer, folks line up out the door to indulge in this stuff. Grand Ole Creamery is open daily.

Izzy's Ice Cream Cafe $
2034 Marshall Avenue, St. Paul
(651) 603-1458
www.izzysicecream.com
Izzy's serves an amazing variety of homemade ice cream, including blueberry cheesecake, green tea, Mexican chocolate fiesta, mango, ginger, hot brown sugar, Guiness, crème de menthe, pineapple, Oreo cookie, and coffee, the latter flecked with coffee grounds. The beauty of it all is that if there's another flavor that you weren't really sure on but would like to try, you can ask the server to make that flavor your izzy—a small scoop added to the top of your first choice. Izzy's also offers malts, shakes, floats, sundaes, and egg creams. Izzy's is open daily.

Grand Ole Creamery on Grand Avenue in St. Paul.
TODD R. BERGER

Just Truffles $
1363 Grand Avenue, St. Paul
(651) 690-0075
www.justtruffles.com
Like its name says, this store carries nothing but truffles: thick, rich, gigantic homemade chocolate truffles kept in a refrigerated glass case until purchase. They are available in dozens of flavors, including Kahlua, raspberry, maple nut, amaretto, and pecan turtle. The edible chocolate boxes are a special and delicious way to send the truffles as a gift. Just Truffles is open Monday through Saturday.

Regina's Candy Shop $
2073 St. Clair Avenue, St. Paul
(651) 698-8603

1905 South Robert Street (Southview Square)
West St. Paul
(651) 455-8864
www.reginascandies.com

Founded in 1926 by a young Greek craftsman and his bride, Regina, and passed on to their children and grandchildren, Regina's uses old-world craftsmanship in making its amazing (and amazingly inexpensive) caramels, chocolates, toffees, and more than 20 flavors of dark chocolate truffles.

Taste of Scandinavia Catering and Bakery $
2900 Rice Street, Little Canada
(651) 482-8876

845 Village Center Drive, North Oaks
(651) 482-8285

401 West 98th Street, Bloomington
(952) 358-7490

3251 Northdale Boulevard NW, Coon Rapids
(763) 421-4749
www.tasteofscandinavia.com
This charming European bakery has luscious desserts spinning inside a glass case—the Scandinavian strawberry torte layers yellow sponge cake with chocolate mousse, fresh banana slices, and raspberry preserves and is covered in strawberries and peaks of cream. Sweets from elegantly decorated layer cakes to muffins and cookies to Finnish cinnamon *pulla* can also be found. On late afternoons the bakery offers many half-price deals, so stop in late and indulge yourself. All four locations are open daily.

COFFEEHOUSES AND TEASHOPS

Minneapolis

Acadia Cafe $
1931 Nicollet Avenue South, Minneapolis
(612) 874-8702
www.acadiacafe.com
If you weren't hungry when you first walked in, a few seconds of standing by the counter and inhaling all the wonderful scents of fresh chocolate croissants and cookies baking is sure to start your stomach rumbling. Aside from all the coffee and espresso drinks you could ever want, Acadia makes fresh soups, sandwiches, store-made bread, yogurt parfaits, and homemade Belgian waffles with fruit and whipped cream that are worth waking up early for. In the evenings, the café transforms into a pub with many unusual beers on tap (SurlyFest, Rogue Nitro Stout, etc.) and live music several days a week.

Blue Moon Coffee Cafe $
3822 East Lake Street, Minneapolis
(612) 721-9230
www.glbt.com
Everything about the Blue Moon breathes comfort and relaxation. The soothing purple and blue color scheme and sparkling strings of white and colored Christmas lights make the cafe the perfect place for a calming evening of quiet revitalization. There are many coffee drinks on the menu and a choice of eight different kinds of coffee, 16 types of tea, homemade biscotti, pastries, sandwiches, and a big ice-cream cooler that carries Häagen-Dazs bars and other treats. Outside seating is available, but the large selection of comfy couches is hard to resist even on the nicest summer evenings. Blue Moon is open daily.

Bob's Java Hut $
2651 Lyndale Avenue South, Minneapolis
(612) 871-4485
www.bobs33.com
This funky little coffee shop stays open late in the summer months and closes earlier depending on how many customers linger in the winter. Don't be intimidated by the odd-looking crowd that hangs out here—they're mostly art students with time on their hands and a budget that includes copious amounts of hair dye. The menu is predominately coffee drinks and juice, with a few baked goods for the morning and lunch crowds. The house specialty is Kool-Aid. No one else in town bothers putting it on the menu, and lots of people who come here order it. On warm days and nights, the large storefront window rolls back to let fresh air and conversation from the outside patio in. Bob's is open daily.

Dunn Bros. Coffee $
201 Third Avenue South, Minneapolis
(612) 692-8530
www.dunnbros.com

This old brick warehouse is the home of one of the numerous Dunn Bros. coffeehouses in town (there are more than 60 throughout the Twin Cities), with live music most summer weekend nights and a beautiful, comfortable interior, furnished with large potted plants that make it feel like it's springtime year-round. The shop serves all the coffee and espresso drinks you could want as well as cookies, muffins, and a changing menu of other treats, depending on the mood of the staff. Dunn Bros. locations have varying opening and closing times, but are generally open daily between 6:00 or 6:30 a.m. and 10:00 p.m. or later. Some locations in downtown Minneapolis and downtown St. Paul close considerably earlier.

Isles Bun & Coffee Company
1424 West 28th Street, Minneapolis
(612) 870-4466

This bakery and coffeehouse at the corner of West 28th Street and Hennepin Avenue South in the heart of Uptown does a brisk business. What people are coming for are the *big,* fresh cinnamon rolls. You can see the bakers at work at this small establishment, so the rolls' freshness is never in doubt. The hefty monsters taste particularly good with an extra dollop of icing from the pot set out for just that purpose. There's limited seating inside and only a few sidewalk tables, so you'll probably want to take your bun to go. For the slightly less decadent-minded, the bakery offers other baked goods—including a vegan scone of the day, cakes, muffins, brownies, biscotti, and dog treats—as well as plenty of java.

La Société du Thé $
2708 Lyndale Avenue South, Minneapolis
(612) 871-5148
www.la-societe-du-the.com

This well-stocked, comfortable teahouse offers more than 100 varieties of specialty and whole-leaf teas sold in three-ounce portions, ranging in price from $4.50 to more than $20. The helpful staff gives careful instructions about heating water, steeping time, and the story behind each particular type of tea, all of which are preserved in airtight canisters. You can also enjoy tea by the cup or the pot in the teahouse. La Société du Thé is open Monday through Saturday.

May Day Cafe $
3440 Bloomington Avenue South, Minneapolis
(612) 729-5627

Situated in the old Powderhorn Co-op grocery spot just off the edge of Powderhorn Park, this small, cozy place is remarkable for its quality coffee and wonderful sweet breads (sweet potato pound cake, cranberry, and zucchini bread in season). The May Day Cafe is open daily.

Muddy Waters $
2401 Lyndale Avenue South, Minneapolis
(612) 872-2232

This long-established coffeehouse, furnished like a college student's first apartment, caters specifically to the quirky hipster crowd, with menu items like Pop Tarts and Spaghetti-Os. There's lots of indoor seating, and in the summertime the crowds of caffeine addicts spill out to fill the tables spread out in front of building. Saturday-morning cartoons are often featured on the TV screens. Muddy Waters is open daily.

Sister Sludge Coffee Café $
4557 Bloomington Avenue South, Minneapolis
(612) 722-3933

330 2nd Avenue South, Minneapolis
(612) 371-4395

This funky little neighborhood coffeehouse serves coffee, espresso, and chai drinks to patrons either crowded into the small shop or spread out comfortably among the tables set outside. The menu is small and consists mostly of Rice Krispie bars, muffins, and cookies, but it's a comfortable place to spend an afternoon or catch a cup of coffee before officially starting your day. Both Sister Sludge locations are open daily.

St. Paul

Ginkgo Coffeehouse $
721 Snelling Avenue North, St. Paul
(651) 645–2647
www.ginkgocoffee.com

By day, Ginkgo is a friendly java joint with mismatched furniture, potted plants, and a few outdoor tables in summer. A couple of nights a week, however, the atmosphere changes, and this coffeehouse on the edge of St. Paul's Hamline University campus becomes a dimly lit, cozy, acoustic-music venue. Ginkgo is open daily.

Lori's Coffee House $
1441 Cleveland Avenue North, St. Paul
(651) 647-9007

Lori's is a nice little corner coffeehouse across the street from the St. Paul campus of the University of Minnesota. Lori's makes wonderful, homemade soups on site and throws a couple of huge slices of also-homemade bread in for free. There's coffee and espresso, cookies, muffins, a good selection of bottled juices to pick from, and fresh-squeezed orange juice. Lots of college kids hang out here, and there's definitely room for them—while the inside is spacious and airy, most summertime loungers opt to sit around one of the many tables spread out on the lawn. Lori's is open daily.

Sarah Jo's Coffee Cafe $
327 West Seventh Street, St. Paul
(651) 224-3890

This establishment caters specifically to the breakfast and lunch crowd, opening earlier than most places in the neighborhood and closing around 5:00 p.m. The menu is wonderfully diverse, with a large selection of hot and cold fresh sandwiches to choose from—including beef French dip and barbecue meatball—as well as homemade soup, smoothies, muffins, and all the usual selections of coffee

and espresso drinks. There's lots of seating space, and the tables are actually big enough for two or three to set down their food and drinks. The coffee shop is also walking distance from the Xcel Energy Center and downtown St. Paul, making it a great place to park and stop before seeing the sights of the area.

Tea Source $
752 Cleveland Avenue South, St. Paul
(651) 690-9822

2908 Pentagon Drive NE, St. Anthony
(612) 788-4842
www.teasource.com

Owner Bill Waddington personally selects the fine teas he sells to customers of all tastes. Although Tea Source sells loose teas in two-to four-ounce bags, you can also stop in either store and enjoy a cup or pot of your favorite tea. With dozens of options among black, green, oolong, tisanes (herbal teas), and blends, you can pick out a few ounces of your favorite or an adventurous alternative to take home. A detailed guide available in the store helps make sense of the inventory, and Tea Source offers similar information in its catalog and online. Tea Source is open daily.

North

The Corner Coffee House $
87 West County Road C, Little Canada
(651) 482-1114

One of the few true coffeehouses in the suburbs, the Corner Coffee House is a big, friendly-looking, yellow two-story house with a large back patio, several cozy rooms inside for neighborhood get-togethers, and lots of lot parking. The menu includes a couple dozen coffee and espresso drinks, huge fresh-fruit smoothies topped with whipped cream, breakfast pastries, and Italian desserts. Art and knickknacks are for sale, most of which are made by local artists, and live musicians stop by to play weekend afternoons and evenings. If you don't feel like stopping in but still want the coffee, there's even a drive-through window in back for a quick pickup.

NIGHTLIFE

A casual drive through the Twin Cities might lead you to think that Minnesotans have a serious drinking problem. There are hundreds of little drinking holes throughout the region, sometimes spaced less than a city block apart from another. The truth is that Minnesotans just like to be together, especially in the winter. Around December the local bar provides a place for people to gather to play Trivial Pursuit, watch TV, and buy tickets to win the traditional bar "meat raffle," which usually consists of some lucky customers winning 10 pounds of bologna or olive loaf. There's no better fun in January than getting bundled up tight as the sun goes down and heading out to the neighborhood bar to meet with friends and neighbors.

If your idea of a night on the town is catching a good live band, you're in luck—nearly all the bars and coffee shops in the Twin Cities metro area offer at least one night of live music every week. There are clubs that cater to just about every musical taste you can imagine. Downtown Minneapolis, particularly the Warehouse District, has the largest concentration of dance clubs. The Uptown area of Minneapolis has many hip bars, some with live music, and the area around the University of Minnesota has numerous, somewhat grittier bars filled with younger, drunker patrons. Downtown St. Paul is much tamer in terms of live music, though brewpubs and bars that have sprung up near Rice Park and around the Xcel Energy Center have certainly livened things up, and the Artists' Quarter jazz club has long made patrons feel as though they'd stumbled upon a subterranean gem. Several elegant drinking establishments inhabit the Selby-Dale area just west of the cathedral, and St. Paul has two excellent spots for live Irish music, Half Time Rec near

Como Park and the Dubliner Pub in the Midway. The numerous pubs in neighborhoods across the Saintly City offer plenty of local color.

ALTERNATIVE MUSIC AND ROCK CLUBS

Minneapolis

The Cabooze
917 Cedar Avenue, Minneapolis
(612) 338-6425
www.cabooze.com
Since 1974 the Cabooze has opened its doors to nationally recognized touring rock, folk, and instrumental acts as well as many local bands. The Cabooze features musical acts Wednesday through Saturday. It has a large dance floor for those who don't feel like just standing around, as well as the largest bar in the Twin Cities.

Club 3 Degrees
113 North Fifth Street, Minneapolis
(612) 781-8488
www.club3degrees.com
Kind of a rarity in the Twin Cities, Club 3 Degrees is an alcohol-free, smoke-free nightclub for audiences of all ages (until 11:00 p.m., when the club allows only those 18 and over). The club mostly books politically correct punk bands and Christian rock, but the occasional acoustic act makes its way in now and again.

Fine Line Music Cafe
318 First Avenue North, Minneapolis
(612) 338-8100
www.finelinemusic.com
Offering a blend of folk music, adult rock, and funk, including many local bands with dreams

of making it big, the Fine Line is an intimate, comfortable club on good nights and extremely packed and uncomfortable on bad nights. A small menu with American basics such as salads, steak, and pasta is available on nights featuring national touring acts.

First Avenue/Seventh Street Entry
701 First Avenue North, Minneapolis
(612) 338-8388
www.first-avenue.com

Yes, this is that place from Purple Rain. Not only did Twin Citian Prince film parts of his movie at First Avenue, he also spent his fair share of time here when the cameras weren't rolling, onstage and in the crowd. The world-famous First Avenue has been a popular hangout for bands, musicians, and club goers since Joe Cocker took the stage on opening night in 1970. Since then the club has featured top-40, alternative, and classic rock acts and has opened its floors to crowds dancing to techno, house music, salsa, hip-hop, reggae, and likely any other type of music you can think of. First Avenue sometimes holds all-ages shows, but the upstairs is always for ages 21-plus. With its own fully stocked bar and a wall-length window providing a view of the action below, upstairs is a great place to retreat from the downstairs crowds. The real beauty of First Avenue is the layout. No matter where you stand in the club, whether on the massive dance floor or upstairs at the bar, you always get a decent view of the stage.

Set in a side room, with its own separate entrance on Seventh Street, the Entry is the more intimate venue. The stage setting is great here, too, and though the room gets packed quickly, on good nights this is about as close to having a major-label act play in your living room as you can get. The dress code is informal, and the bar offers some of the cheapest tap beer you'll find at a live-music venue.

During spring and fall both clubs are booked almost every night. For show and ticket information, pick up a club schedule

i First Avenue/Seventh Street Entry gives out free passes to upcoming shows and events with each ticket purchased. Usually if you buy one ticket, you get enough free tickets to get you into three or four other shows or dance club nights.

(found at any record store in the Twin Cities, both venues are listed on the same schedule), check out the Web site, or just give First Avenue a call.

400 Bar
400 Cedar Avenue South, Minneapolis
(612) 332-2903
www.400bar.com

The bartender's surly, the beer's expensive, and the doorman thinks everybody who comes in is up to no good; but the sound man knows what he's doing, and a lot of touring acts stop here specifically because they sound so incredibly good in this club. The owners' former association with Soul Asylum helped bring people into the club when the band was big, but it's the club's reputation as a good venue to play that brings the bands in now. Everything from alternative rock to folk to blues acts (and everything in between) from all over the world make this club a regular stop on their tours. If you don't get here when the doors open, you probably won't be able to get in because of the huge crowds.

Ground Zero/The Front
15 Northeast Fourth Street, Minneapolis
(612) 378-5115

Ground Zero offers diverse theme nights three times a week. One of the club's most popular dance nights is "Bondage a go-go," where every Thursday and Saturday dancers perform relatively tame S&M; some patrons dress in corresponding attire.

Besides the large dance floor, Ground Zero has a smaller, cozier lounge room, the Front. Theme nights include Funky Friday, with old-school soul, disco, and R&B; and

Astro Lounge, with disco, hip-hop, house, and whatever the DJ feels like playing.

Lee's Liquor Lounge
101 Glenwood Avenue, Minneapolis
(612) 338-9491
www.leesliquorlounge.com
Located in a former industrial area just south of downtown's Warehouse District, Lee's is a little off the beaten path, and the one-way streets in the area sometimes make it tricky to find. It's worth finding. Lee's hosts live music almost every night, and covers generally run $5 or less for the local and touring acts. (Musicians from Austin, Texas, seem to love this place.) The sight lines are good, and the bar is clean and comfortable, despite its slightly rough-around-the-edges roadhouse feel. This is the type of place where you're equally comfortable tossing back a few beers while bobbing your head or doing your thing on the dance floor. And who doesn't benefit from rockin' music, wood paneling, and taxidermy every once in a while?

Mayslacks Polka Lounge
1428 Northeast Fourth Street, Minneapolis
(612) 789-9862
www.mayslacks.com
This place can be the best bang for your buck so far as seeing live music. The cover is rarely more than $3, and bands usually play for a good two or three hours—and for the low cover, you can see anything from a brand-new band made up of neighborhood kids to a major label act. The downside is that there are rarely opening bands for acts, so by the time the headliners are finished playing, they're sometimes panting, out of breath, and usually very drunk. The sound system is better than you might expect from a neighborhood bar. The beer's moderately priced, too, and on football/soccer/hockey/bartender's-in-a-good-mood nights, the lounge has some really great specials.

Terminal Bar
409 Hennepin Avenue East, Minneapolis
(612) 623-4545

Most of the patrons of this bar are people from the neighborhood who like to stop by after work for a beer and college kids coming to see local bands perform on the small stage in the back. The draft beer is a little high priced, but there's a popcorn machine always full of popcorn, and if you ask nicely, you can always sample the bar favorite, a hard-boiled egg on a Ritz cracker with a little mustard. The cover charge, if there is one, is usually very cheap.

The Uptown Bar and Cafee
3018 Hennepin Avenue South, Minneapolis
(612) 823-4719
www.uptownbarandcafe.com
Once known for attracting the loudest national and local acts, the Uptown Bar and Cafee features local bands, mostly composed of roots rock and acoustic music. The bar draws well in Minneapolis's hip Uptown neighborhood and has expanded to live music on Tuesday through Saturday and a DJ on Monday.

Whiskey Junction
901 Cedar Avenue, Minneapolis
(612) 338-9550
www.whiskeyjunction.com
With lots of local music and beer and food specials, Whiskey Junction, just down the street from the Cabooze, attracts a slightly grungy crowd, including plenty of students from the nearby University of Minnesota and Augsburg College. Two bars keep thirsty patrons busy, and the Whiskey has several pool tables and TVs, often flickering with various sporting events (the bar is the base for the unofficial Cleveland Browns Fan Club, making a brave statement in Vikings country). Whiskey Junction has an excellent selection of tap beers, including the local favorite, Summit, as well as rarer finds on tap, such as Beamish Stout, Boddington Cream Ale, Fullers India Pale Ale, and Paulaner Hefe Weizen. The bar also serves bar food, such as burgers, pizza, sandwiches, hot wings, and salads.

The Whole Music Cafe
Coffman Memorial Union
300 Washington Avenue SE
Minneapolis
(612) 625-2272
www.coffman.umn.edu/whole
The Whole, originally called the Gopher Hole, occupies the basement of Coffman Union on the University of Minnesota–Minneapolis campus. The 40-year-old venue has a venerable history, including early days as a coffeehouse featuring folky songsters and poets and later as a haven for new wave, punk, and indie-rock bands and their devoted student (mostly) fans. When Coffman Union underwent a $71 million renovation, improvements to the Whole included such coveted features as bathrooms and a rocking sound system. But the architects wisely left the gritty, down-in-the-cellar atmosphere much as it always has been, a nod to the tradition of this little underground club in the heart of the university.

St. Paul

Christensen's Big V's Saloon
1567 University Avenue West, St. Paul
(651) 645-8472
Christensen's Big V's Saloon features live music from local and national indie bands every weekend and some weekdays, and karaoke on Sunday and Tuesday. The decor of the bar is fabulous—the walls are covered with an old menu from the 1940s, while the bar itself is a classy antique curved wooden affair with a mirrored backdrop. The placing of the stage is a little inconvenient, tucked back where only patrons in the back room can actually see the stage, but considering that the saloon doesn't usually have a cover charge of more than a few dollars, not many people complain.

Station 4
201 East Fourth Street, St. Paul
(651) 298-0173
www.station-4.com
Station 4 features local rock and some national touring bands. The club is divided into two parts, one with a long bar with lots of dartboards and the other for the music. There is a large stage and lots of seating for the young bar crowd, who on weekends fill the club. Station 4 always runs shuttles to Wild hockey games and other big events at Xcel Energy Center. The bar includes separate areas for all ages and for 21+.

Turf Club
1601 University Avenue, St. Paul
(651) 647-0486
www.turfclub.net
Billing itself as the "Best Remnant of the '40s," St. Paul's Turf Club combines upscale sophistication with the feel of an old-fashioned cowboy bar. Local, domestic, and imported beers are on tap, and the club features an elegant, curved wooden bar for customers to perch at, as well as booths and tables throughout the establishment. Long having a reputation for giving local original bands a much-needed performance outlet, the Turf Club is one of the hippest hangouts in the Twin Cities, with music almost every night for ridiculously low cover charges. The Turf Club clientele is refreshingly free of the "beautiful people" crowd found at many downtown Minneapolis dance clubs, and the music here ranges from foot-stomping country to ska. Downstairs is a second bar known as the Clown Lounge, which features local and guest jazz musicians. The lounge retains an intimate, basement-rec-room feel, with wood paneling and taxidermied fish. It's definitely worth checking out if you're around on an evening this downstairs bar is open. It provides a good aural break if the music upstairs doesn't turn out to be your thing.

West

Medina Entertainment Center
500 Highway 55, Medina
(763) 478-6661
www.medinaentertainment.com
About 5 miles west of Interstate 494 in the western suburb of Medina, the Medina Entertainment Center hosts local bands like the disco kings Boogie Wonderland and the White

ℹ️ Students with a valid student ID can get a $2 discount on Thursday night and at 10:30 p.m. shows on Friday and Saturday at ComedySportz.

Sidewalls, a 1950s and 1960s cover band. In addition to live music, the Medina often has poker events.

COFFEEHOUSES

Lori's Coffee House
1441 Cleveland Avenue North, St. Paul
(651) 647-9007
Located near the University of St. Thomas campus, Lori's sometimes hosts live music—swing by and take your chances on who's performing. There's never a cover charge, and this is really a pretty pleasant place to hang out.

White Rock Coffee Roasters
769 Cleveland Avenue South, St. Paul
(651) 699-5448
www.whiterockcoffee.com
This great neighborhood coffeehouse has live local music on Saturday night; usually something acoustic, often a singer-songwriter. The crowd will probably consist of students from the several area colleges as well as nonstudent folk from the neighborhood, who enjoy the coffee shop's caffeinated beverages and wireless Internet service.

COMEDY CLUBS

Minneapolis

Acme Comedy Company
708 North First Street, Minneapolis
(612) 338-6393
www.acmecomedycompany.com
Acme hosts local and national comedians in its Warehouse District space inside the Itasca Building. The club has shows nightly except Sunday, with free open mike on Monday. The on-site restaurant serves pasta, steaks, and ribs, and you have the choice of buying a ticket for the comedy show alone, for $15, or a dinner and show special for $27.

ComedySportz
3001 Hennepin Avenue South (Calhoun Square), Minneapolis
(612) 870-1230
www.comedysportztc.com
Part of the national ComedySportz chain, this club sets up refereed comedy teams that compete for the biggest laughs and the most points for their unscripted, improvisational performances. Audience members are encouraged to heckle the teams as well as throw out suggestions for comedy themes. But make sure your suggestions are clean, or the referee could call the "Brown Bag Foul" on you and you'll end up wearing a paper bag over your head. Shows are every Thursday at 8:00 p.m. and every Friday and Saturday at 8:00 and 10:30 p.m.

DANCE CLUBS

Bar Fly
711 Hennepin Avenue, Minneapolis
(612) 333-6100
www.barflyminneapolis.com
BarFly (tagline: "More quaint than a club. More liberal than a lounge.") sits in the old Skyway Theater on busy Hennepin Avenue downtown. DJs spin for the beautiful people dancing and bellying up to moodily lit bars. This club is open Wednesday through Sunday.

El Nuevo Rodeo
2709 East Lake Street, Minneapolis
(612) 728-0101
www.elnuevorodeo.com
Boasting three hardwood dance floors, two bars, and highly danceable Latin music, El Nuevo Rodeo is one of the biggest and funnest dance clubs in the Cities. The club features live Latin music several nights a week, especially on weekends, and a DJ playing very sexy Latin tunes the rest of the time. At 20,000 square feet, El Nuevo Rodeo is large, but it rarely feels empty when the music is a thumpin'. The club is on East Lake Street a couple of blocks west of the Lake Street/Midtown Station of the Hiawatha Light-Rail Transit line.

Escape Ultra Lounge
600 Hennepin Avenue South, Minneapolis
(612) 333-8855
www.escapeultralounge.com
This 12,000-square-foot 18-plus club is right above the Hard Rock Cafe in the heart of Minneapolis's entertainment district on Hennepin Avenue (there is also a club entrance on First Avenue). A "fashionable" dress code is enforced here, where plasma screens, leather couches, and serious uplighting make for a hip, high-tech mood. Two VIP rooms up the swank factor. Escape is open from 5:00 p.m. to 2:30 a.m. seven days a week and features drink specials and a range of music including hip-hop, latin, R&B, rock, and dance hall.

Spin
10 South Fifth Street, Minneapolis
(612) 333-5055
www.spinmn.com
In Minneapolis's hip Warehouse District, this place is designed for people to see and be seen—and to dance. The sound and the lighting are state-of-the-art amazing, and the ambience can't be beat. There are 40-foot ceilings, a 20-foot water wall, blasts of fog, and the bathrooms—you must visit the bathrooms, where plasma screens perch above the urinals and the stall doors are clear glass that turn opaque when they are closed. Spin's annual November Studio 54 party is totally hot and totally 1970s. The club is open Thursday through Sunday from 9:00 p.m. to 2:00 a.m. Watch for nightly specials, and be aware that the dress code is enforced.

FOLK, IRISH, AND ACOUSTIC MUSIC
Minneapolis

Cedar Cultural Center
416 Cedar Avenue South, Minneapolis
(612) 338-2674
www.thecedar.org
The Cedar Cultural Center is an absolutely amazing place to see musicians perform. The auditorium is designed specifically for listening to music, with beautiful hardwood floors, a large raised stage in the front, excellent acoustics, and a soundman who actually pays attention to musicians' cues. Exciting acts perform at this venue, from traditional Irish bands to folk duos to world-famous acoustic soloists such as Pierre Bensusan and Didier Malherbe. The Cedar is also the home of the annual Nordic Roots festival, a three-day-long event that features elemental, contemporary, and experimental groups from the Nordic countries. The refreshment bar is worth noting, too—this establishment includes cheap, good beer on tap, wine, homemade cookies, and Indian samosas on the menu.

Jitters at the Times
205 Hennepin Avenue East, Minneapolis
(612) 617-1111
Northeast Minneapolis's Jitters features live shows Thursday through Saturday, as well as 99-cent Comedy Night on Wednesday. The decor is interesting; the walls are made of metal siding and silver paint; the couches are covered in red velvet fabric; the tables are small, art deco affairs set with roses in mismatched vases; and the lighting is provided by metal lamps that look as though they were stolen from the Renaissance Faire. There's no admission charge, the beer is cheap, and the music is free. Jitters is closed Sunday and Monday.

Kieran's Irish Pub & Restaurant
330 Second Avenue South, Minneapolis
(612) 339-4499
www.kierans.com
One of the few Irish bars in Minneapolis, Kieran's has a full bar and an excellent menu that includes traditional Irish foods like lamb stew and pot roast with Guinness gravy. The bar usually has live Irish and folk music playing on two different stages Friday and Saturday nights and infrequently during the week, with the occasional open-mike night and scheduled poetry readings on the smaller stage. During the summer, Kieran's sets up an outside bar and lots of tables for clients, with

Care for a Drink?

"Bar time" in Minnesota is 2:00 a.m. although many bars close earlier. Some bars and restaurants, such as First Avenue and Figlio, stay open later but do not continue to serve alcohol. Liquor stores in the Twin Cities can be open from 8:00 a.m. to 8:00 p.m. Monday through Thursday and until 10:00 p.m. Friday and Saturday, as well as on July 3 and New Year's Eve. Liquor stores are closed on Sunday, although some convenience stores sell 3.2 beer on Sunday.

the occasional live band set up outside to serenade both patrons and random passersby.

O'Donovan's Irish Pub
700 First Avenue North, Minneapolis
(612) 317-8896
www.odonovans.com
O'Donovan's is a nice addition to the small Twin Cities Irish pub scene. Unlike the Dubliner Pub or Kieran's Irish Pub, O'Donovan's authenticity to all that is Irish is mostly left to the beautiful decor. The pub was actually built in Ireland and shipped to the Twin Cities in pieces. O'Donovan's draws a young, collegiate crowd, who enjoy the pub's live music selection, which often includes top-40 hits. Location is a prime asset for O'Donovan's—the Target Center and First Avenue/Seventh Street Entry are directly across the street.

St. Paul

The Dubliner Pub
2162 University Avenue West, St. Paul
(651) 646-5551
The Dubliner Pub is an old-style Irish theme bar for its working-class industrial location. The cozy, box-shaped pub is painted green and has a beautiful long bar, where Irish, English, and domestic beers are on tap. There is also a small stage for Irish music on the weekends as well as darts and free popcorn.

Half Time Rec
1013 Front Avenue, St. Paul
(651) 488-8245
www.halftimerec.com
The Half Time Rec is an authentic neighborhood Irish bar that attracts large crowds on the weekends for its live Irish music, numerous ales and stouts on tap, and boccie court in the basement. It features a long, U-shaped bar and an adjoining room with a stage for music Tuesday through Saturday (the show is free Tuesday through Thursday). At the Half Time Rec, patrons vociferously have fun. They frequently sing along with the music or get up and dance to the jig-inspiring Irish music. The Half Time Rec is a few miles from the major thoroughfares, but it is well worth the effort.

GAY BARS

Gay Nineties Theatre Cafe & Bar
408 Hennepin Avenue, Minneapolis
(612) 333-7755
www.gay90s.com
The state's largest gay club, the Gay Nineties features a six-night-a-week (none on Monday) drag show at the La Femme Show Lounge on the second floor. The club has a dedicated straight following as well, who come for the strong mixed drinks and the excellent dance music with no cover charged—Friday and Saturday nights are packed, and there's nearly always a line to get inside. The club has nine different bars on the premises, two discos, a supper club, male strippers, and a game room.

The Saloon
830 Hennepin Avenue, Minneapolis
(612) 332-0835
www.gaympls.com
The Saloon is one of the most popular bars and dance clubs for Twin Cities gay men, featuring a large, dark dance floor with plenty of loud music and a large bar in the back for socializing and imbibing. The Saloon has various themes for the days of the week, including Hard Mondays (hard rock, industrial, and Goth music) and Boys Night Out on Thursdays

(18+ are allowed in), as well as DJs on the weekends.

JAZZ, BLUES, AND R&B
Minneapolis

Bunker's Music Bar & Grill
761 Washington Avenue North, Minneapolis
(612) 338-8188
www.bunkersmusic.com
A popular lunch spot serving soups and sandwiches during the day, this neighborhood bar turns into a blues and rock club at night. The acts booked range from alternative rock bands to blues, R&B, and jazz acts. The cover charge is pretty low—usually under $6—and there are also pool tables and video games.

The Dakota Bar & Grill
1010 Nicollet Avenue, Minneapolis
(612) 332-1010
www.dakotacooks.com
At least once a week, a national headlining jazz act comes through town to play at this club, and while the ticket prices are high (usually around $30) for the area, jazz fans will definitely get their money's worth. The cuisine served is elegant and as improvisational as the music: Caribbean seasoned prime rib of pork, Hawaiian line-caught snapper, and Tabasco-molasses glazed New York strip steak. There's an extensive wine list, a full bar, and a happy hour Monday through Friday from 4:00 to 6:00 p.m. Lighter fare is served in the jazz club.

Famous Dave's BBQ & Blues
3001 Hennepin Avenue South
(Calhoun Square), Minneapolis
(612) 822-9900
www.famousdaves.com
Not only does Famous Dave's have some of the best barbecue ribs and fried catfish in the Twin Cities (especially for a chain restaurant), the Uptown branch also books some of the rawest blues in the area. Bands perform after 9:00 most nights of the week, giving parents time to feed their kids and drop them off at

the sitter's before coming back to sit in on blues sessions. The music is free, and the drinks are reasonably priced.

Sophia
65 Southeast Main Street, Minneapolis
(612) 379-1111
Located right next to the Mississippi River in St. Anthony Main, Sophia serves a wide selection of fairly expensive dishes and has a full bar. Starting around 8:00 almost every night, local jazz acts take the small stage set near the bar and play until closing. There's no cover charge for the music, although there is a two-drink minimum after 9:00 p.m. Nominated by local papers time and again for the best romantic restaurant and best jazz club in Minneapolis, this is an excellent place to take a date you want to impress.

St. Paul

Artists' Quarter
408 St. Peter Street, St. Paul
(651) 292-1359
www.mnjazz.com
The Artists' Quarter's acoustics are great in its small basement space, the stage is big enough to hold a full piano and an accompanying band, and the bar serves cheap tap beer as well as wine and liquor. Primarily a haven for local jazz artists but occasionally featuring a national act, the club is a great place to stop by late at night to unwind—the bartenders are friendly, the cover charge is usually under $5 during the week, and most of the bands that play here are a lot of fun.

LOUNGES, PUBS, AND BREWPUBS
Minneapolis

Brit's Pub & Eating Establishment
1110 Nicollet Mall, Minneapolis
(612) 332-3908
www.britspub.com
This upscale downtown bar is almost always packed on weekends, usually with drinking-

age kids from college or graduate school. The main room is lavishly furnished with mock-Georgian lounges and armchairs as well as beautiful wooden bar stools set next to tables and wall outcroppings to set your beer on throughout the room. During summer Brit's opens its rooftop patio for outdoor libations surrounded by Minneapolis's skyscrapers. You can also watch lawn bowlers practicing their avocation on the rooftop grassy field, the only elevated lawn bowling field in the country. When there is open lawn bowling on the weekends, you can attempt to roll your "bowl" as close as possible to the "jack"—for a small fee. Groups can reserve the green—for a much larger fee—several afternoons and evenings during the week. Brit's is located on Nicollet Mall (buses only) across from Orchestra Hall.

Chatterbox Pub
2229 East 35th Street, Minneapolis
(612) 728-9871

800 Cleveland Avenue S, St. Paul
(651) 699-1154
www.chatterboxpub.net
This bar's big claim to fame is the huge collection of Atari, Nintendo, and Sega Genesis video games available for customers. The bar also makes available vintage board games such as Connect 4 and Yahtzee. If you're hungry in addition to wanting to play games and drink intoxicating beverages, the Chatterbox serves breakfast (St. Paul location only), lunch, several full entree dinners, burgers, and pizza.

Gluek's Restaurant & Bar
16 North Sixth Street, Minneapolis
(612) 338-6621
www.glueks.com
Gluek's is Minneapolis's original brewpub. Since 1902 Gluek's has served Minneapolis with its tasty beer. Located in the historic Warehouse District, Gluek's draws huge crowds with its brew, other domestic and foreign beers, and liquors. Gluek's is across the

street from the Target Center, home of the Minnesota Timberwolves and Minnesota Lynx, and within walking distance of the shops of downtown Minneapolis.

The Herkimer Pub & Brewery
2922 Lyndale Avenue South, Minneapolis
(612) 821-0101
www.theherkimer.com
The Herkimer Pub & Brewery offers a large selection of freshly made beers. Despite its location in the trendy Lyn-Lake neighborhood, the beers made in-house cost less than a bottle of domestic. Each day there are different "Today's Brews" written on a chalkboard, including light lagers and heavier dunkels (German for dark). The Herkimer also serves food and appetizers (burgers, sandwiches, fish and chips, etc.) until midnight.

Lyle's Bar and Restaurant
2021 Hennepin Avenue South, Minneapolis
(612) 870-8183
www.liquorlyles.com
On the edge of Uptown, one would think that Liquor Lyle's, as most area residents call this establishment, would tend toward a hipster crowd. But this neighborhood watering hole attracts everyone from construction workers to artists to its somewhat smudgy, dated-yet-colorful ambience. The booths have vinyl seats, the men's restrooms have trough urinals, and the bouncer is big and hairy; but if you want to share a pitcher of beer and a basket of deep-fried cheese curds with a friend on a day when you haven't taken a shower, Lyle's is hard to beat.

MacKenzie
918 Hennepin Avenue, Minneapolis
(612) 333-7268
www.mackenziepub.com
MacKenzie specializes in Scottish beers and liquors but also has a large selection of American libations, all at reasonable prices. The inside of the bar is decorated with Scottish decor and theater posters on lots of beautiful

The Herkimer Pub & Brewery on Lyndale Avenue South in Minneapolis. TODD R. BERGER

exposed brick. Located next to the historic Orpheum Theatre and within walking distance of several others, MacKenzie is a great stop before or after Hennepin Avenue theater events. The bar has five TVs and shows NFL games whenever one is broadcast.

Mario's Keller Bar
2300 University Avenue NE, Minneapolis
(612) 781-3860
www.gasthofzg.com
Mario's Keller Bar occupies the large and comfortable basement of the Gasthof zur Gemütlichkeit Restaurant. A festive atmosphere overtakes the club, especially on weekends, when fraternity members pack the dance floor and consume massive quantities of beer, which comes as no surprise, considering the excellent selection of German beers on tap and available by the glass, pint, or enormous glass boot. Connoisseurs of German beers will enjoy the bar's selection, which runs

a bit pricey, while many others will revel in the raucous German beer-hall atmosphere.

Triple Rock Social Club
629 Cedar Avenue South, Minneapolis
(612) 333-7499
www.triplerocksocialclub.com
The Triple Rock Social Club is the punk rock bar and restaurant of the Twin Cities. It is owned by Erik Funk, a member of legendary local punk band Dillinger 4. The jukebox is particularly interesting—filled with a surprisingly eclectic range of music, from punk to R&B to metal—patrons' selections never cease to amaze and create an interesting atmosphere. Also of note is the wide selection of beers on tap, a dozen at last count. The Triple Rock's menu contains sandwiches, salads, burgers, and one of the Twin Cities' largest selections of vegetarian and vegan items.

The Summit Brewing Company

The Summit Brewing Company (901 Montreal Circle, 651-265-7800, www.summitbrewing.com) of St. Paul brews some of the finest microbrews around, and most Cities bars and restaurants have at least one Summit beer on tap. The brewery makes Extra Pale Ale, Pilsener, India Pale Ale, ESB, and Porter year-round and seasonal varieties such as Maibock and Winter Ale. The brewery offers tours Tuesday, Thursday, and Saturday at 1:00 p.m. (tours are free, but reservations are required on Saturday).

Whitey's World Famous Saloon
400 Hennepin Avenue East, Minneapolis
(612) 623-9478
Geared somewhat to the college crowd, Whitey's is a neighborhood bar that has weekend specials on Jägermeister shots and about half a dozen domestic and locally brewed beers on tap. The interior is beautiful—the bar is an elegant, curved length of carved wood surrounded by high-backed stools, and in summertime patrons can sit inside the bar or at the tables set outside on the fenced-in patio.

St. Paul

Great Waters Brewing Company
426 St. Peter Street, St. Paul
(651) 224-2739
www.greatwatersbc.com
Great Waters Brewing Company serves flavorful microbrews from its location inside downtown St. Paul's Hamm Building. The brewpub's beers include cask-conditioned ales, served at cellar temperature of 52 degrees F and "hand pulled" from casks in the basement, and pushed beers, which are served at 38 degrees F, similar to other tap beers in the United States. Beers include the Saint Peter Pale Ale, Flying Circus Big Hop Ale, the Knights Who Say "Nee" ESB, and the "Jumby," the latter brewed with wildflower honey, ginger root, and orange peel. Great Waters also brews its own root beer and has an outdoor patio and full menu, featuring several pastas, grilled duck breast, jambalaya, and a top-notch London broil.

O'Gara's Bar & Grill
164 Snelling Avenue North, St. Paul
(651) 644-3333
www.ogaras.com
O'Gara's features a brewpub with several of its own beers, some of which are seasonal; a few specialty brews include Sligo Red, Oktoberfest, Light Amber Ale, and, for more adventurous beer connoisseurs, selections such as Dublin Apricot Wheat, which includes a subtle hint of apricot. If you're sitting in O'Gara's sipping a beer and wondering why there's an entire wall dedicated to the late Peanuts cartoon creator, Charles Schulz, it would be helpful to know that Schulz grew up in one of the apartments above O'Gara's, and his father also worked at a barbershop that today is part of O'Gara's Bar.

Sweeney's Saloon
96 North Dale Street, St. Paul
(651) 221-9157
www.sweeneyssaloon.com
Sweeney's is a local pub with beautiful woodwork and a secluded (though usually packed) patio bar open during the summer. With many excellent beers on tap, lots of booths, and a pub-food menu, Sweeney's attracts young, cute singles and attached (or not) 30-somethings looking for a pint or a pitcher.

MOVIE THEATERS
Minneapolis

Asian Media Access
3028 Oregon Avenue South, Minneapolis
(612) 376-7715
www.amamedia.org

Asian Media Access specializes in the best of Asian cinema from the present and the past. Lacking a theater of its own, the organization rents two local theaters (Riverview and Oak Street) on a regular basis for screenings. Asian Media Access provides action-packed Hong Kong cinema, contemporary Japanese film, Chinese comedies, and more. Be sure to call or check the Web site for details about upcoming events.

Bell Auditorium
U of M Campus, 10 Church Street, Minneapolis
(612) 331-3134
www.mnfilmarts.org
Formerly home to the University Film Society, the Bell Auditorium has long been home to off-beat films. Since its inception, the Bell Auditorium has hosted directors and film scholars of the likes of Robert Altman, Jean-Luc Godard, and Roberto Rosellini. The nonprofit Minnesota Film Arts promotes an appreciation for the art of filmmaking through screenings both at Bell Auditorim and at Oak Street Cinema, and through events such as the Minneapolis–St. Paul International Film Festival.

Block E 15
Block E, 600 Hennepin Avenue, Minneapolis
(612) 338-5900
www.kerasotes.com
The only cinema downtown, the Block E 15 inside the Block E shopping and entertainment complex shows first-run movies in full digital sound with stadium seating. Parking in the complex's underground ramp is only $2 for up to three hours.

Lagoon Cinema
1320 Lagoon Avenue, Minneapolis
(612) 825-6006
www.landmarktheatres.com
Lagoon Cinema is part of Landmark's national art theater chain. Arty, indie, and a few foreign hits are often held over at the Lagoon after playing at its sister theater a couple blocks away, the Uptown. The Lagoon screens smaller-budget films for a longer duration and

others that would not otherwise have been shown. The five theaters in this multiplex are roomy and comfortable, with excellent sound and large movie screens.

Oak Street Cinema
309 Southeast Oak Street, Minneapolis
(612) 331-3134
www.mnfilmarts.org
Oak Street Cinema is the only Twin Cities theater dedicated to classic film revivals. Occasionally new films from famous directors or student films are shown, but beyond that Oak Street Cinema sticks to reviving cinema's illustrious as well as forgotten past. Schedules have included great films of the 1970s, the French New Wave, and the films of directors such as Tarkovsky, Bergman, Mel Brooks, Bunuel, and a host of others. Thematic scheduling such as the best of vampire films or silent films is common. Oak Street Cinema is one of the Twin Cities great artistic treasures. This is one of two venues for Minnesota Film Arts, a nonprofit organization that seeks to foster an appreciation for the art of filmmaking through screenings.

Parkway Theater
4814 Chicago Avenue South, Minneapolis
(612) 822-3030
One of the few one-screen theaters surviving in the Twin Cities, this south Minneapolis theater has a knack for consistently showing the best of second-run indie and mainstream films. Despite the Parkway's less than spectacular ambience, this old mom-and-pop theater more than makes up for it in value. Ticket prices are low, and concession prices are a steal. If you are curious about what is playing at the Parkway, give the theater a call; the message on the answering machine is always homey and interesting.

Riverview Theater
3800 42nd Avenue South, Minneapolis
(612) 729-7369
www.riverviewtheater.com
The Riverview Theater presents second-run

Close-up

The Heights

Once considered an eyesore in an already rundown part of town, the Heights Theatre has been reborn as the centerpiece of a cultural revolution in the Columbia Heights suburb of Minneapolis. Under the guidance of proprietors Tom Letness and Dave Holmgren, who bought the theater in 1998 and funded the renovation with profits from the Dairy Queen franchise they own right next door, the tacky turquoise aluminum siding facade was stripped to reveal the beautiful brickwork underneath. Inside, the garish green walls were replaced with red velvet drapes and a deep purple coat of paint. The sound system and projectors were replaced with up-to-date equipment as well as an antiquated 70mm projector. With this new hardware it's now possible for the Heights to screen silent Frank Capra classics, the original 70mm prints of *Lawrence of Arabia,* and an amazing selection of Bollywood Hindi-language action films that have packed the 410-seat theater to capacity on a regular basis. They put in a restored Wurlitzer theater organ, and classic silent films now have the live organ accompaniment they did when they were first screened.

Aside from the wide selection of art house, classic, and foreign films it shows, the Heights holds special, irregularly scheduled events where independent filmmakers passing through town come into the theater to speak about their work and sign autographs. In 2000 Lloyd Kaufman of Troma Films stopped in on his way to the Sundance Film Festival to lecture, sign copies of his book about the history of his company, and give out free T-shirts and video copies of his movies to audience members. The event was accompanied by a weeklong

movies in one of the Cities' most beautiful theaters. The Riverview is a fine example of art deco architecture and furnishings. The lobby is of particular distinction—appearing today as it probably did 50 years ago—decorated with art deco lamps and sofas.

Films screened at the Riverview are usually popular second-run films. There are occasional deviations. *The Wizard of Oz* and other cinema classics have been shown at this Minneapolis gem. Prices for tickets are a bargain ($3 for most evening shows; $2 for matinees), and concessions are much cheaper than at the suburban multiplexes, especially if you purchase a combo.

St. Anthony Main Theatre
115 Southeast Main Street, Minneapolis
(612) 331-4723
This theater is in Minneapolis's beautiful St. Anthony area. It is also within walking distance of Nicollet Island and the Stone Arch Bridge and across the river from downtown Minneapolis. St. Anthony Main Theatre has much more charm than your average suburban multiplex. The individual theaters and seating are comfortable and the concessions comparable to other theaters in town. Go for a walk and enjoy the grandeur and the sights of downtown and St. Anthony, then stop by the theater for a movie.

film retrospective of Troma classics. The Heights also hosts the Minnesota Film Festival in conjunction with the area's annual spring Art-A-Whirl gallery tours as well as the annual late summer Minneapolis/St. Paul International Film Festival. All during the holiday season (starting with Halloween), holiday-specific classics and new films are shown.

The neighborhood the Heights is nestled in has undergone a similar reawakening. With the influx of immigrants coming into the Twin Cities metro areas, everything from Balkan coffee shops serving Bosnian foods to Middle Eastern restaurants and grocery stores have taken root and blossomed in northeast Minneapolis. Gone are the days when the main sources of entertainment were tiny diners and bowling alleys huddled in the shadows of the giant cereal factories and industrial warehouses—northeast Minneapolis today is a true, working melting pot of customs and cultures.

Despite being an art house theater on par with those in uptown Minneapolis, the Heights retains its everyman's appeal. With its more-than-reasonable door prices (usually $5 per adult), cheap concessions, and free street parking, the Heights has managed to keep itself accessible to the working-class Columbia Heights neighborhood, which only recently started having coffee shops that were more than greasy spoons. The Heights doesn't pretend to be a highbrow establishment, either. It mixes black-and-white horror and science fiction classics with popular second-run films and true art films. The theater has a loyal core crowd of locals who show up to see everything it runs, and, depending on what's on for the night, the rest of the audience comes from every imaginable walk of life to the suburban theater.

Suburban World Theatre
3022 Hennepin Avenue South, Minneapolis
(612) 822-9000
www.suburbanworldtheatre.com
The historic Suburban World Theater was renovated into a one-screen cinema and restaurant. The menu includes the usual burgers and pizza as well as wraps, salads, tapas, and sandwiches, plus wine and beer—all served during shows.

The Suburban World first opened in 1927 as the Granada Theatre. It was and is an example of Spanish-Moorish architecture, adorned with stucco facades of balconies, plants, and statues. The combination of the food and the architecture makes this an interesting place to see a revival or second-run film. The theater also hosts special television sports events, concerts, and live performances.

Uptown Theatre
2906 Hennepin Avenue South, Minneapolis
(612) 825-6006
The Uptown Theatre features art and indie cinema debuts. Films frequently are screened exclusively at the Uptown, owned by Landmark Theatres before moving a block away to Landmark's Lagoon Cinema and farther afield to suburban theaters.

In the heart of Minneapolis's hip Uptown neighborhood, the Uptown Theatre is a stunning piece of architecture. Since the 1930s it has been the best single-screen theater in the area, in part because of its size—as large as most of the suburban multiplexes. The balcony is huge and the seating is comfortable. The Uptown Theatre remains one of the most enjoyable movie venues in the Twin Cities.

St. Paul

Grandview Theater
1830 Grand Avenue, St. Paul
(651) 698-3344

Two neighborhood theaters showing first-run movies survive in St. Paul, and the Grandview, opened in 1933, lives on at its Grand Avenue location near Macalester College and the University of St. Thomas. The theater has two screens, a large theater downstairs and a smaller room upstairs (originally the theater's balcony). Designed in the art moderne style, the classic theater is a neighborhood treasure. Today part of the Mann Theatres chain, the Grandview shows first-run movies.

Highland Theater
760 Cleveland Avenue South, St. Paul
(651) 698-3085

This 1938 art deco theater in St. Paul's Highland Park neighborhood shows first-run movies (like the Grandview, the Highland is owned by the Mann Theatres chain). Competition from suburban megacomplexes has hit many one- and two-screen cinemas in the Cities hard over the years. The Highland is a holdover from another era.

The Suburbs

AMC Mall of America 14
401 South Avenue, Mall of America,
60 East Broadway, Bloomington
(952) 851-0074

A megaplex inside the MegaMall, the AMC Mall of America 14 has large and comfortable theaters with huge screens and clear sound. AMC Mall of America occasionally is the site for local and even national premieres as well as quirky bookings. The "Terror at the Mall" Halloween series is one great example, when recent and classic horror films were shown at midnight during the month of October. If you like the Mall of America, you'll like this megaplex.

Heights Theatre
3951 Central Avenue NE, Columbia Heights
(763) 788-9079
www.heightstheater.com

Once a dilapidated theater, the Heights was transformed into one of the most beautiful theaters in the Twin Cities when the inside and outside were painted, comfortable new seats installed, and a vintage theater organ put in place. The organ allows silent film classics to be scored for the audience's pleasure.

Besides occasional silent film revivals, the Heights books second-run and classic films as well as special events such as Tromafest, a festival dedicated to the kitschy horror of Troma Studios (see "The Heights" close-up). For adventurous film lovers the Heights is one of the most interesting movie theaters in the Twin Cities.

Regal Brooklyn Center Stadium 20
6420 Camden Avenue North
(763) 560-6300
www.regalcinemas.com

The gigantic Brooklyn Center Stadium 20 theater megaplex offers stadium seating, high-back adjustable chairs, digital sound in all of its theaters, and, obviously, many film choices. Despite its size, Regal feels more comfortable due to its design, which includes larger individual theaters decorated with minimalistic murals. The complex includes a cafe stocked with coffees and ice creams and a video arcade.

Roseville 4 Theatres
1211 Larpenteur Avenue West, Roseville
(651) 488-4242

Roseville 4 shows all the Hollywood blockbuster hits—and does it for cheap. Tuesday night tickets are only $1, and concessions are reasonably priced. These bargains make Roseville 4 a perennially favorite hangout for teens in the Twin Cities. The theater is located near the busy Roseville shopping area.

Showplace 16 Theatres
5567 Bishop Avenue, Inver Grove Heights
(651) 453-1916
www.kerasotes.com
One of the first mammoth megaplexes in the Twin Cities, Showplace 16 Theatres offers some of the largest movie screens in the area and comfortable stadium seating.

SPORTS BARS

Minneapolis

Big Ten Restaurant & Bar
606 Washington Avenue SE, Minneapolis
(612) 378-0467

1106 Main Street, Hopkins
(952) 930-0369

1045 Frontage Road, Owatonna
(507) 451-2090
www.big10restaurant.com
The Big Ten Restaurant & Bar is a University of Minnesota institution, known both for good subs and for covering Minnesota Golden Gophers athletics. The Washington Avenue restaurant and bar is filled with memorabilia from Gophers sports; included are numerous autographed photos of triumphs in football, basketball, and hockey. For atmosphere alone, this is the place to catch a Gophers game, not to mention the beer and the excellent bar food. The Big 10 has expanded to the suburbs, with locations in Hopkins and Owatonna.

City Billiards Bar & Cafe
25 North Fourth Street, Minneapolis
(612) 338-2255
City Billiards is the pool hall for downtown Minneapolis. Though smaller than its suburban counterparts, it has the advantage of being situated in the shadows of Minneapolis's skyline. Available at City Billiards are beer, sandwiches, and pizza. The prices are reasonable for the normally pricey Warehouse District, and specials are available for pool, food, and drinks.

Dubs Pub & Grill
412 14th Avenue SE, Minneapolis
(612) 331-4111
Over the years this has been the site of numerous restaurants, bars, and grills. All have served as a principal watering hole for the student population of the University of Minnesota. Dubs is a popular place to watch Minnesota Golden Gophers basketball, football, and hockey games. The big-screen television and the cheap burgers and subs are also big draws.

William's Uptown Pub & Peanut Bar
2911 Hennepin Avenue South, Minneapolis
(612) 823-6271
If you are looking for variety in domestic and imported beers, William's is the place. This Uptown establishment boasts more than 300 different bottled beers from around the world, including Russia, Thailand, Africa, Finland, and Greece. An additional 70+ beers are on tap. In addition, William's offers plenty of daily specials on domestic beers and appetizers. William's is divided into a pub on the first floor and a more casual peanut bar in the basement where, not surprisingly, peanuts and popcorn are complimentary. Despite the sophisticated beer selection, the clientele at William's is mostly the young Uptown set, who enjoy the billiards and darts available on both floors.

St. Paul

Billy's on Grand
857 Grand Avenue, St. Paul
(651) 292-9140
www.billysongrand.com
The rooms at Billy's on Grand provide unlimited possibilities, from sports bar to lodge to patio seating in the summer. The bar features 29 TVs, including 2 big screens and 6 plasma screens. Also available is a full menu, which includes burgers and prime rib. Billy's is extremely busy on weekends.

Tom Reid's Hockey City Pub
258 West Seventh Street, St. Paul
(651) 292-9916

The name of this pub says it all. Hockey returned to Minnesota in 2000 at the Xcel Energy Center in St. Paul; in its wake, many new bars and restaurants have sprung up. And who better to open a pub than Tom Reid, a former National Hockey League player with the Minnesota North Stars (now the Dallas Stars) and current Minnesota Wild broadcaster? Not only does the pub broadcast the game on television screens, but it also hosts a radio pregame on KFAN, the local sports radio station.

The Suburbs

Biff's Sports Bar & Grill
7777 NE Minnesota Highway 65,
Spring Lake Park
(763) 784-9446

Biff's provides inexpensive pool, darts, food, and sports viewing for the northern suburbs. Televisions range in size from big to bigger screens at Biffs, where you can watch all your Vikings game-day action. Besides the sports bar there are more than 25 pool tables, where suburbanites play in organized pool leagues and enjoy the many beer specials at Biffs.

Billiard Street Café/Two Stooges Bar & Grill
7178 University Avenue NE, Fridley
(763) 574-1399
www.billiardstreet.com

Since 1988 Billiard Street Café has served as a pool hall with a cafe and a proshop, and in 2005 it added the Two Stooges Bar & Grill. It is inconspicuously located in a strip mall; despite this, it is one of Minnesota's largest billiard clubs, with more than 40 pool tables. In-house nine-ball leagues make the Billiard Street Café busy, and it is sometimes difficult to reserve a table on weekday evenings, although they are usually available after a

wait. The late night/early morning hours also provide ample opportunity for billiards.

Joe Senser's Sports Grill & Bar
2350 Cleveland Avenue, Roseville
(651) 631-1781

4217 American Boulevard West, Bloomington
(952) 835-1191

3010 Eagandale Place, Eagan
(651) 687-9333

16605 County Road 24, Plymouth
(763) 559-1990
www.sensers.com

Joe Senser's Sports Grill & Bar is a popular spot for Minnesota Vikings fans. All four locations feature a ring of big-screen, high-definition TVs encircling the bar, as well as numerous smaller monitors. Joe Senser, a former Minnesota Viking, is the local legend/owner and also participates in a Vikings postgame show, *Vikings Unsensored* (on sports radio station KFAN), after each game. In addition, Senser's features college football and basketball, as well as professional basketball, baseball, and hockey. Offering a wide selection of beers, Senser's also has plenty of food to accompany the suds.

Park Tavern
3401 Louisiana Avenue, St. Louis Park
(952) 929-6810
www.parktavern.com

The Park Tavern is one of the Twin Cities' premier sports bars. Twin Citians come in hordes to watch sports on the big-screen televisions and enjoy the kitchen's excellent food. This is where Park Tavern has the competition beat. Many other sports bars treat the food as secondary, but the Park Tavern excels, with delicious burgers and sandwiches, not the everyday bar fare. Plus it has some of the best beer specials in town during Vikings games.

UNIQUE TO THE TWIN CITIES

Grumpy's Downtown
1111 Washington Avenue South, Minneapolis
(612) 340-9738
www.grumpysbar.com/downtown.html
Although Grumpy's looks kind of divey from the outside, it is an interesting bar to check out. Intermittently, tables are moved around to make way for performance artists, poets, and acoustic and electric bands to set up in one corner, or a movie screen and projector are brought in and art house films, black-and-white classics, and new films from local film-makers are showcased, including those from those ex-Minnesotans, the Coen brothers. There are several pool tables and an ATM on the premises. About a dozen beers are on tap and a decent selection of food on the menu—especially for a bar—and the waitstaff is attentive and friendly.

Nye's Polonaise Room
112 Hennepin Avenue East, Minneapolis
(612) 379-2021
www.nyespolonaise.com
Now this is a fun place to drink. Nye's, a St. Anthony tradition since 1949, features live polka music in one half of the bar and a piano bar on the other side, and everyone comes here to dance. The crowd is about as mixed as you can get, with senior citizens manning the accordions in the band and barely 21-year-old hipsters hopping on the dance floor. The bar looks much the same as it did when it first opened, with scarlet walls and carpets and dark, polished wood accents everywhere. The bar serves Polish and American food that's good enough to come in for even if you don't want to polka.

SHOPPING

"Shopping trip" means so many different things when in the Twin Cities. It could mean a sunny, summer walk down picturesque Grand Avenue in St. Paul, where beautiful two-story Victorian houses have been converted into antiques shops, custom clothiers, or flower shops with multihued wares spilling out onto the sidewalk. It could mean window-shopping in busy downtown Minneapolis, where importers, clothiers, and jewelers have set up shop in the ornate storefronts of 100-plus-year-old buildings. It could mean braving the immense Mall of America, the largest indoor mall in the country.

But whatever "shopping trip" means to you, you're sure to find satisfaction shopping in the Twin Cities. There are tiny neighborhood shops, heady metropolitan areas, and suburban malls that carry everything from sports to celebrity memorabilia; specialty grocery complexes that sell novelty items and foods from around the world; and stores that carry everything you'd ever need to have a successful and beautiful wedding, professional social event, or child's theme birthday party. Here is a taste of what the Twin Cities has to offer the independently wealthy, those with plenty of revolving credit, and teenagers with ready access to Mom and Dad's money.

ANTIQUES SHOPS

Minneapolis

City Salvage and Antiques
505 First Avenue NE, Minneapolis
(612) 627-9107
citysalvage.squarespace.com
Mantels, archways, buffets, stained glass, and other high-end items salvaged from pre-1950s

buildings fill this architectural-salvage store. The changing inventory has at times included Charlie the Tuna lamps, a full pub complete with booths, and church pews. Owner John Eckley has more than two decades' experience in architectural salvage.

St. Paul

Wescott Station Antiques
226 West Seventh Street, St. Paul
(651) 227-2469
Wescott Station Antiques is a family-run business offering seven rooms full of antique furniture, glassware, lamps, and more. Literally thousands of antiques and collectibles line the walls of this tightly packed store, making a visit here as much a treasure hunt as it is a shopping spree.

West

Battlefield Military Antiques
3915 Minnesota Highway 7, St. Louis Park
(952) 920-3820
www.battlefieldstore.com
Battlefield Military Antiques is absolutely packed with war memorabilia, including rows and rows of books, magazines, and unopened boxes of model soldiers, frontiersmen, warplanes, and boats. The books, new and used, cover every era of combat from Hadrian's Wall to Vietnam, in incredible levels of both technical and strategic detail. What catches the eye first, though, are the neatly racked and displayed antiques: a clothing store's worth of old uniforms, helmets worn by both good guys and bad guys, blue and green caps topping the shelves in perfect rows, ribbons, and medals. Collectors will also appreciate the selection of limited-edition G.I. Joes.

ℹ️ Most downtown Minneapolis restaurants and stores participate in the "Do the Town" parking program, where a $20 purchase after 4:00 p.m. and all day on weekends will get you a parking validation.

Blake Antiques
901 Main Street, Hopkins
(952) 930-0477
www.carlsonantiques.com
Blake Antiques carries refinished antique furniture ready to bring home and display without even needing to be dusted. The store also carries fine sterling jewelry and flatware, original oil paintings, Oriental rugs, fine porcelain (including unusual arts and crafts–movement designs), pottery, and an eclectic collection of costume and fine jewelry. In 2005, Blake Antiques moved to its current location on Main Street in downtown Hopkins.

BOOKSTORES

Minneapolis

Amazon Bookstore Cooperative
755 Chicago Avenue South, Minneapolis
(612) 821-9630
www.amazonfembks.com
Amazon opened in the late 1960s, making it the oldest independent feminist bookstore in the country. The bookstore in south Minneapolis stocks some 10,000 fiction and nonfiction titles as well as gifts, music, and art all by, for, and about women. The bookstore, which specializes in titles from small feminist presses, is a worker cooperative, and the friendly staff will steer you to titles of interest.

The American Swedish Institute Museum Shop
2600 Park Avenue, Minneapolis
(612) 871-4907
www.americanswedishinst.org
Located inside the beautiful American Swedish Institute building, the Museum Shop sells books, prints, cards, gift items, compact discs, and cassette tapes relating to Sweden and Scandinavia. Titles are available in both English and Swedish.

B H Biermaier's Books
809 Fourth Street SE, Minneapolis
(612) 378-0129
Bill Biermaier has been selling used books from his Minneapolis location for a quarter century and is proud of his success in locating hard-to-find copies of out-of-print or obscure books. Arts, literature, and children's books dominate the store's collection in sheer number, but Biermaier's is a good source for just about any genre of book, including rare and collectors' editions. With ceiling-high stacks and books spilling out into the aisles, this place practically begs you to browse for hours. Finding a specific book can become a daylong challenge, but if you need to get out in a hurry, Bill can find it for you awfully quick.

Big Brain Comics
1027 Washington Avenue South, Minneapolis
(612) 338-4390
This small, well-stocked comic book store focuses more on unusual and underground comic books and magazines than the superhero type that Marvel and DC put out. There are lots of imported comics in the stacks, as well as American independent and collectible comic books.

Book House in Dinkytown
429 14th Avenue SE, Minneapolis
(612) 331-1430
www.bookhouseindinkytown.com
The Book House has been a mainstay of the U of M's Dinkytown area for more than 30 years, carrying used hardcover and softcover books. With more than 150,000 volumes in stock, this store has bookshelves that run from floor to ceiling and has excellent fiction, drama, and poetry sections, not to mention rows and rows of foreign language material and an entire basement level dedicated to scholarly works. Book House buys tons of used books, so it's worth checking back regularly to see what's new in stock.

Close-up

Nicollet Mall

Nicollet Mall is Minneapolis's main artery. The 12-block stretch of stores, restaurants, and hotels between Washington Avenue and Grant Street hums year-round. This is a pedestrian mall—no cars allowed, although Metro buses can drive on the mall. It's all about people here.

In spring, people, after being cooped up all winter, descend from their offices in the Minneapolis skyscrapers and exit the skyways to savor the season on Nicollet Mall. In summer they stroll along the mall, pick up dinner ingredients or flower bouquets at the bustling farmers' market, and eat on streetside patios. In winter it's true that a lot of the action stays indoors, but you can count on the Holidazzle Parades to draw people back out. On cold, snowy days, well-insulated folks line Nicollet Mall up to an hour before the nightly twinkle-lit parades begin, which are held from just after Thanksgiving until Christmas. After each parade, the spectators turn into holiday shoppers flitting in and out of businesses along the parade's mall route.

Visitors and new Twin Cities residents, remember the "no cars allowed" rule. It's easy to get caught up in finding your way around downtown and make a wrong turn onto the mall. Cars were banned from Nicollet Mall in the 1960s as part of a broader plan to keep people shopping in the city. By eliminating cars and adding wide sidewalks, trees, and places to sit, Minneapolis encouraged people to shop, dine, and socialize downtown. The fact that the mall exists today shows that the plan worked.

There's a two-story Target here (the discount store's headquarters are on the mall, too) and name-brand stores await in the stretch's shopping centers: Neiman Marcus, Macy's, Saks, and lots of smaller stores you'd find in any major shopping center. There are a few independent stores here, too—though if that's what you're primarily seeking, you're better off walking a few blocks to the Warehouse District, where storefront rents are cheaper and independents thrive.

In the last few years, city promoters gave the mall a nickname: Restaurant Row. It's easy to see why. One of the coolest things about the mall is that the dining options run the gamut from fancy fusion to basic deli to Irish pub food. As soon as Nicollet crosses Grant Street, on its southwestern end, it changes from Restaurant Row to Eat Street, well established and known for its range of ethnic restaurants.

BookSmart
2919 Hennepin Avenue South, Minneapolis
(612) 823-5612
BookSmart is the place to go to buy cheap used books, with a huge selection of mysteries and a great biography section. Turnover is quick, so if you see something you want in stock, you'd better buy it or someone else will.

Cummings Books
417 14th Avenue SE, Minneapolis
(612) 331-1424
www.cummingsbooks.com
This is a used bookstore for book lovers. The variety of books includes literary criticism, special interest, and Canadian history. If you can't find what you're looking for, Cummings Books's friendly staff can help.

Outdoor dining on Nicollet Mall. GREATER MINNEAPOLIS CONVENTION & VISITORS ASSOCIATION

Activities, too, draw people to Nicollet Mall, and those go beyond the street performers and the biweekly farmers' market. Peavey Plaza, next to Orchestra Hall, has lots of free concerts throughout the summer and a Rockefeller Centeresque ice-skating rink in the winter. Macy's continued the traditions of its predecessor, Dayton's, Minnesota's old school department store born on Nicollet Mall. These include a spectacular garden show every spring and a storybook holiday show each winter, both free, and both Twin Cities family traditions. Branch out just a block or two from the mall and you've got the clubs of the Warehouse District, the theaters of Hennepin Avenue, the events of Target Center, and more.

DreamHaven Books & Comics
912 West Lake Street, Minneapolis
(612) 823-6161
www.dreamhavenbooks.com
In addition to Jupiter-size selections of new and used books, DreamHaven is a dream destination for fans of comic books, Japanese anime, kung fu movies, and everything pop-cultural, from Dr. Who to Asterix. An online catalog and a mail-order service mean that even out-of-state patrons can enjoy Dream-Haven. DreamHaven is also responsible for putting on some of the larger science fiction and fantasy fan conventions in the Twin Cities and holds many in-store science fiction and fantasy author signings.

Lien's Bookstore
507 Hennepin Avenue East, Minneapolis
(612) 362-0763

First editions and rare, out-of-print, and gorgeous art and history volumes live in this picturesque corner-store collection. The store holds 4,000 square feet of books and specializes in European and American history, with a particular emphasis on military books as well as classic literature. If Lien's doesn't have the book you seek, they can track it down for you.

Magus Books & Herbs
1309½ Fourth Street SE, Minneapolis
(612) 379-7669 or (800) 99-MAGUS
www.magusbooks.com

Magus Books sells new books on tai chi, Wicca, magic, tarot, astrology, alchemy, Buddhism, Taoism, midwifery, UFOs, Bibles, and aphrodisiacs, to name a few. The bookstore also sells herbs, candles, incense, scented oils, jewelry, and meditation and New Age tapes and CDs. The informed staff can help you find whatever it is you're looking for.

Paperback Exchange
2227 West 50th Street, Minneapolis
(612) 929-8801
www.paperbackexchange.com

Paperback Exchange carries more than 300,000 used paperback books covering pretty much any subject, from pulp mystery to criticism, depending on what's in their current, quick-turnover stock. You can get a better discount on your book purchase if you bring in paperback books to trade. The store also rents hardcover books for nominal charges, many of which are brand-new and not yet available at local libraries.

Present Moment Books & Herbs
3546 Grand Avenue South, Minneapolis
(612) 824-3157
www.presentmoment.com

A major purveyor of herbs and homeopathic remedies, Present Moment also offers more than 36,000 new and used book titles. Whether your New Age and wellness needs run to *Cooking with Herbs* or *The Spirit of Place: A Workbook for Sacred Alignment,* you'll find it at Present Moment. Their specialties include books on alternative health, world religions, New Age, Wicca, and yoga, as well as women's studies and environmental issues.

St. Martin's Table Bookstore
2001 Riverside Avenue, Minneapolis
(612) 339-3920
www.communityofstmartin.org

St. Martin's Table Bookstore shares a space with St. Martin's Table (see the Restaurants chapter), with racks of books devoted to peace, religion, and social-justice issues. The bookstore holds Friday-night readings and performances September through May. The bookstore is closed during the summer.

Uncle Edgar's Mystery Bookstore/ Uncle Hugo's Science Fiction Bookstore
2864 Chicago Avenue South, Minneapolis
(612) 824-6347 or (612) 824-9984
www.uncleedgar.com, www.unclehugo.com

Specialization is the name of the game for many independent booksellers in these days of giant chain bookstores, but Uncle Edgar's/ Uncle Hugo's was at it long before the trend began in the late 1980s. Uncle Hugo's opened in 1974, and Uncle Edgar's opened in 1980. The two shops merged into one location in south Minneapolis in 1984. With a huge selection of their respective genres, both new and used, they sponsor many author readings every month. Check their Web sites for information about upcoming events.

St. Paul

Common Good Books
165 Western Avenue North, St. Paul
(651) 225-8989
www.commongoodbooks.com

Garrison Keillor has done a lot for Minnesota, and the love the public radio icon has for St. Paul is evident at his bookstore, Common Good Books in the city's Cathedral Hill neighborhood. Until the late 1990s and early 2000s, St. Paul was home to such legendary bookstores as Hungry Mind (later known as Ruminator Books) and Odegaard's, but such independents closed their doors one by one. Suddenly, this well-educated city of colleges, Catholics, and government found itself without an independent bookstore selling new titles. Keillor, a prolific author as well as host of radio's *Prairie Home Companion,* fixed that by opening Common Good Books in November 2006. The 2,200-square-foot store is in the cellar beneath Nina's Coffee Cafe and has plenty of choices, whether you are in the mood for "classic American literature or quality trash," as the store says. Local authors are given emphasis, but the store has all the big-name authors as well. Common Good Books is a delightful bookstore, ideal for leisurely browsing.

Midway Used & Rare Books
1579 University Avenue West, St. Paul
(651) 644–7605
www.midwaybook.com
Midway Books has three stories of used and rare books, including huge pulp fiction and small-press poetry sections. The Web site offers some of the store's stock online, but far more titles are available in their store in St. Paul's Midway neighborhood. In addition to books, the store has a wide selection of vintage comics and magazines.

The Red Balloon Bookshop
891 Grand Avenue, St. Paul
(651) 224-8320
www.redballoonbookshop.com
This spacious bookstore, specializing in educational and fun books for kids, is located in a beautiful converted Victorian house on St. Paul's Grand Avenue. The store carries books, audiobooks, DVDs, and selected toys for young people from birth to junior high age. The store also carries a small section of popular books for adults.The bookstore offers non-profit discounts, takes mail and phone orders, and hosts in-store events featuring children's book authors and educators.

There is no sales tax on clothing in Minnesota.

Sixth Chamber Used Books
1332 Grand Avenue, St. Paul
(651) 690-9463
www.sixthchamber.com
Sixth Chamber Used Books is a well-organized and spacious used book store featuring hardcover and paperback editions in most major categories. Especially notable is the used science fiction and fantasy section, which takes up several ceiling-to-floor shelves in the back of the store. Sixth Chamber holds irregular in-store book signings and author readings.

CLOTHING STORES
Minneapolis
Hubert White
747 Nicollet Mall, IDS Crystal Court, Minneapolis
(612) 339-9200 or (800) 776-3920
www.hubertwhite.com
Hubert White carries brand-name, high-end men's contemporary, casual, and formal wear, including Gran Sasso, Bobby Jones, Scott Barber, Canali, Oxxford, Tallia, and Burberry. The professional staff is helpful in both assisting with selecting purchases and arranging alterations at the last minute.

Lava Lounge
3037 Lyndale Avenue South, Minneapolis
(612) 824-5631
www.lavalounge.com
Lava Lounge's inventory makes it a one-stop shop for club clothes. Beyond the staples—shiny, leathered, glittery, synthetic clothes—it also carries an impressive array of cuffs, handbags, and eyewear, with brand names like Miss Sixty, Betty Blush, and Merc stocked for all seasons. Lava Lounge's annual patio sale occurs during the Lyn-Lake Festival in August, when prices on the store's hip clothes are significantly dropped.

Nate's Clothing Company
27 North Fourth Street, Minneapolis
(612) 333-1401

A fixture in the Minneapolis Warehouse District since 1916, Nate's carries a staggering collection of worsted wool, nubby tweed, and linen suits and shirts. The store carries suits and sportcoats from designers like Bill Blass and Ralph Lauren, and Nate's expert staff can find something sharp and classy for even hard-to-size guys. The store's sales are legendary, so sign up for Nate's mailings for the inside scoop on sale dates.

Top Shelf Clothiers & Consultants
3040 Lyndale Avenue South, Minneapolis
(612) 824-2800
www.topshelfinc.com

Located inside a turn-of-the-20th-century former home, Top Shelf is divided into many small, friendly rooms that are perfect for the personalized business of creating custom clothing. A formal dining room now acts as the library for a collection of the finest offerings of suit, sportcoat, pant, and topcoat materials from the woolen mills of England, Italy, Spain, and the United States. Well-known fabric lines such as Zegna, Loro Piana, Roger La Viale, Scabal, Reda, Barberis, Cerruti, Holland, Sherry, and many others are available for custom designs, including shirts.

St. Paul

C'est Fou Showroom
1128 Grand Avenue, St. Paul
(651) 602-9133

This French boutique–style retail store carries one-of-a-kind and custom-made clothes as well as elegant shoes and eclectic and glamorous jewelry and accessories. The store offers free alterations on all clothes purchased here, with an emphasis on creating a flattering fit for customers. The store displays and sells a rotating stock of artwork and jewelry created by local artists.

Coat of Many Colors
1666 Grand Avenue, St. Paul
(651) 690-5255

This Grand Avenue store specializes in natural fabric women's clothing in a wide range of sizes, as well as jewelry and gifts from around the world. Most of the jewelry is handmade, focusing on sterling silver set with semi-precious stones, bone, seeds, and metals. Coat of Many Colors is a socially and environmentally conscious store that returns 20 percent of its profits to Third World development projects.

Grand Jete
975 Grand Avenue, St. Paul
(651) 227-0331
www.grandjete.com

Grand Jete is a retail store carrying dancewear for children and adults, including dance tights, leotards, and skirts, and ballet, pointe, tap, and jazz shoes in a full range of sizes. The store staff is especially helpful in assisting customers in the selection and proper fit of pointe shoes.

West

Whymsy
3360 Galleria, Edina
(952) 924-4176
www.whymsy.com

Whymsy is a retailer of creative attire and accessories for women, including distinctive one-of-a-kind and limited-edition items. The store is full of brand-name lines of upscale, coordinated women's clothing and accessories, with a focus on elegant casual and special occasion attire for the nontraditional woman.

FARMERS' MARKETS

Aldrich Arena Farmers' Market
1850 White Bear Avenue, Maplewood
(651) 227-8101
www.stpaulfarmersmarket.com
8:00 a.m. to noon Wednesday, May through November.

At the Farm
8880 East Minnesota Highway 5, Waconia
(952) 442-4816
www.atthefarmwaconia.com
10:00 a.m. to 4:30 p.m. daily, Memorial Day
through Halloween.

Axdahl's Garden Farm/Greenhouse
7452 Manning Avenue, Stillwater
(651) 439-2460
www.axdahlfarms.com
Call for hours. Open mid-April to October and
during the Christmas season.

Brooklyn Park Farmers' Market
5600 85th Avenue, Brooklyn Park
(763) 493-8154
www.brooklynpark.org
3:00 p.m to 7:00 p.m. Wednesday, late June to
mid-October.

Burnsville Farmers' Market
Diamondhead Senior Campus, 200 West
Burnsville Parkway, Burnsville (Saturday)
Mary, Mother of the Church,
3333 Cliff Road East, Burnsville (Thursday)
(952) 227–8101
www.stpaulfarmersmarket.com
7:00 a.m. to noon Saturday (June to October),
noon to 5:00 p.m. Thursday (May to October).

Cal's Market and Garden Center
6403 Egan Drive, Savage
(952) 447-5215
www.calsmarketandgardencenter.com
8:00 a.m. to 8:00 p.m. Monday through
Saturday, 10:00 a.m. to 6:00 p.m. Sunday,
year-round.

City of White Bear Lake Farmers' Market
Corner of Minnesota Highway 61 and 4th
Street, White Bear Lake
(651) 429-8566
8:00 a.m. to 1:00 p.m. Friday, late June to late
October.

Excelsior Farmers' Market
16 9th Avenue South, Excelsior
(952) 474-5330
www.excelsioronline.com
2:00 to 6:00 p.m. Thursday, May to October.

Falcon Heights Farmers' Market
2025 Larpenteur Avenue, Falcon Heights
(651) 227-8101
www.stpaulfarmersmarket.com
7:30 a.m. to noon, Tuesday, May to October.

Hopkins Farmers' Market
16 Ninth Avenue South, Hopkins
(952) 936-9458
www.mfma.com
7:30 a.m. to noon Saturday, mid-June
to October.

Jordan Ranch
6400 Upper Afton Road, Woodbury
(651) 738-3422
Call for hours.

Marketfest
4701 Minnesota Highway 61, White Bear Lake
(651) 429-8537
www.marketfest.org
6:00 to 9:00 p.m. Thursday, mid-June to the
end of July.

Mill City Farmers' Market
Chicago Avenue South and 2nd Street
South, Minneapolis
(612) 341-7580
www.millcityfarmersmarket.org
8:00 a.m. to 1:00 p.m Thursday and Saturday,
mid-May to mid-October.

Minneapolis Farmers' Market
312 Lyndale Avenue North, Minneapolis
(612) 333-1737
www.mplsfarmersmarket.com
6:00 a.m. to 1:00 p.m. daily, mid-April to
December 24.

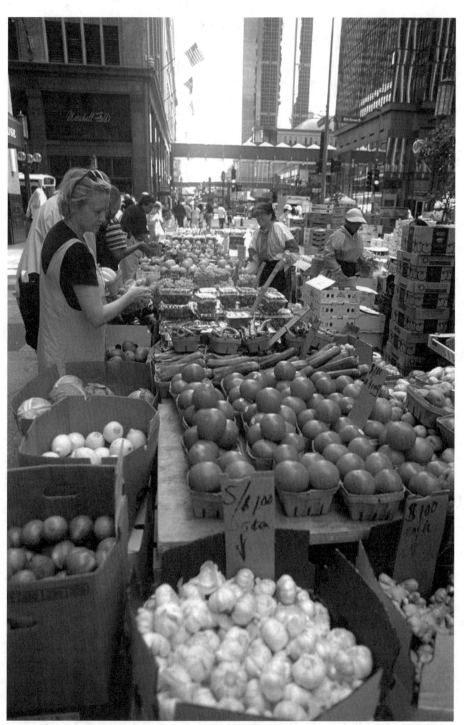

Minneapolis Farmers' Market on Nicollet Mall. GREATER MINNEAPOLIS CONVENTION & VISITORS ASSOCIATION

Minneapolis Farmers' Market on Nicollet Mall
Nicollet Mall between 5th and 12th Street,
Minneapolis
(612) 333-1737
www.mplsfarmersmarket.com
6:00 a.m. to 6:00 p.m. Thursday, mid-April to
early November.

Pahl's Market
6885 West 160th Street, Apple Valley
(952) 431-4345
www.pahls.com
9:00 a.m. to 7:00 p.m. Monday to Saturday,
9:00 a.m. to 6:00 p.m. Sunday, year-round.

Peterson Produce
8910 Minnesota Highway 12, Delano
(763) 972-2052
9:00 a.m. to 7:00 p.m. daily, late April
to October 31.

Richfield Farmers' Market
6335 Portland Avenue South, Richfield
(612) 861-9385
www.richfieldfarmersmarket.org
7:00 a.m. to noon Saturday, May to October.

Seventh Place Mall Farmers' Market
7th Street and Wabasha Street, St. Paul
(651) 227-8101
www.stpaulfarmersmarket.com
10:00 a.m. to 2:00 p.m. Tuesday, mid-June to
September, and Thursday, 10:00 a.m. to 2:00
p.m., mid-June to mid-October.

St. Luke's Farmers' Market
1079 Summit Avenue, St. Paul
(651) 227-8101
www.stpaulfarmersmarket.com
1:15 to 5:00 p.m. Friday, May to October.

St. Paul Downtown Farmers' Market
5th Street and Wall Street, St. Paul
(651) 227-8101
www.stpaulfarmersmarket.com
6:00 a.m. to 1:00 p.m. Saturday, 8:00 a.m. to
1:00 p.m. Sunday, April to November (call for
winter hours).

i Farmers' markets and roadside produce spring up just about everywhere during summer and early fall.
Check for official summer opening dates
and business hours, as they're subject to
change and are dependent on growing
seasons.

West St. Paul–Signal Hills Market
Signal Hills Shopping Center, Butler and
Robert Street, West St. Paul
(651) 227-8101
8:00 a.m. to noon Friday, late June to late
October.

Woodbury Farmers' Market
Central Park/YMCA lot on Radio Drive
Woodbury
(651) 227-8101
www.stpaulfarmersmarket.com
8:00 a.m. to 1:00 p.m. Sunday, July
to October.

FLOWER AND GARDEN SHOPS
Minneapolis
Brown & Greene
4400 Beard Avenue South, Minneapolis
(612) 928-3778
www.bgfloral.net
Brown & Greene floral designer Lyn Williams
has been creating beautiful, nontraditional
arrangements from her historic neighborhood
store since 1989. Her designs are centered
around customers' color choices and feature
unusual flower combinations, like gerberas
and black calla lilies with roses and other
more conventional flowers.

Indulge & Bloom
651 Nicollet Mall, Gaviidae Common,
Minneapolis
(612) 343-0000

701 East Lake Street, Wayzata
(952) 473-2282
www.indulgeandbloom.com
Indulge & Bloom carries beautiful, unusual
flowers and plants from all over the world,

including Ecuadorian roses, orchids, and topiaries. Wedding arrangements are their specialty. The store also features home-decor items, Waterford crystal, bath-and-body products, garden-related items, ornaments, books, cards, truffles, and children's gifts.

St. Paul

Laurel Street Flowers
1129 Grand Avenue, St. Paul
(651) 221-9700
www.laurelstreetflowers.com
Located in a cottage house on historic and picturesque Grand Avenue, this store's arrangements fit perfectly into its surroundings. The shop's guiding style leans to English and French provincial, and typical arrangements include fresh blooms such as tulips and lilies of the valley in spring and summer to boutonnieres shaped as miniature Christmas wreaths for winter weddings. Owner and designer Paula Flom uses a European hand-tie method in her bouquets instead of plastic holders, and her creations often include such unusual choices as mixed fruits in dark colors dripping from centerpieces and viney garlands hanging from chandeliers.

Stems & Vines
917 Grand Avenue, St. Paul
(651) 228-1450

401 Robert Street North, St. Paul
(651) 224-9641

386 West Bernard Street, West St. Paul
(651) 451-9539
www.stemsandvines.com
Stems & Vines designs flower bouquets and events around personalities instead of colors and styles. The store's designers are booked well in advance; it's recommended that reservations be made no later than nine months prior to your event date. Stems & Vines is a sponsor of the Twin Cities Bridal Association and holds exhibitions at every bridal and floral event in town.

GROCERY CO-OPS

The Twin Cities feature one of the highest concentrations of independent food cooperatives in the United States, with stores throughout the Cities and in the suburbs. Co-ops are member (customer) owned and governed, and most specialize in natural, local, and organic foods; environmentally sensitive products; sustainable goods; and bulk whole foods. Some offer membership, which entitles shoppers to discounted prices and a role in the governance of the co-op, and some require members to volunteer a certain number of hours monthly to keep the co-op running. Co-ops are an easy way to buy healthy whole foods in an increasingly megastore culture.

Minneapolis

Eastside Food Co-op
2551 Central Avenue, Minneapolis
(612) 788-0950
www.eastsidefood.coop

Linden Hills Co-op
2813 West 43rd Street, Minneapolis
(612) 922-1159
www.lindenhills.coop

North Country Co-op
1929 South Fifth Street, Minneapolis
(612) 338-3110
www.northcountrycoop.com

Seward Co-op Grocery & Deli
2111 East Franklin Avenue, Minneapolis
(612) 338-2465
www.seward.coop

The Wedge
2105 Lyndale Avenue South, Minneapolis
(612) 871-3993
www.wedge.coop

St. Paul

Mississippi Market Natural Foods Co-op
1810 Randolph Avenue, St. Paul
(651) 690-0507

622 Selby Avenue, St. Paul
(651) 310-9499
www.msmarket.coop

South

Valley Natural Foods
13750 County Road 11, Burnsville
(952) 891-1212
www.valleynaturalfoods.com

East

River Market Community Co-op
221 North Main Street, Stillwater
(651) 439-0366
www.rivermarket.coop

West

Lakewinds Natural Foods
17501 Minnetonka Blvd., Minnetonka
(952) 473-0292

1917 Second Avenue South, Anoka
(763) 427-4340

435 Pond Promenade, Chanhassen
(952) 697-3366
www.lakewinds.coop

HOMEBREWING AND WINEMAKING SUPPLIES

St. Paul

Northern Brewer
1150 Grand Avenue, St. Paul
(651) 291-8849
www.northernbrewer.com
Northern Brewer is the place to go to get everything you need to brew your own beer. It might take a couple of tries to get it right, but for the most part, if you can follow a recipe and careful instructions, you'll be tip-ping a tankard-full of your own brew just a few weeks after a stop at this store. And surprisingly, the prices are about the same or better than buying the equivalents in quality and quantity at a liquor store. All of the equipment you need is here, including carboys, bottling buckets, thermometers, brew kettles and fermentation locks. You can buy things individually or get everything you need in a starter kit. As for the beer ingredient kits, the St. Paul Porter, German Alt, and India Pale Ale are particularly notable. The store also carries many specialty kits, such as Dark Cherry Stout and Peach Wheat, as well as traditional American lagers. If you know what you're doing already, you can buy individual ingredients—including hops, malt extracts, grain malts, and yeast—to craft your own unique brew. Northern Brewer is open daily.

West

Midwest Homebrewing and Winemaking Supplies
3440 Beltline Blvd., St. Louis Park
(952) 925-9835 or (888) 449-2739
www.midwestsupplies.com
Midwest Homebrewing and Winemaking Supplies can get you started making your own beer, but the store also carries everything you need to make your own wine. The store features several "clone" kits designed to make beer that tastes like high-quality commercial brands, including local-favorite Summit Pale Ale, as well as Foster's Lager, Watney's Cream Stout, and Redhook ESB. If your tastes lean more toward reds and whites, Midwest has various winemaking equipment kits, as well as wine kits for many popular varieties, including Cabernet Sauvignon, Merlot, Pinot Grigio, and Chardonnay. You can also buy ingredients to make fruit wines, ranging from apple to plum. Midwest is open daily.

MUSIC STORES

Cheapo Discs
5151 Central Avenue NE, Fridley
(763) 574-2308

71 Snelling Avenue North, St. Paul
(651) 644-8981

1300 West Lake Street, Minneapolis
(612) 827-8238
www.cheapodiscs.com
Cheapo is the Twin Cities' largest seller of new and used CDs. The first store opened decades ago as Cheapo Records but moved into the more popular CD format for recorded music—although not completely (Cheapo Records stores are located next to the Cheapo Discs stores in St. Paul and Minneapolis). Today Cheapo Discs has three Twin Cities locations, where new and used rock, country, R&B, and much more are bought and sold 365 days a year until midnight. Applause, Cheapo's new and used classical and jazz CD stores, are located across the street from the St. Paul store, at 71 North Snelling Avenue (651-644-5115), and next to the Minneapolis store (612-827-8992). Cheapo stocks a large selection of local music and is the place for hardcore fans to pick up new releases on Monday at midnight.

Electric Fetus
2000 Fourth Avenue South, Minneapolis
(612) 870-9300
www.efetus.com
Electric Fetus carries a wide selection of CD releases in all genres. It stocks a superb selection of rock and pop as well as jazz, blues, country, reggae, and ska. Electric Fetus stocks a large selection of CDs by local and independent artists, including many heard on the U's alternative station Radio K. Also available are used CDs, clothing, gifts, and tobacco-related accessories. The store offers frequent sales.

Extreme Noise Records
407 West Lake Street, Minneapolis
(612) 824-0100
www.extremenoise.com

Extreme Noise Records is a co-op specializing in punk rock records and CDs. The store sells its merchandise at lower prices because of the all-volunteer staff and offers many punk titles not available at other Twin Cities music stores. Whether you are looking for classic Buzz-cocks, the Ramones, the Germs, or GG Allin, or more recent punk stars such as local boys Dillinger 4, Extreme Noise usually will have it. Punk records and CDs are available from throughout the world. The store also features "zines," books, and videos about the punk rock lifestyle.

Landspeed/Roadrunner Records
4304 Nicollet Avenue South, Minneapolis
(612) 822-0613
www.landspeedrecords.com
Landspeed/Roadrunner Records specializes in new and used vinyl records in all genres of music, including hard-to-find titles. The largest selection can be found in the rock area; however, the store also features jazz, punk, and world music. The store also stocks a limited number of new and used CDs, particularly strong in world music.

ODDS 'N' ENDS

Minneapolis

Colección y Elegancia
1515 East Lake Street,
Mercado Central, Minneapolis
(612) 728-5416
Colección y Elegancia, a small store tucked into Mercado Central, carries beautiful music boxes, snow globes, porcelain figurines, and other objets d'art. The prices are reasonable for the quality of work, and inventory moves quickly.

Golden Leaf, Ltd.
3032 Hennepin Avenue South, Minneapolis
(612) 824-1867
Golden Leaf carries premium cigars from the leading companies in the industry. The walk-in humidor contains more than 250 brands of the freshest and best-priced cigars in Minnesota.

Other products for sale include accessories, humidors, pipes, tobacco, newspapers, lighters, and other smoking accessories. The former Calhoun Square store is now located across Hennepin Avenue from the mall.

Ingebretsen Scandinavian Gifts & Foods
1601 East Lake Street, Minneapolis
(612) 729-9333
www.ingebretsens.com
Ingebretsen carries Norwegian pewter, Scandinavian crystal (Hadeland, iittala, Nybro), dinnerware from Porsgrund, candles and holders, housewares, linens, Norwegian sweaters, wood carvings, and rosemaling and other folk art. The jewelry case holds beautiful pieces wrought in silver, pewter, bronze, leather, porcelain, enamel, and wood. At the needlework shop next door, you can find fabrics, kits, books, and supplies for Danish counted cross-stitch, Hardanger embroidery, Norwegian Klostersøm needlepoint, lace making, and Norwegian knitting. The select food section includes such Scandinavian delights as lutefisk and lefse, Swedish meatballs and sausage, herring, cheeses, lingonberries, chocolate, and flat bread.

Kitchen Window
3001 Hennepin Avenue South, Calhoun Square, Minneapolis
(612) 824-4417 or (888) 824-4417
www.kitchenwindow.com
Kitchen Window is filled with such brands as All Clad, Calphalon, and Le Creuset cookware; Wusthof Trident, Chef's Choice, and Lamson cutlery; Rosle kitchen tools; and Cuisinart, Kitchen Aid, Krups, and Panasonic small appliances. Kitchen Window features espresso machines and coffeemakers, teamakers, mugs, carafes, and press pots. It also carries items for ethnic cooking that range from lefse griddles and krumkake irons to pasta makers, tortilla presses, sushi mats, and gadgets of all kinds. Kitchen Window holds cooking classes. Check the Web site (click on Upcoming Events) or call for more information.

i Bibelot means "small decorative object," and you'll discover a lot of these at eclectic Bibelot stores found all around the Twin Cities. This is a good place to purchase a last-minute gift for just about anyone. Check the phone book for the Bibelot closest to you.

Patina

1009 Franklin Avenue West, Minneapolis
(612) 872-0880

5001 Bryant Avenue South, Minneapolis
(612) 821-9315

2305 18th Avenue NE, Minneapolis
(612) 788-8933

2057 Ford Parkway, St. Paul
(651) 695-9955
www.patinastores.com
Patina offers stylish and relatively inexpensive gift options—many under $25. This is the type of place where you can find a present in nearly any price range for nearly anyone—and lose track of time doing so. There's lots to look at: contemporary photo frames, bed-tent tops for kids, trendy jewelry, designer stationary, leather passport cases, trout staplers, Band-Aids that look like bacon, and a cheeseboard shaped like France. Patina now has online shopping.

Sister Fun
1604 West Lake Street, Minneapolis
(612) 672-0263
Sister Fun is amazingly fun to poke around in. File cabinet drawers reveal everything from tiny plastic airplanes to tin trains with wind-up cranks, baby doll parts, and cheap novelty key chains. On the shelves can be found 3D renditions of The Last Supper, coin purses with pictures of the Pope on them, Elvis paraphernalia, snow globes containing tiny nuns, Brady Bunch lunchboxes, reissues of Godzilla movies, mood rings, miniature tin carousels, etc., etc., etc. Everything is priced much, much lower than you'd expect, despite being such a chic, campy, and popular shopping stop for college kids, artists, and creative adults.

St. Paul

Ax Man Surplus
1639 University Avenue West, St. Paul
(651) 646-8653

1021 East Moore Lake Drive, Fridley
(763) 572-3730

8008 Minnetonka Boulevard, St. Louis Park
(952) 935–2210
www.ax-man.com
Ax Man has everything you want that you never thought you wanted at more than reasonable prices, including iron lungs, ancient airplane models, antiquated TI-80 computer keyboards, beads, buttons, Pogs, snail shells, seashells, remote control wiring, police tape, public address horns, maps, huge bags of shredded money, rock videos, test tubes, copper cable, bar magnets, refrigerator magnets, transformers, all sizes of electrical motors, music box innards, marbles, bicycle tires, and doll heads. The stock is constantly changing, and some truly strange things wind up for sale, including school bus fenders and fake cheese.

The Bead Monkey
867 Grand Avenue, Victoria Crossing Mall, St. Paul
(651) 222-7729

3717 West 50th Street, Minneapolis
(952) 929-4032
www.thebeadmonkey.com
With two Twin Cities locations, the Bead Monkey is the place to go to buy pipes of inexpensive glass beads, charms, jewelry-making supplies, beading needles and wire, and semiprecious stones. If you are interested in beading but aren't sure how to go about a project, the knowledgeable staff can either help you on the spot or refer you to one of the many beading classes for all ages.

The Crossroads Shoppe of Crocus Hill
619 Grand Avenue, St. Paul
(651) 225-4467
The Crossroads Shoppe presents Red Wing Stoneware and heirloom-quality Amish hand-crafted quilts and furniture. Some of the Amish-crafted items sold here include gorgeously embroidered wall hangings, table runners, thick quilts, braided and woven rugs, straw baskets, and cloth dolls.

Garden of Eden
867 Grand Avenue, St. Paul
(651) 293-1300
www.gardenofedenstores.com
This luxury bath shop carries soaps, oils, perfumes, bath candles, and aromatherapy items. Soaps include handmade bars of glycerin with ribbons of flowers and herbs in them to novelty bars with "Satan Be Gone" emblazoned across the package. While most of the items here are aimed at women, the shop also carries aftershave and other men's products.

Irish on Grand
1124 Grand Avenue, St. Paul
(651) 222-5151 or (888) IRISH-55
www.irishongrand.com
Irish on Grand offers Irish products, including clothing, music, books, food, teas, crystal, china, artwork, and more. Aside from the usual T-shirts with shamrock themes, Irish on Grand carries beautiful woolen capes and throws, sweaters, mittens, scarves, and hats, as well as fine silver and gold jewelry.

Legacy Art & Gifts
1209 Grand Avenue, St. Paul
(651) 221-9094
Legacy Art & Gifts carries items created by local artists showcased in a fabulous converted Victorian house. The shop features pottery, etchings, handblown glass, watercolors, textiles, wood boxes, one-of-a-kind jewelry, and more.

St. Patrick's Guild
1554 Randolph Avenue, St. Paul
(651) 652-9767 or (800) 652-9767
www.stpatricksguild.com
St. Patrick's Guild, established in 1949, is a huge Catholic-themed store that carries religious books, rosaries, medallions dedicated to different saints, holy water bottles, reli-

gious figurines, children's Bibles, and concrete garden statues.

Stogies on Grand
961 Grand Avenue, St. Paul
(651) 222-8700
www.stogiesongrand.com

Stogies on Grand is a premier tobacconist that also offers a comfortable smoking lounge, complete with big-screen TV, newspapers, and board games, for those who want to immediately try out the cigars and tobacco they just purchased. Stogies carries more than 300 premium cigars in their large walk-in humidor and a wide selection of pipes, tobacco, humidors, lighters, cutters, and other tobacco-related accessories.

Ten Thousand Villages
867 Grand Avenue, St. Paul
(651) 225-1043
www.tenthousandvillages.com

Ten Thousand Villages, located in Victoria Crossing West shopping mall, is a nonprofit shop featuring handcrafted jewelry, gifts, clothing, and home furnishings from around the world, with many pieces contributed by artists in developing nations. The profits from purchases made at Ten Thousand Villages go directly back to the artists of these nations in an effort to provide them with a fair living income for their work.

Twin Cities Magic & Costume
250 East Seventh Street, St. Paul
(651) 227-7888
www.twincitiesmagic.com

There is really no place like Twin Cities Magic & Costume. The store has just about everything you need to embark on your career as a magician or for those days you need to be disguised as a gorilla, Little Bo Peep, or Dracula. Costumes, theatrical supplies, and special effects equipment are for sale and rent, including fog machines, strobe lights, explosive paper and powders, wigs, hats, boas, fake mustaches and teeth, tiaras, and more.

West

Ampersand
3445 Galleria, Edina
(952) 920-2118
www.ampersandstores.com

Ampersand carries everything you might possibly need for a party, whether it be a very formal affair or a casual lawn party. Ampersand has boxed invitations for every event under the sun, including birthdays, weddings, showers, anniversaries, barbecues, and cocktail parties, as well as silver olive forks, Italian pottery, designer cork tops, hand-painted dishware, flatware, elegant crystal punchbowls, and a huge selection of candles.

Gabberts Furniture & Design Studio
3501 Galleria, Edina
(952) 927-1500
www.gabberts.com

Gabberts has earned acclaim for its fine home furnishings that suit every lifestyle and span the spectrum of design from traditional to casual to contemporary. The stock changes with the seasons and times and is always amazing—hand-painted desks, tables, and chairs with farm motifs or ocean scenes, or primary-color furniture that looks like adult versions of a kid's playset. Gabberts also carries lush, soft leather couches, beautiful lamps, chandeliers, and pretty much anything else you need to make your home truly yours. Gabbert's also has an Odds & Ends outlet (952-920-0284) in the Galleria, which offers deals on unique pieces of furniture, lighting fixtures, works of art, and more.

General Store of Minnetonka
14401 Highway 7, Minnetonka
(952) 935-7131
www.generalstoreofminnetonka.com

With more than 20,000 square feet of retail space and an inventory that ranges from a Me-ow Me-ow Cat Bowl to a Loon Whirly-Gig, you're bound to find something you just have to have or the perfect gift at the General Store of Minnetonka. Items tailored to men, women, children, and even pets crowd the huge floor space, with particular attention paid to the whimsical and the downright weird. For example, the general store sells an Octodog Hot Dog Converter, which cuts a hot dog from the short end into eight long slices of tantalizing hot dog meat; the book *How to Talk Minnesotan;* a Body Crayon Book (with crayons); and a pillow on which to rest your wooden stir spoon in between swirls. The store also has the General Store Cafe, with a menu that changes daily but includes salads, deli sandwiches, homemade soups, and desserts such as chocolate chip cookies and bread pudding.

Que Sera
3580 Galleria, Edina
(952) 924-6390

This eclectic store, identified in front by a detailed chipped-tile mosaic, carries vintage-inspired home furnishings, lighting, beautiful costume jewelry, and knickknacks of all sorts. Que Sera offers custom upholstery and slip-covered sofas and chairs incorporating vintage fabrics, hand-painted furniture, custom iron and wood beds, custom bedding, hand-blown glass chandeliers, table lamps, candles, mirrors, frames, and more.

SPECIALTY GROCERS
Minneapolis
Holy Land Bakery, Grocery and Deli
2513 Central Avenue NE, Minneapolis
(612) 781-2627

820 East Lake Street, Midtown Global Market, Minneapolis
(612) 872-4041
www.holylandbrand.com

This Mediterranean deli and grocery store sells everything you need to make your own lamb kabobs, hummus, spinach pie, and falafel, although chances are you probably won't be able to make them quite as well as the Holy Land deli counter does. The store stocks items such as pita (made fresh in the bakery every day), meats, gigantic bags of basmati rice, roasted and dried chickpeas, at least six types of feta cheese, black and green olives, specialty coffees, and a wide selection of Middle Eastern cookies, candies, and specialty chocolates.

Midtown Global Market
920 East Lake Street, Minneapolis
(612) 872-4041
www.midtownglobalmarket.com

Opened in 2006, the Midtown Global Market is a colorful and tasty collection of Hispanic, Arabic, Hmong, African American, Scandinavian, and Tibetan, among others, markets, shops, and casual eateries in the heart of south Minneapolis. There is no other place in the Twin Cities where you can eat jerk chicken, buy hand-sewn Hmong wall hangings, and learn to salsa in quick succession. The thriving marketplace has quickly become a gathering place for Twin Citians, and it is a particularly good spot to find unusual gifts (tree-trunk sculpture and stretchy, frilly, tube-top-like shirts, for example) and to shop for spices and foods from Latin America, the Middle East, Southeast Asia, and elsewhere. It is also a great place to get your watch fixed or your trousers let out a couple inches.

Shuang Hur Oriental Market
2710 Nicollet Avenue South, Minneapolis
(612) 872-8606

654 University Avenue West, St. Paul
(651) 251-2196

Shuang Hur carries thousands of products from China, Taiwan, and Thailand. The full-service grocery store has a large fresh-produce section with melons, bean sprouts, and crates of aged duck eggs; freezers full of egg roll and spring roll wraps and desserts; and a Chinese BBQ deli that carries whole roasted pigs and BBQ duck and chicken meat. In the dry goods sections are rows and rows of dried mushrooms, noodles, soups, spices, rice, and shrimp crackers.

Surdyk's
303 East Hennepin Avenue, Minneapolis
(612) 379-3232
www.surdyks.com
This Minneapolis shop is a wine connoisseur's dream come true. Surdyk's carries a wide selection of wines and other spirits, plus a gourmet cheese shop that makes this the place to consider when planning cocktail or dinner parties. Cigar smokers will appreciate the large humidor, which was a part of the store long before puffing cigars became trendy.

St. Paul

El Burrito Mercado
175 Cesar Chavez Street, St. Paul
(651) 227-2192
www.elburritomercado.com
El Burrito Mercado is an all-purpose Mexican and Latin grocery store located in the District del Sol neighborhood on St. Paul's West Side. The immense store features a bakery where you can purchase fresh pastries, fruit turnovers, breads, and cookies; a meat counter that carries fresh seafood, shredded pork, chicken, and beef, as well as gigantic fried pork rinds; a restaurant that whips up tacos, quesadillas, and burritos as quick as most fast-food restaurants, except the ingredients here are fresh, spicy, and good for you; and a full-service grocery carrying everything from Mexican coffees and candies to fresh, homemade corn chips and statues of tiny, sombrero-wearing skeletons playing guitars.

Spiros Mediterranean Market
2264 University Avenue West, St. Paul
(651) 645-4607
This wonderful deli and grocery carries Greek staples such as frozen beef and lamb for gyros, *tzatziki* (cucumber) sauce, and a good selection of cheeses. The grocery section has Mediterranean candies, coffees, beans, pastas, fruit preserves, nuts, flour, jars of olives, pickled squid, and anchovy paste. The deli counter has delicious baklava, as well as hummus and Greek salad, and makes gyros and other sandwiches fresh to order. In the freezer section

are trays of moussaka and frozen spinach pies made fresh in the store.

SPORTS AND RECREATION OUTFITTERS

Minneapolis

Alternative Bike & Board Shop
3013 Lyndale Avenue South, Minneapolis
(612) 374-3635
www.altbikeboard.com
Alternative Bike & Board Shop carries all the respected bicycle, skateboard, and snowboard brands like Burton, Clicker, Nitro, and K2. It also carries clothing, accessories, and gear and has a knowledgeable staff that can help set you up with anything you need to get out on the road or on the slopes. The store also offers bike repairs.

Erik's Bike Shop
1312 Fourth Street SE, Minneapolis
(612) 617-8002
www.eriksbikeshop.com
Eleven additional Twin Cities locations
This chain of local shops offers an excellent selection of equipment and a knowledgeable staff. Cyclists will find an extensive assortment of mountain, road, touring, and BMX bikes from such companies as Cannondale, Specialized, and Haro, as well as accessories, including car racks, helmets, parts, and apparel. Winter sports enthusiasts will be pleased by Erik's selection of snowboards, clothing, and boots. Erik's also has a full-service bike shop for quickie to major repairs.

Freewheel Bike
1812 South Sixth Street, Minneapolis
(612) 339-2219
www.freewheelbike.com
Freewheel Bike carries mountain, road, and tandem bikes from Trek, Fisher, LeMond, Schwinn, Univega, Bontrager, Klein, and Santana, but its best feature is arguably the Public Shop, where, for under $10 an hour you can use the store's racks and tools to fix your bike—if you get in over your head, the staff is

on hand to offer assistance. Freewheel also hosts maintenance classes jointly with the University of Minnesota's Open U, rents bikes, and sponsors riding groups and teams.

Midwest Mountaineering
309 Cedar Avenue South, Minneapolis
(612) 339-3433 or (888) 999-1077
www.midwestmtn.com
Midwest Mountaineering takes up nearly an entire block of Cedar Avenue on the University of Minnesota's West Bank and is one of the most complete retail stores for brand-name outdoor adventure gear (including a giant outdoors-related book section) and one of the few outfitters to rent kayaks, canoes, and other paddling gear. The store's bouldering cave allows novices and seasoned climbers to try out equipment or practice their skills. Once you sign a waiver, you're free to hit the walls. The store's staff is extremely helpful and can direct you to some of the better climbing, rafting, or hiking opportunities in the region.

St. Paul

Finn-Sisu
1841 University Avenue West, St. Paul
(651) 645-2443 or (888) FINN-SISU
www.finnsisu.com
This tiny Midway shop stocks recreational, racing, and skate cross-country skis, as well as equipment and supplies by all the top makers. The staff is very good at matching people with just the right gear. The store is also conveniently located near Como Park, giving you a chance to try out your new toys mere minutes after leaving the store.

i Thrifty Outfitters (612-339-6290 or 800-866-3162), located upstairs inside the Midwest Mountaineering store, sells new and used outdoors equipment, clothing, and boots at steep discounts. Thrifty outfitters also repairs outdoors equipment, from tents to backpacking stoves.

Stillwater's P. J. Asch Otterfitters has a climbing wall inside its converted-grain-elevator retail space. TODD R. BERGER

Joe's Sporting Goods
33 Country Road B, St. Paul
(651) 209-7800 or (888) GO-TO-JOES
www.joessportinggoods.com
Joe's carries a solid selection of top-of-the-line fishing equipment, from rods, reels, and flies to clothes, boots, and hats, as well as a complete array of hunting, camping, and gear for snow sports, such as downhill and cross-country skiing, and snowboarding.

East

P. J. Asch Otterfitters
413 East Nelson Street, Stillwater
(651) 430-2286
www.pjaschotterfitters.com
The owners of P. J. Asch Otterfitters converted four old grain bins in downtown Stillwater into

four cozy climbing rooms, then added an outdoor-sports store to augment the climbing facilities. The store carries a wide variety of climbing gear, skis, snowshoes, kayaks (including used rentals at discounted prices), shoes and clothing for outdoor activities, and camping equipment. The store offers climbing, skiing, and kayaking lessons, and rents sea kayaks for use on the nearby St. Croix River.

VINTAGE CLOTHES AND THRIFT STORES
Minneapolis
Corner Store
900 West Lake Street, Minneapolis
(612) 823-1270
Corner Store specializes in brand-name jeans and Western apparel such as cowboy boots, brass belt buckles, and fringed suede jackets, as well as motorcycle jackets, costume jewelry, and sequined clothing. For more elegant occasions, Corner Store has vintage tuxedos for rent.

Everyday People Clothing Exchange
323 14th Avenue SE, Minneapolis
(612) 623-9095

2912 Hennepin Avenue South, Minneapolis
(612) 824-3112
www.everydaypeopleclothing.com
This vintage and resale store, with locations in Dinkytown and Uptown, carries an eclectic (and sometimes hilarious) collection of disco clothes, old band T-shirts, go-go boots, comfortably broken-in Levis, and studded leather and plastic belts.

Tatters
2928 Lyndale Avenue South, Minneapolis
(612) 823-5285
Originally called Tatters and Platters, a retailer selling apparel and vinyl records, Tatters has been a Twin Cities retro-alternative clothing establishment for many years. Tatters offers freshly laundered used and vintage clothing that spans decades, carrying seasoned

motorcycle and letter jackets, Hawaiian and bowling shirts, party dresses from the 1940s onward, and lots and lots of Levis. It also stocks new apparel ranging from partywear to T-shirts and underwear.

St. Paul
Lula
1587 Selby Avenue, St. Paul
(651) 644-4110
Lula boasts beautiful vintage clothes and accessories, including especially large and eclectic collections of women's dresses, men's shirts, and coats and jackets. The reasonably priced clothing moves quickly, and it's largely from the 1980s and earlier. The owner has been known to load up dressing rooms with all sorts of possibilities you may have overlooked. Trust this woman. She's totally into selling you vintage clothes that make you look and feel incredible.

Jerabek's New Bohemian
63 West Winifred Street, St. Paul
(651) 228-1245
www.jerabeks.com
If you're looking for vintage clothes or housewares, try Jerabek's New Bohemian, a coffee shop tucked into St. Paul's West Side that's been around for 100 years. Not only is Jerabek's famous for its homemade pastries, it doubles as a vintage shop.

Unique Thrift Store
1657 Rice Street, St. Paul
(651) 489-5083
Two additional Twin Cities locations
All three Unique Thrift Store locations are the place to go to get beautiful, barely worn summer dresses, business suits, boots and shoes, ice skates, in-line skates, leather jackets, winter coats, and kids' stuff at unbelievable prices. You can pretty much buy a fashionable, brand-name wardrobe for your son or daughter for a whole growing season, including shoes and a coat, for under $50; prices on adult clothes and shoes are just as reasonable.

ATTRACTIONS

There is never a reason to be bored in the Twin Cities. The metro area is host to amusement parks, a bevy of hands-on historical exhibits, one of the largest zoos and one of the best free zoos in the country, and lots of interesting spots to just hang out for the day. In winter, flocks of teenagers and adults head to the Mall of America to spend the day walking among the still-green trees and surreal landscape that make up the always-summery Camp at MOA, or to the tropical canopies of wild orchid displays that fill Como Park's spectacular Marjorie McNeely Conservatory. In summer there's no excuse for staying inside on the weekend—bike trails await and several water parks are nothing but cool, watery roller coasters, wave machines, and swimming pools.

PRICE CODE

The following price code is based on the cost for general admission for one adult. Most sites offer considerably discounted tickets for children and seniors, and some allow discounts or even free entry for employees, members of the military, and certain organizations.

$ .... $5 and under
$$ .... $6–$15
$$$ .... $16–$30
$$$$ .... $31 and up

AMUSEMENT AND WATER PARKS

The Park at MOA $$$
Mall of America, 5000 Center Court, Bloomington
(952) 883-8600
www.theparkatmoa.com

Located at the center of Mall of America, this seven-acre indoor theme park offers more than 25 rides and attractions. The largest indoor theme park in the nation, the Park at MOA sits right on top of the old Metropolitan Stadium (home of the Minnesota Twins from 1961 to 1981) site—in place of a baseball diamond are 400 live trees, artificial cliffs meant to evoke the St. Croix River valley, and all of those rides and attractions. Unlike outdoor amusement parks such as Valleyfair!, a stroll through the Park at MOA costs you nothing (in fact, cutting through the park is often the fastest route between stores at the mall). Rides require tickets, which you can buy at booths or at automated machines. Tickets for rides and attractions are based on a point system. A point is worth 80 cents, with rides and attractions costing three to six points each. You can also purchase Ticket Point Packages and all-day wristbands, two money-saving options if the little ones (or you) plan to get on a lot of rides.

For small children, there's the Americana Carousel, a hand-painted contemporary version of the classic carousel, and Lil' Shaver, a smaller, slower version of the roller coaster that circles the park (the Ripsaw Roller Coaster). For everyone else, there's the Skyscraper Ferris Wheel that takes visitors 74 feet high, Paul Bunyan's Log Chute—a watery ride that includes a drop over a 40-foot waterfall—and more than enough other rides and attractions to take your mind off shopping. There's also a full-service child care facility, Kids Quest, which charges by the hour and entertains kids with toys, nonviolent video games, karaoke, and more.

Valleyfair! Amusement Park $$$$
1 Valleyfair Drive, Shakopee
(952) 445-6500 or (800) FUN-RIDE
www.valleyfair.com
With more than 75 rides and attractions, the upper Midwest's largest theme park has something to offer the littlest kid and the bravest adult alike. You can enjoy a relaxing inner tube ride down a gently sloping canal; bumper cars and electric car tracks; exciting water rides like the Flume, which sends passenger boats off a 50-foot drop at the end of the ride; and the Excalibur, a high-speed wooden roller coaster with a 105-foot drop and lots of quick twists and turns. The Steel Venom impulse coaster plummets at speeds up to 68 mph, corkscrewing you straight toward the ground before veering to a horizontal ride just before impact. For those with no fear of heights, the 275-foot Power Tower will take you high in the air and then, well, drop you. There are lots of rides for the really little guys, too, from bumble bee–shaped electric cars to a multilevel foam-ball factory to an antique carousel. An IMAX theater is an added attraction to the park and a great place to hide out during sudden late-summer showers. The amusement park is open mid-May through September.

Valleyfair! also has Whitewater Country, a three-and-a-half-acre waterpark with multiple water slides, raft rides, and such attractions as Raging Rapids, Splash Station, and Giggle Run. The waterpark is open late May through late August, and has different hours than the amusement park. Call ahead for more information.

The separate Challenge Park (which has separate fees and different hours than the amusement park) will get the adrenaline and competitive juices flowing with such rides as RipCord (which lifts you up in the air 180 feet and spins you, then drops you, simulating flying and freefall), Adventure Golf, Go-Karts, and Bumper Boats.

i Get half-price tickets to Valleyfair! by buying Starlight admission after 5:00 p.m. Check the park's hours of operation on the day you wish to go, as Valleyfair! is only open until 6:00 p.m on some days early and late in the season (although until midnight on weekends during the heart of the summer).

Water Park of America $$$
1700 East American Blvd., Bloomington
(952) 854-8700
www.waterparkofamerica.com
Adjacent to the Mall of America, the Water Park of America offers the only surfing simulator in Minnesota, a wave pool, a ten-story raft ride, swimming pools, and more. Arrive early during warm summer weekends as the waterpark often fills to capacity. The waterpark is open seasonally and hours vary (call ahead for details). The waterpark complex includes a game arcade with many different prizes for winners, a hotel (see the listing in the Accommodations chapter for more information on the hotel), a spa, and two restaurants.

ANIMALS AND PLANTS

Como Zoo/Marjorie McNeely
Conservatory at Como Park   Free
1225 Estabrook Drive, St. Paul
(651) 487-8200
www.comozooconservatory.org
This year-round zoo offers intimate exhibits housing reticulated giraffes, black-footed penguins, snow leopards, yellow-rumped caciques, blue-eyed black lemurs, gray wolves, and more. One of only four free metropolitan-area zoos in the country (although a small donation is requested), Como Zoo has been an institution in St. Paul for more than a century. The first Siberian tigers successfully bred in captivity were born here in 1958, and the big cat display is still one of the best features of the zoo, including

ℹ️ For a reasonable charge, kids can buy Dixie cups of fish to throw to the seals at Como Zoo.

a breeding pair of lions that has had several healthy pairs of cubs over the past decade.

Located right next door to the zoo is the Marjorie McNeely Conservatory at Como Park, the region's largest botanical garden. The Victorian-style, glass-domed conservatory features hundreds of plants from throughout the world and is divided into eight sections featuring palms, ferns, tropical food plants, bonsai trees, seasonal flowers, orchids, Japanese landscapes, and butterfly-friendly plants. In summer a side door opens into the Como Ordway Memorial Japanese Garden, a *sansui* (mountain and water) design created by St. Paul's sister city, Nagasaki, Japan, for the park.

The antique wooden Cafesjian's Carousel is beautifully restored, and the brightly painted and mirrored wooden animals are available to ride throughout the summer for a nominal charge. Como Town, the park's newest addition, is an amusement park for little ones.

Both the Como Zoo and the Marjorie McNeely Conservatory at Como Park are open year-round. The zoo and conservatory in Como Park can be found about halfway between Interstate 94 and Minnesota Highway 36 off of Lexington Avenue. Call ahead or visit the Web site for further directions.

Minnesota Landscape Arboretum $$
3675 Arboretum Drive, Chaska
(952) 443-1400
www.arboretum.umn.edu
Minnesota is a fertile place. The diversity of flora that thrives in the cool northern climate is simply astonishing, and one of the best places to go to get a feel for the woodsy, prickly, shady, pretty, and pungent side of the Twin Cities is the Minnesota Landscape Arboretum. Minnesota's largest public garden, the arboretum is maintained by the University of Minnesota. But it is not the outdoor equiv-

alent of a musty plant textbook, although an industrious sort could probably research one here. From the Three-Mile Drive and its sampler of trees, flowering plants, grasses, and shrubs to the new Maze Garden, the arboretum is an intriguing and fun place at which both adults and kids will find much to love.

The arboretum features 1,000 acres of public gardens, including spectacular annual and perennial display gardens, collections of plants developed for northern climates, natural and native areas, and demonstration gardens. The arboretum grounds include miles of summer hiking trails and winter cross-country ski and snowshoe trails that take you through northern woodlands, native prairies, and natural marshes. In spring, summer, and fall, trams can be boarded for a guided tour around the beautiful Three-Mile Drive (you can also follow the route in your car), and volunteer-guided walking tours can be taken through the many display gardens for free. Visitors can also take a self-guided audio walking tour of the demonstration gardens (equipment is available in the lobby of the Snyder Building for no extra charge).

The new Maze Garden along Three-Mile Drive is a great place for kids to burn pent-up energy. Adults too will get a kick out of the plethora of dead-ends, swirly footpaths, walls of plants and shrubs, and playful signage. Visitors make their way by trial and error through the maze in an attempt to reach the Lookout Tower, which temptingly looms in the distance and can actually be reached—if you're patient and persistent, or if you're following a kid.

The arboretum is open daily (except for Thanksgiving and Christmas Day) at varying hours depending on the season and the day of the week; call for details. To get to the Minnesota Landscape Arboretum, follow Minnesota Highway 5 west from I-494 in the southwest part of the Metro. After approximately 10 miles, you'll reach the intersection with Minnesota Highway 41. Continue straight ahead on Highway 5 and follow the directional signs to the arboretum.

Minnesota Zoo $$
13000 Zoo Boulevard, Apple Valley
(952) 431-9200 or (800) 366-7811
www.mnzoo.org

Located in the southeastern suburb of Apple Valley and housing approximately 500 species of animals from five different continents, the Minnesota Zoo and its IMAX theater see a million visitors per year. The zoo's 500 acres include an indoor Tropics Trail, populated by gibbons, tapirs, tree kangaroos, hissing cockroaches, and endangered red pandas. The newly redesigned Minnesota Trail, also an indoor walk, is home to gray wolves, porcupines, great horned owls, river otters, and other Minnesota residents. At Discovery Bay, dolphins officially perform for audiences every afternoon and unofficially any time enough people gather around their huge, glass-walled tank; a walk-through aquarium has sharks, fish, and deep-sea plants; and there is a hands-on area where kids (and adults) can pet different kinds of sharks, rays, and starfish. Outside the main exhibit building, you can find ducks and swans, a prairie dog town, wild horses, camels, tigers, and many, many other animals. Domesticated animals like pigs and chickens get their day in the sun at the Wells Fargo Family Farm exhibit. Daily cow milkings are a kick for us city folk to watch. It's worth the extra few dollars to ride the Monorail around the zoo, as it is the least strenuous way to see many animals requiring room to roam, including endangered and extremely rare Mexican wolves, musk oxen, and Siberian tigers.

The zoo also features the 600-seat Great Clips IMAX theater and the Weesner Family Amphitheater, which hosts concerts all summer long.

To reach the zoo, follow Interstate 35E south from I-494 in the southeast Metro, exit at Minnesota Highway 77, and follow the signs.

Underwater Adventures Aquarium $$–$$$
Mall of America, 120 East Broadway
Bloomington
(952) 883-0202 or (888) 348-3824
www.underwateradventures.net

Underwater Adventures is a huge (1.2 million gallons) walk-through aquarium located under the Mall of America. The facility features more than 4,500 different sea creatures from around the world in eight different displays. For a one-time admission charge, visitors can walk through a 300-foot glass-walled tunnel that leads them through the middle of the three freshwater exhibits: Touch of the Wild Woods, Fisherman's Hollow, and the Wild Amazon, and five ocean exhibits: Shark Cove, Rainbow Reef, Seacrits of Hollywood, Circle of Life, and Starfish Beach, where children can touch harmless sharks and stingrays.

CASINOS AND RACETRACKS

Canterbury Park Racetrack and Card Club
1100 Canterbury Road, Shakopee
(952) 445-7223 or (800) 340-6361
www.canterburypark.com

Canterbury Park, located about 25 miles south of both downtown St. Paul and Minneapolis, hosts live horse racing with on-site pari-mutuel betting early May through the beginning of September. In addition, the Canterbury Park Race Book offers year-round on-site betting on simulcast horse races around the country. Canterbury also has a Card Club, including the Poker Room, with 34 tables featuring such games as Texas hold 'em, seven-card stud, and Omaha hi-lo, and the Casino Games Room, with games like blackjack, Caribbean stud, and Let It Ride, as well as additional poker games. The entire facility is smoke free. To reach the racetrack and card club, follow I-494 in the southwest Metro and exit at U.S. Highway 169 South. Follow US 169 to Canterbury Road and turn right (north).

Mystic Lake Casino
2400 Mystic Lake Boulevard, Prior Lake
(952) 445-9000 or (800) 262-7799
www.mysticlake.com

Besides its trademark high-stakes bingo, Mystic Lake Casino has nearly 4,000 slots and 100 blackjack tables as well as restaurants,

Rice Park

Rice Park is one of the most lovely urban green spaces in the Twin Cities. It is one preserved block carved out of St. Paul's core, surrounded by cobblestone streets and towering buildings and replete with benches and trees. One of St. Paul's oldest parks, the square was donated to the city in 1849, the same year St. Paul was incorporated as a town and nine years before Minnesota became a state. The man who donated the park, Henry Mower Rice, was first a fur trader, and then a businessman and one of the town's first cheerleaders. If only Henry knew what his gift would become.

Benches around the huge circular fountain at Rice Park's center make nice spots to eat lunch or listen to a concert in the square. There's a statue of F. Scott Fitzgerald, who wrote and published *This Side of Paradise* (1920) while living on Summit Avenue, the grand St. Paul street full of Victorian mansions. (Incidentally, Henry Rice built one of the first homes on this prime stretch of real estate.) During the Winter Carnival each year, Rice Park holds the festival's ice-sculpting contest. Massive frosty sculptures glow amid trees dressed in twinkling white lights for as long as the weather allows.

But the park is defined as much by what's around it as what's in it. On the north side, along Fifth Street, sits the Landmark Center, built in 1902. It has huge stone towers, the tallest of which holds a clock. Landmark Towers was originally the federal courthouse and post office for the upper Midwest, during which time it saw the trials of many big-name gangsters. Take a peek inside. Now a National Historic Landmark, the building holds lots of offices of nonprofit organizations and is open for tours. The atrium is amazing, and some of the courtrooms and judges' chambers have been restored to their original grandeur.

Along the park's south side, the stately marble Italian Renaissance revival rectangle that is the St. Paul Central Library inspires awe from its spot on Fourth Street. It cost $1.5 million dollars (and that's in 1917 dollars) to construct. It's still a library today, and thankfully, it recently benefited from a $15.9 million restoration. The St. Paul Central Library is also on the National Register of Historic Places. Inside, it's all handsome stone and wood, and there's even a nice little coffee shop and store to visit.

On the park's west side, along Market Street, is one of the premier accommodations in all of the state, the Saint Paul Hotel. It was the luxurious brainchild of St. Paul businessman Lucius Pond Ordway, designed to wow back in 1910 with a grand ballroom, a fine dining room, and guestrooms with scenic views. This is the kind of hotel with a doorman in a top hat, afternoon teas by the fire, and huge arrangements of fresh flowers everywhere. The hotel regularly attracts stars, politicians, and royalty—Calvin Coolidge, Bill Clinton, Bing Crosby, and Bill Murray are among recorded visitors. The hotel's St. Paul Grill is still

Landmark Center of Rice Park. GREATER MINNEAPOLIS CONVENTION & VISITORS ASSOCIATION

known around the Cities as a premier dining spot, the ballroom still hosts events, and the view is still—well, try to get a room overlooking Rice Park.

Directly across from the Saint Paul Hotel, on Washington Street, is the Ordway Center for the Performing Arts, which opened in 1985. Sally Ordway Irving, Lucius's granddaughter, is behind this theatrical gem. By far Rice Park's newest structure, its creators met the architectural challenge of fitting in with the neighbors. The Ordway doesn't pretend to be old, and it holds up yet defers to its surrounding—the low-lying building's soaring glass-walled lobby gives audiences a reason to linger over a spectacular view.

Despite all this history and elegance, Rice Park is a wonderfully and comfortably low-key spot. It gets nice and quiet here, especially at night after the Ordway show has let out and the fancy St. Paul Grill diners have finished and the carriage that waits outside the hotel has gone home. You can practically feel the city's breath in this park, its heart. Depending on the angle, Rice Park could be now or 65 years ago, but it's unquestionably St. Paul, with its best foot forward.

i Down in History motorcoach tours (651-292-1220), led by costumed actors, are a fun way to get oriented to the Twin Cities and learn a little in the process. The Saint Paul Gangster, Historic Cave, Twin Town Tacky, and Uff Dah! Tours are among your choices.

including a huge buffet. The gaming facility offers concerts, celebrity shows (recent shows include Alan Jackson, Tony Bennett, and Kenny G), a hotel, and free daily shuttles across the Twin Cities. It is operated by the Shakopee Mdewakanton Sioux Community. The casino is smoke and alcohol free. Mystic Lake Casino is about 6 miles south of Canterbury Park and about 30 miles from either downtown St. Paul or downtown Minneapolis. It is the closest full casino to the Twin Cities.

Treasure Island Resort and Casino
off Minnesota Highway 61
Red Wing
(800) 222-7077
www.treasureislandcasino.com
Located 45 minutes southeast of St. Paul near the Mississippi River town of Red Wing, tropical-themed Treasure Island features 2,500 slots, 44 blackjack tables, 10 poker tables, bingo, video poker, video keno, and video roulette. The casino has smoking and non-smoking gambling areas and does not serve alcoholic drinks. Guests can take a cruise down the scenic Mississippi River aboard the Spirit of the Water, the casino's 150-passenger yacht. The Indigo Bay Showroom features live comedy and music; recent shows featured Rodney Carrington and Wanda Sykes. You can delay your drive back to the Cities by booking a room in the casino's 250-room tropical-themed resort or by parking your Airstream at the casino's 95-pad RV park.

Should you get hungry, there are plenty of great places to eat at Treasure Island, including the Tradewinds all-you-can-eat buffet, Java's Restaurant for meals ranging from steak to seafood, and several other options serving sandwiches, coffee and pastries, and burgers.

GUIDED EXCURSIONS

The Hitching Company $$$–$$$$
25200 Elmira Street NE, Stacy
(612) 338-7777
www.thehitchingcompany.com
Romantic horse-drawn carriage tours of downtown Minneapolis cover, depending on the tour, such sites as the Stone Arch Bridge, the new Guthrie Theater, the Mississippi riverfront, the Warehouse District, Loring Park, the Basilica of St. Mary, Nicollet Mall, and more. Tours range from 15 minutes to an hour, and the carriages seat up to six, less romantic but great fun for families. Operating year-round (The Hitching Company provides blankets when the mercury drops), the carriage can pick you up at numerous spots in downtown Minneapolis. Call ahead for reservations.

Padelford Packet Boat
Company, Inc. $$–$$$$
Harriet Island Regional Park, St. Paul
(651) 227-1100 or (800) 543-3908
www.riverrides.com
Hop on one of five riverboats leaving from Harriet Island in St. Paul for a Mississippi River excursion. These paddleboat river tours offer an excellent way to experience the river up close.

One of the riverboats is one of the few truly authentic sternwheelers on the Mississippi River. The all-steel *Jonathan Padelford* is named for the tenth great maternal grandfather of Capt. William D. Bowell Sr., founder of the Padelford Packet Boat Company, Inc. The engines are identical to the old steam engines but run hydraulically.

Padelford Packet Boat Company offers two narrated daily public excursions seven days a week in June, July, and August and at 2:00 p.m. every Saturday and Sunday, May and September. Elegant evening dinner cruises depart Fridays, June through September. A Sunday brunch cruise, a lunch cruise, a showboat cruise, a birding cruise, a fall color cruise, private charters, and more are also available.

Segway Magical History Tour $$$$
Saint Anthony Main, 125 Main Street SE,
Minneapolis
(800) 749-5584 or (952) 888-9200
www.humanonastick.com
One of the neater and funnier-looking ways to
tour the historic sites of the Minneapolis riverfront is aboard a Segway, a perfectly balanced
scooterlike device that travels up to 10 mph.
After some brief certified training on how to
drive a Segway, a guide-led convoy departs
Saint Anthony Main and tours such sites as
the Stone Arch Bridge, Saint Anthony Falls,
Mill Ruins Park, the Hennepin Avenue Bridge,
and Nicollet Island. The five-mile tour includes
a loaner helmet, free admission to and
refreshments at the Mill City Museum, and
discounts at area restaurants.

HISTORICAL ATTRACTIONS

Alexander Ramsey House $–$$
265 South Exchange Street, St. Paul
(651) 296-8760
www.mnhs.org/ramseyhouse
Completed in 1872, this is one of the country's best-preserved Victorian homes. The
Ramsey House is one of the most detailed
and intimate historical sites in the Twin Cities.
The only owners were the Ramsey family, and
so the history stayed in the house. More than
90 percent of the furnishings are original,
which is rare for historical sites.

Costumed guides lead visitors on a tour
of the impressive home of Alexander and
Anna Ramsey. Alexander Ramsey was Minnesota's first territorial governor and the second state governor, and he held many other
prominent positions in public life.

The Ramsey House features original furniture, crystal chandeliers, carved walnut woodwork, and marble fireplaces. The costumed
interpreters play out vignettes showing life in
the late 1800s. Free fresh-baked cookies are
handed out by the "servants." There are special events and tours throughout the year,
particularly during holidays. Tours run year-
round on Friday and Saturday between 10:00

a.m. and 3:00 p.m., with expanded hours during summer and the holiday season.

American Swedish Institute $–$$
2600 Park Avenue, Minneapolis
(612) 871-4907
www.americanswedishinst.org
Set in a spectacular, 33-room turn-of-the-20th-
century mansion that looks more like a castle
than a former residence, the American
Swedish Institute is the largest and oldest
museum of Swedish culture, arts, and history
in the country. Completed in 1908, the
châteauesque structure is all ornately carved
Indiana limestone on the outside. The inside
is a marvel of hand-carved wood, with intricate designs lining the walls, and each
sculpted plaster ceiling is a work of art.
There's also a *kakelugnar* in each of eleven
rooms, which is basically a colorful, porcelain-
wrapped Swedish fireplace. Once the home of
Swan J. Turnblad, publisher of North America's foremost Swedish-language newspaper,
the house was donated in 1929 to the American Institute for Swedish Arts, Literature, and
Science, which later changed its name to the
American Swedish Institute. Also exhibited at
the museum are Scandinavian artifacts from
the Turnblad family.

While taking in the decor, expect also to
be taken with tales of immigrants who left
Scandinavia to settle in Minnesota, which
bears similar scenery, albeit sans mountains
and fjords. The museum is a rich resource for
local history as well as a showcase for artwork
by Swedish and Swedish-American artists and
artisans. There are concerts and theater performances in the upper rooms and lectures
and other events in the modernized lower
level. (It's a special treat to visit when the
mansion is decked out at Christmastime.)
There are also fiddling and dancing groups
that come through to entertain visitors, special festivals with music and food, and
Swedish language classes for kids and adults.

Tours of the institute are available Tuesday through Sunday.

The Ard Godfrey House   Free
50 University Avenue NE, Minneapolis
(612) 870-8001 (tours are arranged through
the Woman's Club of Minneapolis)
www.ardgodfreyhouse.com
Built in 1848, the Ard Godfrey House was the
family residence for the millwright who
helped build the first dam and sawmills to put
the waterpower of the Falls of St. Anthony to
use. The oldest wood frame house in Minneapolis, this Greek revival structure was
restored and refurbished by the Woman's
Club of Minneapolis as a gift to city residents.

The Godfrey House was reopened to the
public in 1979. Today the house is available
for guided tours Friday, Saturday, and Sunday
June through September and for private tours
by appointment year-round.

Fort Snelling $–$$
Minnesota Highways 5 and 55, St. Paul
(612) 726-1171
www.mnhs.org/fortsnelling
First established in 1819 as a military encampment, Fort Snelling was built on a bluff overlooking the Mississippi and Minnesota Rivers
in 1825. The fort was once the westernmost
U.S. outpost in the mostly unexplored wilds of
the Northwest Territory (encompassing eastern Minnesota and many of the future states
of the Upper Midwest) and was the center of
frontier commerce and government on the
upper Mississippi. At the time, an outpost on
the confluence of the Minnesota and Mississippi Rivers meant control of river traffic
throughout the region; British fur traders,
American outlaws, and warring American
Indian nations could be held in check. Today
themed tours provide insight into what life
was like at the fort, with costumed guides
reenacting scenes from military, civilian, and
Native American life of the 1800s. Not only
are these some of the oldest surviving buildings in the state, but both Twin Cities trace
their pedigrees to the fort. Soldiers from the
fort built the first sawmill at St. Anthony Falls,
and the first residents of St. Paul were moved
there after being sheltered as immigrants.

This reconstruction of the first permanent
settlement in Minnesota is open May through
October and is staffed by costumed guides
portraying fort life in 1827. Events at the fort
include demonstrations, historical skits, practice military drills, watching or joining in with
residents of the 1820s military post as they
prepare the harvest for storage and winter
use, and book readings and lectures from
Minnesota authors and historians. Contact
the fort directly to hear about special events
year-round.

Gibbs Museum of Pioneer
and Dakotah Life $–$$
2097 West Larpenteur Avenue
Falcon Heights
(651) 646-8629
www.rchs.com/gbbsfm2.htm
Near the farm fields that make up the northern border of the University of Minnesota's
agriculturally focused St. Paul campus, you'll
find this quaint little barn and farmhouse,
which date from 1854. They're preserved in
their original state (additions to the original
cabin were constructed in 1867 and 1873) as
an educational opportunity for those who
would like to step back in time. On summer
weekends expect to see people in period
dress doing farm chores like churning butter
on the porch. Interpreters share the process
and results of their extensive archeology of
this site, displaying excavated artifacts and
explaining their historic significance to the
public. The Gibbs Museum's medicine and
vegetable gardens are especially interesting,
with many native plants that no longer exist
naturally in the area but were especially
important to the Dakotah (Dakota) people and
pioneer settlers.

A point of interest is that the history
most spoken about at this archeological site is
that of Jane Gibbs, a young woman raised by
missionaries and used as an interpreter
between the Dakotah and settlers for many
years, and not that of her husband, Heman
Gibbs, who helped build the two houses on
the property as well as the barn in back. The

Gibbses, who first moved to the Minnesota property in the 1840s from Illinois, lived for five years in a tiny sod house—replicated in astounding detail and now a part of the tour—before building the main house. Guided tours cover the existing buildings, the excavations of the sod house, and a replica "soddy." The Gibbs Museum is open early May through early October.

Henry Sibley House Historic Site $
1357 Sibley Memorial Highway, Mendota
(651) 452-1596
www.mnhs.org/sibleyhouse

Henry Hastings Sibley, an American Fur Company regional manager and Minnesota's first governor, lived in a limestone home amid a trading post in the riverside hamlet of Mendota. Today visitors can walk through three of the structures in one of Minnesota's oldest European-American settlements, including the home of Sibley and his neighbor, Jean Baptiste Faribault. Sibley's restored house is full of fur trade stuff and the trappings of frontier gentility—pelts, muskets, and loads of blue china. The guides' stories of Sibley and company are vivid snapshots of the difficulties faced by these tough frontiersmen living in a wild world.

The Sibley House offers many theme tours and events, including Children's Day—where kids can learn about Dakota techniques used since the 1680s for turning natural materials into tepees, bowstrings, and fishing lines—and the 1850 Holiday Theme Tours, where visitors of all ages can tour the Sibley and Faribault Houses decorated as they were for the winter holidays in 1849–50. During the Holiday Tours, guides discuss the different celebrations by Yankees and French-Canadians, upper and lower classes, Presbyterians and Catholics, and the Dakota peoples. There's even an Irish Wolfhound Day (those bringing a dog of any kind get a discount), when visitors can learn more about and meet wolfhounds, an ancient hunting breed that was a favorite of Sibley's. The site is open weekends May through October and by appointment the rest of the year.

John H. Stevens House $
4801 Minnehaha Avenue South, Minneapolis
(612) 722-2220
www.johnhstevenshouse.org

The John H. Stevens House, built in 1849 and originally located in the present-day riverfront spot of the Minneapolis Post Office, is the first permanent settler's home in Minneapolis. The home of Col. John H. Stevens and his family served as the social and civic hub of the new city. People met here to discuss a name for the city and to organize local schools and government. It was here that John Stevens drew up the original territorial boundaries for Hennepin County. The first county elections were held here in 1852.

The house was reopened to the public in 1985 after being closed since the turn of the last century. It was pulled to Minnehaha Park in 1896 by more than 10,000 schoolchildren (working in seven separate relay teams and aided by horses, large steel wheels, and 400-foot ropes) in the first act of historic preservation in the state of Minnesota, but lack of funding prevented it from being anything but a curious landmark in the park for decades. Now an interpretive museum, exhibits, and tour guides inside the house tell the story of the city, founding father Stevens, and the importance of this little white house. The John H. Stevens House is open Memorial Day weekend through mid-September on Saturday, Sunday, and holidays.

The house is in south Minneapolis's Minnehaha Park on Minnehaha Avenue just south of East Minnehaha Parkway. It is across the street from the 50th Street Light-Rail Transit station.

Mill City Museum $–$$
704 South Second Street, Minneapolis
(612) 341-7555
www.millcitymuseum.org

Minneapolis was once known as the "Flour Capital of the World," and much of that rich heritage is on display at the Mill City Museum, which opened in 2003 on the city's riverfront. The museum is constructed around the ruins of the Washburn A Mill, originally constructed in 1874. The first mill exploded and burned to the ground on May 2, 1878, killing 18. The mill was rebuilt and reopened in 1880, and during its busiest years, the Washburn A ground enough flour every day to make 12 million loaves of bread. The mill continued to grind flour until 1965, but a 1991 fire severely damaged the abandoned mill. The remarkable Mill City Museum incorporates the stabilized limestone ruins of the mill into its design and includes many of the old mill's features, including milling machinery, flour bins, the engine house, and more. The museum also features a waterpower laboratory and an eight-story "Flour Power" ride that carries riders through Minneapolis' flour-milling history. In the museum's Baking Lab, visitors can grind wheat and bake bread. There is also an entertaining film "Minneapolis in 19 Minutes Flat," which features local radio personality Kevin Kling and his Monty Pythonesque and brief retelling of Minneapolis' history.

The museum can be found just north of the Metrodome in downtown Minneapolis along the Mississippi River. The museum is open Tuesday through Sunday.

Minnesota State Capitol   Free
75 Rev. Dr. Martin Luther King Jr. Boulevard
St. Paul
(651) 296-2881
www.mnhs.org/statecapitol
Soaring domes, monumental arches, columns, statues, and symbolic murals dominate the scene for visitors today as they did when the Minnesota State Capitol was completed in 1905. The first two capitols, one destroyed by fire and one outgrown, were in downtown St. Paul. The current structure is the stark, white capitol topped by a magnificent marble dome and the four golden horses—the Quadriga—that are usually what people remember after their visit to this masterpiece of Italian Renaissance architecture.

Today the State Senate, House of Representatives, and Supreme Court have been restored to their original appearances, as has the Rathskellar Cafe, now open to the public during the legislative session. Guided tours of the capitol leave every hour; self-guided tour brochures are available at the front entrance. (Groups of ten or more, please call ahead for reservations.) The State House and Senate are easily accessible to visitors, and if your timing's right, you can hear important issues being decided. The tours showcase amply captioned oil portraits of Minnesota governors around the rotunda, and go on to give insight to the history of the building, including information on the Civil War, and on architect Cass Gilbert's role in selecting art and furnishings for the building. The capitol is open daily year-round.

Murphy's Landing $–$$
2187 East Highway 101, Shakopee
(763) 694-7784
**www.threeriversparkdistrict.org/outdoor_
ed/murphys_landing/**
Murphy's Landing is a living-history site that preserves and interprets 19th-century life in the Minnesota River Valley. More than 40 period buildings were moved here from 1969 to 1972 with the intent of re-creating a 19th-century village; today the village includes a fur trading post, a homestead, and a storefront, all of which are arranged in chronological order by date of construction. Costumed interpreters demonstrate the rigors of the daily life of Minnesota's settlers, from metalsmiths to weavers and merchants. Special seasonal events are planned around the holidays for history buffs of all ages. Murphy's Landing is open daily late May to early September, and on some special-event weekends the rest of the year. You can reach Murphy's Landing from I-494 in the southwest Metro, exiting at US 69 South, and then exiting on Minnesota Highway 101 West. Murphy's Landing is about 4 miles west on the right side of MN 101.

Wabasha Street Caves $–$$$
215 South Wabasha Street, St. Paul
(651) 292-1220
www.wabashastreetcaves.com

Burrowed into the sandstone bluffs that line the Mississippi River on St. Paul's West Side (across the river from downtown), this is the site of the late Castle Royal nightclub, which was a speakeasy during the days of Prohibition and, before that, a mushroom farm. There's a lot of St. Paul history here, especially for those interested in the city's incarnation as a gangster mecca. Considering that the city of St. Paul was built around a cave (Pig's Eye Parrant's cavern and tavern), a cave is an appropriate dwelling for a night out. Dancers come to the caves on Swing Night, held every Thursday as well as select Fridays and featuring live big bands. The Historic Cave Tour covers the history of the Wabasha Street Caves, while the St. Paul Gangster Tour stops at several sites outside the caves where infamous crimes took place. Each October motorcoach tours depart from the caves to deliver St. Paul's haunted history. The caves are also a great spot for wedding receptions. The caves are open year-round (call for tour times and reservations).

INDOOR RECREATION

Hubert H. Humphrey Metrodome
900 South Fifth Street, Minneapolis
(612) 332-0386
www.msfc.com
This multipurpose facility, home of the Minnesota Vikings and Twins (the latter until their new stadium opens in 2010), and the U of M Gophers football team (until their new stadium opens in the fall of 2009), features events year-round. First-time visitors to the Metrodome are awed by its interior volume; regular fans sometimes feel they're watching theater, not sports. The Metrodome is big enough to host motocross events and monster-truck rallies as well as football games, occasional rock concerts, and in-line skaters.

During evenings November through March, when there's no previously scheduled event, the Metrodome turns into the Rollerdome—hordes of skaters take over its half-mile concourses, taking advantage of the tremendous workout the field provides. Skaters addicted to speed zoom around the upper concourse, while less-rabid skaters enjoy the Dome's smooth skating surface on the lower concourse. It's a great cure for cabin fever.

No one gets turned away wearing traditional skates, but Rollerdome is In-line Central. Rollerblade sponsors these skating sessions, where free protective gear is dispensed on a first-come, first-served basis and safety teams patrol to keep in-liners in line.

Parking for Rollerdome and the Metrodome is free in the Metrodome lot, which you can enter at the intersection of South Fifth Street and 11th Avenue. Enter the Dome at Gate D. No cameras, recording devices, or outside cans, bottles, coolers, or containers are allowed at the Metrodome or Rollerdome, but concessions are available inside on weekends in case you get peckish.

Mall of America   Free
60 East Broadway, Bloomington
(952) 883-8800
www.mallofamerica.com
This gigantic mall says only one thing about the state of American shopping: Fantasy moves product. And at this cement-and-plastic Bloomington behemoth, there's a lot of product to move. The largest shopping and entertainment complex in the United States, the megamall—at 4.2 million square feet—is the size of seven Yankee Stadiums and home to more than 520 stores, 50 restaurants, a 14-screen movie theater, an indoor amusement park, and an aquarium. To make your shopping experience more pleasurable, the mall rents strollers, wheelchairs, shopping carts, and lockers. In case you change your mind about shopping and decide to get married instead, there's a wedding chapel conveniently located inside the mall. Phase II of the Mall of America, including an NHL-sized skating rink, numerous upscale shops and restaurants, a 6,000-seat performing arts center, a boutique hotel, and much more is scheduled to open, in part, in 2008.

MUSEUMS

The Bakken Library and Museum $–$$
3537 Zenith Avenue South, Minneapolis
(612) 926-3878
www.thebakken.org

Established in 1976 by Earl E. Bakken, inventor of the first transistorized cardiac pacemaker and cofounder of Medtronic, a Twin Cities company on the cutting edge of electrocardio technology, this Tudor-style mansion houses an incredible collection of rare books, manuscripts, and scientific thingamajigs that are all related to the role electricity plays in life.

One of the most popular exhibits is "Frankenstein: Mary Shelley's Dream," in which visitors step back to the early 1800s for a dramatic multimedia immersion into Victor Frankenstein's laboratory and Mary Shelley's study. The "Electric Heart" exhibit teaches visitors about the electrical impulses of their own hearts, including allowing people to create music timed to their heartbeats.

The Bakken Museum is open Tuesday through Saturday; the museum's research library, with 11,000 rare books and 2,500 scientific instruments, is open Monday through Friday. The museum and library are on the west side of south Minneapolis' Lake Calhoun on Zenith Avenue South just north of West 36th Street.

Bell Museum of Natural History $
University of Minnesota
10 Church Street SE, Minneapolis
(612) 624-7083
www.bellmuseum.org

The Bell preserves an impressive collection of stuffed creatures that would interest 19th-century taxidermists as well as current students of the natural sciences. The animals are displayed in simulated natural environments, with background murals painted by landscape artist Francis L. Jaques. These scenes are curious testaments to the exotic hobbies of scientists of the past, especially in regard to the exhibits displaying passenger pigeons and other now-extinct creatures.

The exhibits of stuffed birds, mammals, and fish are extremely clean and tastefully exhibited, with beautiful painted backdrops of seascapes and woodlands for the animals on display. The exhibits are primarily Northland animals and confined to North America, with emphasis on Minnesota wildlife including porcupines, bears, moose, and ground squirrels. There is also a temporary exhibit hall that features artwork, animal remains, and fossils from around the world, changing approximately every two months.

The Touch and See Room, located on the second floor of the museum, is a veritable paradise for children interested in the natural sciences. Living snakes, turtles, and lizards are on display in tanks around the room, and with assistance from one of the friendly attendants, children can even hold some of these creatures. The room is full of horns, antlers, bones, fossils, and rocks, all for the handling—there's even a big, leathery elephant ear for kids to pick up and examine. There's also a rain-forest plant exhibit and a hall for traveling exhibits and artwork.

The Bell Museum is closed Monday and major holidays. Admission is free every Sunday and to Bell members, University of Minnesota faculty, and U of M students. The museum is on the northern side of the university's Minneapolis Campus at the intersection of Church Street SE and SE University Avenue.

Hennepin History Museum $
2303 Third Avenue South, Minneapolis
(612) 870-1329
hennepinhistory.org

Founded by the Hennepin County Territorial Pioneers Association in 1858, the Hennepin History Museum has long been dedicated to preserving the history of Hennepin County. Today the Hennepin History Museum serves as a gateway to historical resources. Housed in the George H. Christian mansion, designed by Hewitt and Brown, the museum offers a series of rotating exhibits focusing on everything from toys to technology. Past exhibits have highlighted Ojibwe and Dakota cultures, toys, quilt making, the creations of local artists, medical instruments, and historic wedding dresses. City Kids' Gallery is one place where touching the artifacts is not only allowed but encouraged.

The Hennepin History Museum is open varying hours Tuesday through Saturday. The museum is on Third Avenue South a block and a half south of West Franklin Avenue.

Minnesota Air Guard Museum $
Air National Guard Base
Off Minnesota Highways 62 and 55
Minneapolis–St. Paul International Airport
(612) 713-2523
www.mnangmuseum.org
This small but historically important museum displays vintage aircraft and memorabilia of the Minnesota Air National Guard. The memorabilia—airplane pictures, portraits, helmets, patches—is crowded into a couple of cramped rooms in a hangar. The museum's focus is on local flyboys, but 22 cool old planes are on display on the tarmac outside, including fighter jets, transports, and the terrifying black A-12, the CIA's favorite superfast spy plane.

Because the museum is located on an active military base, visitors must arrive by vehicle (rather than light-rail transit) and must show a photo ID. It's open most Saturdays (call for tours on other days) from late April until the end of September. The museum is in a corner of the National Guard Base, and it is best to check the Web site, call ahead, or ask at the guard station for directions.

Minnesota Children's Museum $$
10 West Seventh Street, St. Paul
(651) 225-6000
www.mcm.org
Einstein said that "play was the highest form of research," and if you have children, you will appreciate the diversion this museum can offer your kids. Traveling exhibits have included items on Peter Rabbit and Mister Rogers, while permanent exhibits are interactive and give children a chance to crawl through simulated ant colonies, create paper from gooey slop, or

i An admittance stamp at the Minnesota Children's Museum lets you come and go from the building all day, so you can sneak out and get a decent lunch and still come back and play for no extra charge.

take the stage in a TV studio. This is an especially popular place for graduate students to take their kids, as it keeps the youngsters entertained while letting education-minded parents comfortably take a study break. Recommended for children six months to 10 years of age and for parents looking to entertain their brood during the winter.

The Minnesota Children's Museum is open Tuesday through Sunday, closed Mondays and major holidays. The museum is at the intersection of West Seventh Street and Wabasha Street in downtown St. Paul.

The Minnesota History Center $–$$
345 West Kellogg Boulevard, St. Paul
(651) 259-3000 or (800) 657-3773
www.mnhs.org/places/historycenter
The Minnesota History Center is an architectural masterpiece constructed from Minnesota-quarried Rockville granite and Winona limestone. The view of the city from several vantage points inside the museum is breathtaking—as is the building itself. Exhibits touch on all aspects of Minnesota history. Encounter early settlers in "Tales of the Territory" or learn the facts about our storied weather in "Weather Permitting." The Minnesota History Center has a gigantic library of Minnesota-related books and historic photographs, as well as information on family genealogy; visitors are allowed to pore through the collection for free.

A few of the permanent exhibits are particularly kid friendly. Grainland includes an authentic 24-ton boxcar and a model grain elevator that children can climb through as they learn how grain gets to the marketplace. Juke boxes, interactive kiosks, and recording equipment keep kids busy in "Sounds Good to Me: Music in Minnesota."

The museum also presents a lecture series and book readings from local historians and authors. The Minnesota History Center museum is open Tuesday through Sunday year-round and on Mondays during the summer and on Monday holidays; the research library is open Tuesday through Saturday year-round.

The center sits at the corner of Kellogg Boulevard West and John Ireland Boulevard in downtown St. Paul.

Minnesota Transportation Museum $–$$$
various locations
(651) 288-0263
www.mtmuseum.org

Discover the history of transportation at the museum's exhibit sites. Among other things, visitors may ride diesel-powered trains in Osceola, Wisconsin; or view locomotive restoration up close at Jackson Street Round-house in St. Paul.

Minnesota Transportation Museum's Osceola and St. Croix Valley Railway's trains start at the Osceola, Wisconsin, depot (715-755-3570) about an hour northeast of the Twin Cities. There are two available trips: one to Marine on St. Croix, Minnesota, and one to Dresser, Wisconsin. Trains run weekends and holidays, April through October. In addition, the railway operates special events all season long.

The Jackson Street Roundhouse, located at 193 East Pennsylvania Avenue in St. Paul (651-228-0263), is the first railroad maintenance shop in Minnesota of the oldest known railroad in St. Paul—not bad for a city whose history has been dominated by railroading. Here, train lovers can climb aboard train cars of varying eras and styles and learn the state's railroad history through vintage posters and railroad maps. There's a gift shop, a working turntable (used to turn the locomotives), a kids' play area, and a working repair shop.

The museum also maintains several historic train depots around the state and in Wisconsin. The 1875 Milwaukee Road Depot at Minnehaha Park in south Minneapolis is one such station, open Sunday and holidays between Memorial Day and Labor Day. Although no longer in operation, the station was known as "The Princess," where over-heated Twin Citians once disembarked to enjoy the cool waters of Minnehaha Creek in summertime.

The Science Museum of Minnesota $$
120 West Kellogg Boulevard, St. Paul
(651) 221-9444 or (800) 221-9444
www.smm.org

With eight indoor acres of both permanent and temporary exhibits that include an extensive collection of dinosaur, mammal, insect, and fish fossils, plus a set of T. rex jaws you can operate, there's lots of interaction at this museum. In the Cell Lab, kids don lab coats and check out what their cheek cells look like under the microscope. In the Mississippi River Gallery, kids pretend to drive a real tugboat as they look out over the river. There are river views everywhere, both from the museum's patios and soaring glass windows and from the new exhibits on the museum's 10 outdoor acres. The nine-hole minigolf course is actually a lesson in river science, and the prairie maze is made from native Minnesota plants and grasses.

The Science Museum has traveling exhibits and a very cool IMAX Theater that shows films in front of, to either side, and above you all at the same time as you relax nearly flat on your back in comfy chairs. Both the traveling exhibits and the IMAX Theater have admission fees that can be purchased separately or as a package with admission to the museum.

The Museum of Questionable Medical Devices can also be found in the Science Museum. Located in the Collections Gallery, level four, about a dozen items from the original 300-piece collection give visitors a peek at machines from the past 100 years that were designed to "cure" what ails the average human. In some cases these failed remedies were honest mistakes, but many others were deliberate frauds. A few examples include the phrenology machine, which looks like an old-

The Minnesota History Center in St. Paul. TODD R. AND BONNIE S. BERGER

fashioned, hood-style hair dryer and suppos-
edly "reads" the bumps on your head to tell
you about your personality; a fluoroscope, a
shoe-fitting X-ray machine; and the Kellogg
Vibratory Chair, an electric-powered chair that
shook violently and was reputed to cure con-
stipation and improve respiration.

The Science Museum of Minnesota is
located at the intersection of Kellogg Boulevard West and Washington Street, just east of
the Xcel Energy Center in downtown St. Paul.

Twin City Model Railroad Museum $
Bandana Square, 1021 Bandana
Boulevard East, St. Paul
(651) 647-9628
www.tcmrm.org
Since 1939 this museum has featured the role
played by railroads in the history and development of Minnesota. An extensive collection of
railroad artifacts and art is available, including
a changing photo exhibit in the museum

ℹ️ The Science Museum of Minnesota
sits atop its parking ramp, which is
easiest to reach from Chestnut Street several stories below Kellogg Boulevard
West. From Kellogg, turn west on Eagle
Street and then turn left on Chestnut.

focusing on a different historic train or train
line each month.

The centerpiece of the museum is the
scale-model railroad of the re-creation of the
Twin Cities pre-1950. Up to six trains at once
glide through the depots and tunnels of the
incredibly detailed model, while miniature
streetcars seen running back and forth over
the Third Avenue Bridge model are sometimes brought out to run on the tracks as well.
The museum is closed Monday.

You can find the museum in Bandana
Square on Energy Park Drive halfway between
Lexington Avenue and Snelling Avenue in the
Midway area of St. Paul.

KIDSTUFF

In some ways, the Twin Cities were designed with kids in mind. In both Minneapolis and St. Paul, neighborhoods are centered around parks with community centers, swimming pools, and, in winter, ice-skating rinks. Public schools have initiated many after-school programs to help parents who can't be at home when the school day officially ends, and during summer these same schools offer fun classes for kids that include swimming lessons and summer sports.

From science- and nature-oriented attractions to water parks and bumper cars, your kids won't get bored in the Twin Cities. Luckily, even most museums and art events are fully prepared to receive and entertain children.

As for dining options, you're welcome to bring your kids into plenty of Twin Cities establishments—bars that double as restaurants in the daytime welcome underage patrons (accompanied by adults) until just before happy hour. The restaurants in this chapter try to make children feel comfortable, from the menu to service to decor. Most are also easy on the wallet.

PRICE CODE

The following price code is based on the cost for general admission for one adult. Most sites offer discounted tickets for children and seniors, and some allow discounts or even free entry for members of their respective organizations.

$ .... $5 and under
$$ .... $6–$15
$$$ .... $16–$30
$$$$ .... $31 and up

AMUSEMENT AND WATER PARKS

Cascade Bay $$
1360 Civic Center Drive, Eagan
(651) 675-5577
www.cascadebay.com
Seven-acre Cascade Bay in the St. Paul suburb of Eagan is the largest outdoor municipal water park in the Midwest. Its lazy river, multiple slides, sand beach, and more are extremely popular with just about any kid. Guests under 42 inches tall and those older than 62 get in at a reduced price.

Como Town $$$
1301 Midway Parkway, St. Paul
(651) 487-2121
www.comotown.com
Como Town is a small-but-nice amusement park, with 17 attractions geared toward kids ages 2 to 12, who can fight pretend fires with a personal truck and water cannon, navigate ministreets by kiddie car, and climb, swing, and bounce their way through a mega–jungle gym called Hodge Podge Park. A couple of rides have some height and speed, too. Admission to the park is free, then you buy rides with one to four 75-cent tickets. You can buy ticket packages that will help get the price down if you're planning on hitting a bunch of the rides.

Grand Rios $$–$$$
6900 Lakeland Avenue North, Brooklyn Park
(763) 566-8855
www.grandrios.com
Grand Rios is located inside the Grand Rios Hotel in the Minneapolis suburb of Brooklyn

Park. At 45,000 square feet, it's one of the biggest indoor water parks in this neck of the woods. Grand Rios is a Caribbean-themed affair with water basketball, spas, a lazy river, a 500-gallon dumping bucket, and multiple tube slide, one of which dumps into Hurricane Plunge. Check the Water Park Calendar on the Web site, as the prices fluctuate dramatically depending on what day and at what time you'd like to visit.

The Park at MOA $$$
Mall of America, 5000 Center Court
Bloomington
(952) 883-8600
www.theparkatmoa.com
Located at the center of the Mall of America, the Park at MOA, the largest indoor amusement park in America, has more than 25 rides and attractions for kids and adults alike. For the little guys, there's the Americana Carousel, a hand-painted contemporary version of the classic carousel, and Lil' Shaver, a smaller, slower version of the roller coaster that circles the park (the Ripsaw Roller Coaster). For everyone else, there's the Skyscraper Ferris Wheel that takes visitors 74 feet high in the air, the Log Chute—a watery ride that includes a drop over a 40-foot waterfall—and plenty of other rides and attractions to take your mind off of shopping. Admission to the park is free; you purchase points or a wristband for rides. If you like to sneak some kid-free shopping in, drop the little ones off at Kids Quest in the Park at MOA. The child care facility charges by the hour, and there's plenty for kids to do here, including read books, sing karaoke, and play nonviolent video games.

Valleyfair! $$$$
1 Valleyfair Drive, Shakopee
(952) 445-6500 or (800) FUN-RIDE
www.valleyfair.com
With more than 75 rides and attractions, Valleyfair! is the upper Midwest's largest theme park, with something to offer the littlest kid or the bravest adult. Take an inner tube down a

i Twin Cities parents love Toddler Tuesday at the Mall of America for its great deals, including free meals and activities.

gently sloping canal for a relaxing, meditative ride on Ripple Rapids, or take a boat off a 50-foot drop on the Flume. The park is packed with twists, turns, flips, and freefalls, from the classic wooden High Roller to the Xtreme Swing, like your typical playground version on steroids, new in 2006. There are also many rides for the really little ones, too, from bumble bee–shaped electric cars to a multilevel foam-ball factory to an antique carousel. If it's hot out, don't miss Whitewater Country, a three-and-a-half-acre waterpark with multiple water slides, raft rides, and attractions with names like Raging Rapids, Splash Station, and Giggle.

Water Park at the Depot $$$
225 Third Avenue South, Minneapolis
(612) 758-7873
www.thedepotminneapolis.com
With 15,000 square feet, this locomotive-themed water park includes a three-story waterslide, multiple pools, and a slide/train that sprays water. It's pretty pricey for its size (or lack thereof), but it's connected to hotels that offer package deals and it's downtown, near many other attractions.

Water Park of America $$$
1700 East American Boulevard, Bloomington
(952) 854-8700
www.waterparkofamerica.com
Adjacent to the Mall of America, the Water Park of America offers the only surfing simulator in Minnesota, a wave pool, a ten-story raft ride, swimming pools, and more. Arrive early during warm summer weekends as the water park often fills to capacity. The water park is open seasonally and hours vary (call ahead for details). The water park complex includes a game arcade with many different prizes for winners.

Children love Cafesjian's Carousel at Como Zoo in St. Paul. SAINT PAUL RCVA

ANIMAL ADVENTURES

Como Zoo   Free
1225 Estabrook Drive, St. Paul
(651) 487-8200
www.comozooconservatory.org
One of only four free (donation requested)
metropolitan-area zoos in the country, Como
Zoo has been an institution in St. Paul for more
than a century. The zoo offers intimate
exhibits housing reticulated giraffes, black-
footed penguins, snow leopards, yellow-
rumped caciques, blue-eyed black lemurs,
gray wolves, and more. There is a great pri-
mate display, with about a dozen ring-tailed
and brown lemurs, spider monkeys, a couple
of breeding pairs of tamarins, orangutans, and
gorillas. There are bears, giraffes, zebras, buffalo, and the ever-popular Sparky the Sea Lion
show, held Memorial Day through Labor Day.

But it doesn't stop at the animals. There's
also an antique wooden carousel, Cafesjian's
Carousel, for kids and adults to ride in a building near the entrance of the zoo, and in summer check out the amusement park Como
Town. In late October the zoo opens in the
evening for its annual "Zoo Boo," where kids
come in their Halloween costumes and are
given candy and gifts by more than 300
volunteers.

Minnesota Zoo $$
13000 Zoo Boulevard, Apple Valley
(952) 431-9200 or (800) 366-7811
www.mnzoo.org
Located in the southeastern suburb of Apple
Valley and housing some 500 animal species
from five different continents, the Minnesota
Zoo and its IMAX theater see a million visitors
per year. The zoo's 500 acres include an
indoor Tropics Trail, populated by gibbons,
tapirs, tree kangaroos, hissing cockroaches,
and endangered red pandas. The newly
redesigned Minnesota Trail, also an indoor
walk, is home to gray wolves, porcupines,

great horned owls, river otters, and other Minnesota residents. At Discovery Bay, dolphins officially perform for audiences every afternoon and unofficially any time enough people gather around their huge, glass-walled tank; a walk-through aquarium with sharks, fish, and deep-sea plants; and a hands-on area where kids (and adults) can pet different kinds of sharks, rays, and starfish. Outside the main exhibit building, you can find ducks and swans, a prairie dog town, wild horses, camels, tigers, and many, many other animals. Domesticated animals like pigs and chickens get their day in the sun at the Wells Fargo Family Farm exhibit. Daily cow milkings are a kick for us city folk to watch. It's worth the extra few dollars to ride the Monorail around the zoo, as it is the least strenuous way to see many animals requiring room to roam, including endangered and extremely rare Mexican wolves, musk oxen, and Siberian tigers.

The zoo also features the 600-seat Great Clips IMAX theater and the Weesner Family Amphitheater, which hosts concerts all summer long.

To reach the zoo, follow Interstate 35E south from Interstate 494 in the southeast Metro, exit at Minnesota Highway 77, and follow the signs.

Underwater Adventures Aquarium $$–$$$
Mall of America, 120 East Broadway
Bloomington
(952) 883-0202 or (888) 348-3824
www.underwateradventures.net
Underwater Adventures is a huge (1.2 million gallons) walk-through aquarium featuring more than 4,500 different sea creatures from around the world in eight exhibits. For a one-time admission charge, visitors can walk through a glass tunnel that leads them underneath the three freshwater exhibits:Touch of the Wild Woods, Fisherman's Hollow, and the Wild Amazon, and five ocean exhibits: Shark Cove, Rainbow Reef, Seacrits of Hollywood (with famous fish like Nemo), Starfish Beach, and Circle of Life, where children can touch harmless sharks and stingrays.

BERRY PICKIN'

Driving out to the country to pick fresh strawberries, blueberries, or apples is a Minnesota-childhood staple. For a small per-bucket fee, the following farms let visitors pick as much fruit as they can carry home, and there are often bonus attractions such as petting zoos, wagon rides, and gift shops. For apples, we suggest you stop by **Aamodt's Apple Farm,** 6428 Manning Avenue North, Stillwater (651-439-3127; www.aamodtsapplefarm.com); the **Afton Apple Orchards,** 14421 South 90th Street, Hastings (651-436-8385; www.afton apple.com); or **Sponsel's Minnesota Harvest Apple Orchard,** 8251 Old Highway 169 Boulevard, Jordan (952-492-7753; www.minnesota harvest.net). For strawberries and blueberries, try either the **Bauer Berry Farm,** 10830 French Lake Road, Champlin (763-421-4384; www.bauerberry.com); or **Covered Bridge Farm,** 18655 Forest Boulevard North, Forest Lake (651-464-0735). For a comprehensive list of basically anything grown in the state that you can buy directly from farms, contact **Minnesota Grown** (651-201-6539 or 800-657-3878; www.minnesotagrown.com).

ARTS AND CULTURE

The Children's Theatre Company $$$
2400 Third Avenue South, Minneapolis
(612) 874-0400
www.childrenstheatre.org
Since 1965 the Tony Award–winning Children's Theatre Company and its cast of incredibly talented children and professional adult actors have been putting on performances at its two-stage theater in south Minneapolis. Most of the performances are based

Parents with young children can buy Lap Passes for young kids (three and under) for some Children's Theater Company performances. Costing only $10, a Lap Pass gets your youngster in to see all the fun without cleaning out your wallet.

Underwater Adventures Aquarium offers a chance to walk underneath sharks and other sea creatures.
GREATER MINNEAPOLIS CONVENTION & VISITORS ASSOCIATION

on children's stories and fairy tales, such as *Alexander and the Terrible, Horrible, No Good, Very Bad Day* by Judith Viorst, but there's a healthy dose of impressive original works as well.

In the Heart of the Beast Puppet and Mask Theatre $$
1500 East Lake Street, Minneapolis
(612) 721-2535
www.hobt.org

Unusual masks and large, fantastical puppets teach themes of natural and cultural understanding here. Outside of regular original performances and the much-lauded May Day parade, Heart of the Beast offers kids' performances every Saturday morning for $3, with a $2 discount if you're from the neighborhood.

Minneapolis Sculpture Garden   Free
725 Vineland Place, Minneapolis
(612) 375-7600
www.walkerart.org

Located across the street from the Walker Art Center, this beautiful collection of large sculptures made by local and internationally known artists is a great place to take kids because it's outside, it's interesting, and it's free. Kids can run around and enjoy the 11-acre grounds without worrying about keeping silent while the grown-ups enjoy art—and who knows? They might learn something about art appreciation themselves. The Minneapolis Sculpture Garden features one of the most photographed spots in Minnesota: the gigantic *Spoonbridge and Cherry* by Claes Oldenburg and Coosje van Bruggen, conveniently

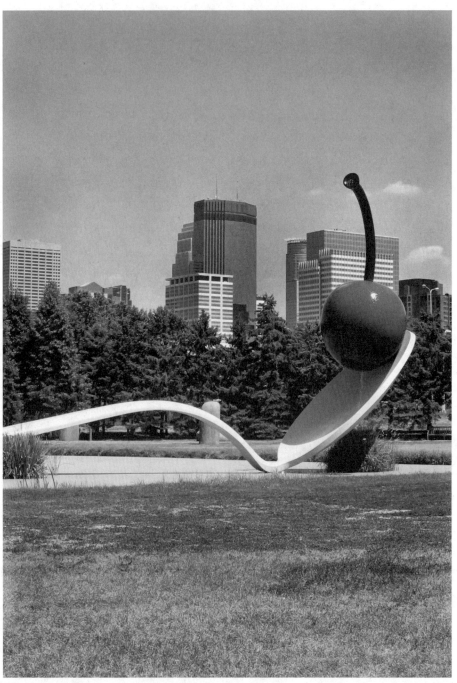

Spoonbridge and Cherry *by Claes Oldenburg and Coosje van Bruggen in the Minneapolis Sculpture Garden is popular for photos.* TODD R. AND BONNIE S. BERGER placed for pictures of the sculpture against the Minneapolis skyline. In all, more than 40 works of art spread out on the lawns of the sculpture garden. Right across another street is Loring Park, with restrooms, a wading pool, a playground, and lots of sunny spots for a relaxing summer picnic.

Minnesota Center for Book Arts $$
1011 Washington Avenue South, Suite 100
Minneapolis
(612) 215-2520
www.mnbookarts.org
The Minnesota Center for Book Arts, the largest independent book arts facility in the nation, offers classes to children, teens, families, and adults on making paper, binding books, and working in a printing-press studio. Kids can take their literary creations to the next level by making a beautiful cover out of found objects and binding their books using traditional methods, or they can create their own newspapers in the letterpress studio using both modern and antiquated letterpress equipment.

MUSEUMS AND HISTORICAL ATTRACTIONS

The Bakken Library and Museum $–$$
3537 Zenith Avenue South, Minneapolis
(612) 926-3878
www.thebakken.org
It starts in the lobby, where kids dive into the shocker machine, thought a cure-all in the 1920s, while parents read about the museum's founder, Earl E. Bakken, inventor of the first portable pacemaker. The rest of the electricity-related thingamajigs throughout this Tudor-style mansion are often hands-on—adults tend to hog the theremin, that instrument that makes B-movie UFO sounds, and kids really like the crack and spark that comes from cranking out 60,000 volts. Nine informational exhibits include the popular "Frankenstein: Mary Shelley's Dream." Recommended for ages six and above. Make-and-take proj-

ects are held weekly on Family Science Saturday from 10:00 a.m. to 4:00 p.m.

Bell Museum of Natural History $
University of Minnesota, 10 Church Street SE,
Minneapolis
(612) 624-7083
www.bellmuseum.org
While most museums of taxidermied animals have fallen out of favor, this is one of the more pleasant traditional natural history museums in the country. The Bell Museum is designed to preserve the past, protect the future, and bring people closer to nature. How else is your kid going to get the chance to pet a Kodiak bear? The Touch and See Room lets children handle history, such as a 10,000-year-old woolly mammoth tusk; various fossils, bones, and rocks; and live animals including lizards and turtles. The museum has two floors of diorama-style exhibits featuring North American mammals and birds, with an emphasis on Minnesota wildlife, including a bald eagle, moose, and squirrels. There's also a rain-forest plant exhibit and a hall for traveling exhibits and artwork. On the second Saturday of each month, the museum offers hands-on programs for families with children under four, and on the first Thursday of every month, the museum hosts Nature Tots for toddlers and preschoolers—and their parents (for the latter, registration is required; call 612-624-9050). In October, the museum also offers two-day Fall Camps, one for kids in kindergarten through second grade, and one for kids in grades three through five.

Fort Snelling $–$$
Minnesota Highways 5 and 55, St. Paul
(612) 726-1171
www.mnhs.org/fortsnelling
Established on a bluff overlooking the Mississippi and Minnesota Rivers in 1819, Fort Snelling was once the last American outpost in the mostly unexplored wilds of the north and was the center of frontier commerce and government on the upper Mississippi.

Themed tours provide insight into what life was like at the fort, with costumed guides reenacting scenes from military, civilian, and American Indian life of the 1800s. Kids can join in the fun by taking up a musket and pretending to be a soldier, scraping hides with fur traders, or "working" in the laundry or kitchen of the fort. New programming includes day camps and kids' activities.

The Jackson Street Roundhouse $
193 East Pennsylvania Avenue, St. Paul
(651) 228-0263
www.mtmuseum.org
It's all about trains here at the first railroad maintenance shop in Minnesota, part of the Minnesota Transportation Museum. Climb aboard train cars of varying eras and styles. Learn the state's railroad history through vintage posters and railroad maps. There's a gift shop, a kids' play area, and a working shop, too, where locomotives are restored. Choo-choo-loving youngsters will love it here.

Mill City Museum $$
704 South Second Street, Minneapolis
(612) 341-7555
www.millcitymuseum.org
Tell your kids you're taking them to a flour-milling museum in a former working mill and you might not hear cheers of excitement. But then tell them about the ride. The Flour Tower takes you on an eight-story-high journey that relates the history of this mill in employees' words. And mention the explosion. Mill explosions were common at the turn of the 20th century, when Minneapolis produced more flour than any city in the world, and here you can watch a small explosion and find out why it happened. From the top of the building, look down at St. Anthony Falls, the only waterfall along the Mississippi, which provided the power that drew the mills in the first place. Lots of hands-on, kid-friendly exhibits here make Minneapolis's flour-milling saga intriguing for both child and adult. Seeing the building itself is worth the trip. A fire nearly destroyed the mill, and the museum was built around the ruins.

Minnesota Children's Museum $$
10 West Seventh Street, St. Paul
(651) 225-6000
www.mcm.org
The great thing about this museum, which is geared toward children six months to 10 years, is that all the exhibits are hands-on. While in the World Works Gallery, kids can operate a crane to pick up blocks, build a house foundation out of rubber masonry, or learn how to make art out of recycled newspaper. The Earth World Gallery has a giant anthill (populated by giant ant statues and nests) that kids can crawl through, pulley-operated clouds that can be moved across the ceiling by remote control, and a beaver dam and a giant hollow log that kids can climb in and out of.

For toddlers ages six months to four years, there's a wonderful playroom, the Habitot, that's set up like a nature preserve, with a giant "pond" playpen filled with plush lily pads and frog, turtle, and fish puppets at one end and a padded crawl-through cave filled with more stuffed animals and puppets at the other end. Changing rooms are connected to the exhibit, too, so parents don't have to rush to the other end of the building to take care of emergencies. Performances and activities take place in the second-floor atrium at scheduled intervals throughout the day.

The Minnesota History Center $$
345 Kellogg Boulevard West, St. Paul
(651) 259-3000 or (800) 657-3773
www.mnhs.org/places/historycenter
A few of the permanent exhibits at the Minnesota History Center are particularly kid friendly. Grainland includes an authentic 24-ton boxcar and a model grain elevator that children can climb through as they learn how grain gets to the marketplace. Juke boxes, interactive kiosks, and recording equipment keep kids busy in the "Sounds Good to Me: Music in Minnesota" exhibit.

Murphy's Landing $$
2187 East Highway 101, Shakopee
(763) 694-7784
www.threeriversparkdistrict.org/outdoor
_ed/murphys_landing/
This living-history site preserves and inter-prets 19th-century life in the Minnesota River Valley. More than 40 period buildings were moved here from 1969 to 1972 with the intent of re-creating a 19th-century village. The village includes a fur trading post, a homestead, and a storefront. The site is peopled by "villagers" who are clothed in period costumes and perform such duties as weaving, metal-smithing, and farming—visitors are encouraged to ask questions about what villagers are doing. Kids can play house 1880s-style in the Pioneer Kids' Play Area.

Science Museum of Minnesota $$
120 West Kellogg Boulevard, St. Paul
(651) 221-9444 or (800) 221-9444
www.smm.org
Cool fossils and dinosaur skeletons, including a set of T. rex jaws you can operate, are at the heart of the Science Museum of Minnesota. But there's lots more interaction among the eight indoor acres of permanent and tempo-rary exhibits. In the Cell Lab, kids don lab coats and check out what their cheek cells look like under the microscope. In the Missis-sippi River Gallery, kids pretend to drive a real tugboat as they look out over the river. There are river views everywhere, from the museum's patios and soaring glass windows and from the new outdoor exhibits—the nine-hole minigolf course is actually a lesson in river science, and the prairie maze is made from native Minnesota plants and grasses. There's an IMAX theater, too, as well as one-shot kids' and family classes with activities such as fossil hunting, robot building, and experimenting with dry ice.

In both Minneapolis and St. Paul, there's a park in nearly every neighborhood for you to stop and let the kids get out and stretch their legs.

Twin City Model Railroad Museum $
Bandana Square, 1021 Bandana Boulevard East, St. Paul
(651) 647-9628
www.tcmrm.org
A great treat for children and adults alike, this museum will particularly impress anyone even slightly interested in history, railroads, or miniatures. In existence in one form or another since 1939, the Model Railroad Club has been educating and entertaining the pub-lic with model locomotives, building its incredible panoramic sets to scale to com-plete the illusion. The museum is set inside a former passenger-train repair shop that houses a wonderful scale model of the Twin Cities and the surrounding communities, including parts of the Mississippi River and the old Mill District in Minneapolis prior to 1950, when trains were still the main means of transporting goods throughout the coun-try. Up to six different trains run at once through the model, disappearing into tunnels and climbing through the tree-filled land-scapes with their tiny headlights blazing. The exhibit changes monthly—miniature street-cars run back and forth over the Third Avenue Bridge model, or steam engines like the *Mil-waukee Hiawatha* pull passenger cars in and out of the 1914 Great Northern passenger depot. In the winter, the museum stays open a little later on Saturday to show off the spe-cial "Night Trains" exhibit, where all the lights are turned off in the museum and the lights on the trains and miniature buildings become the only source of illumination in the room.

PARKS (FAVORITES OF LITTLE INSIDERS)

Edinborough Park $
7700 York Avenue South, Edina
(952) 832-6790
www.edinboroughpark.com
This densely landscaped, indoor one-acre park has a huge playground, pathways, an amphitheater, a junior Olympic–sized pool, and more than 6,000 plants, trees, and flowers.

ℹ️ The Greater Minneapolis Convention and Visitor's Association has a new Web site for visitors with children. See www.minneapolis-kids.com for information about discounts, family-friendly hotels, and kid-approved sights.

Adventure Peak, one of the largest indoor play structures in the country, features a tree to climb, tubes to crawl through, a climbing wall to scale, and a Great Hall to play with bouncy balls. It's hard to drag kids out of Edinborough. The park has scheduled activities and concerts, too, and they are never rained out.

Harriet Island Regional Park   **Free**
West of Wabasha and Water Streets
St. Paul
(651) 632-5111
www.stpaul.gov/depts/parks/specialservices/Harriet_Island/index.html
In the shadow of St. Paul sits the largest urban river park in North America. Seems there's always an event going on at Harriet Island, such as the summer children's concert series and the Taste of Minnesota, the state's popular annual Independence Day celebration (both of which are free, by the way). The Padelford Packet Boat Company launches riverboat tours from here. And you'll find, among other things, a riverboat-themed playground, the floating River Boat Grill, and big, wide steps that head right down into the Mississippi.

Lake Calhoun   **Free**
3000 Calhoun Parkway, Minneapolis
(612) 230-6400
www.minneapolisparks.org
Lake Calhoun is part of Minneapolis's inner-city chain of lakes, which are immensely popular year-round, especially with families. This particular lake has a little bit of everything, including sandy beaches, a fishing dock, picnic areas, walking and biking paths, and a tot lot. You can rent canoes, kayaks, and paddleboats at the Lake Calhoun Pavilion on the east side of the lake. The waterside pavilion houses a restaurant called Tin Fish, with all kinds of seafood, snacks, and kid-friendly items such as hot dogs, grilled cheese, fish-and-chips, and root-beer floats.

RESTAURANTS THAT LIKE KIDS (AND VICE VERSA)

Convention Grill & Fountain
3912 Sunnyside Road, Edina
(952) 920-6881
The Convention Grill & Fountain is an authentic diner that's thankfully light on kitsch as well as on the pocketbook. Choose a booth seat or one at the stainless-steel counter overlooking the double-wide grill. The jukebox plays as servers zip around with vanilla Cokes, hamburgers, skin-on fries, and malts served as they should be—with a long spoon and the overflow in the metal cup each malt was made in.

Cupcake
3338 University Avenue SE, Minneapolis
(612) 378-4818
This is the kind of place you wave in front of your kids as a reward for good behavior, never letting on that you want to go as badly as they do. Cupcakes, people. The cafe/coffeehouse rotates randomly through about 50 tried-and-true cupcake recipes, and you'll find up to 12 varieties offered on any given day. One kid favorite is the Betty Crocker, if solely for its swirly pink frosting and pretty pastel sprinkles, but look for Boston Crème, Red Velvet, Lemon Sunshine, S'More, and Coco Loco as well. The menu holds soups, sandwiches, pizzas, PB&J, and egg salad, too.

Galactic Pizza
2917 Lyndale Avenue South, Minneapolis
(612) 824-9100
www.galacticpizza.com
Superheroes deliver the pizza from Galactic. Generic superheroes, not Spidey or Superman, but spandex and capes are involved. Delivery service, by electric vehicle, is limited to southwest Minneapolis, though it does

extend to downtown Minneapolis during lunch. Travelers can order pizza delivered to their hotels. Or they can opt to eat on-site. The clean, multicolored storefront has brightly colored, child-height tables outdoors, retro Formica kitchen tables inside, and some toys older kids might like, including pick-up sticks, dominoes, and chess. Galactic is more kid friendly than kid oriented, though, and the nighttime crowd is primarily adult. The restaurant theme is social responsibility—you'll see a lot of words like hormone-free, recycled, and organic on the menu. The pizza can be plain or exotic, meaty or vegan, whatever you want. (The Paul Bunyan, with bison sausage, morel mushrooms, and wild rice is surprisingly delicious.) Give the kids a heads-up: Your server will not be wearing a superhero outfit, alas, but you'll catch glimpses of the caped ones as they head off on their pizza-delivery missions.

Pop! A Neighborhood Restaurant
2859 Johnson Avenue Northeast, Minneapolis
(612) 788-0455
www.poprestaurant.com
Pop! possesses hard-to-find qualities in a restaurant: a casually upscale atmosphere that welcomes children, gourmet food at reasonable prices, and a drink menu that holds both a solid wine list and an even bigger selection of pop, the preferred word for sweet, carbonated beverages here in Minnesota. There's more than a hint of Latin America in the menu, where tamales and empanadas exist alongside pasta and burgers, and where smoked jalapeño mayo and avocado find their way onto the chicken sandwich. Try to save room for dessert.

WE ALL SCREAM FOR . . .

Grand Ole Creamery
750 Grand Avenue, St. Paul
(651) 293-1655
www.grandolecreamery.com
Do not be deterred by the line snaking out the door, spilling out onto the sidewalks of Grand

Avenue. This ice cream is worth the wait. The waffle cones are made fresh daily and plugged with a malted milk ball to prevent sticky hands and ice-cream-smeared shirts. There are 200 flavors, and the 31 available on any given day tend toward the seasonal—strawberry kiwi sorbet in the summer, German chocolate and pumpkin apple strudel in the fall, and choices like egg nog and Winter Wonderland (loaded with peppermint candy) in the winter.

Izzy's Ice Cream Cafe
2034 Marshall Avenue, St. Paul
(651) 603-1458
www.izzysicecream.com
Izzy's is a local favorite not only for its kid friendliness but also for its namesake feature: An "izzy" is the extra one-ounce scoop of ice cream that tops your single- or double-scoop cone here. With 31 of Izzy's 100-plus artisan options spread out before you, it's hard enough to choose a flavor, let alone decide which izzy would be the best complement. Kids go gaga over the bubble gum and the blue cotton candy flavors. The one-ounce izzy cone is a nice size for young children, and it costs just over a dollar.

SHOPPING KID-STYLE

Creative Kidstuff
4313 Upton Avenue South, Minneapolis
(612) 927-0653
Five additional Twin Cities locations
www.creativekidstuff.com
This neat little local toyshop chain offers educational and creative toys for both kids and parents to salivate over. Hands-on is the motto here. Lots of toys have been removed from their packaging and scattered about the store for kids to try out. There are three big sales a year—a storewide event in June and clearance sales in July and after Christmas. Creative Kidstuff holds in-store kids' events throughout the year, too.

Kiddywampus

4402½ France Avenue S, Edina
(952) 926-7871
www.kiddywampus.com

Opened in 2006, this unusual toy store carries things to monkey with from all over the world (not just China) and has a built-in play area. Products include an Alien Pizza-Making Kit (with green crust and purple pizza sauce), an Insect Color Paint and Draw Kit (not for use on real bugs), and a Balloon-Powered Boat (perfect for bath time). Kiddywampus actively courts parents looking for a birthday party venue and will host such gatherings, and the store also offers Abrakadoodle art classes for kids as young as 20 months.

Pacifier

310 East Hennepin Avenue, Minneapolis
(612) 623-8123 or (888) 623-8123
www.pacifieronline.com

Pacifier stocks an offbeat and artistic collection of clothes, wooden toys, diaper bags, gifts, and much more for the baby of the family and the baby's parents. The store features clothing from Global Mamas, high-quality handmade dresses and onesies made by Ghanan women who are guaranteed a fair wage for their work.

The Red Balloon Bookshop

891 Grand Avenue, St. Paul
(651) 224-8320
www.redballoonbookshop.com

Located in a house on St. Paul's cozy Grand Avenue, the Red Balloon has been turning kids on to books since 1984. The selection is comprehensive, with classics past and future, and the staff obviously loves what they do—they're ready with suggestions if you need ideas. There's nearly always an event scheduled, whether it be a story hour or an author reading or lecture.

Siji Kids

370 Snelling Avenue South, St. Paul
(651) 699-5290
www.sijikids.com

This combination children's clothing boutique and photo studio is a great spot to find stylish clothing for junior, including outfits from Baby Soy, Mimi + Maggie, and Wes & Willy, among others. For bored kids, Siji has a train table and a bunch of toys to keep reluctant shoppers busy while the parents browse. Siji Studios (651-442-5917; www.sijistudios.com) in the basement of the storefront offers professional "journalistic" photography of kids either in studio or on location. Photographer Kyle Johnson specializes in photographing "kids being kids," and he creates lovely images that go well beyond the blue-background posed mall shots most parents choose by default.

Wild Rumpus Books for Young Readers

2720 West 43rd Street, Minneapolis
(612) 920-5005
www.wildrumpusbooks.com

The front door of this 2,000-square-foot bookstore hints at what's to come. It actually holds a door within a door, giving kids an entrance that's their own size rather than the same old adult-height doorway. This place is definitely designed for kids. The name, plucked from Maurice Sendak's Where the Wild Things Are, fits. Animals are everywhere—chickens, cats, birds, ferrets, tarantulas, geckos, fish, and even a rat, whose cage is appropriately placed in the floor of the scary books reading shack. You'll find old and new favorites as well as lots of books from smaller presses that you simply can't find at your local chain bookstore—one of many refreshing ways this bookshop differentiates itself from the big guys.

ANNUAL EVENTS AND FESTIVALS

Festivals abound year-round in the Twin Cities. In the winter, elaborate festivities like the Holidazzle Parade and the St. Paul Winter Carnival stave off cabin fever. With the coming of spring, just about anything can kick off a festival, from an abundance of wildflowers blooming to charitable functions and building restoration projects. Entire city blocks are roped off for block parties in the summer, and the streets are filled with cars decorated with seashells, ribbons, sculptures, and big painted flowers. Just about every tiny town in the state holds at least one spring and summer festival, complete with parades, concession and merchandise kiosks, and live music.

The following calendar lists only events that have been around for a while and that we expect will continue to be around.

JANUARY

St. Paul Winter Carnival
Various locations around St. Paul
Last week of January through first week of February
(651) 223-4700
www.winter-carnival.com
The St. Paul Winter Carnival is by far the coolest celebration in the Midwest and one of the oldest winter festivals in the country. More than 50 events—including amazing snow and ice-sculpture exhibits, live music, and sporting events such as a 5K run and half marathon, and softball on ice—are a part of this annual festival, with the crowning events

i The Twin Cities Infoline (612-379-CALL) provides an automated list of events, arts and entertainment, restaurants, sports scores, and other happenings throughout the Twin Cities metro area.

being the King Boreas Grande Day Parade and the more decadent evening Vulcan Victory Torchlight Parade.

FEBRUARY

Kidfest
RiverCentre/Touchstone Energy Place
175 Kellogg Boulevard, St. Paul
(651) 265-4800
Kidfest, in January or February, is Minnesota's longest-running children's event, with multiple stages of live entertainment, dozens of free activities and games for kids of all ages, and Minnesota's largest inflatable playground (featuring a superslide, Velcro wall, maze, sports challenges, and much more), all guaranteed to keep your kids busy for at least a day, maybe two. The Saturday and Sunday festival features celebrity visits from national childrens' artists (usually of Nickelodeon fame). In addition, there's the perennial favorite, the petting zoo, a rain-forest stage filled with exotic creatures, and pony rides.

Twin Cities Food & Wine Experience
Minneapolis Convention Center,
1301 Second Avenue South, Minneapolis
A mid-February weekend
(612) 371-5800
www.foodwineshow.com
Although tickets for this annual event get into the pricey range (over $50), you are likely to get your money's worth even if you come hungry. About 300 Twin Cities restaurants; local, national, and international wineries; and other exhibitors serve up their gourmet specialties to the masses. Additional events (at an additional charge) include wine seminars and wine lunches at restaurants throughout the Metro.

MARCH

St. Patrick's Day Parade
Downtown St. Paul
(651) 292-3225
St. Paul's annual St. Patrick's Day Parade picks up at Fourth and Wacouta Streets and heads west all the way down Fourth Street, ending at Rice Park. The parade features Irish music and performers, and food, drink, and merchandise kiosks are set up along the parade route for the remainder of the day.

The parade is all part of St. Paul's annual Irish Celebration, paying homage to the many Irish immigrants who settled in the city. Entertainment, crafts, Irish foods, and beer (Irish and otherwise) are all part of the festivities, centered around Landmark Center in downtown St. Paul.

APRIL

Minneapolis/St. Paul International
Film Festival
Various locations
Three weeks in April
(612) 331-3134
www.mspfilmfest.org
In 20-plus years, Minnesota Film Arts' Minneapolis–St. Paul International Film Festival has gone from a weekend-long event to the present high-water mark where about 150 flicks from more than 60 nations are screened during three full weeks in April. The festival's participating theaters include the Oak Street Cinema, Bell Auditorium, Riverview Theater, Crown Theatres Block E, and other Twin Cities film houses.

Ironman Bicycle Ride
Lakeville High School, Lakeville
Last Sunday of April
(651) 251-1495
www.ironmanbikeride.org
An annual event for more than 40 years, the Ironman Bike Ride takes 5,000 participating bicyclists through 30-mile, 62-mile, or 100-mile scenic tours through the Minnesota countryside.

MAY

Festival of Nations
175 Kellogg Boulevard West, RiverCentre, St. Paul
(651) 647-0191
www.festivalofnations.com
Founded in 1932 and held generally in late April or early May, the Festival of Nations has been an event of the people who helped create it for their pleasure and the ethnic values they treasured. Its underlying philosophy has been that as Americans of all backgrounds— native citizens and naturalized citizens alike— share experiences, their differences become less significant and barriers to understanding are removed. Today Minnesota's largest multicultural event showcases more than 100 ethnic groups through food, dance performances, cultural exhibits, folk art demonstrations, an international bazaar, and more.

Cinco de Mayo Fiesta
District del Sol, St. Paul
First week in May
(651) 222-6347
www.districtdelsol.com
The Cinco de Mayo Fiesta lights up the District del Sol on the west side of St. Paul, across the Robert Street Bridge from downtown (for visitors, the "west" side of St. Paul is actually south of downtown). More than 100,000 people fill the streets of the Hispanic neighborhood to take in Mexican entertainment and food and to watch the Cinco de Mayo Parade.

In the Heart of the Beast
May Day Parade
Powderhorn Park, 3400 15th Avenue South, Minneapolis
First Sunday of May
(612) 721-2535
www.hobt.org

The Cinco de Mayo Fiesta in the District del Sol across the Mississippi from downtown St. Paul brings many smiles. SAINT PAUL RCVA

For more than 30 years, In the Heart of the Beast Puppet and Mask Theatre's annual May Day Parade has been as true a sign of spring returning to the Twin Cities as robins choosing their mates. The brilliantly colored ensemble of friendly and scary creatures on stilts, children dressed as flowers, and other magical images travels along Minneapolis's downtown Bloomington Avenue and ends in a colorful pageant in Powderhorn Park, where puppets sail across the pond in boats. This funky celebration of spring will fill an entire day with dance, music, fun, and food all along the parade route.

JUNE

Alive After Five Concert Series
Peavey Plaza, 11th Street and Nicollet Mall,
Minneapolis
(612) 338-3807
Unwind after the workday with good food and music on the mall throughout June. Local and touring bands can be seen at the plaza for free, and drink and food kiosks are set up close to the stage.

Grand Old Day
Grand Avenue, St. Paul
First Sunday of June
(651) 699-0029
www.grandave.com
More than 200,000 people show up for this granddaddy of Twin Cities celebrations with everything from a Strongest Man and Woman on Grand contest to local bands performing on multiple stages. Lots of food vendors and merchant kiosks, and various family attractions are featured during the event, as well as the 10:00 a.m. Kiddie Parade followed at 10:30 by the Grand Old Day parade.

The festival engulfs 30 city blocks and is packed with more than 150 outdoor vendors offering every delicacy imaginable, from Cokes, pizza, and corn dogs to gyros, egg rolls, and Jamaican beef.

Edina Art Fair
50th and France, Edina
First weekend in June
(952) 922-1524
www.50thandfrance.com
More than 400 local, regional, and national artists whose works include clothing, dolls, woodcarving, and more are featured at this annual festival.

Red Hot Art Festival
Stevens Square Park, Second Avenue and 18th Street, Minneapolis
First weekend in June
(612) 879-0200
www.redhotart.org
Works by local emerging artists are showcased at this event, along with food, music, and other entertainment.

St. Anthony Main Summer Music Series
219 Southeast Main Street, Minneapolis
(612) 378-1226
www.saintanthonymain.com/musiccalendar.shtml
Throughout the summer, weekends, and July 4, you can catch live music for free on the stage outside Tuggs Tavern, located right across the street from the Mississippi River.

St. Anthony Park Arts Festival
Como Avenue, St. Anthony Park neighborhood, St. Paul
First Saturday of June
(651) 642-0411
www.stanthonyparkartsfestival.org
More than 100 Midwestern artists showcase their goods annually in one of St. Paul's prettiest neighborhoods, with food and music available all along Como Avenue from Carter to Luther Seminary. You can find spectacular deals on truly unusual items at this juried art show.

Tater Daze
Downtown Brooklyn Park
A weekend in June
(763) 493-8013
www.brooklynpark.org/taterdaze
Tater Daze celebrates Brooklyn Park's potato-growing heritage. The weekend festival kicks off with a parade on the first night and is followed by a host of events, including live music and lots of family activities.

Art on the Lake
Downtown Excelsior
A weekend in June
(952) 474-5000
For more than 20 years, Excelsior's juried Art on the Lake has showcased the work of local and national artists through art competitions, demonstrations, and other related activities. Food, live music, and other entertainment are almost as important a part of this festival as the art itself.

Father Hennepin Festival
Downtown Champlin
Second weekend in June
(763) 421-2820
This is a family-oriented festival, featuring fireworks, powerboats, personal watercraft races, and amusement park rides.

South St. Paul Kaposia Days
Various locations, South St. Paul
(651) 451-2266
www.kaposiadays.org
This family-oriented festival includes a street dance, a treasure hunt, a grand parade, children's activities, a flea market and craft sale, royalty pageants, bingo, water war games, fireworks, a Kiss the Pig contest, and athletic tournaments.

St. Louis Parktacular
Various locations, St. Louis Park
(952) 924-2550
www.parktacular.org
St. Louis Park's annual community celebration features a carnival, live music, a parade, food vendors, a silent auction, and an art fair.

Stone Arch Festival of the Arts
Mississippi Riverfront, Old St. Anthony Main, Minneapolis
Father's Day weekend
(612) 378-1226
www.stonearchfestival.com
More than 250 artists, along with vendors, bands, and street performers, congregate along the riverfront, making this a fun festival to either take Dad to for the afternoon or to shop for a present for him. The festival also features free dance, theater, and music performances; kids' art projects; free cooking demonstrations; and an "Art of the Car" car show, featuring many vintage vehicles.

Midsommar Celebration
American Swedish Institute, 2600 Park Avenue South, Minneapolis
Mid-June
(612) 871-4907
www.americanswedishinst.org
Celebrate Midsommar in the Swedish tradition with music, folk dance, and food. Join the museum's costumed guides and performers in this traditional festival that celebrates everything good about summer.

Midsommar Dag
20880 Olinda Trail, Scandia
Third Saturday in June
(651) 433-5053
www.gammelgardenmuseum.org/midsommar.shtm
Midsommar Dag kicks off the festival season in the picturesque town of Scandia, located east of the Twin Cities a few miles north of Marine on St. Croix. Sponsored by the Gammelgården Museum, the festival is a bright affair of parades, traditional Scandinavian dancing and costumes, and lots of food.

Buckhorn Days
Long Lake
A weekend at the end of June
(952) 476-1408
www.longlake-orono.org/buckhorn_days.html
This weekend-long festival in the western suburb of Long Lake features live music, dancing, carnival games, fishing contests, "mad scientist" exhibits, and concession stands.

Earle Brown Days Festival
Downtown Brooklyn Center
Last week of June
(763) 569-3400
This annual festival, honoring civic leader and activist Earle Brown, features a parade, fireworks, arts and crafts fair, ice-cream social, live music and entertainment, and special events aimed at kids and teens, including a kids' fishing contest and lots of games.

Minnetonka Summer Festival
Various locations, Minnetonka
Last Saturday in June
(952) 939-8200
www.eminnetonka.com
This citywide festival includes family-oriented activities for all ages: live entertainment, rides, games, food vendors, and fireworks.

MSRA's Back to the '50s Weekend
Minnesota State Fairgrounds, St. Paul
End of June
(651) 641-1992
www.msra.com
Every year, the Minnesota Street Rod Association (MSRA) heads to the state fairgrounds to show off its members' street rods, classic

cars, and custom cars. More than 11,000 show cars can be seen at the event, which also features food and merchandise kiosks, commercial exhibits, and live music.

Twin Cities GLBT Pride Festival
Various locations, Minneapolis
Two weeks at the end of June
(612) 305-6900
www.tcpride.org
The largest and probably the oldest annual gay/lesbian/bi/transsexual pride festival in the upper Midwest includes a parade, music, food, and more. An estimated 400,000 people show up for the festival over the course of two weeks.

JULY

Basilica Block Party
Corner of Hennepin Avenue and 17th Street
Basilica of Saint Mary, Minneapolis
Beginning of July
(612) 317-3511
www.basilicablockparty.org
Proceeds from this annual outdoor festival go to restore the historic Basilica of Saint Mary, which in turn offers outreach and charitable programs to poor and impoverished people throughout the state. More than 20,000 people of all ages and denominations come to this event, which features big-name bands, food, and drink.

Taste of Minnesota
Harriet Island Regional Park, St. Paul
Five days ending July 4
(651) 772-9980
www.tasteofmn.org
This huge event offers food prepared by more than 40 of the Twin Cities' best restaurants, and dozens of national and regional performers. Each night concludes with fireworks.

i The Taste of Minnesota festival is a good way to sample many local restaurants in one place.

Eden Prairie's Fourth of July "Home Town" Celebration
Round Lake, 7550 Constitution Avenue
Fourth of July
(952) 949-8450
www.edenprairie.org
This celebration finishes with spectacular fireworks at the Eden Prairie Center. Daytime activities at Round Lake Park include a kiddie parade, youth baseball tournament, live music, games, and concession stands.

Minneapolis Riverfront Fourth of July Celebration
Old St. Anthony Main, Minneapolis Riverfront
Fourth of July
(612) 378-1226
www.mpls4thofjuly.com
This is one of the best Fourth of July fireworks displays in the Twin Cities, with music and self-guided tours of the area's Mississippi River bridges. The best seat in the house is anywhere on Nicollet Island, where the fireworks seem to explode directly overhead.

Pan-o-Prog
Downtown Lakeville
First week of July
(952) 985-9558
www.panoprog.org
Since 1967 Lakeville has celebrated its Panorama of Progress festival, now called Pan-o-Prog, which features family entertainment including races, picnics, pet shows, dances, a scholarship pageant, Fourth of July fireworks, and a parade.

Anoka Riverfest & Craft Fair
Historic Downtown Anoka
Second Saturday of July
(763) 421-7130
www.anokariverfest.com
This all-day riverfront festival includes a craft/artisan fair, historical society events, live music, youth activities, and, of course, lots of food.

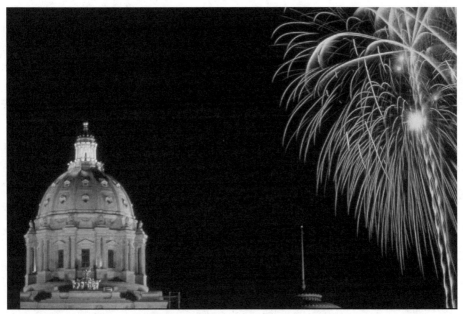

Fireworks over the State Capitol during the Taste of Minnesota. GREATER MINNEAPOLIS CONVENTION & VISITORS ASSOCIATION

Sommerfest
Minnesota Orchestra
Peavey Plaza, downtown Minneapolis
Mid-July to early August
(612) 371-5656 or (800) 292-4141
www.minnesotaorchestra.org

The Minnesota Orchestra's annual Sommerfest features a series of concerts on Peavey Plaza (corner of South 12th Street and Nicollet Mall) adjacent to Orchestra Hall. The festival opens with Macy's Day of Music, a 24-hour, free music marathon with dozens of bands, singers, and ensembles playing from noon one day to noon the next. Numerous concerts follow, some played by the Minnesota Orchestra but also with many guest artists performing everything from opera to Zydeco.

Summer Music and Movies
Loring Park, 1382 Willow Street, Minneapolis
(612) 375-7622
www.walkerart.org

Every Monday night from mid-July through August, free live music is followed by a movie in downtown Minneapolis's Loring Park. This is a collaboration between the Walker Art Center and the Minneapolis Park and Recreation Board.

Subway Block Party
Nicollet Mall between Third and Fourth Streets, Minneapolis
Second weekend in July
(612) 376-7669
www.aquatennial.com

Part of the Minneapolis Aquatennial Celebration, this free outdoor concert always features big-name bands and even bigger crowds.

Minneapolis Aquatennial
Various locations around Minneapolis
Third full week of July
(612) 376-7669
www.aquatennial.com

Royalty pageants, parades, milk carton boat races, and other events are featured in this citywide celebration nicknamed the 10 Best Days of Summer. The Aquatennial has the

i In 1978 millionaire and philanthropist Percy Ross rode in the Minneapolis Aquatennial's Torchlight Parade and threw $16,500 worth of silver into the crowd. This would get Percy in big trouble today—throwing objects from parade floats is now illegal in Minneapolis.

Torchlight Parade, a huge fireworks show, sand castle competitions, a triathlon, programs for juniors and seniors, and tons of family-oriented activities. One of the highlights of the celebration, the milk carton boat races, invites participants of all ages to create full-size boats out of hundreds of sealed milk cartons and race on Lake Calhoun.

Lumberjack Days
Lowell Park, Stillwater
Second to last weekend of July
(651) 430-2306
www.lumberjackdays.com
This huge, weekend-long event features live concerts from local and regional artists, tons of concession stands, Minnesota's fastest 10-mile and 5K runs, kids' events, a huge parade, and Minnesota's biggest fireworks display—all located in historic downtown Stillwater. Wine tasting, ice-cream socials, lumberjack exhibits, logrolling and pie-baking contests are just a few of the events that you can expect to be torn between, not to mention the annual Treasure Hunt.

AUGUST

Uptown Art Fair
Lake Street and Hennepin Avenue South, Minneapolis
First full weekend of August
(612) 823-4581
www.uptownminneapolis.com
The Uptown Art Fair is the largest art fair in Minneapolis, featuring work from hundreds of local and national artists as well as food and live music. Painting, photography, sculpture,

jewelry, ceramics, and fiber are on display and for sale at the event.

Loring Park Art Festival
Loring Park, Oak Grove Street and Hennepin Avenue South, Minneapolis
First full weekend in August
(612) 203-9911
www.loringparkartfestival.com
Held at the same time as the Uptown Art Fair and Powderhorn Art Fair, the Loring Park Art Festival features more than 130 artists showing (and selling) their work on the grassy lawn surrounding Loring Lake. The juried show includes all manner of media, and the festival also has food booths, musicians wandering through the crowds, and stage performances.

Powderhorn Art Fair
Powderhorn Park, 3400 15th Avenue South, Minneapolis
First weekend of August
(612) 729-0111
www.powderhornartfair.org
The popular Powderhorn Art Fair, which usually runs concurrent with the Uptown Art Fair and the Loring Park Art Festival, is a winning attraction for crafts-fair fans. The weekend-long festival—originally billed as an alternative to the "big one down the street"—has developed a flavor of its own, exposing an eclectic variety of both artwork and artists to the public. Free bus service connects it with the Uptown Art Fair and Loring Park Art Festival.

Minnesota Fringe Festival
Various venues in Minneapolis
First two weeks of August
(612) 872-1212 (office);
(651) 209-6799 (tickets)
www.fringefestival.org
This annual celebration of offbeat live stage performances and visual art has hundreds of shows in multiple venues throughout Minneapolis. The venues range from well-known theaters, such as the Southern and the Bryant-Lake Bowl, to esoteric venues, such as the

downtown YWCA swimming pool and the condo of one of the performers. Musicals, puppetry, dance, theater, spoken word, and performance art are just some of the events during the festival. All performances are 60 minutes or less, and all are selected for inclusion in the festival by a lottery system, rather than a juried competition, allowing an unbiased and decidedly unsnooty process to prevail.

Old Time Harvest Festival
Fairview Lane, across from the Scott County Fairgrounds, Jordan
First weekend of August
(952) 492-2062
www.scottcarverthreshers.org
This family-oriented festival has a vintage tractor show, a flea market, an antiques auction, and an antique car show, as well as demonstrations of threshing, sawing, spinning, and quilting. There's even a vintage farm equipment parade each afternoon.

Minnesota Irish Fair
Harriet Island, St. Paul
Second weekend of August
(952) 474-7411
www.irishfair.com
From bagpipes to bodhrans, corned beef to ceilis, this free three-day celebration of Irish culture features Irish music, dance, theater, exhibits, sports, a marketplace, genealogy information, and a special children's area.

Minnesota State Fair
State Fairgrounds, 1265 Snelling Avenue North, St. Paul
Twelve days ending on Labor Day
(651) 288-4800
www.mnstatefair.org
More than 1.6 million people attend the Minnesota State Fair—usually drawing crowds of over one hundred thousand a day. The fair has big-name entertainment, exhibits, competitions, food, demonstrations, horse shows, auto races, a huge midway carnival, and lots of food on a stick. There's also a bust of the festival's princess sculpted in butter, farm animal shows and competitions, a huge garden show, a vintage tractor display on Machinery Hill, and juried arts and crafts from state elementary, high school, and college students.

Woodbury Days
Ojibway Park, Woodbury
Last weekend of August
(651) 714-3500
www.woodburydays.com
Woodbury Days is a community event with lots of activities for the whole family, including carnival rides, games, food, the Woodbury Days Annual Bike Ride, inflatable slides, water fights, a petting zoo, the Rod & Custom Car Club Car Show, fireworks displays, a daily parade, and live music.

Stiftungsfest
Downtown Norwood Young America
Last full weekend of August
(952) 467-1812
www.stiftungsfest.org
There's something for everyone at this celebration of German heritage and culture: German choirs, dancers, polka bands, arts, crafts, ethnic foods, and beverages. Stiftungsfest, founded in 1861, is the oldest festival in Minnesota.

Minnesota Renaissance Festival
3 miles south of Shakopee on Minnesota Highway 169
Mid-August through the end of September
(952) 445-7361 or (800) 966-8215
www.renaissancefest.com
Jump back in time to experience life in the 16th century, or at least the fun parts of it. Food, fun, sword fights, games, comedy, dancers, singers, music, multiple stages of continuous entertainment, and royalty are regular staples of this annual event, which is open weekends in mid-August and through the end of September, as well as on Labor Day. The food choices are extensive, with some of the more notable including Turkey

Drumsticks, Rice Krispie Kabobs, and Bangers & Mash. Wash it all down with a tankard of mead. The site of the Minnesota Renaissance Festival is a bustling 16th-century village filled with hundreds of costumed villagers, period buildings, and a huge marketplace.

SEPTEMBER

Excelsior Apple Day
Downtown Excelsior
First Saturday after Labor Day
(952) 474-6461
Excelsior Apple Day is a main street festival with antiques, crafts, apples, produce, entertainment, food, and the children's Red Wagon and Doll Buggy Parade.

Sunbonnet Day
Riley-Jacques Barn, 9096 Riley Lake Road, Eden Prairie
Second Sunday in September
(952) 949-8450
Each September, Eden Prairie steps back in time on Sunbonnet Day, with old-fashioned wagon rides, pony rides, a farmers' market, and games of Pennies in the Hay.

Johnny Appleseed Bash
Utley Park, 50th Street West & Woodale Avenue, Edina
Third weekend of September
(952) 920-0595
www.ststephens.com/stst/the_bash
This annual benefit for St. Stephen's Episcopal Church takes place in Utley Park. Food, live entertainment, a silent auction, a petting zoo, and pony rides are just a few of the things you can expect at this community-oriented festival.

Lone Oak Days
Historic Holz Farm, 4665 Manor Drive, Eagan
End of September
(651) 675-5500
www.eaganmn.com
Hayrides, farming demos, games, and self-guided tours of 1940s-era farm life at Holz Farm highlight Eagan's heritage festival.

Harvest Festival
Gibbs Museum of Pioneer and Dakota Life
2097 Larpenteur Avenue West, Falcon Heights
Late September or early October
(651) 646-8629
www.rchs.com/gbbsfm2.htm
At this annual event with food, music, and square dancing, guests can participate in crop gathering, kitchen duty, and other farm activities. The festival also features craft demonstrations.

OCTOBER

Twin Cities Marathon
Minneapolis and St. Paul
First weekend of October
(763) 287-3888
www.twincitiesmarathon.org
The Twin Cities Marathon's unique scenery and aesthetics have earned it the distinction as the most beautiful urban marathon in America. It's also ranked as one of the nation's top marathons. The 26.2-mile course begins near the Metrodome in Minneapolis and finishes at the State Capitol on John Ireland Boulevard in St. Paul. The course is easy to navigate, mostly asphalt, and very scenic with mile after mile of parkways, lakes, rivers, and tree-lined boulevards. Prospective runners should register early for the race, as this race attracts contestants from around the world. Good viewing spots include the Lake Harriet Rose Garden, Minnehaha Falls, and along Summit Avenue.

Anoka Halloween
Downtown Anoka
Mid-October through Halloween
(763) 421-7130
www.anokahalloween.com
Anoka celebrates almost 90 years as the Halloween Capital of the World with three parades and many other activities for young and old alike. The celebration begins with a football game dubbed "the Pumpkin Bowl." Other events include cemetery tours, a house-decoration contest, ghost stories, cos-

tume contests, a haunted house, and a 5K Grey Ghost Run.

NOVEMBER/DECEMBER

Samhain Celtic New Year
Newell Park, Fairview Avenue and Pierce Butler Route, St. Paul
November 1
(651) 641-0485
This celebration consists of traditional Irish music, food, storytelling, dancing, and games.

Autumn Festival: An Arts and Crafts Affair
Canterbury Park, 1100 Canterbury Road, Shakopee
November
(952) 445-7223
The largest crafts show in the upper Midwest, the Autumn Festival draws more than 500 vendors from all over the country.

Victorian Christmas
at the Historic Courthouse
101 West Pine Street, Stillwater
Weekend before Thanksgiving
(651) 275-7075
Fine handmade crafts by local artists are displayed at the elegantly decorated Stillwater courthouse. The building, beautifully decorated in Victorian style, resounds with laughter and music, while vendors in costume offer their wares to the public. Volunteers in period clothing offer jail tours, an exhibit, an old-fashioned tearoom, and music of the season.

i If you call ahead of time (612-616-7669), you can volunteer to march in the Holidazzle. The Holidazzle organizers offer a variety of costumes to volunteers, from elfin outfits to Old Saint Nick himself. Call early for the best costumes and your preferred date. And don't forget the long underwear.

Holidazzle
Nicollet Mall, Minneapolis
Friday after Thanksgiving through December 23
(612) 376-SNOW
www.holidazzle.com
Costumed children, adults, and festooned floats covered with one million colored lights make up the Holidazzle. These free, 30-minute night parades head down Nicollet Mall from 12th to 5th Streets, beginning at 6:30 p.m. Wednesday through Sunday. Fairy tale–themed floats, marching bands, celebrity grand marshals, and, of course, Santa in his sleigh can be seen in the parade.

Old-Fashioned Holiday Bazaar
Landmark Center, 75 West Fifth Street, St. Paul
A weekend in November or December
(651) 292-3230
www.landmarkcenter.org
Stroll through a marketplace of more than 80 exhibits featuring beautiful and unique gift items, all handcrafted by the area's finest artisans. Participating in this annual event is considered an important tradition by many, who get their holiday shopping done here.

THE ARTS

The Greater Twin Cities have been dubbed a "cultural Eden on the prairie," where people widely support more than one hundred theater companies and classical music ensembles. Sir Tyrone Guthrie pumped up the theatrical boom back in 1963, enrolling large-scale local assistance to establish the classical repertory company named after him. The Cities now have more theater seats per capita than any Metropolitan area in the United States apart from New York City.

Minneapolis and St. Paul are also serious museum towns, with a number of important collections housed in several world-famous buildings. Many, many more little galleries spread throughout the metro area take up any slack the major museums might have missed, displaying everything from concrete anatomy molds to metal mechanical sculptures.

More than 100 performing arts groups and organizations flourish in the Twin Cities area, ranging from tiny neighborhood-based production companies to full-fledged touring troupes.

No matter what your artistic passions are, you are likely to have them stoked and satisfied in Minneapolis–St. Paul.

ALL ABOUT BOOKS

Open Book
1011 Washington Avenue South, Minneapolis
(612) 215-2520
www.openbookmn.org
The first literary arts complex of its kind in the nation, this renovated historic building opened in 2000. Visitors can watch the book printing and binding process from beginning to end, explore the exhibitions gallery, or simply stretch out on the sofa in the literary commons with a good book from the center's library. Other amenities include occasional live performances, literary readings, writing workshops, family reading space, and a cafe. Located in the building is the Minnesota Center for Book Arts, the largest independent book arts facility in the nation; the Loft, which offers classes on writing and publishing; a performance space for visiting authors and lecturers; Milkweed Editions, a nationally known nonprofit literary publisher; and Rosalux Gallery, an artist collective exhibiting a wide range of artistic styles and media. Open Book is fun to just walk around in, as so much of the original structure and facades were preserved in the restoration process, including pieces of the original wallpaper, staircases that go nowhere, and ancient bakery and factory signs painted on the brickwork itself.

ART GALLERIES

AZ Gallery
Northern Warehouse Building, 308 Prince Street, St. Paul
(651) 224-3757
www.theazgallery.org
This prominent Lowertown St. Paul gallery holds opening receptions on the first Friday of each month, hosting artwork premieres of two featured artists plus a group exhibit. The 2,000-square-foot gallery also puts on performing arts events throughout the year.

CIRCA Gallery
210 North First Street, Minneapolis
(612) 332-2386
www.circagallery.org
CIRCA Gallery's mission is to provide awareness and appreciation of contemporary styles, media, and expressions. The gallery represents 40 regional and national artists,

with an exhibition rotation approximately every five weeks.

Dolly Fiterman Fine Arts Gallery
100 University Avenue Southeast, Minneapolis
(612) 623–3300
Dolly Fiterman Fine Arts represents American and European contemporary artists in a turn-of-the-20th-century landmark marble building. The gallery's collection emphasizes sculptures, painting, drawings, and graphics, and the gallery is known globally for its advanced and avant-garde international scope.

Groveland Gallery
25 Groveland Terrace, Minneapolis
(612) 377-7800
www.grovelandgallery.com
Groveland Gallery represents the work of nearly 50 regional artists and specializes in contemporary representational painting and drawing. Established in 1973, this elegant gallery is located in a restored 1890s mansion and carriage house on the edge of downtown Minneapolis. On the premises is a second gallery, the Annex, which features work by emerging local artists. Exhibitions in both galleries change every six weeks.

Inside Out Gallery
Interact Center for the Visual and Performing Arts, 212 Third Avenue North, Suite 140, Minneapolis
(612) 339-5145
www.interactcenter.com
Interact is a studio for actors and artists with physical and mental disabilities. The organization's Inside Out gallery has four exhibitions each year that are open to the public. Interact's theater company, supported by professional actors as teachers and peers, produces two major shows per year.

Intermedia Arts
2822 Lyndale Avenue South, Minneapolis
(612) 871-4444
www.intermediaarts.org
The graffiti on Intermedia's facade isn't just a nice concession to local taggers—giving them the space is part of the gallery's mission. More than perhaps any other gallery in town, Intermedia is dedicated to being a neighborhood space, with shows often focusing on the work of artists from the semibohemian streets of Lyn-Lake. (An annual show called 55408 accepts only artists from this local zip code.) As a result, Intermedia's exhibits lack the gloss and commercial appeal of other galleries' shows, but they do offer a compelling artistic window into the soul of a community.

Katherine E. Nash Gallery
Regis Center for Art, 405 21st Avenue South, Minneapolis
(612) 624-6518
www.nash.umn.edu
The mission of the Katherine E. Nash Gallery is to create an accessible environment for University of Minnesota faculty and students to exhibit their work, as well as to show art in various media by regional, national, and international artists.

Minnesota Center for Photography
165 13th Avenue NE, Minneapolis
(612) 824-5500
www.mncp.org
The Minnesota Center for Photography offers works from local and national artists. The gallery encourages strong community involvement and is a good place for budding photographers to begin exploring the professional side of their craft. The center offers many classes, workshops, and seminars in the photographic arts.

Northern Clay Center
2424 East Franklin Avenue, Minneapolis
(612) 339-8007
www.northernclaycenter.org
Northern Clay Center's mission is the advancement of the ceramic arts. Ongoing

i Almost every arts venue in town offers a discount to students with a valid student ID.

programs include classes and workshops for children and adults at all levels of proficiency, more than 10 exhibitions a year of functional and sculptural work by regional and national clay artists, studio facilities and grants for artists, and a sales gallery representing many of the top ceramic artists across the region and country.

The Soap Factory
518 Second Street SE, Minneapolis
(612) 623-9176
www.soapfactory.org
The Soap Factory is an exciting, and expanding, nonprofit arts organization that supports emerging artists, raises the public's understanding and appreciation of their artistic expressions, and fosters strength and vitality within the arts, cultural, and education communities of the Twin Cities. The gallery is particularly supportive of experimentation in the visual arts. Each year, the Soap Factory presents several large-scale visual exhibitions featuring a wide range of media from local, national, and international emerging artists as well as performance art, film, video, and spoken-word events.

Vern Carver & Beard Art Galleries
LaSalle Plaza, 800 LaSalle Avenue, Minneapolis
(612) 339-3449
www.verncarverbeard.com
Vern Carver & Beard is the oldest gallery in the Twin Cities. Founded in 1886, the gallery features fine original art by regional artists of past and present, antique prints, and art glass (stained glass, blown glass, etc). The gallery also provides custom framing for prints and paintings.

ART MUSEUMS

Frederick R. Weisman Art Museum
333 East River Road, Minneapolis
(612) 625-9494
www.weisman.umn.edu
The Weisman is impossible to miss—it's the huge metal structure on the east side of the

Washington Avenue Bridge that either looks stunningly beautiful or stunningly pretentious, depending on your mood, your architectural sensitivities, and the time of year. On the outside the museum faces the Mississippi River with an undulating, dramatic facade covered in stainless steel, especially beautiful at sunset. In comparison the interior is surprisingly conservative, and the modestly scaled and wonderfully lit galleries inside are so attractive that the *New York Times* called them "possibly the five best rooms for viewing art in the world."

The mostly 20th-century permanent collection contains the world's largest assemblage of works by Marsden Hartley and Alfred Maurer as well as paintings and prints by Georgia O'Keeffe, Arthur Dove, and Robert Motherwell, among others. The entrance is dominated by Roy Lichtenstein's *World's Fair Mural.* Be sure to take in the river view from the tiny balcony, located one floor above the galleries.

A teaching museum for the university and the community, this sculptural stainless-steel and brick landmark building designed by architect Frank Gehry provides a multidisciplinary approach to the arts through programs and a changing schedule of exhibitions. Gehry designed an expansion of the museum (including a new gallery wing and a cafe), which is scheduled to be completed in 2009.

The Weisman is on the campus' East Bank where Washington Avenue crosses over East River Parkway. Admission is free, although the parking garage will set you back a few bucks.

The Minneapolis Institute of Arts
2400 Third Avenue South, Minneapolis
(612) 870-3131 or (888) MIA-ARTS
www.artsmia.org
The Minneapolis Institute of Arts, one of the outstanding art museums in the country, features art and artifacts from around the world, from ancient sculptures to photography and film. Housed in a 1915 Beaux-Arts marble building designed by McKim, Mead, and White near downtown Minneapolis, the museum contains a world-class collection of nearly 100,000 objects representing artistic

traditions and treasures spanning 5,000 years. Unlike many big-city art museums, which have the tendency to overwhelm casual visitors, the MIA can be easily explored in a few hours—and, unlike many big-city museums, no admission fee is charged.

Highlights of the museum include a small but exceptional collection of French impressionist and postimpressionist paintings, including works by Monet and van Gogh; an extensive collection of carved Oriental jades; *Lucretia,* considered by art historians to be the best Rembrandt in the country; and works by old masters Titian, El Greco, and Poussin as well as 19th- and 20th-century American and European artists. There're amazing collections of tapestries, photography, and prints as well.

The Minnesota Museum of American Art
50 Kellogg Boulevard West, St. Paul
(651) 266-1030
www.mmaa.org

The Minnesota Museum of American Art—St. Paul's art museum—recently moved from its home at Landmark Center to a new 6,000-square-foot riverfront space just a few blocks away. (Look for the big ART HERE sign at the corner of Kellogg and Market Street.) The museum features American art by national and regional artists from the 19th century to contemporary times. Special exhibitions highlight significant American artists and movements. This is a place for the traditional and the unconventional. The diversity of art and artists past, present, and emerging is revealed through music, performance, dance, fashion, painting, film, and sculpture.

Schubert Club Museum of Musical Instruments
Landmark Center, 75 West Fifth Street, St. Paul
(651) 292-3267
www.schubert.org

Considering how small this museum is, its collection of keyboards, phonographs, and musical instruments is amazingly complete. Owned and operated by the Schubert Club,

Minneapolis Institute of Arts. GREATER MINNEAPOLIS CONVENTION & VISITORS ASSOCIATION

this museum is a popular stomping ground for music aficionados of all types, local and otherwise.

Walker Art Center/Minneapolis Sculpture Garden/Cowles Conservatory
1750 Hennepin Avenue, Minneapolis
(612) 375-7600
www.walkerart.org

For years the Walker's been the foremost modern art museum in the state. The museum is the only place in town to consistently bring in artists who tweak, poke, or outright stab at comfortable Midwestern sensibilities, organizing concept-centered shows with a sociopolitical awareness. The displays include a permanent collection of 20th-century American and international art, including works from Willem de Kooning, Andy Warhol, Sol LeWitt, and Dan Flavin; the Walker also sponsors vanguard music, dance, theater, film, and video

Walker Art Center. GREATER MINNEAPOLIS CONVENTION & VISITORS ASSOCIATION

events throughout the year, as well as innovative education programs and visionary new media initiatives. Artists and filmmakers from around the globe have lectured and performed at the Walker, including filmmaker John Waters and composer Philip Glass. The popular monthly After Hours parties offer previews of new shows, live music, and cocktails.

Located right next to the Walker Art Center is the Minneapolis Sculpture Garden's beautiful collection of large sculptures made by local and internationally known artists. The 11-acre garden holds more than 40 sculptures, including works by George Segal, Jenny Holzer, and David Nash, set among tree-lined courtyards. The garden is one of the most-visited sites in Minneapolis, for good reason—the works of art combined with the ever-changing landscape make it a year-round delight.

The garden's entrance is framed by a pair of monumental granite columns titled *Ampersand* by the sculpture's creator, Martin Puryear. The Minneapolis Sculpture Garden features one of the most photographed spots in Minnesota: the gigantic *Spoonbridge and Cherry* by Claes Oldenburg and Coosje van Bruggen, conveniently placed for pictures of the sculpture against the Minneapolis skyline. The glass-walled Cowles Conservatory, located in the garden, is a perfect place to hide from gloomy weather, with a changing display of blooming plants and a palm court dominated by Frank Gehry's *Standing Glass Fish.*

Cinema—Art House and Specialty Theaters

Bell Auditorium
University of Minnesota Campus, 10 Church Street SE, Minneapolis
(612) 331-3134
www.mnfilmarts.org
Formerly home to the University Film Society, the Bell Auditorium has long been home to offbeat films. Since its inception, the Bell Auditorium has hosted many directors and film scholars, including Robert Altman, Jean-Luc Godard, Roberto Rosellini, and countless others. The nonprofit

Minnesota Film Arts promotes an appreciation for the art of filmmaking through screenings both at Bell Auditorium and at Oak Street Cinema; and through events such as the Minneapolis–St. Paul International Film Festival.

The Heights Theatre
3951 Central Avenue NE, Columbia Heights
(763) 788-9079
www.heightstheater.com

The Heights is one of the last of the great one-screen theaters. Renowned for showing first-run films that are actually interesting, the Heights is a classic place to catch a film. The Heights introduces movies with Wurlitzer organ music on Friday and Saturday night. As an added bonus, refills on soda and popcorn are always free.

Landmark's Lagoon Cinema
1320 Lagoon Avenue, Minneapolis
(612) 825-6006
www.landmarktheaters.com

If you're into art house, indie, or critically acclaimed film fare, chances are you'll end up here. Lagoon Cinema is part of the Landmark franchise, which consistently snatches up the best new films and markets them aggressively to a niche of art houses. The facilities are relatively distinctive for a cineplex, with swirled carpet and abstract light trees. Even more impressive, the theater is designed for optimum viewer friendliness—cushy yet supportive seats, no center aisles, and sharp floor inclines.

Oak Street Cinema
309 Southeast Oak Street, Minneapolis
(612) 331-3134
www.mnfilmarts.org

What more could you want from a repertory house? Oak Street offers films ranging from mainstream classics to obscure art house fare, with room to include work from all over the globe, too. Oak Street's not too stuffy to include edgy crowd-pleasers but still serious enough to give a fair share of time to Antonioni and Hitchcock films.

i Admittance to the Walker Art Center is free every Thursday and the first Saturday of every month.

Riverview Theatre
3800 42nd Avenue South, Minneapolis
(612) 729-7369
www.riverviewtheatre.com

The first impressive thing about this king of all budget movie theaters is the cool 1950s lobby straight out of *The Jetsons*. And then there's the popcorn—it's one of the few places where you buy the popcorn because it tastes good—there's even a discount on takeouts. The Riverview has a lot going for it, and you'll pay only $3 ($2 for matinees) to take it all in.

Uptown Theatre
2906 Hennepin Avenue South, Minneapolis
(612) 825-6006
www.landmarktheaters.com

Uptown is the granddaddy of all local single-screen theaters, boasting the biggest screen around and some of the roomiest seats. This place not only stands out as a great space to see films but also ranks as one of Minneapolis's landmarks. The movie fare includes independents, art house flicks, and other offbeat films.

DANCE

James Sewell Ballet
528 Hennepin Avenue, Suite 205, Minneapolis
(612) 672-0480
www.jsballet.org

Founded in New York City in 1990 by James Sewell, the James Sewell Ballet relocated to Minnesota in 1993. The ballet specializes in original contemporary ballet, and the beautiful performances run the gamut from classical choreography to improvisation of entire movements. In the Twin Cities, the James Sewell Ballet performs at the O'Shaughnessy Auditorium on the College of St. Catherine's campus in St. Paul.

Ragamala Music and Dance Theater
711 West Lake Street, Suite 309, Minneapolis
(612) 824-1968
www.ragamala.net
Ragamala presents original works of dance, music, and poetry based on the ancient classical dance of southern India, Bharatanatyam. The cross-cultural performances of the company have developed a strong reputation for innovation, and the company's school offers classes from introductory to advanced levels. Ragamala performs at the O'Shaughnessy Auditorium on the College of St. Catherine's Campus in St. Paul and at the Southern Theater in Minneapolis.

Zenon Dance Company
528 Hennepin Avenue, Suite #400, Minneapolis
(612) 338-1101
www.zenondance.org
Zenon commissions original works of modern and jazz dance from emerging choreographers in Minnesota as well as established masters. The high-energy performances of the company appeal to communities not regularly reached by dance troupes. Zenon performs regularly in the Twin Cities at the Guthrie Theater and the Southern Theater, and operates a school teaching modern, jazz, hip-hop, tap, break dancing, and yoga.

MUSIC ENSEMBLES AND COMPANIES

Greater Twin Cities Youth Symphonies (GTCYS)
528 Hennepin Avenue, Suite 404, Minneapolis
(612) 870-7611
www.gtcys.org
GTCYS boasts six youth orchestras and a student body with 600-plus members. While pursuing its mission of educating future musicians, it presents fall, winter, and spring concerts and the Young Soloists' Concerto Showcase. GTCYS sponsors a summer orchestra program as well.

Minnesota Chorale
528 Hennepin Avenue, Suite 211, Minneapolis
(612) 333-4866
www.mnchorale.org
Under the artistic direction of Kathy Saltzman Romey, the Minnesota Chorale has become the state's preeminent symphonic chorus and ranks among the best in the nation. At around 150 voices, the chorale is the principal chorus for the Minnesota Orchestra and the St. Paul Chamber Orchestra. Its nationally recognized Bridges series seeks to build musical and social bridges through artistic collaboration.

The Minnesota Opera
620 North First Street, Minneapolis
(612) 333-2700
www.mnopera.org
The Minnesota Opera, founded in 1963, stages performances at the Ordway Center for the Performing Arts in St. Paul from November through May. An anchor tenant at the acoustically perfect Ordway, the Minnesota Opera also offers classes at its Minnesota Opera Center in the Minneapolis Warehouse District. Walk-ins are welcome.

The Minnesota Orchestra
1111 Nicollet Mall, Minneapolis
(612) 371-5656 or (800) 292-4141
www.minnesotaorchestra.org
The Minnesota Orchestra performs nearly 200 concerts each year ranging from classical to pops. Performances are scheduled in Minneapolis' Orchestra Hall. The orchestra's award-winning concert broadcasts, produced by Minnesota Public Radio and distributed by American Public Media to more than 120 radio stations nationwide, reach approximately 200,000 people each week.

The Minnesota Youth Symphonies
790 Cleveland Avenue South, Suite 203, St. Paul
(651) 699-5811
www.mnyouthsymphonies.org

The Minnesota Orchestra in Minneapolis's spectacular Orchestra Hall. GREATER MINNEAPOLIS CONVENTION & VISITORS ASSOCIATION

The Minnesota Youth Symphonies are open to students from elementary school through high school. Co–music directors Claudette and Manny Laureano oversee four advanced orchestras. The MYS presents major concerts at Orchestra Hall in Minneapolis. Auditions are held at the end of August of each year.

The St. Paul Chamber Orchestra
408 St. Peter Street, St. Paul
(651) 291-1144
www.stpaulchamberorchestra.org
As the only full-time professional chamber orchestra in the United States, the SPCO presents more than 150 concerts annually and reaches millions more through radio broadcasts and regional, national, and international touring. The chamber orchestra performs at St. Paul's Ordway Center for the Performing Arts, Minneapolis's Ted Mann Concert Hall, and at other locations throughout the Twin Cities.

The Schubert Club
Landmark Center, 75 West Fifth Street, St. Paul
(651) 292-3267
www.schubert.org
The Schubert Club is Minnesota's oldest arts organization, presenting world-renowned artists and local and regional musicians to Twin Cities audiences through various grants and private funding. The Schubert Club Museum of Musical Instruments is located in Landmark Center as well.

VocalEssence
1900 Nicollet Avenue, Minneapolis
(612) 547-1451
www.vocalessence.org
VocalEssence is recognized internationally as one of America's premier choral arts organizations. The chorus offers innovative programming under the direction of founder Philip Brunelle.

THEATERS AND PERFORMANCE SPACES

In addition to the following theater troupes and venues, various local, regional, national, and international shows are regularly staged at St. Paul's Roy Wilkins Auditorium (175 West Kellogg Boulevard, St. Paul, (651-265-4800, www.theroy.com) and Xcel Energy Center (199 West Kellogg Boulevard, St. Paul, 651-989-5151, www.xcelenergycenter.com), as well as Minneapolis's Northrop Auditorium on the University of Minnesota Campus (84 Southeast Church Street, Minneapolis, 612-624-2345, www1.umn.edu/umato) and Target Center (600 First Avenue North, Minneapolis, 612-673-0900, www.targetcenter.com).

Minneapolis

Acadia Cafe Cabaret Theater
1931 Nicollet Avenue South, Minneapolis
(612) 874-8702
www.acadiacafe.com
This space wasn't necessarily designed to

hold theater performances—it's a second room within the Acadia Cafe, equipped with riser seating and a permanent stage. But any eccentricities fade away when the shows start. Seven nights a week, Acadia hosts a performance—music, improv, comedy, poetry, or performance art—anything at all, so long as it's original (no cover songs allowed). The space has the perk of being within a cafe, which offers food and a 24-rail tap (see the Restaurants chapter for more information on the Acadia Cafe). And while it may not be the best theater space in town, it holds some of the most intense productions to be found.

Brave New Workshop Theatre
2605 Hennepin Avenue South, Minneapolis
(612) 332-6620
www.bravenewworkshop.org
The country's longest-running satirical comedy theater, founded by Dudley Riggs in 1958, features original comedy shows and late-night improvisation on Friday and Saturday for just a dollar. The Brave New Workshop is known for its satirical takes on pop-culture icons and news-dominating factoids of the moment, from YouTube to FEMA to Blue States, bringing cutting-edge shows like *Happiness for Dummies: An Idiot's Guide to the Soul* and *Sweet Violence: An American Reality.* The theater also offers classes on improvisation, acting, and writing.

Bryant-Lake Bowl Theater
810 West Lake Street, Minneapolis
(612) 825-3737
www.bryantlakebowl.com
The Bryant-Lake Bowl Theater has become a mainstay of local performance acts, bringing live music (including opera), dance, comedy, and theater to an intimate stage tucked behind the bowling alley. On any given night you may wander in and find the tiny performance area packed in support of local talent. No matter where you decide to sit, make sure to take advantage of the extensive beer and wine lists.

Cedar Cultural Center
416 Cedar Avenue South, Minneapolis
(612) 338-2674
www.thecedar.org
The Cedar offers an eclectic selection of folk, blues, jazz, indie rock, and world music. Some past performers include French guitar virtuoso Pierre Bensusan and American performer Ani DiFranco. The Cedar is also host to the annual Nordic Roots Festival, which brings Nordic and Nordic-style performers from around the world to play the weekend event.

Children's Theatre Company
2400 Third Avenue South, Minneapolis
(612) 874-0500
www.childrenstheatre.org
Since 1965 the Children's Theatre Company (CTC) and its cast of incredibly talented actors and actresses, young and old, have been performing at the 746-seat facility—recently remodeled to include a second stage. Most of the performances are based on children's stories and fairy tales, such as A Year With Frog and Toad. There's a healthy dose of impressive original works as well, such as *Korczak's Children,* a story about the Holocaust through children's eyes, and *The Monkey King,* based on a 500-year-old Chinese story about a trickster on a quest with pious monks to recover sacred scrolls. One of the country's leading theater groups for youths, the Tony Award-winning CTC produces an annual season featuring hundreds of mainstage performances and a touring production that performs throughout the Midwest.

Guthrie Theater
818 South Second Street, Minneapolis
(612) 377-2224
www.guthrietheater.org
Anyone who knows American theater knows the Guthrie, the Minneapolis theater founded in the early 1960s by legendary director Sir Tyrone Guthrie. The company's metier has always been intriguing interpretations of classic drama. The largest nonprofit theater between New York and San Francisco, the

Guthrie is renowned for its productions of classic, comedic, and contemporary plays.

In June 2006, the Guthrie moved into a new building designed by French architect Jean Nouvel, and the building has risen to the level of architectural masterpiece, a fitting home to a world-class theater. With three stages, the restaurant Cue (see the Restaurants chapter for more information), and a lounge, the new facility is more than three times as big as the Guthrie's former home. The dark blue building along the Minneapolis riverfront features the Endless Bridge, a seemingly unsupported appendage sticking out 178 feet from the main building toward the Mississippi River.

The mainstay of Twin Cities professional theater, the Guthrie features shows and performers such as *Jane Eyre* and the Royal Shakespeare Company, as well as smaller-scale, more offbeat performances in the Dowling Studio, one of the three theaters in the new Guthrie.

Hennepin Theatre District
805 Hennepin Avenue, Minneapolis
(612) 339-7007
www.hennepintheatredistrict.org
Downtown Minneapolis's Hennepin Theatre District comprises three historic theater venues and two smaller stages all within a short walk of each other, as well as the hotels, restaurants, sports venues, and other attractions of downtown. The district's theaters include the Orpheum (910 Hennepin Avenue), the State (805 Hennepin Avenue), and the Pantages (710 Hennepin Avenue), as well as the Hennepin Stages (824 Hennepin Avenue) and the Music Box Theatre (1407 Nicollet Avenue South). Each hosts everything from full-scale Broadway musicals to rock concerts. At times, Broadway musicals have opened at one of the Minneapolis theaters to work out the kinks and fine tune a production for its debut under the Big Apple's brighter spotlight. If you're looking for big-time entertain-

i At 10:00 a.m. on the last Saturday of every month, tours of the Hennepin Theatre District depart from the State Theatre Box Office at 805 Hennepin Avenue. The tour includes a backstage look at one of the historic theaters. Tickets are $5 and can be purchased at the State Theatre Box Office or through Ticketmaster (612-673-0404; www.ticketmaster.com).

ment in the Twin Cities, check out the district's Web site for upcoming shows.

In the Heart of the Beast Puppet and Mask Theatre
1500 East Lake Street, Minneapolis
(612) 721-2535
www.hobt.org
In the Heart of the Beast's unique theater production is marked by elaborate costuming; stories are told through puppets or actors hidden behind gigantic masks, giving performances a mystical and magical quality. The theater company uses the ancient traditions of puppet and mask theater to explore issues, events, and values of contemporary society. Though some performances are adaptations of children's stories, all shows are a wonder for eyes of any age. Puppets are hand-hewn by those involved with the shows, and the traveling company stages shows both regionally and nationally.

Jungle Theater
2951 Lyndale Avenue South, Minneapolis
(612) 822-7063
www.jungletheater.com
The Jungle Theater has a reputation for straightforward performances scripted by lesser-known or more poetic playwrights, offering a year-round season of plays from classic and contemporary sources in an intimate, 150-seat theater. The theater company has put on plays by Dylan Thomas, Tennessee Williams, and David Mamet, and has staged many world premieres since its founding in 1991.

Mixed Blood Theatre
1501 South Fourth Street, Minneapolis
(612) 338-0937
www.mixedblood.com
Mixed Blood is a professional theater company whose mission is to expose and promote the Twin Cities cultural melting pot. Founded in 1976 by Jack Reuler to provide voice and venue for actors of color, Mixed Blood has branched out into the working world to tackle hot topics like race, culture, gender, sexual orientation, and disability. The main stage is housed in a turn-of-the-20th-century brick firehouse, while the touring company itself performs in schools and organizations throughout the region.

Mu Performing Arts
2700 NE Winter Street, Suite 4, Minneapolis
(612) 824-4804
www.muperformingarts.org
Mu Performing Arts includes both Theater Mu, an Asian-American theater company, and Mu Daiko, a Japanese taiko drumming group. Dedicated to staging performances that showcase Asian and Asian-American plays, Theater Mu hosts three productions annually, while Mu Daiko stages one production. Mu Performing Arts also performs in outreach programs throughout the Twin Cities. The organization sponsors several Artist Development Festivals to support, encourage, and give experience to young directors, playwrights, and taiko students. Mu Performing Arts also offers taiko drumming classes.

Orchestra Hall
1111 Nicollet Mall, Minneapolis
(952) 371-5656 or (800) 292-4141
www.minnesotaorchestra.org
The Minneapolis counterpart to St. Paul's Ordway, Orchestra Hall is the place to go to hear the Minnesota Orchestra. The modern exterior can put you off a little, but once inside, visual distractions are kept to a minimum. The minimalist auditorium, which seats 2,400, has a large main floor with three balconies symmetrically girding it. Behind the natural wooden stage and on the ceiling loom what look like enormous sugar cubes hurled by some mythical giant. These blocks provide hundreds of surfaces that deflect sound, making Orchestra Hall among the most acoustically perfect theaters in the nation. The hall lobby opens to Peavey Plaza, which holds the orchestra's popular outdoor summer music festival.

The Playwrights' Center
2301 East Franklin Avenue, Minneapolis
(612) 332-7481
www.pwcenter.org
This former church converted into theater space stands in the middle of the Seward neighborhood on Franklin Avenue. If people know about it, it's because they read the name in another theater's playbill—usually because the Playwrights' Center supported the performance through a fellowship, residency, commission, or other funding. Plays supported by the center have been featured at the Guthrie and other local theaters, as well as on national and international stages. Behind the scenes this membership organization helps actors and writers workshop their creative ideas. It also hosts the occasional performance.

Rarig Center
Univeristy of Minnesota Campus,
330 21st Avenue South, Minneapolis
(612) 624-2345
www.theatre.umn.edu
The Rarig Center, located on the West Bank of the University of Minnesota's Minneapolis campus, hosts University Theatre and Xperimental Theater productions throughout the year in four theaters: a proscenium, a thrust, an arena, and a black box. The Mainstage shows are usually the more popular ones, and the smaller theater spaces offer experimental shows. The X Theater productions are directed and performed exclusively by undergraduate U of M students. At University Theatre, student and professional actors,

designers, and directors write and direct musicals, comedies, and dramas. The Minnesota Centennial Showboat offers performances each summer aboard a sternwheeler riverboat anchored at Harriet Island in St. Paul.

Red Eye Theater
15 West 14th Street, Minneapolis
(612) 870-0309
www.redeyetheater.org
The intimate Red Eye Theater features experimental works, including plays developed at the theater. Just off Nicollet Avenue, the Red Eye's theater space hosts film and video productions and dance events, both local and imported, but its main thrust is theater. The venue itself has hosted Fringe Festival performances over the last few years, an example of how Red Eye is committed to energizing and establishing artists' work.

Southern Theater
1420 Washington Avenue South, Minneapolis
(612) 340-1725
www.southerntheater.org
The Southern has increasingly become a venue for dance due to its rebuilt stage floor. Many local dance companies perform here, and everything from flamenco to classical Indian dance to modern dance can be seen in this venue. Exposed-brick walls enclose the auditorium, lending a comfortable warehouselike feel to the performance experience. Every January the Southern co-hosts (with the Walker Art Center) Out There, a notably high-quality series of theatrical performances. Saturdays at midnight the Southern hosts BALLS, described as "experimental cabaret" and essentially an uncensored open mic with those who have something to say getting five to seven minutes each to speak. Some of the speakers use their amplified freedom to bump and grind through their five to seven minutes, while others will deepen your thinking, make you laugh, or make you cry. The name, incidentally, comes from the cabaret's founder, Leslie Ball.

Theatre de la Jeune Lune
105 North First Street, Minneapolis
(612) 333-6200
www.jeunelune.org
The Theatre de la Jeune Lune is located in the Warehouse District of downtown Minneapolis and is known for its elaborate and poignant commedia-style productions. This theater ensemble is known for its highly physical, visually spectacular productions. The space itself is justification for buying the first ticket; after that most theatergoers are hooked. The facade of the building was designed by renowned architect Cass Gilbert, and the theater is listed on the National Register of Historic Places.

Theatre in the Round Players, Inc.
245 Cedar Avenue, Minneapolis
(612) 333-3010
www.theatreintheround.org
Theatre in the Round, the oldest community theater in the Twin Cities, performs drama and comedy on a unique arena stage. Because the audience surrounds the stage entirely, sets are minimal, making the action between the actors more intense. Props are also very important because of the lack of stage settings. Most of the plays presented are classics, but the players perform a few well-done area premieres each year.

St. Paul

The Fitzgerald Theater
10 East Exchange Street, St. Paul
(651) 290-1200
fitzgeraldtheater.publicradio.org
Opened in 1910 as the Schubert Theater and long known as the World Theater, this comfortable classic structure was renamed in 1994 after St. Paul's famous literary figure and social gadfly, F. Scott Fitzgerald. The man behind the restoration and renaming of the theater is its well-known tenant, Garrison Keillor, host of *A Prairie Home Companion* radio show. As St. Paul's oldest surviving theater space, now restored to its former elegance,

The Fitzgerald Theater in St. Paul is the home of A Prairie Home Companion, *the wildly popular radio show of Garrison Keillor.* SAINT PAUL RCVA

the Fitzgerald Theater presents its shows in a two-balcony, 1,000-seat hall with excellent acoustics and sightlines. The theater's many pleasant features make it popular with touring acts that could probably sell out much larger venues. The theater schedules classical, jazz, folk, country, and pop music events as well as film screenings and theater productions.

Ordway Center for the Performing Arts
345 Washington Street, St. Paul
(651) 224-4222
www.ordway.org
While Minneapolis's Orchestra Hall is modern and glassy like the downtown around it, St. Paul's Ordway is elegant and old world, fitting in without quite conforming to the high and somewhat stuffy standards set forth by its older neighbors, Landmark Center, the Saint

Paul Hotel, and the St. Paul Public Library. Both the hall and the lobby are tastefully designed, with the wooden walls of the auditorium making for outstanding acoustics, especially for a relatively small ensemble like the St. Paul Chamber Orchestra, as well as for touring Broadway productions like Andrew Lloyd Webber and Jim Steinman's *Whistle Down the Wind*. The Ordway also features more contemporary performances (such as *Stomp*) and a dance series with performances by ballet, modern dance, and international touring groups. Rich in contemporary details, the handsome 1,900-seat theater is laid out in the manner of a European opera house (it is home to the Minnesota Opera), with spacious lobbies overlooking Rice Park from a continuous, three-story bank of windows.

Park Square Theatre
20 West Seventh Place, St. Paul
(651) 291-7005
www.parksquaretheatre.org
Located in the heart of downtown St. Paul in the center of Park Square—a block-long brick street that's for pedestrians only—Park Square Theatre offers great professional theater in a not intimate but not huge 344-seat theater. The sets and costumes are beautiful, and there are no bad seats in the house. The shows range from contemporary plays to classical works.

Penumbra Theatre
270 North Kent Street, St. Paul
(651) 224-3180
www.penumbratheatre.org
As the only professional African-American theater company in Minnesota, the Penumbra has a large following and a great reputation. Founded by artistic director Lou Bellamy with the mission of creating artistically exceptional productions that address the African-American experience, the troupe has a rich history of excellence that has included two-time Pulitzer Prize–winning playwright August Wilson, who got his start at Penumbra.

West

Chanhassen Dinner Theatres
501 West 78th Street, Chanhassen
(952) 934-1525 or (800) 355-6273
www.chanhassendt.com
The Chanhassen Dinner Theatres complex is the nation's largest professional dinner theater, featuring four stages under one roof including its 541-seat Main Dinner Theatre, and producing one lavishly costumed Broadway musical comedy after another year-round. This facility is also the largest restaurant in the state.

Old Log Theater
5175 Meadville Street, Excelsior
(952) 474-5951
www.oldlog.com
At the Old Log Theater on the shore of Lake Minnetonka, you'll find American and British comedies with all of the slamming doors, mistaken identities, and double-entendres inherent in the genre. Typically running for months at a time, the productions are crowd-pleasers for conservative audiences but are usually not adventurous enough for those who enjoy theater with an edge.

Plymouth Playhouse
2705 Annapolis Lane North, Plymouth
(763) 553-1600
www.plymouthplayhouse.com
The Plymouth is the flagship space of Troupe America, which specializes in dinner-theater productions long on laughs and music. *Nunsense, Pump Boys* and *Dinettes,* and revues featuring the Twin Cities' own Lovely Liebowitz Sisters have had extended runs here. Their popular long-running production, *How to Talk Minnesotan,* was adapted for the stage by the book's author, Howard Mohr. More recently, *Church Basement Ladies* poked similar fun at the stereotypical Minnesotan.

Stages Theatre Company
1111 Main Street, Hopkins
(952) 979-1111
www.stagestheatre.org
Stages' produces a full season of plays for young audiences. Housed in the Hopkins Center for the Arts, it offers acting, singing, and directing classes for youth ages 5 through 18. The theater often hosts plays featuring well-known kid-favorites such as Charlie Brown and Winnie the Pooh.

PARKS

The Three Rivers Park District, formerly Hennepin Parks, is an independent park district established by the state legislature in 1957 and is responsible for maintaining most of the parks around the Twin Cities metro area. As a special park district, Three Rivers is charged with acquiring, developing, and maintaining large park reserves, regional parks, and regional trails for the benefit and use of the citizens of suburban Hennepin County, Scott County, the metropolitan area, and the state of Minnesota. Three Rivers' policy for planning and management of natural resources distinguishes it from other park and recreation agencies in Minnesota. The policy specifies that no more than 20 percent of a park reserve may be developed for active use and that at least 80 percent of a park reserve shall be restored to and retained in a natural state. As a result, once-rare osprey, bald eagles, sandhill cranes, and trumpeter swans are now nesting in the park reserves. Woodland and prairie restorations have been accomplished using native wildflowers, shrubs, and trees produced from seeds collected in the park reserves.

Twin Citians have the luxury of being able to walk past wetlands full of migratory waterfowl and turtles on their way to downtown Minneapolis, or through thickly forested areas housing species of native animals and birds just minutes outside St. Paul. Kids who grow up in the Twin Cities share in pleasures usually reserved for children in the country, whether it be fishing in one of the many regularly stocked urban lakes, berry picking, or just being surrounded by trees, songbirds, and wildflowers. Even in the dead of winter, you'll find people outside cross-country skiing, snowshoeing, or ice fishing in the many city and suburban parks around the Cities. Take a trip to any of the following, and you'll soon see why we Minnesotans are rabidly protective of our wilderness areas.

MINNEAPOLIS

Boom Island
Plymouth Avenue and Northeast
Eighth Street, Minneapolis
(612) 230-6400
www.minneapolisparks.org
Boom Island Park is a jewel of the Minneapolis parks system. The island is a part of the Minneapolis Riverfront District, a series of parks that stretch from Plymouth Avenue to Interstate 35W. Situated above historic Main Street, Nicollet Island, and the St. Anthony Lock and Dam, Boom Island is a popular destination for picnicking, tossing a Frisbee, sightseeing on a riverboat, launching one's own boat, or simply relaxing by the river on the plaza overlooks.

The park is accessible to persons with disabilities. Low-grade rampways have been integrated into the overlooks and boarding docks. Water fountains and the public telephone all incorporate current accessible features, and level asphalt pathways connect most areas of the park. The park can serve as a nice starting or ending point on a journey on foot or by bike to the nearby Heritage Trail around historic Main Street and St. Anthony Falls or going north up the river to connect with the Mississippi River Regional Corridor Trail.

The boat launch is on the north side of the main parking area in a small, protected channel about 300 feet away from the water's edge and the dock area to the boat slips. Several sets of stairs and a wheelchair-accessible ramp go to the boat slip dock area, and a lovely promenade/plaza is just downriver of the boat dock. This area provides a nice view

The downtown Minneapolis skyline towers over Loring Park, as seen from the Walker Art Center. TODD R. AND
BONNIE S. BERGER

of the river as well as a stunning view of down-town Minneapolis. Another small plaza area with wood decking adjacent to the boat dock affords visitors an opportunity to view the comings and goings of both the riverboats and the private boats being launched nearby.

Boom Island is home to St. Anthony Falls' miniature "lighthouse," which sits on a prominent point overlooking the boat dock and river, although it is no longer operational.

Loring Park
1382 Willow Street, Minneapolis
(612) 370-4929
www.minneapolisparks.org
Modeled after New York's Central Park, although about 800 acres smaller than the real thing, Loring Park is a hip city park with just about everything. There's a large, beautiful pond (Loring Pond) often with mallards, wood ducks, and Canada geese on and around the water; lush, green rolling hills;

and, in summer, free live music and movies in the outdoor amphitheater several nights of the week. There's also a concession cart selling snacks and ice cream parked near the amphitheater most nights. The park is well maintained, with lots of paved trails that take you around the pond and the stunning fountain and bronze sculpture of Norway's esteemed violinist Ole Bull.

A short walk across the street takes you to either the Basilica of Saint Mary or the internationally acclaimed Walker Art Center and its sculpture garden, depending on which way you point your feet.

Mill Ruins Park
704 South Second Street, Minneapolis
(612) 341-7555
www.millcitymuseum.org
Mill Ruins Park on the Mississippi River is next to the Mill City Museum, the historic Crosby A Mill now preserved to celebrate the history of

First-time offenders getting a parking ticket at Minneapolis parks in lots with blue Patron Pass signs can purchase a cheaper annual Patron Pass parking permit in lieu of paying the fine. Check the fine print on your ticket to make sure the citation was issued while parking in a Patron Pass area. You'll have to pay the fine if you're a repeat offender. Call the Minneapolis Park and Recreation Board (612-230-6400) for more information.

the flour mills that built the city of Minneapolis. The park overlooks the locks and St. Anthony Falls, and visitors can watch the barge traffic making its way through the locks and on down the Mississippi. The park connects to the Stone Arch Bridge, a pedestrian and bicycle pathway across the river, and to the bike trail system winding up and down the Mississippi and throughout the Twin Cities.

Minneapolis Chain of Lakes/Rice Creek Regional Parks
Cedar Lake, 25th Street West and Cedar Lake Parkway

Lake Calhoun, Calhoun Parkway and Lake Street

Lake Harriet, 4135 Lake Harriet Parkway East

Lake Nokomis, Minnehaha Parkway East and Cedar Avenue

Lake of the Isles, 25th Street West and Lake of the Isles Parkway East
(612) 230-6400
About 2,500 acres of parkland surround Minneapolis's Chain of Lakes, which includes Lake Harriet, Lake Calhoun, Lake of the Isles, Cedar Lake, and Lake Nokomis. The lakes are connected by Rice and Minnehaha Creeks, which makes canoeing through much of the parkland a fun trip that involves little or no docking to get from lake to lake. Both boat and shore fishing are popular in the Chain of Lakes, and many fishing piers and easily accessed shore fishing sites can be found throughout the parks.

The lakes are surrounded by paved bike and walking trails, and the bike trails connect to the larger system surrounding and cutting across the city of Minneapolis, including the Cedar Lake Trail, the Minnehaha Creek Trail to the Mississippi (which will also get you to the St. Paul bike trail system), and the Midtown Greenway, which follows the railroad tracks along 29th Avenue through south Minneapolis and Uptown.

Thomas Sadler Roberts Bird Sanctuary, located on the north shore of Lake Harriet, consists of 13 acres of unapologetically wild land that attracts more than 200 bird species each year. The sanctuary is named for Thomas Roberts, the late Minneapolis physician and University of Minnesota ornithology professor who in 1932 wrote what remains the definitive work on local avian culture, *Birds of Minnesota.* Created by the Minneapolis Park Board in 1936 as Lyndale Park Bird Sanctuary, its name was changed after Roberts's death to honor the man who led so many field trips here.

Minnehaha Falls and Park
4801 Minnehaha Avenue South, Minneapolis
(612) 230-6400
www.minneapolisparks.org
This historic, heavily used, and recently refurbished 193-acre regional park gives visitors little wonder where Henry Wadsworth Longfellow got the inspiration to write his epic poem *Song of Hiawatha,* which was inspired by accounts the poet had read about Minnehaha Falls, though he never actually visited them. The impressive falls are the primary destination point for most park visitors, with several wonderful overlooks and steps that take you to the base of the falls. From the bottom, you can pick up the Minnehaha Trail and follow it and the river to the Lower Glen area of Minnehaha Park. There you'll find a wide, open field, old stone bridges that cross the water at regular intervals, limestone cliffs, and areas of restored prairie and undeveloped wetlands. Throughout the park are statues, plaques dedicated to historic events, and his-

ℹ️ While Minnehaha Park is beautiful in summer, it's a real treat to go there in winter and see the powerful waterfall frozen solid. Most of the park trails are closed then, but you can still walk down to see the falls.

toric buildings, including the historic Minnehaha Depot, built in 1875 to serve as a recreational gateway for visitors to the falls and as a departure point for soldiers from nearby Fort Snelling, and the Col. John H. Stevens House, which is open to visitors Memorial Day weekend through mid-September.

The main area of the park, around the picnic areas and the falls, can be busy during summer months. There are lots of walkers, bikers, and skaters, so keep one eye out as you go from overlook to overlook. South of the falls, however, you will find quieter, more reflective surroundings in which to relax and enjoy the natural beauty of the park. Benches are strategically placed in and among statuary, gardens, and a unique pergola (covered walk). About 1 mile south of the main park entrance is a hike/bike trail that goes from Minnehaha Falls to Fort Snelling State Park. The trail is mostly paved, with a few sections in disrepair, but it's quiet, little used, and takes bicyclists and hikers all along the upper river bluffs and past a magnificent river overlook at a pedestrian bridge that crosses to the Old Soldier's Home.

The park is also connected to the Minnehaha Creek Bike Trail, which follows the creekbed all the way to Lake Harriet; the Mississippi River Trail leading north to the University of Minnesota; and downtown Minneapolis; and the St. Paul bike trail system via the Ford Parkway bridge.

Nicollet Island Park
40 Power Street (off Historic Main Street at East Hennepin Avenue), Minneapolis
(612) 230-6400
www.minneapolisparks.org
In summertime this little island located in the middle of the Mississippi River is a haven for native wildlife of all sorts, including the occasional deer. In winter the park is converted into a giant ice-skating rink. Year-round the park is a beautiful place for an afternoon or evening stroll—at night the lights of downtown Minneapolis reflect off the Mississippi River, giving one the feeling of being downtown yet still walking through a quaint, small town. Horse-and-carriage rides are available from the nearby Nicollet Inn, and fireworks displays can be seen from the park's rolling green hills on New Year's Eve, the Fourth of July, and during the Aquatennial celebration.

St. Anthony Falls Heritage Trail
Main Street, Minneapolis
(888) 676-6757
www.minneapolisriverfront.com
This amazing stretch of land is often overlooked because the entrance is tucked behind the giant Pillsbury flour mill, next to Minneapolis's historic Main Street retail area directly across the Mississippi River from downtown.

The Heritage Trail is a highly accessible asphalt multiuse trail (bike, hike, jog, and skate) that takes visitors on a 1.8-mile loop, connecting them to most of the historic and natural features of early Minneapolis, including vistas of the tree-lined banks of the Mississippi River as well as many ruined brick arches from the days of the bustling milling industry. The trail is widely interpreted along the way, making this an excellent self-guided trail.

The centerpiece of the park, the Stone Arch Bridge, was built by railway baron James J. Hill in 1883 to speed his trains across the Mississippi. Now beautifully restored, the bridge provides serene transit for walkers, joggers, and bikers. Trail users can cross the river over the historic bridge, which offers a spectacular vista of the river, the downtown Minneapolis skyline, and St. Anthony Falls Lock and Dam. A beautiful promenade parallels the river on its west bank and is a favorite destination of noontime walkers and others who wish to sit, read, or watch the river flow by. There are plenty of overlooks and bench areas on the trail, and water and toilets are located at developed areas on both sides of the river.

Theodore Wirth Park
1339 Theodore Wirth Parkway, Minneapolis
(612) 230-6400
www.minneapolisparks.org
Theodore Wirth Park, or just Wirth Park, as it's usually called, is a huge chunk of land extending from Minneapolis at Glenwood Avenue to Lowry Avenue and from Vincent Avenue into Golden Valley. This beautiful 500-acre park surrounds Wirth Lake, which has a swimming beach as well as a boat launch. There's also an archery range, a playground, tennis courts, the Theodore Wirth Golf Course, and the Eloise Butler Wildflower Garden.

This is a particularly popular park in winter. Behind Theodore Wirth Park's great sledding hill (on the golf course's 10th fairway) is the lighted snow-tubing hill, which isn't too steep and has a tow rope. Cold, hungry snow tubers will appreciate the nearby Swiss Chalet, which has a fireplace and serves fast-food fare such as burgers and fries. Both a skate-skiing course and an intermediate traditional trail start from the chalet. From the top of the skiing hill, downtown Minneapolis's skyscrapers glittering in the afternoon sun may startle you with their closeness. This is known as one of the prettiest places in the Cities for nighttime skiing.

Named for schoolteacher Eloise Butler, who is buried in the bird sanctuary, the 15-acre Eloise Butler Wildflower Garden and Bird Sanctuary is a favorite spot for urbanites to escape the realities of city life and walk among the brilliant, carefully tended wildflower plots. Around the turn of the 20th century, Eloise Butler feared that the wild beauty of Minnesota would be destroyed the way the old-growth hardwood forests near her childhood home in Maine had been. After her retirement from teaching in 1911, Butler was appointed curator of what was then called the Minneapolis Wild Botanic Garden. Butler allowed the native plants to grow with minimal interference to re-create natural conditions. The garden was renamed in her honor in 1929. In addition to the beautiful summertime wildflowers, the park draws crowds of native and migratory songbirds, including meadowlarks, red-wing blackbirds, and finches.

ST. PAUL

Battle Creek Regional Park
2300 Upper Afton Road East, St. Paul
(651) 748-2500
www.co.ramsey.mn.us/parks
Battle Creek Regional Park, consisting of 1,840 acres in the southeast corner of St. Paul and southern Maplewood, provides a large natural area in a highly developed urban environment. The park's extensive areas of woods, wetlands, and grasslands provide habitat for many species of wildlife, including deer, foxes, herons, egrets, and hawks. In summer, the park offers biking and hiking trails. Winter visitors can tour the park on groomed cross-country trails. A large picnic pavilion accommodates groups of up to 500 people, and smaller picnic shelters are also available. In summer the park has a weekly concert series that showcases everything from local alternative acts to acoustic jazz combos.

Como Park
1360 North Lexington Parkway, St. Paul
(651) 632-5111
www.stpaul.gov/depts/parks
This 450-acre urban park is one of the most visited sites in the Twin Cities, offering large picnicking areas, a conservatory, a zoo, a Japanese garden, a small amusement park with pony rides, and summer concerts and plays. There's also an 18-hole golf course that turns into a cross-country ski area in the winter; seasonal equipment rentals and refreshments are available at Como Lakeside Pavilion.

In the middle of a tough Minnesota winter, there's no palliative like a visit to the lush, green-filled Marjorie McNeely Conservatory at Como Park, which houses such exotic plants as 125-year-old palm trees and papaya trees.

Outside, the teahouse in the Como Ordway Memorial Japanese Garden offers a traditional chanoyu tea ceremony several times throughout the summer. Look for the beautiful goldfish pond stocked with giant, colorful fish. (See the Attractions chapter for information on Como's zoo and conservatory.)

The historic Cafesjian's Carousel can be found just south of the conservatory. The carousel and its beautiful antique horses are available to the public during the summer, and a ride on the carousel is a great way to end a day at the park.

Hidden Falls Park
East Mississippi River Boulevard, St. Paul
(651) 632-5111
www.stpaul.gov/depts/parks
Hidden Falls Park dates from 1887, when the area was identified as one of four major park sites for the city of St. Paul. The park got its name from the small, spring-fed waterfall hidden deep inside the park. Today hiking and biking trails run along shady, wooded bottomlands next to the river and along the marshes of the lake before connecting to the trails along Mississippi River Boulevard. The park features a well-developed picnic area with pavilion and modern toilet facilities, a boat launch ramp, and picnic sites. Panfish can be caught in the Mississippi River.

The hiking/biking trail, which converts to a cross-country ski trail in the winter, takes users along the Mississippi River, where the flora and fauna of river life can be observed up close. Songbirds migrate and nest nearby, and deer and rabbits can be seen in the thick wooded areas around the park. At points along the trail, historic Fort Snelling can be seen on the high bluffs across the river.

Fort Snelling State Park
101 Snelling Lake Road, St. Paul
(612) 725-2724
www.dnr.state.mn.us/state_parks
For hundreds of years before Europeans arrived, generations of Dakotas lived in villages along the Mississippi and Minnesota Rivers that meet in what's now Fort Snelling State Park. The river confluence was believed to be the place of origin and center of the earth by the bands of Mde-wa-kan-ton-wan Dakotas, the "Dwellers by Mystic Lake." By the late 1600s Europeans had visited the area. In the 1820s Fort Snelling was built on the bluff above the two rivers to control the exploration, trade, and settlement on these waterways.

Established as a state park in 1962, the 3,400-acre Fort Snelling State Park is located in the Mississippi River Sandplains Landscape Region at the confluence of the two great rivers. Most of the park is on the Minnesota River floodplain and is thickly wooded with large cottonwood, silver maple, ash, and willow trees along the braided channels of the Minnesota River. Picnic sites, a beach, and river and lake fishing invite visitors to enjoy the recreational opportunities offered by this historic and beautiful park nestled in the shadow of city freeways and airport flyways. The swimming beach is a popular summertime attraction, and the park offers miles of hiking, biking, and cross-country skiing trails, including a trail that leads up to historic Fort Snelling on the bluff above the confluence.

The Pike Island Interpretive Center hosts exhibits concerning historic Fort Snelling and the region in general. Golf equipment and canoes are available for rent in the park, and naturalist programs ranging from bird-watching tours to nature and snowshoe hikes are offered year-round.

Indian Mounds Park
Earl Street and Mounds Boulevard, St. Paul
(651) 632-5111
www.stpaul.gov/depts/parks
Enshrining six 2,000-year-old Hopewell Indian burial mounds, Mounds Park occupies what was the choicest residential land in St. Paul in the 1860s, when this park was set aside. Today the bluffs of the park give visitors one of the best "aerial" views of the Twin Cities, with the Minneapolis skyline on the left, the St. Paul skyline on the right, and the Mississippi River below. The mounds are sur-

rounded by metal rail fences but are easily seen and approached—the remains have long since been removed, but the mounds are still standing as a sacred memorial. Visitors are not permitted to climb on the mounds. A brass plaque describing the site stands near the brick pavilion. The park is also the site of the first visit by Europeans to the Twin Cities area; Father Louis Hennepin and two other Frenchmen were brought here in 1680.

The park is actively used by families, groups, skateboarders, cyclists, hikers, and others. It is a well-worn park with old restrooms and access routes developed before accessibility regulations were in place, but there are plenty of picnic areas and play spaces for people of all ages and accessible parking spaces at many points in the park.

Lilydale Park/Harriet Island Park/Cherokee Park
South side of Mississippi River at Wabasha, St. Paul
(651) 632-5111
www.stpaul.gov/depts/parks
The river-oriented Lilydale and Harriet Island Parks include the natural area of the Lilydale portion below the river bluffs and Harriet Island itself. Harriet Island, situated on the Mississippi River across from downtown St. Paul, was one of the first recreational sites in the city. Named for pioneer schoolteacher Harriet Bishop, the park was a true island separated from the mainland by a channel of water until 1950, when the channel was filled. At the top of the bluffs is Cherokee Park, which has picnic grounds and good spots overlooking Harriet Island, the Mississippi, and downtown St. Paul's skyline.

Harriet Island has long been a playground for St. Paul citizens who come alone or with friends and family to fish, launch their boats, cruise on a historic riverboat, picnic, take walks, and simply enjoy nature. The park has landscaped river edges, beautiful flower gardens that attract native and migratory songbirds, and a marina from which park visitors

can board several large paddleboats to tour the waterways.

Lilydale, formerly a residential community, extends to the west of Harriet Island and is now an undeveloped floodplain. It used to be the site of former Twin City Brick Co.'s mining operations, until the company exposed extensive fossil beds, making the area well known among professional and amateur paleontologists, who are sometimes allowed to accompany professionals on guided digs at the park. A connected pond and about 200 acres of marsh and woodlands provide habitat for varied flora and fauna.

Mears Park
366 Sibley Street, St. Paul
Located near Galtier Plaza in the distinctive, anachronistic Lowertown neighborhood of St. Paul, Mears Park serves as the neighborhood's village commons. The park is a popular lunchtime and evening gathering spot and is filled with trees, flowers, benches, sculpture, and even a rippling creek. Summertime brings outdoor concerts, performances, events, and festivals. In winter the park's many trees are covered with hundreds of thousands of twinkling lights.

Phalen Park
Off Wheelock Parkway and East Larpenteur Avenue, St. Paul
(651) 632-5111
www.stpaul.gov/depts/parks
Founded in 1899, Phalen Park surrounds the quiet residential area around Phalen and Round Lakes in northeast St. Paul, with 3.2 miles of paved trails, an amphitheater, a beach, an 18-hole golf course, and a picnic shelter and pavilion. The park is named for Edward Phelan (whose name was spelled various ways), the earliest settler of the land around Phalen Creek. The park's trails connect to the Gateway State Trail, a paved biking and walking trail stretching from downtown St. Paul to Pioneer Park, north of Stillwater.

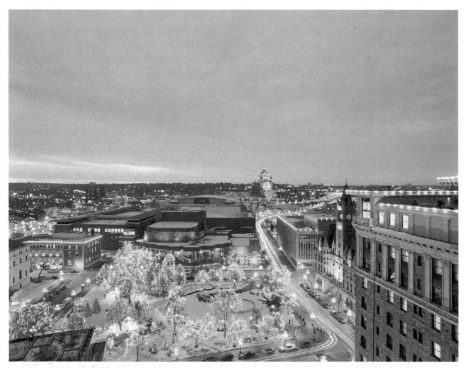

Elegant Rice Park is one of the many small parks in St. Paul. SAINT PAUL RCVA

Rice Park
140 Washington Street, St. Paul

In the shadow of Landmark Center, the Ordway Center for the Performing Arts, the St. Paul Public Library, and the Saint Paul Hotel, St. Paul's Rice Park is a restful yet active square of greenery and monuments. Young trees provide a little shade during the day, but the park is at its best for summer concerts and as the ice sculpture hub of the annual St. Paul Winter Carnival.

North

Bald Eagle–Otter Lakes Regional Park
5800 Hugo Road, White Bear Township
(651) 748-2500
www.co.ramsey.mn.us/parks

Bald Eagle–Otter Lakes Regional Park, comprising 884 acres, is located in White Bear Township in the northeast corner of Ramsey County. The park features extensive woods, wetlands, and grasslands. The park is home to many species of wildlife, including red foxes, deer, woodcocks, herons, turtles, minks, beavers, osprey, otters, and muskrats. More than 3 miles of paved and woodchip-covered hiking trails offer visitors the opportunity to experience nature up close. Fishing—both when the park's lakes are liquid and when they are frozen—is popular here.

The Tamarack Nature Center offers a variety of programs, including bird-watching tours, syrup making, guided summer hikes, and winter snowshoe walks. Inside the nature center itself are mounted displays of many animals native to the area.

i Rice Park and Mears Park in downtown St. Paul are picturesque stroll-worthy urban pockets, especially in winter, when they're decorated with myriad white lights.

Coon Rapids Dam Regional Park
10360 West River Road, Brooklyn Park
(763) 694-7790
www.threeriversparkdistrict.org

Situated on the banks of the Mississippi River, the 610-acre Coon Rapids Dam Regional Park offers visitors the chance to see our nation's greatest river up close. The centerpiece of this large park is the refurbished Coon Rapids Dam, which spans the Mississippi River. A wide dam walkway, usable by pedestrians, bicyclists, and in-line skaters, allows visitors a unique opportunity to walk across a working dam, with a scenic view of the riverway above and below the dam.

Interpretive signs describing the history of the dam and natural features line the bridge; the visitor center provides outstanding exhibits focusing on the economic, cultural, and environmental impact the Mississippi River has on the lives of people who live and depend on the river. Boating is allowed north of the visitor center, with a boat launch for accessing the north Mississippi River waterway through a naturally sheltered backwater. Fishing is allowed from the fishing deck on the western end of the dam.

Trout fishing is also allowed in Cenaiko Trout Lake, a beautiful lake stocked with rainbow and brook trout (Minnesota fishing license with State Trout Stamp affixed required), located on the eastern side of the park. Bait and tackle supplies can be purchased at the visitor center. Bicycle and in-line skate rentals are available at the visitor center for use on many of the paths.

The stunning Native Prairie Restoration Area is on the nearby banks of the river, just past the visitor center entrance and extending to the picnic plaza. The park has two well-developed and conveniently linked and accessible asphalt bike/hike trails—all part of the extensive Mississippi River Trail Corridor that leads users south into Anoka Regional Park and eventually connects users with the Minneapolis Parkway Trail System at Boom Island and the Heritage Trail at historic Main Street in Minneapolis.

Crow-Hassan Park Reserve
11629 Crow-Hassan Park Road, Rogers
(763) 694-7860
www.threeriversparkdistrict.com

It's hard to imagine an endless sea of grass flowing from Minnesota to the Rocky Mountains now that trees, crops, houses, and billboards muddy the view. But one of the best places in the Twin Cities to catch a glimpse of that sweeping landscape is Crow-Hassan Park Reserve, where 600 acres of old farm fields have been transformed back into prairie.

The reintroduction of native grasses and forbs began here in 1969, using seeds from a two-acre remnant of virgin prairie located in the park near Prairie Lake. Other sources were also tapped to complete the collection of nearly 100 species that have been planted over the years, and with the reintroduction of native grasses and plants, native animals have slowly made their way back to the land as well.

For pet owners, more than 40 acres are open for dogs to run off leash; a special permit is required and is available from Three Rivers Park District Headquarters for $30 per year or $5 per day. This is also a popular park for horseback riders, with more than 10 miles of trail dedicated for just this purpose. In winter cross-country skiing and snowmobiling bring crowds of enthusiasts. The beauty of Crow-Hassan, though, is that in between the rolling hills, the deep prairie grass, and the thick tree cover, you can be as completely alone as you want to be, even if the park is at peak season.

Elm Creek Park Reserve
13351 Elm Creek Road, Osseo
(763) 694-7894
www.threeriversparkdistrict.org

The Elm Creek Park Reserve, located northwest of Osseo, is a beautiful and varied park and nature reserve. A swimming beach, creative play area, and a concession stand with volleyball, horseshoe, and bike rentals are located on the premises, and horse trails, cross-country ski trails, hiking trails, and bicycle paths interlace the park.

At 4,900 acres, Elm Creek Park Reserve is the largest in the Three Rivers system. Wildlife is abundant in Elm Creek because of the numerous streams and marshes: Herons, ducks, and beavers can be viewed from miles of trails. Coyotes are also known to roam the wilds of Elm Creek, though your chances of seeing one are slim. Five lakes, three streams and wetlands, a hardwood forest, and reclaimed farmland provide plenty of elbow room for wildlife and parkgoers alike.

The Eastman Nature Center includes displays giving a concise overview of the reserve's habitat. From here hikers can go on self-guided tours ranging from wildflower walks to a trip through turtle country. If the displays don't move you into the woods, the enthusiastic naturalists and creative courses (on tagging monarch butterflies, for example) offered will. On late afternoon weekend days in January and February, Eastman packs them in to view the white-tailed deer that come to feed.

Lake Maria State Park
11411 Clementa Avenue NW, Monticello
(763) 878-2325
www.dnr.state.mn.us/state_parks
Lake Maria State Park includes a native stand of maple, oak, and basswood, remnants of the Big Woods that once covered much of south-central Minnesota. The park offers hiking, backpacking, horseback riding, and cross-country ski trails. Backpack sites are located on remote lakes and ponds throughout the park. Log camper cabins, also located near lakes and ponds, provide bunk beds for six people and a table and benches.

The park maintains more than 20 miles of summer hiking trails, 16 miles of groomed cross-country ski trails, and 3 miles of winter hiking trails. Snowshoeing is permitted anywhere in the park except on groomed ski trails, and snowshoes can be rented at the visitor center. Boat and canoe rentals are available through the visitor center in summer. You can also make campsite and cabin reservations at the visitor center or on the park's Web site.

Interpretive programs are available year-round. The marshes, potholes, and lakes here provide excellent habitat for wildlife, especially birds during seasonal migrations. Lake Maria is also one of the last remaining natural habitats of the endangered Blanding's turtle, easily identified by the bright yellow spots on its shell.

Long Lake Regional Park
1500 Old Highway 8, New Brighton
(651) 748-2500
www.co.ramsey.mn.us/parks
The 218 acres of Long Lake Regional Park include frontage on Long Lake and cattail marshes, oak woods, and restored prairie around Rush Lake. The park features a 3-mile hiking and biking trail, a beautiful swimming beach, and a large picnic area near the swimming beach. After a dip in Long Lake, make tracks to the beach house for snacks, restrooms, changing rooms, and showers. A large picnic pavilion is complete with kitchen and public restrooms, and the group picnic area features a game field, a volleyball court, hiking/biking trails, and a wheelchair-accessible play area. On the south end of Long Lake, you can launch your boat and park your trailer—or just fish off the pier. The pier has a parking area, restrooms, a clean water source, and seated angler stations.

Riverfront Regional Park/Islands of Peace
5100 East River Road, Fridley
(763) 757-3920
www.anokacountyparks.com
This Anoka County park's biking, hiking, and ungroomed cross-country skiing trails offer nice views of the Mississippi River all along the trails. Canoes can be rented from the park, and fishing is permitted from the shore and the river. If you're lucky enough to hook some lunch, grills and picnic shelters are also available.

The Islands of Peace segment of the park, located north of Interstate 694, has been developed by the Foundation for Islands of Peace. A reception center has a fireplace, restrooms, a library, a lounge, and meeting rooms. A walk bridge and paved trail link the center to Chase's Island facilities, which include paved trails, shelter, river viewing, and picnic facilities—all with wheelchair access. The 57-acre Durnam Island segment, located in the Mississippi River west of Chase's Island, has accessible nature trails and a boat shuttle service.

Riverfront Regional Park also acts as a trailhead for the trail segment to the south along East River Road, connecting the Minneapolis trail system and the trail segment to the north to Islands of Peace in Fridley. An additional trail link to Brooklyn Center exists as well, with a trail crossing over the I–694 bridge.

Wild River State Park
39797 Park Trail, Center City
(651) 583-2125
www.dnr.state.mn.us/state_parks
Wild River State Park's name is derived from the fact that the St. Croix River was one of the original eight rivers protected by the U.S. Congress through the Wild and Scenic Rivers Act of 1968. The park has 18 miles of shoreline along the St. Croix.

Wild River State Park attracts people who enjoy camping, hiking, horseback riding, canoeing, interpretive programs, self-guided trails, and cross-country skiing. Day visitors can enjoy a leisurely paddle down the St. Croix River from the Sunrise River access to the southern park river access. The park provides opportunities for drive-in camping, group camping, backpack camping, and canoe camping. (Winter camping is also available here.) Visitors who want modern amenities can reserve the guesthouse, which provides a living room, dining room, kitchen, and fireplace. The park also has two camping cabins, with bunk beds, a table, and benches. An all-season trail center is a great spot to relax after hiking, riding horses, biking, or cross-country skiing on the park's trail system. A visitor center with exhibits and environmental education programs is open year-round.

Naturalist programs at the park are available to individuals as well as schools and other groups upon request. The park maintains 35 miles of hiking and groomed cross-country ski trails, 18 miles of horse trails, 2.6 miles of paved biking trails, and 1.5 miles of snowshoe trails—snowshoeing is permitted anywhere in the park except on groomed ski trails. Guided snowshoe tours include a visit to a beaver pond, identifying and following animal tracks, or a challenging trip down a short, steep slope to a hidden prairie (basic instructions on how to snowshoe are covered before the hikes, and snowshoes are provided at no charge for participants). The park also offers one-day classes on tapping maple trees for sap and making maple syrup.

South

Cleary Lake Regional Park
18106 Texas Avenue, Prior Lake
(763) 694-7777
www.threeriversparkdistrict.org
The 1,045-acre Cleary Lake Regional Park, southwest of Burnsville, is a popular year-round recreation spot in the southern metro area. A distinctive three-season pavilion, available by reservation, is great for large group gatherings, while golfers find challenge in the par 3, nine-hole golf course and driving range. Water sports available include swimming, boating, and fishing in Cleary Lake. Winter activities include cross-country skiing on groomed trails and snowshoeing anywhere in the park except the ski trails. Boats, bicycles, in-line skates, and cross-country skis are available for rent at the visitor center; reservation picnic areas and campsites are also available.

Hyland Lake Park Reserve
10145 Bush Lake Road, Bloomington
(763) 694-7687
www.threeriversparkdistrict.org
The 1,000 acres of parklands at Hyland Lake Park Reserve, which include prairie lands, deciduous woods, and Normandale, Hyland, and Bush Lakes, have more than 9 miles of trails for hiking, an additional 8.5 paved miles

for bicycling, and, in winter, 8 miles of groomed trail for cross-country skiing. The first cross-country ski trail in the Twin Cities was cut here, near the old Bush Lake ski jump in the winter of 1965–66. Hyland Lake Park Reserve is now one of the finest and most popular cross-country facilities in the area.

On the lakes there's a boat landing with a rental/storage facility for canoes, rowboats, and paddleboats, as well as a large fishing pier for shore fishing. Bush Lake has a clean swimming beach with picnic shelters nearby. Skis, bicycles, paddleboats, and seasonal recreation equipment can be rented at the visitor center for reasonable rates.

The Richardson Nature Center, located inside the park, is home to deer, pheasants, and wild songbirds. Richardson's spacious center focuses especially on raptors and raptor recovery, with programs on eagles, owls, hawks, and falcons. You can see ospreys banded and meet live owls, hawks, and kestrels.

Lebanon Hills Regional Park
860 Cliff Road, Eagan
(651) 554-6530
www.co.dakota.mn.us/parks
Less than 30 minutes from both downtown Minneapolis and St. Paul, this Dakota County park covers more than 2,000 acres of lakes, marshes, beaches, and trails. Open year-round, the park is divided into east and west sections connected by an immense network of trails. Nearly every outdoor activity is available—swimming in Schultz Lake (one of the few local beaches with lifeguards present), RV and tent camping, hiking, picnicking, horseback riding, mountain biking, and cross-country skiing. Fishing and all nonmotorized boats are allowed on Jensen Lake, and in winter ice fishing is allowed on the lake as well.

Lebanon Hills is a popular destination for winter sports enthusiasts. The park has two great ski areas: the 2-mile skate-ski offers long, tough uphills and fast, winding downhills (not recommended for beginners), and several other park trails are tracked for classic cross-country skiing. The trail system was

originally laid out for hiking and horse paths, so some downhill corners can be awkward for skiers. Cross-country ski and snowmobile trails snake through the park's wooded, hilly terrain, and hot cocoa and snacks are available at the warming house at Schulze Lake.

Minnesota Valley National Wildlife Refuge and Recreation Area
3815 American Boulevard, Bloomington
(952) 854-5900
www.fws.gov/midwest/MinnesotaValley
Only minutes from the Twin Cities and the airport, the Minnesota Valley National Wildlife Refuge is dedicated to preserving the wildlife of Minnesota River habitats. This archipelago of river-valley land parcels functions as a federally managed nature preserve, particularly for waterfowl and migrating birds using the Minnesota River flyway. All told, 14,000 acres are at your disposal, including the Minnesota Valley Trail, which links Fort Snelling State Park and units of the Minnesota Valley National Wildlife Refuge to waysides and other public lands. The area is ideal for hiking, biking, cross-country skiing, mountain biking, canoeing, snowshoeing, camping, and snowmobiling. Wildlife observation and bird-watching are also popular activities year-round. The landscapes are just as diverse as the trail system and include wetlands, floodplain forest, remnants of farmlands settled in the late 1800s, and blufftop oak savanna.

In the state-managed Minnesota Valley Recreation Area, you can see the only remaining building from the town of St. Lawrence, visit the Jabs Farm Homestead, or ride your bike across a 1900s railroad bridge. The interpretive center in the recreation area contains engaging displays of Minnesota River Valley human history and natural history. Naturalists offer field trips to the woodcock dancing grounds in spring and to the heron rookery in winter via cross-country skis. The wildlife refuge occupies about half of the larger Minnesota Valley Recreation Area, which stretches 75 miles from historic Fort Snelling to Le Sueur.

Murphy-Hanrehan Park Reserve
15501 Murphy Lake Road, Savage
(763) 694-7777
www.threeriversparkdistrict.org
Murphy-Hanrehan Park Reserve is a largely undeveloped park. The park's hilly terrain attracts mountain bikers, horseback riders, and endurance hikers in summer and cross-country skiers and snowmobilers in winter. Boaters with oars, paddles, or electric-trolling motors can launch into Murphy Lake from the boat launch off County Road 75; the lake has been stocked with everything from bullheads to walleye.

East

Afton State Park
6959 Peller Avenue South, Hastings
(651) 436-5391
www.dnr.state.mn.us/state_parks
Five miles south of the town of Afton, Afton State Park is a 1,695-acre wilderness area set along the St. Croix National Scenic Riverway. The park is located in a landscape of rolling glacial moraines and rocky bluffs, surrounded by thick hardwood and pine forests, with protected remnants of original prairie being restored by park management. Throughout the park visitors get picture-perfect glimpses of the slow-moving St. Croix River.

Afton State Park has more than 20 miles of paved and groomed trails for horseback riding and hiking in spring and summer. In winter many of these trails are left open for cross-country skiers and snowshoers to explore. Many activities are offered throughout the year by volunteers who lead snowshoe hikes, demonstrate bird-banding practices, and teach visitors how to identify many of the birds that visit the park. There are also several primitive camping sites with

i A $40 season pass is required to cross-country ski in most of the parks in the Three Rivers Park District. Call the park district at (763) 559-9000 or visit their Web site (www.threerivers parkdistrict.org) for more information.

nearby access to hiking trails—reservations are needed from April to November but not from November to April. Bird-watching, swimming, sledding, and fishing are other popular activities at Afton State Park.

Cottage Grove Ravine Regional Park
9940 Point Douglas Road, Cottage Grove
(651) 430-8240
www.co.washington.mn.us
This handsome 506-acre park stays pretty quiet except when the high school teams are practicing. The park name refers to the nearby town (organized in May 1858) and the wooded ravine that was formed in glacial times and may once have been a channel of the St. Croix River. The park is home to native Minnesota wildlife, including the pileated woodpecker. These spectacular birds have a flaming red crest and can reach 16 inches in height. If a loud jackhammering sound breaks the silence, you'll know they are close by.

In winter this is a great park for the experienced cross-country skier, with almost 150 feet in elevation change and some great downhill runs through heavily wooded, dramatic ravines. It is also a popular spot for ski skaters.

A new fishing pier on the eastern side of Ravine Lake, which has recently been stocked with walleye and bluegill, beckons the angler.

Interstate State Park/Glacial-Pothole Trail
On Minnesota Highway 8 in Taylors Falls
(651) 465-5711
www.dnr.state.mn.us/state_parks
Carved by glacial meltwater, Interstate State Park follows the cliffs and bluffs bordering the beautiful St. Croix River. Established in 1895 when Minnesota and Wisconsin created separate parks across the river from each other, this was the first example of an interstate park collaboration in the country.

The main attraction of the park, besides the St. Croix, are the unusual basalt formations and potholes and the greenstone cliffs that were formed before there was any complex life on Earth. The Pre-cambrian basalt boulders make up the Glacial-Pothole Trail, a rough-hewn pathway through the maze of "potholes"—deep, perfectly circular holes carved into the hard basalt by glaciers—some of which are hundreds of feet deep (the deepest known glacial potholes in the world are here). During the summer a park naturalist leads tours along the Glacial Pothole Trail and offers programs detailing the natural history of the area. The colorful park features wildflowers in spring, and Interstate, like much of the St. Croix River valley, is a prime spot to be when the leaves turn in autumn. There is much to do at Interstate State Park. Cliff climbing, kayaking, canoeing, camping, hiking, picnicking, and playing volleyball (equipment is available in the park office) all forestall boredom.

The park has a 22-acre campground with 37 drive-in sites (including some without electricity) located near the Glacial-Pothole Trail that fills up quickly in the summer months—reservations are highly encouraged. You can also camp here in the winter, although you'll have to break out the snowshoes or cross-country skis to get to the campground: The park does not plow the campground roads in winter. Canoes can be rented at the nearby boat dock and can be reserved by calling the park.

Lake Elmo Park Reserve
1515 Keats Avenue, Lake Elmo
(651) 430-8370
www.co.washington.mn.us

The Lake Elmo Park Reserve is 2,165 acres of forest, wetlands, and prairie restoration lands. Eighty percent of the parkland is set aside for preservation and protection, and because of this, Lake Elmo is home to a huge variety of native animals, birds, reptiles, and fish. People come to Lake Elmo year-round for both shore and boat fishing, canoeing, hiking, swimming, and cross-country skiing. There are also three campgrounds with a total of 103 campsites, restroom facilities, lighted picnic shelters with electricity, hand pumps for water, and a two-acre swim pond that's regularly maintained by the park.

St. Croix Bluffs Regional Park
10191 St. Croix Trail South, Hastings
(651) 430-8240
www.co.washington.mn.us

Five miles south of Afton, this 579-acre park is made up of rolling hills, blufftop hardwood forests, and nearly a mile of scenic St. Croix River shoreline. Woodlands and ravines cut through tight bluffs to the riverbank, making great bird-watching areas for everything from eagles to wild turkeys. Swimming is not allowed in the St. Croix, but boating, fishing, and ice fishing are. The park features a fishing pier and a boat launch, as well as trails for hiking and cross-country skiing. The park has a large campground suitable for both tent and RV campers.

St. Croix National Scenic Riverway
401 North Hamilton Street, St. Croix Falls, WI
(715) 483-2274
www.nps.gov/sacn

The St. Croix River stretches more than 150 miles and partially forms the boundary between Minnesota and Wisconsin. It is the only river in the world that's protected along its entire length. Beginning near Gordon, Wisconsin, the Upper St. Croix flows southerly to St. Croix Falls. The Lower St. Croix flows from St. Croix Falls dam to Prescott, Wisconsin, where it joins the Mississippi River. The Lower St. Croix is deeper, wider, and slower moving than the Upper St. Croix, making it a great place to fish, canoe, water-ski, and swim. Hot air balloon rides are available year-round. Winter activities include ice fishing, downhill and cross-country skiing, tubing, snowmobiling, and sledding. Nearby Lake St. Croix is formed by a dam on the Mississippi River and is popular for water recreation.

Spring Lake Park Reserve
13690 Pine Bend Trail, Rosemount
(651) 438-4660
www.co.dakota.mn.us/parks

This lovely park is criss-crossed with scenic hiking or skiing trails that wind through the woods and along the bluffs high above the ℹ️ Three Rivers Park District's 25-foot climbing wall regularly moves to different parks in the park system—contact Three Rivers (763-694-7718; www.threeriversparkdistrict.com) to find out its current location.

Mississippi River. Spring Lake Park Reserve provides a scenic and peaceful setting for nature lovers to appreciate, as well as a model airplane flying field and a challenging archery trail. A youth campground with a heated lodge and an outdoor classroom is available to youth groups. The park also has 66 garden plots available for seasonal rental on a first-come, first-served basis.

Square Lake County Park
15450 Square Lake Trail North, Stillwater
(651) 430-8370
www.co.washington.mn.us
The 27-acre Square Lake County Park is known for having one of the clearest lakes in Minnesota, making it a popular spot for scuba divers, swimmers, and anglers alike. The lake is regularly stocked with trout and has a 950-foot clean sand beach, a concession stand where food and fishing supplies can be purchased, and restrooms with showers. The park also has a boat launch, a fishing pier, and a picnic area.

William O'Brien State Park
16821 O'Brien Trail North, Marine on St. Croix
(651) 433-0500
www.dnr.state.mn.us/state_parks
A great "getaway" park only 45 minutes from the Twin Cities, the 1,520 acres of William O'Brien State Park provide a beautiful setting along the banks of the St. Croix River. The park is named for a pioneer lumberman in the St. Croix River Valley, and its human-made lake is named for O'Brien's daughter, Alice, who donated an additional 180 acres to the park in 1945.

O'Brien is an extremely popular camping spot, and in the summer the first-come, first-served campsites fill up quickly, especially on weekends; campsite reservations are strongly encouraged. The lower campground offers great river views, while the upper has both sunny, open spots and heavily wooded ones. The park has 124 drive-in campsites, 2 walk-in sites, 7 wheelchair-accessible sites with wheelchair-accessible flush toilets and showers, 4 group campsites, and one camping cabin available to the public. Conveniently, the park's open picnic shelter sells firewood and ice to campers, and public phones are also available for campers' use.

Hiking/skiing trails offer quiet exploration of the park's rolling, wooded hills. For anglers, the channels of the St. Croix have northerns, walleye, bass, and trout. Ideal for canoeing, the river is also a migratory pathway that offers visitors an exciting diversity of sights and sounds. Canoes can be rented from the park for an outing on the St. Croix or on Lake Alice. Swimming in the river isn't allowed, but Lake Alice has a sandy beach and shallow water close to shore. On clear days you can see Taylors Falls from one overlook, and, although the park is heavily used, the 12 miles of hiking/skiing trails are rarely crowded. Snowshoeing is permitted anywhere in the park except on groomed ski trails. The park also has a warming house for huddling in after playing in the snow.

West

Baker Park Reserve
2301 County Road 19, Maple Plain
(763) 479-2473
www.threeriversparkdistrict.org
Located on Lake Independence in central Hennepin County, Baker Park Reserve's 2,700 acres offer a 210-site campground, golfing at the Baker National Golf Course, swimming and boating in Lake Independence, and a playground for kids. The kids' playground area is truly spectacular, almost fortresslike. Kids scramble over ramps, platforms, and paths made of recycled rubber mats that protect against minor falls and bumps and bruises.

In winter a sledding hill, a cozy warming chalet, and snowmobile, mountain biking, and groomed cross-country ski trails are opened. In summer paved hiking and biking trails wind through one of the remnants of a Big Woods forest. Boats, bikes, snowshoes, and skis are available for rent at the park's visitor center.

Baylor Regional Park
10775 County Road 33,
Norwood Young America
(952) 466-5250
www.co.carver.mn.us/parks

Baylor Regional Park is located in the extreme southwest corner of the Twin Cities metro area, so far removed from the bright lights of the downtowns that it's a favorite observation point for junior astronomy clubs and amateur stargazers. Perched on the shoulder of Eagle Lake and surrounded by farmers' fields, Baylor preserves a rich mix of native habitats, from the large grove of mature maple trees that are tapped in early spring each year for maple syrup, to the floating boardwalk that carries visitors over wetland marshes to get a glimpse of turtles, waterfowl, and wildflowers.

The park offers a 50-site tent and RV campground with shower facilities, as well as a swimming beach and bathhouse on Eagle Lake, two large picnic shelters, tennis courts, and 4 miles of hiking trails. A community room in the park barn is available for group use with reservations in advance. In winter the hiking trails turn into neatly groomed cross-country ski trails, and a warming house is available for outdoor enthusiasts from 8:00 a.m. to sunset daily.

Bryant Lake Regional Park
6800 Rowland Road, Eden Prairie
(763) 694-7764
www.threeriversparkdistrict.org

Bryant Lake Regional Park is located in Eden Prairie south of Minnesota Highway 62 and west of Shady Oak Road on Rowland Road and has a three-season concession plaza, three-season pavilion, a paved boat launch, a fishing pier, a swimming beach, boat rentals, and 3 miles of turf and paved hiking/biking trails. The 170-acre park also provides habitat for deer, waterfowl, and songbirds; fishing, boating, swimming, and ice fishing are popular activities here. The park is set in a vista of rolling hills that block out the surrounding city lights and sounds, making it a perfect spot for an urban escape.

Carver Park Reserve
7025 Victoria Drive, Victoria
(763) 694-7650
www.threeriversparkdistrict.org

Carver Park Reserve is one of the crown jewels of the Three Rivers Park District, with 3,500 acres and lakeshore frontage on six major lakes. One of the most popular places in the reserve is the Lowry Nature Center, which offers programs that focus on Carver's abundant natural resources, ranging from fall bird migration and waterfowl watches to the springtime activity of maple-syrup making and summertime stargazing, as well as tracking mink, voles, and foxes and building snow-caves. The park itself is home to deer, foxes, owls, hawks, and many other animals that can be seen from roads and trails. Wetland animals can be seen from the more than 1,700 feet of boardwalk that takes you through tamarack marshes. For small children, Habitats, a creative education play area, features larger-than-life flowers to climb on, dragonfly eyes to peer through, and a beaver lodge to sit in.

Park facilities include a boat launch and a campground at Lake Auburn. Four of the park's lakes are open for canoeing, fishing, and ice fishing, and the park has miles of trails for hiking, horseback riding, cross-country skiing, snowmobiling, and snowshoeing. On winter weekends the park turns a wood-heated barn into a warming house, with snack counters and restroom facilities conveniently located nearby. Cross-country skis, Norwegian kick sleds, and bicycles can be seasonally rented from the park.

French Regional Park
12605 County Road 9, Plymouth
(763) 694-7750
www.threeriversparkdistrict.org
French Regional Park, usually shortened to "French Park" by locals, was named for the first superintendent of the Hennepin County park system, Clifton E. French. Located on 310 acres on Medicine Lake, French Regional Park features many water-based activities. A self-guided canoe trail through the backwaters of the beautiful lake provides intimate views of wetland wildlife. Rental canoes, paddleboats, rowboats, and kayaks are available at the visitor center, and you can also rent a slip or wintertime lift storage to park your sailboat (under 20 feet only). Monthly outdoor education programs feature such activities as maple syruping, bird-watching, and guided hikes to beaver lodges. The open landscape of rolling glacial hills is broken along the lake and lagoons with second-growth forest. This is not a place to come for wintertime solitude. The park's central location attracts more than 20,000 skiers—half at night—during a good season.

The visitor center rents other equipment, from cross-country skis to volleyballs. A creative play area is available, and a shuttle tram runs throughout the summer season between the visitor center and the swimming beach. French Park's playground is usually humming with childhood energy, and the park features several miles of biking, hiking, and cross-country skiing trails. In winter, a lighted sledding hill lets everyone hug their inner luger.

Lake Minnetonka Regional Park
4610 County Road 44, Minnestrista
(763) 694-7754
www.threeriversparkdistrict.org
This 292-acre park features picnic areas, a visitor center, a fishing pier, a boat launch, a unique 1.75-acre upland swimming pond with chlorinated water, and a wheelchair-accessible swimming ramp that extends into the pond. The visitor center, which was formerly a private residence, contains meeting rooms, a

The Big Deal about the Big Woods

The Big Woods was a forest that once occupied 3,030 square miles in south-central Minnesota. The forest was composed of maple, basswood, white and red elm, red oak, tamarack, and red cedar on the banks of numerous lakes. The trees were so thick that sunlight couldn't penetrate to the forest floor in some places. French explorers who came to the area called the forest "Bois Grand," or "Bois Fort," which was later amended by English settlers to "Big Woods." Today farms, towns, suburbs, and industry have replaced much of the Big Woods. Fortunately, the 1,590 acres located in Lake Maria State Park at the northern edge of what was once the Big Woods retain a remnant of the grandness of these original forests.

reception area, exhibits concerning the area around Lake Minnetonka, and a garden containing a huge variety of native medicinal and herbal plants.

The park has a nice fishing pier, with two seated angler stations. There's a concession stand next to the changing rooms/bathrooms by the picnic area with accessible tables where folks can purchase goodies while enjoying the water. The beach is well maintained, with large umbrellas located around the water for families to use to keep themselves cool on the hottest summer days.

Lake Minnewashta Regional Park
6900 Hazeltine Avenue, Chanhassen
(952) 466-5250
www.co.carver.mn.us/parks
Lake Minnewashta Park contains remnants of the Big Woods that once covered this area. Some of the oak trees here are so old that

they're more than 12 feet in circumference. An ambitious reforestation project that included the planting of 25,000 new hardwoods was completed a few years ago but will realistically take many years to re-create the leafy canopy that once covered the park.

This park is tucked away and is visited mostly by locals, and at times you probably have a better chance of seeing deer than people while visiting. Lake Minnewashta is a popular fishing lake, allowing powerboats, canoes, and sailboats in summer and ice fishing in winter. The park also has a fishing pier and 5 miles of hiking/skiing trails.

Lake Rebecca Park Reserve
9831 County Road 50, Rockford
(763) 694-7860
www.threeriversparkdistrict.org
From canoeing on the Crow River to boat and ice fishing on Lake Rebecca, this 2,200-acre park offers outdoor activities in settings that suggest you are much farther away from the metropolitan area than you actually are. Lake Rebecca Park Reserve's gently rolling landscape, with numerous wetland areas, provides a haven for wildlife, including deer, beavers, and waterfowl. This reserve is also one of the sites for the trumpeter swan restoration program; you can often see the swans from the park's trails. The park has trails for mountain biking, road biking, hiking, cross-country skiing, dog walking, and horse riding. Boats are available for rent from the park's visitor center, and nonmotorized boat launching is permit-

i Dogs are permitted on Regional Trail corridors and on designated turf trails in all parks. Pets must be on a leash no more than 6 feet long, and owners must clean up after pets and dispose of pet feces in a sanitary manner.

ted. Reservation picnic areas and group campsites are available. The park also features a fishing pier and swimming area.

Noerenberg Memorial Gardens
2865 North Shore Drive, Orono
(763) 559-6700
www.threeriversparkdistrict.org
In 1972 the last surviving child of Frederick and Johanna Noerenberg—heirs to the Grain Belt brewery fortune—bequeathed the family lakeside estate to Hennepin County. The bequest stipulated that the 73 acres of flower beds, shade trees, and ornamental grasses be opened to the public.

Today the park features beautifully sculpted flower gardens that include unusual annuals and perennials, an assortment of grasses, and a large daylily collection. The park is a beautiful spot to stroll through and enjoy the flowers—however, part of the bequest of the Noerenberg family states that no picnics or boating activities are to be permitted on the premises, so light hiking and sightseeing covers the range of what park visitors can do here. The gardens are a very popular spot for weddings.

SPECTATOR SPORTS

People in the Twin Cities love sports. It is, however, a love tempered by regional priorities and perspectives on life. There are sports fanatics in the cities, men and women whose hearts bleed the purple of the Minnesota Vikings football team or have not missed a Twins game in decades, but most Twin Citians practice a little more restraint. They love the local teams but also value a summer trip "up north" to the cabin at the lake or a night at the other entertainment options the Cities offer.

Twin Cities sports fans love winners. Win or lose, the teams receive support, but when they win, the area erupts. The Twins' two world championships in 1987 and 1991 created a colossal public outpouring of local pride. St. Paul and Minneapolis streets were flooded with happy citizens waving their "homer hankies" and celebrating their team.

The metro area is also home to two NASCAR racetracks and one venue for live and simulcast horse racing.

A rather interesting fact of life in the Twin Cities is that the metropolitan area is a mecca for many northern and western Wisconsinites who move to the big city for school or jobs or just for kicks. Fans from Wisconsin are equally rabid about their sports teams. When these teams come to town, you can expect to see a huge following for the Wisconsin teams (some speculative and wholly unsupported guesstimates figure as much as 50 percent of Metro residents may be rooting for the Cheeseheads). Native Minnesotans may pooh-pooh such heresy, but attending a Golden Gophers football game against the Badgers in recent years will reveal a packed stadium dominated by red-clad Wisconsin fans singing "On Wisconsin" at the top of their lungs and polkaing to the Budweiser song seemingly unendingly. And if you think Minneapolitans and St.

Paulites are from different worlds, try finding common ground between beer-soaked Vikings and Packers fans when Green Bay plays at the Dome.

Tradition, rivalries, a long list of world-class athletes, fierce competiveness, massages by nuns and enthusiastic fans are all part of the Twin Cities sports scene.

AUTO RACING

Elko Speedway
26350 France Avenue, Elko
(952) 461-7223 or (800) 479-3630
www.elkospeedway.com
For nearly 25 years, Elko Speedway has been affiliated with NASCAR. Elko Speedway is one of only 60 short racetracks in the nation sanctioned by NASCAR, and it is a member of the Whelan All-American Series and the Weekly Racing Series Presented by Dodge. The ⅜-mile track has an asphalt and granite aggregate surface and high banking. Elko Speedway usually has races from April through October, with races beginning in the evening on Friday and Saturday (most races are on Saturday).

Raceway Park
1 Checkered Flag Boulevard, Shakopee
(952) 445-2257
www.goracewaypark.com
Raceway Park also offers NASCAR racing in the Whelan All-American Series. This track has had racing for more than 50 years. The most talented local drivers race at Raceway Park. There are also racing events at the track geared toward children, including such oddball events as school-bus races and figure-8 trailer races. Racing is usually on Sunday, but the track also races on select Fridays and Saturdays, and on major holidays during the

summer. The track stays open late April to the end of September.

BASEBALL

Minnesota Twins
Metrodome, 34 Kirby Puckett Place,
Minneapolis
(612) 375-7454 or (800) 33-TWINS
minnesota.twins.mlb.com
The Twins currently play at the Hubert H. Humphrey Metrodome ("the Dome" in local parlance), a large concrete structure capped with an expansive Teflon bubble located in downtown Minneapolis and surrounded by parking lots. Fans of the Dome enjoy its steady temperature, in the low 70s. Detractors find the Dome's environment sterile and dull and at times incredibly loud. But such arguments are about to become moot.

On August 30, 2007, after a more than 10-year battle to approve funding for a new Twins ballpark, ground was finally broken on an outdoor baseball stadium for the Twins alone (they currently share the Dome with the Minnesota Vikings and the University of Minnesota Golden Gophers football and baseball teams), now under construction near downtown Minneapolis' Warehouse District. The new stadium is scheduled for completion in 2010.

Twins tickets are readily available for most games. For the 2008 season, ticket prices ranged from $7 for outfield upper deck general admission to $50 for the "lower club" area behind home plate. Prices are a little higher for Premium Games, which are any in which the New York Yankees, Boston Red Sox, or Milwaukee Brewers are the opponents. These prices are subject to change.

The Twins have many special offers and promotional events. One is Twins Kids Days games. Kids Days allow a paying adult to bring children to games for free. The free seats are always upper level general admission.

Twins tickets are available on the team's Web site, by phone, and in person. The Twins ticket office is located on the west side of the Dome facing the Minneapolis downtown sky-

> **i** In downtown Minneapolis, light-rail and buses are convenient ways to travel to and from the major sporting venues. Buses are available to get to and from the Xcel Energy Center in downtown St. Paul. If your starting point is in either downtown, the fare is a mere 50 cents within the downtown zones. Visit www .metrotransit.org or call (612) 373-3333 for schedules and route information.

line. Twins tickets can also be purchased at Twins Pro Shops in Apple Valley and Roseville.

St. Paul Saints
Midway Stadium, 1771 Energy Park Drive,
St. Paul
(651) 644-6659
www.saintsbaseball.com
The Saints create an ambience reminiscent of the glory days of baseball. Each of the 6,329 seats at Midway Stadium has a great view of the game. There are also good concessions and the omnipresent tailgating. Because of long and harsh winters, Twin Citians love outdoor baseball—a beer, a hot dog, summer sun, and baseball.

The St. Paul Saints are a hot ticket in the Twin Cities. Tickets may be purchased at the stadium ticket office, by phone, or on the team's Web site. Keep in mind that games can and frequently do sell out.

Ticket prices are reasonable, considering there is not a bad seat at Midway Stadium, and are generally in the range of $4 to $12, with special discounts for seniors and children ages 14 and younger.

Parking is readily available for a small fee in the large parking lot abutting Midway Stadium. Feel free to bring some food and your

> **i** The St. Paul Saints offer outdoor baseball at its best, but there's a lot besides baseball going on at the ballpark—get a massage by a nun, watch the between-game antics, or rent the hot tub seating in left field.

In 1997 the Saints received national exposure when they signed Ila Borders, the first woman to pitch in an all-men's professional baseball league. She was traded to Northern League rival Duluth-Superior after seven games.

favorite beverage for tailgating. The parking lot opens three hours before gametime.

BASKETBALL

Minnesota Golden Gophers
Men's Basketball
Williams Arena, 1925 University Avenue SE, Minneapolis
(612) 624-8080 or (800) U-GOPHER
www.gophersports.com
The Twin Cities are a great place to be if you're a basketball fan. The area boasts both men's and women's professional teams as well as the collegiate Big Ten men's and women's teams, the University of Minnesota Golden Gophers.

Since the 1895–96 season the Minnesota Golden Gophers men's basketball team has played in one of the most august and competitive conferences in collegiate sports, the Big Ten. Current and former NBA stars, such as Joel Przybilla, Mychal Thompson, and Kevin McHale, wore the Gophers' maroon and gold. Today coach Tubby Smith, lured north from the fabled University of Kentucky program, brings new hope to the Golden Gophers.

The Gophers play at Williams Arena, a great place to watch basketball. It is a beautifully renovated brick building that feels comfortable yet electric because of the U of M students and alumni who attend games at "the barn."

You may purchase Gophers tickets by phone, online, or in person at Williams Arena. The University of Minnesota accepts Visa, MasterCard, Novus, and American Express. There is plenty of parking for Gophers basketball in lots on Oak Street Southeast and Fifth Street Southeast.

Minnesota Golden Gophers
Women's Basketball
Williams Arena, 1925 University Avenue SE, Minneapolis
(612) 624-8080 or (800) U-GOPHER
www.gophersports.com
Under coach Pam Borton, who took over the Minnesota Golden Gophers women's basketball team in 2002, the future of Golden Gophers women's basketball looks bright. Each year under Coach Borton, the team has had a winning record, something that was quite rare under previous coaches.

Golden Gophers women's basketball has been in action since 1973 and has competed as part of the Big Ten since 1982. The intense games of the grueling Big Ten season bring numerous hard-fought battles to Williams Arena. Tickets are available by phone, online, or in person at Williams Arena.

Minnesota Lynx
Target Center, 600 First Avenue North, Minneapolis
(612) 673-8400
www.wnba.com/lynx
The Minnesota Lynx have built a strong fan base with the Women's National Basketball Association's (WNBA) brand of basketball. The WNBA may not be as flashy as the NBA, but it shines on many other levels. Women's basketball is more team oriented, with plenty of well-executed passes, set plays, and teamwork.

The Lynx share the Target Center with the Timberwolves; the season begins in late May and ends in early August. There are many seating options. Tickets are available in person at the Target Center, by phone, or on the Lynx's Web site. There is ample parking in the several municipal ramps behind the arena.

Minnesota Timberwolves
Target Center, 600 First Avenue North, Minneapolis
(612) 673-1600
www.nba.com/timberwolves
Professional basketball has a long history in Minnesota, going back long before the Tim-

Historic Williams Arena, home of the University of Minnesota Golden Gophers basketball teams. TODD R. BERGER

berwolves. From 1947 to 1960, the Twin Cities were home to the Minneapolis Lakers, a team that won six league championships during its time in Minnesota, including the first NBA championship after that league formed for the 1949–50 season. The team has been called the "forgotten dynasty," as it would go on to greater fame and success when the owners moved the team to Los Angeles after the 1959–60 season.

Minnesota remained without an NBA franchise for nearly 30 years. But the expansion Minnesota Timberwolves appeared on the scene for the 1989–90 season, finally returning NBA basketball to the Twin Cities.

The Target Center was constructed for the Wolves and opened in October 1990 as a single-sport arena. The Target Center was the first Twin Cities facility for one major-league franchise. Today, the Wolves share the Target Center with the Minnesota Lynx WNBA team.

The Target Center is ideally located on the edges of the Warehouse District and the Hennepin Theater District in downtown Minneapolis. The structure fits tightly on its lot and almost spills out onto the street. It is comfortable on the inside, despite its size. Target Center has a capacity of nearly 20,000 for basketball.

Individual tickets for Wolves games range from $10 to $1,700 (the latter is for courtside seating next to the bench). Tickets are available in person at the Target Center, by phone, or through Ticketmaster (www.ticketmaster .com; 800-4-NBA-TIX). There is ample parking in the municipal ramps behind the arena.

i When Minnesota was awarded an NBA franchise in 1987, the name-the-team contest turned up possibilities such as the Flakes, the Purple Cows, and the Fighting Norsemen. "Timberwolves" was chosen because Minnesota has more of the animal than any state in the Lower 48.

FOOTBALL

Minnesota Golden Gophers Football
Metrodome, 34 Kirby Puckett Place,
Minneapolis
(612) 624-8080 or (800) U-GOPHER
www.gophersports.com

Long before the Minnesota Vikings arrived as an NFL expansion team, the Gophers were the Twin Cities' principal football team. They play in one of the premier NCAA conferences, the Big Ten, which has presented a significant hurdle for the team. The football team, like their basketball counterparts, lacks the recruiting base of many other Big Ten schools. Nevertheless, in recent years the Gophers football squad has improved but has a ways to go to reach the upper tier of the Big Ten.

The Gophers currently play at the Hubert H. Humphrey Metrodome. But a new on-campus, outdoor stadium is under construction at 2009 University Avenue Southeast, and what will be known as TCF Bank Stadium is scheduled to open in August 2009. Tickets for Gophers football games are available by phone, online, or in person at the Mariucci Arena ticket office on campus at 4 Oak Street SE, Minneapolis. You cannot buy Gophers football tickets at Metrodome ticket outlets. Single game tickets for the 2007 season ranged from $10 to $70.

Minnesota Vikings
Metrodome, 34 Kirby Puckett Place
Minneapolis
(612) 338-4537
www.vikings.com

Are the Vikings among the NFL's elite or aren't they? And what's in store now that former owner Red McCombs sold the team to Zygi Wilf in 2005? It's anybody's guess. Despite the uncertainty, and despite sometimes less than stellar performances, the Vikings are wildly popular with Minnesota sports fans.

The Vikings play at the Hubert H. Humphrey Metrodome. The Dome is a multi-purpose stadium that the Vikings, Twins, and the University of Minnesota's football and baseball teams currently call home; however,

i A new feature on the Minnesota Vikings' Web site (www.vikings.com) known as TicketExchange allows people searching for single-game tickets to connect with season ticket holders looking to unload tickets for specific games.

the seats have better sight lines for football than baseball. When modified for football, the Dome seats 64,121 fans. The Vikings have a tremendous home-field advantage at the Dome. Dome Vikings fans cheer loud enough to create a near-deafening din. The Vikings' "Dome field advantage" acts as the twelfth man on the field at Vikings home games.

Minnesota Vikings tickets are available through Ticketmaster (651-989-5151; www.ticketmaster.com) or in person at the Metrodome ticket office. A limited number of single-game tickets go on sale in mid-July, but they sell out quickly. There is plenty of parking, with tremendous variation in prices. The lots next to the Dome are expensive, but north of Washington Avenue there is ample reasonably priced parking.

HORSE RACING

Canterbury Park Racetrack and Card Club
1100 Canterbury Road, Shakopee
(952) 445-7223 or (800) 340-6361
www.canterburypark.com

Canterbury Park has been the state's only horse track since 1985. Canterbury Park's horse racing is also the only sport in the Metro where gambling is legal. Live racing from Thursday through Sunday (plus major holidays) begins in mid-May and runs through the beginning of September. The track is open year-round for simulcast racing with pari-mutuel betting.

Admission is $5 for adults. Anyone under age 18 must be accompanied by an adult and is admitted free of charge. Seniors (60+) can get in for $3. Besides horse racing, the track also has a card club (see the Attractions chapter for more information). Parking at the track is free.

Canterbury Park is approximately 25 minutes from downtown Minneapolis and 15 minutes from the Mall of America.

HOCKEY

Minnesota Golden Gophers
Men's Hockey
Mariucci Arena, 1901 Fourth Street SE,
Minneapolis
(612) 624-8080 or (800) U-GOPHER
www.gophersports.com

The Golden Gophers men's hockey team has a rich tradition at the University of Minnesota. It is the only Western Collegiate Hockey Association (WCHA) team in the Twin Cities and the largest university team in the area. In a state with so many sports entertainment options, Gophers fans are diehards. They have been rewarded with a team that has consistently played high-caliber hockey in one of college hockey's toughest conferences, the WCHA.

The year 2002 brought glory back to Golden Gophers hockey, when, for the first time since 1979, the Golden Gophers reigned as NCAA National Champions. The team, amazingly, was able to repeat as champions in 2003.

The Gophers play at beautiful Mariucci Arena, a facility built specifically for the team. Here they have a significant home advantage behind the enormous enthusiasm of students and alumni.

Regular-season ticket prices were $30 in 2008. Tickets can be purchased by phone, online, or in person at Mariucci Arena. Plenty of parking for Gophers hockey is available in the lots across from Mariucci Arena on Oak Street Southeast.

Minnesota Golden Gophers
Women's Hockey
Ridder Arena, 1815 Fourth Street SE
Minneapolis
(612) 624-8080 or (800) U-GOPHER
www.gophersports.com

The Golden Gophers men's hockey team is not the only hockey team on the U of M

i Minnesota is arguably the hockey capital of the United States. In fact, Minnesotan's love of hockey mirrors that of our neighbor to the north, Canada.

campus, nor is it the only team with a recent national championship. Women's hockey is blossoming in Minnesota, from young kids all the way to Division I athletics. Wildly successful, the Gophers women's hockey team won the NCAA National Championship in 2000, 2004, and 2005.

The Golden Gophers women's hockey team is the only women's hockey team in the country with an arena built specifically for it. Ridder Arena, a gorgeous 3,400-seat arena next door to Mariucci Arena, opened for the 2002–03 season and is considered by many to be the finest women's collegiate hockey arena in the country.

Tickets are available by phone, online, or in person at the Mariucci Arena ticket office. Tickets are a relative bargain, ranging from $4 to $10 for the 2007–08 season. Parking is widely available at lots and ramps near Ridder Arena.

Minnesota Wild
Xcel Energy Center, 175 West Kellogg
Boulevard, St. Paul
(651) 222-WILD
www.wild.com

The Minnesota Wild were an expansion team for the 2000–2001 NHL season. However, a lot of work went into luring professional hockey back to Minnesota after losing the North Stars to Dallas in 1993. In fact, the NHL decision to come to St. Paul was incumbent on a new hockey-only facility. Efforts by city officials and fans led to the state-of-the-art Xcel Energy Center.

The Xcel Energy Center is located in downtown St. Paul. It is equipped with four 9-foot by 16-foot, high-definition scoreboards as well as two 16-foot by 24-foot, high-definition marquees outside the arena. A truly spectacular ribbon board circles the entire arena at the suite level, showing statistics and ads in 16.7 million shades of color. When the

Close-up

Dome Souvenir Plus & The Original Baseball Hall of Fame Museum of Minnesota

When you walk down Third Street en route to the Hubert Humphrey Metrodome, it's just about impossible to miss the building. A loudspeaker mounted on the outside of Ray Crump's deceptively small establishment invites passersby in, warning them that they'll be paying twice as much for the same souvenirs inside the Metrodome.

Few people passing by the brick storefront would confuse the building for the National Baseball Hall of Fame in Cooperstown, New York, but on entering the store, they'll be amazed by the wealth of local and national baseball history. The museum houses an impressive Wall of Celebrities, featuring a rotating display of the store's 10,260 signed photos, baseballs, and bats. The museum is free, and the adjoining Dome Souvenir Plus stocks extensive sports souvenirs and team-related merchandise for all the Twin Cities sports teams at reasonable prices.

Ray Crump arrived in Minnesota after the Twins relocated from Washington, D.C., for the 1961 season. Crump's career in Major League Baseball began as a batboy for the Washington Senators, where he would later assume the position of equipment manager. His career spanned 36 years with the Senators and then the Twins, where he was able to acquire the unique sports memorabilia found at the museum. An affable and insightful man, Ray Crump has written and published a book detailing his professional baseball experiences, *Beneath the Grandstands*.

Vintage Minnesota Twins collectibles are prominently displayed at the Original Baseball Museum, including the complete uniforms of retired Twins stars Harmon Killebrew, Tony Oliva, and Rod Carew. There is a special section dedicated to former Twins great Kirby Puckett, as well as plenty of Twins 1965, 1987, and 1991 World Series memorabilia. Included is a prominent display focusing on the Washington Senators relocation to Minnesota. Unique displays include baseballs autographed not only by baseball stars but also by a wide array of nonsports stars; e.g., Jerry Lewis, Hubert Humphrey, and Louis Armstrong. The Elvis Corner displays personal items from the King of Rock 'n' Roll.

Crump's Wall of Celebrities includes autographed photos of such stars as Muhammad Ali, Hulk Hogan, Liberace, and Bill Cosby shown posing with a younger Ray Crump. Many of the photos were autographed long before the

Wild score a goal, the lighthouse in the northeast corner of the arena sounds its foghorn, and the Wild fans go nuts.

Seating in the facility is comfortable and all seats have an excellent view of the action. There are 18,600 seats in the arena, with ticket prices ranging from $22 to $96 for the 2007–08 season. Tickets can be purchased for individual games through Ticketmaster at (651) 989-5151 or www.ticketmaster.com. They may also be bought at the box office at the Xcel Energy Center. Wild tickets are a hot personalities became stars. "When I got the photo taken with Bill Cosby, no one knew who he was," says Crump. "He was some guy who had done a Jell-O commercial. I also have a baseball signed by Frank Sinatra, except he signed it 'Francis Sinatra.' Years later this woman who worked for him told me he never signed anything except business papers 'Francis,' and that he never signed autographs with anything but 'Frank.'"

When Ray Crump opened the museum and store, there was no Wall of Celebrities. These autographed photos of the stars were considered personal and cherished by the Crump family. Crump decided to display the autographs after making an observation: Many women seemed bored at the museum while their husbands refused to leave. He quickly realized displaying the celebrity photos made the museum more fun for the entire family.

And the focus of the museum is on family fun. "This is a family business," explains Crump. "My wife's right back there behind the counter most days, and my two sons frequently help me up front or in the snack bar. I like working at the snack counter better than the front of the store because it gives me a chance to talk to people more. I really enjoy talking to customers about the museum and all the souvenirs we've got here." At least one Crump family member will be available when the museum/store is open to serve the needs of Minnesota sports fans.

The amiable Crump gushes with interesting stories and minutiae about memorabilia and Major League Baseball. How many people can give you a detailed explanation of the differences between the National and American Leagues' methods for taking attendance, or know that the Vikings lease at the Dome does not expire until 2011? If you have any questions about sports at all, Crump probably knows the answer or can tell you who does. As far as souvenir shopping goes, Dome Souvenir Plus has a huge selection of items at reasonable prices. Whether you are looking for a Twins hat, Vikings barbecue sauce, or a collectible bobblehead doll, Dome Souvenir Plus has it.

Dome Souvenir Plus & The Original Baseball Hall of Fame Museum of Minnesota is conveniently located 1 block directly north of the Dome, across from gate A (910 South Third Street, Minneapolis). For further information call (612) 375-9707 or, to order merchandise, (888) 375-9707. They also can be visited at www.domeplus.com.

commodity in the Twin Cities, and you may have difficulty finding tickets at any price level after the season begins. When tickets become available for an upcoming game, the Wild typically run ads in the sports sections of the *StarTribune* and *St. Paul Pioneer Press*. There are many readily available parking options in downtown St. Paul within walking distance of the arena. The arena is connected to the extensive downtown skyway system.

SUMMER RECREATION

Minnesotans know how to make use of warm weather. It seems like every day free of winter's cold is spent in the great outdoors. Casual visitors to the Twin Cities are often amazed by how much space inside the metro area is left unpaved and untouched, that near downtown Minneapolis the high-bluff banks of the Mississippi are covered with greenery and lined with thick forests. In St. Paul the bird sanctuary of Harriet Island can be found just across the Mississippi from the bustling downtown area, set in a beautiful flower garden that just doesn't feel like it's in the middle of a city.

In short, the best way to describe what to do in the Twin Cities during the summer is "Go outside." In this chapter we list not only where to go to play but also the local associations responsible for organizing many of the outdoor recreational events. We also list some of the more reasonable places to rent gear, from bicycles to canoes to scuba equipment. Whether you're looking for something for the whole family to do or seeking a quiet, beautiful spot to escape from city traffic and shopping malls, you're sure to find it in the Twin Cities.

BIKING

Minnesota has more miles of paved trails than anywhere else in the country. Mountain biking trails wind their way through forests and along cross-country ski trails in the off-season. Lakes, creeks, waterfalls, bluffs, rivers— you can bike near them all without ever having to leave the metro area.

Inside the Cities proper, there are numerous paved bike trails to choose from. In Minneapolis the **Grand Rounds Parkway** follows the perimeter of the Chain of Lakes and encircles the city. Considered the crown jewel of metropolitan biking, this 50-mile scenic and

urban trail traces the shorelines of Lake Nokomis, Lake Hiawatha, Shingle Creek, Bassett Creek, Minnehaha Creek, and the Mississippi River.

Minneapolis is also home to the newly completed **Midtown Greenway** bike trail, which runs 5.7 miles from Chowen Avenue South just west of Lake Calhoun all the way to the Mississippi River. The trail connects to the Grand Rounds Parkway trails in the Uptown neighborhood in the west and the West River Parkway Trail section of the Grand Rounds in the east. You can also cross the Mississippi at Ford Avenue, Lake Street, Franklin Avenue, or Washington Avenue to connect with the East River Parkway Trail in St. Paul.

Commuters in the western suburbs can make use of the **Cedar Lake Trail,** which runs 3.6 miles from the intersection of 12th Street and 2nd Avenue in downtown Minneapolis to Minnesota Highway 100 near Cedar Lake Road South. The Cedar Lake Extension Trail continues west another 4.3 miles to Hopkins.

The other three trails are located in St. Paul. **Como Park**'s 1.7-mile bike trail circles Como Lake and heads toward the Como Park Zoo and Conservatory area. **Hidden Falls/ Crosby Farm**'s 6.7-mile bike path follows the shady, wooded bottomlands along the banks of the Mississippi and is an especially pleasant ride to take during the dog days of summer. **Phalen Park**'s 3.2-mile bike trail circles Lake Phalen and its beautiful swimming beach, a layout that makes it oh-so-convenient to stop riding and go in for a dip. St. Paul's **East River Parkway Trail** traces along the east bank of the Mississippi from downtown St. Paul all the way to the University of Minnesota's Minneapolis Campus.

The Cities also have extensive bike lanes along major thoroughfares, and the bike lanes and trails in the Twin Cities link to recreational trails stretching far into the suburbs, including the Gateway Trail from St. Paul to Stillwater, the Bruce Vento Regional Trail from St. Paul to Maplewood, and the Southwest LRT Trail from Minneapolis to Victoria, among others.

Parks in the metro area with paved biking trails include Anoka County Riverfront, Baker Park Preserve, Bryant Lake, Bunker Hills, Burlington-Northern Regional Trail, Carver Park Preserve, Central Mississippi Riverfront, Cleary Lake, Coon Rapids Dam, Elm Creek Park Reserve, Fish Lake, French, Hyland-Bush-Anderson Lakes, Lake Elmo Park Reserve, Lake Minnetonka Regional Park, Lake Rebecca Park Reserve, Lebanon Hills, Lilydale/Harriet Island, Long Lake Regional Park, Minnehaha Parkway, Mississippi Gorge, Murphy-Hanrehan Park Reserve, North Hennepin Trail Corridor, Rice Creek–West Regional Trail, Rum River Central, Snail Lake, Southwest Regional LRT Trail, Theodore Wirth, and the Wirth-Memorial Parkway (see the Parks chapter for details about many of these parks). For more information about biking in the Twin Cities, call the **Minnesota Community Bicycle Safety Project** at (612) 625-9719, the **Minnesota Safety Council** at (651) 291-9150, or the **Minnesota Office of Tourism** at (888-TOURISM), or visit the latter's Web page at www.explore minnesota.com.

There are several good places in the metro area to rent bicycles and get geared up. In Minneapolis you can rent bicycles at reasonable prices from **Calhoun Rental** (612-827-8231) at 1622 West Lake Street, **Campus Bikes** (612-331-3442) at 213 Southeast Oak Street, or from **Kenwood Cyclery** (612-374-4042) at 2123 West 21st Street.

Several in-town organizations hold annual bike-riding marathons worth checking out. One example: the **Minnesota Chapter of the Multiple Sclerosis Society** (612-335-7900; www.mssociety.com) holds three separate MS Bike Tours in the Cities each summer to raise funds for multiple sclerosis research and treatment.

The **Minnesota Cycling Federation** (www.mcf.net) comprises bicycle racing clubs in the upper Midwest, whose purpose is the education and promotion of bicycle racing skills and safety and the promotion of races for bicycle racers. The federation provides cycling enthusiasts with the most current information about area race calendars, race results, MCF member clubs, the NCS Velodrome, and the Youth Cycling League.

CAMPING

Camping sites in the metro area are scarce and quickly snatched up, so it's a good idea to reserve a site at least two weeks in advance. To make camping reservations, call the campgrounds directly. For a free copy of the Minnesota Alliance of Campground Operators' Minnesota Campgrounds and RV Parks, call the **Minnesota Department of Tourism** (888-TOURISM; www.exploreminnesota.com).

Baker Park Reserve (763-694-7662; www.threeriversparkdistrict.org) Campground is on Lake Independence, 20 miles west of Minneapolis on County Road 19, between U.S. Highway 12 and Minnesota Highway 55. There are 210 sites, including 98 with electricity. Each has a picnic table and fire ring and can accommodate two tents or one tent and one RV, with a maximum of six people per campsite. There are showers and flush toilets (wheelchair accessible) and an RV dump station. Daily fee: $17 per site, $22 per site with electricity.

Lake Auburn Campground is in **Carver Park Reserve** (952-443-2911; www.threerivers parkdistrict.org), near Victoria on County Road 11 between Minnesota Highway 5 and Minnesota Highway 7. Each site at Lake Auburn has a picnic table and fire ring and can accommodate two tents or one tent and one RV, with a maximum of six people per campsite. There are 54 sites plus 2 hike-in sites. This is rustic camping—there are pit latrines (wheelchair accessible), a hand pump, no showers, and no electricity. There is an RV dump station (for a fee). Daily fee: $11 per site.

The Red Pine Hike-In Family Camping Area is in **Cleary Lake Regional Park** (763-694-7777; www.threeriversparkdistrict.org), near Prior Lake on County Road 27 (Texas Avenue) just south of County Road 21. Red Pine has five sites with fire rings and picnic tables and can accommodate tent camping only. There are pit latrines (wheelchair accessible), a water pump nearby, no showers, and no electricity. Daily fee: $11 per site.

There are beautiful state parks with campsites within an hour's drive or so of the Twin Cities. Among the most popular are **William O'Brien** (651-433-0500), northwest near Marine-on-St. Croix; **Interstate** (651-465-5711), northwest near Taylors Falls; and **Afton** (651-436-5391), southwest near Hastings. Check out the parks online at www.dnr.state.mn.us/state_parks or contact the DNR reservations center (866-85PARKS, www.stayatmnparks.com). You'll need a day permit ($5) or an annual permit ($25), available at the parks, for your vehicle. Fees range from $11 to $18 per night, depending on the remoteness of the site and the amenities.

CANOEING AND KAYAKING

The benefits of canoeing and kayaking are immeasurable. Not only are they great ways to stay in shape, but they're also a pleasant way to get close to nature without noisy motors or worrying about getting hung up on waters too shallow for outboard motors. In the Cities several parks are perfect for canoes and kayaks. **Lake Calhoun** in Minneapolis is a popular canoeing and kayaking lake surrounded by swimming beaches and fishing piers. The lake has a great view of the downtown Minneapolis skyline and is absolutely

i Three Rivers Park District (763-559-9000; www.threeriversparkdistrict .org) sells gift cards that can be used to purchase services, programs, or merchandise (rounds of golf, ski lessons, and books, for example) at park district facilities that accept credit cards.

spectacular at sunset. Connected to Lake Calhoun is **Lake of the Isles,** an especially beautiful place to take a canoe or kayak, with narrow waterways overhung with old stone bridges, wide areas full of friendly ducks and geese, and a small forested island in the middle of the lake. A city-run building on the Lake Calhoun grounds rents canoes and sailboats to park visitors.

Adjacent and connected to Lake Calhoun, is **Lake Harriet,** a wide-open lake heavily used by canoes, kayaks, sailboats, peddle boats, and motorboats alike. The lake has several public swimming beaches and a refreshment stand on its northwestern shores—the perfect place to stop after a heavy workout on the water.

Other metro area parks that have waterways suitable for canoeing and kayaking include Anoka County Riverfront, Baker Park Preserve, Bald Eagle–Otter Lakes, Bryant Lake, Carver Park Preserve, Cleary Lake, Como, Coon Rapids Dam, Crow-Hassan, Fish Lake, French, Hidden Falls-Crosby Farm, Hyland-Bush-Anderson Lakes, Lake Byllesby, Lake Elmo Park Reserve, Lake George, Lake Minnewashta, Lake Rebecca Park Reserve, Lebanon Hills, Lilydale/Harriet Island, Long Lake Regional Park, Martin-Island-Linwood Lakes, Minneapolis Chain of Lakes, Nokomis Hiawatha, Phalen-Keller, Rice Creek/Chain of Lakes, Rice Creek–West Regional Trail, Rum River Central, Snail Lake, and Theodore Wirth (see the Parks chapter for more parks information). Canoeing is also popular in Interstate State Park in Taylors Falls and on other sections of the Lower St. Croix National Scenic Riverway east of the Metro.

The **Minneapolis Rowing Club** (612-729-1541; www.mplsrowing.org) has participated in regattas around the country almost every year since its founding in 1877. The club sponsors classes on rowing for youths of all ages as well as beginning adult rowers.

To rent canoes in the Cities, try **Aarcee Rental** (612-827-5746; www.aarceerental .com) at 2910 Lyndale Avenue South in Minneapolis, Wheel Fun Rentals (612-823-5765;

www.wheelfunrentals.com) at 3000 Calhoun Parkway East, or specific parks in the **Three Rivers Park District** (763-559-6700; www.three rivers parkdistrict.org). There are also many canoe rental places along the St. Croix River, particularly in Taylors Falls and Stillwater. Visit www.dnr.state.mn.us/canoeing/outfitters.html and scroll down to the St. Croix River section for a complete list.

Some of the best canoeing in the world is available three to four hours north of the Twin Cities in the **Boundary Waters Canoe Area Wilderness** (BWCAW), a protected area in the Superior National Forest with thousands of lakes linked by streams and canoe portages. You can enter the Boundary Waters only with a permit for your specific entry point. It is best to plan well in advance for a trip to the Boundary Waters, as the most popular entry points are scooped up quickly when permits become available the previous winter. Some are available only through a lottery system, which means you may not get your preferred entry point even if you're the first to get your registration in; plan alternate routes to improve your chances. For more information about the Boundary Waters, permits, routes, and more, call (877) 550-6777 or visit www .bwcaw.org. Detailed maps and books on the BWCAW can be found at REI stores in Bloom-ington (952-884-4315), Maple Grove (763-493-7861, and Roseville (651-635-0211), as well as at Midwest Mountaineering (612-339-3433; www.midwestmtn.com) in Minneapolis.

CAR SHOWS

For more than 30 years, the **Minnesota Street Rod Association** (MSRA; 651-641-1992; www.msra.com) has been sponsoring car shows in and around the Twin Cities area. More than 13,000 enthusiasts belong to the MSRA, a fact that's never more apparent than when the association's annual Back to the '50s show comes to town in June and the streets of St. Paul are filled with beautifully restored vintage hot rods.

i Friends of the Boundary Waters Wilderness (612-332-9630; www .friends-bwca.org), based in Minneapolis, is a nonprofit membership organization dedicated to helping protect, preserve, and restore the wilderness character of the BWCAW. Check out their Web site or give them a call for more information about how you can help.

DISC GOLF

Sort of a combination of Frisbee and golf, disc golf is available throughout the metro. The rapidly growing sport involves throwing a spe-cial golf disc down a fairway with the aim of dropping it in a basket on a pole on the "green."

In St. Paul, the **Highland Park Disc Golf Course** (651-632-5111) has eight holes on what is considered a challenging course over rolling terrain. There are no disc golf courses in Minneapolis proper as of this writing.

There are numerous courses in the Twin Cities suburbs, including at Bryant Lake Regional Park in Eden Prairie, Hyland Ski and Snowboard Area in Bloomington, Alimagnet Lake Park in Apple Valley, Oakwood Park in Cottage Grove, Lakewood Hills Park in White Bear Lake, Acorn Park in Roseville, Bassett Creek Park in Crystal, Central Park in Brooklyn Park, Plymouth Creek in Plymouth, and Rosland Park in Edina. To find out more and to locate courses near you, visit the Professional Disc Golfers Association Web site at www.pdga .com or the Minnesota Frisbee Association at www.mfaonline.org.

FISHING

Many of the 1,000-plus lakes in the Twin Cities metro area have either been stocked with fish by the Department of Natural Resources or are naturally just great fishing holes. For more information about licensing requirements and where to drop your line, see the Hunting and Fishing chapter.

ℹ The Minnesota Department of Natural Resources has publications dealing with camping, fishing, hunting, and boating in Minnesota. Call (800) 285-2000 to have information mailed to you about any of these activities.

FOOTBALL

Cities Sports Connection (CSC; 612-929-9009; www.cscsports.com) offers coed and men's outdoor and indoor touch football leagues for all skill levels. CSC touch football leagues are offered year-round. CSC is open to all adults 18 or older—no membership or nonmember fees are charged to participate in CSC leagues.

GOLF

With hundreds of acres of flat, open plains and gently rolling hills, Minnesota is naturally home to some exceptional golf courses. The Twin Cities region alone has more than 175 courses. Telephone reservations are highly recommended for all of the golf courses listed here. For more information about these courses and others in the metropolitan area, including amenities, tee fees, course features, and more, visit www.golfminnesota.com.

Minneapolis has five public golf courses scattered throughout the city, including Theodore Wirth Golf Course (763-522-4584) at 1301 Theodore Wirth Parkway, Columbia Golf Course (612-789-2627) at 3300 Central Avenue Northeast, Francis A. Gross National Golf Course (612-789-2542) at 2201 St. Anthony Boulevard, Hiawatha Golf Course (612-724-7715) at 4553 Longfellow Avenue South, and Meadowbrook Golf Course (952-929-2077) at 201 Meadowbrook Road. The city also has several private courses.

St. Paul has six public golf courses, including Phalen Golf Course (651-778-0413) at 1615 Phalen Drive, Como Golf Course (651-488-9673) at 1431 North Lexington Parkway, Fort Snelling Golf Course (612-726-6222) on Taylor Avenue in Fort Snelling State Park,

Highland 18-Hole Golf Course (651-695-3774) at 1403 Montreal Avenue, Highland 9-Hole Golf Course (651-695-3708) at 1797 Edgcumbe Road, the University of Minnesota Les Bolstad Golf Course (612-627-4000) at 2275 Larpenteur Avenue West, and Keller Golf Course (651-766-4170) at 2166 Maplewood Drive.

The suburbs are a fertile place for gold courses as well. Some of the more notable courses include Baker National Golf Course, located in the Baker Park Preserve at 2935 Parkview Drive, Medina (763-494-7640); Glen Lake Golf & Practice Center (763-694-7824) in Glen Lake Park at 14350 County Road 62 in Minnetonka; Cleary Lake Golf Course (763-694-7777) in Cleary Lake Regional Park at 18106 Texas Avenue, Prior Lake; River Oaks Golf Course (651-438-2121; www.riveroaks munigolf.com) at 11099 South Minnesota Highway 61, Cottage Grove; and Falcon Ridge Golf Course (651-462-5797; www.falconridge golf.net) at 33942 Falcon Avenue, Stacy.

HIKING

Just about every park in the Twin Cities metro area has at least one hiking trail that wanders in and out of forests, follows rivers and streams, passes close by natural waterfalls, or winds along the banks of the Mississippi River. Area parks with easy to moderate paved and turf hiking trails include Anoka County Riverfront, Baker Park Preserve, Bald Eagle–Otter Lakes, Battle Creek, Baylor, Bryant Lake, Bunker Hills, Burlington-Northern Regional Trail, Carver Park Preserve, Central Mississippi Riverfront, Cleary Lake, Como, Coon Rapids Dam, Cottage Grove Ravine, Crow-Hassan, Elm Creek Park Reserve, Fish Lake, French, Hidden Falls–Crosby Farm, Hyland-Bush-Anderson Lakes, Lake Byllesby, Lake Elmo Park Reserve, Lake George, Lake Minnewashta, Lake Rebecca Park Reserve, Lebanon Hills, Lilydale/Harriet Island, Long Lake Regional Park, Martin-Island-Linwood Lakes, Minneapolis Chain of Lakes, Minnehaha, Minnehaha Parkway, Mississippi Gorge, Murphy-Hanrehan Park Reserve,

Nokomis Hiawatha, North Hennepin Trail Corridor, Rice Creek/Chain of Lakes, Rice Creek–West Regional Trail, Rum River Central, St. Croix Bluffs, Snail Lake, Southwest Regional LRT Trail, Spring Lake, Springbrook Nature Center, Theodore Wirth, Wirth-Memorial Parkway, and Wood Lake Nature Center (see Parks chapter for the parks listings).

For more experienced hikers, **Fort Snelling State Park** in St. Paul (612-725-2389), at 101 Snelling Lake Road, has 18 miles of turf hiking trails that wind through the park's nature preserve, and **Minnesota Valley State Recreational Area** in Jordan (952-492-6400), at 19825 Park Boulevard, has 47 miles of turf and paved hiking trails to explore.

If you're interested in meeting other hikers, **Friends of the Mississippi River** (651-222-2193; www.fmr.org) organizes bird-watching tours and wildflower hikes at different spots along the Mississippi River. For women who don't like hiking in the backwoods of Minnesota alone, the Department of Natural Resources' **Becoming an Outdoors Woman in Minnesota** (651-296-6157) organizes group hikes for women as well as other solo and group gender-specific outdoors experiences ranging from canoeing to big-game hunting.

HORSEBACK RIDING

Many of the parks in the metro area allow horses to share paved and dirt paths with cyclists and pedestrians. The trick is finding a place to rent horses. Tourists and residents alike can rent horses or arrange for guided rides at many locations throughout the metro area suburbs for an average of $15 an hour.

North of the Twin Cities, horses can be rented at **Brass Ring Stables,** 9105 Northwest Norris Lake Road, Elk River (763-441-7987); **Valley View Horse Ranch,** 5168 County Road 33, Buffalo (651-682-2928); **Bunker Park Stables,** 550 Bunker Lake Boulevard, Coon Rapids (763-757-9445; www .bunkerparkstable.com); and **Roselawn Stables,** 24069 Rum River Boulevard NW, St. Francis (763-753-5517).

i The Minnesota Department of Natural Resources requires horse riders to carry a DNR Horse Pass to use state trails, state forests, or state parks. In the metro area, this would apply to riding in such places as Afton, Wild River, and St. Croix state parks; along the Gateway State Trail; on the Luce Line State Trail; and in the Minnesota Valley State Recreation Area. Other areas may also require the permit. For more information, contact the DNR (651-296-6157 or 888-646-6367; www.dnr.state.mn.us/horseback_riding/index.html).

In the eastern suburbs, horses can be rented at the **Diamond T Riding Stable,** 4889 Pilot Knob Road, Eagan (651-454-1464); **Rockin' R Ranch,** 8540 Kimbro Avenue North, Stillwater (651-439-6878); the **Windy Ridge Ranch,** 2700 Manning Avenue South, Woodbury (651-436-6557); and **Woodloch Stable & Tack,** 5676 North 170th Street, Hugo (651-429-1303).

South of the Twin Cities and just outside Carver, horses can be rented at **River Valley Ranch,** 16480 County Road 45 (952-361-3361).

Parks in the metro area with specified horse paths are Baker Park Preserve, Carver Park Preserve, Crow-Hassan, Elm Creek Park Reserve, Lake Rebecca Park Reserve, and Murphy-Hanrehan Park Reserve (see the Parks chapter for more information).

HOT AIR BALLOONING

Balloon Adventures (952-474-1662) in Chanhassen and **Aamodts Balloons** (651-351-0101; www.aamodtsballoons.com) in Stillwater offer balloon adventures from champagne rides to daylong trips. Call companies for specific takeoff times and sites. To learn how to pilot one of these big colorful beasts by yourself, **Wiederkehr Balloon Academy** in Lakeland (651-436-8172), located at 130 North St. Croix Trail, offers classes in balloon navigation.

IN-LINE SKATING

Both cities have plenty of paved paths open to in-line skaters. Some of the parks that allow in-line skates to share paved walking paths are Lilydale/Harriet Island, Minneapolis Chain of Lakes, Hiawatha, and Theodore Wirth (see the Parks chapter for listings). Two other particularly nice places to skate are along Lake Calhoun and Lake of the Isles; both the trails follow the lakeshore all the way and are wide enough that you don't have to worry about knocking pedestrians over or being hung up behind them for too long. There are also extended paved trails along both banks of the Mississippi in southwestern Minneapolis and southeastern St. Paul, and the newly completed Midtown Greenway is great for skating through south Minneapolis between Uptown and the Mississippi River.

Skate parks have their place here, too, and the most impressive one is in the western suburb of Golden Valley. **Third Lair Skatepark** (763-79-SKATE; www.3rdlair.com), 850 Florida Avenue, has indoor and outdoor parks plus a really good skate shop. The **Tri-City Skate Park** at the Southdale YMCA (952-835-2567; www.ymcatwincities.org/skatepark/skatepark .htm), at 7355 York Avenue South in Edina, has a skate park, too—the first all-concrete, in-ground, continuous-bowl skate park in the upper Midwest. You can sign up for summer skateboarding classes, too.

For more information about in-line skating events around town, contact the **Minnesota In-line Skate Club** (612- 827-3205; www.skate minnesota.com). This club has trail information and organizes weekly skates.

KICKBALL

Cities Sports Connection (CSC; 612-929-9009; www.cscsports.com) organizes coed kickball leagues for players ages 18 and over. Teams consist of players with lower to average and decent skill proficiency and game knowledge, with a focus on sportsmanship, having fun, and getting a good workout. No membership or nonmember fees are charged to participate in CSC leagues, and teams play events all over the metro area. CSC provides paid officials for all league action and free T-shirts for participants.

MINIATURE GOLF

St. Paul's Como Park has a nice course at **Putt'er There** (651-488-0277; www.putterthere .com) at 1300 Midway Parkway (across the street from the zoo). **Adventure Gardens Miniature Golf** (612-861-9169), at 6335 Portland Avenue South in Bloomington, is the largest of the bunch. In Eagan, **Grand Slam Sports and Entertainment Center** (651-452-6569), at 3984 Sibley Memorial Highway, has a midsize golf park that makes for a fun night out.

NATURE INTERPRETATION AND BIRD-WATCHING

Many of the metro area parks have ongoing wildlife conservation projects open to the public, which are a great way to get an up close look at Minnesota's wildlife. Bald eagles, hawks, egrets, deer, porcupines, and the occasional skunk are just a few of the animals you might see, especially in outlying parks. Raccoons and Canada geese are plentiful along the banks of the Mississippi River. Some of the metro area parks that have specific areas set aside for nature interpretation include Bald Eagle-Otter Lakes, Baylor, Bunker Hills, Carver Park Preserve, Como, Coon Rapids Dam, Elm Creek Park Reserve, French, Harriet Island, Hidden Falls-Crosby Farm, Lake Minnetonka Regional Park, Lebanon Hills, Minneapolis Chain of Lakes, Noerenberg, Memorial Park, Rice Creek/Chain of Lakes, Springbrook Nature Center, Theodore Wirth, and Wood Lake Nature Center (see the Parks chapter).

Part of the **Minnesota River Valley Birding Trail** (651-739-9332; www.birdingtrail.org) lies in the southern Twin Cities, and many parks have bird-watching hikes. Check with **Three Rivers Park District** (763-694-7750;

www.threeriversparkdistrict.org), **St. Paul Parks and Recreation** (651-266-6400; www .stpaul.gov/depts/ parks), and the **Minneapolis Park and Recreation Board** (612-230-6400, www.minneapolisparks.org) seasonally for more information.

PAINTBALL

You have your choice of outdoor or indoor paintball arenas at **Adventure Zone** in Burnsville (952-890-7981; www.theadventure zone.net) at 13700 Nicollet Avenue South, and at **Splatball Inc.** (612-378-0385; www .splatball.com), at 2412 University Avenue SE in Minneapolis. The biggest outdoor paintball center is **Splat Tag** (651-488-7700 or 866-775-2882; www.splattag.com), at 835 County Road E, Hudson, Wisconsin. The park is open to groups of six or more (up to 24 participants per group), although walk-ons are sometimes okay, especially on weekends. See the Web site for more information and for detailed directions to Splat Tags "battle courses."

SAILING AND SAILBOARDING

There's really nothing quite as pretty as the white triangles of sailboats bobbing in the placid waters of Minnesota's wide blue lakes. There's also nothing quite as pleasant as actually being on one of the boats, enjoying the hot summer sun as you dangle your fingers and toes in the cool, clear water. Many lakes in the metro area are perfect for sailing and sailboarding alike, including Lake Harriet in Minneapolis, White Bear Lake in White Bear Lake, Keller Lake in St. Paul, Lake Minnetonka in Minnetonka, Medicine Lake in Plymouth, and Lake Nokomis in Minneapolis.

Parks in the metro area that allow sailboats and sailboards in their lakes (and provide convenient boat launches for the same) include Baker Park Preserve, Bald Eagle-Otter Lakes, Bryant Lake, Carver Park Preserve, Cleary Lake, Fish Lake, French, Hyland-Bush-Anderson Lakes, Lake Byllesby, Lake Elmo Park Reserve, Lake George, Lake Min-

newashta, Long Lake, Martin-Island-Linwood Lakes, Minneapolis Chain of Lakes, Nokomis Hiawatha, Phalen-Keller, Rice Creek/Chain of Lakes, and Snail Lake (see the Parks chapter).

The **Minneapolis Park and Recreation Board** (612-230-6400) offers sailing classes and events throughout the summer, as does **Lake Calhoun Yacht Club and Sailing School** in Minneapolis (612-927-8552; www.lakecal houn.org), at 3000 East Calhoun Parkway; and **Scuba Center** (612-925-4818; www.scuba center.com), at 5015 Penn Avenue South in Minneapolis and 1571 Century Point in Eagan (651-681-8434).

SCUBA DIVING

Yes, there is scuba diving in Minnesota. Divers from around the world come to Minnesota to dry-suit dive in the frigid waters of Lake Superior, where hundreds of shipwrecks, including the famous *Edmund Fitzgerald,* can be found miles off the coast, and underwater life found only in this region can be studied up close. If you feel like exploring the bottom of a less cold and much less deep lake, pretty much any lake that has a swimming beach is fine for diving and snorkeling. Classes on scuba diving, scuba certification, and gear rental are provided by **Scuba Center** (612-925-4818; www.scubacenter.com), at 5015 Penn Avenue South, Minneapolis and at 1571 Century Point, Eagan (651-681-8434); and **Scuba Dive and Travel** (612-823-7210; www.scubadive andtravel.com), at 4423 Nicollet Avenue South in Minneapolis. **FantaSea Scuba & Travel** (952-890-3483; www.fantaseadivers .com), at 3429 East Minnesota Highway 13 in Burnsville, offers both classes and certification and arranges international scuba adventure packages.

SKYDIVING

The **Minnesota Skydivers Club** (507-351-7001; www.mnskydive.com) offers static line and tandem airplane jumps as well as free-fall jumps to those who have satisfactorily completed five static line jumps. Ground training is provided for beginning jumpers, with instruction given by jumpmasters and instructors who have been certified by the United States Parachute Association. Skydive Twin Cities (715-684-3416 or 800-SKYDIVE; www.skydive twincities.com), based 30 minutes from the Twin Cities in Baldwin, Wisconsin, also offers ground training and tandem jumping for first-time parachuters. More experienced jumpers have additional options that progress in the skills used as you complete each training level.

SOCCER

Cities Sports Connection (612-929-9009; www.cscsports.com) offers coed outdoor and indoor soccer leagues at various skill levels. CSC soccer leagues are offered outdoors in spring (May–July), summer (June–August), and fall (September–December). CSC also runs two indoor leagues, one in late fall (October–January) and the other in winter (January–March). CSC is open to all adults 18 or older; no membership or nonmember fees are charged to participate in CSC leagues.

SOFTBALL

Cities Sports Connection (612-929-9009; www.cscsports.com) organizes coed softball leagues at all skill levels. CSC softball leagues are offered in the spring (April–June) and summer (June–August). CSC is open to all adults 18 or older; no membership or non-member fees are charged to participate in CSC leagues.

If you're looking to form your own softball team, the Amateur Softball Association (612-230-6487; www.asasoftball.com) can help. Another option is to contact the United States Slowpitch Softball Association (763-571-1305; www.mnusssa.com), which can help you put together a slow-pitch softball team. The association will send you the information you need or at least get you in touch with your local park and recreation department.

RUNNING

The Twin Cities Marathon, Inc. (763-287-3888; www.mtcmarathon.org) is a nonprofit corporation that organizes and directs the annual Twin Cities Marathon, TC 10 Mile, and Saturday events as a community service for the Minneapolis–St. Paul area. The Twin Cities Marathon is often referred to as the most beautiful urban marathon in America and runs alongside the Mississippi River and through many metro area parks.

The Minnesota Distance Running Association (MDRA; 952-927-0983; www.runmdra .org) promotes running, stages many races and fun runs, and serves as a resource for runners in Minnesota. For a $25 membership fee, members of MDRA receive a subscription to the organization's magazine, RunMinnesota, the Running Minnesota Annual with details about running events throughout Minnesota, and the chance to participate (for free) in the many training runs the association sponsors year-round to help runners get in shape for distance runs.

SWIMMING

Summertime is beach weather, and all together there are more miles of swimming beaches in Minnesota than in California and Florida combined. There are more than 1,000 lakes throughout the seven counties in the Twin Cities metro area alone. In Minneapolis swimmers are welcome at Lake Calhoun, Lake Harriet, Cedar Lake, Lake Hiawatha, and Lake Nokomis. In St. Paul, swimmers can take to the water at Lake Phalen and Josephine Lake. White Bear Lake in White Bear has five public areas set aside for swimming, and in Minnetonka the 1,500-acre Lake Minnetonka is surrounded by swimming beaches and boat launches. Plymouth's Medicine Lake has two public beaches with lifeguards and has an on-site outfitter that rents small boats and canoes. Parks in the metro area with swimming beaches are Baker Park Preserve, Bald Eagle–Otter Lakes, Baylor, Bryant Lake, ℹ️ One popular 5K race for runners (and walkers) of all levels is named after a beer. September's James Page Blubber Run has a halfway stop at a bar and ends at a party on Peavey Plaza in downtown Minneapolis. For more information, call (651) 238-2651.

Bunker Hills, Cleary Lake, Como, Elm Creek Park Reserve, French, Hyland-Bush-Anderson Lakes, Lake Byllesby, Lake Elmo Park Reserve, Lake George, Lake Minnetonka Regional Park, Lake Minnewashta, Lake Rebecca Park Reserve, Lebanon Hills, Long Lake Regional Park, Martin-Island-Linwood Lakes, Minneapolis Chain of Lakes, Nokomis Hiawatha, Phalen, Rice Creek/Chain of Lakes, Snail Lake, Square Lake Park, and Theodore Wirth (see the Parks chapter for more information).

If you want to take a quick dip in a pool, nearly every neighborhood park in the Twin Cities has a free wading pool for kids and adults to splash around in, while several parks have full-size pools for public use. In Minneapolis full-size public swimming pools can be found at **North Commons Water Park** (612-370-4945), at 1701 Golden Valley Road;

Rosacker Pool (612-370-4937), at 1520 Johnson Street NE; and **Webber Pool** (612-370-4915), at 4300 Webber Parkway. In St. Paul full-size public swimming pools can be found at **Como Pool** (651-489-2811), in Como Park at Como Avenue and Lexington Parkway; **Highland Aquatic Center** (651-695-3773), at 1840 Edgcumbe Road; and Oxford Pool (651-647-9925), at North Lexington Parkway and Iglehart Avenue.

VOLLEYBALL

Cities Sports Connection (612-929-9009; www.cscsports.com) offers indoor and outdoor (sand and grass) coed volleyball leagues at all skill levels. CSC volleyball leagues are offered indoors in the fall (September–December), winter (January–March), and spring (March–May). CSC leagues move outdoors for early summer on sand (May–July) and on grass (May–July), and for late summer (July–September, sand). CSC is open to all adults 18 or older; no membership or nonmember fees are charged to participate in CSC leagues.

WINTER RECREATION

Minnesota is transformed during winter. Familiar landmarks are completely obliterated by giant piles of soft, white snow, and the horizon stretches out seemingly forever, no longer blocked by the lush green foliage of the spring and summer landscape.

With the change in scenery comes a change in the mood and activities of the people. Summer streets are always packed with pedestrians, and the parks are full of picnicking families and nature lovers. However, when the temperature drops below 20 degrees F—and in January and February, below 0 degrees F—many of these same people couldn't be pried out of their houses for anything but the absolutely necessary drive to work or trip to the grocery store. Those who do venture outside engage in ice-skating, sledding, snowmobiling, ice hockey, and skiing. Many others take up indoor activities, such as bowling, broomball, working out at health clubs, and yoga. Provided you dress for conditions, there's no real weather-related reason to settle in for months of boring inactivity; winter, in a sense, is a state of mind.

BALLROOM AND SQUARE DANCING

What better way to chase away the winter blues and meet new people than dancing? Several clubs in the Twin Cities area bring like-minded dance partners together, including the **Twin Cities Rebels Swing Dance Club** (952-941-0906; www.tcrebels.com), which has regular West Coast Swing classes and dances all over the Metro area, and the **Twin Town Twirlers Square Dancing Club** (763-502-8898, www.tripletdance.com), which holds weekly dances on Mondays and offers square dancing classes at various times of the year. To find out about a variety of dance classes and events, contact the Minnesota Chapter of the **U.S. Amateur Ballroom Dancers Association** (651-483-5467, www.usabda-mn.org).

BOWLING

A great winter sport, bowling gets you out of the house and in someplace warm and friendly. Leagues and tournaments take place in bowling centers throughout the metro area. Stop in at your local lanes to inquire.

If you just want to bowl a couple of games with friends, there are dozens of bowling alleys to choose from. The **Brunswick Zone Eden Prairie** (952-941-0445; www.bowl brunswick.com), located at 12200 Singletree Lane in Eden Prairie, has 40 lanes and is open until midnight Sunday through Wednesday and 2:00 a.m. Thursday through Saturday. This is the original Twin Cities home of Cosmic Bowling, during which the lights fade to black, pins glow, fog machines blow, and laser lights keep time to 1950s through 1990s dance music. There are also pool tables, video games, and dartboards, as well as the largest bar in Eden Prairie.

Memory Lanes (612-721-6211; www .memorylanesmpls.com), at 2520 26th Avenue South in Minneapolis, is where cosmic hipsters come to toss glow-in-the-dark bowling balls and drink reasonably priced fancy mixed drinks. Things get quite interesting on Punk Bowl Mondays and during Thursday-night Electrobowl (featuring electronica and other dance-club mix tunes), the latter fueled by College ID Night with cheap drinks for students in the hours up to and during the beginning of Electrobowl. Memory Lanes also has a full-service kitchen and 14 TVs in the bar—a hot spot on Sunday during football season thanks to its NFL package in high-definition format.

Park Tavern in St. Louis Park (952-929-6810; www.parktavern.net), located at 3401 Louisiana Avenue, is another hot bowling spot. Every Friday and Saturday night beginning at 10:00 p.m., the Park Tavern holds Cosmic Rock and Bowl (for ages 21 and over) with black lights, lots of music, and a flat fee for shoes and unlimited bowling. Be sure to show up early to reserve a lane on these nights, because the 20 in-house lanes are booked fast.

Bryant-Lake Bowl (612-825-3737; www.bryantlakebowl.com), 810 West Lake Street in Minneapolis, is a throwback to bowling alleys of the past. The 1950s-era lanes in this small bowling alley provide loads of atmosphere, and the Bryant Lake Bowl does not have electronic scoring, so you get to practice scoring by hand, something many of us haven't done since childhood. Bowling is cheap here, but the lanes are first-come, first-served, and no reservations are accepted. Expect to wait on busy weekend nights, although the numerous microbrews on tap will make the wait enjoyable.

BOXING

Boxing is no longer a sport confined to men alone, and boxing rings have sprung up at health clubs all over the metro area, while those that have been long established have found new participants and audiences of both genders. In St. Paul, Brunette Boxing Gym (651-779-6248), at 1135 Arcade Street, is the oldest boxing gym in the metro. It hosts boxing competitions and offers personal training for men and women of all ages and skill levels, from beginner to professional. Uppercut Boxing Gym (612-822-1964; www.uppercutgym.com), at 1324 Quincy Street NE in Minneapolis, provides boxing training for all fitness levels, amateur to professional.

BROOMBALL

Similar to hockey, except using brooms instead of sticks and an actual ball instead of a puck, broomball is becoming a popular sport throughout the world and here in the Midwest. The Minneapolis Parks and Recreation Board (612-230-6475) organizes broomball teams for competitions and informal meets. Cities Sports Connection (612-929-9009; www.cscsports.com), offers coed and men's outdoor broomball leagues of all skill levels each winter (December–February).

CROSS-COUNTRY SKIING

There's nothing quite as exhilarating as exploring the Minnesota backwoods on a pair of cross-country skis. Nearly every park in the metro area has well-groomed ski trails, taking skiers through everything from heavily wooded tracked forest paths to gently sloping open spaces with incredible views of frozen waterfalls, lakes, and streams. On top of that, nearly every golf course in the metro area doubles as a cross-country ski park as soon as there's sufficient snow to do so. In the Cities, St. Paul's Como Park, at 1431 North Lexington Parkway, has a 5K trail that loops around the park. Cross-country ski lessons are offered at the park's pavilion on an irregular basis—call (651) 488-9673 for details. Also in St. Paul are Fort Snelling State Park (612-725-2389), which is located at 101 Snelling Lake Road and offers 12 miles of groomed trails for cross-country and skate-ski use; Hidden Falls/Crosby Regional Park (612-632-5111), at Crosby Farm Road and Shepard Road, which has 13.9K of trails for ski use; Highland Nine Hole Golf Course at 1797 Edgcumbe Road, which has a 5K groomed track for experienced skiers and a 3K loop across the street for beginners; and Phalen Golf Course at 1615 Phalen Drive, which has 10K of groomed track for cross-country skiers. For more information on these and other St. Paul trails, call St. Paul Parks and Recreation at (651) 266-6400.

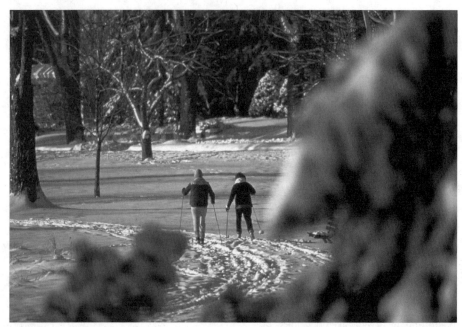

When the snow falls, cross-country skiers shush around Minneapolis's Chain of Lakes. GREATER MINNEAPOLIS CONVENTION & VISITORS ASSOCIATION

Metro area parks with groomed trails for cross-country skiers include Baker Park Preserve, Carver Park Preserve, Cleary Lake, Coon Rapids Dam, Cottage Grove Ravine, Elm Creek Park Reserve, French, Hyland-Bush-Anderson Lakes, Lake Minnewashta, Lebanon Hills, Murphy-Hanrehan Park Reserve, and Theodore Wirth, Wirth-Memorial Parkway. (See the Parks chapter for more park information.)

Cross-country ski gear can be rented or purchased in Minneapolis at **AARCEE** at 2910 Lyndale Avenue South (612-827-5746) and at **Midwest Mountaineering** at 309 Cedar Avenue South (612-339-3433). In St. Paul ski gear can be rented or purchased at either **Finn-Sisu** at 1841 University Avenue West (651-645-2443) or **Joe's Sporting Goods** at 33 East County Road B in Little Canada (651-488-5511).

CURLING

Resembling a combination of ice hockey and shuffleboard, curling has gone from a popular sport confined mostly to Canada and the United Kingdom to an Olympic event and a well-loved, albeit still relatively obscure, winter sport. The **St. Paul Curling Club** (651-224-7408; www.stpaulcurlingclub.org), the largest member-owned curling club in the country, organizes curling matches and practices at its home at 470 Selby Avenue in St. Paul.

DOGSLEDDING AND SKIJORING TRAILS

Dogsledding and skijoring—the latter in which a skier is pulled along by a horse or a vehicle—are permitted on designated trails in some metro area parks. With the exception of the multiuse trail at Baker Park Reserve, a special-use permit and a Park Patron permit are required for both activities; call the **Three Rivers Park District** reservations office at (763) 559-6700 for further information, permits, and maps.

Sections of snowmobile trails at Crow-Hassan Park Reserve and Elm Creek Park Reserve are open for skijoring and dogsledding on weekdays during the day and weekends and holidays from 5:00 a.m. to 10:00 a.m. Crow-Hassan Park Reserve, located west of Rogers on Sylvan Lake Road, has 5.5 miles of trail designated for dogsledding/skijoring use; Elm Creek Park Reserve, located northwest of Osseo on County Road 81, has 11 miles of trail designated for dogsledding/skijoring use; the North Hennepin Trail Corridor, connecting the Coon Rapids Dam Regional Park in Brooklyn Park to Elm Creek Park Reserve in Maple Grove, has 6 miles of trail designated for dogsledding/skijoring use. These trails are usually packed, so be prepared for lots of company.

Murphy-Hanrehan Park Reserve, located near Prior Lake on County Road 75, has 3 miles of trail designated for dogsledding and horseriding—no snowmobiles are allowed. The trail is open all week during daylight hours and is not usually heavily used.

Baker Park Reserve, located 20 miles west of downtown Minneapolis on County Road 19, has 4 miles of trails set aside for dogsledding, skijoring, mountain biking, and snowshoeing.

DOWNHILL SKIING AND SNOWBOARDING

In the immediate Twin Cities metro area, there aren't a lot of options for downhill skiing or extreme snowboarding. But let's face it—this is farm and lumber country, and mountains don't really figure into our natural geography. For real downhill skiing, you have to make the three- to four-hour trek up to Duluth and the North Shore, where you'll find the **Giants**

Ridge Golf & Ski Resort (218-865-3000 or 800-688-7669; www.giantsridge.com), in the town of Biwabik off County Road 138; **Spirit Mountain** (218-628-2891 or 800-642-6377; www.spiritmt.com), at 9500 Spirit Mountain Place in Duluth; and **Lutsen Mountains** (218-663-7281; www.lutsen.com) found between Duluth and the Canadian border on Ski Road Hill near Lutsen. All three ski areas are also resorts, and discounts are offered seasonally on rooms and lift tickets for those who purchase a combination of both—advance reservations are highly recommended.

Closer to home—but not as tall or as steep as the North Shore slopes—are **Buck Hill** in Burnsville (952-435-7174; www.buckhill.com) located at 15400 Buck Hill Road; **Hyland Ski Area & Snowboard Area** in Bloomington (763-694-7800; www.hylandski.com), at 8800 Chalet Road; **Afton Alps** (651-436-5245 or 800-328-1328; www.aftonalps.com), located near Afton off County Road 20; **Welch Village Ski and Snowboard Area** (651-222-7079; www.welchvillage.com), located in Welch on Minnesota Highway 61 and County Road 7; and **Wild Mountain Ski and Snowboard** (651-465-6315 or 800-447-4958; www.wildmountain.com), located off Minnesota Highway 8 near Taylors Falls at 37200 Wild Mountain Road.

FENCING

The **Twin Cities Fencing Club** (651-225-1900; www.twincitiesfencing.com) is one of the top fencing clubs in the country. Head coach Roberto Sobalvarro has coached U.S. National Teams at the World Championships, World Cup competitions, and the U.S. Olympic Festival. The club serves fencers of all ages and all levels of experience, from beginner to national champion. Kid, teen, and adult classes, as well as training and practice nights, will get you dodging, parrying, and thrusting in no time.

HEALTH CLUBS

The Twin Cities proper have many gyms and health clubs to choose from, many of which offer free child care and youth programs such as swimming lessons and martial arts. **Lifetime Fitness** (www.lifetimefitness.com) has two locations in St. Paul—at 2145 Ford Parkway in the Highland Park neighborhood (651-698-5000) and at 340 Cedar Street (651-227-7777), downtown. There is also a downtown Minneapolis branch for executive members only at 615 Second Avenue South (612-752-7000) in the Grand Hotel Minneapolis and one for all types of members in Target Center (612-486-3600), and several locations in the suburbs, including the women-only location at 2480 Fairview Avenue North in Roseville (651-633-4444). The facilities include Cybex, Nautilus, Gravitron, and ski machines as well as stair-climbers. Aerobics, dance, and karate classes are offered, as are massage, tanning beds, personal training, nutrition seminars, and free child care.

There are **YMCA** locations (www.ymca twincities.org) in downtown Minneapolis (612-371-9622) at 30 South Ninth Street and in downtown St. Paul (651-292-4143) at 194 East Sixth Street, as well as in other neighborhoods in both cities and throughout the suburbs. In addition, there are YWCA locations in both cities, including in downtown Minneapolis (612-332-0501, www.ywca-minneapolis .org) at 1130 Nicollet Mall and in St. Paul (651-225-9922, www.ywcaofstpaul.org) at 375 Selby Avenue in the Cathedral Hill neighborhood. Another notable location is the relatively new Midtown YWCA (612-215-4333, www.ywca-minneapolis.org) at 2121 East Lake Street near the Hiawatha Light Rail Station. This beautiful facility is the largest YWCA in the country. Equipment, facilities, and classes vary by location.

Los Campeones Fitness & Body Building, 2721 Franklin Avenue East in Minneapolis (612-333-8181), features free weights and cable machines, treadmills and other cardio machines, a juice bar, and an on-site pro shop offering items including vitamin supplements.

Special student and couple rates are available. The **Sweatshop Health Club** in St. Paul (651-646-8418; www.sweatshopfitness.com), located at 167 Snelling Avenue North, offers personal weight-training programs, kickboxing, spinning, and Pilates mat and reformer classes and has a child care facility on the premises. **The Firm** (612-377-3003; www.the firmworkoutstudio.com), located at 245 Aldrich Avenue North in Minneapolis, is known for its trendsetting, urban approach to fitness—classes like striptease and funk aerobics add spice to the core necessities you'd expect from any top-notch gym.

HOCKEY

Kids in Minnesota start playing hockey about as soon as they can walk, and both boys and girls participate in the sport with equal fervor. Every winter, parks in the Twin Cities metro area are flooded to make ice-skating rinks for skaters and hockey players, and formal and informal hockey teams are formed among children and adults alike. During hockey season, large amounts of television time are blocked off on more than one station to bring live coverage of local high school and college hockey playoffs.

Traditionally St. Paul has been a much more dedicated hockey town than Minneapolis, and it shows. St. Paul has the Minnesota Wild's Xcel Energy Center arena and is home to groomed ice hockey rinks (some indoor, some outdoor), including **Conway Recreation Center Rink** (651-501-6343) at 2090 Conway Avenue, **Desnoyer Recreation Center Rink** (651-298-5753) at 525 Pelham Boulevard, **Edgcumbe Recreation Center Rink** (651-695-3711) at 320 South Griggs, **Griggs Recreation Center Rink** (651-298-5755) at 1188 Hubbard Avenue, **Langford Recreation Center Rink** (651-298-5765) at 30 Langford Park, **Linwood Recreation Center Rink** (651-298-5660) at 860 St. Clair Avenue, and **Merriam Park Ice Skating Rink** (651-298-5766) at 2000 St. Anthony Avenue. For more indoor and outdoor locations and information, contact **St.**

Paul Parks and Recreation at (651-266-6400) or www.stpaul.gov/depts/parks.

But if you find yourself in Minneapolis and want to take to the ice, there are options. You can lace up your hockey skates at the **Palace Ice Garden** (612-370-4846) at 600 Kenwood Parkway and the **Northeast Ice Arena** (612-370-3920) at 1306 Central Avenue NE. For more information on these as well as outdoor rinks across the city, contact the **Minneapolis Parks and Recreation Board** (612-230-6400, www.minneapolisparks.com).

There are dozens of suburban ice rinks as well. You can track down ones near you by visiting www.arenamaps.com/arenas/Minnesota.htm.

ICE FISHING

Ice fishing entails setting up camp on top of a frozen lake, cutting a hole in the ice, and waiting for some sluggish fish to come along and snap up your bait. There are lots of fancy variations on this, including bringing portable houses, space heaters, and televisions out onto the ice with you, but this is basically the blueprint to every ice fishing trip. Pretty much every lake in the metropolitan area is a potential ice fishing bonanza, although some are more fruitful than others. Also remember the standard that ice be at least 6 inches thick to support a person and a foot thick to support a vehicle, and keep in mind ice thickness may vary on a given body of water. For more information, see the chapter on Hunting and Fishing.

ICE-SKATING

Just about every park in the Twin Cities metro area, if not every park in Minnesota, has a picturesque area that gets flooded every winter and turned into a free neighborhood ice-skating rink. One great example is the **Wells Fargo WinterSkate** (651-291-5608) on Landmark Plaza at St. Peter and Fifth Streets in downtown St. Paul from late November to late February, depending on conditions. **Rice**

Winter Car Safety

The **American Red Cross** and other organizations sometimes sell winter car safety kits that include a flashlight and batteries, a snack food item, flagging tape, a candle, matches, a pencil and notepad for messages, a guide for safe winter travel, and other roadside necessities. But you don't have to wait for these occasional special offers—you can compile your own emergency car kit. For tips on how to make one, contact **Minnesota's Division of Homeland Security and Emergency Management** (651-201-7400; www.hsem.state.mn.us) or the **Minnesota Safety Council** (651-291-9150; www.mnsafetycouncil.org).

Park's white lights twinkle nearby as you skate in the shadow of the massive old courthouse that is now Landmark Center. There is no fee to use the rink, skate rental is $2 (or free if you produce your Wells Fargo credit or check card), and there's a warming tent with hot chocolate and snacks.

In St. Paul, you can find well-groomed skate rinks (some indoor, some outdoor) at **Conway Recreation Center Rink** (651-501-6343) at 2090 Conway Avenue; **Desnoyer Ice Skating Rink** (651-298-5753) at 525 Pelham Boulevard; **Eastview Recreation Center Rink** (651-772-7845) at 1675 East Fifth Street; **Edgcumbe Ice Skating Rink** (651-695-3711) at 320 South Griggs; **Griggs Recreation Center Rink** (651-298-5755) at 1188 Hubbard Avenue; **Hazel Park Recreation Center Rink** (651-501-6350) at 945 North Hazel Avenue; **Langford Recreation Center Rink** (651-298-5765) at 30 Langford Park; **Linwood Recreation Center Rink** (651-298-5660) at 860 St. Clair Avenue; **Merriam Park Recreation Center** Rink (651-298-5766) at 2000 St. Anthony Avenue; **North Dale Recreation Center Rink**

i A nice winter date is indoor ice-skating at the Depot, a historic glass-walled rink in downtown Minneapolis. There are bars and restaurants nearby to complete the night.

(651-298-5812) at 1414 North St. Albans; and **Northwest Como Recreation Center Rink** (651-298-5813) at 1550 North Hamline. There are many more options. Contact St. Paul Parks and Recreation for information at (651) 266–6400 or www.stpaul.gov/depts/parks/specialservices.

Minneapolis skating rinks include **Lake Harriet** (612-230-6475) at 1300 42nd Street East; **Bryn Mawr Park** (612-230-6400) at 1905 Mt. View Avenue; **Longfellow Park** (612-370-4957) at 3435 36th Avenue South, (612-370-4957); and **Loring Park** (612-370-4929) at 1382 Willow Street (612-370-4929). **The Depot Ice Rink** (612-339-2253, www.thedepotminneapolis.com/rink.htm) in the refurbished 1899 Milwaukee Road Train Station is one of the most beautiful, with its floor-to-ceiling windows and turn-of-the-20th-century atmosphere. Skate rentals are available.

For more information on Minneapolis rinks, contact the **Minneapolis Park and Recreation Board** at (612) 230-6400 or www.minneapolisparks.com. You can find additional indoor and outdoor rinks in both cities and the suburbs by visiting www.arenamaps.com/arenas/Minnesota.htm.

ROCK CLIMBING

While there aren't any mountains in the Twin Cities metro area, there are many bluffs in the region and several organizations that can put together mountaineering excursions for solo or group climbers. A few gyms and retail stores offer indoor climbing walls for varying skill levels.

REI (952-884-4315; www.rei.com), located at 750 West American Boulevard in Bloomington, has information on REI's annual trips to such destinations as the Summit Challenge in Nepal and the Kilimanjaro Climb. Staff can also direct you to local climbing spots. REI is a complete gear shop and can hook you up with anything you need to prep yourself for any level of climb. The Bloomington store has an indoor climbing wall available free to members (for a one-time fee of $15) and for $10 to nonmembers. (Note there are no climbing walls at REI's Roseville and Maple Grove stores.)

Midwest Mountaineering (612-339-3433, www.midwestmtn.com), located at 309 Cedar Avenue South in Minneapolis, is another great gear shop with clinics and information about local climbing spots for all levels of climbers. The store has erected an on-site climbing cave that's free and open to the public during store hours.

Other indoor climbing options include **Vertical Endeavors** (651-776-1430, www.verticalendeavors.com), at 845 Phalen Boulevard in St. Paul, has practice climbing options for all skill levels as well as on-site climbing instructors. The gym currently has more than 18,000 square feet of climbing space. It also holds clinics and organizes trips.

For outdoor climbing, you can head to **Interstate State Park** (651-465-5711) near Taylors Falls an hour northeast of the Twin Cities and climb 30–70-foot bluffs along the St. Croix River. There are also good climbing areas along the Mississippi River near Red Wing, an hour southeast of the Twin Cities, and fantastic wintertime ice climbing at Duluth and on the North Shore of Lake Superior, two to four hours north of the Cities. St. Paul offers ice climbing in some of the city's parks, particularly at Lilydale Regional Park along the Mississippi River. Ice climbing in St. Paul parks requires a permit; contact **St. Paul Parks and Recreation** (651-632-5111, www.stpaul.gov/depts/parks/userguide/iceclimbing.html) for more information.

SLEDDING/TOBOGGANING

There aren't really rules regarding or areas set aside for sledding or tobogganing—most Twin Cities metro parks have great sledding hills. Use your common sense and don't pick a hill that bottoms out at a busy street, and don't try to take your sled on a ski or snowboard slope. **Como Park** in particular has great areas built up especially for sledding/tobogganing—call (651) 488-9673 for more information.

SNOWMOBILING

An incredible sense of freedom comes with riding a snowmobile, and Minnesota has 18,000 miles of public and private snowmobile trails that cross wide-open frozen lakes and follow paths cut through thick Minnesota forests. With a few commonsense rules, this is a great way to see the outdoors in Minnesota. You can download a copy of the Snowmobiler's Safety Laws, Rules & Regulations from the **Department of Natural Resources** Web page at www.dnr.state.mn.us/snowmobiling, or call the DNR at (651) 296-6157 for a copy by mail. Maximum speed in Minnesota for snowmobiles is 50 mph. All resident snowmobiles must be registered with the DNR.

You are allowed to ride snowmobiles anywhere within the seven-county metro area on your own land (although you'd better be on good terms with your neighbors if you try it in the Cities), on land that has signs posted saying snowmobiles are allowed, and on land where you have written or spoken consent from the owner or lessee. Parks within the metro area that have trails specifically groomed for snowmobiles include Baker Park Preserve, Carver Park Preserve, Cleary Lake, Crow-Hassan, Elm Creek Park Reserve, Lake Rebecca Park Reserve, Lake Theodore, Lebanon Hills, Minnetonka Regional Park, and

ℹ️ A Snowmobile State Trail Sticker is required for all snowmobiles being operated on state trails. For more information, contact the Minnesota Department of Natural Resources at 800-MINN DNR or http://www.dnr.state.mn.us/licenses/snowmobile/trailpermit.html.

Murphy-Hanrehan Park Reserve (see the Parks chapter for complete park listings). Additional information on trails, trail maps, and snowmobiling events can be obtained by calling the **Minnesota United Snowmobilers Association** at (763) 577-0185 or www.mnsnowmobiler.org.

SNOWSHOEING

Snowshoeing is an ideal means of transportation after a fresh snowfall. The wide, flat paddles make it possible to walk safely over the top of snowdrifts. Once you've mastered walking in snowshoes, you will practically glide over the soft snow.

The following parks have areas and trails set aside for snowshoers: Baker Park Preserve, Carver Park Preserve, Coon Rapids Dam, Crow-Hassan, Elm Creek Park Reserve, French, and Murphy-Hanrehan. Individual parks hold events like full-moon and naturalist-led hikes.

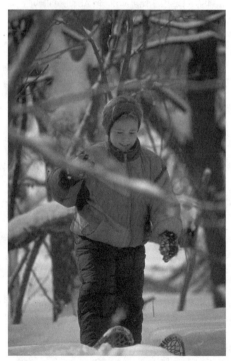

A young snowshoer high-steps through the powder.
GREATER MINNEAPOLIS CONVENTION & VISITORS ASSOCIATION

Call ahead or check out the activities listed with **Three Rivers Park District** (763-694-7750; www.threeriversparkdistrict.org), **St. Paul Parks and Recreation** (651-266-6400; www.stpaul.gov/depts/parks), or **Minneapolis Park and Recreation Board** (612-230-6400; www.minneapolisparks.com).

SNOW TUBING

Unlike sledding or tobogganing, you need to have a decent hill to get real speed on an inner tube. Some of the places that have designed and built special hills for snow tubing are **Eko Backen** (651-433-2422; www.eko backen.com), at 22570 Manning Trail in Scandia; **Green Acres** (651-770-6060; www.green acresrec.com), at 8989 55th Street North in Lake Elmo; **Trapp Farm Park** (651-675-5511), at 841 Wilderness Run Road in Eagan; **Valley-wood Golf Course and Park** (952-953-2323), at 4851 125th Street West in Apple Valley; and **Theodore Wirth Park** (612-230-6400), at 1301 Theodore Wirth Parkway in Minneapolis. Inner tubes can be rented at all of the aforementioned facilities for a nominal fee.

i If venturing onto frozen lakes, watch for thin-ice warning signs, brightly colored buoys, or anything else that seems out of place. Minnesotans are intensely aware of the dangers of thin ice, and if nobody else is playing on a frozen public lake, it's a good idea to steer clear of it yourself.

YOGA

Depending on how you approach it and what you want to get out of it, yoga is a religion, an exercise routine, or a great way to forget about frigid outdoor temperatures. There are many different types—Hatha, Vinyasa, Ashtanga, and more. Find your style in Minneapolis at **Grasshopper Yoga Studio** (612-724-7311; www.grasshopperyogastudio.com), 810 West 31st Street, or **One Yoga Studio** (612-872-6347; www.one-yoga.com), 2100 B Lyndale Avenue South. Or in St. Paul at **Yoga Center** (651-644-7141; www.stpaulyogacenter.com) 1162 Selby Avenue, or **Sol Yoga & Massage** (651-224-8800; www.sol-yoga.com), 758 Grand Avenue.

HUNTING AND FISHING

Hunting and fishing have been important parts of many Minnesotans' lives and the state's economy since nomadic indigenous peoples and, later, European explorers discovered the dense, rich hardwood forests that harbored whitetailed deer, black bear, and moose, or the lakes and streams that teemed with fish and furbearing animals like otter and beaver. Much, much later, wealthy socialites from Chicago made annual treks to Minnesota to swim and fish in the clear waters, giving rise to vacation and health resort towns all along the banks of Lake Superior, Lake Minnetonka, and many other Minnesota lakes.

These traditions stand today. There are hundreds of hunting and fishing resorts all over the state, many of which can sell you your hunting or fishing licenses right on the premises, as well as bait, ammunition, and rod and boat rentals. **Hospitality Minnesota** (651-778-2400; www.hospitalitymn.com) and the **Minnesota Office of Tourism** (888-TOURISM; www.exploreminnesota .com) issue an annual booklet that lists resorts in detail and will mail you a free copy if you call or contact them through either Web site.

Hunters and anglers are encouraged to be ethical, safe, and responsible. Minnesota's Department of Natural Resources (DNR), has been working since 1931 to make sure that there will always be game and fish for future generations, and strict fines and imprisonment are some of the penalties imposed on poachers and careless hunters who disregard the laws. The DNR offers many valuable resources to hunters and anglers, including information booklets on the best places to go hunting and fishing, a regularly updated Web site (www.dnr.state.mn.us) with specific information about breeding and stocking programs for game animals and fish, the convenience of applying for hunting and fishing licenses over the telephone or on the DNR's Web site, regulations, and information about hunting seasons for specific game and for specific types of hunting.

HUNTING

Hunting is a heavily regulated sport in Minnesota, requiring specific licensing dependent on game targeted, whether you're hunting with firearms or bow and arrow, the area you plan to hunt in, and the age of the hunter. If you purchase a small-game license but do not specify that you plan to hunt migratory birds (waterfowl, woodcock, snipe, rails, etc.), you are not allowed to hunt those birds; you must reapply for the same license and specify that you do plan to hunt migratory birds. Deer and other big game licenses are awarded on a lottery basis depending on how many animals the Minnesota DNR considers an expendable excess.

Trespassing laws are rigidly enforced, and if you're caught hunting on private property or on land that is not zoned for hunting, you'll be fined. (Fines vary by county.) Exceptions to the trespassing laws include entering private land on foot and without a weapon to retrieve a wounded animal that was lawfully shot or to retrieve a hunting dog. If a landowner does not allow you onto his land to retrieve a wounded animal, you must leave the private property immediately without the game animal.

Hunting dogs are not allowed to chase down, wound, or kill big-game animals. A dog that is observed doing so may be legally killed by a person other than a DNR conservation officer between January 1 and July 14. Hunting dogs may not be killed by anyone other than a DNR conservation officer any other time, as many hunters legally use dogs to track upland game, waterfowl, rabbits, raccoons, foxes, and coyotes.

For current licensing rates for game hunting, call the **Minnesota DNR** at (651) 296-6157 or (888) 646-6367, or check out the Web site at www.dnr.state.mn.us. Most licenses, both hunting and fishing, can be picked up at almost any bait shop or convenience store near the popular hunting areas, but the DNR can immediately issue small-game licenses electronically if you call (651) 296-4506 or (888) MINN-DNR, or if you apply through the DNR's Web site. Hunters are encouraged to apply for all licenses early, as the number of licenses issued is dependent on game availability.

Animal poaching is a serious crime in Minnesota. Turn In Poachers (TIP), Inc., is a non-profit organization founded by hunters and concerned citizens to stop poaching in Minnesota. TIP offers cash awards for information leading to a poacher's arrest; all tipsters remain anonymous. For more information call the toll-free **TIP hotline** at (800) 652-9093.

The following listings are only general rules that apply to hunting and trapping game in Minnesota. Most parks and wildlife preserves have specific rules and restrictions regarding hunting and trapping, and it's important to check with both the DNR and with the specific park/preserve in question before going out.

Big Game

When hunting big game (deer, moose, bear, etc., as dictated by law) in Minnesota, the minimum caliber of rifle, shotgun, muzzleloader, or handgun that can be used is at least .23 caliber, and only single-projectile ammunition can be used. It's illegal to harvest big game with a bow and arrow while in possession of a firearm, with the exception of hunting bear, where possession of a firearm while in possession of archery equipment is allowed. Bows must have a minimum pull of 40 pounds at or before full draw in order to effectively kill big game. Arrowheads used must have a minimum of two sharp metal cutting edges and be barbless. Crossbows are not allowed for either big- or small-game hunting, except by special permit given only to disabled hunters. Big game may only be hunted from one-half hour before sunrise to one-half hour after sunset.

Bear

Bear hunting is legal in much of northern and north-central Minnesota. Residents and non-residents can obtain bear hunting licenses, which are usually made available by mid-March, from the DNR. More than 13,000 bear hunting permits are issued annually, with numbers adjusting annually depending on the bear population.

Deer

Open season for deer hunting generally begins in early November and lasts through early December. Archery season for deer traditionally begins in mid-September. Muzzleloader season typically begins in late November. Minnesota also offers an All-Season deer hunting license that allows a hunter to hunt in the archery, firearm, and muzzleloader seasons. Call the DNR for specific dates, as they vary from year to year. Any deer harvested by a hunter must be tagged according to DNR specifications. Brochures on proper tagging procedures are available at any of the 1,800 licensing stations across Minnesota or from the **DNR Information and License Center** at 500 Lafayette Road, St. Paul, MN 55155-4040, www.dnr.state.mn.us, (888) 646-6367.

A limited number of Special Area Permits are issued each year to hunters in places where the number of hunters must be limited to control the harvest or for public safety. Permits are awarded by a lottery system dependent on a head count and estimation of expendable deer available. Hunters who receive Special Area Permits may also hunt deer outside that Special Area if they apply to do so and have it specifically punched on their hunting license. Laws can change signifiℹ️ The Minnesota Deer License, Site Tag, and Registration Slip now come as a three-part form—the upper half is the Site Tag to be attached to the deer; the bottom half includes your hunting license and a Registration Slip to exchange for a Possession Tag at an official deer registration station.

cantly from year to year. For the most current deer hunting regulations, contact the **Minnesota DNR** at (888) 646-6367 or look online at www.dnr.state.mn.us.

Elk

Minnesota has a tiny population of elk primarily near the town of Grygla in the northwestern part of the state. During years when elk hunting is permitted, the season is open only to residents of Minnesota, and hunters must apply in parties of two. Elk hunting permits are not issued every year; contact the DNR to find out more about whether there will be a hunt and for more information about applying for permits. Permits are issued by random drawing, and the hunt is a once-in-a-lifetime event.

Moose

Minnesota's annual moose hunt is open only to Minnesota residents and is a once-in-a-lifetime event—each hunter is allowed to take down only one moose in his or her lifetime. Moose licenses are awarded annually on a lottery basis determined by actual animal populations. Some years no moose permits are issued. Generally the moose hunting season runs from late September to mid-October. Contact the DNR for more specifics.

Small Game, Waterfowl, and Migratory Birds

It's no accident that Minnesota has an abundance of wildlife in its parklands, wildlife preserves, and even in the Twin Cities. Careful monitoring of habitats and hunter/game interaction by Minnesota conservation officers has been an important facet of state government for more than a century, with the goal of creating safe hunting opportunities for residents and visitors while preserving as much of the native Minnesota wildlife as possible. Limits on migratory birds and many species of small game are strictly enforced.

Beaver, mink, muskrat, and otter

It is unlawful to trap any furbearing animals within any state-owned game refuge without first obtaining a permit from the appropriate wildlife manager. Most of the state parks and state wildlife refuges allow trapping of furbearing small game as long as you get prior permission and have a small-game hunting license.

Foxes, raccoons, squirrels, rabbits

A small-game hunting license is required, unless you are hunting on your own land.

Migratory waterfowl

A State Migratory Waterfowl Stamp (State Duck Stamp), purchased from the DNR for a nominal fee, is required for hunting geese, ducks, and mergansers. All hunters—resident and nonresident—between the ages of 18 and 65 are required to have a valid State Duck Stamp in their possession while hunting migratory waterfowl, with the exception of those taking down waterfowl on their own property or who are in the U.S. Armed Forces and are stationed outside Minnesota with official military leave papers on their person.

Waterfowl hunting seasons and bag limits are set in late summer, and season dates are announced in early September. Contact the DNR for more information.

A special permit is also required for hunting Canada geese in season. During early Sep-

ℹ️ Parts of Beltrami, Lake of the Woods, Koochiching, Roseau, and St. Louis Counties are Ojibwe territories and are closed to nonband hunters and anglers except by special permission from the tribal council. Consult the DNR regarding specific contact information and how to acquire permission.

tember and late December, the entire state is open to hunting geese. Daily bag limits range from two to five geese per hunter, depending on the DNR-specified hunting zone, and shooting hours last from one-half hour before sunrise to sunset every day. Possession limits are double the daily bag limits. Migratory waterfowl must be transported in an undressed condition (with head and wings attached) at all times until delivery to either the hunter's home or to a commercial processing facility.

It is unlawful to take geese, ducks, mergansers, coots, or moorhens with lead shot or while having any lead shot in your possession. Only nontoxic shot approved by the U.S. Fish and Wildlife Service may be used. These nontoxic shot restrictions are responsible for preventing lead poisoning of more than 400,000 wild ducks nationwide each year.

Wild turkey

Spring and fall (check with the DNR for specific dates) are open for hunting wild turkey in Minnesota. Generally application deadlines for Wild Turkey Stamps are five or six months before the season begins. Smaller, quicker, and smarter than domestic turkeys, these Minnesota birds can also fly up into trees to hide, making them a competitive target for firearm and bow hunters alike. Although a small-game license is not necessary for taking wild turkey, you must purchase a Wild Turkey Stamp from the DNR to legally hunt the birds. Bag limit is one bird of either sex in the fall season per hunter and one male bird per hunter in spring.

Only fine shot size number 4 and smaller may be used to hunt turkey, and nothing smaller than a 20 gauge shotgun can be carried on turkey hunts. Bows must have a pull of no less than 40 pounds, and arrows must be sharp, have at least two metal cutting edges, and be at least 7/8 inch in diameter. Poison- or explosive-tipped arrows may not be used to hunt any game animal or bird in Minnesota. Hunting dogs and electronic tracking devices

are not allowed on turkey hunts. Every hunter who takes a wild turkey must personally present the bird for registration at one of the 1,800 registration stations throughout Minnesota; the feathers, head, and feet must remain on the bird until it is officially registered.

Protected Animals

There is no open season for hunting bobwhite quail, prairie chickens, cranes, swans, hawks, owls, eagles, herons, bitterns, cormorants, loons, grebes, or any other species of birds except specified game or unprotected birds. Crows may be taken without a license in season (September 1 through February 28) or at any time when they are doing or are about to do damage. There is also no open season for hunting caribou, pronghorn, gray wolf, wolverine, cougar, or spotted skunk ("civet cat").

Unprotected Species

Minnesota residents are not required to have a license to hunt unprotected species. Weasels, coyotes, gophers, porcupines, striped skunks, and all other mammals for which there are no closed seasons or are not under protected status may be hunted year-round. They may be taken in any manner, except with the aid of artificial lights or by using a motor vehicle to chase, run over, or kill the animal. Poisons may not be used except in accordance with restrictions stated by the Minnesota Department of Agriculture.

House sparrows, starlings, common pigeons, chukar partridge, quail other than bobwhite quail, mute swans, and monk parakeets are all unprotected and may be hunted year-round.

No person may take a wild animal with a firearm or by archery from a motorized vehicle except a disabled person with an appropriate permit on a stationary vehicle. Also, it's against the law to transport an uncased firearm or shoot from any motorized vehicle in Minnesota.

FISHING

In the Land of 10,000 Lakes, it's no surprise that fishing is one of the most popular summer recreational activities. To meet the demand of thousands of dedicated anglers, the Minnesota DNR runs fisheries all over the state that are in charge of keeping some of the most popular lakes and fishing holes well stocked with walleye, pike, muskellunge, trout, bass, catfish, crappie, bluegill, and, in Lake Superior, salmon. Fishing licenses are available at any of the 1,800 licensing agents located at convenience stores, bait shops, and sports outfitters across the state. Since March 2000 the DNR has also been issuing fishing licenses electronically over the telephone (call 888-MNLicense for more information) and through its Web site at www.dnr .state.mn.us.

Regulations for fishing areas change per year according to species populations, so it's a good idea to call the DNR to request a current fishing guide or to ask about a specific fishing spot before heading out. The DNR's Web site regularly posts updated fishing information and regulation changes, if any.

Common Catches in the Twin Cities Area

Northern pike

Although walleye is the most popular fish in Minnesota, the most widely spread game fish in the state is the northern pike. With its abundance of marshes and shallow streams, Minnesota has as much as or more northern pike habitat than any other state. Given relatively clean water, an adequate food supply, and enough shoreline marshes and wetlands to spawn in, northern pike will propagate in abundance all on its own.

Northern pike does so well on its own, in fact, that stocking lakes with the fish is usually unnecessary. The feisty carnivorous fish, which can grow to weigh 20 pounds, will eat just about any other fish, and lakes with an abundance of northern pike tend to have low populations of all other fish. Eventually the food supply runs out, and pike populations start dropping off as well.

This practice of allowing pike populations to grow on their own has problems. It's every sport angler's dream to catch a giant trophy northern pike, but it usually takes at least 15 years for a northern pike to grow to weigh 20 pounds and another 10 to reach 30 pounds. You can usually count on a few 20-plus pounders to be caught each year, but most northern pike caught are only two or three pounds on average. The DNR encourages anglers to view the northern pike as a trophy fish only, and that all small fish carefully caught and released can be caught again year after year for sport until they are big enough to be mounted.

Pike are a fun sport fish for all levels of angler, as they are fearless, toothy creatures and will snap at just about any bait you use. This makes catch-and-release tactics especially practical, as northern pike can be lured with harmless artificials as easily as live bait and tend to release their grip on artificials a lot easier than they do tasty organic bait.

Northern pike season generally runs mid-May through mid-February of the following year. Contact the DNR for specific season dates. A possession limit of three is in effect, and only one pike longer than 30 inches can be taken each day.

Northern pike are best caught in cool waters, so winter, early spring, and late fall are the best times to pursue these fish.

Bass

Bass are some of the scrappiest, most wildly gymnastic fish in Minnesota's waters and can fight an angler after being hooked for several hours before either wearing out or breaking free. Because of their aggressive reaction to being hooked, catch-and-release fishing is often not viable; these fish literally throw themselves into the air and against boats and rocks trying to escape, sometimes ripping hooks completely out of their bodies while

i Minnesota actually has 11,842 lakes of 10 or more acres and thousands of smaller bodies of water to angle in, adding up to significantly more than the 10,000 the state's motto proclaims.

doing so. Both smallmouth and largemouth bass are very strong for their size, and anglers should expect a good fight no matter what size the catch.

Largemouth bass are especially adaptable and prolific fish. They live and successfully spawn in a variety of conditions, and only very few stocked bass are required to populate a large body of water. Male largemouth bass viciously guard largemouth fingerlings until they're old enough to leave the nest, which almost guarantees that many of the tens of thousands of largemouth eggs laid each year will someday become full-grown fish. Consequently, stocking plays a very small role in largemouth bass management.

Largemouth bass are a warmwater fish and do best in waters that are as warm as 80 and 90 degrees. In winter, largemouth bass go into a state of near-hibernation, settling lethargically near the bottom of lakes until temperatures rise to 60-degrees-plus again.

Smallmouth bass don't usually get much larger than two or three pounds, although those who catch them swear they're at least twice that big in the water because of their incredible strength. A native Mississippi watershed fish, smallmouth are abundant throughout the Mississippi River and its tributaries. The smallmouth is also naturally found in many Minnesota lakes, though it is far less common than are largemouth bass. Unlike largemouth bass, smallmouth bass prefer to live in cool water and need to be in 60-degree or colder water in order to spawn. Like the largemouth bass, though, smallmouth males guard their nests until the fingerlings are at least two weeks old, guaranteeing a successful population in any area they find comfortable enough to settle.

Stream-based smallmouth bass are migratory fish, and in late fall these migrations take them 50 miles or more from their spawning grounds to their "hibernacula"—places where large groups of smallmouth bass crowd together under the ice, eating and moving little while they wait out the winter.

Largemouth and smallmouth bass season generally runs mid-May through mid-February of the following year; the dates change year to year and depend on what part of the state you intend to fish and which fish you are after. Contact the DNR for specific season dates. A six-fish possession limit of combined smallmouth and largemouth bass is in effect.

In the Metro, largemouth bass can be found in most Twin Cities–area lakes. Smallmouth bass are primarily found in the Mississippi River and its tributaries, and in some lakes in the outlying suburbs.

Catfish and bullheads

Catfish and their close cousin, the bullhead, are incredibly hardy fish that can live on just about anything. Both fish, especially bullheads, are often stocked in urban ponds and lakes that have low oxygen levels due to high concentrations of algae or detritus, where they can be fished for fun by kids and those with limited mobility. Minnesota has two native catfish species, channel and flathead, and three species of bullheads—black, brown, and yellow. Found throughout the state, the fish prefer fertile waters but respond well to stocking programs that put them in waters other than where their populations would naturally occur. During winter catfish and bullheads seek deep waters where boulders or logs provide refuge from currents, and they sink into a torpor so deep that silt often collects on their bodies.

Catfish have sharp spines along the leading edges of their dorsal (top) fin and the two pectoral (side) fins. Dispute rumors that such spines are poisonous, they are not; however, it is wise to be careful when handling a catfish to avoid the pain of getting poked by one or more spines.

Flathead catfish, also called "mud cat" or "yellow cat," are most commonly found in

Minnesota's large, slow-moving rivers, such as the Minnesota River, the St. Croix at Taylors Falls, and the Mississippi River below the Coon Rapids Dam. Distinguished by the broad, flat head from which it got its name, it is the largest catfish in Minnesota and has been reported to grow up to 100 pounds. Flatheads occupy deep pools with dense cover, such as logjams, and feed primarily on other fish—because they eat such great numbers of other fish, fish managers sometimes introduce them to lakes with large numbers of undesirable fish, such as carp, to try to control those populations. They have an acute sense of smell and therefore don't generally go for artificial lures, dead bait, or "stink bait," preferring live bait instead.

Channel catfish are steel gray and peppered with dark spots that disappear with age. Similar in appearance to the flathead, their distinguishing characteristic is their deeply forked tail. Much smaller than flatheads, rarely growing to exceed 20 pounds and usually averaging one to four pounds, channel cats can navigate much better in the faster waters of the Mississippi, St. Croix, Red, and St. Louis Rivers than flatheads do. While channel cats prefer deep, still, clean waters, they often move to murky waters to spawn, as the limited visibility protects their fry from predators.

Bullheads are the toughest of the catfish, requiring nothing but a puddle of warm water and some wet grass to survive. Ideally, though, these omnivorous fish prefer weedy, deep lakes and ponds with bottom cover (logs, thick weeds, etc.) for them to lay their eggs. All bullheads are relatively small members of the catfish family—yellow bullheads, found in southern Minnesota, weigh about a pound on average, while black bullheads and brown bullheads, naturally found in the Mississippi, Minnesota, St. Croix, and Red Rivers, usually don't grow to be longer than 10 inches.

Catfish are plentiful throughout the Metro and are not usually stocked in lakes or streams unless they're put there to control other fish populations; some are also stocked in inner-city ponds to give kids and those with limited mobility a chance to enjoy the sport of fishing.

Currently, the season for both bullhead and catfish is year-round. The DNR sets possession limits of 100 bullhead and 5 catfish. Contact the DNR for more information.

Crayfish

Licensed anglers and children under age 16 may take home up to 25 pounds of crayfish for personal use during crayfish season, as determined by the DNR. Crayfish cannot be sold as bait or for aquarium use, but you can use them for bait in the same body of water in which you caught the crayfish. Some areas—including the St. Croix National Scenic Riverway and Voyageurs National Park—do not allow fishing with live crayfish, even if caught there.

Muskie and tiger muskie

The muskellunge is one of the largest and most elusive fish in Minnesota and is also one of the most prized trophy fish sought by sport anglers. Closely related to the northern pike, muskies can grow to more than 40 inches long and weigh 30 pounds or more. Light-colored with dark bars running up and down their bodies, muskies can be silver, green, or brown, with large, strong, tooth-lined jaws for grasping prey.

As with northern pike, stocking lakes and waterways with muskies is unnecessary. They prefer larger fish as prey, so introducing them to a fishing lake only guarantees the eventual annihilation of the already-existing bass and trout populations. Muskies are also very particular about their environment, requiring well-oxygenated, cool water (60 degrees and cooler) that's clear enough for these sight-feeding fish.

Because muskies are perceived as trophy fish only, and because large muskies are scarce and usually very old, Minnesota imposes a possession limit of one muskie per licensed angler, with a minimum length of 40 inches on most lakes, but 48 inches on some, including some lakes in the metropolitan area.

i For information on which fish species are in Metro-area lakes, visit the DNR's Fish in the Neighborhood program on the Web at www.dnr.state .mn.us/fishing/fin/7_county.html.

See the DNR fishing regulations online for the latest updates on size limits. The muskie season generally runs early June through mid-February of the following year. Contact the DNR for specific season dates.

Tiger muskie, a sterile hybrid of the northern pike and the muskellunge, has characteristics of both parents. Tiger muskies have distinct bars that run along their light-colored bodies similar to the bars on a full muskie, fins and tail lobes rounded like a northern pike's, and cheekscale patterns that fall somewhere between those of both fish. The hybrid grows slightly faster than either pure-strain parent and can exceed 30 pounds in less than 10 years. Because of their quick maturation rate and because they are sterile, tiger muskie are often stocked in heavily fished lakes and streams throughout Minnesota, including some Metro area lakes.

Panfish

Panfish are not actually any particular species of fish but a blanket term referring to any number of small food fishes, especially those caught with hook and line and generally not available on the market. Minnesota has quite a few good-tasting "panfish," and it's common practice to take home a few of them to eat to make up for all the undersized trophy fish you caught and had to let go.

Crappies and bluegills—two of the most well-known and populous panfish in the Twin Cities—are probably caught for eating more often than any other fish in Minnesota. Crappies are easy to catch and produce sweet-tasting fillets, and they travel in schools, which make them even easier to find and catch. Bluegills are Minnesota's biggest and most popular panfish, found in about 65 percent of Minnesota's lakes and slow streams,

including the backwaters of the Mississippi and most lakes in the Metro. Though they occasionally exceed a pound, an 8-inch bluegill is considered a big fish.

Black and white crappies are among Minnesota's most popular panfish. Black crappies are much more widely distributed than white crappies and can be found in most lakes in the Twin Cities area. The two fish are very similar in appearance—in fact, the only real difference in appearance is that the black crappies are a slightly darker gray color than white crappies. Both fish rarely grow to weigh more than two pounds, and both species travel in large schools that are easy to spot.

Rock bass are stout and heavy compared with sunfish and crappies, measuring 10 inches on average and weighing around a pound. With red eyes and brassy-colored, black-spotted flanks, a rock bass is easy to identify when caught. Rock bass live in many streams and lakes in the Metro, generally preferring well-oxygenated, hard-water walleye lakes with boulder and sand bottoms.

The season for most of Minnesota's panfish runs year-round, with varying bag limits. Contact the DNR for more details.

Walleye, sauger, and perch

Walleye is the most sought-after fish in Minnesota, and anglers and restaurant patrons alike go crazy over the thick-filleted perch. Each year anglers in Minnesota catch and keep almost four million pounds of walleye, keeping the DNR's hands full stocking Minnesota lakes and rivers with the elusive fish.

The average walleye weighs one to two pounds, although some specimens caught have weighed in at as much as 10 pounds. The fish is torpedo shaped, with opaque, pearly eyes (for which the fish is named), and its color ranges from dark olive-brown to yellowish gold. Unlike its near cousin, the sauger, the walleye lacks spots on its dorsal fin, except for a dark patch on the rear base of the fin, which the sauger does not have. Also, the lower tip of the walleye's tail is white, while the lower lobe of the sauger's tail is all dark.

Both the walleye and the sauger are native fish, although walleye is much more commonly found in Minnesota's waterways than the sauger. Because of its popularity as a game and food fish, the walleye has been introduced to waterways all over the state and now occupies more than 1,600 lakes and 100 warmwater streams throughout the Midwest, including most of the lakes in the Metro. The walleye's low-level vision and sensitivity to light keep it hidden in the deep parts of lakes until dawn and dusk, at which point walleyes come to the shallows to feed. Their diet consists almost solely of other fish, and their biggest prey is yellow perch, which can't see well in the dark and are easily caught by the night-feeding walleye. Because of their sensitivity to light, walleyes are best caught at dawn or dusk, or when the skies are overcast.

Sauger are similar to walleye in appearance and habits, although their distribution throughout Minnesota is more limited. In the Metro, you are unlikely to catch one in most of the area's lakes, but there is a sauger presence in the Minnesota River, particularly around Fort Snelling State Park. Saugers seldom exceed three pounds and are generally much slimmer than walleye.

Yellow perch, cousin to both walleye and sauger as well as a shared common prey, are also found throughout the lakes and streams of the Twin Cities. They're often infected with parasites, and even the healthy ones are usually too small to reasonably consider eating. Walleye and yellow perch populations often coincide with each other, and lakes where the yellow population is strong are also home to big, healthy walleye—who may not be hungry enough to be interested in bait.

The season for walleye and sauger generally runs mid-May through mid-February of the following year, with a limit of six fish. The opening of walleye season is an annual event

i Kids under age 16 do not need a license to fish in Minnesota when accompanied by an adult with a fishing license.

i Don't know what you've caught? The DNR can send you free information describing in detail how to tell which fish is which, describing species' markings to the minutest detail to avoid confusion. Similar information is available on their Web site, www.dnr.state .mn.us.

in Minnesota, opened with much fanfare by the governor casting a line in a chosen out-state lake with cameras clicking and TV cameras rolling. Perch season is year-round, with a limit of 10 fish per day. Contact the DNR for more details.

Harmful Aquatic Species

Several plant and animal species introduced to Minnesota waters over the past century have caused severe damage to native species populations. Among these are zebra mussels, Eurasian watermilfoil, ruffe, and round goby.

Eurasian watermilfoil is a water plant similar in appearance to duckweed that reproduces quickly in shallow water and can interfere with water recreation as well as harm oxygen levels in lakes and ponds. Even the tiniest of fragments clinging to boats and trailers can spread the prolific plant from one body of water to another. Zebra mussels, originally from Asia, can quickly displace native mussels, disrupt lake ecosystems, and clog industrial equipment. Their microscopic larvae can accidentally be transported in bait buckets or by moving a boat from one confined body of water to another. The best way to prevent the spread of Eurasian watermilfoil and Zebra mussels is to make sure you drain or pump *all* water from your boat before moving it from one body of water to another, and dump bait buckets on land and dry them thoroughly before putting them back in water. If you leave your boat in the water for more than a day in areas with zebra mussels (including the St. Croix River in the eastern Metro), you must wash your boat with a high-pressure hose and hot water and remove any attached mussels.

Ruffe is a small, perchlike fish from Europe that has taken over parts of Duluth harbor, displacing many native fish. Also from Europe is the bottom-dwelling round goby, which has displaced many fish in Minnesota lakes and is a serious threat to the fisheries in the Great Lakes, which it has already entered. The spread of both fish can be attributed to being transported from one body of water to another in bait buckets and livewells.

Ice Fishing

Ice fishing is a longtime tradition in Minnesota. The basic principle of ice fishing is to walk out on a deep lake with enough ice cover to safely support your weight (ice should be a minimum of 6 inches thick for walking, a foot or more for vehicles), cut a hole in the ice with an ice auger, and sink a hook through it with hopes of luring the few fish that aren't in a state of torpor to take your bait. Over the years this simple idea has expanded to include portable ice fishing houses for anglers to sit in comfort while waiting for fish to bite, equipped with televisions, suspended heating elements, radios, furniture, and the requisite cooler stuffed with beer.

Your best bet in ice fishing is to stake out lakes and rivers known for having good muskie populations, as these fish actually get more energetic as the weather grows cooler.

Some Metro-area parks with lakes deep enough (and enough lively coldwater fish) for ice fishing include Baker Park Preserve, Bald Eagle–Otter Lakes, Bryant Lake, Carver Park Preserve, Como, Coon Rapids Dam, Fish Lake, French, Hidden Falls–Crosby Farm, Lake Byllesby, Lake George, Lake Minnewashta, Lake Rebecca Park Reserve, Lebanon Hills, Long Lake Regional Park, Martin-Island-Linwood Lakes, Minneapolis Chain of Lakes, Nokomis Hiawatha, Phalen, Rice Creek/Chain of Lakes, Snail Lake, and Theodore Wirth (see the Parks chapter for individual park listings).

Metro Fishing

Both Minneapolis and St. Paul have a surprising number of good fishing lakes within city limits, as do their nearby suburbs. More than 100 lakes and rivers in the Metro area are regularly stocked and monitored by the Minnesota DNR, with the purpose of providing safe, fun fishing lakes for urbanites, children, and those with limited mobility.

Some of the best fishing lakes in Minneapolis are Lake Calhoun, Lake of the Isles, Cedar Lake, Lake Harriet, and Lake Nokomis. Lake Calhoun, located about 3 blocks west of Lake Street and Hennepin Avenue South, is a deep (82 feet deep in spots) fishing and boating lake with largemouth bass, northern pike, crappie, sunfish, tiger muskie, walleye, perch, catfish, and carp swimming in its waters. Rental canoes are available at the concession stand, which also sells fast food but no bait. Calhoun has a couple of great fishing piers and three swimming beaches.

Connected to Lake Calhoun by a canoe-navigable channel is Lake of the Isles, located by land just south of Franklin Avenue and 1 mile west of Hennepin Avenue. Many of the same types of fish as in Lake Calhoun are in these waters, with a huge population of sunfish and crappies, much to the delight of the many species of waterfowl that also frequent the lakes.

Cedar Lake, located just south of Interstate 394 and east of Minnesota Highway 100 and connected to Lake of the Isles by a winding channel, is stocked with largemouth bass, northern pike, crappie, sunfish, tiger muskies, perch, carp, and catfish and is a great shore fishing spot due to the deep water right next to shore. Anyone willing to bushwhack along the brushy banks can usually find some good-size largemouth bass hanging out along the lake's north shore.

Lake Harriet, another great Minneapolis fishing and boating lake with waters as deep as 87 feet in places, is located 1 mile west of Lyndale Avenue just north of 50th Street and just south of Lake Calhoun. Shore fishing at Lake Harriet is surprisingly good, considering that most of the really deep water is near the middle of the lake. Muskies, bass, sunfish, perch, catfish, and walleye can be caught here. The lake has a fishing pier and a boat rental facility nearby as well as a swimming beach and playground.

Lake Nokomis, located south of Minnehaha Parkway between Cedar and Hiawatha Avenues, is one of the best crappie lakes in the Twin Cities. Because it gets more sun and warms up quickly, the north shore fishing pier is the best spot to stake out in the spring. Also found in Lake Nokomis are northern pike, sunfish, tiger muskie, carp, bullhead, perch, and walleye.

St. Paul has a couple of excellent fishing spots for more serious anglers—meaning no picnic area, no playground, and little or no paved paths leading down to the water. Hidden Falls Regional Park, located just south of Ford Parkway, is an excellent summer fishing spot for walleye, catfish, crappie, sunfish, white bass, smallmouth and largemouth bass, northern pike, and carp. If the water level is high, anglers can fish from the grassy picnic area, but if it's low you must descend a steep bank to reach the water.

Pike Island and Snelling Lake, both located in St. Paul's Fort Snelling State Park, are two rustic yet excellent fishing holes. Pike Island is good for early-season walleye fishing, as the fish pass here while moving upstream to spawn below Ford Dam. The best fishing is where the channel north of Pike Island meets the Mississippi River, where you can catch carp, catfish, smallmouth bass, walleye, sauger, white bass, and crappie. Snelling Lake has some nice paved paths leading to the shoreline, although to get to the best fishing areas, you have to stand in the marsh. There's also a good fishing pier here, from which you can catch largemouth bass, crappie, sunfish, northern pike, carp, and bullhead.

Other metro area parks that have areas set aside for fishing include Anoka County Riverfront, Baker Park Preserve, Bald Eagle–Otter Lakes, Baylor, Bryant Lake, Carver Park Preserve, Central Mississippi Riverfront, Cleary Lake, Como, Coon Rapids Dam, Fish Lake, French, Lake Byllesby, Lake Elmo Park Reserve, Lake George, Lake Minnetonka Regional Park, Lake Minnewashta, Lake Rebecca Park Reserve, Lebanon Hills, Lilydale–Harriet Island, Long Lake Regional Park, Rice Creek/Chain of Lakes, Rice Creek–West Regional Trail, Rum River Central, Snail Lake, and Theodore Wirth.

Becoming an Outdoors Woman in Minnesota (888-646-6367), based in the DNR at 500 Lafayette Road in St. Paul, and **Women Anglers of Minnesota** (www.womenanglers mn.com) offer angling, ice fishing, and shore fishing classes for women interested in either taking up the sport or finding other women to fish with.

DAY TRIPS AND WEEKEND GETAWAYS

Any way you point your vehicle, you're sure to end up somewhere extraordinary. Minnesota is dotted with hundreds of little towns settled in the early days of the state, and just about all of them are worth exploring. Although there are more than enough attractions and sights in the Twin Cities to fill up your time, there's nothing like a good, long road trip through the countryside to clear one's mind of the hustle and bustle of the Metro.

The best time to hit the road is early spring, the last two weeks of April and the first two weeks of May, or when autumn is in full swing, the last two weeks of September and the first two weeks of October. There is nowhere better to see the changing of the seasons than out in the country, amid the old hardwood forests that line the state highways and the charming old farmhouses that dot the gently rolling fields and coulees outside the Cities. Here is a sampling of the road trips well worth taking from the Twin Cities.

DULUTH

Located on the shore of Lake Superior and a major shipping port, Duluth was once the fastest-growing city in the country and was expected to surpass Chicago in size by 1870. When Jay Cooke, the wealthy Philadelphia land speculator, picked Duluth as the terminus of the Northern Pacific, Lake Superior, and Mississippi Railroads, Duluth's future appeared prosperous. Unfortunately, Jay Cooke's empire crumbled when the stock market crashed in 1873, and Duluth almost disappeared from the map. By the late 1800s, with the continued boom in lumber and iron mining and with the railroads completed, this shipping port again bloomed. By the turn of the 20th century, there were almost 100,000 inhabitants, and it

was again a thriving community. At its economic height, more millionaires lived in Duluth than anywhere else in the world.

Much of this history is reflected in present-day Duluth, both in the beautiful architecture and in the huge ships that serve as floating museums. The signs that Duluth is once again experiencing an economic revival have never been more obvious. Most of the old warehouses by the Maritime Center and along the harbor have been converted into picturesque shopping centers and family-owned restaurants, many with the original facades left intact. Uphill from busy Canal Park Drive, the streets are lined with row houses and redbrick churches, many of which have been closed up but left intact. While driving up the steep roads in Duluth is a little nerve-racking (especially in winter), the harbor looks absolutely stunning from the heights. An incredible stretch of blue water dotted with white sailboats and gigantic ore boats greets you, while the far, far North Shore of Lake Superior is barely visible even on the clearest days.

For more information on the sights and attractions of Duluth, call the **Duluth Convention & Visitor Bureau** at (218) 722-4011 or (800) 4-DULUTH, or check out its extensive Web page at www.visitduluth.com.

Getting There

Getting to Duluth from the Twin Cities is easy. Just take Interstate 35E north or Interstate 35W north (depending on where you are in the Twin Cities). Note: Until construction is completed on the new I-35W bridge just north of downtown Minneapolis, use Interstate 94 East to Minnesota Highway 180 north until it merges with I-35W north. The highways merge into I-35 north of the Metro, and the interstate shoots straight north 150 miles to Duluth.

Attractions

Most of Duluth's attractions are located around the Duluth Harbor, so it's easy to walk from one to the next to make a full day of sightseeing. **The Great Lakes Aquarium** (GLA) at 353 Harbor Drive (218-740-FISH; www.glaquarium.org) houses the largest freshwater aquarium in America. While the main focus of the GLA is the gigantic aquarium that is home to every known species of fish from Lake Superior (including several giant sturgeons), there are also many hands-on exhibits geared toward children. One of the favorites is a joystick-operated microscope hooked up to a video monitor that's focused on a tank full of fish. Kids also love the very friendly otter on the first floor that shows off for visitors.

Right next door to the aquarium at 301 Harbor Drive is the S.S. *William A. Irvin* (218-727–0022; www.williamairvin.com), a giant ore ship turned museum. The ship is open for tours Memorial Day through mid-October, with a special "Ship of Ghouls" exhibit around Halloween. For serious maritime buffs there's also the **Lake Superior Maritime Visitor Center,** 600 Lake Avenue South (218-720-5200; www.lsmma.com), owned and operated by the U.S. Army Corps of Engineers. Movies, model ships, and rotating exhibits are housed both inside and outside the free museum year-round. The museum also hosts a boat watchers' hotline (218-722-6489) and has a Web cam trained on the harbor.

At 506 West Michigan Street inside the depot is the **Lake Superior Railroad Museum** (218-722-1273; www.lsrm.org), which houses a rotating exhibit of historic railway cars, locomotives, and engines, most of which can be boarded for a close-up view of turn-of-the-20th-century machinery. On permanent display is a dining car china exhibit, the William Crooks (Minnesota's oldest engine), and the oldest known rotary snowplow in existence. The depot is also home to the **Duluth Chil-**

i The University of Minnesota–Duluth offers reasonably priced accommodations for senior citizens during the summer months. Call the campus at (218) 726-8222 for more information and rates.

dren's Museum (218-733-7543; www.duluthchildrensmuseum.org). The depot is full of hands-on exhibits for kids as well as education programs and tours, the Duluth Art Institute, the St. Louis Historical Society, and a performing arts wing where community and touring ballet companies, plays, and concerts take place throughout the year.

At 72nd Avenue West and Grand Avenue is the **Lake Superior Zoo** (218-730-4900; www.lszoo.org), home to more than two dozen endangered and threatened species from around the world. Admittedly on the small side, the zoo is a preservation project and educational tool as well as a tourist attraction.

For a little highbrow entertainment, check out the **Karpeles Manuscript Library Museum** at 902 East First Street (218-728-0630; www.rain.org/~karpeles). This museum displays a rotating selection of original manuscripts from all over the world, including the original draft of the Bill of Rights and Einstein's description of his general theory of relativity. The **Tweed Museum of Art,** located on the University of Minnesota–Duluth campus at 1201 Ordean Court (218-726-7823; www.d.umn.edu/tma), features nine separate galleries and exhibits with artwork dating from the 15th century. For a glimpse of what life was like for the well-to-do during the Iron Range boom, the historic **Glensheen Estate** at 3300 London Road (888-454-GLEN; www.glensheen.org), holds tours of its seven-acre grounds throughout the year (call for times and reservations).

For wintertime fun head to **Spirit Mountain** (800-642-6377; www.spiritmt.com), just outside Duluth, for cross-country and downhill skiing and, of course, snowboarding. Spirit Mountain has five chairlifts (including a covered one for skiers wanting to take a little break from the cold), and the 175-acre site

Duluth's historic lift bridge allows freighters from all over the world to reach the city's inner harbor.
TODD R. BERGER

has 23 separate downhill runs geared for all levels of skiers and two huge freestyle parks, one for skiers and one for snowboarders. Spirit Mountain has all sorts of package plans for extended stays in the area, including discounts on lodging, meals, and lift tickets. Call area hotels and motels directly for package information.

Accommodations and Camping

Right on the waterfront and steps away from Canal Park Drive, the following hotels are relatively new buildings designed with easy access to the hot spots of Duluth in mind. **The Canal Park Lodge,** at 250 Canal Park Drive (800-777-8560; www.canalparklodge.com), features an indoor heated pool and hot tub, and all guests receive a complimentary breakfast each morning. The **Hampton Inn** at 310 Canal Park Drive (218-720-3000 or www .hamptoninn.com) offers the same amenities with a full hot breakfast, while the **Inn on**

Lake Superior at 350 Canal Park Drive (218-726-1111 or 888–668–4352; www.innonlake superior.com) offers a lakefront view with its balcony suites. Downtown lodging is more affordable than the lakefront hotels. At 131 West Second Street is the **Best Western Downtown** (218-727-6851 or 800-570- 9802; www.bestwestern.com), located close to the skyway system that connects downtown Duluth. Two blocks away at 200 West First Street is the **Holiday Inn** (218-722-1202 or 800-477-7089; www.hiduluth.com), which has two pools and a sauna on the premises. Also downtown is the **Radisson Hotel** at 505 West Superior Street (218-727-8981 or 888-201- 1718; www.radisson.com/duluthmn), **Fitger's Inn** at 600 East Superior Street (218-722-8826 or 888-FITGERS; www.fitgers.com), and the **Voyageur Lakewalk Inn** at 333 East Superior Street (218-722-3911 or 800-258-3911; www .visitduluth.com/ voyageur).

Duluth has many beautiful bed-and-breakfasts designed to make guests feel right at home. In town is the **Mathew S. Burrows 1890 Inn** at 1632 East First Street (218-724-4991 or 800-789-1890; www.1890inn.com), the **Ellery House** at 28 South 21st Avenue East (218-724-7639 or 800-355-3794; www.elleryhouse.com), and the **Firelight Inn** on Oregon Creek at 2211 East Third Street (218-724-0272 or 888-724-0273; www.firelightinn.com). All of these establishments are historic landmarks built around the turn of the 20th century and furnished with period antiques.

While there aren't any campsites in Duluth proper, there are several notable ones right outside the city limits. Ten miles south of Duluth is **Buffalo Valley Camping**, located at 2590 Guss Road, Proctor (218-628-7019; www.buffalohouseduluth.com), which has a full bar and restaurant at the campground as well as showers and electrical, sewer, and water hookups. Take exit 239 off I-35 and you'll find the **Knife Island Campground** at 234 Minnesota Highway 61, Esko (218-879-6063), located right in the middle of the ghost town of Slateville and the adjacent abandoned logging camp. Water and electrical hookups are available at almost all of the 30 available sites, and firewood is provided by the campground.

Shopping

Unless you're just out for groceries, most of your Duluth shopping is going to take place around the museums and walkways in the Canal Park Drive and Lake Avenue area. Here original warehouse structures from Duluth's manufacturing past have been converted into shopping malls and restaurants, while new structures have been built to integrate perfectly with the brickwork of the older buildings.

If you're into antiquing, the **Canal Park Antique Mall** at 310 Lake Avenue South (218-720-3940) is your best bet. The largest antiques and collectibles mall in Duluth is where you're sure to find that perfect knick-knack for yourself or souvenir to take home to family and friends. If you prefer collecting old literature, **Old Town Antiques & Books** at

102 East Superior Street (218-722-5426) is a good place to stop.

And while you're on Superior Street, try out **Torke Weihnachten Christmas & Chocolates** at 637 East Superior Street (218-723-1225 or 800-729-1223) for both specialty candies and European Christmas ornaments. Check out the wonderful **Electric Fetus,** 12 East Superior Street (218-722-9970), for the best selection of records, CDs, and tapes in this part of the state (visit its sister store in Minneapolis when you come back).

Along the Canal Park area is the **DeWitt-Seitz Marketplace** at 394 Lake Avenue South, home to both **Hepzibah's Sweet Shoppe** (218-722-5049), with its wonderful homemade and imported candies, and toy and gift store **J. Skylark Company** (218-722-3794). Outside the mall and along Lake Avenue are even more gift shops—this is a great place to catch up on your window-shopping in the summer.

Restaurants

Traditional American fare dominates the restaurant scene in Duluth, with steakhouses on the high end of the scale and hamburger and french-fry joints at the low end. In the **Fitger's Brewhouse** complex at 600 East Superior Street is **Fitger's Brewhouse Brewery and Grill** (218-279-BREW; www.brewhouse.net). The casual brewpub offers live music entertainment most nights, home-brewed beer, and gourmet sandwiches. For something a little more exotic, try **Taste of Saigon** in the Dewitt-Seitz Marketplace at 394 Lake Avenue South (218-727-1598)—its food and selection are as good as the portions are large and generous. For late-night dining and carousing, the **Top of the Harbor** at the Radisson Hotel on 505 West Superior Street (218-727-8981) is a rotating restaurant that gives you a full view of the city every 72 minutes. The Radisson also has the **Fifth Avenue Lounge** at street level.

An invaluable resource to pick up when in Duluth is the local free paper, *Ripsaw*—each issue has dining information and a calendar of events that is informative to even the most experienced of Duluth visitors. Well written and fun to read even if you don't need help picking out something to do for the day, *Ripsaw* is available at most retail centers and newsstands around town.

NEW ULM

Founded in 1857 by two German immigration societies, New Ulm reflects the town's German heritage. The shadow of the **Hermann Monument,** set high on a hill just outside the business district, rises in the distance and is visible from just about anywhere in town. Often referred to as the "City of Charm and Tradition," New Ulm's colorful history is reflected in its attractions and many seasonal festivals.

Getting There

New Ulm is easily accessible by taking U.S. Highway 169 south from the Twin Cities to Minnesota Highway 99 west. From there, go west on U.S. Highway 14 (the Laura Ingalls Wilder Highway), which will take you into downtown New Ulm. The town is about 100 miles from the Metro.

For further information, brochures, or directions, be sure to visit the **New Ulm Area Chamber of Commerce/Visitors Information Center** at 1 North Minnesota Street (507-233-4300 or 888-4639856; www.newulm.com), located a short walking distance from most of the area attractions, shopping, and restaurants.

Attractions

At the forefront of New Ulm's attractions is the **Hermann Monument.** Representing the Teutonic hero, Hermann Arminius of Cherusci, the monument overlooks the city from the bluff on Center and Monument Streets. Dedicated in 1897, the monument stands 102 feet tall in Hermann Heights Park—a beautiful park with a panoramic view of the city below. The Hermann Monument is open Memorial Day through Labor Day and costs a nominal fee of $1, but you may visit the adjoining Hermann Heights Park year-round for free.

Another attraction is the **Glockenspiel/ Schonlau Park** at Fourth and Minnesota Streets. The glockenspiel is one of the few freestanding carillon clock towers in the world. The glockenspiel chimes at noon, 3:00, and 5:00 p.m. daily and features a revolving stage of 3-foot-high characters that depict the city's history.

Brown County Historical Society and Museum at Center and Broadway Streets (507-233-2616; www.browncountyhistory mnusa.org) provides an excellent overview of the history of the New Ulm area. The building was once the New Ulm Post Office, and it was placed on the National Register of Historic Places in 1976. The Brown County Historical Society houses three floors of regional history: a Dakota Indians exhibit, a Brown County settlers area called "Made in Brown County," seasonal displays, and much more. All of the information is insightfully presented with great detail.

New Ulm is filled with beautiful historic homes, but the **John Lind Home,** at the intersection of Center and State Streets (507-354-8802), is especially aesthetically pleasing and historically significant. This lovely structure is an excellent example of Queen Anne–style architecture and was the home of the 14th governor of Minnesota and the first Swedish member of the United States Congress, Minnesota representative John Lind. Afternoon tours are held daily in summer, Friday through Sunday in spring and fall, and by appointment in winter.

Beer brewing was New Ulm's first industry. The **August Schell Brewing Company,** 1860 Schell Road (507-354-5528 or 800-770-5020; www.schellsbrewery.com), was founded in 1860, and since its inception Schell's has produced premium-quality crafted and specialty beers. Tours of the brewery, gardens, and park are available daily Memorial Day through Labor Day, and on weekends the rest of the year. Schell's now owns the Grain Belt brand of beer, a well-known Minnesota brew of American lager formerly made in the Twin Cities. If you can't make it to Schell's Brewery, be sure to visit one of New Ulm's restaurants and bars for a bottle or draught of Schell's Bock, Dark, or Original, or of the 1919 Root Beer it also produces.

New Ulm has a wealth of additional attractions. For lovers of the classic children's book *Millions of Cats,* author Wanda Gag's childhood home, the **Wanda Gag Home,** 226 North Washington Street (507-359-2632), is open on weekends in June, July, August, and December and during the rest of the year by appointment.

Yet another attraction of historical significance is the **Turner Hall,** at the intersection of First Street South and State Street (507-354-4916). The New Turnverein opened in 1856 and was dedicated to improving the health of New Ulmers through gymnastics and exercise. Parts of the Turner Hall building date from 1865, including 70 feet of murals in the Ratskeller, a bar and restaurant. The Turner Hall is free and open daily.

New Ulm has a full slate of annual festivals and events. New Ulm celebrates Christmas with traditional German hoopla. Included are the **Christmas Parade of Lights,** which celebrates the arrival of Santa Claus on the Friday evening after Thanksgiving and the traditional German St. Nicholas Day, December 6; **Fasching,** a German version of Mardi Gras, occurs annually in late February or early March concurrent with Schell's **Bock Beer Fest.** Summer has an active festival schedule with both **Bavarian Blast and Polka Days** at the end of July, plus **River Blast** in Riverside Park over Labor Day weekend, which features a floating parade. **Oktoberfest** in October features traditional German food, music, and, of course, beer.

Accommodations

New Ulm has ample accommodations, including bed-and-breakfasts as well as hotels. As with all other aspects of New Ulm, most of the accommodations have a German flavor.

The Holiday Inn, at 2101 South Broadway Street (507-359-2941 or 877-359-2941; www .holidayinn.com), is the largest hotel in New Ulm. It hosts Oktoberfest for two weekends each fall and has a swimming pool, restau-

rant, and cocktail lounge. The **Budget Holiday Motel,** 1316 North Broadway Street (507-354-4145), was renovated in 2002. Another New Ulm hotel is the **Colonial Inn** at 1315 North Broadway Street (507-354-3128 or 888-215-2143), a relatively small, 24-unit hotel that offers free HBO during your stay.

The New Ulm area has many bed-and-breakfasts. The **W. W. Smith Inn** at 101 Linden Street SW in nearby Sleepy Eye (507-794-5661 or 800-799-5661), for example, is located 14 miles from New Ulm. The W. W. Smith Inn has much to offer lovers of bed-and-breakfasts. Listed on the National Register of Historic Places, this elegant Queen Anne structure was constructed in 1901 for a wealthy area banker. In New Ulm, **Deutsche Strasse B&B** at 404 South German Street (507-354-2005 or 866-226-9856; www.deutschestrasse.com), offers five rooms, two with queen-size beds and three with full-size beds, and all with private baths. Also included is a full breakfast.

Shopping

If you're looking for specialty shops with a German flair, you'll find them in New Ulm. New Ulm boasts businesses devoted to antiques, crafts, sweets, dolls, and sausages. The vast majority of shops are conveniently located on Minnesota and Broadway Streets, in the heart of beautiful old downtown. **Edelweiss Flower Haus,** 304 North Minnesota Street (800-881-8898; www.edelweissflower haus.com), specializes in flowers, and shoppers can watch floral artists create arrangements before their eyes. In addition, there's **NadelKunst, Ltd.,** 212 North Minnesota Street (507-354-8708), specializing in knitting, crocheting, beading, and cross-stitch.

Of course, New Ulm has stores that specialize in German merchandise: the **Guten Tag Haus,** 127 North Minnesota Street (507-233-4287; www.gutentaghaus.com), and **Domeier's New Ulm German Store,** 1020 South Minnesota Street (507-354-4231). Unlike the aforementioned businesses, Domeier's is located 10 blocks south of the downtown business district.

i New Ulm shops have limited hours, with many closing as early as 5:00 p.m., so call ahead or arrive early to maximize your New Ulm shopping experience.

The Christmas Haus, 203 North Minnesota Street, and **Lambrecht's**, 119 North Minnesota Street, share an owner, a phone, and a Web site (507-233-4350; www .lambrechtsgifts.net). The former specializes in German and seasonal goodies, and the latter has two entire floors of flowers and gift items, from greeting cards and framed prints to lace, lamps, and shirts. At **August Schell's Brewing Company**, 1860 Schell Road (507-354-5528; www.schellsbrewery.com), there is something for every shopper. Naturally, there are many Schell and Grain Belt clothing items and collectibles, plus gourmet food and novelty gifts.

Restaurants

Surprisingly, German food does not dominate New Ulm's restaurant options. German food is often included with traditional American fare. Certainly the place to start when discussing New Ulm's restaurants is **Veigel's Kaiserhoff**, 221 North Minnesota Street (507-359-2071). The Kaiserhoff's most popular dish is the barbecue ribs. The menu also includes many German favorites such as bratwursts, schnitzels, landjaeger, and German chocolate cake. Don't forget to wash down the Kaiserhoff's cuisine with a delicious Schell's beer, brewed in New Ulm. Another restaurant with heavy German influences is **Otto's Feierhaus and Bier Stube** at 2101 South Broadway Avenue (507-359-5300). Otto's is conveniently located for travelers in the New Ulm Holiday Inn and serves American food and German specialties.

Traditional American food is popular in New Ulm. **Hy-Vee's Kitchen** in a grocery store at 2015 South Broadway Avenue (507-354-8255), is a local cafe-style restaurant. The **Ulmer Cafe**, 115 North Minnesota Street (507-354-8122), is right in the middle of New Ulm's shopping area and features breakfast and lunch in a hometown cafe.

For families, **Happy Joe's**, 1700 North Broadway Street (507-359-9811), specializes in food kids and adults love, such as pizza and chicken. There is also a smorgasbord at Happy Joe's, which outside Minnesota is called an all-you-can-eat buffet. **DJ's**, 1200 North Broadway Street (507-354-3843), is another family diner featuring lunch and dinner specials daily.

Main Jiang House is a Chinese restaurant at 400 North Minnesota Street (507-354-1218). New Ulm also has several sandwich, burger, pizza, and taco chain restaurants.

NORTH SHORE SCENIC DRIVE

The North Shore Scenic Drive, officially U.S. Highway 61, is lined with rental cottages, bed-and-breakfasts, RV parks, and motels, while the shore is dotted with rent-by-the-day boat docks and marinas. The first town outside Duluth is Two Harbors, a virtual mecca of restaurants and gift shops, while the residences themselves are relatively new and tucked away some distance from the downtown area. Two Harbors is a good place to sit down and get a bite to eat or rest for the night before heading on to the beautiful parks that make up the attractions in this area, or to pick up a bag of regionally grown wild rice, fresh honey, fruit preserves, or a lighthouse-shaped refrigerator magnet.

Getting There

The North Shore Scenic Drive begins in Duluth and stretches 154 miles to Grand Portage, near the Canadian border. To reach the drive from the Twin Cities, take either I-35W or I-35E north to I-35 all the way to Duluth. I-35 ends at Minnesota Highway 61, which is the North Shore Scenic Drive. The beginning of the drive is about 150 miles from the Twin Cities.

Attractions

Thirteen miles northeast of Two Harbors on US 61 is **Gooseberry Falls State Park** (218-834-3855; www.dnr.state.mn.us/state_parks), which holds an amazing series of relatively untouched waterfalls that are open to the public to walk out on—literally. This is not recommended for those struggling with a fear of heights, as it's possible to climb to the very top of the waterfalls via hiking trails and walkways and walk right to the edge of the rocky face to peer over the edge—without the presence of handrails or safety mesh. A visitor center features exhibits on Lake Superior and the history of the park itself.

Split Rock Lighthouse State Park (218-226-6377; www.dnr.state.mn.us/state_parks), also on US 61 about 20 miles northeast of Two Harbors, surrounds the lighthouse that has been a landmark on the Lake Superior shore since 1910. Now a state-run historic site, it and the neighboring lighthouse keeper's houses and fog signal building have been restored to 1920s appearance and opened to visitors and tour groups. Call the lighthouse directly for tours. The attached History Center shows films and exhibits on the lighthouse, commercial fishing, and shipwrecks through most of the summer.

For more energetic travelers, the **Superior Hiking Trail** winds through the forested ridgeline of the coast for 200 miles. There are many small and midsize fishing lakes and tiny craft shops to be found all along the drive that parallels the trail—for more information, contact the Superior Hiking Trail Association in Two Harbors: (218) 834-2700; www.shta.org.

Accommodations and Camping

The Lighthouse Bed & Breakfast, at the harbor in Two Harbors (218-834-4814 or 888-832-5606; www.lighthousebb.org), is one of the few B&Bs on the Great Lakes housed inside a working lighthouse, built in 1892. The B&B has four rooms decorated with period antiques, and all have a view of Lake Superior. For more pedestrian comforts, **AmericInn Lodge and Suites,** 1088 US 61 West, Two Harbors (218-834-3000), offers guests an indoor pool, hot tub, and sauna, while just outside Two Harbors on the shoreline is the **Grand Superior Lodge,** 2826 US 61 (218-834-3796 or 800-627-9565), a beautiful resort with individual log homes, an on-site restaurant and cocktail lounge, and an indoor pool and spa.

Shopping

It's a Minnesota tradition to make the trek up to the North Shore every summer for one reason—wild rice. The tiny one-quarter pound bags of wild rice you get at the supermarket in the Cities usually cost you a couple of dollars, while just about every store in Two Harbors on up sells four-pound bags for around $8. Wild rice is much richer than your typical white variety rice and adds a wonderful, hearty dimension to soups, poultry stuffing, and anything else that calls for rice.

All along the North Shore Drive can be found tiny houses converted into shops where you can buy anything from jars of wild clover honey to homemade preserves to lighthouse-shaped refrigerator magnets and, of course, fish bait. One is **Beaver Bay Agate Shop and Museum,** 1003 Main Street in Beaver Bay (218-226-4847), which is exactly what it sounds like, with jewelry and key chains made from agates found along the Lake Superior shoreline as well as permanent displays of man-made artifacts and geological marvels found in the area.

The remote shops in the small towns dotting the North Shore Highway all the way to the Canadian border often sell unique and memorable items and are worth a browsing stop. In particular, the beautiful town of Grand Marais, about 110 miles northeast of Duluth on US 61, is a haven for many artists, and the downtown region is alive with galleries and studios.

Restaurants

If you're more comfortable dining at familiar restaurant chains, then Two Harbors is the place to stop before heading on up the Lake Superior coast. Pretty much every fast-food chain in America is represented here, including Dairy Queen, Pizza Hut, and Culvers. If you're more interested in sticking to family owned-and-run establishments, there are plenty of those to choose from, too, either in ℹ️ Keep an old plastic credit card–type hotel key in your wallet in case you find yourself with an ice-covered windshield and no scraper.

Two Harbors or along the North Shore Drive. For burgers and sandwiches, and breakfast all day long, try **Judy's Cafe** at 623 Seventh Avenue, Two Harbors (218-834-4802), or for traditional North Shore smoked fish as well as pickled herring, salmon spread, and cheese, head to **Lou's Fish House,** 1319 US 61, Two Harbors (218-834-5254). For a north woods dining experience, try the **Northern Lights Restaurant** on US 61 in Beaver Bay (218-226-3012), with wild game and Scandinavian dishes, and for informal, family-style meals, there's **Our Place** on Minnesota Highway 1, Finland (218-353-7343). **Vanilla Bean Bakery and Cafe,** 812 Seventh Avenue, Two Harbors (218-834-3714), is a cozy bistro for designer coffees or meals.

RED WING

Perhaps best known as the home of the Red Wing Shoe Company, Red Wing is a charming Mississippi River town with a beautiful, regal downtown composed of refurbished old warehouse buildings and absolutely amazing churches that date from 1855. Set deep in the river valley surrounded by beautiful fishing lakes, scenic hilltop views, streams, picturesque farms, and apple orchards, Red Wing has the added advantage of being populated by some of the most genuinely friendly and helpful people you'll ever meet.

Getting There

There are several ways to get to Red Wing. The principal ways are via US 61 from St. Paul, which is quite scenic south of Hastings, or via

ℹ️ No tickets are sold at the Red Wing Amtrak station, so make sure you buy a round-trip ticket at the Twin Cities station.

train from the Amtrak station in St. Paul (730 Transfer Road; 800-872-7245) all the way to the historic **Old Milwaukee Depot** at 420 Levee Street in Red Wing. You may want to stop by the depot while in Red Wing anyway, since it doubles as the visitor center and there are lots of maps, brochures, and free local newspapers with restaurant coupons and information on events and happenings around town. The depot, established in 1904, is located next to downtown Red Wing and all its sights, too, so there's no need to worry about transportation unless you have plans outside of town.

If you opt to drive, a nice alternative to US 61 is to cross the river just before Hastings and jump on Wisconsin Highway 35 south at Prescott. Follow WI 35 to Bay City, and then turn on to U.S. Highway 63 west to cross the Mississippi to Red Wing between Hager City and Bay City. WI 35 is a two-lane highway that passes through beautiful old hardwood forests and gently sloping farmlands dotted with old farmhouses, stone silos, and shallow creeks. It also roughly follows the Mississippi River here, providing spectacular views of the waterway and the bluffs across the river on the Minnesota side.

For more information about the area, contact the **Red Wing Visitors and Convention Bureau,** 420 Levee Street; (651) 385-5934 or (800) 498-3444; www.redwing.org.

Attractions

A good place to start exploring Red Wing is **Bay Point Park** on Levee Street. Located right on the Mississippi River, this is also the home of **Boathouse Village,** one of the only remaining "gin pole" boathouse installations in the country. The village looks just like a bunch of little houses floating in the water, with floating walkways connecting the "neighborhood." Close by is **Levee Park,** located just behind the historic 1904 Milwaukee Depot. Both parks have picnic tables and play areas for kids.

At the corner of Third Street and East Avenue at 443 West Third Street is the historic **Sheldon Theatre** (651-388-8700 or 800-899-5759; www.sheldontheatre.org). First opened in 1904, the theater was such an unabashed collection of sculpture, arches, marble columns, and gilded plaster detail, it was once described as a jewel box. Nowadays the 466-seat theater is used for everything, including children's plays, concerts, acrobats, and films. If you just want to walk in and look at the inside of this beautiful building, the helpful men and women at the ticket counter will gladly let you in to take a peek. Guided tours are offered on Saturday. Call ahead for tour times.

Red Wing has its share of museums, including the somewhat unconventional **Red Wing Shoe Museum,** 314 Main Street (651-388-8211; www.RedWingshoe.com). Owned and operated by Red Wing Shoes, the museum treats visitors to exhibits imparting the history of the company as well as an interactive display that helps you learn the process of making a pair of shoes. There are other displays, too, including a kiosk in which you can match occupation to shoe. About 9 blocks away at 1166 Oak Street is the **Goodhue County Historical Museum** (651-388-6024; www.goodhuehistory.mus.mn.us), which contains more than 150,000 paintings, photographs, geological and natural history displays, and artifacts concerning Goodhue County from prehistory to the present.

At the end of East Fifth Street is majestic **Barn Bluff,** immortalized by Henry David Thoreau in 1861 after he hiked to the top. The bluff is listed on the National Register of Historic Places, and a marked stairwell is available to hikers. An even easier climb (or drive) to the top of the bluffs is in **Memorial Park,** located at the end of East Seventh Street. On your way to the top of **Sorin's Bluff,** you'll find hiking trails, bike paths, and caves that may or may not be wise to explore. From either bluff, you get a great view of Red Wing and the Mississippi River, as well as the beautiful valley and tree-covered bluffs that stretch around the town. For another view of the valley, **River Boat Rides,** located at the Levy Wall (651-592-

i Bald eagles on their annual migration congregate in Red Wing's Colvill Park from November through the end of March. Often multiple eagles can be spotted in a single tree, looking for abundant shad in the Mississippi River.

3494), offers relaxing, one-hour-plus boat rides along the rugged bluffs of the Mississippi River. Be sure to bring your binoculars, as everything from deer, beavers, bald eagles, and wild turkeys have been seen on these rides. Passengers are encouraged to pack a picnic lunch to take with them for the trip.

In wintertime Red Wing and its neighbor, Welch, become ski country. Twelve miles northwest of town, just off US 61, is the **Welch Village Resort** (651-222-7079; www.welchvillage.com), which features some of the best downhill skiing in the state. Right next door, **Welch Mill,** at 14818 264th Street Path (800-657-6760; www.welchmillcanoeandtube.com), offers canoe and inner tube rentals and to-and-from shuttle service to the Cannon River in spring, summer, and fall. For cross-country skiers, there's the **Cannon Valley Trail** (507-263-0508; www.cannonvalleytrail.com) in Cannon Falls, stretching through nearly 20 miles of countryside, following the original Chicago Great Western Railroad line that once connected Cannon Falls and Red Wing. A Wheel Pass is required to bike, inline skate, or skateboard on the trail April through November. Passes are available by calling the trail office or at trailside pay stations.

Ten miles north of Red Wing and just off US 61 is the glamorous **Treasure Island Resort and Casino** (651-388-6300 or 800-222-7077; www.treasureislandcasino.com), a tropical-themed casino and hotel that features 44 games tables, 2,500 slot machines, a 10-table poker room, and a 40-foot waterfall, and smoking and nonsmoking gambling areas. The casino is decorated with palm trees, and the slot machines and gambling tables are spread far enough apart that the casino never feels too crowded. The attached hotel has an indoor pool with another waterfall, a fitness room, and a child care facility, while outside is a RV park with 95 pull-through sites and a 137-slip marina.

Accommodations and Camping

If you plan to spend the night in Red Wing, you have many options. The most elegant of the hotels in the area is downtown Red Wing's historic **St. James Hotel** at 406 Main Street (651-388-2846 or 800-252-1875; www.st-james-hotel.com), established in 1875 and a member of the National Trust's Historic Hotels of America. The elegant hotel has only 61 guest rooms, so you'll want to call ahead of time to make reservations.

Many beautiful old houses in Red Wing have been converted to bed-and-breakfasts and inns. Most of them are on the National Register of Historic Places, and many were former residences of Red Wing Shoe Company tycoons. The **Golden Lantern Inn** at 721 East Avenue (651-3883315 or 888-288-3315; www.goldenlantern.com), was home to three former presidents of the Red Wing Shoe Company. The Golden Lantern has since added whirlpools and fireplaces to some of the rooms and offers a full breakfast each morning to visitors. At 1105 West Fourth Street is the **Moondance Inn** (651-388-8145 or 866-388-8145; www.moondanceinn.com), which offers a five-course gourmet brunch to weekend guests and rooms with private bathrooms and double whirlpools.

For more conventional lodging, there's an **AmericInn Motel** at 1819 Old West Main (651-385-9060), which offers guests a free continental breakfast and has a pool and sauna on the premises; a **Best Western Quiet House & Suites** across the highway from Pottery Place Mall off US 61 (651-388-1577; www.quiethouse.com), offering both indoor and outdoor pools as well as complimentary coffee in every room; a **Super 8 Motel** at US 61 and Withers Harbor (651-388-0491), which has an indoor pool and allows pets to stay with guests for a small additional fee; and the **Parkway Motel** at 3425 US 61 west (651-388-8231

or 800-762-0934), which features snowmobile trails, hiking trails, fishing lakes, and a golf course within walking distance.

If you're more happy "roughing it" while on vacation, there's the **Hay Creek Valley Campground** (651-388-3998 or 888-388-3998), located 6 miles south of Red Wing on Minnesota Highway 58. The campground has a heated swimming pool and a restaurant, the Old Western Saloon, on the premises and borders a stocked trout stream. Right next to the campground is the **Hardwood State Forest** with trails laid out for horseback riding, hiking, snowmobiling, and areas set aside for in-season hunting.

Shopping

Antiques addicts beware—Red Wing has some amazingly good deals on antique furniture, toys, jewelry, and collectibles in general. The two main shopping areas in town are situated near each other, too. There's the Downtown District, which is composed of beautiful old warehouse buildings and storefronts that have been refurbished and turned into antiques stores, thrift stores, and restaurants, while about 12 blocks away, down Old West Main Street, is the Historic Pottery District, where you can buy antiques from **Al's Antique Mall** at 1314 Old West Main Street (651-388-0572), or shop at antiques and outlet stores in what was once a pottery factory at the **Historic Pottery Place Mall** at 2000 Old West Main Street (651-388-1428; www.rwpotteryplace.com).

The Downtown District has the widest variety of shops to choose from. At **Memory Maker Antiques** in the Boxrud Building at 415 Main Street (651-385-5914), you can find everything from 50-cent postcards to vintage dishes to antique wardrobes. **Twigges of Galena** at 415 Main Street in the St. James Hotel's shopping court (651-388-3033) has lots of twig furniture as well as home items such as Yankee Candles and quilts. At Main and Bush Streets is the **Uffda Shop** (800-4883332) selling all things Scandinavian, such as gnomes, Norwegian sweaters, lefse grills, porcelain, solje jewelry, and, of course, Ole and Lena joke books.

Restaurants

While the majority of Red Wing's restaurants can be categorized as traditional American fare, quite a few add a unique twist to those traditional dishes. The **Staghead Restaurant** at 219 Bush Street (651-388-6581) offers a changing and eclectic menu of steak, Italian dinners, and specialty sandwiches; the restaurant has a huge wine list and more than 30 imported and domestic beers on tap. Former Staghead chef and Hüsker Dü bassist Greg Norton now owns and cooks at the **Norton's** (715-792-2464; www.thenortonsrestaurant .com) with his wife, at W7171 135th Avenue, across the river in Bay City, Wisconsin. The upscale menu has a little something for everyone. The incredible food and the quaint wooded location make this place worth the trip. **Fiesta Mexicana,** 2918 Service Drive North (651-385-8903), serves authentic Mexican food for the lunch and dinner crowd and is quite possibly the only nonchain Mexican restaurant you'll find within a 50-mile radius. **Bev's Cafe** at 221 Bush Street (651-388-5227) offers classic home-style meals from hash to roast beef dinners and a fish fry on Friday. For a very elegant evening, the historic St. James Hotel's restaurant, the **Port** (651-388-2846; 800-252-1875; www.port-restaurant.com) serves a limited but tantalizing dinner menu. Call ahead for reservations.

If you just want a cup of coffee and something to munch on while you read the paper, you're in luck. Red Wing has several cozy little nooks to grab a cup of java, including **Lily's Coffee House & Flowers** at 419 West Third Street (651388-8797; www.lilyscoffeehouse .com), which serves soups, sandwiches, pastries, coffee, and espresso drinks; **Braschler's Bakery and Coffeeshop** at 410 West Third Street (651-388-1589) makes its own pastries and muffins to accompany its large menu of caffeinated beverages; **Tale of Two Sisters**

Tea Room and Gift Shoppe at 204 West Seventh Street (651-388-2250) offers a full English tea or just a cup of coffee to patrons.

For the sports bar fan, **Andy's Bar** at 529 Plum Street (651-388-4471), has 10 TVs with satellite hookups to accompany its menu of beer, appetizers, burgers, and chicken dinners, while in downtown proper, the **Barrel House,** at 223 Main Street (651-388-9967), serves light food, pizza, and beer, with daily happy hour specials.

In the Area

Twenty-three miles south of Red Wing across the Mississippi River on WI 35 is the historic town of Pepin, Wisconsin. Named after the Pepin brothers, who were two of the first French trappers in the area, the village was settled in 1846 and was known for years as a steamboat boomtown and a vacation spot for wealthy Chicago socialites who summered on Lake Pepin. This is the place to visit if you're interested in fishing, boating, or birdwatching—the 13,000-acre **Tiffany Wildlife Area,** right next to Lake Pepin, is a regular roosting spot for bald eagles and hawks, while Lake Pepin itself has several beautiful marinas with public docking ramps.

Perhaps the most famous of Pepin's residents was Laura Ingalls Wilder, immortalized in *Little House on the Prairie*. Every September, Pepin celebrates **Laura Ingalls Wilder Days** with events including a Laura knowledge contest, a parade, demonstrations of traditional crafts and industries, and bus tours of Wilder's birth site. For more information about Laura Ingalls Wilder Days, contact the Laura Ingalls Wilder Days Committee at (800) 442-3011.

STILLWATER

Stillwater is technically considered a Twin Cities outer-ring suburb, but it's a good half hour's drive from St. Paul. Long in competition with the Twin Cities for everything from being the state's logging and industry capital to making a bid for the state capital itself, Stillwater is a beautiful riverside city with much to offer antiques shoppers, architecture connoisseurs, book collectors, and nature lovers. There's more than enough to do in the Stillwater area to make it at least a day trip, if not a relaxing weekend getaway.

That the economy is on an uphill climb in Stillwater has never been more apparent— everywhere you go, brick-and-wood storefronts have been restored and repainted, and specialty stores, wineries, and espresso bars have set up shop where there were once just thrift shops and diners. With all of its parks and bicycle trails, Stillwater is sure to offer something that appeals to you and your family.

For more information about Stillwater, check out www.ilovestillwater.com, or call the Stillwater Chamber of Commerce at (651) 439-4001.

Getting There

Take Minnesota Highway 36 east until you reach Stillwater.

Accommodations and Camping

Stillwater boasts bed-and-breakfasts housed in Victorian mansions and quaint old hotels listed on the National Register of Historic Places as well as modern hotels with the expected amenities. **The Water Street Inn** at 101 South Water Street (651-439-6000; www.waterstreetinn.us) is a beautiful red-brick building that's located right next to the St. Croix and is furnished with turn-of-the-20th-century period pieces. The **1849 Brunswick Inn** at 114 Chestnut (651-430-8111) features gas fireplaces and double Jacuzzis in the rooms. Another fine choice is the **Elephant Walk** at 801 West Pine Street (651-430-0359 or 888-430-0359; www.elephantwalkbb .com), where each room is decorated with exotic finds from around the world. You're welcomed with a complimentary bottle of wine, cheese, fruit, and homemade crackers in your room.

The newer hotels and motels are clustered along MN 36 southwest of downtown.

Options include the **Holiday Inn Express** at 2000 Washington Avenue (651-275-1401; www.hiexpress.com); **Days Inn Stillwater,** 1750 West Frontage Road (651-430-1300; www.daysinn.com); and the **Super 8 Motel** at 2190 West Frontage Road (651-430-3990; www.super8.com).

For RV campers, there's the **Golden Acres RV Park & Picnic Area** at 15150 North Square Lake Trail (651-439-1147), which has 54 campsites with water, electrical, and sewer hookups available (no tent camping allowed). The campground, located on the shore of Square Lake, has a nice swimming beach and good fishing.

Shopping

Stillwater is antiques central, with shops that sell everything from collector's dolls and teddy bears to handmade Amish quilts and furniture. In Main Street Square at 124 South Main Street, you can buy pottery, jewelry, and vintage clothing at **Country Charm Antiques** (651-439-8202) or consignment clothing at **Nearly New** (651-430-1188). **Seasons Tique** at 229 South Main Street (651-430-1240) carries beautiful Christmas tree ornaments and decorations from around the world all year long. For the larger budget, **Enigma** at 213 South Main Street (651-439-2206) carries new and antique furnishings from Europe and Asia, and the **J. P. Laskin Company** at 306 East Chestnut Street (651-439-5712) carries handmade American goods made by Amish people and Native Americans, as well as handblown glass artifacts.

Stillwater has several independent bookstores to choose from. **St. Croix Antiquarian Booksellers** at 232 South Main Street (651-430-0732; www.booktown.com/stcroixbooks), carries more than 50,000 books on history, art, philosophy, Americana, and everything in between, while **Loome Theological Booksellers** in the Old Swedish Covenant Church at 320 North Fourth Street (651-430-1092; www.loomebooks.com) specializes in secondhand and out-of-print books on theology, religion, and philosophy. The **Valley Bookseller,**

i In 1994 Stillwater was declared America's first "Book Town," an international designation sponsored by Welshman Richard Booth to honor notable book-friendly towns worldwide. Stillwater's multiple antiquarian and new booksellers line Main Street downtown. For more information about Stillwater's bookstores, visit www.booktown.com.

217 North Main Street (651-430-3385; www .valleybookseller.com), is an independent bookstore selling new titles. The beautiful store is bright and sunny and features a strong children's section, a large selection of fiction and local history titles, and an exotic bird aviary in the middle of the store.

Restaurants

Stillwater has no shortage of coffeehouses and espresso bars. At the **Dreamcoat Cafe,** 215 South Main Street (651-4300615), you can order sandwiches or ice cream to go with your coffee—on weekend nights, local acoustic acts perform at this neighborhood cafe. At the other end of Main, **Supreme Bean Espresso Cafe** at 402 North Main Street (651-439-4314) serves delicious sandwiches and pastries that you can take outside to eat on the patio.

There are just as many places to go for dinner in Stillwater, too. Featuring a beautiful view of the St. Croix as well as traditional American fare is the **Dock Cafe** at 425 East Nelson Street (651-430-3770; www.dockcafe .com). **Brine's** at 219 South Main Street (651-439-7556; www.brines-stillwater.com) serves hot deli sandwiches, soups and salads, and the famous "Brine Burger," which is a heck of a lot better than it sounds. For German food, try the **Gasthaus Bavarian Hunter** at 8390 Lofton Avenue North (651-439-7128; www .gasthausbavarianhunter.com), which features live accordion music Friday and Sunday evenings.

For more refined dining, the historic **Lowell Inn** at 102 North Second Street (651-439-1100; www.lowellinn.com) serves elegant dinners in a variety of themed rooms.

Stillwater is also the home to two wineries with on-site tasting rooms, including **Saint Croix Vineyards** at 6428 Manning Avenue (651-430-3310; www .scvwines.com) and **Northern Vineyards Winery** at 223 North Main Street (651-430-1032; www.northernvineyards .com). Call ahead for an appointment at either place, just in case they're already booked.

In the Area

Just south of Stillwater and across the St. Croix River is the city of **Hudson, Wisconsin,** which is basically a little Stillwater. There are plenty of antiques stores, jewelry stores, and coffee shops, as well as beautiful storefronts and turn-of-the-20th-century architecture throughout the downtown area. On the west end of Coulee Road is the turnoff to **Birkmose Park,** which, if you take the drive to the top, gives you a great view of the harbor as well as a few imposing-looking Native American burial mounds. Hudson is also the home of the **San Pedro Cafe** at 426 Second Street (715-386-4003; www.sanpedrocafe.com), which features excellent dishes with a Caribbean flair, such as jerk chicken and rubbed, slow-roasted BBQ pork.

North of Stillwater on Minnesota Highway 95 is the **Boomsite,** a large body of water where fresh-cut trees once poured in through the river mouth and were then collected by the hardworking men of Stillwater's logging past. Now the Boomsite is a wonderful park surrounded by forest with an easily accessible path down to the beach. This is a beautiful, well-maintained park, a fun place to stop and relax and let the kids run around before getting back on the road.

TAYLORS FALLS

In order to properly appreciate autumn in Minnesota, a drive to Taylors Falls on the St. Croix River in the last two weeks of September or the first two weeks of October is absolutely necessary. During autumn, the leaves of the trees growing in the mineral-rich soil turn fluorescent shades of scarlet, gold, and yellow, looking more like bright springtime flower petals than dying tree leaves.

But don't just visit in the fall. Taylors Falls is just as beautiful in springtime, with millions of tiny purple, white, and blue wildflowers springing up between even the smallest of sidewalk cracks. In the warm months, birdwatching is a popular pastime all along the St. Croix River, and canoes can be rented at Interstate State Park for those who want to get a closer look at the cliffs that line the river. For more information, you can call the Taylors Falls Chamber of Commerce at (800) 447-4958 or visit its Web page at www.taylorsfalls chamber.org.

Getting There

If you take I-94 east to MN 95 north to Taylors Falls, you'll be treated to scenes of beautiful old hardwood forests and the St. Croix River all the way. If you just want to get to Taylors Falls, the quickest route is to take either I-35E north or I–35W north (depending on where in the Twin Cities you are) to I-35, then take I-35 north to U.S. Highway 8 east and follow US 8 all the way to Taylors Falls. It's a little less scenic, but you'll travel through the cute towns of Chisago City, Lindstrom, and Center City, and you can still get a glimpse of the beautiful St. Croix Valley along the last few miles.

Attractions

Taylors Falls attractions run the gamut of breathtaking, cliffside views of a landscape carved out by Ice Age glaciers to wild water park rides to self-guided tours through a historic neighborhood with houses dating from the 1850s. You can take a trip down the St. Croix on your own in a rented canoe or get on a steamboat for a relaxing luncheon tour.

The centerpiece of the Taylors Falls, Minnesota, and the St. Croix Falls, Wisconsin, border is **Interstate State Park** (651-465-5711; www.dnr.state.mn.us/state_parks), just off US 8 in Taylors Falls, known for its rare flora and fauna. Perhaps the most distinguishing features of the park, however, are the dark gray

basalt formations scattered throughout the region. Believed to once be full-size mountains, the dense stone was slowly eroded by glaciers into solitary pillars, winding towers, and the deepest glacial potholes in the world. The potholes are really something to see. It's nearly impossible to glimpse the bottom of the deepest ones. It's amazing how thousands of years of erosion can shape even the densest rock into these near-perfect, soft-edged circles that curve their way nearly 100 feet down through solid basalt.

Aside from the unique geological formations, Interstate State Park is crisscrossed with nature trails that lead visitors through thick forests (breathtaking in the height of autumn), up into the greenstone cliffs and Precambrian basalt flows that encircle the Minnesota side of the park, and then into open fields of tiny purple trilliums and other native wildflowers. Bird-watching is another popular pastime in the park. Eagles and their hatchlings can be seen almost every summer. For another view of the park and its wildlife, catch a ride on the riverboat *Taylors Falls Princess*. The boat dock is located right next to the entrance to Interstate State Park, and you can buy tickets at the dock. For more information, call (651) 465-6315 or visit www.taylorsfallsboat.com.

For human-made entertainment, head over to **Wild Mountain** (651-465-6315 or 800-447-4958; www.wildmountain.com). To get there, follow MN 95 north to County Road 16, go right onto CR 16 to Wild Mountain. Park visitors can play on one of the giant waterslides, float down an 800-foot lazy river in an inner tube, splash around Wild Adventure Island (an interactive water playground), slide down one of the two 1,700-foot-high alpine slides, or race around on the park's go-kart track. In winter Wild Mountain becomes a ski and snowboard park.

While most of the historic houses in Taylors Falls are private residences and not open to tourists, you can stop by the **Folsom House Museum** at 272 West Government Street (651-465-3125). Listed on the National

Register of Historic Places, along with the rest of the Angel Hill neighborhood, the Folsom House is a five-bedroom Greek revival home furnished with the original furniture, books, family pictures, and memorabilia belonging to Minnesota state senator W. H. C. Folsom and his family in the 1800s. The home is open to tour groups Wednesday through Monday from Memorial Day weekend to mid-October each year.

Accommodations and Camping

A few of the historic houses in Taylors Falls have been converted to bed-and-breakfasts. The **Cottage Bed & Breakfast,** 950 Fox Glen Drive (651-465-3595; www.The-Cottage.com), was designed in the style of an 18th-century English country house and offers guests a spectacular view of the St. Croix River. The house is furnished with English and French country period pieces and is minutes away from several state parks and Wild Mountain. Even more interesting—especially from a historical perspective—is the **Old Jail Bed & Breakfast** at 349 Government Street (651-465-3112; www.oldjail.com). Exactly what it sounds like, the Old Jail has three furnished suites available to rent, each with its own private bathroom, kitchen, sitting room, and entrance. The Old Jail is located a short walk from the St. Croix River, Interstate State Park, and downtown Taylors Falls. For modern hotel/motel options, search across the river in St. Croix Falls, Wisconsin, which has several chain motels.

For campers, Interstate State Park (651-465-5711; www.dnr.state.mn.us/state_parks) offers woodsy camping with some sites along the St. Croix River. There are sites for both tents and RVs, and some of the sites have electric hookups. The campground also has showers and flush toilets. The brave and well-insulated can camp here in the winter, but you'll have to snowshoe or ski into the campground as the road is not plowed. **Wildwood RV Park & Campground,** 1 mile west of Taylors Falls off US 8 (800-447-4958; www.wildwoodcamping.com), offers sunny or shaded campsites for both tents and RVs, with immediate access to hiking and bicycle trails, a swimming pool, and a miniature golf course. The campground also has well-maintained showers and flush toilets, as well as water, electrical, and sewer hookups.

Restaurants

The Drive In Restaurant at 572 Bench Street (651-465-7831) is a quaint, 1950s-style drive-in with wonderful burgers, shakes, and homemade root beer served by waitresses in hoop skirts wearing roller skates. Patrons of the Drive In also get to enjoy a great view of the St. Croix and the steamboats passing by while they eat either in their cars or at one of the picnic tables set up outside the restaurant.

For indoor dining, stop by **Romayne's** on Main, a sports bar and grill at 391 Bench Street (651-465-4405).

If you're just looking for a cup of coffee, stop by **Coffee Talk,** 479 Bench Street (651-465-6700). The cafe is in a beautifully renovated Victorian house with a small front porch and a gigantic, beautiful flower garden with lots of comfortable, quaint wicker furniture and chairs spread around in the back. The menu includes espresso and coffee drinks and fresh pastries.

In the Area

While driving up to Taylors Falls on MN 95, a stop at the little village of **Marine on St. Croix** is a must. The community, composed of stately old houses surrounded by fantastic flower gardens and ancient hardwood and conifer forests, is so still and quiet and beautiful it feels completely apart from the rest of the world. Established in 1838 as a lumber town, Marine has kept the look of a 19th-century settlement while becoming less an industrial town and more an out-of-the-way retreat for artists and writers. Inspired by the forests, ancient stone silos, and farmhouses that pepper the landscape and, of course, by the St. Croix River, they create their art. Writer Garrison Keillor once compared Marine to his mythical hometown of Lake Wobegon, while the directors of such films as *Grumpier Old Men, Beautiful Girls* (which was also shot in nearby Stillwater), and *The Cure* all chose to film on location here.

Marine on St. Croix is mostly made up of residences, but there are several places worth stopping by. The 2-block downtown district on Judd Street, now on the National Register of Historic Places, has a gas station and general store, perfect for making pit stops, and the **Village Scoop** ice-cream parlor. The **Brookside Bar and Grill,** 140 Judd (651-433-5132), has a natural spring-fed stream that runs through its basement and keeps the beer cool. There are also plenty of cross-country skiing and hiking trails that start in town and head out into the forests.

If you take US 8 across the river to Wisconsin, you'll come to **St. Croix Falls, Wiscon-sin** (715-4833580; www.stcroixfallschamber .com). Located on the east side of the St. Croix River, the historic downtown area has many antiques shops and farm stores that sell knickknacks and produce. The countryside around the town is dotted with llama and ginseng farms, ancient farmhouses, and about a dozen abandoned one-room schoolhouses that date from the time when wealthy landowners built schools on their land for their own as well as their employees' children.

If you take US 8 all the way to US 63, you'll reach the town of **Turtle Lake, Wisconsin,** home of the St. Croix Casino & Hotel, 777 US 8 and US 63 (800-U-GO- U-WIN; www.stcroix casino.com). An easy-paced, almost neighborly feeling casino decorated like a north woods lodge, the St. Croix has live entertainment every weekend.

RELOCATION

Minneapolis–St. Paul has always been an attractive place for relocation, given the region's consistently strong economy, the high quality of life, access to world-class educational resources, the numerous corporations based in the Metro, the lower crime rates than comparable metropolitan areas, and its vibrant cultural scene. Not surprisingly, many persons relocating to Minneapolis and St. Paul come from neighboring states, new Twin Citians accustomed to the cold. In recent years, however, thousands of Hispanic, Hmong, Somali, and Russian immigrants have chosen to come to Minnesota, adding new faces and languages to the Twin Cities community.

Although some of the quirks inherent to the Twin Cities may be hard for newcomers to understand (ice fishing, annual New Year's Day swims in area lakes, Twin Citians' inability to merge smoothly into freeway traffic, "snow emergencies," and the rivalry between Minneapolis and St. Paul), the friendly nature of Minnesotans and the conveniences of the 15th largest metropolitan area in the country will quickly make just about anyone feel at home.

This chapter is designed to aid newcomers to the Twin Cities, with details about looking for work, buying real estate, renting, and choosing neighborhoods. We then give you listings for useful resources such as libraries, motor vehicle departments, and tourism bureaus (which can send you relocation packets in addition to comprehensive area info). If you don't find what you are looking for here, ask a native; 9 times out of 10, the famous quality of "Minnesota Nice" will come through and he or she will steer you in the right direction.

FINDING A JOB

The Twin Cities is a mecca for jobs in manufacturing, banking, retail, airlines, information technology, medicine, law, publishing, state government, insurance, and many other fields. The following are a few sources to consult as you look for your perfect job.

Temp Agencies

Temp agencies can often provide short- or long-term employment in a variety of fields. They can be very useful for newcomers to an area who have not yet secured a full-time job. All the national temp agency chains have offices in the Twin Cities, as do many local agencies and specialized businesses that hire temp workers only in certain industries. The following are a few places to get you started.

Adecco: The Employment People
900 Second Avenue South, Suite 270, Minneapolis
(612) 339-1153

U.S. Bank Center, 101 East Fifth Street, Suite 206, St. Paul
(651) 224-4040
www.adeccousa.com
Multiple additional locations in the Twin Cities
Adecco specializes in clerical, financial, technical, engineering, administrative, and light industrial jobs.

Allied Professionals
3209 West 76th Street, Edina
(952) 832-5101
www.alliedprofessionals.com
Allied focuses on medical and dental temporary positions, including jobs for nurses, X-ray

technicians, dentists, medical secretaries, and home care assistance.

Celarity: Staffing Creative Professionals
7835 Telegraph Road, Bloomington
(952) 941-0022
www.freelancecreative.com
Celarity matches workers with jobs in creative fields, including graphic design, marketing, technical writing, editing, proofreading, and Web design.

Pro Staff
40 South Seventh Street, Suite 104
Minneapolis
(612) 339-2220

55 East Fifth Street, St. Paul
(651) 291-7811
www.prostaff.com
Multiple additional locations in the Twin Cities
Pro Staff is a national company specializing in hiring temps for companies looking for workers in the fields of accounting, creative services, office support, finance, and light industrial.

Strom Engineering
10505 Wayzata Boulevard, Minnetonka
(952) 544-8644 or (800) 205-8732
www.stromengineering.com
Strom Engineering finds temporary and permanent positions in engineering, technical, industrial, personnel, consulting, support services, and more.

Teachers on Call
3001 Metro Drive, Suite 485, Bloomington
(952) 703-3719
www.teachersoncall.com
Educational professionals can get their foot in the door with the help of Teachers on Call.

Employment Agencies

Of the many employment agencies in the Twin Cities, some specialize in certain fields, while others place candidates in nearly every kind of job. Some employment agencies charge a substantial fee to help you find a job; others charge their fee to the employer that hires you. Ask questions before you sign anything.

Robert Half Legal
800 Nicollet Mall, Suite 2700, Minneapolis
(612) 349-2810
www.affiliates.com
Robert Half Legal specializes in helping workers in the legal field find jobs, including lawyers, legal secretaries, and support staff.

Career Professionals
7301 Ohms Lane, Suite 200, Edina
(952) 835-9922
www.gocpi.com
Career Professionals focuses on recent college graduates, finding entry-level positions in customer service, marketing, financial industries, sales, retail, and administrative settings.

Creative Group
800 Nicollet Mall, Suite 2700, Minneapolis
(612) 333-7990
www.creativegroup.com
Creative Group serves clients looking for work in marketing or advertising, including art directors, copywriters, graphic designers, Web site developers, marketing managers, and similar positions.

Thomas Moore, Inc.
1221 Nicollet Mall, Suite 710, Minneapolis
(612) 338-4884
www.thomasmooreinc.com
Thomas Moore matches accountants, financial professionals, and information technology specialists with jobs at Twin Cities companies.

State Agencies

Minnesota WorkForce Center
777 East Lake Street, Minneapolis
(612) 821-4000

540 Fairview Avenue North, St. Paul
(651) 642-0363
www.MNWorkForceCenter.org
Multiple additional locations in the Twin Cities
The Minnesota WorkForce Center is operated by the state. It offers free or inexpensive serv-

ices, including access to its huge database of available jobs, help with resumes and interviewing skills, free local faxing, and free computer usage. After registering with the agency, you can have descriptions of available jobs of interest e-mailed directly to you. Positions run the full spectrum of the Twin Cities economy, including education, human services, state government, and executive management.

Classified Ads

The two major dailies in the Twin Cities, the *St. Paul Pioneer Press* and the *StarTribune,* have exhaustive classified job listings, particularly in their Sunday editions. The listings in the *StarTribune* are generally more extensive, although the *St. Paul Pioneer Press* is stronger in listings for jobs in the East Metro. Both newspapers allow you to search the classifieds on their Web sites for free (visit www .startribune.com or www.twincities.com).

Several national Web sites allow you to search for jobs in the Twin Cities based on specific criteria. Some allow you to post your resume to the site for free, and some will e-mail job openings that match your criteria to you.

BUYING A NEW HOME

The Twin Cities have recently seen an explosion in the value of homes and skyrocketing rents. The median price of a home has risen to nearly $240,000 in the metropolitan area, double what it was in the mid-nineties. At the time of this writing, the explosive growth has stabilized and prices have even declined in some areas of the Metro. Buying real estate is almost always a good bet, but most will not

i To find other people to enjoy the outdoors with, Twin Cities Transplants (not a singles' club), www.imnot fromhere.com, has been matching newcomers with residents for more than 10 years to help new residents get acclimated to the Twin Cities.

see the kind of growth in value seen in the decade up to 2007. The following are a few places to get you started on your search for a new home in the Cities.

Real Estate Agencies

Here are some of the major, national agencies that work through franchised operations in the Twin Cities metro area, as well as the larger independent agencies that are based here. Many allow you to search for houses through their Web sites.

Century 21–Luger Realty
4536 France Avenue South, Edina
(952) 925-3901
www.century21luger.com
Century 21 is one of the largest residential real estate franchisers in the world, with more than 100,000 independently owned and operated franchised broker offices. Its local, independently owned branch, Century 21–Luger Realty, has achieved the highest honor conferred by Century 21, the Centurion Award, ranking it among the top 3 percent of all Century 21 offices worldwide. Luger Century 21 represents the entire Twin Cities metro area, including the outlying suburbs.

Coldwell Banker
Burnet-Minneapolis Lakes, 3033
Excelsior Boulevard, #100, Minneapolis
(612) 920-5605

Burnet-Highland Park, 1991 Ford
Parkway, St. Paul
(651) 698-2481
www.cbburnet.com
Several additional Twin Cities locations
The Minnesota division of Coldwell Banker national, Coldwell Banker Burnet makes a genuine effort to make buying and selling homes as convenient as possible for clients, connecting potential buyers with local, accredited mortgage companies and payment plans specifically suited to each individual. More than 25 Coldwell Banker Burnet offices serve the Twin Cities metro area, both the Cities and the surrounding suburbs.

The Minneapolis Lakes office is Coldwell Banker's No. 1 office nationally and is equipped to handle relocation needs, set up mortgages, and refinance existing properties in the entire Twin Cities metro area, with an emphasis on properties in Minneapolis and St. Paul proper. In St. Paul the Highland Park office deals with properties in St. Paul, Mendota Heights, Highland Park, Lilydale, Inver Grove Heights, and Eagan. Both locations are dialed into strong intraoffice networking and communication with other offices and brokers, ensuring that your needs are broadcast to the largest possible audience of buyers and sellers.

Counselor Realty

7250 France Avenue South, Suite 300 Edina
(952) 921-0911
Several additional Twin Cities locations
www.counselorrealty.com
Established in 1964, Counselor Realty is a local Minnesota company with strong ties to the community and nine branches throughout the metro area. Counselor Realty prides itself on providing superior service tailored to each client's individual needs, as well as total integrity and honesty with clients. The agency has built its reputation through word-of-mouth referrals from satisfied customers and has firmly established itself with the local community by involvement in local charities and causes.

Edina Realty

3270 West Lake Street, Minneapolis
(612) 926-4606

700 Grand Avenue, St. Paul
(651) 224-4321
Several additional Twin Cities locations
www.edinarealty.com
Founded in 1955 by Emma Rovick, a Minnesotan housewife with three kids and a $2,000 loan, Edina Realty Home Services was built on a strict standard of quality and service that lives on today. Now part of a company that is one of the largest real estate

companies in the nation with a mortgage division (Edina Realty Mortgage), a title division (Edina Realty Title), and a relocation division (Edina Realty Relocation), Edina has independently run offices throughout the Metro. Edina realtors pride themselves on being able to match customers with their first-choice, affordable dream house as quickly and efficiently as possible without pressuring customers to settle for anything. The company Web site has many tools available for home buyers to use, including a mortgage calculator and full listings of all of the homes Edina represents.

Prudential Plus

4901 West 77th Street, Suite 125, Edina
(952) 835-4400
Several additional Twin Cities locations
www.prudential.com
With offices all over the Twin Cities metro area, Prudential Plus is part of the Metrowide Group of Prudential Realty, which provides its independently run offices with regional support and national relocation information and services, making it a favorite relocation service among businesses nationwide. All offices have in-house closers and information on mortgages and home insurance on-site, making it an especially complete real estate agency to deal with.

RE/MAX Results

11200 West 78th Street, Eden Prairie
(952) 829-2900

1071 Grand Avenue, St. Paul
(651) 251-4800
www.remax.com
Numerous additional Twin Cities locations
RE/MAX Results specializes in corporate relocations, and, as such, has many highly trained Corporate Relocation Specialists (CRPs) on staff. RE/MAX Results has strategically located offices to service the Metro area's strongest and fastest-growing markets, including Eden Prairie, Plymouth, and Woodbury.

Roger Fazendin Realtors
15550 Wayzata Boulevard, Wayzata
(952) 473-7000
www.rogerfazendin.com
Founded in 1965, Roger Fazendin Realtors is the largest family-owned and operated residential real estate company in Minnesota. The company has more than 30 professional real estate agents to serve you. The company's agents practice broker reciprocity and have good connections within the local financial community. All of their listings are available on their Web site, including color photos and basic floor plans.

Other Sources for Finding Homes

Both Twin Cities newspapers carry extensive listings of homes for sale in the Metro, particularly in their Sunday editions. Pick up a paper, or check out their Web sites: the *StarTribune* at www.startribune.com or the *St. Paul Pioneer Press* at www.twincities.com.

There are general sites on the Internet for searching for homes in the Cities. The following sites allow you to search by city and other specifics, with additional information about finding movers, financing, contacts, and more.

www.realestate.com
www.realtor.com

RENTING

The Twin Cities offer rental properties from historic apartments with hardwood floors, beautiful woodwork, and lots of character to modern apartments in complexes with many amenities. In Minneapolis, one-bedroom apartments average $800 per month; and rent is around $650 per month on average for a similar unit in St. Paul.

There are several ways to find an apartment in the Cities. One easy option is to consult with an agency. Two agencies in the Twin Cities with excellent reputations are **Relocation Central** (2756 Hennepin Avenue South, Minneapolis and other Twin Cities locations, 612-870-0525 or 800-832-7436; www.relocationcentral.com)

and **Apartment Mart** (612-927-4591 or 888-254-5899; www.apartmentmartmn.com). Neither business charges a fee to the renter to locate an apartment.

Both Twin Cities newspapers carry extensive listings of apartments and houses for rent in the Metro, particularly in their Sunday editions. Pick up a paper, or check out their Web sites: the *StarTribune* at www.startribune.com or the *St. Paul Pioneer Press* at www.twincities.com. The Twin Cities' free weekly newspaper *City Pages* (www.citypages.com) also carries extensive rental ads. The newspaper can be found at most businesses throughout the Metro.

Several national Web sites allow you to search for apartments in the Twin Cities. The following sites should provide some good leads.

www.rent.com
www.rentnet.com
www.apartments.com

If you are looking for a roommate, one option is to contact **Roommate Referrals**, 4104 Portland Avenue South, Minneapolis; (612) 827-5565 or (800) 949-7056; www.tc roommates.com. For a fee this company can match you up with persons looking to share their apartments or, if you've already found a place, with persons looking to move in with someone else. You get a list of matches, allowing you to screen potential roommates by telephone.

NEIGHBORHOODS

Each neighborhood in the Twin Cities has a distinct personality, its own churches; often its own religious, ethnic, or social groups; city parks and schools specific to the neighborhood; and independently owned markets and delis, particularly in Minneapolis and St. Paul. Moving from one neighborhood to another is almost like moving to another town at times, with benefits and drawbacks to each location. With more than 80 neighborhoods in

Minneapolis and another 20-plus in St. Paul, new residents have the opportunity to choose exactly what kind of place they'd like to live in, whether it's in swanky, funky Uptown Minneapolis; the vibrant, artistic, mixed-ethnic community of Frogtown in St. Paul; or one of the pleasant suburbs north, south, east, or west of the Cities.

Minneapolis

Como

The Como community of Minneapolis is named after Como Avenue. The thoroughfare continues into St. Paul, where the similarly named Como Park neighborhood is located. The Minneapolis Como neighborhood is filled with middle-income homes. Van Cleve Park is a matter of pride for the community and includes baseball fields, a pool, and a community center. Housing prices tend to be lower than the the city's averages.

Downtown

Downtown Minneapolis is one of the Twin Cities' fastest growing neighborhoods. The area is expanding rapidly as high-rises and renovations replace once vacant or dilapidated properties. Living options in downtown Minneapolis include apartments, condominiums, and lofts. In the past few years all three types of properties have been developed next to the old milling district and in the Warehouse District along the Mississippi riverfront. So you're in luck if you're looking to live downtown; however, remember most properties garner a premium price.

The benefits of living downtown are almost endless. There are numerous employment opportunities without the headache of commuting. The cultural and shopping opportunities abound—where else are so many four-star restaurants, performing arts venues, and varied stores accessible by foot? And when the weather becomes inclement, most buildings downtown are connected by skyways, so a downtown resident often doesn't have to experience the unpleasant elements.

Linden Hills

Linden Hills is nestled between Lake Calhoun and Lake Harriet, two of the City of Lakes' most breathtaking bodies of water. Its location isolates the area from the bustle of Uptown and downtown but allows easy access to the lakes, which offer everything from bicycling and walking to riding a sailboat on a sunny summer day.

Linden Hills' appearance is reminiscent of a small town. Specialty shops and restaurants are located on Linden Avenue. The restaurants offer choices ranging from barbecue to Hmong cuisine. The idyllic shopping district is one of the many selling points of one of Minneapolis's loveliest neighborhoods. Housing prices tend to be considerably higher than Minneapolis averages in this desirable area.

Marcy-Holmes

Marcy-Holmes is named after the two neighborhood parks located within the community. The neighborhood is a healthy mix of students, senior citizens, college professors, and young families. Beautiful Victorian houses sit side by side with apartments in this neighboorhood next to the University of Minnesota.

Marcy-Holmes is also near many of Minneapolis's attractions. The historic St. Anthony neighborhood borders Marcy-Holmes, and the James J. Hill Stone Arch Bridge, now a pedestrian bridge, offers one of the best views and shortcuts to downtown. Home prices are a little higher compared with the rest of the city.

Prospect Park

The Prospect Park neighborhood is recognizable because of its historic water tower, which

> **i** Residents of the Marcy-Holmes neighborhood in Minneapolis have the advantage of living in a quiet residential neighborhood but the convenience of living across the Mississippi River from downtown Minneapolis—located just on the other side of the Third Avenue Bridge.

overlooks the Minneapolis community. The water tower, no longer in use, sits atop the highest point in Minneapolis and is one of the most scenic vistas in the area. The neighborhood is composed mainly of classic, expensive homes that sit on the many winding roads surrounding the water tower. The homes in Prospect Park are some of the most attractive in the Twin Cities. Prospect Park has easy access to all of the Twin Cities major thoroughfares and is centrally located between downtown Minneapolis and downtown St. Paul.

Seward

Seward is the Twin Cities' idealistic, former hippie neighborhood. The area is lined with beautiful old homes, and many have lovely gardens. The neighborhood has many schools and diverse shopping options. Ethiopian restaurants and diners coexist in this neighborhood, where community is emphasized. Churches of various faiths as well as New Age and wellness businesses can be found in this charming community. Housing prices in this neighborhood are slightly less than the city average.

Uptown

The Twin Cities' hippest neighborhood, Uptown is the community that locals visit for fun. Others choose to live in this wonderful cosmopolitan hub because of the numerous cultural amenities. An example of comfortable high-density living, the area is packed with restaurants and retail shops.

A favorite spot for summer recreation and relaxation, Uptown borders Lake of the Isles and Lake Calhoun, each a short walk from the neighborhood's commercial center. The community effervesces with excitement each summer when it hosts the Uptown Art Fair. As a result of the trendiness of the neighborhood, the historic home and apartments available, and the proximity to the Chain of Lakes, rents and home prices are generally expensive.

St. Paul
Como Park

Not to be confused with the Como neighborhood in Minneapolis, St. Paul's Como Park neighborhood is centered around Como Park, Como Zoo, and Como Lake. Residents here enjoy many pleasant neighborhood coffeeshops and restaurants, and many of the bungalows and smaller two-story homes are reasonably priced.

Frogtown

Arguably St. Paul's most ethnically diverse community, the Frogtown neighborhood has been a magnet for poets, artists, and immigrants for many years. With some of the lowest housing prices in the city, who could blame them? Property values for these same houses are on the rise (with the rest of St. Paul), as are the small storefronts and restaurants owned by the Thai, African-American, Vietnamese, Cambodian, and Hmong residents who populate this area.

Highland Park

Highland Park, in the southwestern corner of the city and bordered by the Mississippi River, is a delightful area, with many bungalows, larger two-story homes, and a smattering of upper-tier properties. The area surrounds the shops and restaurants centered at the intersection of Ford Parkway and Cleveland Avenue South, with numerous specialty retailers, bookstores, ethnic restaurants (as well as fast-food fare), and a major grocery store within a short drive from home. Housing prices tend to be significantly higher than St. Paul averages.

i Residents of the Como Park neighborhood often remark about how beautiful it is to hear the wolves at Como Zoo howling at night, especially in winter.

Macalester-Groveland

Macalester-Groveland (Mac-Groveland to locals) is one of the Twin Cities' premier urban neighborhoods. The neighborhood has several excellent schools and is filled with diverse local businesses. The name of the neighborhood is in part derived from Macalester College, a highly respected liberal arts institution of higher learning, which has a significant presence in the area. The neighborhood borders the Mississippi River to the west. Home prices tend to be much higher than St. Paul averages but some reasonably priced rental units in historic buildings can be found here.

Merriam Park

This attractive St. Paul neighborhood just north of Mac-Groveland and bordering the Mississippi River to the west is ideally located roughly halfway between downtown St. Paul and Minneapolis. An important part of the neighborhood is the University of St. Thomas. Housing prices tend to be significantly higher than city averages.

North

Forest Lake

Founded in 1855 by Louis Scheil, a German immigrant, this area has long been a summer haven for tourists from Chicago and beyond and is now known as one of the most popular resort towns in the area. The city has managed to keep its small-town charm even with the introduction of many big-city conveniences, especially the outstanding medical care and the many businesses that have moved into the area. Activities in Forest Lake are centered around Lakeside Memorial Park, where outdoor concerts and other cultural events take place at the gazebo in summer. Ice-skating and ice fishing are popular in winter. Housing prices are on par with St. Paul city averages.

New Brighton

The land around New Brighton was originally inhabited by the Dakota and Ojibwe tribes. They were drawn to the area for its rich farmland and abundant wetlands, which were perfect for growing wild rice. French and English settlers first came to the area in the mid-1800s, looking for land to homestead and farm. By 1858 the settlement was named Mounds View Township, which was later broken up into the communities of New Brighton and Mounds View. Today New Brighton has a population just over 22,000, and many of the residents work within the city limits at the industries that have been established here. Housing prices tend to be somewhat higher than Twin Cities averages.

Roseville

Rose Township was originally named for Isaac Rose, one of the first white settlers in the area. Rose and his family settled on a claim near what is now St. Anthony Road and Fairview Avenue—look for the historical marker if you happen to pass by.

Today Roseville is a residential community and thriving commercial district of pleasant houses with expansive gardens, specialty shops, a major mall, many big box retailers, and restaurants. The city of Roseville has 23 park sites, ranging in size from 2 to 220 acres, including a large concert amphitheater in Central Park. The Guidant John Rose Minnesota Oval & Roseville Ice Arena have outdoor and indoor rinks available for hockey, figure skating, open skating, and speed skating.

Most of the residential areas are filled with split-level ramblers and bungalows in this suburb, with housing prices a little higher than those in the Twin Cities.

Shoreview

Socrates A. Thompson, the first white settler on the land that makes up present-day Shoreview, came to the area from St. Paul looking for a good place to farm. He decided on the east shores of Turtle Lake and was soon joined by other settlers from as far away as Germany and Switzerland.

In 1941 the U.S. government opened the Army Arsenal plant on the west side of Shoreview, bringing many new workers into the area. This expanse of residential property turned Shoreview from a small, lakeside, rural community into a Twin Cities suburb, and the township was officially made a city on January 1, 1974.

Today Shoreview is surrounded by expanses of farmland, lakes, and woods. Residents enjoy proximity to the Twin Cities as well as a strong sense of community, and housing prices are similar to averages in Minneapolis.

Vadnais Heights

Since its humble roots as a small rural farming community, Vadnais Heights has grown into the successful, thriving residential suburb and business community it is today. Within the city limits can be found many open, protected wetlands, lakes, and ponds, around which have sprung idyllic neighborhoods with relatively expensive houses. A solid industrial core and many service manufacturing jobs employ more than 5,000 residents, while many others make the easy commute into the Twin Cities. Housing prices are a little above St. Paul averages.

South

Apple Valley

Originally a small farming community named Lebanon, Apple Valley and its low-cost farmland first started drawing city developers as early as 1960. When the city was incorporated in 1968, the area was renamed Apple Valley for developer Orrin Thompson Homes's habit of putting an apple tree on every residential lot. Located a dozen or so miles south of Minneapolis and St. Paul off Minnesota Highway 38, Apple Valley today is a small business and residential community. Apple Valley is also home to the Minnesota Zoo, one of the state's best-known attractions. Housing prices tend to be a little lower than Minneapolis averages.

Bloomington

With its proximity to the Minneapolis–St. Paul International Airport and more than 30 hotels,

Bloomington is often the first and last stop of visitors to the Twin Cities. Home of the Mall of America and several prestigious golf courses and country clubs, as well as more than 85,000 residents, Bloomington is a city in the middle of an economic boom. Because of Bloomington's proximity to Minneapolis and St. Paul, this is a choice community for those who don't want to live in the Cities but have to commute there for work. The city is surrounded by open country and maintained parklands. Housing prices tend to be a little higher than Twin Cities averages.

Eagan

Aside from its rich agricultural history, Eagan has a thriving business community. Major employers in the area include Cray Research, Blue Cross–Blue Shield, Northwest Airlines, Thomson West Publishing, and Coca-Cola. Eagan borders several beautiful, large parks, including Lebanon Hills Regional Park and the Caponi Art Park, which features an outdoor sculpture garden. Housing prices are near Twin Cities averages.

Eden Prairie

Eden Prairie is a refuge for commuters who want a quiet, beautiful town to escape to after a busy day at work. It's surrounded by parklands, including Bryant Lake Regional Park and its boating and fishing lake. Housing prices are far above Twin Cities averages.

Prior Lake

Located in the southwestern Metro area, Prior Lake is centered around the 16-square-mile lake that shares its name. Of Prior Lake's attractions, perhaps the best known is Mystic Lake Casino, Minnesota's largest gaming and entertainment establishment. Prior Lake is also home to the world-class Wilds Golf Club'With its many swimming beaches and boating marinas, Prior Lake is a favorite recreation spot for watersport enthusiasts. Lakeside living, however, is linked with expensive homes; the farther you get away from the waterfront, the more reasonably priced the houses get. On average, housing prices in Prior Lake are well above Twin Cities averages.

Savage

The city of Savage is a dynamic community offering many housing options, all with easy access to the surrounding urban areas. An interesting mix of older homes and new construction, Savage is the fastest-growing and most populated community in Scott County. Housing prices are somewhat higher than Twin Cities averages.

East

Afton

Nestled between wooded river bluffs and the St. Croix River, the historic town of Afton is a rural community of approximately 3,000. Located on the eastern edge of Washington County along the St. Croix River, the quiet residential community has a small business district composed of restaurants, marinas, unique shops, and services. The village is surrounded by parks, farms, and nature preserves, and the residential area is made up of mostly upper-bracket houses. This highly desirable community has housing prices more than double Twin Cities averages.

Bayport

Settled more than 150 years ago, Bayport, known as South Stillwater until 1922, was known as a bootlegger's paradise during Prohibition. Today the small community on the St. Croix River boasts a charming downtown area, including a park, several marinas, and quaint little shops and restaurants in a downtown made up of turn-of-the-20th-century brick-and-wood buildings. Formerly a center of the lumber industry, today Bayport's main employer is Andersen Windows, one of the country's largest producer of windows and patio doors. Housing prices are somewhat higher than Twin Cities averages.

Lake Elmo

With the growth of the Twin Cities metro area, city dwellers seeking the quiet life have found Lake Elmo. Located on the old mail trail between Stillwater and St. Paul, the city boasts a big blue lake of the same name and eight other smaller lakes as well. Lake Elmo is a historic town that has kept its quaint, turn-of-the-20th-century feel. Because it has resisted growth as its neighbors have expanded, it has retained its small-town feel. Downtown Lake Elmo is made up of old brick-and-wood buildings and an old grain elevator, which have been turned into restaurants, antiques shops, and other businesses. Lake Elmo is also home to the Washington County Fairgrounds and an annual August county fair. The town's population is around 7,000 residents. Housing prices in Lake Elmo tend to be far higher than averages for the Twin Cities.

Mahtomedi/Grant

Founded in the mid-1800s as a Methodist summer colony, Mahtomedi soon became a desirable location for summer homes and resorts due to its proximity to beautiful White Bear Lake. Both Mahtomedi and the nearby former township of Grant, one of Minnesota's newest cities, are dotted with hobby farms and working farms as well as natural areas set aside for parkland. White Bear Lake is deep enough for waterskiing and boating in the summertime and is a popular ice fishing spot in the winter.

Many of the homes in Grant are located on the rolling acres of hobby, horse, or agricultural farms, while Mahtomedi offers more variety, including town houses, condominiums, and newer residential developments centered around small parks.

Housing prices in both areas tend to be considerably higher than Twin Cities averages.

Maplewood

Maplewood's three most distinct features are the Maplewood Community Center—containing a fully appointed fitness center with a pool, a senior lounge, and a craft center—the Maplewood Mall, and the worldwide corporate headquarters of the 3M company, a major employer in the area.

Like many other Twin Cities suburbs, Maplewood is rich in parks and recreation areas. The city-funded Maplewood Nature Center offers environmental programs for children and adults, with interactive displays and marked trails for seasonal use.

Maplewood housing prices are generally on par with Twin Cities averages.

North St. Paul

North St. Paul manages to combine the benefits of a bustling commercial and industrial district with the feel of a quiet residential area, with tree-lined neighborhoods, a historic downtown area, and many community events along the shores of Silver Lake. Housing prices tend to be somewhat lower than Twin Cities averages.

Stillwater

Stillwater on the St. Croix River is home to some of the finest examples of 19th-century residential architecture in the state. A short drive from the downtown area are homes built in the Queen Anne, second empire, and stick styles of the 1800s as well as the prairie style of the 1900s. Many of the older homes have been restored and reopened as bed-and-breakfasts.

Given the beautiful setting and vibrant community, Stillwater properties are some of the most expensive in the region, particularly if you have your heart set on a Victorian masterpiece with a turret and big front porch.

White Bear Lake

Set along the clear waters of White Bear Lake and located just 20 minutes from St. Paul, the city of White Bear Lake has a beautiful, turn-of-the-20th-century downtown area with modern residential areas situated around parks and wetlands. Golf courses, beaches, lakes, and nature trails can be found within the city limits, and White Bear Lake itself is the largest lake within the metropolitan area, making it a great place for boating and fishing in the summer and cross-country skiing and ice fishing during the winter.

Housing prices tend to be slightly higher than Twin Cities averages.

Woodbury

With both beautiful residential neighborhoods and a thriving business community, Woodbury has enjoyed a population explosion over the past 15 years. Commercial development has helped create a strong community with a high quality of life, making Woodbury a great place to live and do business. Although most of Woodbury is strictly residential, the city is also home to businesses from large corporations to small businesses and retail outlets.

Citizens of Woodbury enjoy four community parks: the Bielenberg Sports Center, Carver Lake, Ojibway, and Tamarack Nature Preserve, the latter three offering more than 120 acres of parkland connected by paved and turf trails. Woodbury has many neighborhood parks, too, with amenities such as basketball courts and ballfields.

Housing prices in Woodbury tend to be considerably higher than Twin Cities averages.

West
Deephaven

A small city surrounded by protected bays and woodlands, Deephaven is located on the south shore of Lake Minnetonka. The city is so close to the water, in fact, that few of its residents live more than 1 mile from the beaches of this beautiful lake. Deephaven has more than 76 acres of parkland, with Thorpe Park being the largest, offering picnic areas, a lighted hockey rink, basketball courts, and many flower gardens.

Housing prices tend to be considerably higher than Twin Cities averages.

Excelsior

The historic town of Excelsior is a perfect blend of the old and the new, combining a villagelike atmosphere of antiques shops and inns with modern hotels and restaurants. First settled in 1853, downtown Excelsior is full of old buildings and houses that date from the turn of the 20th century. Excelsior borders

Carver Park Reserve and its 3,500 acres of parkland, campgrounds, and horseback and snowmobile trails, as well as Minnewashta Regional Park and its public swimming beach.

Housing prices in Excelsior are far higher than Twin Cities averages.

Minnetonka

Residents of this Twin Cities metro suburb may just have the best of both worlds—a thriving, competitive business community set in a beautiful residential area along the shores of Lake Minnetonka. Minnetonka has more than 40 city parks and is set close to the shores of Lake Minnetonka. Careful city planning over the years has allowed its beautiful woodlands, wetlands, and creeks to survive intact inside the city itself.

A highly desirable area, Minnetonka housing prices are far above Twin Cities averages.

Orono

This picturesque residential community is surrounded by many neighborhood and city parks, including Noerenberg Memorial Park, and five public marinas. City ordinances require minimum sizes for residential lots, so each home owner has at least two acres of land, and many home owners own five acres of land.

Housing prices tend to be far higher than Twin Cities averages.

Wayzata

Pronounced "why-ZEH-tah," Wayzata is a small city located on the north shore of Lake Minnetonka. The name comes from the Dakotas' god of the north, a giant who blew cold winds from his mouth. Today this area is a beautiful spot for a weekend retreat as well as a luxurious residential area with access to many downtown specialty shops, restaurants, and boutiques. The town has the only free trolley service in the Twin Cities, which takes visitors and residents around town spring through fall.

Housing prices are well above Twin Cities averages.

LIBRARIES

Hennepin County Library
17524 Excelsior Boulevard, Minnetonka
(952) 847-5725
www.hclib.org
Twenty-five additional locations in Hennepin County suburbs

The suburban Hennepin County Library system has locations throughout the Minneapolis suburbs. Borrowing privileges are available to suburban Hennepin County residents. In addition to the general library collections, the Hennepin County Library offers an eLibrary through its Web site and at branch libraries, with many databases available in languages commonly spoken in the seven-county metro area, including Hmong, Somali, Russian, and Spanish. The library also has KidLinks and TeenLinks collections of electronic resources for children, including children's search engines and word processing, as well as easy electronic information about the library's holdings of materials for children and teens.

The Hennepin County Library's hours vary widely by location; call for more information. At the time of this writing, the Hennepin County Library system and the Minneapolis Public Library system were considering merging, perhaps as soon as 2008.

Minneapolis Public Library
300 Nicollet Mall, Minneapolis
(612) 630-6000
www.mplib.org
Fourteen additional locations in Minneapolis

The new central Minneapolis Public Library opened to the public on May 20, 2006, and the Cesar Pelli–designed masterpiece is a spectacular building worth a visit even if you're not looking for a book. For casual browsers, the new library has nearly 100 percent of its collection accessible to the public, a noticeable improvement from the 15 percent that was available in the old library. The transparent building is extremely energy efficient and allows readers to page through their finds under natural lighting. The windows are

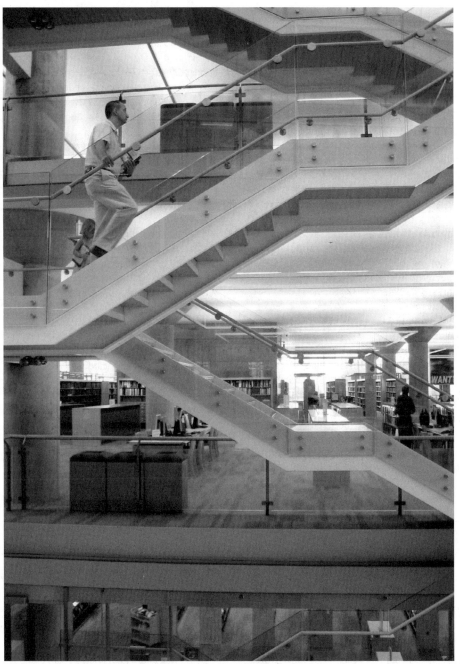

The downtown Minneapolis Public Library is an architectural masterpiece. TODD R. AND BONNIE S. BERGER specially designed to avoid damage to fragile books from ultraviolet light. The building includes numerous meeting rooms, an auditorium, areas specifically for young children and teens, a New Americans Center for non–English-speaking immigrants, a cafe, a bookstore, vast computer services, and a connection to the Minneapolis Skyway System. The library will also be home to the Minnesota Planetarium and Space Discovery Center, scheduled for completion in 2010. Satellite libraries can be found throughout Minneapolis, and as of this writing, the Minneapolis Public Library system was exploring a merger with the Hennepin County Library system, perhaps as soon as 2008.

Ramsey County Library
4570 North Victoria Street, Shoreview
(651) 486-2300
www.ramsey.lib.mn.us
Six additional locations in Ramsey County suburbs
The Ramsey County Library allows residents of the St. Paul suburbs of Arden Hills, Maplewood, Mounds View, North St. Paul, Roseville, Shoreview, and White Bear Lake convenient access to books and other materials. The seven libraries house more than one million items, and patrons can also access the Internet from library terminals, use Microsoft Word at all branches, and enjoy such amenities as a Dunn Bros. cafe in the Roseville branch library. Any resident of the seven-country metropolitan area can get a library card.

St. Paul Public Library
90 West Fourth Street, St. Paul
(651) 266-7000
www.stpaul.lib.mn.us
Twelve additional locations in St. Paul
The elegant St. Paul Public Library building in downtown St. Paul dates from 1917. Having reopened in 2002 after a $15.9 million renovation, the beautiful Italian Renaissance revival building brashly shows off its historical and artistic interior. The renovation included

restoration of the building's detailed hand-painted ceilings, Mankato stone and plaster details, and compressed cork floors, as well as updating the library's telecommunications connections to allow high-speed Internet access. The library building is connected to downtown Saint Paul's skyway system via a tunnel between the Saint Paul Hotel and RiverCentre. Other features include an enlarged children's room, larger public browsing areas, a cafe on the first floor, and a new entrance from Kellogg Boulevard. St. Paul Public Library cards are available to residents of St. Paul, but nearly all residents of Minnesota can borrow books from the library using their home library card.

University of Minnesota Libraries
Wilson Library, 309 19th Avenue South,
West Bank Campus, Minneapolis
(612) 626-2227
www.lib.umn.edu
The University of Minnesota–Twin Cities Libraries contain the largest collection of materials in the state, including some 6 million books, 37,000 periodical subscriptions, 2.6 million government documents, and 400,000 maps. The library system's extensive holdings are housed in five major libraries and 14 branch locations on the U of M's campuses in Minneapolis and St. Paul. In addition to the main Wilson Library general collection, the system includes such specialized collections as the Veterinary Medical Library on the St. Paul campus, the Science and Engineering Library within Walter Library on the East Bank of the Minneapolis campus, and the Eric Sevareid Journalism Library in Murphy Hall on the East Bank. The U of M Library is also the regional depository for Minnesota and South Dakota of all publications produced by the U.S. Government Printing Office, and the library boasts more than one million full-text journal articles stored in electronic databases.

University students, faculty, staff, and research assistants enjoy free borrowing privileges to the library's collections. The general public can borrow books and other materials from the library by joining the Friends of the Libraries, with a minimum donation of $80 annually, or by requesting an interlibrary loan at a public library. The hours of Wilson Library and the other libraries and collections on campus vary widely, depending on the individual library's policies and the academic schedule of the university. Call Wilson Library for more information.

MOTOR VEHICLE REGISTRATION AND DRIVER'S LICENSES

Minnesota Department of Public Safety Driver and Vehicle Services
445 Minnesota Street, Suite 168, St. Paul
(651) 297-2005
www.dps.state.mn.us/dvs
Numerous locations throughout the Twin Cities metro

As a new resident of Minnesota, you have 60 days after moving to the Twin Cities to register your vehicle and obtain a driver's license if your vehicle is registered in another state and/or you have a driver's license from another state. Commercial vehicle drivers have 30 days to obtain a commercial driver's license.

To obtain Minnesota plates and register your vehicle, you will need the current vehicle registration card or certificate of title, your insurance information, the odometer reading from your vehicle, a driver's license (or other valid form of identification) and, if you are leasing your vehicle, a copy of the leasing agreement. The cost to register your vehicle is based on set fees for plates, filing, public safety tax, and title, as well as on the value of your vehicle for the registration tax. The registration tax for first-time registration of a vehicle in Minnesota is based on the value of the vehicle and can run as high as $189. Subsequent renewals are capped at $99. The tax for cars older than 10 years is set at $35 for new registration and renewals.

i You don't need to be a resident of the town or county in which the Motor Vehicle Registrar Office is located to obtain a driver's license or vehicle plates there, and it is often a much shorter waiting time at suburban offices than at the main offices in Minneapolis and St. Paul. For a full list of Twin Cities registrar offices, contact the Minnesota Department of Public Safety at (651) 297-2005 or www.dps.state.mn.us.

If you have a valid driver's license from another state, you will need to pass a knowledge test and vision check to obtain a Minnesota driver's license. If your license from another state has been expired for more than a year or you move to Minnesota from another country, you will also need to pass a skill (road) test. You will need to present your current driver's license when applying for a Minnesota license. A regular driver's license for adults over 21 costs $41.25; for those under 21, it's $21.25.

Motor Vehicle Registrar Offices are located throughout the seven-county metropolitan region. The following offices serve Minneapolis and St. Paul.

Driver and Vehicle Services
Government Center, 300 South Sixth Street, Minneapolis
(612) 348-8240

Driver and Vehicle Services
Sears, 425 Rice Street, St. Paul
(651) 292-9791

TOURISM BUREAUS

Both Minneapolis and St. Paul have convention and visitor bureaus with a wealth of information about the Cities, on such topics as relocation, current arts and sporting events, restaurants, real estate agents, neighborhoods, and many other resources.

The **Greater Minneapolis Convention and Visitors Association,** 250 Marquette Avenue South, Minneapolis (612-767-8000 or 888-676-MPLS; www.minneapolis.org), offers a visitor guide, a complete listing of visitor and resident resources, travel/hotel reservations, events calendars, and discounted tickets to certain events.

The **Saint Paul RiverCentre Convention and Visitors Authority,** 175 West Kellogg Boulevard, Suite 502, St. Paul (651-265-4900 or 800-627-6101; www.stpaulcvb.org), offers detailed information about the city's attractions, restaurants, hotels, neighborhoods, and more. A free visitor kit, with much information useful to new Twin Citians, is available through the bureau.

SENIOR SCENE

The Twin Cities and its suburbs are home to more than 100 retirement communities and nursing homes, many of which are located on scenic lakefronts or surrounded by parklike grounds. This chapter covers just a few of the residences senior citizens have to choose from in the greater Twin Cities metro area and is in no way meant to be all-inclusive. For more information about nursing homes, contact the **Minnesota Department of Health** (651-201-5000; www.health.state.mn.us), **Care Providers of Minnesota** (952-854-2844; www.careproviders.org), the **Minnesota Health and Housing Alliance** (651-645-4545; www.mhha.com), or the **AARP** (866-554-5381; www.aarp.org/states/mn).

Today, more and more emphasis is placed on senior citizens receiving assisted care in their own homes instead of relocating to a group nursing home. With tens of thousands of senior citizens in Minnesota in need of day-to-day care, many nursing homes are filled to capacity, and most opt to stay relatively small and intimate in order to provide quality care to residents. To accommodate the growing senior population in the state, many hospitals and managed care facilities offer assisted living options to seniors that are covered by either Medicare or their own insurance plans. These services range from having a nurse stop by on a regular basis to having a home care worker live full-time with seniors, helping out with everything, including grooming, medication, shopping, and housekeeping.

Senior citizens are a vital force in the Twin Cities, as evidenced in many successful political campaigns that have run primarily on senior concerns and issues. This is in no small part because of the Twin Cities being home to some of the most dynamic senior rights advocacy groups, including the Gray Panthers, the AARP, the Minnesota Senior Federation, and many of the other lesser-known organizations that are listed in this chapter. These groups have effected positive change in the way government, employers, and businesses view senior citizens. They have also changed for the better the way all adults are treated in nursing homes and medical facilities across the country.

RETIREMENT COMMUNITIES

Alterra Sterling House
1005 Paul Parkway, Blaine
(763) 755-2800

5891 Carmen Avenue East
Inver Grove Heights
(651) 306-0919

305 East Thompson Avenue, West St. Paul
(651) 453-1803
www.assisted.com
Alterra Sterling House, which recently merged with Brookdale Senior Living, offers assisted living to older adults who want to retain their independence while receiving the personal services they need. The three Metro communities emphasize freestanding residences specifically designed for individuals with memory impairments such as Alzheimer's disease. Residents live in their own private apartments, complete with kitchens and private bathrooms, receiving individual care and personal assistance in a cheerful, homelike atmosphere. This allows residents to enjoy privacy yet still have access to a full-time professional staff that caters to their personal needs.

Bethany Covenant Village
2309 Hayes Street NE, Minneapolis
(612) 781-2691
www.covenantretirement.com
Located in northeastern Minneapolis, Bethany
Covenant Village is a 16-room Christian facility
that provides care to senior citizens who need
assistance in their day-to-day living. Their supportive and sensitive staff provides assistance
with such activities as dressing, bathing, medication management, and anything else that
may be needed to help residents retain their
independence. A licensed nurse supervises
medical management; rehabilitation services
include physical, occupational, speech, and
intravenous therapy.

Studios and one-bedroom apartments are
furnished and decorated by the residents.
Each unit has a private bathroom, carpeting,
drapes, individual climate control, master TV
antenna, telephone outlets, and an emergency call system.

The Commons on Marice
1380 Marice Drive, Eagan
(651) 688-9999
www.commonsonmarice.com
The Commons on Marice is an elegant senior
living community offering independent and
assisted living, a progressive memory center,
and intergenerational learning opportunities.
The luxurious apartments include a full kitchen
and a private bathroom with a walk-in shower
equipped with grab bars. The residents' common grounds feature a two-story atrium
where residents can tend a garden, enjoy
entertainment, or simply gather for conversation with neighbors. The library, fireplace,
lounge, and billiards room provide residents
with additional opportunities to gather.

The Commons' main claim to fame is fine
dining—meals are prepared from scratch by
an executive chef using only the finest ingredients. All meals are chosen by residents from
a changing and extensive menu, and meals
are taken when the resident chooses to do so
and not on any predetermined schedule.

i For up-to-date information about
retirement communities in the Twin
Cities, *New Lifestyle* magazine has a great
Web site at www.NewLifeStyles.com listing regularly updated community
overviews.

There's also an ice-cream parlor, a chapel, and
a Wellness Center offering everything from
massage to aromatherapy. The Commons
offers around-the-clock staffing, a 24-hour
emergency call system, and programs aimed
at three levels of living, from independent residences to assisted living to a Memory Center
for residents with Alzheimer's.

Covenant Village
5800 St. Croix Avenue North, Golden Valley
(763) 546-6125 or (800) 296-4114
www.covenantretirement.com
Covenant Village is the first accredited
continuing-care retirement community in Minnesota—one of only 260 in the nation to
achieve this honor. Loving care is the essence
of Covenant Retirement Communities, from
assistance with daily activities to rehabilitative
care following injury or illness to long-term
skilled nursing care. Established in 1886,
Covenant Village provides homes to more
than 5,000 senior adults in 14 retirement
communities found throughout the country.

Apartments of various sizes include a full
kitchen and balcony, and some are equipped
with dens and fireplaces. Housekeeping, maintenance, dining services, and amenities such
as recreational facilities all contribute to residents' comfort, and regular group activities
are scheduled. Residents enjoy the comforts
of a community that cares for them physically,
socially, emotionally, and spiritually. Wellness
programs, exercise facilities and programs,
dietary services, and residential and nursing
services are all a part of the Covenant facilities, and everything from assisted living to
rehabilitative care is available from a licensed
skilled nursing facility located on the grounds.

Lake Ridge Care Center and Lake Ridge Manor
310 Lake Boulevard South, Buffalo
(763) 682-1434
www.elimcare.org/lrcc.htm
Located just 30 minutes west of Minneapolis in a quiet rural community, Lake Ridge Care Center (short- or long-term nursing care) and Lake Ridge Manor (assisted living) combine exceptional professional health care with personal attention to help residents achieve their highest level of ability and independence. Providing a family-like, Christian community, the care center and manor's gracious common grounds overlook beautiful Lake Buffalo. A licensed nurse supervises medical management; rehabilitation services include physical, occupational, and speech.

Residents are in charge of personally furnishing their single or double (private or semi-private) residences. Each apartment has a private bathroom, carpeting, draperies, individual climate control, a master TV antenna, telephone outlets, and an emergency call system.

RidgePointe
12600 and 12800 Marion Lane West
Minnetonka
(952) 540-6200
www.ridgepointeseniorliving.com
RidgePointe offers one- and two-bedroom apartments surrounded by gardens to active, independent seniors and adults. The complex is located conveniently near shopping centers, restaurants, medical facilities, theaters, and cultural centers. The complex itself has a group dining room, a fitness center, a hair salon, a convenience store, and hobby rooms on-site. There's also daily scheduled transportation to shopping, medical appointments, and church services for residents; and amenities figured into the apartment rent include weekly housekeeping, a complimentary continental breakfast, all utilities except telephone and electric, basic cable television, individual climate control, and centrally located elevators in each apartment building. For recreation, there's a card room, a complete library, a billiards room, and a tropical atrium and art gallery connecting the resident buildings.

Twin Lake North
4539 58th Avenue North, Brooklyn Center
(763) 533-1168
langnelson.com/twinlakenorth.html
Twin Lake North's independent living six-apartment townhouses are surrounded by beautiful grounds that allow residents country-like comfort with city convenience. One- and two-bedroom apartments are available, and rent includes utilities plus an attached garage. Many apartments have private balconies. Additional amenities include daily activities, garden plots, a fitness center, a clubhouse, a heated pool, and free van service.

SERVICES AND PROGRAMS IN THE METRO AREA

Many organizations in the Twin Cities are concerned with protecting the welfare of our senior community. These organizations deal with everything from helping senior citizens and their families choose a suitable retirement community to matching grandparentless children with volunteer senior citizens. For more information about senior advocacy groups in the Twin Cities, contact the AARP at (866) 554-5381 or www.aarp.org/states/mn.

Alzheimer's Association, Minnesota/North Dakota Chapter
4550 West 77th Street, Suite 200, Edina
(952) 830-0512
www.alzmndak.org
Formed by family caregivers who sought support and help, the nonprofit Alzheimer's Association is available to answer questions about

i For informed referrals to medical programs, specially trained personnel, or special housing arrangements, contact the Minnesota Home Care Association at (651) 635-0607 or www.mnhomecare.org.

Alzheimer's disease and to direct you to services, educational workshops, support groups, and information in the Twin Cities.

CARELINK
www.carelinkusa.com
CARELINK is an interactive resource to connect families with long-term care facilities throughout Minnesota. Up-to-the-minute information gives caregivers current resources to better define individual plans of care for senior citizens.

DARTS
1645 Marthaler Lane, West St. Paul
(651) 455-1560
www.darts1.org
DARTS (Dakota Area Resources and Transportation for Seniors) provides professionally coordinated transportation and in-home services for Dakota County seniors and their families. As a volunteer-based, nonprofit organization, DARTS offers services that support the full participation of seniors in community life, seeking out group activities and volunteer opportunities for seniors in the metro area and providing transportation to those functions.

Elderhostel
(800) 454-5768
www.elderhostel.org
Elderhostel is dedicated to providing extraordinary learning adventures for people age 55 and older. About 3,000 programs are offered in sites around the world, including some in Minnesota. Elderhostel's learning vacations provide opportunities for older adults to take noncredit courses in many subjects—history, culture, food and wine, the outdoors, and more—while enjoying extracurricular activities with others who share similar interests. This is learning just for the pleasure of learning. Visit Elderhostel's Web site or call them to be put on Elderhostel's mailing lists.

Estates in Transition, Inc.
5427 Pompano Drive, Minnetonka
(952) 938-5253
Estates in Transition, Inc., has been helping individuals with household organization, financial management, and personal and care management since 1982. It is particularly concerned with senior advocacy in all the aforementioned cases.

Evercare Minnesota
9900 Bren Road East, Minneapolis
(800) 905-8671
www.evercareonline.com
Evercare provides health care services to both Medicare and Medicaid recipients and offers programs to keep frail individuals living independently as long as possible. Started in 1987 by two nurse-practitioners in Minnesota, Evercare has grown from a small Medicare pilot program to an international, award-winning health care organization that's the largest organization of its kind in the country.

Gentle Transitions
7346 Ohms Lane, Edina
(952) 944-1028
www.gentletransitions.com
Gentle Transitions is a fully insured moving company that provides moving services for relocating senior citizens, offering premove planning, sorting, and packing, through to unpacking and settling into a new home.

Twin Cities Gray Panthers
3249 Hennepin Avenue South, Minneapolis
(612) 822-1011
www.graypantherstwincities.org
The long-established Gray Panthers have worked on local, state, and national levels to fight ageism, press for legislation that promotes age equality, and to advocate social justice issues of concern to seniors such as health care and family security. Call to find out about what's going on in your local network.

HandyWorks
Greater Minneapolis Council of Churches
1001 East Lake Street, Minneapolis
(612) 721-8687
www.gmcc.org/handyworks
HandyWorks provides assistance to older
adults and people with disabilities with household chores and minor home repairs to help
people continue to live independently in their
own homes. For some, HandyWorks is a solu-
tion to a temporary situation—an illness or
recovery from an injury. For others, Handy-
Works becomes an essential service to help
them to remain in their homes by providing
assistance with such things as routine cleaning, yard work, and snow removal.

Home Instead Senior Care
2580 White Bear Avenue, #104, St. Paul
(651) 747-8722
6 additional Twin Cities locations
www.homeinstead.com
Home Instead Senior Care is the world's
largest provider of comprehensive compan-
ionship and home care services for seniors.
From a few hours a day, up to 24 hours' care,
seven days a week, Home Instead helps with
everyday tasks to enable older adults to live
independently.

Jewish Family and Children's Services (JFCS)
of Minneapolis
13100 Wayzata Boulevard, Suite 400
Minnetonka
(952) 546-0616
www.jfcsmpls.org
Jewish Family and Children's Services of Minneapolis is dedicated to helping older adults
maintain their autonomy, independence, and
safety. The Older Adult Services staff includes
social service and nurse case managers who
are specialists in the field of aging and are
knowledgeable about community resources—
the staff also includes professionals who
speak Yiddish and Russian. One phone call to
JFCS puts you in touch with a case manager
who will answer your questions and schedule
a time for an in-home visit. Some of the services offered include housecleaning, personal
grooming, Kosher Meals on Wheels, in-home
health services, transportation to medical and
dental appointments, grocery shopping, con-
sultation with family and caregivers, household financial management, volunteer visitors,
and individual and family counseling. Fees are
based on income and ability to pay.

Keystone Community Services
2000 St. Anthony Avenue, St. Paul
(651) 645-0349
www.keystonecommunityservices.org
Keystone Community Services provides activities for mind and body, Meals on Wheels, jobs
and training, and supportive services that help
seniors overcome obstacles to independence.

Lutheran Social Service of Minnesota
2485 Como Avenue, St. Paul
(651) 642-5990 or (800) 582-5260
www.lssmn.org
Senior programs through Lutheran Social
Service, one of Minnesota's largest statewide
nonprofit charitable organizations, include
assisted living, nonmedical in-home respite,
counseling, debt counseling, foster grandpar-
enting, grandparents raising grandchildren
support, conservatorship, senior compan-
ions, Meals on Wheels, and healthy living
workshops.

Metropolitan Area Agency on Aging, Inc.
2365 North McKnight Road, Suite 3,
North St. Paul
(651) 641-8612
www.tcaging.org
This state-designated agency advocates and
educates on issues of aging, as well as plans,
coordinates, and offers services that help
older adults remain in their homes. This is a
great resource that offers a range of help or
links to help for everything from teaching seniors how to use the Internet, home-delivered
meals, senior employment, and in-home
assistance and care to counseling, prescrip-
tion, and community service hotlines.

The Minnesota Board on Aging
540 Cedar Street, St. Paul
(651) 431-2500
www.mnaging.org
The Minnesota Board on Aging is committed
to providing leadership to ensure that the
needs of the state's older citizens are met.
The board provides many opportunities and
programs to enhance quality of life. Programs
include the Senior LinkAge Line® (800-333-
2433) that provides information about and
assistance with a variety of senior issues,
Eldercare projects, legal advocacy, coordinated health insurance, counseling, congregate housing services, nutrition programs,
and services as an ombudsman for older Minnesotans.

Minnesota Department
of Veterans Affairs (MDVA)
20 West 12th Street, Room 206C, St. Paul
(651) 296-2562
www.mdva.state.mn.us
The Minnesota Department of Veterans
Affairs provides information to seniors on
benefits for former armed forces personnel in
Minnesota. The MDVA also operates LinkVet
(888-LINKVET), which provides referrals,
immediate crisis intervention, and psychologi-
cal counseling 24 hours a day.

The Minnesota Relay Service
(651) 602-9005 or (800) 657-3775 (both TTY
or Voice)
The Minnesota Relay Service connects those
who are deaf, hard of hearing, deaf-blind, or
speech impaired to hearing people via the
telephone, 24 hours a day, 365 days a year.
Either party can initiate the call. One service is
CapTel, where specially trained operators
type the telephone users' verbal responses,
relaying conversations to the CapTel user
almost simultaneously with the spoken word.
All calls are confidential.

Minnesota Senior Federation (MnSF)
1885 University Avenue, Suite 171,
St. Paul
(651) 645-0261 or (877) 645-0261
www.mnseniors.org
The Minnesota Senior Federation is dedicated
to maintaining a democratic, grassroots
organization that trusts in the common sense
of its members. Uniting seniors and their own
organizations, the MnSF acts as a body of
peers, leaders, and decision makers, influenc-
ing state policies regarding seniors and providing community information and services to
benefit people of all ages with an emphasis
on health, housing, retirement planning, and
legal issues. The MnSF publishes a monthly
newspaper for members.

Osher Lifelong Learning Institute
250 McNamara Alumni Center
200 Oak Street SE, Minneapolis
(612) 624-7847
www.cce.umn.edu/olli
OLLI is a voluntary, noncredit education and
service program for older adults. It is an affiliated program of University College at the University of Minnesota College of Continuing
Education. The organization offers courses,
luncheon programs, informal summer programs, educational tours, service opportunities, and special events. Courses are offered
for an eight-week session each fall and spring
and a six-week session each winter that meet
weekly for one-and-a-half- to two-hour sessions. Courses focus on a wide range of interests—literature, psychology, world cultures,
history, politics, economics, science, wellness, and the arts.

Outfront Minnesota
Sabathani Center
310 East 38th Street, Suite 204, Minneapolis
(612) 822-0127 or (800) 800-0350
www.outfront.org
Visit Outfront Minnesota's Web site for information on resources for older gays and les-

ℹ️ Children of Aging Parents (CAPS) offers advice on all aspects of senior care, as well as support for those facing difficult decisions. Call (800) 227-7294 or visit them on the Web at www.caps4caregivers.org.

bians for yourself, family, or friends. Information available includes several social groups, family and individual support, medical and mental health, housing, employment (volunteer, stipended, and paid), job search help, and many other services.

Recovery, Inc.
(612) 824-5773
Recovery, Inc. organizes and sponsors free self-help groups throughout the Twin Cities to help people regain and maintain mental health when dealing with mood and personality disorders such as depression, anger, frustration, fear, and anxiety.

RSVP
2021 East Hennepin Avenue, Suite 200
Minneapolis
(612) 331-4063
The Retired and Senior Volunteer Program invites persons 55 and older to make volunteering a part of their lives. RSVP provides free assistance in locating volunteer opportunities, along with supplemental insurance and limited reimbursement of travel expenses. Volunteer opportunities are available throughout the eleven counties.

Saint Paul Parks and Recreation
300 City Hall Annex, 25 West Fourth Street,
St. Paul
(651) 266-6378
www.stpaul.gov/depts/parks/seniorcitizen
Saint Paul Parks and Recreation's Senior Citizen Recreation Program invites adults at least 50 years of age to spring into new activities. Bimonthly, the program publishes *The Pioneer Spirit,* a newsletter listing upcoming activities and registration materials—call the

above phone number to get a copy mailed to you. There are special events and weekly groups with activities such as craftmaking, bowling, cards, movies, senior choir, and senior exercise.

St. Louis Park Senior Program
6715 Minnetonka Blvd., St. Louis Park
(952) 928-6444
www.stlouispark.org/experience/senior_programs.htm
The St. Louis Park Senior Program organizes dozens of outings, guest speakers, and special events. Events include such things as trips to the Minnesota History Center, State Capitol, Chanhassen Dinner Theater, Lunch and Learn sessions with speakers discussing issues of interest to seniors, holiday concerts, and flu shot clinics. Their Web site lists the latest happenings.

Senior Community Services
10709 Wayzata Boulevard, Suite 111
Minnetonka
(952) 541-1019
www.seniorcommunity.org
Senior Community Services provides in-home counseling and case management to frail seniors and their families throughout suburban Hennepin County to help older adults remain independent as long as possible. Its services include transportation, homemaking, medical care, and assistance with health insurance. The staff meets with seniors in their own homes to identify and connect with the combination of services that will fit their specific needs.

TeleFriends
2021 East Hennepin Avenue, Suite 200,
Minneapolis
(612) 331-4063
Senior volunteers provide reading support, encouragement, and assistance to grade-school children via the telephone. TeleFriends provides age-appropriate books to volunteers and students.

Volunteers of America
5905 Golden Valley Road, Minneapolis
(763) 546-3242
www.voamn.org
Volunteers of America has several programs under Senior Services. Options include meals at various locations and home-delivered meals; mental health services for seniors; the Park Elder Center with numerous programs and classes; legal services; Experience Corps, which involves seniors in tutoring and mentoring roles with kids in Kindergarten through third grade; assistance to caregivers of seniors; assisted living programs; and much more. The Wellness Initiative provides strength and flexibility classes, grocery shopping assistance, and one-on-one nutritional counseling by a registered dietitian. And the new Nutrition Education Web site helps seniors access nutrition education through current articles, links, and activities.

SUPPORT PROGRAMS

Adult Day Programs
2021 East Hennepin Avenue, Suite 200, Minneapolis
(612) 331-4063
Adult Day Programs offers long-term, daily support for seniors, including transportation and day care for adults with social activities, lunch, field trips, and more.

Elder Ride
(612) 332-9544
Elder Ride provides van rides for seniors to medical and nonmedical appointments.

Hennepin County Coordinated Transportation
(952) 541-1019
HCCT plans, develops, promotes, and coordinates transportation resources for older adults in Hennepin County.

CHILD CARE

There are hundreds of child care providers and preschools in the Twin Cities metro area, ranging from small, home-based day care centers that cater to infants and toddlers to public schools that have specialized programs for children as young as two years old. Minnesota law has specific guidelines for child care providers. Minnesota's licensing procedure for potential child care providers is a strict one, too, requiring thorough background checks, drug testing, proof of completion of a child development course and a family day care training program, and unannounced site inspections that continue long after the license is granted. Minnesota law dictates that each day care must adhere to specific adult-to-child/infant ratios, usually of no more than six preschool-aged children per adult or two infants per adult.

The upside of this is that parents are able to rest much easier knowing their children are placed in such rigidly monitored day care facilities. Most day care centers in the Twin Cities have large, fenced-in play areas attached; serve one or two hot, homemade meals that meet USDA guidelines; and are run by people willing to go through rigorous screening procedures to become day care providers. The downside is that child care expenses in the Twin Cities are easily above the national standard, costing parents between $4,000 and $22,000 per year per child, with an average monthly bill of about $700. The following listings are by no means exhaustive but should give you a good foundation for your search for child care.

AFTER-SCHOOL CARE

Almost every school in Minneapolis and St. Paul offers some sort of after-school program for children, continuing education classes for adults, or weekend activities open to both children and adults as part of their continuing effort to both get parents involved in school and to keep public schools an important focus of their community. For information regarding after-school activities in your neighborhood, contact Minneapolis Public Schools at (612) 668-0000 or www.mpls.k12.mn.us, or the St. Paul Public Schools at (651) 767-8100 or www.stpaul.k12.mn.us.

MONTESSORI SCHOOLS

Founded by Dr. Maria Montessori in 1907, Montessori education has gained favor with the public over the past two decades. In Minnesota many Montessori schools have been incorporated into the public school system, bringing their tradition of encouraging independent thinking and cultural literacy to inner-city children who might otherwise not have the financial option of attending the formerly private schools. As Montessori schools generally allow children as young as three to attend classes, a Montessori education is a viable alternative to traditional day care.

When choosing a Montessori school for your child to attend, it's important to remember that no two Montessori schools are exactly alike. One might emphasize arts and crafts, while another might concentrate on math and science. Curriculums are subject to change, too, so the only way to know for sure what type of Montessori school is in your neighborhood is to personally check it out—which the schools strongly encourage anyway, as parent involvement is just as vital a part of the system as the students and teachers themselves. *NOTE*: Montessori preschool classes fill up quickly, and parents are encouraged to apply to their school of choice at least six months in advance.

In Minneapolis, Montessori schools that have specifically pre-K (from one year old on up) and kindergarten classes are **Bernie's Montessori School** (612-333-5460) at 115 Second Avenue South and **Children's Village Montessori** (612-378-7730) at 2929 University Avenue SE. In St. Paul there is **Children's House Montessori** (651-690-3403) at 1194 Randolph Avenue and **Oak Hill Montessori School** (651-484-8242) at 4665 Hodgson Road.

GROUP DAY CARE CENTERS

New Horizon Child Care
111 Marquette Avenue, Minneapolis
(612) 332-7866

401 Robert Street North, St. Paul
(651) 224-4256
www.newhorizonchildcare.com
Numerous additional Twin Cities locations
One of the largest child care providers in the Twin Cities with more than 50 branches in the metro area alone, New Horizon Child Care aims to give children under their care a safe place to play as well as a head start on their future academic careers. New Horizon has a curriculum for children, based on their age and developmental levels, which includes art, drama, computer, music, reading classes, field trips, lots of storytelling, and indoor and outdoor exercise (depending on weather). Infants as young as six weeks old are accepted into the program, as well as children as old as 12.

KinderCare Learning Center
807 Second Street SE, Minneapolis
(612) 379-0857

2070 Burns Avenue, St. Paul
(651) 731-1815
www.kindercare.com
With some 72 locations in the Twin Cities metro, this all-purpose day care is extended to children as young as six weeks old to kids

i The Greater Minneapolis Day Care Association (612-341-1177) connects parents to day care centers and child care providers in the Twin Cities metro area.

as old as 12. The facilities offer transportation to and from home, and meals are provided three times a day.

NANNIES

The state-required screening process for nannies and the potential hiring parents, as well as the extra screening completed by the individual agencies themselves, ensures a roster of child care professionals. Nanny care is not just for infants—the agencies listed below have nannies qualified to take care of infants and children up to age 14.

Nannies from the Heartland
5490 Balsam Lane North, Minneapolis
(763) 550-0219
www.nanniesheartland.com

Nanny Professionals
2456 Arkwright Street St. Paul
(651) 221-0587
www.nannyprofessionals.com

CHURCH-BASED CARE

Many of the hundreds of churches in the Twin Cities metro area offer weekday and/or weekend day care for young children. It would be difficult to list every church that offers day care, just because these programs are sometimes offered only in the summer or are even canceled due to lack of community support. Your best bet is to call the churches directly to find out if they are offering day care—church-based care generally costs about $150 per week for full-time care.

Lexington Kids Christian Child Care (651-646-6484; www.stmatthewsluth.org/lexington.html), located at 701 North Lexington Parkway in St. Paul, is a Christian-oriented day care that offers children six months to school age a playground, computer labs, and various monthly activities. **Calvary Lutheran Pre-Kindergarten** (763-545-5659; www.calvary.org/pre-k), located at 7520 Golden Valley Road in Golden Valley, is a Christian-oriented preschool for children ages two to five, with an academic curriculum that encourages children to start reading and writing prior to entering the public school system. Calvary has a full-time kindergarten as well.

SPECIAL NEEDS

Ronald McDonald House
818 Fulton Street SE, Minneapolis
(612) 331-5752
www.rmhtwincities.org
The Ronald McDonald House of the Twin Cities is a home away from home for families who have children with cancer or other life-threatening illnesses and are accessing a local medical treatment facility. The purpose of the Ronald McDonald House of the Twin Cities is to support and strengthen families during times of medical crisis for children.

Crisis Nursery of Anoka
County–Childrens Home
1400 131st Avenue NE, Blaine
(763) 785-9222
Crisis Nursery offers emergency care family services, including help for battered women, teen parents, and abused or neglected children. Families are encouraged to call ahead to set up a meeting, in either home or at Crisis Nursery's office, to see what action would be most beneficial. Referrals are available, so call with any problem and the staff will do their best to direct you to the most appropriate organization.

SUPPORT GROUPS

Chrysalis—A Center for Women
4432 Chicago Avenue South, Minneapolis
(612) 871-0118
www.chrysaliswomen.org
Chrysalis holds classes and workshops for women, with a special emphasis on helping couples with children deal with divorce or separation—these meet the county requirements that divorcing families must attend. Child care is available during counseling and classes (Chrysalis has a child care program as well), and counseling is extended to children ages 6 to 17 whose parents are separating or divorcing.

ℹ️ The University of Minnesota's Center for Early Education & Development (612-6253058; cehd.umn.edu/ceed) keeps a database of early childhood programs throughout the Twin Cities.

Prevent Child Abuse Minnesota
1821 University Avenue West, Suite 202-S, St. Paul
(651) 523-0099 or (800) 621-6322
www.preventchildabusemn.org
Prevent Child Abuse Minnesota provides support groups for children and parents—adults talk about challenges and ideas while, in a different room, children learn new coping skills. Weekly meetings are offered around the metro. The organization also provides materials on preventing and coping with abuse, advocates strength-based family services and policies, and gives guidance to families in crisis.

Resource Center for Fathers and Families
1201 89th Avenue NE, Blaine
(612) 783-4938
www.resourcesforfathers.org
With locations in Minneapolis, St. Paul, Blaine, Crystal, Burnsville, and New Hope, the Resource Center for Fathers and Families has programs aimed at single, married, or divorced fathers who want to improve their relationship with their children, including anger management groups, parent education classes, and support groups. The center also has information for fathers on legal issues, including referrals and up-to-date information on public policy and child support issues.

Southside Family Nurturing Center
2448 18th Avenue South, Minneapolis
(612) 721-2762
www.ssfnc.org
Southside Family Nurturing Center offers parenting classes to men, women, and couples alike. The program features classes on the prevention of abuse and neglect, parent and child activity nights, anger management, and therapeutic group discussions and individual counseling.

EDUCATION

Education is a matter of considerable civic pride in the Twin Cities and is viewed as essential to the area's continued success. The area's school districts strive to incorporate the entire community in improving the quality of learning, and the influence of K–12 education is felt beyond the confines of the students in the classroom in important areas such as parent involvement, athletics, and local school boards. The State of Minnesota places a premium on education, and therefore an astounding number of local residents are directly or indirectly involved in the school system. The end result is one of the best educational environments in the nation.

This section's focus is on metro area public education, particularly Minneapolis and St. Paul. In addition, there are profiles of a few of the area's private preparatory schools, both nonsectarian and parochial, and profiles of institutions of higher education.

PUBLIC SCHOOLS

Organization

The organization of Minnesota public education (K–12) is based on a stable and efficient school board government. A significant issue with state school districts is consolidation, especially in rural areas. As Minnesota's population has swelled, the number of school districts has shrunk. Many suburban school districts have rapidly expanded to immense megadistricts, but they have shrewdly avoided the political difficulty of dividing districts. Today the state of Minnesota has 541 school districts, from traditional K–12 districts to charter districts. All the different types of school districts have missions and objectives specified by the State of Minnesota.

All districts are subject to review and are granted powers by the state legislature and government. When school districts are negligent, their powers may be rescinded and inspected by the Minnesota School Board Association (MSBA). The MSBA frequently serves as a surrogate for direct state intervention in the school districts.

Minnesota school boards' size and lengths of elected terms differ, and they are frequently authorized to make personnel, curriculum, and budget decisions. The Minneapolis school district is the largest in the state, with 38,532 students enrolled in 2006, and is governed by seven "at large" elected school board members, who serve four-year terms. School District 623, the Roseville Area School District, in contrast, elects six members every odd year.

Both state and local government make enormous financial appropriations to Minnesota public education. The state serves approximately 830,000 K–12 students annually. The state is fervently committed to providing a quality education for all students. The Twin Cities have an important organization dedicated to improving Twin Cities K–12 public education, the Association of Metropolitan School Districts (AMSD), which represents 280,000 students from Minneapolis, St. Paul, and many of the Twin Cities' suburbs. AMSD's mission is to advocate for state education policy that enables metropolitan school districts to improve student learning. Organization is an essential component of Minnesota and Twin Cities K–12 public education, and efforts are continually made to better serve the area's children.

Grade Level

Most area school districts are divided into elementary (K–6 or K–5), junior high (7–8 or 7–9) or middle school (6–8), and high school (9–12). The state's two largest school districts, Minneapolis and St. Paul, differ in matters of grade level. Minneapolis has a standardized districtwide system of elementary (K–5 or K–8), middle school (6–8), and high school (9–12). St. Paul's demarcation of grades includes elementary (K–8 or 1–8), middle school (6–8), junior high (7–8), high school (9–12), as well as innovative 4–6, K–12, and 4-year-old programs. Twin Cities suburban public schools frequently use a system similar to Minneapolis for grade levels, and although junior highs continue to persist, middle schools have become much more prevalent over the past couple of decades.

Standards

Minnesota, unlike many other states, did not develop statewide graduation standards until 1993. Because Minnesota consistently has had a 90 percent graduation rate (18- to 24-year-olds), many argued against the trend toward state graduation standards. At the beginning of the 1990s, the legislature and what is now the Minnesota Department of Education jointly initiated a statewide graduation standards program. The resulting Minnesota State Graduation Standards, approved in 1993, had two distinct components: basic skills tests and the profile of learning. These standards were replaced in 2006.

Under the new standards students have to pass basic skills tests and Minnesota Comprehensive Assessments, and complete a certain number of credits in various subjects, in order to graduate. The Minnesota Comprehensive Assessments (MCA-IIs) were developed to help schools and districts measure student progress in mastering the state's new reading, writing, and mathematics standards. They are gradually replacing the basic skills tests. Students begin taking the MCA-IIs in grade 3 and their performance on these statewide assessments can be used as one of multiple criteria to determine grade promotion or retention. To graduate, students will have to pass the MCA-II written composition test given in grade 9, the MCA-II reading test given in grade 10, and the MCA-II math test given in grade 11 (beginning in 2008). All public schools and charter schools must administer the tests.

Teachers

Minnesota has one of the nation's premier public education systems. Central to the state and the Twin Cities success are the 52,796 teachers statewide. Funding and class size are important, but nothing can overshadow passionate, well-educated, committed, student-centered teachers. Education Minnesota, the state's teachers' union, espouses and promotes only the highest caliber of members in its ranks. The strength of teaching in Minnesota can be attributed to a number of factors, from the Department of Children, Families, and Learning to individual school districts.

Requirements for teaching in Minnesota are more rigorous than in many other states. First, in order to receive a license, prospective teachers must attend an institution accredited by the state. Then they must successfully complete classes in a specific area of study; e.g., English, social studies, mathematics, or science. In addition, the state has designated requirements for teachers, which vary depending on the grade levels in which the license can be used. All licensed teachers in the state must pass a course in human relations. Since 1973 each teacher's education institution has been required to provide a course addressing race, culture, socioeconomic status, and general interpersonal communication. Specific licenses have additional requirements. For example, in social studies, and most prospective grade 6–12 disciplines, teachers must take a number of state-specified courses in teaching technology, assessment, kinesiology, special education, and drug and alcohol abuse. Beyond academic requirements, passing a relatively simple test of general knowledge, the Praxis I, is required. Finding employment as a teacher in the Twin Cities is highly competitive, especially in liberal arts subject areas such as social studies and English. Math, science, and special education teachers, in contrast, are in high demand.

Education Minnesota represents the teachers of the state. Education Minnesota developed after the first merger at the state level of the nation's two largest unions of the Minnesota Federation of Teachers (affiliate of the American Federation of Teachers) and the Minnesota Education Association (affiliate of the National Education Association). The 1998 merger was completed to improve the bargaining position of Minnesota's teachers.

Almost 37 percent of Minnesota teachers have received advanced degrees. The average salary among Minnesota teachers is $46,906 annually, and statewide the student/teacher ratio is 16:1.

Special and Gifted/Talented

Over the past couple decades local educators have moved toward integrating special education students in the classroom to reflect society at large. The largest school district in the state, Minneapolis, has developed an approach to special education that is followed by most school districts statewide.

Both St. Paul and Minneapolis emphasize diagnosing and beginning special education students as early as possible. Both schools have early-childhood special education programs, which follow the proscriptions of state law: Students who are assessed to require additional educational enrichment prior to K–12 education receive it. St. Paul addresses these students with the Early Childhood Special Education program (ECSE). Minneapolis has a similar pre-K–12 program and promotes job seeking and job retention skills for high school special education students. Twin Cities special education integrates these students in the classroom so that they can fully participate in the community as adults.

Minnesota special education is among the best in the nation because of the stringent requirements of its teachers. Statewide, master's degrees or greater are required for all special education teachers. The University of Minnesota sponsors special education outreach programs, such as the Institute on Community Education, which provides social support to individuals with developmental problems.

Gifted and talented students in the Twin Cities also have access to specialized programs to meet their educational needs. St. Paul addresses gifted education at the elementary level with DISCOVER, where students are assessed and identified for enriched education. Most elementary districts have Schoolwide Enrichment Models (SEMs), with programs for gifted students and teachers to meet their needs. At the senior high level, the International Baccalaureate program provides a challenging liberal arts curriculum. For Minneapolis talented students there is the Gifted Catalyst Program, which develops the strengths and talents of this important student group. Another essential part of gifted education statewide is a postsecondary option, where Minnesota high school students enroll in college and university classes and earn coursework toward graduation.

Alternative Education

Alternative education programs lead to degrees for nontraditional students who have dropped out of school or require a more flexible learning experience. The state features 145 area learning centers (ALCs), with many other options available within the Twin Cities. From night school GED programs to charter schools, the state has always been an innovator in education for every student.

School Choice

The Twin Cities have without great commotion implemented school choice programs. Integration in the Twin Cities has been relatively civil over the past few decades; compliance has occurred largely through districtwide magnet programs in both St. Paul and Minneapolis, which provide all area students with extensive choices in public education.

Minnesota state statute allows students to attend the public school of their choice, regardless of the community they live in and where their parents pay taxes. If the student is of low socioeconomic status, in some cases transportation may be provided free of charge. As long as there is space in the school, and the student completes registration before individual district's deadlines, then he or she is ensured admittance. Because of the success of open enrollment, the idea of vouchers has only been bandied about but not considered a serious public education option. The success of Minnesota school choice can in part be attributed to the relative parity in funding between Twin Cities school districts. If this condition did not exist, local public education expert Joe Nathan of the nationally recognized Center for School Change argues that school choice would surely fail. Minnesota is proud of the equitable school choice system developed by the state, which offers educational opportunity to every child.

Magnet schools are a major component of Twin Cities school choice. Minneapolis has a combination of magnet and community schools, where specific magnet programs and comprehensive options are available. Comprehensive takes a general, wide-breadth approach to curriculum, whereas the magnets feature a wide array of options. Some of the programs included at the high school level are travel and tourism, aviation and aerospace, communication and technology, education, international baccalaureate, automotive and liberal arts, and several more specific areas of study. There are also magnets available beginning in kindergarten, as well as community schools, which make it easier for families to participate in their particular elementary school's education policies. Minneapolis school choice provides almost infinite options for Minneapolis's children.

The St. Paul district's magnet system is similar to Minneapolis's, with some minor differences. In the jargon of St. Paul public education, there are magnet/citywide and neighborhood schools. Again, the system is developed as a voluntary form of desegregation and offers numerous educational opportunities in specific and broad areas of study.

In both districts magnet programs admission is competitive; however, the majority of students get into the program they desire during their first application. Magnet programs are an important part of the Twin Cities' school choice program, which offers specialized education for every area student.

Charter Schools

Minnesota passed the nation's first charter school law in 1991, and since then, both locally and nationally, there has been an exponential growth of charter schools.

As a laboratory for innovation in education, Twin Cities charter schools have distinguished themselves. Charter schools are independent educational entities, where experiments are permitted in the classroom. Minneapolis alone sponsors 35 charter schools. The charter schools vary widely in curriculum and environment. The Cyber Village Academy is a school dedicated to serving students with "a serious challenge to learning." Annually, approximately 150 homebound students participate in this program for students who may otherwise fall behind or drop out of school. The Oh Day Aki (Heart of the Earth) Charter School serves Twin Cities American Indians in a K–12 school. St. Paul has 30 charter schools to meet the needs of specific student groups, including Hmong Academy, which is a school that emphasizes Hmong culture for students whose first language is Hmong , and City Academy, where "hard to teach learners" receive an education. City Academy, founded in 1992, was the first charter school in the United States.

ℹ️ Extensive homeschooling information is available from the Minnesota Homeschoolers Alliance, P.O. Box40486, St. Paul, MN 55104; (612) 288-9662 or (888) 346-7622.

Homeschooling

Homeschooling is another sector of Minnesota education to experience significant growth in the past couple decades. Numerous organizations have developed to meet the requirements of homeschoolers and the complex labyrinth of local, state, and federal laws with which they must comply.

Minnesota has several laws that protect students from being denied a compulsory education, which also set minimum curriculum requirements for schools across the state, including homeschools. Other statutes ensure that homeschool teachers are competent and address other issues relevant to quality of education. Homeschool students are required annually to successfully complete a state exam to prove that they are being provided with a sufficient education. For the most part, homeschool students have scored well academically compared with their peers. Homeschooling is yet another option for Twin Cities students, requiring substantial planning and hard work by parents and teachers.

Athletics

Athletics play a significant role in Twin Cities education. The number of sports available for both boys and girls varies greatly across school district boundaries. Most schools have boys' baseball, soccer, football, basketball, and hockey. For young women sports include soccer, softball, basketball, gymnastics, and hockey. Girls' hockey is by far the fastest-growing sport in the state, the result of the sport becoming available in the last decade at most large Minnesota high schools. Over the years, the Twin Cities have produced a number of outstanding athletes of both genders.

Local residents support their area athletic teams with an outpouring of enthusiasm. March in Minnesota is tournament time, when high school sports fans become captivated with state championships over three successive weeks. Minnesotans love high school hockey. The Minnesota High School Hockey Tournament draws sellout crowds, and enormous television ratings, as the Twin Cities and greater Minnesota schools engage in annual rivalries. The men's and women's basketball tournaments are also well received throughout the state, as is the annual state football championship the day after Thanksgiving, the Prep Bowl.

The Minnesota State High School League (MSHSL) is the organization that oversees the state's interscholastic athletics and fine arts programs. As a nonprofit, the MSHSL promotes fairness and good sportsmanship by standardizing rules and acts as a bureaucratic force protecting the integrity of statewide athletics. Each year more than 200,000 students participate in MSHSL-sanctioned events.

Parent Involvement

Parents are encouraged to actively participate in their child's education, whether it's in the classroom or in local school board elections. In fact, Minneapolis has one of the nation's most proactive programs for parent involvement.

The first place parents can involve themselves is at the local polling place. There they can support school board members who espouse an agenda most closely resembling their own. In addition, school districts periodically have levies or referenda regarding funding. Twin Citians are usually willing to support more taxes if they believe it will markedly improve K–12 public education.

The Twin Cities school districts have specific initiatives for parent involvement. In 1996 the Minneapolis school district adopted family involvement standards. The program bridges the gap between students, parents, and the community to promote learning. Training and access to resources help families enrich their student's educational experience. Parent involvement creates an important link between Twin Cities children and the community.

English Language Learners (ELL)

In the past decade the Twin Cities have undergone a transformation in student composition, particularly in the two largest urban districts, Minneapolis and St. Paul. English Language Learners have always been a significant part of student demographics. In the late 19th and early 20th centuries, large groups of Czech, German, Swedish, Norwegian, Polish, Jewish, and other immigrant children entered Twin Cities public schools. Today ELL programs have been established to make the transition easier for Hmong, Somali, Tibetan, Bosnian, Hispanic, Amharic (Ethiopian), Russian, and other students whose first language is not English. The Minneapolis K–12 school guide is an excellent example of the school's commitment to ELL education; on the very first page, seven languages ask, "Do you speak a language other than English?"

Minneapolis is the most diverse school district in the state, with school attendance figures for 2006–07 at 53 percent African American, 2 percent Asian American, 5 percent Hispanic American, 5 percent Native American, and 36 percent Caucasian. Minneapolis schools have 31 percent ELL students or approximately 12,000 in the district. An ELL student must meet two requirements: The student's first language is not English, and he/she scores poorly on an English reading or language proficiency test. Throughout the district specific ELL programs are available at most schools. For example, the Ericcson Community School has Hmong and Spanish ELL programs.

PRIVATE SCHOOLS

The Twin Cities are home to nationally respected private schools. Many of the schools are denominational parochial institutions, but in most cases they include children of diverse faiths in their student body.

The area also features schools with innovative academic programs, which mirror charter schools with one exception—tuition. Many of these schools are quite expensive; however, many do offer scholarships for children with low socioeconomic status. Admission is another difficult matter, since some of the schools have fairly rigid admission requirements for K–12 education.

Minneapolis

DeLaSalle High School
1 DeLaSalle Drive, Minneapolis
(612) 676-7600
www.delasalle.com
DeLaSalle is the only Catholic high school in Minneapolis. The school was founded in 1900 by Archbishop John Ireland, who stipulated that it be run by the Brothers of the Christian Schools, a Roman Catholic congregation of religious laymen founded in 1680 by St. John Baptist de La Salle. Because of this Lasaillian underpinning, DeLaSalle emphasizes education for students from a variety of economic levels, academic abilities, racial communities, and ethnic backgrounds. Ninety percent of DeLaSalle graduates go on to college, an impressive number when compared to the statewide average of 66 percent.

Minnehaha Academy
3100 West River Parkway, Minneapolis
(612) 729-8321
www.minnehahaacademy.net
Minnehaha Academy offers a pre-K–12 education with a distinctly Christian orientation. The school's approach to teaching and curriculum does not endorse a particular Christian denominational outlook but does emphasize "challenging minds and nurturing souls."

Minnehaha Academy has three campuses: one in suburban Bloomington and two Minneapolis campuses, idyllically located on West River Parkway overlooking the Mississippi River. Founded in 1913, Minnehaha Academy continues its mission of providing an excellent education rooted in faith.

St. Paul

Cretin-Derham Hall
550 South Albert Street, St. Paul
(651) 690-2443
www.cretin-derhamhall.org

Cretin-Derham Hall (CDH) is one of the premier private high schools in the Twin Cities area. The school is recognized throughout the area for providing a disciplined Catholic education. CDH is also respected statewide as an athletic powerhouse, especially in football and baseball, where students almost annually compete in state championships.

Cretin-Derham Hall's roots date from 1871. The Brothers of the Christian Schools founded Cretin High School exclusively for young men, and in 1905 the Sisters of St. Joseph Carondelet founded Derham Hall. The schools did not merge until 1987, creating a much larger coeducational Catholic high school. After all these years Catholic values remain central to the school's academic experience. CDH inculcates in its students such values as leadership, service, diversity, and equity.

Friends School of Minnesota
1365 Englewood Avenue, St. Paul
(651) 917-0636
www.fsmn.org

A school developed by parents, educators, and members of the Quaker community, the Friends School of Minnesota is in the fine tradition of Quaker education nationally. The Friends School prepares children with a specific Quaker curriculum in grades K–8.

The curriculum at the Friends School is characterized by several teaching techniques. One important aspect of the school's academic experience is a weekly silent meeting, where students and staff reflect on the events of the day. As a part of the Quaker tradition, students also have daily moments of reflection. The curriculum emphasizes hands-on education, especially with young children. The school has a community focus in the classroom, and group gatherings are a regular component of the curriculum, where students discuss group dynamic problems. Essential to the educational experience at the Friends School is the inquiry process, which encourages students to be thirsty for answers when learning.

St. Paul Academy and Summit School
1150 Goodrich Avenue, Goodrich Campus, St. Paul
1712 Randolph Avenue, Randolph Campus, St. Paul
(651) 698-2451
www.spa.edu

St. Paul Academy and Summit School provides a private education on two beautiful campuses in St. Paul. The school's mission is to prepare students for life by providing academically challenging programs.

Another area private school that developed as the result of a merger, St. Paul Academy and Summit School are the result of consolidation to create a coeducational school. St. Paul Academy was founded in 1900 to educate young men, and Summit School first opened its doors in 1917. The two schools have been one since 1969 and have provided an excellent college preparatory education in beautiful, historic facilities.

North

Totino-Grace
1350 Gardena Avenue NE, Fridley
(763) 571-9116
www.totinograce.com

Totino-Grace, a private Catholic high school, serves the northern Twin Cities suburbs. The school's mission centers on learning, faith, service, and community. As the second largest of the 13 Catholic high schools in the Archdiocese of St. Paul and Minneapolis, the school has an annual enrollment of more than 1,000. Totino-Grace was founded in 1965 to meet the needs of the rapidly expanding Twin Cities north suburban area.

i Totino-Grace High School is named in part for Jim and Rose Totino, owners of Totino's frozen pizzas, who made a large donation to the private Catholic school.

South

Academy of Holy Angels
6600 Nicollet Avenue South, Richfield
(612) 798-2600
www.ahastars.org
The Academy of Holy Angels, one of the Twin Cities' most picturesque campuses, sits on 26 acres in suburban Richfield, where the school actively pursues a diverse student population. The 850 students in grades 9–12 have ample academic resources available. Amenities include a theater, computer labs, and a library with more than 12,000 books. The school has excellent athletic facilities, which include a domed football stadium, two gyms, and a weight room with modern exercise equipment. The Academy of Holy Angels specializes in a Catholic education with state-of-the-art education facilities.

The International School of Minnesota
6385 Beach Road, Eden Prairie
(952) 918-1800
www.ism-sabis.net
The International School of Minnesota (ISM) is a private preparatory school for pre-K–12. The school is a member of the SABIS School Network that includes 50 schools worldwide and traces its history back to 1886 in Lebanon.

Located in Eden Prairie, a southern suburb of Minneapolis, ISM has an impressive 55-acre campus beside Bryant Lake. The school was founded in 1986 with an enrollment of only 24 students; since then the school has rapidly expanded to over 500 students. High school students at ISM have advanced placement programs in many academic fields, such as art, biology, history, French, English, and several more college-level courses.

East

Hill-Murray School
2625 Larpenteur Avenue East, Maplewood
(651) 777-1376
www.hill-murray.org
Hill-Murray is a respected Catholic private school for the east metropolitan Twin Cities.

The school enrollment is just under 1,000 students for grades 7–12, and it has an impressive 14:1 student/teacher ratio. Academics with a moral perspective are emphasized at Hill-Murray, and the results show in student standardized test performance. On average, 94 percent of the school's graduates attend college.

Athletics are another important aspect of a Hill-Murray education. There are 23 varsity sports teams, and the Pioneers excel in many, especially hockey, where they have regularly competed in state high school tournaments. Hill-Murray has provided an excellent Catholic education for 50 years.

West

Blake School
Blake Campus, 110 Blake Road, Hopkins

Highcroft Campus, 310 Peavey Lane, Wayzata

Northrop Campus, 511 Kenwood Parkway, Minneapolis
(952) 988-3420
www.blakeschool.org
Blake School is one of the area's elite private preparatory schools and provides a nonsectarian, coeducational experience. The school features two campuses in the western Twin Cities metropolitan area and one next to the Walker Art Center in Minneapolis.

The Blake School's academic programs are challenging and intensive. Though the school is nonsectarian, it does promote a specific set of values, which include respect, love of learning, integrity, and courage. All students participate in artistic, academic, and athletic activities designed to prepare Blake students for higher education.

Breck School
123 Ottawa Avenue North, Golden Valley
(763) 381-8100
www.breckschool.org
The Breck School is recognized as one of the Twin Cities' finest private schools. The school offers Episcopalian values in the curriculum and is coeducational. Breck has a beautiful

campus just outside Minneapolis and features 37 acres for school activities.

HIGHER EDUCATION

It's hard to imagine a metropolitan area with more diverse higher education options than the Twin Cities, from nationally recognized colleges and universities to esteemed community colleges and technical institutes that transcend the traditional notion of trade schools to prepare students to participate in the area's dynamic economy.

The area's higher education institutions have long, storied histories. The University of Minnesota was founded in 1851, and throughout its history the school has shaped the quality of public education in the state and has provided a relatively inexpensive undergraduate education through significant state subsidies. The area's community colleges are evenly distributed throughout the Twin Cities to serve as a feeder system for the University of Minnesota and the Minnesota state colleges and universities. Another feature of Twin Cities' higher education is the many nationally recognized private colleges located in the area.

Continuing education has become an increasingly essential component of most school's missions. Area colleges and universities have extensive, flexible continuing education programs to satisfy the needs of nontraditional students and adult learners. "Distance learning" is an innovative means for busy adults to complete undergraduate and professional degrees.

Numerous Twin Cities graduate programs and schools are nationally recognized for educational excellence and professional training. For more information on specific educational programs, most area higher education institutions have Web sites. *Peterson's 4-Year Colleges* is also a good source of information on Minnesota institutions. Several area institutions are mentioned in *The 331 Best Colleges* by *Princeton Review.*

Minneapolis

Augsburg College
2211 Riverside Avenue South, Minneapolis
(612) 330-1000
www.augsburg.edu

Located approximately 1 mile from downtown Minneapolis, Augsburg College is the Twin Cities' Evangelical Lutheran institution of higher learning. The college provides a distinctly secular education, though it retains its affiliation. The college, founded in Marshall, Wisconsin, in 1869, relocated to Minneapolis in 1872. Since then Augsburg has grown in scope and enrollment, with annual enrollments of nearly 4,000 students.

Teaching students (rather than publishing research) is at the core of an Augsburg education, and it is reflected in many programs and activities. Professors concentrate on teaching, and the average class size is only 15. Another asset is the plentiful multicultural support programs, ranging from Pan-Afrikan and Pan-Asian to Hispanic/Latino student services.

Augsburg offers programs in most disciplines. For many majors the college has an area of emphasis, such as "Sociology-Crime and Community" or "Social Psychology." Augsburg also offers majors not found at some other institutions of higher learning, e.g., Nordic Area Studies, which reflects the heritage of the region and the continuing influence of Scandinavian Lutheran culture.

Activities abound at Augsburg and enrich students' educational experience. With nine male and eight female intercollegiate sports, the "Auggies" are members of Division III of the NCAA in the MIAC (Minnesota Intercollegiate Athletic Association). More than 50 clubs and organizations are on campus, including forensics, cheerleading, and the student newspaper.

Capella University
225 South Sixth Street, 9th Floor, Minneapolis
(888) 227-2736
www.capella.edu

Capella University was the Twin Cities' first "distance learning" undergraduate and gradu-

E-learning is a rapidly expanding service area of the economy; Minneapolis-based Capella reflects this trend, and was named one of the 500 fastest growing companies by *Inc.* magazine.

ate school, primarily offering courses online but also offering directed studies programs. About 20,000 students are enrolled at the school in more than 20 nations worldwide.

Since receiving accreditation in 1997, the school has received significant media attention for its high-tech version of higher education. The school offers 870 accredited online classes, which are accessible anywhere and anytime a computer is available. Capella offers the online "cybrary," the school's Internet version of a library. The university has five primary schools: Undergraduate Studies, Technology, Psychology, Human Services, and Education, plus 116 specialized areas of study. Conferred degrees at Capella University include B.S., Ed.S., M.S., MBA, Ph.D., and Psy.D. Adult students are the most common group in the student body.

Dunwoody College of Technology
818 Dunwoody Boulevard, Minneapolis
(612) 374-5800
www.dunwoody.edu

Dunwoody College of Technology is an excellent Twin Cities unified trade school. The institute is a nonprofit that offers more than 20 technical programs. Founded in 1914, Dunwoody has trained more than 250,000 students for technical careers. Located next to the breathtaking Walker Art Center's Minneapolis Sculpture Garden, the school sits on the edge of downtown Minneapolis and has one of the most panoramic views of the city, where many of its students move on to successful careers in various trades.

Dunwoody is recognized as one of the premier trade schools in the nation. Among the programs offered at Dunwoody are construction, accounting, electronics, technology, auto collision repair, heating and cooling

systems, and welding. There are continuing education and Web-based technical classes, such as night classes offered for construction industry trades.

Minneapolis College of Art and Design
2501 Stevens Avenue South, Minneapolis
(612) 874-3700 or (800) 874-MCAD
www.mcad.edu

Minneapolis College of Art and Design (MCAD) is the leading art educator in the Twin Cities. Since 1886 MCAD has served area art students. Today the art college shares a large portion of the state-of–the-art Minneapolis Institute of Arts (MIA) building. MIA is one of three excellent art museums in Minneapolis, all within a few miles of MCAD.

MCAD programs are available in more than 20 fields, which include comic art, advertising, and photography, plus business-friendly areas of art, such as furniture design and advertising design. Besides the rigorous studio art portion of most majors, important foundation and liberal arts courses are required.

MCAD confers many specialized graduate degrees. Offered are masters of fine arts programs as well as one-year postbaccalaureate and certificate programs in design, fine arts, and media arts. MCAD's continuing education courses are open to the general public, and include distance learning and design programs.

Minneapolis Community and Technical College
1501 Hennepin Avenue, Minneapolis
(612) 659-6000 or (800) 247-0911
www.minneapolis.edu

The focus at Minneapolis Community and Technical College (MCTC) is on creating an environment where recent high school graduates, working adults, and continuing education students are comfortable and excel together in various educational fields. The college has 12,000 students with an average age of 29.

Diversity is a major commitment at MCTC. As the state's most ethnically diverse school of higher education, MCTC has an important mission: providing a quality education to students who speak more than 80 languages and dialects. In part this is accomplished by the English as a Second Language program, which serves these frequently skilled students, who may need to improve their English language proficiency. MCTC offers programs that lead students into successful careers. A few of the most popular programs are liberal arts disciplines, law enforcement, nursing, and computer support. Associate in arts (AA) and Associate in science (AS) degrees are popular at MCTC, as are technical certificate programs.

MCTC abuts Loring Park, one of the Twin Cities' most beautiful parks, and is within walking distance from all downtown Minneapolis's attractions and employers.

The University of Minnesota–Twin Cities
231 Pillsbury Drive SE, 240 Williamson Hall, Minneapolis
(612) 625-2008
www1.umn.edu/twincities
The University of Minnesota–Twin Cities pervades all aspects of the area's culture from sports, education, research and development to medicine, law, politics, and business. Known in the Twin Cities as the U, the institution is the flagship of Minnesota public higher education and a matter of tremendous civic pride. The University of Minnesota–Twin Cities has an undergraduate, graduate, and nondegree student enrollment of more than 50,000, making it the largest university in the country.

The University of Minnesota public education system includes five campuses. Outstate campuses are located in Crookston, Duluth, Morris, and Rochester. The University of Minnesota–Twin Cities has two campuses. The vast majority of programs are on the Minneapolis campus, where the administration is housed. The St. Paul campus is much less urban, with 155 acres of beautiful property devoted to agriculture and natural resources programs.

The academic options at the U of M are seemingly endless. From architecture to zoology, the university offers fields of study for just about any academic or professional interest.

> **i** Bob Dylan attended the University of Minnesota and lived and performed in the adjoining Dinkytown neighborhood from 1959 to 1960. Many of Dylan's former stomping grounds still stand in the area.

The two largest colleges are the College of Liberal Arts (CLA) and the Institute of Technology (IT). Eleven U programs are ranked in the top 10 in the nation, including Chemical Engineering, Psychology, Geography, Economics, and Forestry. In addition to the 16 distinct colleges of the U, there is University College, the continuing education program, which is important in serving Twin Cities nontraditional students.

University of Minnesota alumni appear in almost every imaginable field. Two vice presidents and Democratic Party nominees for president of the United States, Hubert H. Humphrey and Walter Mondale, attended the U. The school counts five alumni in the Pro Football Hall of Fame: Bud Grant, Leo Nomellini, Alan Page, Bobby Bell, and Bronko Nagurski. The list of alumni includes Seymour Cray, the founder of Cray Research and an important figure in the development of the supercomputer; Earl Bakken, who created the first battery-operated pacemaker and founded Medtronic; and 1998 Nobel Prize winner Dr. Louis Ignarro, who was instrumental in the development of Viagra. Another U Nobel Prize winner is Norman Borlaug, who received the award in 1970 for engineering the "green revolution," which resulted in unprecedented food yields for feeding the third world. University of Minnesota alumni have had enormous impact on the Twin Cities by creating 1,500 technological companies, which contribute $30 billion annually to the state economy.

The U's newspaper, the *Minnesota Daily*, has operated for more than a century and is regarded as one of the nation's best college newspapers. The university's radio station, KUOM, better known as Radio K, provides student radio programming—including the best variety of alternative music in the Twin

The College of St. Catherine in St. Paul. TODD R. BERGER

Cities—from dawn to dusk daily. The U plays intercollegiate sports in the Big Ten conference and has been particularly successful in recent years in men's hockey, women's hockey, and men's wrestling, with the university's teams hauling in eight national championships since 2000. The Golden Gopher football team hasn't had as much success lately (the maroon-and-gold last won a national championship and went to the Rose Bowl in 1960), but they are looking forward to a new home. In the fall of 2009, the Gophers will move back outdoors onto their own field, TCF Bank Stadium, ending a long association with the climate-controlled Metrodome that never felt quite right for the pageantry and tradition of college football Saturdays.

St. Paul

The College of St. Catherine
2004 Randolph Avenue, St. Paul
(651) 690-6000 or (800) 945-4599

601 Second Avenue South, Minneapolis
(612) 690-7700 or (800) 945-4599
www.stkate.edu

Located on an idyllic 110-acre wooded campus 5 miles from downtown St. Paul (the college has a second location in downtown Minneapolis), the College of St. Catherine champions the cause of women's higher education. The school is the largest Catholic college for women in the country.

The College of St. Catherine, or St. Kate's, has a notable history. The college was founded in 1905 by the Sisters of St. Joseph Carondelet, whose mission is improving women's educational opportunities. That said, St. Kate's does offer limited programs for men at its much smaller campus in Minneapolis as well as at the graduate school.

St. Kate's emphasizes a distinctly Roman Catholic spiritual and ethical approach to education. St. Kate's curriculum emphasizes depth and breadth and is reflected in critical inquiry, multicultural studies, and interdisciplinary teaching in the classroom. Offered at the college are nearly 50 different majors, from art and biology to theater and theology. Nursing is the most popular area of study, although there are many liberal arts programs. The College of St. Catherine is the Twin Cities' oldest and largest health care educator and includes highly regarded programs in nursing, occupational therapy, and pre-med.

One of St. Kate's greatest educational innovations was the creation of "Weekend College" in 1979. Weekend College is designed to meet working women's needs for a college education. Classes meet every other weekend on Friday evening, Saturday, and Sunday. Fifteen practical, career-oriented majors are offered in the Weekend College program, including elementary education, accounting, communication, healthcare management, and nursing.

Concordia University–St. Paul
275 Syndicate Street North, St. Paul
(651) 641-8230 or (800) 333-4705
www.csp.edu
Concordia University (not to be confused with Concordia College in Moorhead, Minnesota) provides higher education in a Christian environment. The origins of Concordia date from 1893, when the Lutheran Church–Missouri Synod created a high school to prepare students for its ministry. The school became coeducational in 1950 and began granting bachelor's degrees in elementary education in 1962 for the first time as a college.

Today educational opportunities are available in numerous fields. Liberal arts, business, and health care are popular areas of study, including 45 undergraduate degree programs and 12 M.A. programs. The college continues to offer many specialized career majors in the ministry, such as directors of church, parish music, Christian outreach and Christian education, as well as preseminary studies. Concordia's School of Continuing Study offers many classes in the evenings, on weekends, and online. The school has an enrollment of a little more than 2,000 students.

Hamline University
1536 Hewitt Avenue, St. Paul
(651) 523-2800
www.hamline.edu
Hamline University is Minnesota's oldest university. The United Methodist Church organized the school in 1854 in Red Wing. Shortly thereafter, it relocated 50 miles north to its present site in St. Paul. Hamline was the third coeducational college in the United States. The cornerstone of Hamline's curriculum is liberal arts.

Hamline offers degrees and majors in numerous areas of study. Undergraduate bachelor's degrees in liberal arts disciplines are the most popular certificates granted. Also conferred are master's, doctoral, and law degrees. The campus is composed of approximately 4,600 undergrad and graduate students in areas of study ranging from art history to women's studies. The university offers nearly 40 undergraduate majors. Besides the Hamline Law School, there are several additional graduate programs: the Graduate School of Education and the Graduate School of Liberal Studies, including M.A.s in Teaching English as a Second Language and M.F.A.s in Writing .

Luther Seminary
2481 Como Avenue, St. Paul
(651) 641-3456 or (800) LUTHER3
www.luthersem.edu
Luther Seminary educates ministers for the Evangelical Lutheran Church in America (ELCA). It is the largest of eight ELCA seminaries in the United States. The seminary expanded and merged with other seminaries over nearly 150 years to its present size after the consolidation of six area institutions serving a similar function. The campus is located on a pastoral bluff in St. Paul, where they provide graduate degree programs in several religious areas of study and confer Master of Divinity for those wishing to become pastors. Luther also offers D.Min. (Doctorate of Ministry) and Ph.D. degrees, the latter in select fields of study related to the Lutheran Church.

Macalester College
1600 Grand Avenue, St. Paul
(651) 696-6000
www.macalester.edu

Macalester College is a preeminent private liberal arts college conferring undergraduate degrees on some of the world's brightest students. The college is respected locally, nationally, and internationally for maintaining high academic standards and championing internationalism and multiculturalism. Macalester is the recipient of enormous endowment monies, particularly from the DeWitt-Wallace fund, which helps underwrite the costs of tuition, through scholarships and other awards, for students of low socioeconomic status.

Macalester was founded in 1874 by the Reverend Dr. Edward Duffield Neill. A former superintendent for Minnesota Territory Schools, Neill did not move the college to its present site until 1885. In its early years the college received significant financial support from philanthropist Charles Macalester, for whom the college was named.

Macalester College's diversity is reflected in the exceptional students it attracts from the nation and abroad. Macalester is the alma mater of both former Vice President Walter Mondale and former Secretary General of the United Nations Kofi Annan, and the school is highly selective. Nestled on a leafy campus in the exquisite Macalester-Groveland neighborhood, the college creates an excellent learning environment. Macalester's demographics consistently have represented one of the most diverse schools of higher education in the nation. The roughly 1,900 full-time undergraduates come from 49 states, D.C., and around the world—16 percent are from more than 92 countries. There are 39 majors and minors offered at Macalester, including geography, Russian, and classics, as well as African-American studies, women's and gender studies, urban studies, and several interdepartmental fields. A major area of focus at Macalester is the arts, particularly music and theater. Macalester hosts four or five theater productions a year. In addition, the college features numerous organized music groups, which include: Symphony Orchestra, Mac Jazz, New Music Ensemble, Festival Chorale, Flying Fingers (a traditional bluegrass group), the Electric Guitar, and several other diverse music organizations.

Metropolitan State University
700 East Seventh Street, St. Paul
1450 Energy Park Drive, St. Paul
1501 Hennepin Avenue, Minneapolis
(651) 793-1300
www.metrostate.edu

Metropolitan State University provides flexible and affordable education to nontraditional students in the Twin Cities. Convenience is emphasized in offering the chance to earn bachelor's and graduate degrees.

Metro State has served the Twin Cities since 1971. The university's original objective was to offer a program for working adults. This has remained Metro State's focus, though the university has broadened its objectives. In 1983 the first graduate program, master of management and administration, was launched. Today Metro State's enrollment is approximately 8,900 and the school continues to support education of diverse and underserved student populations.

Metro State offers more than 60 majors. Most majors are training toward occupations, such as accounting, social work, law enforcement, and nursing, although students can also study liberal arts areas such as English, sociology, ethnic studies, and anthropology. Metro State accounting students frequently distinguish themselves by annually placing in the top 10 percent on the CPA exam.

Metro State campuses are conveniently located to facilitate greater academic success. The Dayton's Bluff neighborhood, just outside downtown St. Paul, is the largest campus. Two additional campuses are in the heart of downtown Minneapolis and in St. Paul's Midway area. In addition, Metro State offers classes at other colleges and at businesses throughout the Twin Cities, which minimizes the time students spend getting to school and brings classes closer to their homes.

St. Paul's Metropolitan State University. TODD R. BERGER

Northwestern College
3003 Snelling Avenue North, St. Paul
(651) 631-5100 or (800) 692-4020
www.nwc.edu

Northwestern College is a nondenominational, conservative, private Christian college. The college has nearly 3,000 students studying nearly 50 different majors, and the college serves many nontraditional students with its adult degree completion program, Focus, and the Center for Distance Learning.

Northwestern College began as the Northwestern Bible and Missionary School in Minneapolis in 1902. Over time educational and vocational opportunities have been greatly expanded, with the creation of the Northwest Theological Seminary in 1935 and the College of Liberal Arts founded in 1944. Then the college acquired a former Roman Catholic seminary in 1970; the large, wooded, gated campus was renovated and reopened as Northwestern College in 1972.

Christian doctrine is central to the educational mission at Northwestern College. Unlike with many of the Twin Cities commuter campuses, 63 percent of students live on campus, and, reflecting current higher education trends, the college student body is composed of 61 percent women. Northwestern College offers a distinctly conservative Christian education option.

St. Paul College
235 Marshall Avenue, St. Paul
(651) 846-1600 or (800) 227-6029
www.saintpaul.edu

Formerly St. Paul Technical College, St. Paul College is a remarkable educational institution. Foremost among its accomplishments is its astounding job placement statistics; since 2000, 84 to 92 percent of its students annually find positions in their field of study. Technically trained employees are highly sought by Twin Cities employers. St. Paul College provides education in more than 70 occupational fields, which include formal trades such as cabinet-making, carpentry, and auto body repair, as well as numerous medical and computer service occupations, e.g., medical laboratory technician and computer programmer. Deaf education is another prominent field of study. St. Paul College offers an affordable education in numerous fields and places graduates in frequently high-paying and rewarding trades.

University of St. Thomas
2115 Summit Avenue, St. Paul
(651) 962-5000
www.stthomas.edu

In 1885 Archbishop John Ireland founded St. Thomas Aquinas Seminary. This higher education institution quickly grew beyond the bounds of its original purpose, as a high school, college, and seminary, with only two departments, Theology and Classics. However, the Twin Cities' largest Catholic university was prepared to gradually expand into numerous other areas of study.

The first four-year baccalaureate degrees were conferred by then St. Thomas College in 1910. The college increased its liberal arts emphasis and broadened its demographic in 1977 when it became coeducational and accepted women for the first time. Today the school is composed of 51 percent undergraduate women.

St. Thomas has evolved into a private Catholic university with a liberal arts emphasis. The school offers 96 majors ranging from theology, Latin, and classical languages to history, English, and geography. The annual enrollment at St. Thomas is approximately 11,000 students. St. Thomas offers graduate education in numerous areas, including engineering, education, social work, business, psychology, and law.

Continuing education is another paramount focus at St. Thomas. Since New College opened in 1975, the needs of part-time, adult, and nontraditional students have been readily met with innovative methods, such as off-campus classes to make convening easier.

St. Thomas boasts several campuses. The main campus is 78 acres approximately halfway between downtown Minneapolis and St. Paul, on the western edge of historic Summit Avenue. In addition, the downtown Minneapolis campus is home to the Graduate School of Professional Psychology, the School of Education, the Opus College of Business, and the School of Law. St. Thomas also owns smaller campuses in out-state Owatonna and Rome, Italy.

Student activities abound at St. Thomas. Students can choose from a large slate of intercollegiate sports, such as basketball, swimming, cross-country running, and men's and women's hockey. The seminary also publishes *Catholic Digest,* a world-renowned Catholic magazine.

William Mitchell College of Law
875 Summit Avenue, St. Paul
(651) 227-9171 or (888) WMCL-LAW
www.wmitchell.edu

Founded in 1900, what is today known as the William Mitchell College of Law has had many different names, but the goal has remained the same: providing a quality legal education for recent college graduates or, more frequently, students returning to school after a long absence. William Mitchell began as a night school, and it was prescient in creating flexible schedules where nontraditional students could succeed.

Alumni of William Mitchell are an important group in Twin Cities government and law. The school's most famous graduate was Supreme Court Chief Justice Warren E. Burger of St. Paul, who attended one of the four predecessor law schools of William Mitchell. The Warren E. Burger Library was built in 1990 in his honor and is one of the finest law-school libraries in the nation.

The school is small (approximately 1,200 students) and moderately selective, and the student body is 53 percent female. The J.D. program emphasizes what it calls "practical wisdom," to train lawyers to not only to practice law, but to work constructively with other people, to think about the law with breadth and depth, and to learn from legal experiences.

North

Anoka-Ramsey Community College
11200 Mississippi Boulevard NW, Coon Rapids

Cambridge Campus
300 Spirit River Drive South, Cambridge
(763) 433-1100
www.an.cc.mn.us

Anoka-Ramsey Community College (ARCC) has served the north metropolitan Twin Cities since 1965. As the suburbs of Minneapolis and St. Paul have expanded, Anoka-Ramsey has grown to meet the area's needs.

After opening the first campus in Coon Rapids, presently one of the Twin Cities' fastest growing suburbs, the college added the Cambridge Campus in 1978 and shrewdly anticipated an area that would undergo significant urbanization.

Numerous programs can be started, and in some cases completed, at Anoka–Ramsey. They range from accounting, art, astronomy, music, and law enforcement, to Spanish, sociology, mathematics, and zoology. The community college offers associate in arts (A.A.) and associate in science (A.S.) degrees. Anoka-Ramsey was developed as a feeder school for students to begin their educations and then move on to a four-year college to complete their degrees, but it also offers many programs to train for practical careers in physical therapy, business, computer networking and telecommunications, nursing, and other specific trades.

Bethel College and Seminary
3900 Bethel Drive, Arden Hills
(651) 638-6400
www.bethel.edu

Bethel College offers a four-year liberal arts education with an evangelical Christian perspective. Approximately 5,600 students attend the college, nestled on 214 wooded acres on the shore of Lake Valentine.

The Baptist General Conference created Bethel Seminary in 1871. Preceding Bethel College was a secondary academy and a junior college, before the liberal arts college was formed in 1948. Today, Bethel offers programs in more than 100 different fields, from art to youth ministry. It also offers graduate programs in many fields, including divinity, business administration, counseling psychology, education, nursing, and more. The Baptist seminary offers graduate degrees with various concentrations from M.A. and M.Div. (Master of Divinity) to D.Min. (Doctorate of Ministry).

North Hennepin Community College
7411 85th Avenue North, Brooklyn Park
(763) 488-0391 or (800) 818-0395
www.nh.cc.mn.us

North Hennepin Community College (NHCC) serves the northern Twin Cities. The 80-acre campus has an annual enrollment of more than 9,000 students. NHCC has many liberal arts programs, which earn credit toward bachelor degrees. Associate in arts (A.A.) and associate in science (A.S.) are transferable to all Minnesota State Colleges and Universities (MnSCU) schools as well as the University of Minnesota. Also offered at NHCC are career-oriented programs, such as nursing and accounting, and professional development and enhancement classes. Continuing education is another important part of NHCC's mission; it is reflected in the 5,000 part-time students enrolled at the community college. Numerous classes are offered to enrich people's lives in the community.

United Theological Seminary
3000 Fifth Street NW, New Brighton
(651) 633-4311
www.unitedseminary-mn.org

United Theological Seminary (UTS) is the Twin Cities' ecumenical theological school. Although chartered by the United Church of Christ, more than 20 denominations are represented at UTS—just about everything from Unitarian Universalist to Muslim. The school focuses on tolerance, empathy, and diversity in its educational program. Also of paramount importance to UTS is supporting students of diverse racial, ethnic, sexual orientation, and denominational traditions.

UTS's history is fairly brief in the Twin Cities, but its antecedents are rooted in the

Evangelical and Reformed Church Seminary of Plymouth, Wisconsin (founded in 1862), and the Yankton School of Theology, which began serving the German Congregational churches in South Dakota in 1869. Not until 1960 did the seminaries merge and form UTS.

A progressive theological education is provided at UTS. Instruction reflects recent developments in curriculum, and the educational experience at UTS includes both field learning and classroom study.

UTS offers programs in ordained ministry, lay ministry, and some academic vocations, as well as continuing education programs. Degrees include conferred master's degrees in divinity, arts in religion and theology, religious leadership, and women's studies. Doctorate in ministry is also offered. There are specialized programs, which are available at few other seminaries, including Indian ministries, rural ministries, and religion and arts.

East

Century College
3300 Century Avenue North, White Bear Lake
(651) 779-3300 or (800) 228-1978
www.century.mnscu.edu
Students of all ages attend Century College based on their needs, whether to build a foundation for a four-year degree, solely for the joy of learning as a continuing-education student, or to learn a trade. There are classes to satisfy almost everyone's interest. With more than 12,000 students, Century is the largest two-year community college in Minnesota.

Century College was created when Lakewood Community College and Northeast Technical College merged in 1996. Both institutions had long histories serving the area. Since 1967 Lakewood provided an inexpensive education for many students who otherwise wouldn't have been able to afford to go to college. Northeast Technical College performed a similar function from its inception in 1968.

More than 80 technical, academic, and occupational programs are offered at Century

College, as well as more than 100 degrees, certificates, and diplomas. Students with limited financial means may begin a four-year degree program in numerous subject areas, such as English, geography, and biology by earning associate of arts (A.A.) and associate of science (A.S.) degrees. When students complete their A.A. or A.S. and transfer to the University of Minnesota system or the Minnesota State Colleges and Universities (MnSCU), all credits are accepted toward a B.A. or B.S.

Another important function of Century College is continuing education. Century College serves more continuing-education students than any other college in Minnesota, making up 55 percent of the student body.

Minnesota School of Business and Globe University
8089 Globe Drive, Woodbury
(651) 730-5100

5910 Shingle Creek Parkway, Brooklyn Center
(763) 566-7777

1401 West 76th Street, Richfield
(612) 861-2000

1455 County Road 101 North, Plymouth
(763) 476-2000

3680 Pheasant Ridge Drive NE, Blaine
(763) 225-8000

1200 Shakopee Town Square, Shakopee
(952) 345-1200
www.msbcollege.edu
Minnesota School of Business has six Twin Cities campuses, as well as campuses in St. Cloud and Rochester, and resource centers for online students in Fargo, North Dakota, and Sioux Falls, South Dakota. At all locations Globe University offers a quick track to many careers in business as well as technical fields. Degree programs include accounting, software development, e-commerce design, nursing, digital video and media production, massage therapy, and many more. In addition to regular classroom instruction, Globe University also offers distance education, which allows students to take classes online.

South

Argosy University
1515 Central Parkway, Eagan
(651) 846-2882 or (888) 844-2004
www.argosy.edu

Medicine is an important part of the Twin Cities economy, and Argosy University has the most comprehensive allied health care associate programs in the area. Students can pick from numerous health care programs. Here are a few of the associate degree programs available: histotechnology, radiologic technology, dental hygiene, medical laboratory technician, veterinary technology, and radiation therapy. Argosy also offers programs in psychology, education, and business.

Brown College
1440 Northland Drive, Mendota Heights
(651) 905-3400 or (888) 574-3777
www.browncollege.edu

Brown College is an important local technical and trade school. The school boasts many graduates from its programs in local television and radio positions. Brown provides an education that employs its students in their fields of study. Since it opened in 1954, the range of programs at Brown has rapidly expanded. The school has a second campus in Brooklyn Center.

Today Brown College has 14 programs in fields as varied as culinary arts and criminal justice. The culinary arts program is a member of Le Cordon Bleu French cooking school. Le Cordon Bleu began in Paris in 1895; since then, exclusive, limited culinary arts programs have been licensed by the institution. Another important program is the Department of Visual Communications, where students train for such careers as graphic design and Web site design. Also of note at Brown is the radio and television broadcasting program, where students can train to become camera operators, producers, video editors, newscasters, and more. In addition, Brown has digital electronics and computer technology, telecommunications, PC/LAN, and e-commerce programs.

Inver Hills Community College
2500 East 80th Street, Inver Grove Heights
(651) 450-8500
www.inverhills.edu

Inver Hills Community College fulfills the needs of students working toward a four-year degree, to improve job skills, or simply to explore subjects of personal interest. The community college serves the south and east suburbs of St. Paul.

It offers numerous programs for degrees and certification. The associate in arts, or A.A. degree, is a popular stepping-stone toward four-year degrees in more than 50 academic areas, which include sociology, economics, and nursing, as well as more uncommon major fields, such as fish, game, and wildlife, and public health education. Another important two-year degree is the associate in science, or A.S., which is more career oriented (e.g., accounting, criminal justice, aviation, and construction management). The associate in applied science is a two-year degree aimed at immediate employment upon completion, and includes medical secretary, building inspection, and management/marketing. Finally, Inver Hills offers several vocational certificates. The certificates qualify students for various vocations or can be used to improve jobs already held. Many high-demand technical degrees are available, including desktop publishing, medical-office systems, computer applications, and many others.

Normandale Community College
9700 France Avenue South, Bloomington
(952) 487-8200 or (866) 880-8740
www.normandale.edu

Normandale Community College serves the needs of the southern Twin Cities by offering associate degrees, certification programs, and classes for personal enrichment. The community college is easily accessible from Interstate 494 and is located on a 90-acre site, complete with the beautiful Normandale Japanese Garden. Founded in 1968, the school has an enrollment of 10,000 students.

Normandale offers programs in occupational fields, including law enforcement, radiologic technology, hospitality management, dental hygiene, and computers/information management. Other popular programs include two-year liberal arts degrees.

Northwestern Health Sciences University
2501 West 84th Street, Bloomington
(952) 888-4777
www.nwhealth.edu
Northwestern Health Sciences University offers classes in a frequently overlooked portion of medicine: natural approaches to health and health care. There are programs in acupuncture and herbal studies, professional massage, integrative health and wellness, and chiropractics. The university also offers master's programs in Oriental medicine and professional acupuncture.

The university's undergraduate programs are approximately two years in duration. Programs are also offered for nontraditional and/or adult learners. As medical technology increases, Northwestern Health Sciences University's programs have experienced growing importance.

HEALTH CARE AND WELLNESS

Minnesota has been a medical industry hub and site of health care innovation for decades, even before the founding of such illustrious facilities and companies as the Mayo Clinic, Medtronic, and Hazelden. Ironically, a good deal of this reputation came from rumors started by PR agents in territorial times, who were horrified to find that the rest of the country likened Minnesota to an American Siberia. With the hordes of health-challenged immigrants who moved to the state in the 1850s to 1870s to follow these claims of rejuvenation came doctors and scientists who were just as willing to test the healing powers of Minnesota's climate, including Dr. William W. Mayo, whose sons founded the Mayo Clinic in Rochester, and Dr. Brewer Mattocks, who wrote the highly partisan book *Minnesota as a Home for Invalids.*

Minnesota's health care system has been at the top of the field for many, many years. A strong emphasis on research ensures that hospitals and treatment facilities in the Twin Cities and throughout Minnesota will remain far ahead of the times.

HOSPITALS AND HOSPITAL COOPERATIVES

Abbott Northwestern Hospital
800 East 28th Street, Minneapolis
(612) 863-4000
www.abbottnorthwestern.com
Abbott Northwestern Hospital has grown to become the Twin Cities' largest nonprofit health care provider, with a tradition of compassionate care, outstanding service, and leadership in education and clinical research. The huge facility treats a wide range of health-related issues, from family practice to cos-

metic medicine and surgery, cancer treatment, neuroscience, and behavioral studies.

CHILDREN'S HOSPITALS AND CLINICS

Children's-Minneapolis, 2525 Chicago Avenue South, Minneapolis
(612) 813-6100

Children's-St. Paul, 345 North Smith Avenue, St. Paul
(651) 220-6000
www.childrenshc.org
Four additional Twin Cities locations
Children's Hospitals and Clinics was created by the merger of the children's hospitals in St. Paul and Minneapolis. With 268 staffed hospital beds at their main Minneapolis and St. Paul campuses, they are the largest children's health care organization in the upper Midwest, with services available in all major pediatric specialties.

Comfort is an important facet of each Children's Hospitals facility, with such amenities as videos available for checkout, computers with games, built-in beds in hospital rooms for a parent to sleep in, and a wheelchair-accessible garden. Playrooms full of toys, colorful play structures, art supplies, and games are on each floor of the hospitals. Special efforts are made to accommodate children who need to stay in their rooms.

i MinnesotaCare (651-431-2670 or 800-657-3739; www.dhs.state.mn .us) provides health care insurance to residents who cannot afford private insurance. Premiums are based on family income and size.

Fairview Health Services
University of Minnesota Medical Center,
Fairview, Riverside Campus,
2450 Riverside Avenue, Minneapolis

University of Minnesota Medical Center,
Fairview, University Campus,
520 Delaware Street SE, Minneapolis
(612) 273-3000
www.fairview.org
Eight additional Twin Cities locations
University of Minnesota Medical Center,
Fairview, is among the most respected teaching institutions in the nation. The medical center balances responsiveness to patients' needs and wishes with access to innovative treatments and technology. Located on two campuses on the east and west banks of the Mississippi River in Minneapolis, the medical center provides comprehensive services from primary care, emergency care, and the delivery of thousands of babies each year to care of patients with the most complex conditions, including organ and blood and marrow transplantation, heart disease, cancer, neurosciences, and behavioral illnesses.

University of Minnesota Children's Hospital, Fairview, is a renowned pediatric teaching and research hospital for children. The hospital is located in the Riverside and University campuses of the University of Minnesota Medical Center, Fairview; it is the primary pediatric teaching hospital for the University of Minnesota Medical School. University of Minnesota Children's Hospital provides a broad range of pediatric programs and services—including mental health, general surgery, imaging, neonatal, and intensive care; plus cardiac, cancer, and cystic fibrosis services; as well as blood, bone marrow, and organ transplantation.

Hennepin County Medical Center
701 Park Avenue, Minneapolis
(612) 873-3000
www.hcmc.org
Four additional Twin Cities locations
Hennepin County Medical Center (HCMC) is a public teaching hospital in downtown Minneapolis affiliated with the University of Minnesota Medical School. HCMC is the centerpiece of Hennepin County's health services system. HCMC provides specialized and general medical care, often through hospital referrals.

Because HCMC serves many patients from the Native American community, an Indian Health Advocate is available to ensure that the special needs or cultural preferences of Native American patients are treated with sensitivity and respect, and that both American Indian health practices and Western medicine can be brought to the care of the patient.

Mayo Clinic Rochester
200 First Street SW, Rochester
(507) 284-2511
www.mayoclinic.org/rochester
The world-famous Mayo Clinic has been a pioneer in medical research and disease treatment for more than a century. While it is located almost 90 miles south of the Twin Cities, the very existence of the hospital is one of the reasons there is such a strong medical community in Minnesota. More than 2,000 physicians and 35,000 allied health staff work in the Mayo system, treating nearly half a million patients annually. Their specialties include (but are far from being limited to) cancer treatment, dermatology, diagnostic radiology, Native American studies and medicine, internal medicine, cardiovascular disease treatment, allergy studies and treatment, plastic surgery, HIV study, and general practice/family medicine.

Mercy Hospital
4050 Coon Rapids Boulevard, Coon Rapids
(763) 236-6000

Unity Hospital, 550 Osborne Road, Fridley
(763) 236-5000
www.allina.com/ahs/mercyunity.nsf
Mercy and Unity Hospitals are nonprofit hospitals that have been serving the northern Minneapolis–St. Paul metropolitan area for more than 40 years. The two hospitals function as

Guided tours of the historic Plummer Building at the Mayo Clinic can be arranged through the hospital, or self-guided tours may be taken during public hours. Call (507) 284-2511 for more information.

virtually one entity, with shared resources to help ensure quality, cost-effective care. Mercy and Unity specialty services include behavioral health, cardiac, emergency, family centered care, oncology, and bariatrics. The hospitals offer medical transportation, health education, and support groups. In addition, Mercy Hospital provides specialized services for senior citizens.

North Memorial Medical Center
3300 Oakdale Avenue North, Robbinsdale
(763) 520-5200
www.northmemorial.com
The independently owned North Memorial Medical Center's history of responding to the health care needs of its communities has lasted for more than five decades and continues to be the main ingredient to its success. North Memorial was an early leader in emergency care and is home to the first totally integrated hospital-based medical transportation system in Minnesota, which now includes two helicopters, 100 ambulances, and 575 employees. North Memorial also founded the I Can Cope cancer education program that is now used by the American Cancer Society and in hospitals throughout the country.

St. Francis Regional Medical Center
1455 St. Francis Avenue, Shakopee
(952) 403-3000
www.stfrancis-shakopee.com
St. Francis Regional Medical Centerspecialties including orthopedics, spine surgery, cardiology, and oncology. Hospital services include the St. Francis Cancer Center, emergency department, St. Francis Sleep Diagnostics Center, St. Francis Family Birth Place, St. Francis Breast Center, St. Francis Children's Pediatric Unit, St. Francis Rehabilitation and

Sports Medicine, St. Francis Health Services, and several primary and specialty clinics. St. Francis is jointly owned and sponsored by the Benedictine Health System, Allina Hospitals & Clinics, and Park Nicollet Health Services.

St. Joseph's Hospital
69 West Exchange Street, St. Paul
(651) 232-3000
www.stjosephs-stpaul.org
The first hospital in Minnesota, St. Joseph's was founded by the Sisters of St. Joseph of Carondelet in 1853. Today the downtown St. Paul Catholic hospital serves patients in the eastern Metro, with specialties in heart care, cancer care, mental health and chemical dependency treatment, and maternity care. St. Joseph's operates a 24-hour emergency room and comprehensive services for inpatient care. The hospital has been a member of the HealthEast Care System since 1987, which operates several hospitals, clinics, and rehabilitation centers throughout the eastern Metro. The respect and compassion routinely shown by staff members at the hospital reflect the vision of the founders of this historic hospital.

United Hospital
333 North Smith Avenue, St. Paul
(651) 241-8000
www.unitedhospital.com
United Hospital is a premier acute care medical facility. A part of the Allina Health System, United's facilities include a birth center, a pain center, the John Nasseff Heart Hospital, and a center for breast care; the hospital specializes in behavioral health studies and treatment, emergency care, heart/lung medicine, oncology, rehabilitation services, and surgery.

REHABILITATION CENTERS
Hazelden Foundation and Renewal Center
15245 Pleasant Valley Road, Center City
(651) 213-4200 or (800) 257-7810
www.hazelden.org
Hazelden has a history spanning nearly 50 years of pioneering leadership in the care of

St. Joseph's Hospital in downtown St. Paul is the oldest hospital in Minnesota. TODD R. BERGER

chemically dependent people and their families. It is internationally recognized for its broad spectrum of interrelated services and continuum of care, which includes assessment and rehabilitation for adolescents and adults, aftercare and family services, renewal services, extended care and continuing care, professional development, counselor training, and clergy training and counseling. A nonprofit organization dedicated to helping people recover from alcoholism and other drug addiction by providing residential and outpatient treatment for adults and young people, Hazelden offers programs for families affected by chemical dependency as well as training for a variety of professionals. Hazelden is also the world's premier publisher of information on chemical addiction and related areas.

New Beginnings
190 Northshore Drive, Waverly
(763) 658-5800 or (800) 487-8758
www.newbeginningsatwaverly.com

New Beginnings is nationally recognized for its treatment of alcohol, cocaine, methamphetamine, and other drug dependencies, providing intensive and individualized treatment programs for adults and adolescents. New Beginnings' program components are designed to help men and women overcome the physical, emotional, spiritual, behavioral, and social aspects of addiction. New Beginnings at Waverly offers intensive individualized treatment programs that include residential and outpatient levels of care. All dimensions of addiction are addressed under the principle that successful treatment demands the efforts of an interdisciplinary team that includes the patient, family, clinicians, and other professionals.

i Earl E. Bakken invented the first wearable cardiac pacemaker in Minneapolis. The company he cofounded, Minneapolis-based Medtronic, continues to be a world leader in medical technology.

HMOS

HealthPartners
8100 34th Avenue South, Bloomington
(952) 883-6000
www.healthpartners.com
HealthPartners is a nonprofit, consumer-governed family of health care organizations focused on improving the health of its members, its patients, and the community. Health-Partners provides health care coverage at numerous HealthPartners Clinic sites across the Twin Cities and at Regions Hospital in St. Paul. Additionally, HealthPartners has a contracted network of thousands of providers in the Twin Cities and throughout the nation.

SPECIALTY CLINICS

Phillips Eye Institute
2215 Park Avenue, Minneapolis
(612) 775-8800
www.phillipseyeinstitute.com
Phillips Eye Institute is a premier specialty center devoted exclusively to the diagnosis, treatment, and care of eye disorders and diseases. The institute integrates the latest technologies in eye care with unprecedented staff expertise. Nearly 8,000 patients a year visit the institute for refractive surgery (LASIK), vision rehabilitation, and other inpatient services. The institute also has an established pediatric ophthalmology department.

HEALTH ASSOCIATIONS

Alzheimer's Association
(952) 830-0512 or (800) 232-0851
www.alzmndak.org

American Cancer Society
Minneapolis (952) 925-2772
St. Paul (651) 644-1224
www.cancer.org

American Diabetes Association
(763) 593-5333
www.diabetes.org

American Heart Association
(952) 835-3300
www.americanheart.org

American Lung Association
of Minnesota
(651) 227-8014
www.alamn.org

American Parkinson's Disease
Association
(612) 863-5850 or (888) 302-7762
www.mnapda.org

American Red Cross
(612) 871-7676
www.redcrosstc.org

Arthritis Foundation of St. Paul
(651) 644-4108
www.arthritis.org

United Way
(612) 340-7400
www.unitedwaytwincities.org

COUNSELING

Catholic Charities of St. Paul and Minneapolis
(612) 664-8500
www.ccspm.org

Jewish Family and Children's Service
(952) 546-0616
www.jfcsmpls.org

Lutheran Social Services of Minnesota
(651) 642-5990 or (800) 582-5260
www.lssmn.org

MEDIA

Much of what a newspaper says about a city goes beyond the printed word. Insight is gleaned by analyzing what's front-page newsworthy, how much (or little) heft the arts section has, and what the classifieds reveal about the cost of homes. In the Twin Cities we have two dailies to analyze as well as plenty of free publications dispensed in business entryways across the Metro. Add two slick city magazines, sold by subscriptions and on newsstands, and the local print media is surprisingly vast and diverse. The radio stations, too, run the gamut, but again, the Twin Cities lean toward the local—Clear Channel has a firm presence, but we've always found our many homegrown personalities more interesting than the for-the-faceless-masses national shows, and we love, love, love our local public radio stations. For TV we have all the standards, plus a professional independent station that puts out some of its own programming.

DAILY NEWSPAPERS

St. Paul Pioneer Press
345 Cedar Street, St. Paul
(651) 222-1111 or (800) 950-9080
www.twincities.com
The *St. Paul Pioneer Press* is Minnesota's oldest newspaper, founded as the *Minnesota Pioneer* in 1849. Today the paper is known as being on the cutting edge of news journalism. The newspaper retains bureaus in Washington, D.C., and at the State Capitol in St. Paul. It also has a Metro West bureau in Minneapolis. While it has a smaller readership and distribution than Minneapolis's *StarTribune*, it has arguably just as good coverage of the area and is only 25 cents on weekdays and $1.00

on Sunday as opposed to the *StarTribune*'s 50 cent daily price tag and $1.75 on Sunday.

StarTribune
425 Portland Avenue, Minneapolis
(612) 673-4000
www.startribune.com
Since 1867 the *StarTribune* has been a part of the Twin Cities community with an outstanding newspaper that's read by 1.5 million people each week and an online network of services that has become the region's preferred source for online information.

Bigger than the *Pioneer Press*, especially in the employment/job search and business sections, the *StarTribune* is considered the leading area paper in sports coverage as well. Their main sportswriter, Sid Hartman, is considered the ultimate "homer"—that is, a Twin Cities–biased booster/sportswriter—and has been with the paper for so long that staffers joke he was there when the first issue hit the streets.

MAGAZINES

Minnesota Monthly
600 U.S. Trust Building, 730 Second Avenue South, Minneapolis
(612) 371-5800 or (800) 933-4398
www.minnesotamonthly.com
Full of interviews with local political figures and celebrities, restaurant reviews, and features ranging from controversial reports on small-town sexual harassment suits to staying healthy longer, *Minnesota Monthly* is a vibrant publication that showcases Minnesota and its people. A monthly publication, it can be bought at most magazine racks and bookstores in the Twin Cities.

Mpls/St. Paul Magazine
MSP Communications
220 South Sixth Street, Suite 500,
Minneapolis
(612) 339-7571 or (800) 999-5589
www.mspmag.com
For 30 years, *Mpls/St. Paul Magazine* has been providing readers with up-to-date information on Twin Cities events and dining, as well as features on local celebrities and important members of the community. The magazine runs travel articles, lodging information outside the metro area, and universally pertinent features concerning health, beauty, child-rearing tips, and everything in between.

Utne Reader
12 North 12th Street, Suite 400, Minneapolis
(612) 338-5040
www.utne.com
The *Utne Reader* is a nationally distributed monthly magazine that reprints articles from thousands of alternative media sources, providing interesting perspectives on current events, environmental issues, lifestyles, politics, books, and the arts. The magazine hosts a popular online discussion room, Cafe Utne (accessible through the magazine's Web site), with postings about many of the topics the magazine covers.

OTHER PUBLICATIONS
Business
Twin Cities Business Monthly
MSP Communications
220 South Sixth Street, Suite 500,
Minneapolis
(612) 339-7571
www.tcbm.com
Twin Cities Business Monthly, published by the same company that publishes *Mpls/St. Paul Magazine,* includes profiles of successful businesspeople and companies in the metropolitan area and information about business education, technology, and other topics of interest to business-oriented readers.

Ethnic Community
Asian American Press
417 University Avenue, St. Paul
(651) 224-6570
www.aapress.com
Asian American Press provides excellent coverage of international and local news geared to Asian populations, from local business profiles to politics to festival information to the struggles recent immigrants have adjusting to life in a new country.

The Circle
3355 36th Avenue South, Minneapolis
(612) 722-3686
www.thecirclenews.org
Approximately 25,000 Native Americans from various tribes live in the Twin Cities, and *The Circle* monthly newspaper is dedicated to publishing news, arts information, community calendars, and resource information for Native Americans in the region.

Gente de Minnesota
Latino Communications Network
1516 East Lake Street, Suite 200,
Minneapolis
(612) 729-5900
www.gentedeminnesota.com
Published in Spanish, *Gente de Minnesota* is a weekly newspaper that serves the Hispanic population of the Twin Cities with local, national, and international news, as well as sports, entertainment, and Spanish-language TV program listings.

Hmong Times
962 University Avenue West, St. Paul
(651) 224-9395 or (888) 229-9577
www.hmongtimes.com
With some 70,000 Hmong residents, the Twin Cities have the largest population of Hmong of any urban area in the world. The community is served by the English-language *Hmong Times,* with news, community information, religion, sports, and agriculture coverage. Published twice a month, the newspaper

Pick up a copy of *City Pages* or *Pulse... of the Twin Cities* to get an idea of what's happening in town. Both weeklies have a good calendar of entertainment events in the Cities.

reaches a wide audience among the community, which began settling in Minnesota after the Vietnam War.

Family Papers

Best of Times
St. Louis Park
(763) 541-9363
www.familytimesinc.com
The sister publication of *Family Times*, the award-winning *Best of Times* (formerly known as *Senior Times*) is geared to the senior community. The paper is full of news about independent living and adjusting to retirement, as well as about senior events and activities around the Twin Cities and surrounding communities.

Family Times
St. Louis Park
(952) 922-6186
www.familytimesinc.com
Family Times is geared toward the entire family. News about children and senior events alike is listed here, as well as wellness information for everyone in the family. There's an extensive theater section in the back and a decent calendar of events for all members of the family.

Good Age
1115 Hennepin Avenue South, Minneapolis
(612) 825-9205
www.mngoodage.com
This senior-oriented monthly publication contains pages of information on health care issues and developments dealing with medical expenses, support groups, and nursing homes, as well as lots of advice and tips on how to stay at your peak physical and mental shape for as long as possible. There's also

information on less age-specific things like filing taxes and shopping for a new house.

Minnesota Parent
1115 Hennepin Avenue South, Minneapolis
(612) 825-9205
www.mnparent.com
Presenting itself both as a support group and a how-to guide to parenting, *Minnesota Parent* contains information on essentials like enrolling your children in school or helping them survive a divorce. The greatest part of this magazine, however, is the exhaustive calendar of events in the back, containing times, prices, and contact info for just about every museum and park in town.

Minnesota Women's Press
771 Raymond Avenue, St. Paul
(651) 646-3968
www.womenspress.com
The biweekly print flagship of Minnesota's Feminist Voices (MFV), the *Minnesota Women's Press* provides a fair and open-minded view of women in politics and feminist issues that affect women and men alike, as well as profiles and interviews with political personalities and prominent women in the Twin Cities. The publication is well written by members and volunteers of MFV as well as outside contributors, many of them prominent local businesswomen and writers.

Food and Entertainment

Buon Gusto
1001 Twelve Oaks Center Drive, Suite 1017, Wayzata
(612) 375-9222
www.buon-gusto.com
This is a fun little food-related publication that's released bimonthly and carried at most gourmet grocery stores and some restaurants. Covering everything from haute cuisine to Minnesota hot dishes and carrying many interviews with local chefs and restaurant owners as well as reviews of local cooking supply stores, this newsletter has information for the weekend cook and professional alike.

It also has great recipes, usually about six in every issue.

City Pages
401 North Third Street, Suite 550, Minneapolis
(612) 375-1015
www.citypages.com

Since the 1970s, when it was called *Sweet Potato, City Pages* has been consistently providing great coverage of local politics, music events, and Twin Cities culture in general. The weekly calendar and A-List deliver the best information on what to do with your spare time, whether it be catching a lecture at the university or seeing a show at your neighborhood coffeehouse, while the interviews with notable Minnesotan artists and musicians are both entertaining and informative. The restaurant reviews are also worth noting, serving up the good and not-so-good news about area eateries. You can find this free weekly all over the Twin Cities, especially in restaurants and bars.

Lavender
3715 Chicago Avenue South, Minneapolis
(612) 436-4660
www.lavendermagazine.com

The Twin Cities are home to the third largest gay, lesbian, bisexual, and transgender (GLBT) community in the United States. The best known of the local GLBT publications, *Lavender* contains interviews, features, events calendars, and book and music reviews of interest to GLBT Twin Citians and visitors. Published biweekly, it's carried in record stores, coffee shops, bars, and many other venues throughout the Twin Cities.

Pulse . . . of the Twin Cities
3200 Chicago Avenue South, Minneapolis
(612) 824-0000
www.pulsetc.com

Founded in 1996, *Pulse* provides good coverage of music, art, and film community activity happening throughout the Twin Cities, as well as many controversial political feature stories. Available at most convenience stores and alternative media venues in the area, *Pulse* officially hits the streets every Wednesday.

Rain Taxi Review of Books
P.O. Box 3840, Minneapolis 55403
www.raintaxi.com

Distributed nationally, this quarterly publication contains tons of book reviews (all genres) as well as interviews with established and up-and-coming authors from around the world.

Twin Cities Blues News
P.O. Box 65671, St. Paul 55165
(612) 642-5170
www.mnblues.com

Full of information about new blues recordings, blues acts coming to town, and reviews of regional blues festivals, this publication contains some of the more interesting music interviews in town with both old and new bluesmen (and women). Released monthly and carried in record stores and coffee shops throughout the area, this is full of essential blues info to even the most casual of enthusiasts.

Health, Religion, and Support Publications

Edge Life
Leap Productions
14590 Bowers Drive NW, Ramsey
(763) 427-7979
www.edgelife.net

Falling somewhere between a New Age and Christian publication, *Edge Life* contains articles about miracles and biblical prophesies and articles about how they've been fulfilled—reincarnation, faith healing, and archeological excavations that may or may not prove the existence of God. The paper is carried at most bookstores in the Twin Cities.

i The satirical weekly *The Onion* (612-370-1372; www.theonion.com) now has a Twin Cities edition available in stores and restaurants throughout the metro.

Essential Wellness
4270 Honey Tree Pass, Danbury, WI
(888) 667-7866
www.esswellness.com
This monthly paper is an excellent source of information about alternative healing techniques, breakthroughs in homeopathic and alternative medicines, and features written by practitioners of alternative medicine. There's information on where to find alternative and homeopathic doctors and treatment centers in the Twin Cities area, from massage therapy to herbal vendors.

FATE Magazine
P.O. Box 460, Lakeville 55044
(800) 728-2730
www.fatemag.com
FATE is a monthly magazine that features accounts of the strange and unknown, from psychics, spiritualists, and "fringe science" to authoritative UFO and paranormal investigations.

Neighborhood Free Publications

Almost every neighborhood in the Twin Cities has a free paper that can be found in neighborhood convenience stores or appears on your doorstep. These papers cover local news, school district announcements, flea market schedules, city council efforts on the part of the district in question, and sometimes news that affects the entire city. Here are just a few of the neighborhood papers and the areas they cover:

Downtown Journal–downtown Minneapolis
Northeaster—northeast Minneapolis
Southwest Journal—southwest Minneapolis
Southeast Angle—southeast Minneapolis
The Villager—St. Paul, Highland Park area
The Riverview Times—Harriet Island
    St. Paul riverside community
Midway/Como Monitor—St. Paul Como Park
    and Midway areas
Grand Gazette—St. Paul Summit Hill/Grand
    Avenue area

Seward Profile—Minneapolis, Seward/
    Cedar-Riverside/Cooper/North Longfellow
    neighborhoods

Sports

Minnesota Motorcycle Monthly
7265 Balsam Lane North, Maple Grove
(763) 315-5396
www.motorbyte.com/mmm
This publication contains everything from reviews of new motorcycle gear to motorcycle vacation tips to travel logs contributed by readers and staff writers. Check out the anti–Harley Davidson "Geezer with a Grudge" column for some really scintillating insight into the mind of a longtime motorcycle owner.

Twin Cities Sports
701 Fourth Avenue South, Suite 500,
Minneapolis
(612) 859-3886
www.twincitiessports.com
This monthly free magazine covers all aspects of personal sports in the Metro, with features on such things as in-line skating at the Metrodome, profiles of athletes, and a very detailed calendar of events. The magazine can be found at many restaurants, bars, grocery stores, and bookstores in the Twin Cities.

RADIO STATIONS
AM Stations

KFAN–1130 AM
1600 Utica Avenue South, Suite 400,
St. Louis Park
(651) 989-1130
www.kfan.com
KFAN is the Twin Cities sports radio leader. The Fan features interesting sports talk and occasional discussions about current affairs. The talk personalities on KFAN are the station's strength. Morning drive host Dan Cole, "the Common Man," is a seasoned veteran of local talk, who offers an offbeat look at various topics. The Fan is also the radio home of the Minnesota Timberwolves basketball games.

ℹ️ A couple stations showcase the thriving local music scene: the University of Minnesota's Radio K (770 AM and 106.5/100.7 FM) and the Current (89.3 FM).

KKMS–980 AM
2110 Cliff Road, Eagan
(651) 405-8800
www.kkms.com
KKMS is a Christian talk radio station owned by Salem Communications. It features the Salem Radio Network and *Family News in Focus*.

KSTP–1500 AM
3415 University Avenue, St. Paul
(651) 646-TALK
www.am1500.com
KSTP is one of many Hubbard Broadcasting Inc. media stations in the Twin Cities. KSTP specializes in sports and political talk radio. The station emphasizes local personalities such as Joe Soucheray, Bob Davis, and Matt Thomas but also carries some national shows such as Paul Harvey.

KTIS–900 AM/98.5 FM
3003 Snelling Avenue North, Roseville
(651) 631-5000
ktis.nwc.edu
KTIS is a religious music and talk station, with frequencies on the AM (900) and FM (98.5) dials.

KUOM–770 AM/106.5 and 100.7 FM
University of Minnesota, 610 Rarig Center, 330 21st Avenue South, Minneapolis
(612) 625-3500
www.radiok.org
The Twin Cities' largest and most popular college radio station is KUOM or, as it is known locally, Radio K. Radio K plays alternative, techno, ska, hip-hop, and much more. It features music from independent labels and local music as well as major label music. Radio K has the most diverse playlist in the Twin Cities. AM radio broadcasts stop at sundown, but the FM stations broadcast 24 hours a day on weekends. Radio K is also available 24-7 online.

KYCR–1570 AM
2110 Cliff Road, Eagan
(651) 405-8800
The New KYCR features conservative talk radio with such hosts as Bill O'Reilly and Dr. Laura Schlesinger.

WCCO–830 AM
625 Second Avenue South, Minneapolis
(612) 370-0611
www.wccoradio.com
WCCO Radio was, until the 1990s, the undisputed leader in news and talk. In the past decade, ratings have slid as demographics aged, yet WCCO remains a vital force on Twin Cities radio. The station continues as the broadcast home of Minnesota Twins baseball as well as University of Minnesota Golden Gophers football and basketball.

FM Stations

KBEM–88.5 FM
1555 James Avenue North, Minneapolis
(612) 668-1735
www.jazz88fm.com
Jazz 88 focuses on light jazz, fusion, classic jazz, and cool jazz but also programs that include exotica, Latin, and bluegrass music. The station is operated by students of the Minneapolis Public Schools system.

KCMP–89.3 FM
480 Cedar Street, St. Paul
(651) 290-1212
www.minnesota.publicradio.org
KCMP, more popularly known as the Current, debuted in 2005, thus driving up the number of Twin Cities Minnesota Public Radio stations to three. The Current plays a broad spectrum of artists, with a strong showing of independent and local music—don't be surprised to hear Frank Sinatra sandwiched between clas-

sic country and local hip-hop. It sounds strange, but it works, as evidenced by the huge listenership the Current has built in its first few years on air.

KDWB–101.3 FM
1600 Utica Avenue South, St. Louis Park
(651) 989-KDWB
www.kdwb.com
KDWB plays contemporary hits, with an emphasis on dance, especially on weekend evenings. The station has been popular with local teens for decades because of its programming.

KFAI–90.3/106.7 FM
1808 Riverside Avenue, Minneapolis
(612) 341-3144
www.kfai.org
Since 1978 KFAI has served the Twin Cities with an extremely wide array of programming. KFAI programming is remarkably diverse. Prominent features of the program schedule are arts, public affairs, world music, community affairs, jazz, and rock. In addition, KFAI hosts several weekly bilingual programs to serve the local immigrant communities. KFAI features Khmer, Hmong, Somali, Eritrean, and Ethiopian programs. The station broadcasts on 90.3 in Minneapolis and the western suburbs and on 106.7 in St. Paul and the eastern suburbs.

KMOJ–89.9 FM
1422 West Lake Street, Minneapolis
(612) 377-0594
KMOJ is the Twin Cities home to soul, jazz, blues, and reggae. It is one of only two area community radio stations. KMOJ gives its community, North Minneapolis, a voice on the air with music and public discussions of issues important to the neighborhood. The station moved into a temporary home in the Uptown neighborhood of Minneapolis in 2007 but is developing a new permanent home on North Minneapolis's West Broadway Avenue.

KNOW–91.1 FM
45 East 7th Street, St. Paul
(651) 290-1212
www.mpr.org
KNOW is the Twin Cities Minnesota Public Radio news, information, and talk station. The programming consists of a mix of local, nationally syndicated, NPR, and BBC broadcasts.

KQQL–107.9 FM
1600 Utica Avenue South, St. Louis Park
(651) 989-2020
www.kool108.com
If you are looking for golden oldies, KOOL 108 is the Twin Cities frequency on the FM dial. The station is known for "good times, great oldies" and plays a surprisingly diverse chunk of rock music.

KQRS–92.5 FM
2000 Southeast Elm Street, Minneapolis
(612) 989-7625
www.kqrs.com
KQ 92 is the Twin Cities' most popular classic rock station. It began as an early FM maverick radio station in the late 1960s but in the 1970s began to take on its classic rock position. Since then KQ has been enormously popular—so popular, in fact, that the KQ Morning Show with Tom Barnard caused the local affiliate with the Howard Stern Radio Show to leave the area and change formats. Beyond the "the KQ Morning Crew" led by Barnard, the station plays a consistent rotation of Pink Floyd, Led Zeppelin, Foreigner, and Tom Petty.

KSJN–99.5 FM
45 East Seventh Street, St. Paul
(612) 290-1212
www.mpr.org
KSJN is Minnesota Public Radio's Twin Cities classical music station.

KSTP–94.5 FM
3415 University Avenue, St. Paul
(651) 989-5795
www.ks95.com
KS 95 has held the honor of being the Twin Cities' favorite top-40 station for decades and continues to play "the best variety of the 1980s, 1990s, and today!"

KTCZ–97.1 FM
1600 Utica Avenue South, St. Louis Park
(612) 989-9797
www.cities97.com
Cities 97 plays alternative music from artists such as John Mayer, Damien Rice, Wilco, and Death Cab for Cutie.

KXXR–93.7 FM
2000 Southeast Elm Street, Minneapolis
(612) 617-4000
www.93X.com
93X is the station for fans of acts like Offspring, Korn, Metallica, and Megadeath. The station serves up nonstop new metal and industrial music.

WLKX–95.9 FM/KBGY–107.5 FM
15226 West Freeway Drive, Forest Lake
(651) 464-6796
www.spirit.fm
WLKX/KBGY is a Twin Cities adult contemporary Christian channel. WLKX reaches the Metro, northern suburbs, and western Wisconsin; KBGY reaches the Metro, southern suburbs, and a wide area of southeastern Minnesota.

WLTE–102.9 FM
625 Second Avenue South, Suite 300, Minneapolis
(651) 989-1029
www.wlte.com
WLTE plays a large selection of light rock; some perennial favorites are Van Morrison, Kenny G, Martina McBride, and Chicago.

TELEVISION STATIONS

TPT2–Channel 2
172 East Fourth Street, St. Paul
(651) 229-1330
www.tpt.org
TPT2 is the Twin Cities public television station that has continually served the community with a healthy mix of national PBS and local public television programming.

TPT2 features more children's television programming than any other Twin Cities station. *Sesame Street* and *Teletubbies* are featured on the daily schedule, as well as *Newton's Apple,* a locally produced science program for nearly 20 years.

For adults TPT2 has national PBS hits such as *Frontline,* the *NewsHour with Jim Lehrer* and countless national public television specials. Additionally, TPT2 has created a wealth of locally produced programming. Local public affairs programs like *Almanac,* and *Newsnight Minnesota* distinguish the station and serve the community.

WCCO–Channel 4
90 South Eleventh Street, Minneapolis
(612) 339-4444
www.wcco.com
The Twin Cities' CBS affiliate WCCO has a long history in television and radio in the Twin Cities. In fact, the acronym, WCCO, stands for Washburn and Crosby Company, the former name of the Twin Cities–based international corporation, General Mills.

WCCO promotes its newscasters as "the Home Town Team," and emphasizes several other programs and initiatives for the community. One is Hometown Heroes, where WCCO-TV encourages Twin Citians to nominate people who make significant contributions to the community; later some of the outstanding local citizens nominated are interviewed and honored on WCCO news. Another WCCO community-based program is Community 4 Kids, where adults in the community mentor troubled area youths.

KSTP–Channel 5
3415 University Avenue, St. Paul
(651) 646-5555
www.kstp.com
ABC-affiliated KSTP is recognized locally and nationally as an innovator in the television industry. KSTP was the first television station in the Twin Cities, signing on the air on April 27, 1948. It also was the first color television station and the first to broadcast daily newscasts in the nation.

News is important to KSTP and its "Eye Witness News Team." KSTP was a local pioneer in investigative journalism and weather reporting. It is also the only affiliated station in the Twin Cities that remains under local ownership, which is reflected in the station's news and programming.

KMSP–Channel 9
11358 Viking Drive, Eden Prairie
(952) 944-9999
www.kmsp.com
KMSP is the Twin Cities' Fox affiliate. Fox News Sunday is the network's competition against such Sunday news institutions as NBC's *Meet the Press* and CBS's *Face the Nation.* The station carries plenty of Twin Cities sports. NFL football and Major League Baseball are featured prominently on the station. In addition, the Twin Cities NHL team, the Wild, is broadcast locally on Fox and also UPN's WFTC.

KARE–Channel 11
8811 Olson Memorial Highway, Minneapolis
(763) 546-1111
www.kare11.com
KARE is the Twin Cities home of NBC. Besides NBC programming, it consistently has the highest-rated news broadcasts at 6:00 p.m. and 10:00 p.m. KARE has created local initiatives such as "11 Who KARE," which recognizes citizens who have made significant contributions for the betterment of the Twin Cities. In addition, KARE produces programs like *Whatever,* aimed at teens. *Whatever* features teen reporters examining subjects of interest to the group, which is frequently underserved by national and Twin Cities media.

WUCW–Channel 23
1640 Como Avenue, St. Paul
(651) 646-2300
www.thecwtc.com
WUCW, which changed its call letters from KMWB in 2006, is the Twin Cities CW network affiliate. WUCW airs CW programs, such as *America's Next Top Model* and *Smallville,* plus syndicated programming, movies, and infomercials. The *Jerry Springer Show* calls WUCW its Twin Cities home. There are also plenty of reruns of recent sitcoms to sate the viewing appetite of Twin Citians.

WFTC–Channel 29
11358 Viking Drive, Eden Prairie
(952) 944-9999
www.wftc.com
After many years as an independent, WFTC is now the Twin Cities Paramount, or UPN, affiliate. The station primarily runs movies and sitcom reruns, with a few original programs.

KPXM–Channel 41
10700 Old County Road 15, Suite 285, Plymouth
(763) 417-0041
www.ionline.tv
KPXM recently became part of the ION Television Network, with a steady diet of reruns.

KSTC–Channel 45
3415 University Avenue, St. Paul
(651) 645-4500
www.kstc45.com
KSTC, a sister station to KSTP but not an ABC affiliate, primarily shows rerun sitcoms and dramas, such as *Scrubs, The Shield,* and *24.*

WORSHIP

An amazing variety of religious groups are represented in the Twin Cities, with hundreds of churches, synagogues, and mosques—many are on the National Register of Historic Places—spread throughout the Twin Cities. Besides established religions such as Catholicism, Judaism, and Islam as well as Evangelist, Lutheran, Mennonite, and Methodist denominations, other traditions, celebrations, and orders have come to the Cities with new waves of immigrants.

Catholicism has long been one of the primary faiths in the area, especially in St. Paul, as evidenced by the many beautiful old Catholic churches throughout the region. Still, during Ramadan, Muslims can be seen walking to mosque dressed in beautiful traditional robes. In December street celebrations of Hanukkah, complete with food and live music, are a regular tradition in both Twin Cities downtown areas. Many cultures and religious groups have found a home here in the Cities.

Churches and other religious centers are an important aspect of Minnesota culture, and vice versa. Most neighborhoods in the Twin Cities were traditionally built around churches, and these churches are an integral component of their neighborhoods. Churches in the Twin Cities remain an active part of the community, setting up soup kitchens and sleeping quarters for homeless people, FoodShare and Food Shelf grocery giveaways, and shelters for battered women, orphans, and runaways. On the lighter side of things, many religious centers in the Twin Cities also double as reasonably priced day care centers during the workweek, and most have regular festivals and picnics open to the general community, sponsor neighborhood rummage sales for charity, and arrange summer camps for kids.

If you're looking for volunteer opportunities, any and all the religious centers in the Twin Cities would be more than happy to have your help. **Loaves and Fishes** (1917 Logan Avenue South, Minneapolis; 612-377-9810; www.loavesandfishesmn.org) is the primary local service for providing free dinners to disadvantaged families. Operating from seven facilities spread throughout the metro, Loaves and Fishes serves hot, nutritious meals to an average of over 2,300 persons each weeknight.

ISAIAH, located at 2720 East 22nd Street in Minneapolis (612-333-1254; www.gamaliel.org/isaiah) provides leadership training and a vehicle for congregations to take action in the public arena to achieve social, economic, and racial justice in our metropolitan and regional communities. ISAIAH is a membership-driven organization of 85 congregations located in the Twin Cities metropolitan and St. Cloud regions.

Lutheran Social Service of Minnesota, located at 2485 Como Avenue in St. Paul (651-642-5990; www.lssmn.org), started in 1865 when a Swedish pastor and his congregation began taking in children orphaned by poverty and tragedy. The congregation soon opened the Vasa Children's Home to serve orphans and from there grew into what it is today: the largest statewide nonprofit social service agency, offering crisis shelters, group homes, counseling, and adoption services for people of all income levels and religious affiliation. The Lutheran Social Service helps more than 100,000 Minnesota children, families, seniors, and people with disabilities each year.

No matter what your religious persuasion, two important stops in the Twin Cities are the Basilica of Saint Mary and the Cathedral of Saint Paul. The **Basilica of Saint Mary,** or just "the Basilica," as locals call it, was the first basilica built in the United States, taking seven years to build before holding its first mass on May 31, 1914. Located at the corner of 17th Street and Hennepin Avenue in Minneapolis (612-333-1381; www.mary.org), the Basilica has ingrained itself firmly into the community around it, organizing events ranging from amazing bell choirs open to the public to a full-scale annual summer rock concert—the Basilica Block Party—of which proceeds go to help maintain the historic building. Rose Ensemble chorale group has an artists residency here. Tours of the building are available—call or check the Web site.

The Cathedral of Saint Paul, located at 239 Selby Avenue in St. Paul (651-228-1766; www.cathedralsaintpaul.org) is impossible to miss once you're in St. Paul's capitol district. It took more than 50 years to complete and is absolutely stunning. The gigantic building, topped by a dome with an exterior height of 307 feet, is filled with carved marble statues of saints, gold accents, painted murals, and large stained-glass windows. The cathedral dome is an important landmark of the city, lending St. Paul a European feel that the rest of the Midwest can only envy. A $35 million renovation of the historic cathedral resulted in replacing the copper domes, cleaning and sealing the granite walls, repairing interior damage, and updating the lighting, heating, and cooling systems. The replacement of the main copper dome involved 60 roofers and more than 100 craftspeople (carpenters, electricians, ironworkers, and plumbers) to put the new 70-ton dome in place. The spectacular results have returned St. Paul's great landmark to its historic state. The cathedral is the working headquarters of the archdiocese and has a regular attending congregation of nearly 3,000. Many regularly scheduled choral and orchestral concerts are held here (the acoustics are spectacular).

OTHER WORSHIP RESOURCES AND ORGANIZATIONS

Archdiocese of St. Paul and Minneapolis
266 Summit Avenue, St. Paul
(651) 291-4400
www.archspm.org

Catholic Aid Association
3499 Lexington Avenue North, Arden Hills
(651) 490-0170
www.catholicaid.com

Good News For Israel
6408 Minnetonka Boulevard, St. Louis Park
(952) 926-7369
www.gnfi.org

Greater Minneapolis Council of Churches
1001 East Lake Street, Minneapolis
(612) 721-8687
www.gmcc.org

Islamic Center of Minnesota
1401 Gardena Avenue NE, Fridley
(763) 571-5604
www.islamiccentermn.org

Joint Religious Legislative Coalition
122 Franklin Avenue West, Minneapolis
(612) 870-3670
www.jrlc.org

Minnesota Zen Center
3343 East Calhoun Parkway, Minneapolis
(612) 822-5313
www.mnzencenter.org

St. Paul Area Council of Churches
1671 Summit Avenue, St. Paul
(651) 646-8805
www.spacc.org

Close-up

Minnesota FoodShare

Minnesota FoodShare is just one example of how the diverse religious and neighborhood communities in the Twin Cities come together to help people in need. FoodShare, one of the region's largest and most successful charities, is the result of what happens when neighborhood religious centers with soup kitchens and grocery giveaways get together to form a community organization. Members of the FoodShare project include Catholic Charities, the Minnesota Rabbinical Association, and the Minnesota Council of Churches, as well as many members of the business community, including several popular nightclubs. Organized officially in 1982, Minnesota FoodShare now delivers literally millions of pounds of food each month to people in need through neighborhood churches, grocery stores, and home delivery programs.

One church that has been an active member of Minnesota FoodShare is Pastor Paul's Mission. For nearly 25 years, Pastor Paul Arnopoulos has been helping feed homeless and disadvantaged Minnesotans through Disciples Ministry Mission in north Minneapolis, an area that even now is still struggling with poverty. Every day staff members hand out bags of groceries and cook hot meals for families in need, distributing approximately 14 million pounds of food each year. More than 12,000 families from Minnesota and Wisconsin depend on the mission for help, and Pastor Paul has dedicated his entire life to making sure they get it.

Supporters of the mission and the FoodShare project come from some unlikely sources. The most well-known one is the Acoustic Garage Sale, a rock benefit put on each year by the First Avenue nightclub. Each January First Avenue brings in several dozen local and national acts to play the Main Room stage, and all door proceeds go directly to Pastor Paul's Mission. Concertgoers have the option of bringing in canned and boxed food in lieu of the door price, and that, too, is taken to the mission. After the show well-known local and national music personalities donate musical instruments, autographed photographs, albums and CDs, and other items to be auctioned off for additional money for the mission.

Minnesota charities all work together to feed those in need. The charities keep in touch with one another, and if one charity is having trouble meeting its neighborhood's needs, another pitches in to bring any surplus. This network of charities makes Minnesota's FoodShare program among the most successful in the country.

Unitarian Universalist Association
122 Franklin Avenue West, Suite 303
Minneapolis
(612) 870-4823
www.psduua.org

Wat Lao Minneapolis
1429 Northeast Second Street, Minneapolis
(612) 789-9382
www.laocenter.org

INDEX

ABOUT THE AUTHOR

Todd R. Berger is a freelance writer and editor presently based in Grand Canyon National Park in Arizona, where he also works as the Director of Publishing for the Grand Canyon Association. A former long-term resident of the Twin Cities (primarily in the Mac-Groveland neighborhood of St. Paul), Berger met his wife, Bonnie, in St. Paul; adopted his cat, Hitchcock, from a no-kill shelter in Hastings; spun out on icy stretches of I-94 in downtown Minneapolis (more than once); and watched the Green Bay Packers win and lose consecutive Super Bowls at Liquor Lyle's. He is the author of *Lighthouses of the Great Lakes,* and the author, co-author, or editor of several additional books and anthologies. He returns to the Twin Cities often to visit family and to work on updates to the *Insiders' Guide to the Twin Cities*.